Artists in Exile

Expressions of Loss and Hope

Frauke V. Josenhans

With essays by
Marijeta Bozovic
Joseph Leo Koerner
Megan R. Luke

And contributions by
Suzanne Boorsch
Nicole Demby
David Ake Sensabaugh
Clara Yang

Yale University Art Gallery
New Haven

Distributed by Yale University Press
New Haven and London

Publication made possible by the Richard Brown Baker, B.A. 1935, Collection Care and Enhancement Fund and the Société Anonyme Endowment Fund.

First published in 2017 by the
Yale University Art Gallery
1111 Chapel Street
P.O. Box 208271
New Haven, CT 06520-8271
artgallery.yale.edu/publications

and distributed by
Yale University Press
302 Temple Street
P.O. Box 209040
New Haven, CT 06520-9040
yalebooks.com/art

Published in conjunction with the exhibition
Artists in Exile: Expressions of Loss and Hope,
organized by the Yale University Art Gallery.

Yale University Art Gallery
September 1–December 31, 2017

Tiffany Sprague,
Director of Publications and Editorial Services

Christopher Sleboda,
Director of Graphic Design

Project director: Madeline Kloss, Assistant Editor

Copyeditors: Heather Brand, Zsofia Jilling
Proofreader: Heather Brand
Indexer: Mark Mastromarino

Set in Canela and Tempera Biblio
Printed at GHP, in West Haven, Conn.

Cover design by Christopher Sleboda

ISBN 978-0-300-22570-9
Library of Congress Control Number: 2017937193

10 9 8 7 6 5 4 3 2 1

Cover illustrations: (front, clockwise from top right) Paul Gauguin, *Parau Parau (Whispered Words)*, 1892 (cat. 1); Shirin Neshat, Untitled, from the series *Rapture*, 1999 (cat. 29); Kurt Schwitters, *47 20 Carnival*, 1947 (cat. 16); (back, clockwise from top left) Matta, Untitled, 1943–44 (cat. 21); George Grosz, *The Filling Station*, 1934 (cat. 24); Mu Xin, *Dawn Mood at Bohai*, 1977–79 (cat. 28); (front flap) Elizabeth Catlett, *My right is a future of equality with other Americans*, 1947 (cat. 26)

Frontispiece: Detail of Shirin Neshat, Untitled, from the series *Rapture*, 1999 (cat. 29)
Pages 13–14: Detail of André Kertész, *Forced March to the Front between Lonie and Mitulen*, from the portfolio *A Hungarian Memory*, 1915, printed 1980 (cat. 13)
Pages 29–30: Detail of An-My Lê, Untitled [Ho Chi Minh City], from the series *Việt Nam*, 1998, printed 2006 (cat. 8)
Pages 85–86: Detail of Lyonel Feininger, *Old Gables V*, 1943 (cat. 15)
Pages 127–28: Detail of Kurt Schwitters, *47 20 Carnival*, 1947 (cat. 16)
Pages 183–84: Detail of Shirin Neshat, Untitled, from the series *Rapture*, 1999 (cat. 29)
Pages 236–37: Detail of R. B. Kitaj, *Amerika (Baseball)*, 1983–84 (cat. 6)

Contents

Home/Mobility

Nostalgia

Transfer/Adjustment

Identity

Director's Foreword

Yale University has a long history of welcoming scholars and students from all over the globe to its campus, and these individuals have enriched the academic community and opened up new fields of research. The history of the University reflects its engagement with past and current issues of immigration, globalization, and diaspora. Particularly during wartime, Yale has welcomed academics from conflict zones, offering them refuge on its campus, and many of them subsequently became major cultural voices in the United States. The Yale School of Art alone hosted the influential German modernist Josef Albers, who was appointed chair of the Department of Design in 1950 and trained generations of students, as well as Jack Tworkov, who immigrated with his family to the United States in 1913 and was chairman of the school from 1963 to 1969. In more recent years, numerous art students fleeing war or persecution have come to the United States and enrolled in the visual arts program at Yale. Four of them, and their artworks that express personal experiences with exile and migration, are featured in this catalogue: Abelardo Morell, M.F.A. 1981; An-My Lê, M.F.A. 1993; Do Ho Suh, M.F.A. 1997; and Ahmed Alsoudani, M.F.A. 2008.

The encyclopedic collection of the Yale University Art Gallery is so rich in part because it mirrors this diversity. It reflects the transfer and movement of objects and people throughout the centuries, and it foregrounds how some of the darkest chapters in human history have engendered some of the most creative artistic responses. The collection of modern and contemporary art in particular illustrates how immigrants have shaped the history of modern art in the United States. The cornerstone of the Gallery's modern art collection is the holdings of the Société Anonyme, Inc., which was founded by Katherine S. Dreier and Marcel Duchamp in 1920 with the aim to introduce modern art to America; it comprises works by artists from Armenia, Austria, Belgium, Bulgaria, Canada, Chile, Cuba, France, Georgia, Germany, Hungary, Iceland, Italy, Lithuania, the Netherlands, Norway, Poland, Romania, Russia, Spain, Sweden, Switzerland, Ukraine, and Uruguay, in addition to the United States. Dreier was one of many American art collectors and museum directors who, during World War II, played a crucial role in helping exiled artists find safe passage to the United States and acquired works by persecuted artists.

Thus it is fitting that the Gallery has undertaken the present project, *Artists in Exile: Expressions of Loss and Hope*, which highlights the significant contributions of disenfranchised individuals to the history of art. Frauke V. Josenhans, the Horace W. Goldsmith Assistant Curator of Modern and Contemporary Art, embarked on this exhibition and publication by intensely researching works in the Gallery's collection. She not only delved into twentieth-century art and the Société Anonyme but also expanded her research to other areas of the Gallery's collection, including the Departments of American Paintings and Sculpture, Asian Art, European Art, Photography, and Prints and Drawings, with a special focus on contemporary artists. Subsequently she settled on a worthy and ambitious goal, that of presenting a broad narrative of the exile experience that encompasses artists from diverse backgrounds— a goal that seems especially important amid current global events.

This exhibition has also facilitated collaborations across different departments on campus. Yale students, at both the undergraduate and graduate level, participate in research projects

across the museum, and two played a major role in
this exhibition and publication. Nicole Demby, a
PH.D. candidate in the Department of the History
of Art, completed in-depth research on many
objects in the exhibition and wrote several object
entries for the catalogue. Similarly, Clara Yang,
B.A. 2017—who, as a Gallery Guide, came to the
project with a solid understanding of the collection—also contributed research and ideas to the
exhibition and publication.

In addition, Marijeta Bozovic, Assistant
Professor of Slavic Languages and Literatures;
Film and Media Studies; and Women's, Gender,
and Sexuality Studies, shared her vast knowledge
of Russian literature and culture in an essay for
the catalogue. Two other essays were authored
by Yale alumni: Joseph Leo Koerner, B.A. 1980,
the Victor S. Thomas Professor of the History of
Art and Architecture and Senior Fellow of the
Society of Fellows at Harvard University, and
Megan R. Luke, B.A. 1999, Associate Professor in
the Department of History of Art and a Faculty
Affiliate of the Visual Studies Research Institute at
the University of Southern California.

Lastly, gifts and loans by numerous alumni,
museum colleagues, and other individuals have
helped make this exhibition possible. The collections of Richard Brown Baker, B.A. 1935, and
Charles B. Benenson, B.A. 1933, now stewarded
by the Gallery, include many works that reflect
the visual and material impact of exile on artists. Exceptional loans by Philip H. Isles and
other private collectors who wish to remain
anonymous—of works by Jacques-Louis David,
Emil Nolde, Max Beckmann, George Grosz, and
Henry Koerner—make a substantial contribution
to this exhibition and the narrative that it puts
forth. I also acknowledge the generous support

the show has received from other museums and
their directors, notably Frank H. Goodyear III
and Anne Collins Goodyear of the Bowdoin
College Museum of Art, in Brunswick, Maine, and
Olivier Meslay of the Sterling and Francine Clark
Art Institute, in Williamstown, Massachusetts.

Above all, the Gallery is enthusiastic about
the opportunity to mount an exhibition that
engages with the theme of exile in a way that
reflects the many faces of the Yale community.
Artists in Exile: Expressions of Loss and Hope seeks
to capture the hybrid emotions, backgrounds, and
experiences of exiles—bolstering this teaching
museum's mission to foster vibrant dialogue and
diverse perspectives within and beyond its walls,
but always grounded in original works of art.

Jock Reynolds
The Henry J. Heinz II Director
Yale University Art Gallery

Acknowledgments

This exhibition and publication grew out of my desire to expand the narrative of exile in art history beyond the twentieth-century European perspective that is the dominant focus of most studies. Given the millions of refugees and displaced people who still seek safe homes around the world, it is clear that the exile experience is not relegated to one part of the world or to the past. Thus, my somewhat utopic idea was to open up the theme of exile to encompass global and temporal diversity—four continents and two hundred years of art history, to be precise. Although this seemed like almost an unrealistic goal at first, it became possible thanks to the resources and incredibly rich collection of the Yale University Art Gallery, and through the invaluable encouragement, feedback, and contributions I received from so many people.

From the moment that the idea for this exhibition was formulated until its realization, I could not have hoped for more support, collaboration, and help from various individuals at the Gallery, across the Yale campus, at other institutions, or in my personal life. I am first and foremost grateful to Jock Reynolds, the Gallery's Henry J. Heinz II Director, for shepherding this project, trusting me with it, and providing me with the means to achieve it. Similarly, I am immensely thankful for the steadfast encouragement of Pamela Franks, Senior Deputy Director and the Seymour H. Knox, Jr., Curator of Modern and Contemporary Art, who advocated this project early on and helped me throughout its inception. Laurence Kanter, Chief Curator and the Lionel Goldfrank III Curator of European Art, played a tremendous role as well, and I appreciated his guidance, and his critiques, that helped to shape this exhibition in many different ways.

My research on exile has been nourished by groundbreaking publications on this topic, the eye-opening work of other scholars, and various archival materials at museums and libraries, which allowed me to follow the artists' itineraries and read between the written lines that documented their lives. Along the way, I was very fortunate to meet and engage with exceptional scholars whose keen interest and understanding enriched this project in too many ways to count. The three authors who wrote essays for this catalogue deserve special thanks: Joseph Leo Koerner contributed his seemingly bottomless knowledge as well as his personal history to this project, resulting in an essay with unique emotional depth. Marijeta Bozovic, during our various discussions, not only added many valuable ideas and thoughts to the project as a whole but also lent a singular perspective to the catalogue. Megan R. Luke immediately jumped on board and embraced the idea for this exhibition when I first mentioned it to her, and her outstanding catalogue essay reflects her profound expertise and superb writing skills.

At the Gallery I am very fortunate to be able to work closely with students and faculty at Yale, and thus I was able to include two skilled and enthusiastic students in this project. Nicole Demby, a PH.D. candidate in the Department of the History of Art, has enriched this exhibition and catalogue through her serious research and excellent ideas, and I feel very privileged to have had her work with me. Sincere thanks are also due to Clara Yang, B.A. 2017, for her many valuable contributions to both the exhibition and the catalogue.

Colleagues across the entire Gallery staff were essential in bringing this exhibition and publication to fruition. In the Department of Modern and Contemporary Art, I am greatly indebted to Alexander Harding, Senior Museum Assistant. He provided logistical and moral support during the past few years, as well as helpful suggestions and feedback, and I am very appreciative of his unflagging assistance, thoughtfulness, and good humor.

The Department of Publications and Editorial Services was a key player in the genesis of this project, and early on I had the support of its director, Tiffany Sprague, to whom I am most thankful. I am equally beholden to the project director Madeline Kloss, Assistant Editor, who has been my partner in crime, shaping the different essays and entries in this catalogue into something coherent and often helping me frame my sometimes abstract ideas in a more concrete way. I thank her for never losing her patience or optimism, and for always being willing to work around challenging schedules. All of the logistics were masterfully taken care of by Julianna White, former Senior Editorial Assistant, and Jennifer Lu, Editorial and Production Assistant. Tamara Schechter, Assistant Editor, has similarly helped with many aspects of the exhibition. Christopher Sleboda, Director of Graphic Design, brilliantly translated the concept of the exhibition into a unique graphic presentation and an inspired design for the galleries, with the help of Chris Chew, Graphic Designer; I am most thankful for all of the inspiring creative discussions we had.

I am deeply indebted to my colleagues in other curatorial departments, particularly Suzanne Boorsch, the Robert L. Solley Curator of Prints and Drawings—another proponent of this exhibition from its beginnings—and David Ake Sensabaugh, the former Ruth and Bruce Dayton Curator of Asian Art, who both agreed to share their rich knowledge by writing entries for the catalogue.

For their collegial support I would like to express my deep gratitude and appreciation to the Department of Prints and Drawings, who enabled me to view and borrow so many works on paper: Elisabeth Hodermarsky, the Sutphin Family Senior Associate Curator of Prints and Drawings; Suzanne Greenawalt, Senior Museum Assistant; and Rebecca Szantyr, the Florence B. Selden Fellow. Immense thanks are also due to Diana Brownell, Senior Museum Technician, for her thoughtful efforts preparing these works for exhibition.

I would also like to express my gratitude to the following curatorial colleagues: Mark D. Mitchell, the Holcombe T. Green Curator of American Paintings and Sculpture, Keely Orgeman, the Alice and Allan Kaplan Assistant Curator of American Paintings and Sculpture, and Janet M. Miller, Museum Assistant; Judy Ditner, the Richard Benson Assistant Curator of Photography and Digital Media, and Gabriella Svenningsen, Senior Museum Assistant; Denise Patry Leidy, the Ruth and Bruce Dayton Curator of Asian Art, Sadako Ohki, the Japan Foundation Associate Curator of Japanese Art, and Ami Potter, Museum Assistant; and Meghan Lynch, former Senior Museum Assistant, and Katharine Luce, Museum Assistant, both in the Department of European Art.

Warmest thanks are due to the Conservation Department, especially Cynthia Schwarz, Associate Conservator of Paintings, with whom I had many inspiring discussions about materials and techniques influenced by the exile experience. I also extend my profound thanks to Ian McClure, the Susan Morse Hilles Chief Conservator; Carol Snow, Deputy Chief Conservator and the

Alan J. Dworsky Senior Conservator of Objects; Theresa Fairbanks Harris, Senior Conservator of Works on Paper; Anne Turner Gunnison, Associate Conservator of Objects; Irma Passeri, Senior Conservator of Paintings; Anna Krez, Paintings Conservation Fellow; Paul Panamarenko, Museum Technician; and Elizabeth Godcher, Senior Administrative Assistant. I would also like to thank Anikó Bezur, the Wallace S. Wilson Director of Scientific Research, as well as Paul Whitmore and Pablo Londero, at the Institute for the Preservation of Cultural Heritage at Yale.

I received an incredible wave of support and help from all of the other different departments at the museum, notably from Heather Nolin, Deputy Director for Exhibitions, Programming, and Education, and Elizabeth Landau, Senior Administrative Assistant. In the Exhibitions Department, I could rely on the invaluable work and aid of Jeffrey Yoshimine, Deputy Director for Exhibition and Collection Management; Andrew Daubar, Exhibition Production Manager; Anna Russell, Museum Assistant; and all of the museum technicians. There are really not enough words to thank my colleagues in the Registrar's Office for managing the loans and logistics surrounding the exhibition, especially L. Lynne Addison, Registrar, and Amy Dowe, Senior Associate Registrar, as well as Anne Goslin, Senior Associate Registrar, and Tiffany Davidson, Assistant Registrar. Thanks are also due to John Pfannenbecker and his exceptional security team.

In the Visual Resources Department, I am most grateful to its director John ffrench; Anthony DeCamillo and Richard House, Senior Photographers; Kathleen Mylen-Coulombe, Rights and Reproductions Coordinator; David Whaples, Visual Resources Coordinator; and Jessica Smolinski, Documentation Photographer. Immense thanks are due to Joellen Adae, Director of Communications, and Janet Sullivan, Communications Coordinator, for masterfully advocating the exhibition and catalogue and spreading the word about it on many different platforms.

I would like to express my sincere appreciation to Jill Westgard, Deputy Director for Advancement, and Brian McGovern, Associate Director of Advancement, as well as to Valerie Richardson, Stewardship Manager. In the Business Office, I am most grateful to Jessica Labbé, Deputy Director for Finance and Administration; Charlene Senical, Operations Manager; and Catherine Sparer-Morales, Operations Manager. In the Director's Office, I thank Lisa Scilipote, Executive Assistant to the Director. I would also like to thank Leonor Barroso, Director of Visitor Services, and Michael Moore, Visitor Services Assistant.

For their thoughtful work, and for the many fruitful exchanges about programming tied to the exhibition, I thank Molleen Theodore, Associate Curator of Programs; Emily Arensman, Programs Fellow; and Elizabeth Harnett, Program Coordinator. In the Education Department, I would like to express my deep gratitude to Ryan Hill, the former Nolen Curator of Education and Academic Affairs, for his creative take on things. I also thank Jessica Sack, the Jan and Frederick Mayer Senior Associate Curator of Public Education; Issa Lampe, the Bradley Senior Associate Curator; Jennifer Reynolds-Kaye, the former Lewis B. and Dorothy Cullman–Joan Whitney Payson Senior Fellow; and Sara Carrigan, Senior Administrative Assistant.

Various colleagues outside the museum have also supported this exhibition. For extremely valuable assistance during the preparation of this exhibition and many inspiring conversations, I would like to thank Stephen K. Scher, who has supported and encouraged me in too many ways to count, for which I am immensely grateful.

Furthermore, I am most appreciative of the help and guidance of the following museum colleagues and other organizations and individuals: Kishwar Rizvi of Yale University; Barbara Plankensteiner of the Museum für Völkerkunde, Hamburg; Ian Wardropper of the Frick Collection, New York; Betsy Rosasco of the Princeton University Art Museum, New Jersey; Timothy O. Benson and Julia Kim of the Robert Gore Rifkind Center for German Expressionist Studies, Los Angeles County Museum of Art; Christiane Zeiller of the Bayerische Staatsgemäldesammlungen, Max Beckmann Archiv, Munich; Stephanie Schrader and Amanda Maddox of the J. Paul Getty Museum, Los Angeles; Julia Drost of the German Institute of Art History, Paris; Lynette Roth of the Harvard Art Museums, Cambridge, Massachusetts; Brenda Danilowitz and the staff of the Josef and Anni Albers Foundation, Bethany, Connecticut; Isabel Schulz of the Kurt Schwitters Archiv, Sprengel Museum Hannover, Germany; Regina Elzner of the Deutsche Nationalbibliothek, Frankfurt; Charles Stuckey of the Yves Tanguy Catalogue Raisonné, Pierre and Tana Matisse Foundation, New York; Halley K. Harrisburg of Michael Rosenfeld Gallery, New York; Sophie Greig of Mona Hatoum Studio, London; Sarah Landry of Galerie Lelong, New York; Laurence Choko of Galerie Intemporel, Paris; Monique Wells of Les Amis de Beauford Delaney; Jason Andrew of the estate of Jack Tworkov; Shaina Larrivee of the Hedda Sterne Foundation, Inc., New York; Jay Vincze of Christie's, London; Stephen Robeson Miller; Najwa Mayer; Alison Oscar; Diana Howard; Tracy Hamilton; and Kelly Pask.

I would like to express my profound gratitude to all the museum colleagues and lenders who have supported this exhibition through exceptional loans: Frank H. Goodyear III, Anne Collins Goodyear, Joachim Homann, and Laura Latman at the Bowdoin College Museum of Art, Brunswick, Maine; Olivier Meslay, Jay A. Clarke, and Chris Hightower at the Sterling and Francine Clark Art Institute, Williamstown, Massachusetts; Philip H. Isles; Mohamad Hafez; and all the private collectors who wish to remain anonymous.

I address my deepest thanks to Édouard Kopp for our many discussions, for his patience and support in times of struggle, and for being my partner on this journey. Finally, this catalogue is dedicated to my parents and grandparents, and to the generations of exiles to whom we are all indebted.

Frauke V. Josenhans
The Horace W. Goldsmith Assistant Curator of Modern and Contemporary Art
Yale University Art Gallery

Note to the Reader

Contributors to the Catalogue Entries

SB Suzanne Boorsch
ND Nicole Demby
FVJ Frauke V. Josenhans
DAS David Ake Sensabaugh

Dimensions
Dimensions are given in inches followed by
centimeters. Height precedes width precedes
depth. Inches have been rounded to the nearest
sixteenth, centimeters to the nearest tenth.

Provenance
Provenance is given in chronological order.
Locations of owners and dates of ownership are
given, if known. When transfer is from one known
owner to another, the names are separated by a
semicolon; when there is a break in ownership, the
semicolon is replaced by a period.

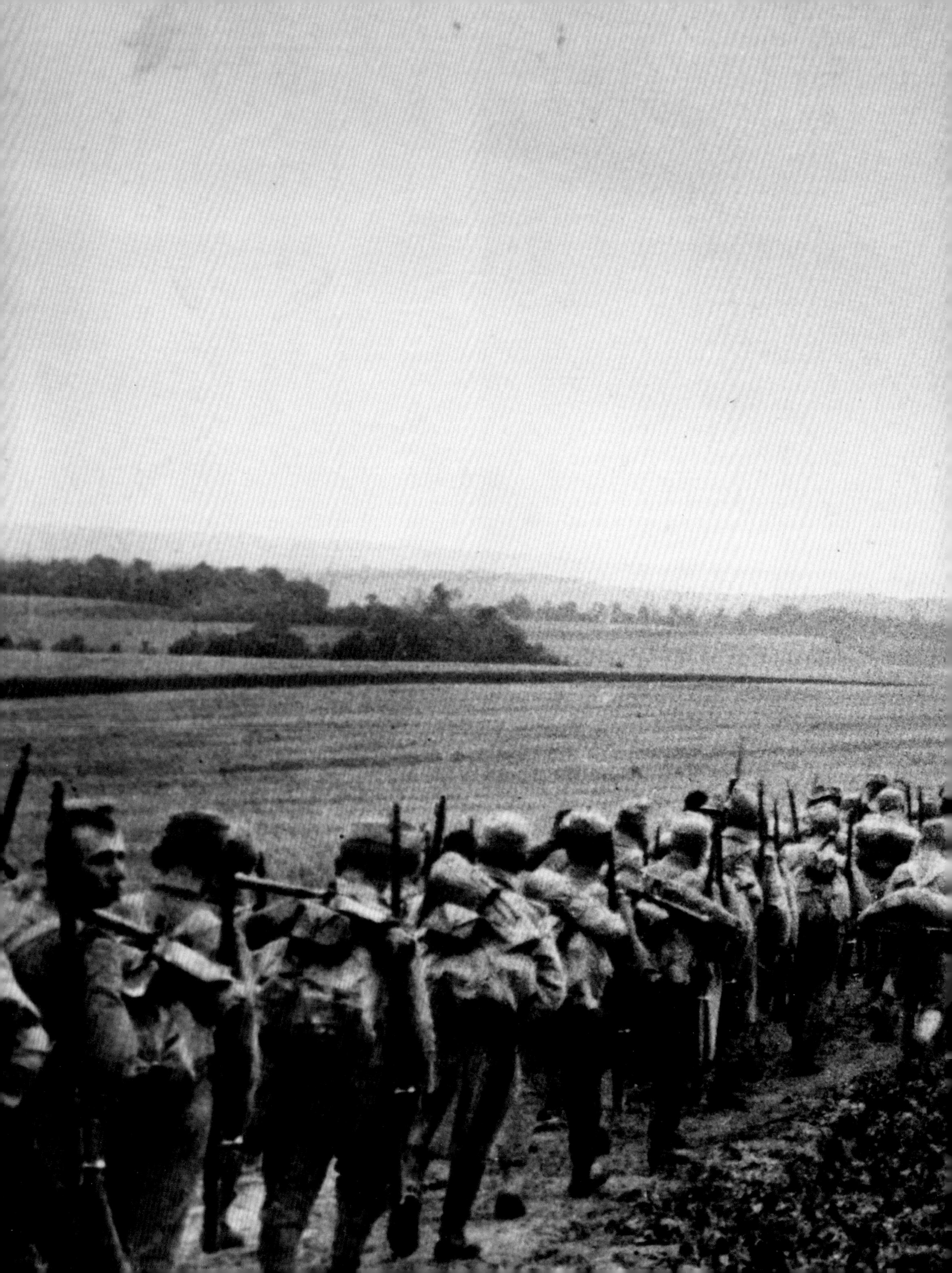

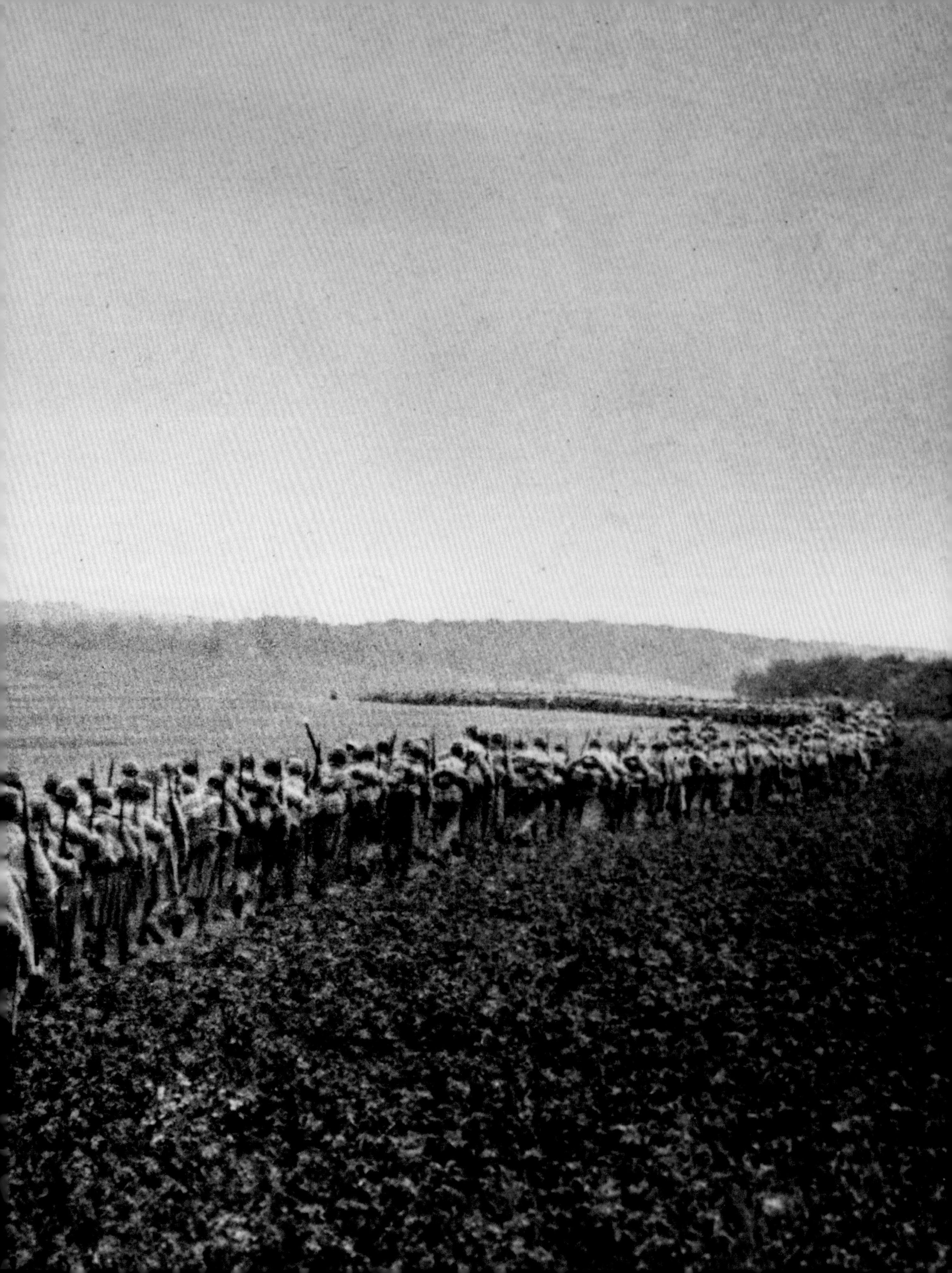

EXILES IN ART, AND ARTISTS IN EXILE

Frauke V. Josenhans

"Exile is life led outside habitual order. It is nomadic, decentered, contrapuntal;
but no sooner does one get accustomed to it than its unsettling force erupts anew."
—Edward W. Said, *Reflections on Exile and Other Essays*, 2000 [1]

The "unsettling force" of exile pervades the history and mythology of civilizations around the world and has had a great impact on visual and literary culture. Nevertheless, studies of exile seem to conspicuously focus only on one of the darkest chapters of modern history—the rise of Nazism and the resulting flight of millions of people to safer shores—and multiple exhibitions and publications have drawn attention to well-known, male artists exiled during that period.[2] In the current age of technology and globalization, with people easily commuting between different cities, countries, and continents, it is essential to look at exile in the visual arts from a new perspective and to reconsider artists who left their countries of birth, or their adopted homes, for a variety of reasons. New avenues of research lead away from the Eurocentric line of most exile studies and ask for a more comprehensive approach that includes a wider scope of artists, notably in regard to national origin, time period, and gender.[3] At the same time, exile should be considered not only as a mental or physical state but also as a catalyst for creativity. For some artists, separation from the familiar, either willing or unwilling, inspired innovations in form and technique. Thus exile, though for many an existential trauma resulting from persecution and alienation, can also provoke a personal and artistic metamorphosis.

Artists in Exile: Expressions of Loss and Hope aims to show these different sides of exile: the profound loss experienced by so many artists, with their work conjuring images of the past and of what they left behind; and, on the other hand, its transformative potential, with new forms of expression resulting from artists' expulsion or departure. The works in this catalogue and the attendant exhibition are for the most part drawn from the encyclopedic collection of the Yale University Art Gallery, enriched by the addition of key objects from other institutions and private collections. While they do not present an exhaustive history, they offer a more nuanced view and expanded narrative of artists in exile.

The origin of the word *exile*, and its literal meaning, lies in the idea of banishment.[4] The person expelled from his or her city, region, or country of birth was supposedly sentenced to a life of misery and loneliness, cut off from his or her own culture and society. In contrast, the notion of exile as a triggering force for creativity emerged only later. One of the most famous exiles in the literary and visual arts, Dante Alighieri, who was banished from Florence in 1302 for his political stance, subsequently made exile an inherent component of his intellectual and poetic oeuvre. Dante notably wrote his masterpiece, the epic poem *Divina commedia* (Divine Comedy), during his exile, relating his imaginary journey through hell, purgatory, and paradise. His life and exile appealed to many Romantics across Europe, and with the revival of Dante's popularity in the nineteenth century, the poet became a widespread motif in the visual arts (fig. 1).[5] Successively, exiled artists began to subvert the negative implications of banishment and instead consciously embrace it for personal or political gain. This shift also echoed aesthetically throughout their work, as suggested by Ewa Lajer-Burcharth in her essay on portraits that Jacques-Louis David painted during his exile in Brussels; she raised the possibility of exile as "a historically, politically, and psychologically specific condition of art making."[6]

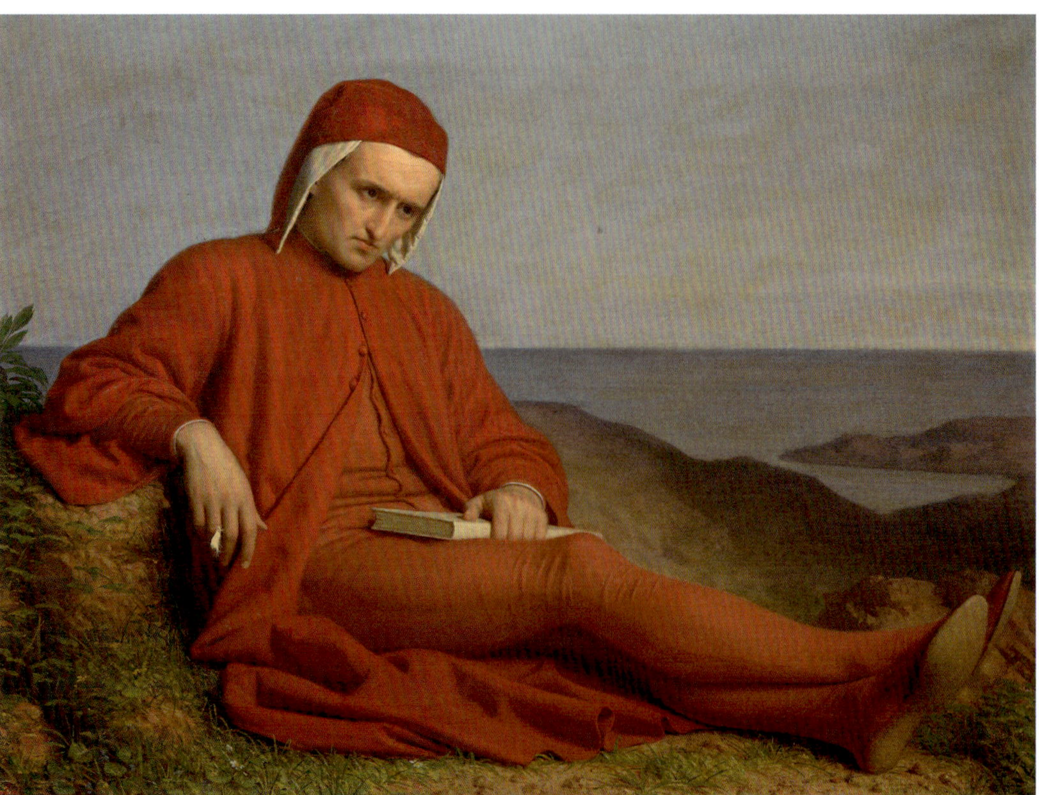

Fig. 1. Attributed to Domenico Peterlini, *Dante in esilio*, ca. 1860. Oil on canvas, 29 9/16 × 38 in. (75 × 96.5 cm). Galleria d'Arte Moderna, Florence

The present exhibition and catalogue thus take as their starting point the nineteenth century, with the radical political and social upheavals—including wars, revolutions, and colonization—that sparked many forced departures, such as those of David and Gustave Courbet from France (cats. 10–12). In the later decades of the century, amid rapid industrialization and changes to the urban structures of cities like Berlin, London, New York, and Paris, artists were lured by the idea of life outside of artistic centers, in close contact with nature; this was the case for Paul Gauguin, for instance, who sought a supposedly unspoiled culture in the South Pacific (cat. 1). Still others were expelled because they held political beliefs at odds with their home governments, and their banishment became tainted with an almost idealized aura; indeed, several celebrated artists and intellectuals of the nineteenth century not only accepted the status of exile but even found that it contributed to their reputation and success. The writers Heinrich Heine, Aleksandr Herzen, Victor Hugo, and Germaine de Staël, to name a few, were all opposed to the governments in place in their respective countries and subsequently faced exile, which ultimately only bolstered their renown.[7] Interestingly, de Staël, the famous French *femme de lettres* who went into exile because of her opposition to Napoléon, was painted in Switzerland by another famous exile, Élisabeth Louise Vigée Le Brun, who had been the primary portraitist of Marie-Antoinette and fled France during the French Revolution (fig. 2). Far away from home, many artists

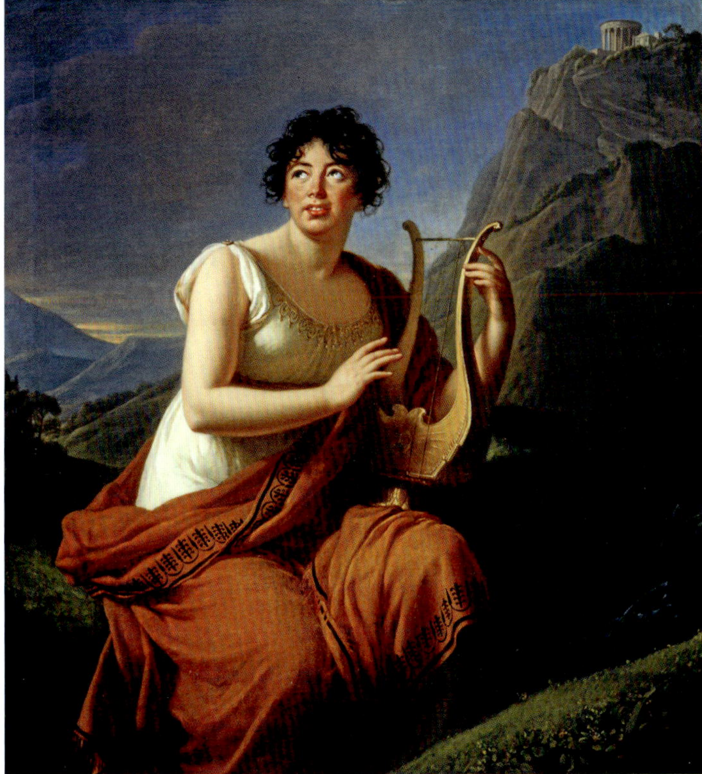

Fig. 2. Élisabeth Louise Vigée Le Brun, *Portrait of Madame de Staël as Corinne*, 1809. Oil on canvas, 55⅛ × 46⁷⁄₁₆ in. (140 × 118 cm). Musée d'Art et d'Histoire, Geneva, Gift of Mme Necker-de Saussure, 1841

searched for proximity to fellow exiles, united by their resistance to the governments that had forced them to leave. Exile was no longer just a punishment that one had to endure—it could be used to forge new alliances.

The dawn of the twentieth century saw pogroms in the Russian Empire; the horrors of World War I, with millions of people killed and displaced; and the Russian Revolution, which caused waves of émigrés to come to Europe and the United States. Only a few decades later, with the rise of totalitarian regimes in Germany, Italy, Russia, and Spain, numerous more departures took place. The year 1933 was particularly momentous, as it marked not only Adolf Hitler's seizure of power but also the beginning of emigration and flight from Germany for citizens who realized early on the danger of the Nazi agenda. Emigration continued in the following years, although many artists remained in Germany in hopes of seeing the fascist regime vanish as quickly as it had risen to power. However, the government swiftly started to target and humiliate modern and communist artists, especially those associated with movements such as Expressionism, Dada, and Cubism. This persecution culminated in the removal of many artists' work from public collections and their inclusion in the infamous *Entartete Kunst* (Degenerate Art) exhibition in 1937, a propaganda show that presented—in an intentionally derogatory and demeaning way—modern artworks that, because of their abstract character or subject matter, were considered "un-German" by the government (see cat. 2, fig. 2).[8] By this point, hope had vanished for a return to a humane and tolerant society, and many artists, such as Max Beckmann (cat. 25) and Lyonel Feininger (cat. 15), sought refuge abroad.[9]

These events caused the number of immigrants and exiles coming to the United States to soar during the first half of the twentieth century. Among this group were numerous artists—such as Anni and Josef Albers (see Luke, "The Trace of Transfer"), George Grosz (cat. 24), and Hans Hofmann (cat. 20)—who then taught in America and influenced younger generations for decades.[10] These years also marked a turning point when exile developed into an intrinsic part of modern art. Despite its implication of loss and abandonment, exile has been described in historical writings of the postwar period as an essential factor of renewal and a generator of modern culture, especially in the United States.[11] The waves of painters, sculptors, architects, filmmakers, intellectuals, and writers who arrived in the 1930s and 1940s—among them Hannah Arendt, André Breton, Marc Chagall, Albert Einstein, Fritz Lang, Thomas Mann, Jean Renoir, and Marguerite Yourcenar—shaped American culture in an unprecedented way and seemingly made the center of the art world shift to New York.[12] The Museum of Modern Art and its founding director, Alfred H. Barr, Jr., played a crucial role in introducing European Modernism to America during this time. In conjunction with the Emergency Rescue Committee, a private agency, and its agent Varian Fry, Barr and his wife, Margaret Scolari Barr, helped many artists—including Breton, Chagall, Max Ernst, Wifredo Lam, and André Masson—escape German-occupied France, and Barr continued to support them by acquiring their work for his museum.[13] Immigrants also contributed to the birth of Abstract Expressionism, namely Hofmann, Arshile Gorky (cat. 14), and Jack Tworkov. However, while abstraction became the leading art form, other artists exiled in New York persisted in a figurative or allegorical vein, returning to a more "traditional" iconography inspired by classical mythology and the apogees of European culture, such as antiquity and the Renaissance. For example, Salvador Dalí depicted Saint George fighting the dragon (fig. 3), a famous motif in Christian iconography, during his exile in New York; Jacques Lipchitz (fig. 4) and Kurt Seligmann (cat. 22) both took inspiration from Greek mythology.

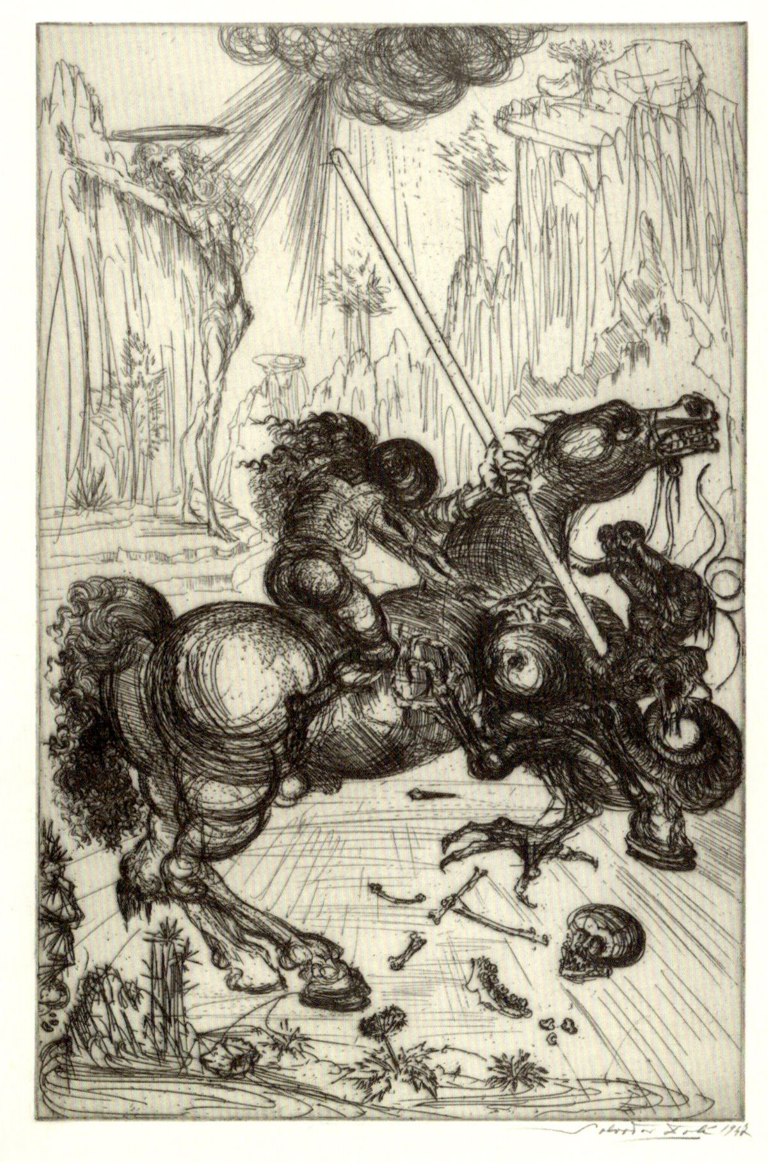

Fig. 3. Salvador Dalí, *Saint George and the Dragon*, 1942. Etching, 17 ⅝ × 11 ¼ in. (44.8 × 28.6 cm). Yale University Art Gallery, New Haven, Conn., Gift of Mrs. Paul Moore, 1959.24.17

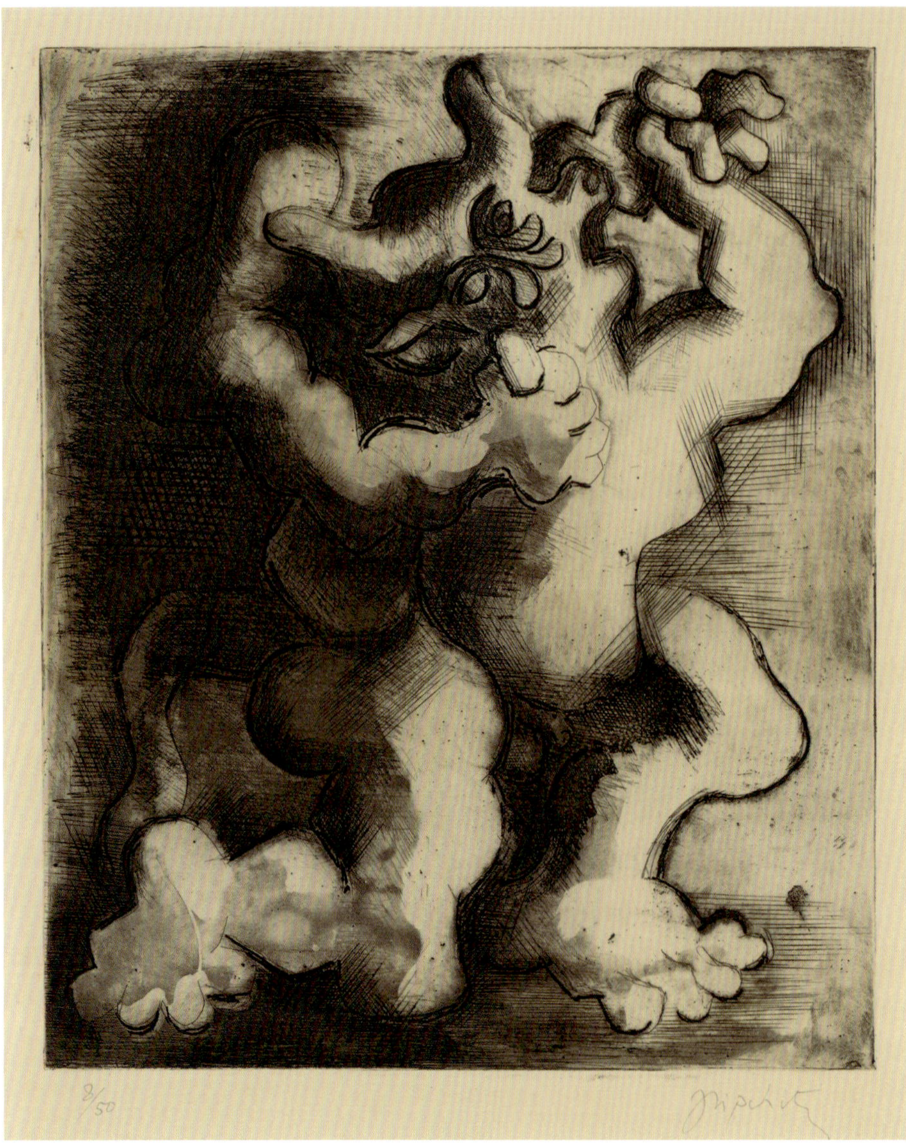

Fig. 4. Jacques Lipchitz, *Theseus and the Minotaur*, ca. 1945. Etching, 13⅞ × 11¼ in. (35.2 × 28.5 cm). Yale University Art Gallery, New Haven, Conn., Everett V. Meeks, B.A. 1901, Fund, 2006.169.2

As Barbara McCloskey remarked in her essay "Cartographies of Exile," World War II marked the cleavage between "modernist" and "post-modernist" exile.[14] The war era and its aftermath witnessed almost a normalization of exile, with millions of people all over the globe forced to seek safer havens. While the Modernist, midcentury iteration of exile comprised departures triggered by national, ethnic, or religious reasons, the Postmodernist counterpart conflates exile with migration and has become part of the human experience in a world where the ideas of nation and home tend to dissolve.[15] Since the end of the twentieth century and the start of the twenty-first, the experience of exile has largely been perceived as generative, implying hope. Edward W. Said, for one, outlined "the pleasures" of exile, proposing that it can lead to an entirely new conception of one's surroundings and awareness of a multitude of cultures and homes, thus instilling an expanded vision of the world and increased empathy for others.[16] It is also true that exile is not only a social or political condition but a universal experience that seemingly everyone has faced at some point—albeit most often on a personal scale—either physically, spiritually, or emotionally.[17] Mona Hatoum is one contemporary artist who captures the movement of people beyond ethnic and political borders, in works like *Routes II* (fig. 5). Others have been drawn to consider and reconsider the notion of home, such as Do Ho Suh (fig. 6), who has lived in New York, London, and Seoul and worked across the globe. Similarly, the term *exile* itself has evolved, with various words now used to designate someone leaving his or her country for different reasons: refugees, émigrés, immigrants, expatriates. These various appellations raise new questions—about the differences between types of exile, whether there is a perceived hierarchy among them, and who decides on these designations. Regardless, more and more artists refuse to be reduced to the label of *exile* and instead see themselves as citizens of the world.

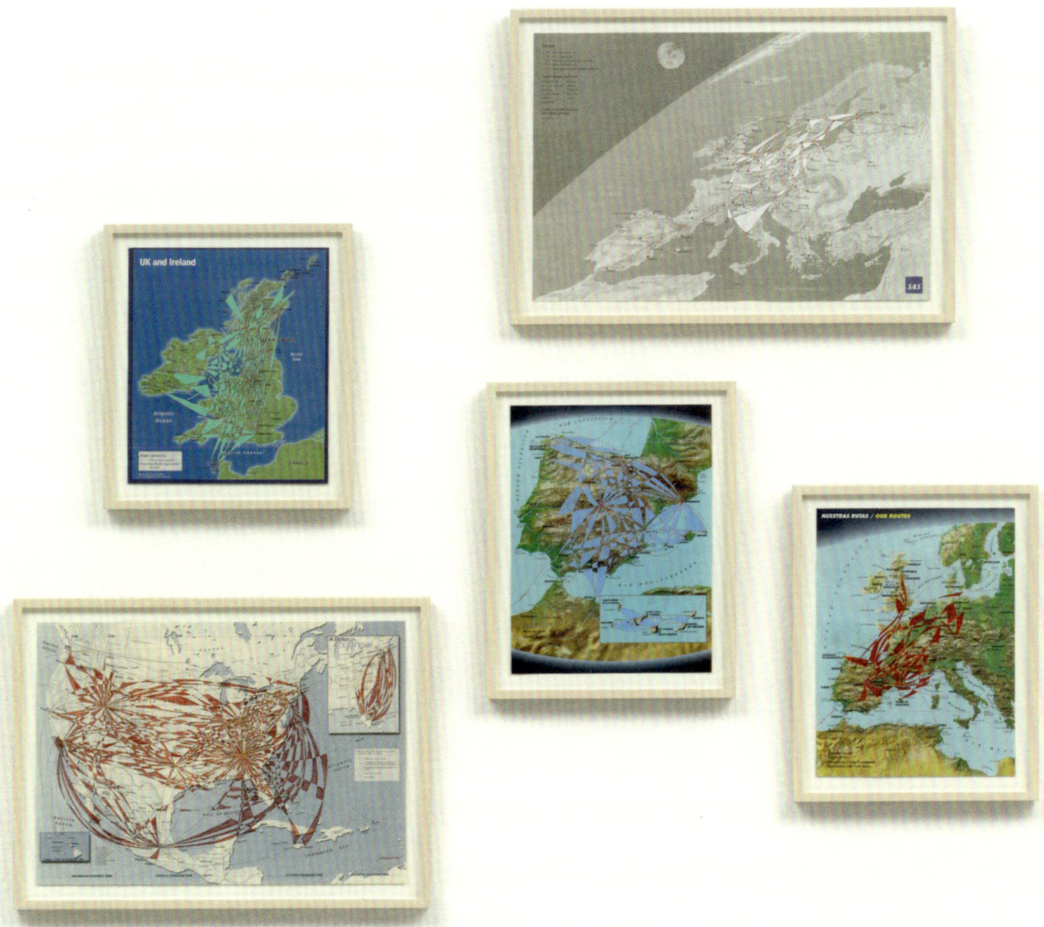

Fig. 5. Mona Hatoum, *Routes II*, 2002. Pen and ink on five printed maps, overall 35½ × 42 in. (90.2 × 106.7 cm). Museum of Modern Art, New York, The Judith Rothschild Foundation Contemporary Drawings Collection Gift, 1832.2005.a–e

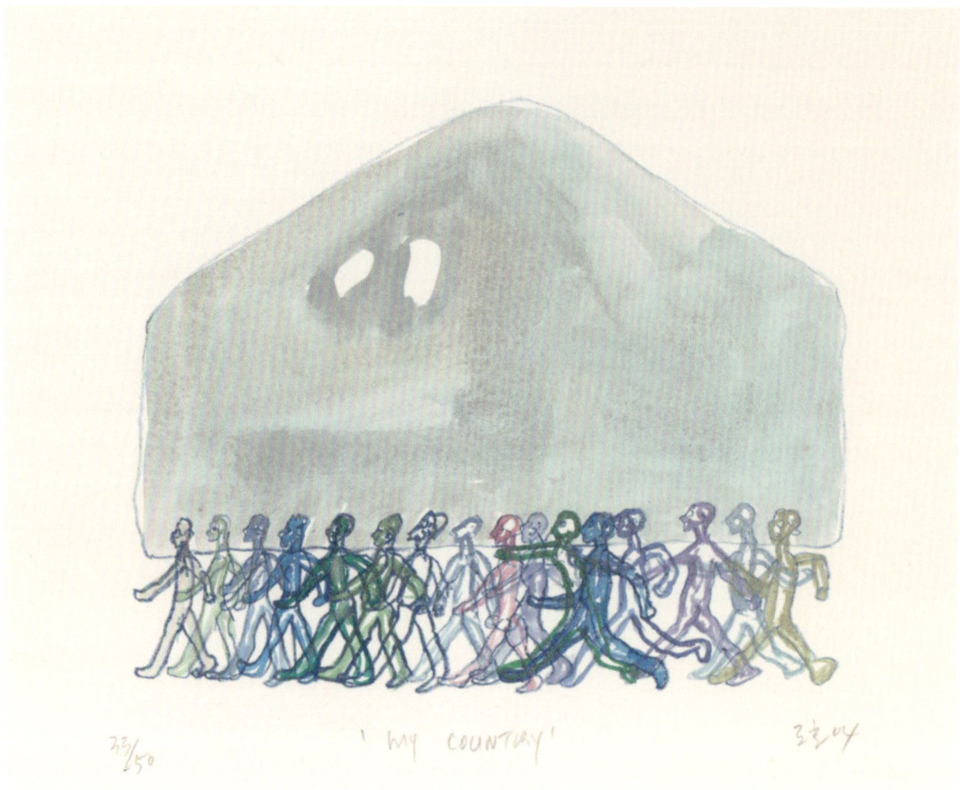

Fig. 6. Do Ho Suh, *My Country*, 2004. Lithograph with hand additions in watercolor, 6 ¹¹⁄₁₆ × 7 ¹⁵⁄₁₆ in. (17 × 20.2 cm). Yale University Art Gallery, New Haven, Conn., Gift of Bruce Christopher Carr, 2009.131.5

Tracing New Narratives of Exile

As mentioned previously, exhibitions and publications have often focused on the Eurocentric, mid-twentieth-century perspective of exile—and rightly so, as World War II had an unprecedented impact on the art world.[18] A picture taken at the opening of the *Artists in Exile* exhibition in 1942 at Pierre Matisse Gallery in New York (fig. 7) represents the emblematic face of (mostly) European exiled artists, an image that dominated in subsequent decades.[19] Yet as this photograph shows, the narrative of exiled European Modernists was itself often limited to the majority male face. It somehow minimized the presence of the numerous female artists—the photographer Lotte Jacobi (cat. 17) and the painter Hedda Sterne (fig. 8), for example—who fled Nazi-occupied countries during the war and brought new artistic approaches with them.[20]

For female artists, exile, in certain cases, was and is a chance to create an artistic identity by breaking free from religious or social boundaries.[21] In the nineteenth century, some female artists chose to leave their native countries and move abroad, more specifically to Paris, where the art world was more liberal; although women were not allowed to attend the official art academy in the city, the École des Beaux-Arts, they could take classes at private academies and sketch at the Musée du Louvre.[22] In the twentieth century and even today, some female artists still seek more freedom abroad. Art historian Linda Nochlin pointed

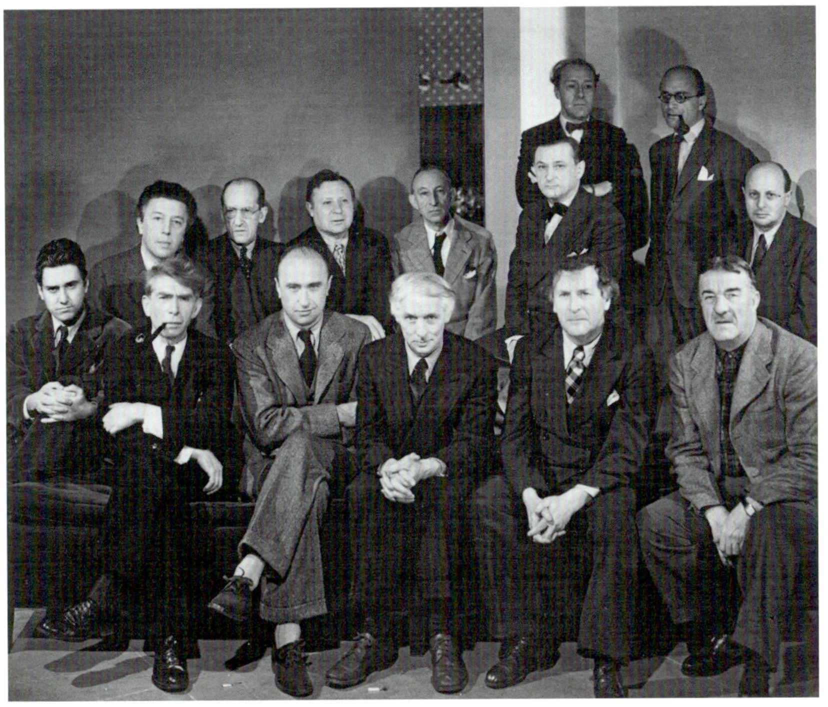

Fig. 7. George Platt Lynes, group photograph for the announcement of the *Artists in Exile* exhibition at Pierre Matisse Gallery, New York, 1942

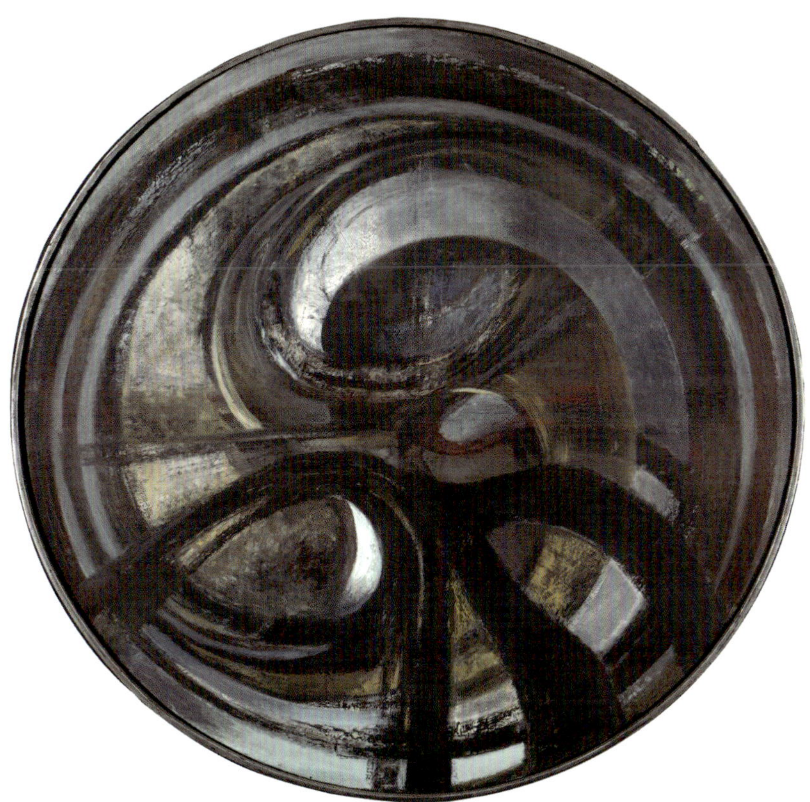

Fig. 8. Hedda Sterne, *Tondo*, ca. 1953. Oil on canvas, DIAM. 30⅜ in. (77 cm). Yale University Art Gallery, New Haven, Conn., Gift of Susan Morse Hilles, 1984.75.7

out that for the Spanish-born artist Remedios Varo, who fled from France to Mexico during World War II, the exile experience fostered the artist's independence and helped her develop a deeply psychological and spiritual body of work (fig. 9).[23] Indeed, the Mexican Revolution of 1910–20 allowed women to take a more active part in the cultural life of the country through teaching and commissions. Immigrant artists such as Varo and the British-born painter Leonora Carrington, who sought refuge in Mexico as well, quickly established new relationships with local artists affiliated with Surrealism, like Frida Kahlo, and showed their work in exhibitions.[24]

Other events in the aftermath of World War II led to the exile of countless artists outside the predominant white and Western sphere. For instance, during the postwar period, the Cold War and the McCarthy era were marked by the increasing nationalism of American society and growing discrimination. This led many African American and leftist artists to leave the United States in search of a tolerant home abroad—Elizabeth Catlett (cat. 26), for example, settled in Mexico, and Harold Cousins (cat. 4) and Beauford Delaney both found a new home in France.[25] At the same time, communist and socialist regimes in China, Cuba, the German Democratic Republic, the Soviet Union, and Vietnam prompted the departures of many others—such as An-My Lê (cat. 8), Ana Mendieta (cat. 5), Abelardo Morell (cat. 7), and Mu Xin (cat. 28)—as did revolutions, dictatorships, and the Arab-Israeli conflict in the Middle

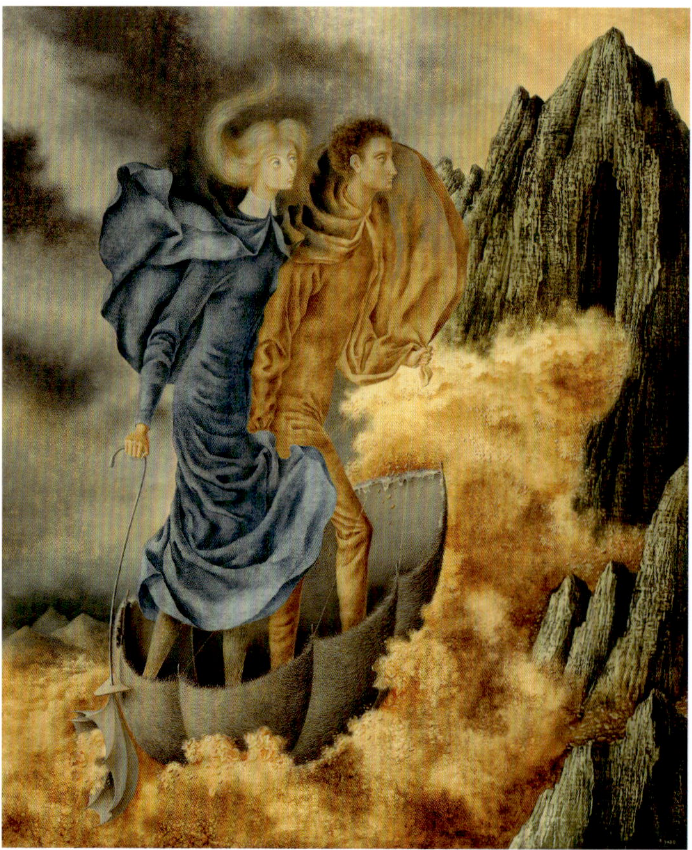

Fig. 9. Remedios Varo, *La huida* (The Escape), 1961. Oil on Masonite, 48⁷⁄₁₆ × 38⁵⁄₈ in. (123 × 98 cm). Museo de Arte Moderno, Mexico City, Collection Isabel Gruen Varsoviano, In Memoriam, Gift of Walter and Anna Alexandra Gruen

East, as illustrated by the exiles of Shirin Neshat (cat. 29), Mona Hatoum (cat. 9), and Ahmed Alsoudani (cat. 30). These histories have often been overlooked in traditional narratives of exile, and the Eurocentric, World War II–focused study is still the one that prevails. Truly, with war, genocide, and terrorism that still today cause waves of refugees and exiles, the paradigm of exile studies in the visual arts requires a new, more global approach.

This exhibition and catalogue examine works by exiled artists from cultures and continents across the globe, spanning 1816 to the present day and a variety of media. The four sections of the publication reflect this multidisciplinary, transcultural, and hybrid approach by focusing on universal themes—home and mobility, nostalgia, transfer and adjustment, and identity— that permeate the artworks and lives of the artists selected. These themes allow us to approach exile not from a unilateral viewpoint but from perspectives that speak instead to general human experiences and conditions.

The essays that follow, one in each section, foreground the different aspects of exile, considering art historical, literary, and personal angles to propose a broader reflection on how exile shaped artists' work. Joseph Leo Koerner, in his essay "Home and the World," examines the migration of artists and artworks throughout history, from antiquity until the twentieth century. He not only demonstrates the impact and importance of leaving one's territorial boundaries but also challenges the contemporary understanding of exile and unravels its many dimensions. In "Russia in Exile: Nostalgia for Other Shores," Marijeta Bozovic reconsiders the politics and aesthetics of exile in Russia, still so strongly colored by the intellectual legacies of the Cold War. She reminds readers that in the nineteenth century, Russian exiles embraced—and inspired—very different politics than émigrés fleeing the Soviet Union, and she suggests that contemporary artistic practice and political thought have much to learn from these predecessors. Megan R. Luke, in her essay "The Trace of Transfer," contemplates how the exile experience of Bauhaus teacher Josef Albers shaped his art and pedagogy in the United States, and led him to challenge ideas of origin, perception, and affiliation to convey a deeper understanding of material and color. In "(Re)Defining the 'I' in Exile," this author considers how one searches for identity through materials and iconography, while being cut off from inherent cultural and social identifiers, by addressing issues of alienation and adaptation to new cultures through the lens of specific exiles from the nineteenth century to today.

Artists in Exile: Expressions of Loss and Hope challenges some of the usual accepted ideas about exile and proposes a reexamination of it through the visual arts. By juxtaposing artists from different continents, countries, and time periods, this catalogue portrays exile as a collective experience that pervades art history and has left its mark on centuries of artists and their work. The objects discussed prompt questions about how exile is defined, and by whom; where it begins and where it ends; and its visual or material imprint on an artwork. Searching for common factors among such a diversity of works yields a reflection of a shared social and cultural history and, at the same time, reveals individual stories of loss and hope.

1. Edward W. Said, *Reflections on Exile and Other Essays* (Cambridge, Mass.: Harvard University Press, 2000), 186.

2. See most notably the following essential studies on European artists in exile: Barbara Stehlé-Akhtar, Stephan Lackner, and Reinhard Spieler, *Max Beckmann in Exile*, exh. cat. (New York: Guggenheim Museum SoHo, 1996); Stephanie Barron, ed., *Exiles and Emigrés: The Flight of European Artists from Hitler*, exh. cat. (Los Angeles: Los Angeles County Museum of Art, 1997); Shulamith Behr and Marian Malet, eds., *Arts in Exile in Britain, 1933–1945: Politics and Cultural Identity* (Amsterdam: Rodopi, 2005); Maurice Fréchuret and Laurence Bertrand Dorléac, eds., *Exils: Réminiscences et nouveaux mondes*, exh. cat. (Paris: Réunion des musées nationaux, 2012); and Susan Tumarkin Goodman, *Chagall: Love, War, and Exile* (New Haven, Conn.: Yale University Press, 2013).

3. Linda Nochlin, "Art and the Conditions of Exile: Men/Women, Emigration/ Expatriation," *Poetics Today* 17, no. 3 (Fall 1996): 317–37; Ursula Hudson-Wiedenmann and Beate Schmeichel-Falkenberg, eds., *Grenzen überschreiten: Frauen, Kunst und Exil* (Würzburg, Germany: Königshausen und Neumann, 2005); Kobena Mercer, ed., *Exiles, Diasporas, and Strangers* (Cambridge, Mass.: MIT Press, 2008); James Harithas and Alan Schnitger, eds., *Iraqi Artists in Exile*, exh. cat. (Houston: Station Museum of Contemporary Art, 2010); and Uwe Fleckner, Maike Steinkamp, and Hendrik Ziegler, eds., *Der Künstler im Exil: Migration—Reise—Exil* (Berlin: De Gruyter, 2015).

4. The term *exile* comes from the French word *exil*, a Latinized version of the earlier Middle French word *essil*, meaning "banishment." Its origins lie in the Latin word *exilium*, which in turn comes from *exul*, meaning "banished person." Exile is defined as "expulsion from one's own country to live abroad, imposed as a sentence or punishment; penal banishment; residence abroad enforced by law or political power." In another sense, it denotes "prolonged residence in a foreign country, either voluntary or imposed by circumstances; expatriation." See *The Shorter Oxford English Dictionary on Historical Principles*, 5th ed. (New York: Oxford University Press, 2002), s.v. "exile"; and *Oxford English Dictionary*, s.v. "exile," accessed October 24, 2016, http:// www.oed.com/view/Entry/66231.

5. Antonella Braida and Luisa Calè, eds., "Introduction," in *Dante on View: The Reception of Dante in the Visual and Performing Arts* (Hampshire, England: Ashgate, 2007), 9–11.

6. Ewa Lajer-Burcharth, "The Self in Exile: David's Portrait of Sieyès," in *David after David: Essays on the Later Work*, ed. Mark Ledbury, conference proceedings (New Haven, Conn.: Yale University Press, 2007), 232–51, esp. 233–34.

7. Heine (1797–1856) was a German poet, critic, and journalist whose works were censored by the German government; Herzen (1812–1870) was a Russian writer who went into exile for his socialist beliefs; Hugo (1802–1885), the French poet and novelist, was opposed to Napoléon III; and de Staël (1766–1817) was a French author who went into exile for her criticism of Napoléon I.

8. The *Entartete Kunst* exhibition opened in July 1937 in Munich at the Hofgarten-Arkaden, with 650 artworks confiscated from 32 museums. It then traveled to other cities in Germany, notably Berlin, as well as to Austria. Many of the exhibited works were later sold abroad, were destroyed, or disappeared.

9. Stephanie Barron, "1937: Modern Art and Politics in Prewar Germany," in *"Degenerate Art": The Fate of the Avant-Garde in Nazi Germany*, ed. Stephanie Barron, exh. cat. (Los Angeles: Los Angeles County Museum of Art, 1991), 9–23.

10. Cynthia Jaffee McCabe, *The Golden Door: Artist-Immigrants of America, 1876–1976* (Washington, D.C.: Hirshhorn Museum and Sculpture Garden, 1976), 22–44.

11. This idea is critically discussed in Sabine Eckmann, "Considering (and Reconsidering) Art and Exile," in Barron, *Exiles and Emigrés*, 30–39, esp. 34.

12. For an in-depth analysis of exiles in music and the performing arts, see Joseph Horowitz, *Artists in Exile: How Refugees from Twentieth-Century War and Revolution Transformed the American Performing Arts* (New York: HarperCollins, 2008); see also Eckmann, "Considering (and Reconsidering) Art and Exile," 35, 39n32.

13. Elizabeth Kessin Berman, "Moral Triage or Cultural Salvage? The Agendas of Varian Fry and the Emergency Rescue Committee," in Barron, *Exiles and Emigrés*, 99–112.

14. Barbara McCloskey, "Cartographies of Exile," in *Exile and Otherness: New Approaches to the Experience of the Nazi Refugees*, ed. Alexander Stephan (New York: Peter Lang, 2005), 135–52, esp. 136–37.

15. Ibid.

16. Said, *Reflections on Exile and Other Essays*, 186.

17. Eva Hoffman, "The New Nomads," in *Letters of Transit: Reflections on Exile, Identity, Language, and Loss*, ed. André Aciman (New York: The New Press, in collaboration with the New York Public Library, 1999), 35–63, esp. 39.

18. Stephanie Barron, "European Artists in Exile: A Reading Between the Lines," in Barron, *Exiles and Emigrés*, 11–29, esp. 11–12.

19. Pierre Matisse Gallery, with essays by James Thrall Soby and Nicolas Calas, *Artists in Exile*, exh. brochure (New York: Pierre Matisse Gallery, 1942).

20. In 1950 Sterne—along with other prominent Abstract Expressionists and avant-garde artists, dubbed "The Irascibles"—signed a notorious open letter to the director of the Metropolitan Museum of Art protesting the conservative juries for group exhibitions. Some of these artists were gathered by *Life* magazine for a group portrait, taken by Nina Leen and published in 1951, in which Sterne was the only female artist pictured.

21. Nochlin, "Art and the Conditions of Exile," 317–37, esp. 318–19.

22. Frauke Josenhans and Nina Struckmeyer, "Les cercles des artistes allemands à Paris autour de 1800," in *Artistes, savants et amaturs: Art et sociabilité au XVIIIe siècle (1715–1815)*, ed. Jessica L. Fripp et al. (Paris: Mare et Martin, 2016), 87–100, esp. 93.

23. Nochlin, "Art and the Conditions of Exile," 319–320.

24. Tere Arcq, "In the Land of Convulsive Beauty: Mexico," in *In Wonderland: The Surrealist Adventures of Women Artists in Mexico and the United States*, ed. Ilene Susan Fort and Tere Arcq, exh. cat. (Los Angeles: Los Angeles County Museum of Art, 2012), 64–87, esp. 64–68.

25. See, for instance, Audreen Buffalo, ed., *Explorations in the City of Light: African-American Artists in Paris, 1945–1965*, exh. cat. (New York: Studio Museum in Harlem, 1996).

Home/
Mobility

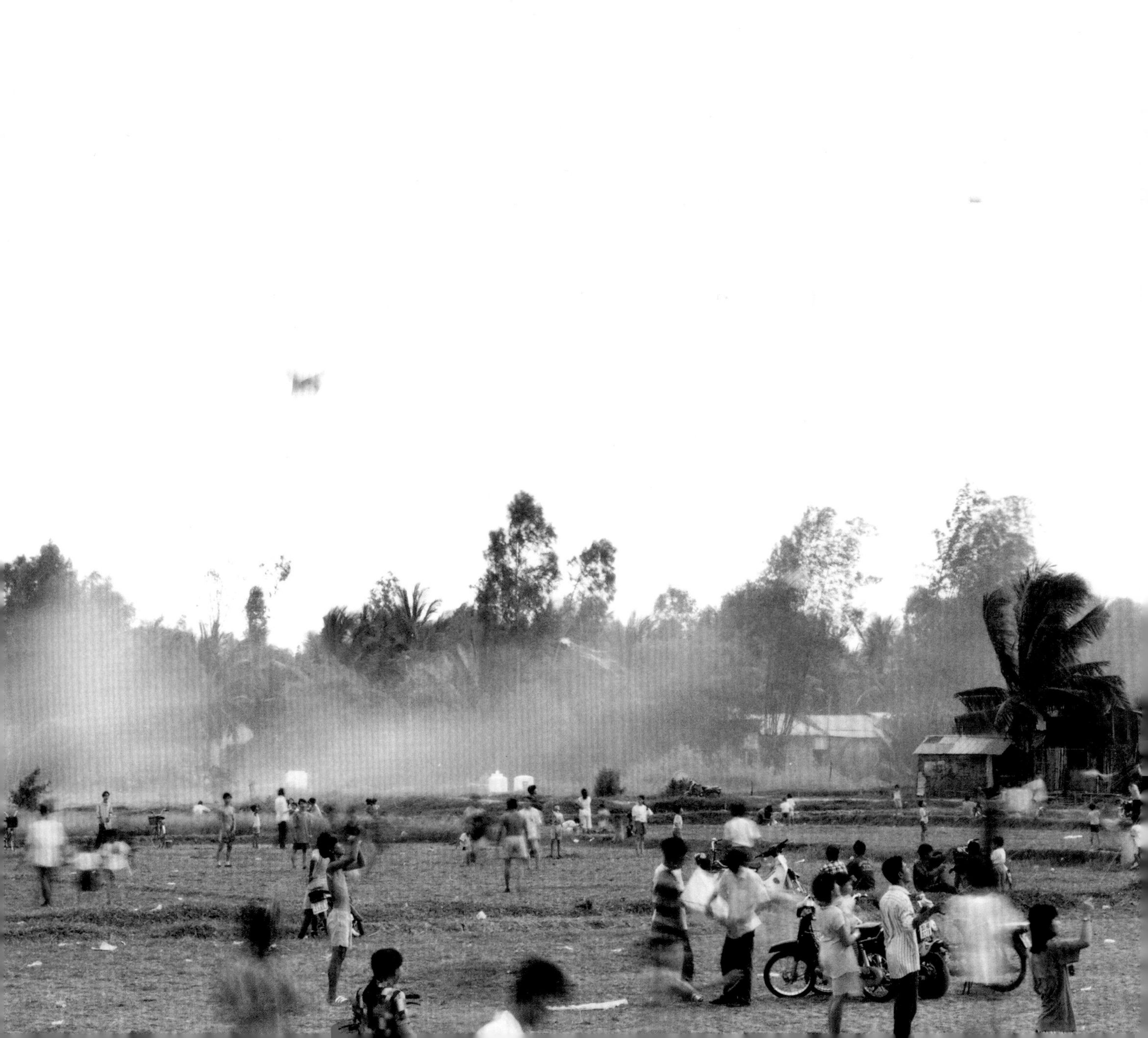

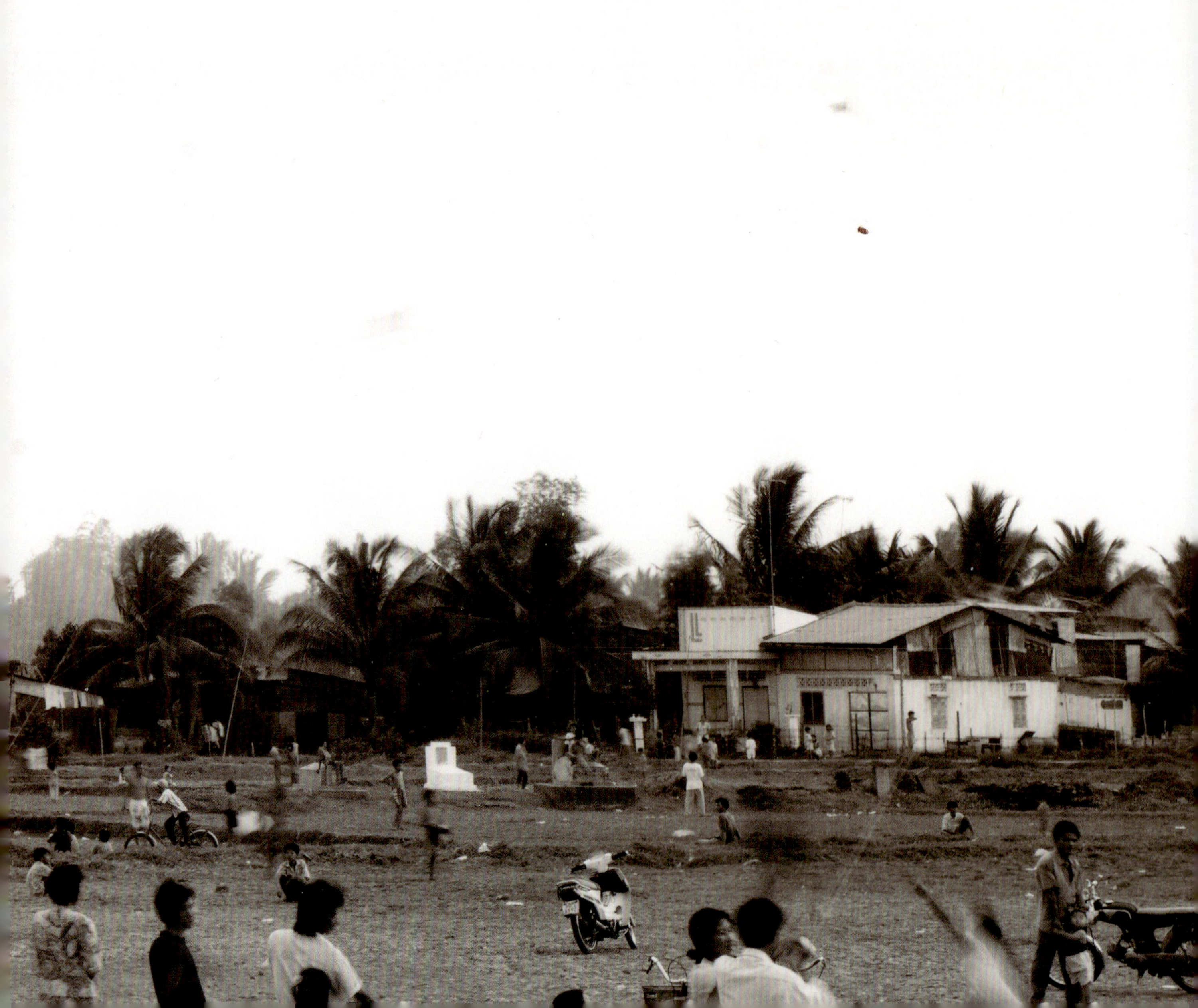

HOME AND THE WORLD

Joseph Leo Koerner

The painting *My Parents I* (fig. 1) always hung above my bed in Pittsburgh, where I was born and raised.[1] Dark and heavily framed, it depicted my father's childhood home in Vienna, with his father asleep and his mother knitting lace. My father, Henry Koerner, painted it all from memory in 1944, far away from Vienna. Thanks to this painting, I could time travel to a lost interior, but what fascinated me most was how the image looked forward to me. Through the window behind my sleeping grandfather, at the end of the narrow street shown plunging into depth, I could glimpse the windows to another, more familiar apartment: the one where my father brought our family to spend summers in Vienna. Our top-floor flat overlooked the Volkertplatz, a run-down market square in the city's Leopoldstadt district. In *My Parents I*, the Volkertplatz, with its single chestnut tree rising from its northeastern corner, becomes the vanishing point of the window's view.

In German, a perspectival vanishing point is called the *Fluchtpunkt*, literally the point of flight or escape. If I stood on my pillow and looked at the painting up close, I could imaginatively escape from my bedroom in Pittsburgh to Vienna via my father's former home. In summer, while we were living in our apartment in Vienna from May through September, the situation was different. The Volkertplatz's chestnut tree—now leafy—still stood where it had decades before, as did all the buildings faithfully recorded in the painting's window view. However, my father's childhood home down the street, the one depicted in the painting, was long gone. Indeed, the whole building at Am Tabor 13 burned down in April 1945, when the Russians took the city. According to city records, the apartment block was destroyed by a bomb, although local lore had it that its part-owner, a fervent Nazi who lived right next door to my father, behind the glass-fronted bookshelves shown on the left side of the painting, had torched it so that no one could claim it after Germany's defeat. Looking out our window back to Am Tabor, I therefore saw just a surrogate. On the empty lot, Vienna's municipal housing authority erected, in the early sixties, a modern six-story apartment block. Its smooth gray facade seemed to deliberately erase any residual sentiments.

In Vienna, I felt banished not just from the painting's lost interior. I felt in exile from Pittsburgh, where my friends were, and where, as an American with an American mother,

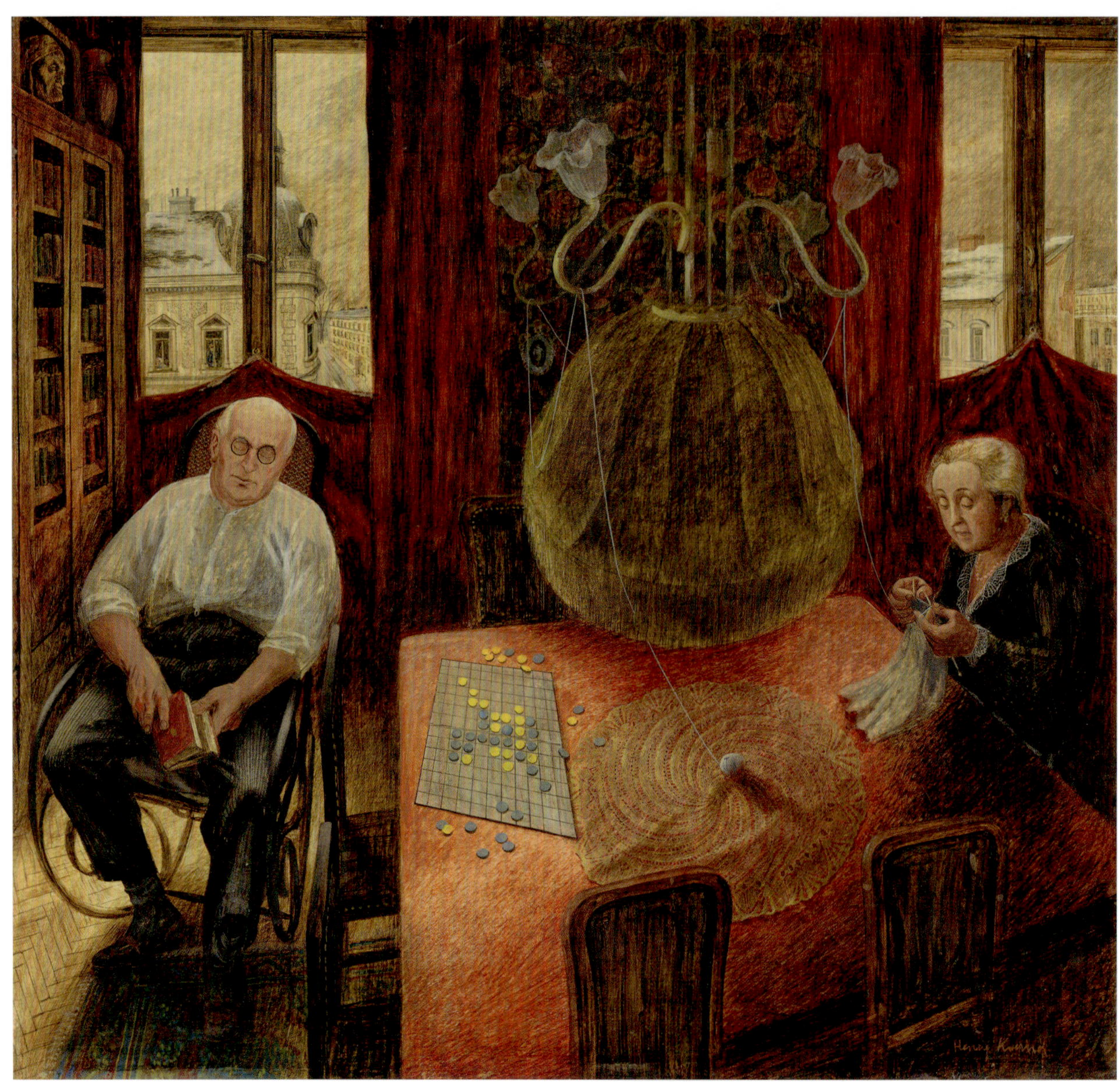

Fig. 1. Henry Koerner, *My Parents I*, 1944. Oil on Masonite, 24½ × 25½ in. (62.2 × 64.8 cm). Private collection

and speaking only English, I felt at home. In our little flat (one common room, a kitchen, and a bathroom shared by neighbors in the hall), I felt out of place and trapped. In the painting, the padded and encased interior felt strange and claustrophobic, too, and I was grateful for the visual escape offered through the windows, for that view showed the enjoyable bit of being in Vienna. We used the flat only for sleeping and spent our waking life almost entirely outside, on exploratory walks through the city and its environs. That was how my father, a professional painter who sold his work on spec, pursued his trade. He was proud to have no studio and painted out-of-doors, always from life, brushstroke by brushstroke, and usually in Vienna. The painting's depicted city view captured—as part for whole—both the Vienna we wandered and the temporal expanse between my father's childhood and mine.

Literature inhabits, primordially, a state of exile. The *Iliad* and especially the *Odyssey* find their heroes far from home. After Odysseus and the other Greeks sack Troy, they try to return to their lands in circuitous and ill-fated adventures. These tales were called *nostoi* in Greek: "returns home." From this word we get our evocative term for homesickness, *nostalgia*. Jewish scripture is a story of exile and homecoming, too. It pivots around the movement of a chosen people out of slavery in Egypt to a promised land—this is the exodus Jews are commanded ritually to remember. The psalms and prophets hinge on a second trauma of exile, when Jews were expelled to Babylon. There they were captives, singing their songs in a strange land: "By the rivers of Babylon, there we sat down and wept, when we remembered Zion" (Psalms 137:1). Behind these displacements, extending them to all peoples, lies Adam and Eve's expulsion from Eden. For Christians, exile described the human condition after the Fall. Either we wander as aliens through a corrupted world or, seduced by its pleasures, we take pleasure in the world, in which case we are damned.[2] The pursuit of life, in this view, is at best a brief, painful pilgrimage from this existence to another.

Exile is not merely a theme of literature. In a sense, it is literature's condition, founded as stories are on the wandering, temporal matrix of plot. Beginning not in the beginning but in the midst of things, and proceeding backward and homeward by way of artfully delaying adventures, the *nostos* models the nomadic space of all narratives. Music is also exilic, especially in its Western forms. It journeys from a tonal center (the "tonic" in the diatonic scale) through permutations (to the dominant, subdominant, and so forth) to a resolution back home in the tonic. The visual arts are different. Grounded in space, not time, they establish place and therefore intensify belonging. Before the era of mechanical reproduction when printing could disseminate copies of them everywhere, crafted images were rooted in one spot. Even if a statue, mural, or altarpiece was created elsewhere, even if its maker was foreign and what it depicted was exotic, distant, or otherwise unavailable, the object itself, the singular thing of wood or stone, nevertheless stood fixed in place. In the temple, church, or market square, or even in the hearth and home, the image both furnished and marked its locality, making it seem more spatially specific, and therefore more homelike. For me, my father's painting belonged more to the fabric of my childhood bedroom in Pittsburgh where it hung than to the home and city it depicted.

The Makapansgat Pebble (fig. 2) is arguably the earliest image and perhaps the oldest surviving human symbol. A small, reddish-brown cobble, it features chipping and wear patterns that look like a portrait of a human face. Not a manufactured artifact (research has proven this), the cobble was evidently somehow transported from some faraway place to the cave where it was found, most probably—it is argued—by one of our distant troglodyte ancestors, *Australopithecus africanus*, who brought it home some three million years ago, perhaps because of its (to already therefore *human* eyes) fascinating, facelike appearance. This originary image, which hardly counts as an image, might also be the oldest extant manuport—the first object moved by deliberate human agency from one locality to another.

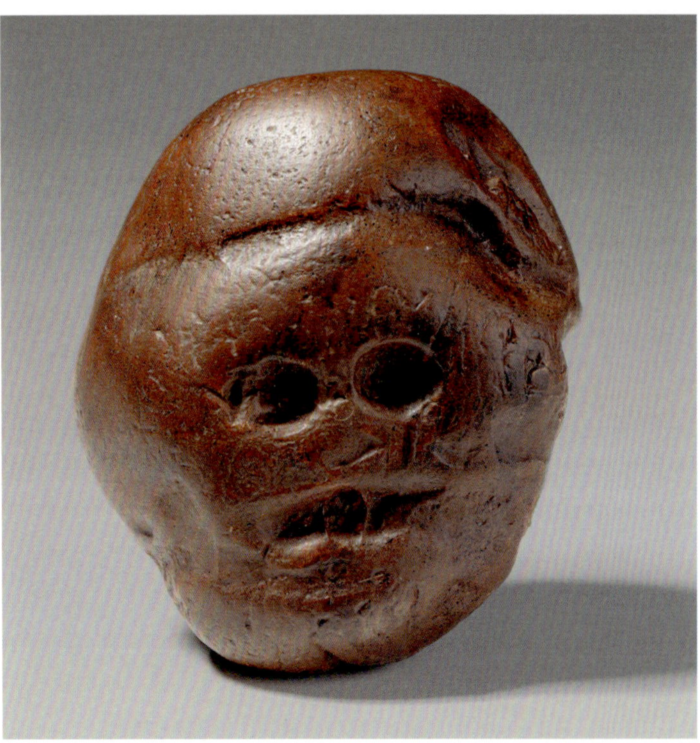

Fig. 2. *Makapansgat Pebble*, South Africa, ca. 3 million B.C.E. Reddish-brown jasperite, DIAM. 2⅜ in. (6 cm). University of Witwatersrand, Johannesburg

The mythic origins of painting lie in displacement. The first-century A.D. Roman author Pliny the Elder, in his *Natural History*, traced one beginning of this art to a girl in Corinth, who, before her love left on a long journey, traced on a wall the fleeting outline of his shadow. Though founded on movement and absence, shadow drawing keeps in place what it represents. Upon my mother's death, I inherited the painting *My Parents I*. Shipped from Pittsburgh to Cambridge, Massachusetts, it now hangs in my home, connecting me to my childhood and to my father's childhood, making its surroundings that much more homelike. Rugs and weavings, like the ones depicted in the painting, performed this function for nomadic cultures. Rolled up, they are robust and portable; rolled out, they turn any locality into a familiar habitat—or at least that is a story we tell about rugs. Sigmund Freud covered his famous couch with Persian carpets and backed it with another weaving (fig. 3), partly to make patients feel cocooned in the therapeutic setting, partly to allow them inwardly to wander via the free association demanded of the talking cure and, via the free-flowing ornaments and arabesques of the couch's coverings and surrounds, back to strange, abandoned corners of their psychic interior, which (according to psychoanalysis) consists largely of memories of one's childhood home. The craze for Oriental rugs began in Vienna in 1873, through the great World's Fair of that year that turned the city into a showcase of exotic cultures, especially the Eastern ones that the Danube city felt it faced. By 1900, when Freud gave shape to the interior of his home and offices, Oriental rugs had become signs of domestic belonging. They turned the treatment room, which in earlier medical practice would have been a cold examination room, into a curious mix of the familiar and the strange. These portable weavings enabled Freud briefly to reconstitute his home and office in London, where he died in 1939, in exile from Vienna after Hitler's takeover.

When artworks travel, they can project a sense of distance wherever they arrive. Artists travel, too, sometimes as a fixed or even mandatory stage of their career. In many parts of Europe until the modern era, guilds required artisans to follow their training and apprenticeship with journeyman years, to acquire new skills and to protect local masters from competition from recent trainees. Craft expertise is an embodied form of knowledge acquired by seeing how something is done and by doing it oneself. You cannot

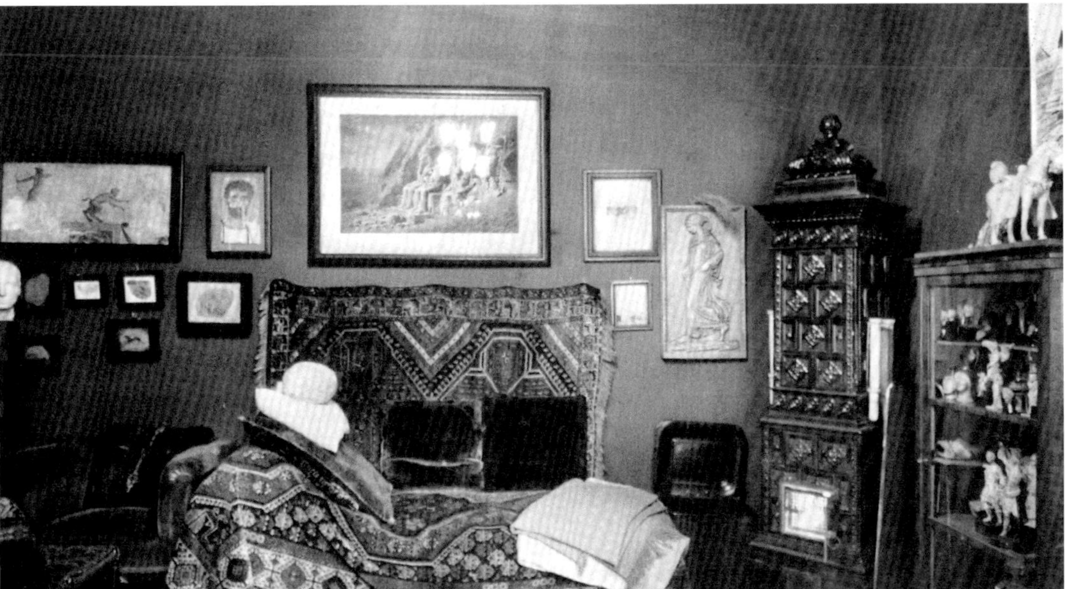

Fig. 3. Edmund Engelman, photograph of Sigmund Freud's consultation room, Vienna, 1938

quite know how a Titian or Rembrandt is made, and certainly you cannot make something like it, simply by looking at the finished work. In the sixteenth century, the painter, biographer, and art theorist Giorgio Vasari established for the future discipline of art history a pronounced localism.[3] He described artists as belonging to distinctive regional schools and celebrated the talents specific to his native Tuscany. But Vasari also preached the virtue of variety. *Varietà* consisted of the plurality of styles in an artist's output. It was acquired through travel, through the encounter with foreign procedures and tasks. Innovation follows from the infusion of new and alien procedures into set ways of doing, which is why today aspiring chefs spend years working in different kitchens throughout the world. To work their magic, artists' processes and materials often become trade secrets, preserved in closed craft enclaves. The glassmakers of Murano, in the Venetian lagoon, were granted privileges, such as immunity from prosecution by the state and the right to bear arms, but were forbidden from leaving the republic for fear they might divulge the tricks of the trade or establish their production elsewhere. To require artists to travel is to wager that they will smuggle foreign craft secrets home, enriching their repertoire and local craft know-how as well.

Albrecht Dürer, for one, owed much of his growth as an artist to travel. When, around 1500, the itinerant Venetian painter and printmaker Jacopo de' Barbari visited Nuremberg, Germany, he showed the young Dürer some idealized nudes he had made. But by Dürer's account, the Italian refused to divulge the secret of their proportions. This sent the German artist to read, or have explained to him, Vitruvius's *De architectura* (a treatise written toward the end of the first century B.C. and rediscovered in 1414 by Poggio Bracciolini) and to track down humanist scholars in Italy who might share more information. Dürer had already crossed the Alps in 1494. Fresh from his journeyman years (or *Wanderjahre*) in Germany, the Netherlands, and Switzerland (1490–94), he became a different artist as a result of this Italian trip. Transformed by contact with Venetian masters and encounters with styles and themes of antiquity, Dürer—through his prints—succeeded in changing Northern art with him. By the later sixteenth century, the stylistic language of European art became an Italianate one. Whereas Dürer's first trip to Italy was somewhat accidental (he probably tagged along with Nuremberg merchants conducting business in Venice, Europe's global trade capital), an Italian journey became standard for Northern artists after him.

This new dependency on foreign models fostered a new, reactive nostalgia for erased vernacular styles. In his paintings of village life, produced mostly in the 1560s, Pieter Bruegel the Elder explored his own local Flemish lifeworld as if it were a foreign country, collecting in his painted imagery peasant customs, games, and wordplay in the manner of an ethnographer. He did this in a deliberately Netherlandish pictorial style, one harking back to Jan van Eyck, Rogier van der Weyden, Hugo van der Goes, and Hieronymus Bosch, and at odds with the Italianizing tendencies of other painters of the region. Bruegel himself became famous as the avatar of the local (hence the epithet "Peasant Bruegel"), but as his first biographer reported in 1604, when during his *Wanderjahre* he first crossed the Alps, it was not Italian art that affected him.[4] Bruegel's style remained—perhaps it even deliberately became—"Northern." What changed him was instead the mountain scenery through which he passed to get to Italy. This he "devoured" with voracious eyes, "disgorging" the Alps onto canvases and panels.[5] Unfamiliar landscapes often change traditions and an artist's way of making because they confound inherited conventions. Italian light changed Northern artists as much as Italian art did. Joseph Mallord William Turner's alpine scenes embodied and enabled the artist's break from the "beautiful" and "picturesque" structures of earlier landscape art (as codified by academic theory); European artists traveling or exiled to Australia were challenged to revise (and sometimes tragically to mourn) their inherited ways of seeing and making in the face of a radically different scenery; and Paul Klee confessed to having become a painter through the color harmonies he experienced in Tunisia.[6]

Artists travel to where they can find work. Engaged in an activity not necessary for basic human survival, they ply their trade where it is wanted and rewarded. The revolutionary master of Northern art, Jan van Eyck, was drawn from his home in the northern Rhineland to the Netherlands, where a new urban economy of trade, commerce, and conspicuous consumption was booming under Burgundian rule. The forefathers of Hieronymus van Aken (alias Bosch) hailed from the German city of Aachen, arriving in the Brabant region about the time of van Eyck's arrival in Bruges. Hans Memling was similarly a German transplant to the Netherlands. Earlier, the great medieval cathedrals were erected by special guilds or corporations, termed "building lodges," which operated in the same town for generations. Drawing on talented makers from elsewhere, and training them in a local idiom, these lodges also enabled the fabulous unity of structure, style, and purpose for which Gothic cathedrals are renowned. Artisans cycling out of one lodge into another brought new ideas and methods, sometimes transforming the tradition. The architect and mason Peter Parler, who designed much of the Prague cathedral, was likely trained in a building lodge of Cologne. He probably arrived in Prague via England, where he would have seen the innovative cathedrals of Wells and Exeter. Prague's cathedral is revolutionary and international as a result, absorbing the know-how of far-flung regions while making eclecticism an aesthetic ideal.

Prague's fourteenth-century flourishing was the result of Emperor Charles IV's residence there. Court culture facilitated internationalism in the arts. Through its wealth and conspicuous consumption, the nobility drew talent to its places of residence while also, through familial alliances across territories, enabling artists easily to move between courts. Born in Cologne to parents from Aachen, trained in Italy, and installed as painter and collection curator at the court of Holy Roman Emperor Rudolf in Prague in the late sixteenth century, Hans von Aachen was an artistic chameleon; whether or not he experienced nostalgia we will never know. He left no writings, and in his period, personal experience was rarely the subject of art. But in the many friendship portraits he made—all likenesses of itinerants, of the artists (such as the Swiss-born painter and architect Josef Heintz, fig. 4), composers, and humanists with whom he became acquainted on his travels—he fashioned a "cosmopolitan" belonging. Sometimes gifting these friendship paintings to their sitters, von Aachen formed an allegiance with a set of outsiders, something that would later become central to artistic self-understanding. We know that Dürer felt more at home in Italy than in Nuremberg. He perceived Venetian culture to be more appreciative of artistic talent. "Here I am a gentleman, at home only a parasite," wrote Dürer from Venice in his last letter to a friend and fellow traveler back in Germany.[7] Soon Protestant iconoclasm would ruin the careers of many Northern artists, sometimes sending them into exile. Returning to iconoclastic Basel, Switzerland, from England, Hans Holbein the Younger, in what may be his most moving portrait, captured the family he had abandoned and would abandon again, with children huddled around his careworn wife (fig. 5). This is what the South African artist William Kentridge called "art in a state of siege," self-exiled from the tumult of the time, but not yet resigned to give up the brush.

Artists bring other artists to certain centers of production, patronage, and reception that come to dominate art making internationally. No seventeenth- or eighteenth-century

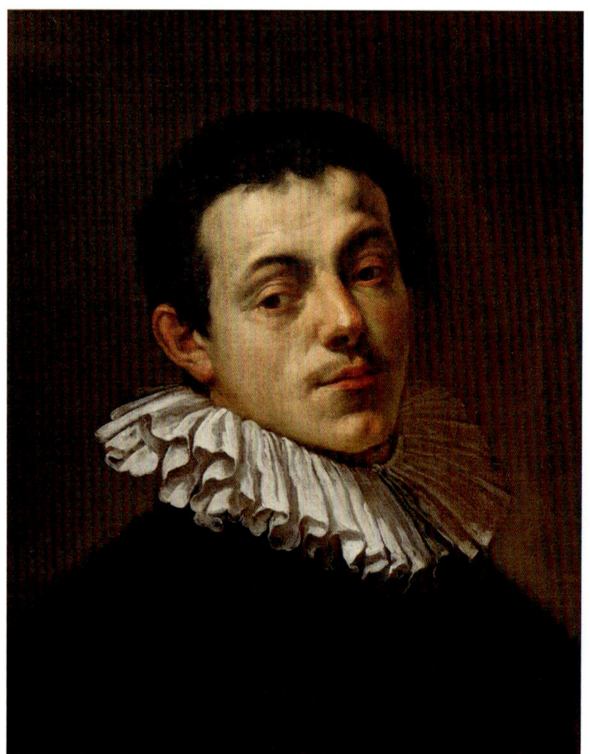

Fig. 4. Hans von Aachen, *Portrait of Josef Heintz*, 1585. Oil on panel, 22⁷⁄₁₆ × 17⁵⁄₁₆ in. (57 × 44 cm). National Gallery, Prague, DO 4326

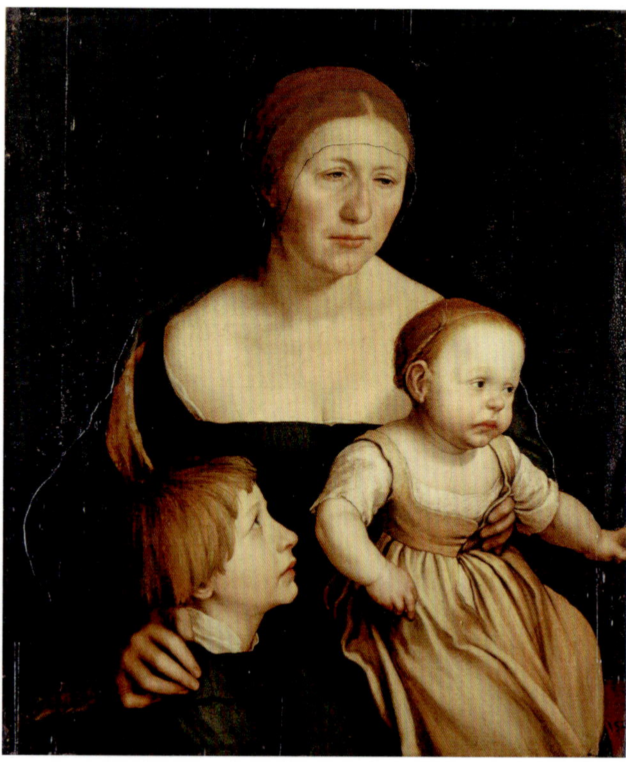

Fig. 5. Hans Holbein the Younger, *Portrait of Elsbeth Holbein (born Binzenstock), Philipp Holbein, and Katharina Holbein*, 1528/29. Oil on paper transferred to panel, 31¼ × 25½ in. (79.4 × 64.7 cm). Kunstmuseum, Basel, Switzerland, Amerbach-Kabinett 1662, inv. 325

artist of ambition could avoid a sojourn in Rome, not only because great art—old and new—was visible there, but also because of the vibrant artistic culture that resulted simply from so many different artists gathering there. Paris became such a magnet city in the nineteenth century, and New York became the twentieth-century center.[8] The global art world of today may have multiple centers, but it remains vital—in career terms—that an artist be exhibited and known in one or, even better, in several of them. As with itinerant court artists of the distant past, high status for contemporary artists often depends on their dexterity in creating site-specific works and installations in the wide range of centers around the world, while at the same time retaining a core identity, preferably an exotic one that underwrites the prevailing value of the global. As children, my sister and I used to joke about my father's bathetic trajectory from Vienna through New York to Pittsburgh, where he settled in 1952 for no good reason, just at the moment when Andy Warhol was fleeing the Steel City for the bright lights of New York.

The power of artistic centers is felt most acutely by those who inhabit the margins. Bruce Nauman's 1967–68 film *Walking in an Exaggerated Manner around the Periphery of a Square* (fig. 6) takes place in the artist's studio, which could be anywhere,

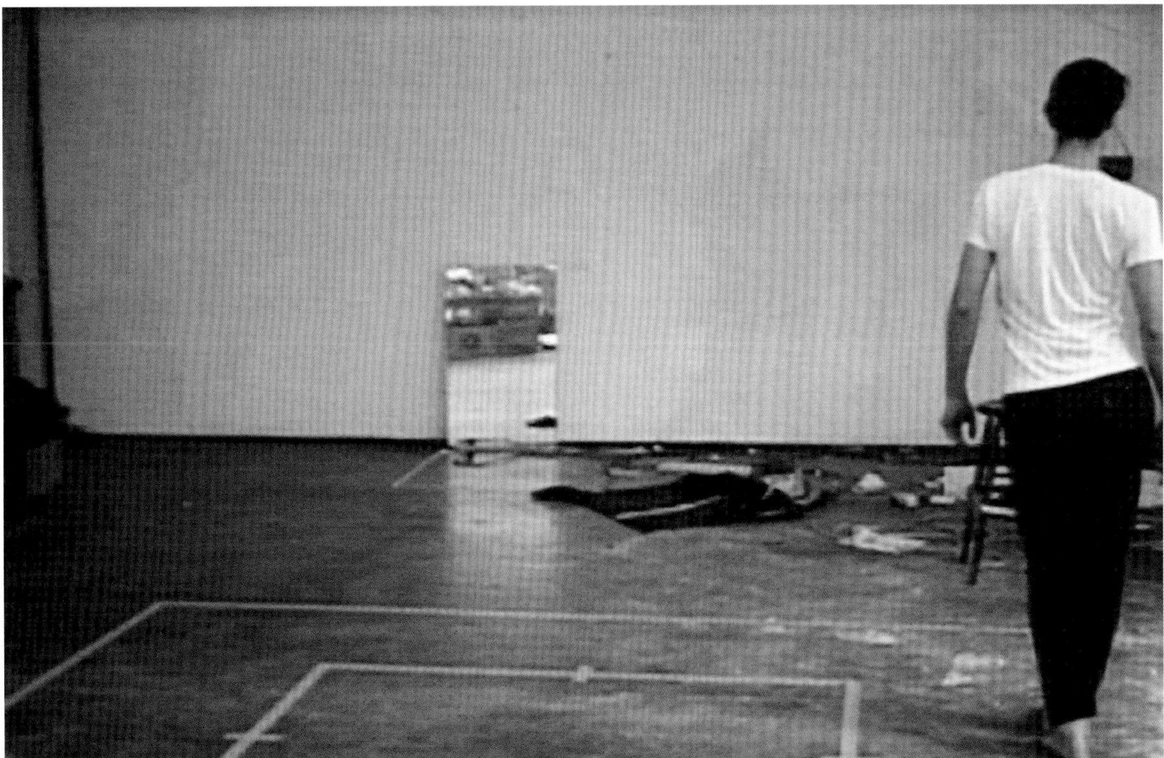

Fig. 6. Bruce Nauman, still from *Walking in an Exaggerated Manner around the Periphery of a Square*, 1967–68. 16mm film viewed as black-and-white VHS projection, 400 ft., 10 mins. Harvard Art Museums/Fogg Museum, Cambridge, Mass., Contemporary Art Department Fund, 2001.288

and defines any action in it as art. "If I was an artist and I was in a studio," reported Nauman in conversation, "then whatever I was doing in a studio must be art."[9] The studio transforms and centralizes what happens in it, hence Nauman's repetition of its square framework as a living sculpture documented on film. Kentridge said that seeing Nauman's film helped him to realize how far from the mainstream he was, working in the political and geographic isolation of apartheid South Africa, where no one would see or care if he walked in a square in his studio in Johannesburg, and where, in the condition of an unjust regime, Nauman's formalism seemed absurd.[10] Kentridge understood that his own art would have to revolve around lives lived on the periphery. The dramas of his first animated film, *Johannesburg, 2nd Greatest City after Paris*, unfold against a backdrop of the ceaseless movement of dispossessed people on foot (fig. 7). Keeping his home and studio in Johannesburg when the rest of his family immigrated to the United Kingdom and Canada, Kentridge maintains his perspective at the periphery, understanding how deeply that anamorphic viewpoint speaks to an art world and a world where exile has become the norm.

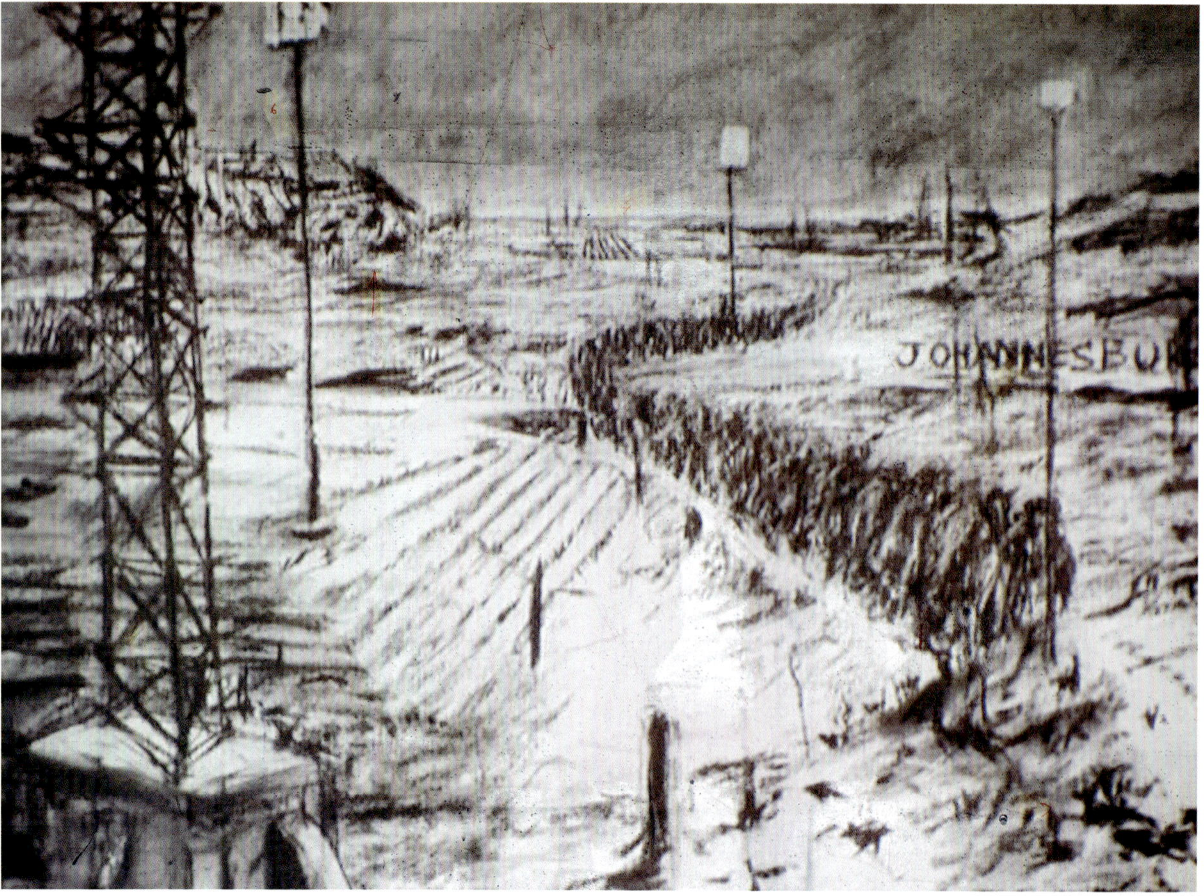

Fig. 7. William Kentridge, still from *Johannesburg, 2nd Greatest City after Paris*, 1989. 16mm film; video and laser disc transfer, 8 mins., 2 secs.

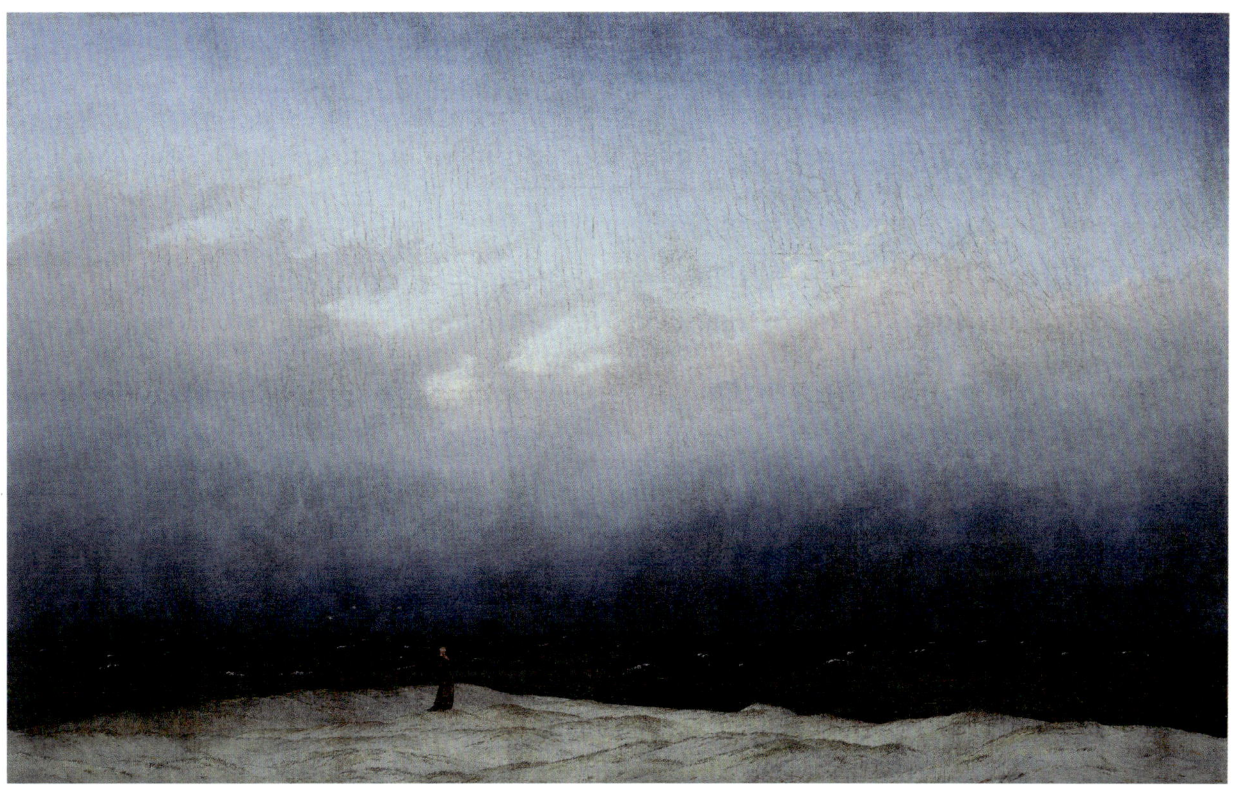

Fig. 8. Caspar David Friedrich, *Mönch am Meer* (Monk by the Sea, after 2015 restoration), 1808–10. Oil on canvas, 43⁵⁄₁₆ × 67½ in. (110 × 171.5 cm). Nationalgalerie, Berlin, NG 9/85

Dürer's experience of himself as a "parasite" in Germany articulates the stance typically taken by the modern artist: that of an outsider at home. In the first decade of the nineteenth century, Caspar David Friedrich portrayed himself isolated and dressed in a Capuchin monk's habit at the edge of a barren seashore (fig. 8). In doing so, he drew on the old Christian metaphor of life as a pilgrimage from the empty, time-bound realm of this world to an eternal beyond. But in his writings, Friedrich also claimed that this alienation relates specifically to his artistic calling; not medieval, it is deeply and symptomatically modern. His persona as monk derived from his being misunderstood by and isolated from the contemporary public.[11] Art required ascetic self-sacrifice in this life not for salvation at the end of time, but for the sake of some audience in the distant but historical (rather than eschatological) future that might understand him. Friedrich projects exile onto the painting's beholder, who, like the monk, stands at the brink of nothingness. Romantic alienation—the condition of the self's distance from the world—gets embedded in the very structure of the image. In John Constable's landscapes, nostalgia mobilizes a new approach to space. His early painting of his father's garden in East Bergholt, England (fig. 9), depicted from the window of his childhood home and painted right after his mother's death, refigures conventions of landscape painting as a measured progression into depth. Barriers and gaps block the painted world, forbidding arrival or return. Aesthetic autonomy (the artwork as something cut off from life) becomes—in this work as in so many works afterward—a symptom of homesickness.

From the late nineteenth century onward, it was expected that artists should scandalize the public and live lives split off from ordinary society. The impulse to reach beyond the European tradition and seek renewal far from home (for example, Paul Gauguin in Tahiti, cat. 1) dramatizes the tendency of "genius"—since the Renaissance the signature aspect of the great artist—to stand apart. Ironically, this expectation of marginality took shape at the centers of art production. Returned from Tahiti and feeling unappreciated, Gauguin went about Paris in Polynesian garb. Oskar Kokoschka, having been rejected by the Viennese public in 1909, shaved his head in imitation of a criminal and published (in Berlin) a likeness of this outsider persona, to great acclaim.[12] Rejection at and by the center verified an artist's centrality. In the provinces, acceptance and rejection were both the kiss of death. World War II displaced countless European artists to the United States, where, after having styled themselves at home as avant-garde outsiders, they experienced a different outsider status: that of critical oblivion. When, after 1945, New York replaced Paris as the place to be, the city produced and

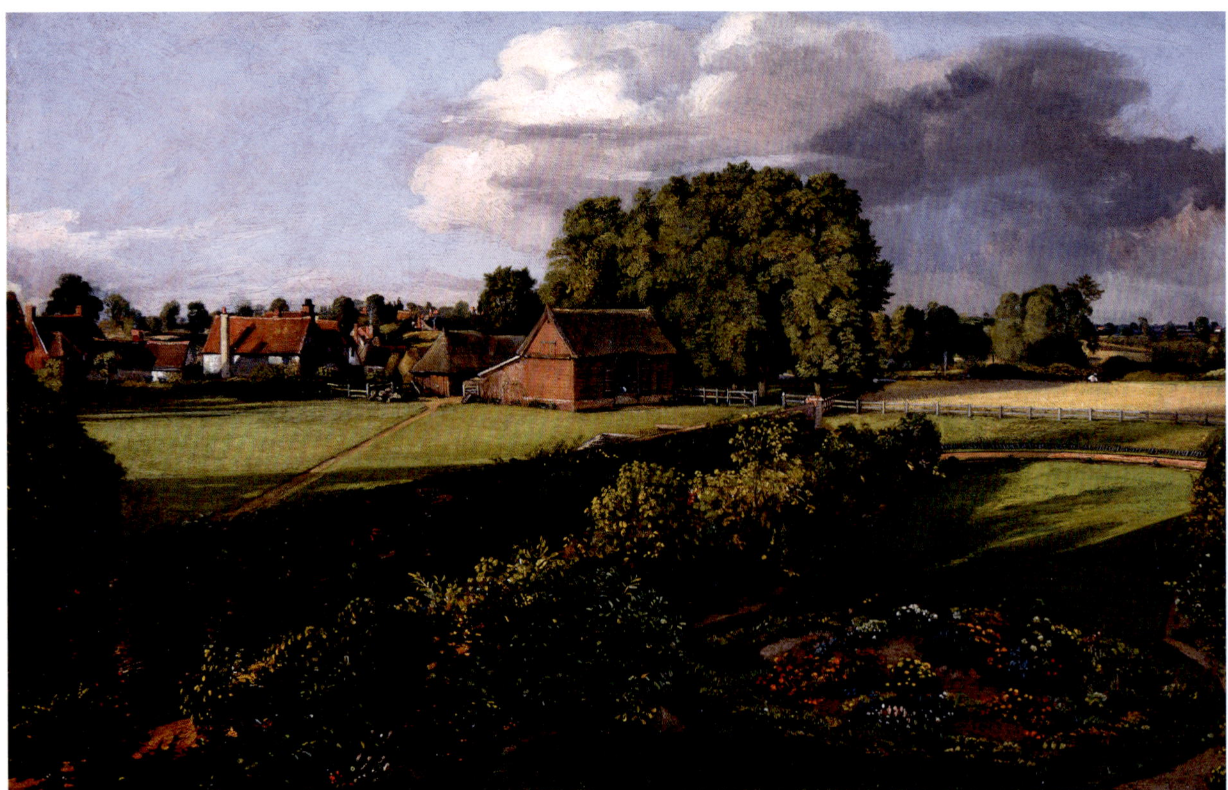

Fig. 9. John Constable, *Golding Constable's Flower Garden*, 1815. Oil on canvas, 13 × 20 in. (33 × 50.8 cm). Ipswich Borough Council Museum and Galleries, Christchurch Mansion, Suffolk, England, Acquired through the Ernest E. Cook Bequest via the National Art Collections Fund

embraced an art deliberately severed from history, requiring immigrant artists to shed their past or be forgotten. Both its champions and its detractors understood Modernist abstraction as reflecting a mobile or nomadic subjectivity for which home could be anywhere and everywhere, and in postwar America, abstraction became a means of assimilation for displaced artists (such as Arshile Gorky [cat. 14], John Graham, and Jack Tworkov) by obviating an irrelevant or obsolete iconography. The influence of Europe continued to act tacitly, via a transplanted art pedagogy (Josef Albers at Black Mountain College and at Yale University, Walter Gropius at Harvard University, László Moholy-Nagy at the New Bauhaus in Chicago) or through critical expectations and vocabulary forged by the European interwar avant-garde. The discovery of an "American Scene" also allowed some transplanted artists, such as George Grosz in New York (cat. 24), to find a place at the center.

My father painted *My Parents I* in 1944, in Washington, D.C., while serving as a graphic artist for the U.S. military's Office of Strategic Services—the precursor to the Central Intelligence Agency. Trained as a graphic designer in Vienna, he fled that city in 1938, after Hitler annexed Austria in March of that year. Arriving in New York, he embarked on a highly successful career designing posters and book jackets, first commercially and then for the Office of War Information, where he worked alongside artists Ben Shahn and Bernard Perlin to create visual images for the U.S. war effort. Just before the Army shipped him to London, my father made *My Parents I* as his "opus one," partly to prove to Shahn that he could paint (he executed his poster designs in airbrush, which annoyed the older artist), partly to come to terms with the realization that his parents and brother had been sent from Vienna to their deaths somewhere in the East. In London and Berlin, by way of the Nuremberg trials (where he drew the defendants from life) and Vienna, he began to paint in earnest, creating a series of figurative works dealing with the war experience. These would be exhibited to considerable international acclaim in Berlin in 1947, in the first postwar art exhibition in Germany's ruined capital. Well known when he returned to New York, he joined a group of celebrated artists (including Ivan Albright, Paul Cadmus, and George Tooker) dubbed "Magic Realists." In 1952 he accepted an invitation to be artist in residence for one year at the Pennsylvania College for Women, now Chatham University, in Pittsburgh. There he met his wife (my mother), and because the city seemed more paintable to him than New York, and because its hills, rivers, and bridges resembled those of Vienna, he decided to settle in Pittsburgh permanently.

My Parents I was not part of his exhibited oeuvre. Kept at home and (uniquely of all of his many thousands of paintings) not for sale, the painting also depicts in meticulous detail the home he had lost. In the painting, my father gives his mother and father—Fanny and Leo—each a window, and he frames them with drapes hooked above the windowsill to keep out drafts. Leo uses the light to read, and Fanny, to knit. The bentwood Thonet rocker is typically Viennese, as are the other chairs. The chandelier has glass flower-shaped lights in Art Nouveau style. Its large bell-shaped shade was his mother's work; she specialized in creating such coverings, gifting or selling them to friends, and it was she who made the mesmerizing lace doily on the table. Leo has dozed off while reading. His finger marks his place in the book. He loved books, especially light fiction—detective and adventure novels—and the fantasies of the German Romantic writer E. T. A. Hoffmann. The Dante mask (in the upper-left corner) appears in another early painting by my father, of a crazy New Yorker named Mr. Lucas.[13] Mr. Lucas had such a mask and recited the lines from the *Inferno* about the inscription on the gates of Hell:

> Through me the way into the suffering city,
> Through me the way to eternal pain,
> Through me the way to the lost people.[14]

These words probably echoed in my father's head when he painted the mask. Just through that wall of books, the next-door neighbor—a certain Josef Riefenthaler—had been one of the founders of the so-called Hitler Movement in Austria in the 1920s, and immediately after the Nazi annexation of Austria in 1938, he seized ownership of the entire apartment building, so Dante's words seem apt.[15]

The board game on the table in the painting was one of Leo's inventions. Made of wood and paper, it had its own set of rules known only to the family. It is shown still in play, with the blues and yellows almost tied. The game conjures the children who played it. My father and his only sibling, Kurt, are also implied by the painting's most puzzling detail. A string rises from Fanny's knitting, up over the branching lights of the chandelier, and down to the ball of thread resting on the table. The brothers teased their mother by tossing her yarn over the chandelier and tangling the whole apartment with string. When she makes the next stitch, the ball will tumble. This string is a sort of lifeline to the painting, evoking what was left behind and imagining a connection and a return. My father once said it is the umbilical cord connecting him to his mother.

The parents live in separate worlds, she absorbed in lacemaking, he asleep, perhaps dreaming of the book's adventures. My father received letters from his parents with comfortable regularity, first in Italy, where he stayed awaiting his visa to the States, then in Brooklyn, where he lived until joining the Army. In these letters, the parents worried about their children, especially about Kurt, who had been deported with his pregnant wife, Olga, to Kielce, Poland, in 1941. They wrote almost nothing about themselves, remarking coolly (when the Nazis forced them from their home) that they were looking for a smaller flat, and urging my father to send what money he could to Kurt and Olga. Painted from an odd position above the table, the board game and ball of thread appear as they might to a child playing. They also have the character of objects in a dream. This builds on the figure of the sleeping father and accords with the painting's mix of distortion and clarity: distortion in the spatial order of the interior, and clarity in the things themselves—the spiral-patterned doily, the game in play, the view down the street.

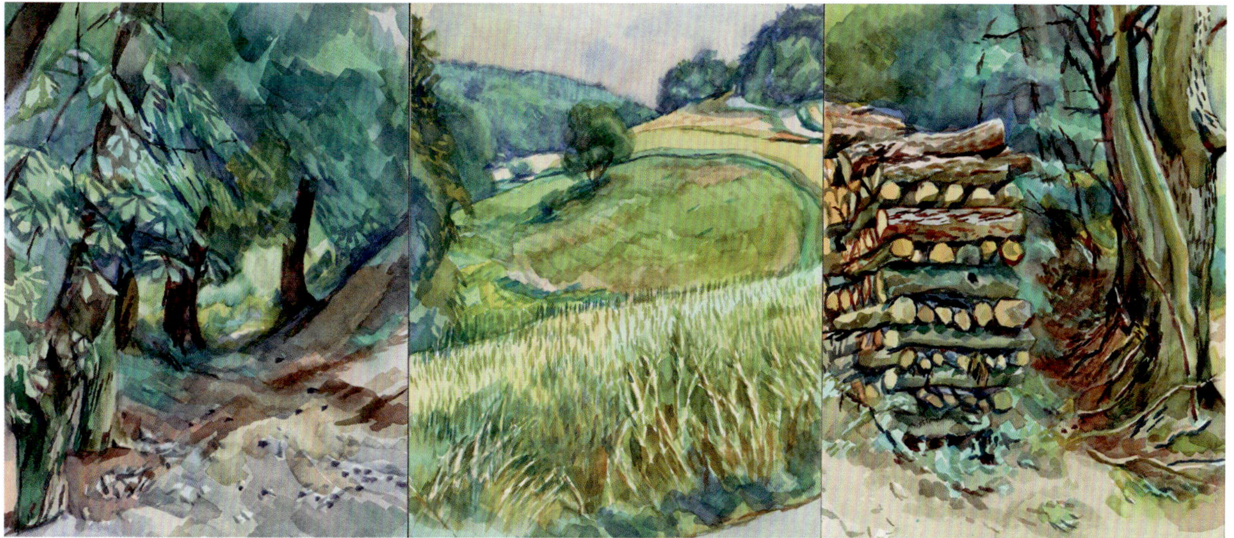

Fig. 10. Henry Koerner, *My Parents IV*, 1984. Triptych of watercolors on paper mounted on cardboard, 18¹⁵⁄₁₆ × 39 in. (48 × 99 cm). Private collection

The painting is like a dream, and so is home. While inside its four thickly padded walls, the denizens rest safe from what happens outside. Leo Koerner's response to Hitler was always, "It will blow over." The drapes hung to keep out the draft convey this idea. But the windows betray the dangerous porousness of home. A man looks directly at us from the opposite building, and the windows resemble the eyes of a face. Am Tabor was tumultuous during the *Anschluss*. On the day before Hitler's arrival, police advised Jewish tenants to close their curtains and stay at home. My father remembers Hitler's motorcade reaching its endpoint at Am Tabor. In fact, Hitler did not arrive at this street until April 9, 1938, when he spoke at a rally in the Nordwestbahnhof train station (a block away, at the end of the street), urging Austrians to vote for joining Germany. But already in the first days of the *Anschluss*, Hermann Göring led a rally in the Nordwestbahnhof. Of the day of Hitler's arrival in Vienna, my father recalls huge searchlights lighting the sky and casting strong shadows on the ceiling of his apartment. He remembers also a sound invading the family home, one he had never heard before and never heard again, the roar of people, tens of thousands of them, in Leopoldstadt, some alone in their apartments, literally crying for joy.

Late in 1945, on his return to Vienna, he confirmed his parents' deportation and deaths. In the painting, in the *Fluchtpunkt* near the windows to our family home, my father imagined his flight from Vienna and his traumatic return. He never again worked from memory but instead sketched and painted from reality, particularly scenes he encountered in Vienna, with his family in tow. Indeed, his painting was the reason for our yearly returns to Vienna. The city and its environs, encapsulated in the pictured terrain between our home and his home, became his uncanny studio. Late in his career, he related this practice of walking and painting beautiful views to its most personal origins. A work from 1984 titled *My Parents IV* (fig. 10) mounts together three ordinary landscape scenes painted in watercolor in the Wienerwald (Vienna Woods).[16] Each is typical of motifs he painted on our family walks. Each depicts a pathway adjacent to a path, but veering toward different vanishing points, and together they evoke the activity of walking through which most of his motifs were found. The triptych's title is cryptic, however. Projecting people into the empty landscapes, it indicates that these views arose out of a compulsive return to the parents, and that, for an exile, home is everywhere anticipated if nowhere attained. Not surprisingly, this personal backstory was lost on critics, who took all my father's plein air paintings to be strange, provincial throwbacks.[17] In *My Parents IV*, he cast himself as an exile both from his origins and from an art world that had no place for him.

46

1. On the painting, see Gail Stavitsky, *From Vienna to Pittsburgh: The Art of Henry Koerner*, exh. cat. (Pittsburgh: Museum of Art, Carnegie Institute, 1983), 13, cat. 3; John Czaplicka and David Mickenberg, *Emigrants and Exiles: A Lost Generation of Austrian Artists in America, 1920–1950*, exh. cat. (Evanston, Ill.: Mary and Leigh Block Gallery, Northwestern University, 1996), 139–40; Joseph Leo Koerner, *Unheimliche Heimat: Henry Koerner 1915–1991*, exh. cat. (Vienna: Österreichische Galerie Belvedere, 1997), 16–19; and Edith Balas, *The Early Work of Henry Koerner*, exh. cat. (Pittsburgh: Frick Art and Historical Center, 2003), 22–23.

2. On the metaphor, see Gerhart B. Ladner, "*Homo Viator*: Mediaeval Ideas on Alienation and Order," *Speculum* 42, no. 2 (April 1967): 233–59.

3. David Young Kim, *The Traveling Artist in the Italian Renaissance: Geography, Mobility, and Style* (New Haven, Conn.: Yale University Press, 2014), 125–60 and passim.

4. Karel van Mander, *The Lives of the Illustrious Netherlandish and German Painters, from the First Edition of the "Schilder-boeck" (1603–1604)*, ed. and trans. Hessel Miedema (Doornspijk, Netherlands: Davaco, 1994), 190.

5. Ibid.

6. On the pictorial and cultural problems posed to European artists by the Australian landscape, see Bernard Smith's remarkable "European Vision and the South Pacific," *Journal of the Warburg and Courtauld Institutes* 13 (1950): 65–100, esp. "The Exile's Vision," 85–90; on Tunisia's impact on Klee and his circle, see most recently Roger Benjamin and Cristina Ashjian, *Kandinsky and Klee in Tunisia* (Berkeley: University of California Press, 2015).

7. Albrecht Dürer to Willibald Pirckheimer, October 13, 1506, in *The Writings of Albrecht Dürer*, ed. and trans. William Martin Conway (New York: Philosophical Library, 1958), 58.

8. Serge Guilbaut, *How New York Stole the Idea of Modern Art: Abstract Expressionism, Freedom, and the Cold War*, trans. Arthur Goldhammer (Chicago: University of Chicago Press, 1983).

9. Ian Wallace and Russell Keziere, "Bruce Nauman Interviewed," *Vanguard* (Canada) 8, no. 1 (February 1979): 18.

10. William Kentridge, "Artists on Artists Lecture Series: William Kentridge on Bruce Nauman," Dia Art Foundation, podcast audio, December 19, 2002, https://soundcloud.com/diaartfoundation/william-kentridge-on-bruce-nauman.

11. Caspar David Friedrich, *Observations on a Collection of Paintings by Living or Recently Deceased Artists*, in *Neoclassicism and Romanticism 1750–1850*, ed. Lorenz Eitner, vol. 2, *Restoration/Twilight of Humanism* (Englewood Cliffs, N.J.: Prentice-Hall, 1970), 56.

12. The self-portrait was published as a color lithograph poster advertising the new issue of *Der Sturm* (1910).

13. The painting dates from 1944 and was formerly in the collection of Henry Koerner's first wife, Kay Kaufmann. See Stavitsky, *From Vienna to Pittsburgh*, cat. 4; and Czaplicka and Mickenberg, *Emigrants and Exiles*, pl. 90.

14. Dante, *Inferno*, canto 3, lines 1–3.

15. Riefenthaler's possession of Am Tabor 13 was contested by Nazi authorities who, because of a legally disputed part-ownership by the building's former Jewish owners, seized half-ownership of the building in 1942. Years later, ownership of the plot of land was restored to its original Jewish owners, who sold it to the city of Vienna in an undocumented settlement.

16. On *My Parents IV*, see Koerner, *Unheimliche Heimat*, 71.

17. For the criticism of Koerner's symbolism as being too personal, see Judith Kaye Reed, "Koerner sans Text," *Art Digest*, April 1, 1950, 14; Belle Krasne, "Koerner's Paradoxes," *Art Digest*, March 15, 1951, 15; and "Private Realist," *Newsweek*, March 19, 1951, 55; on responses to his stylistic shift to Cézanne-inspired facture, see Stavitsky, *From Vienna to Pittsburgh*, 21–22.

47

Pastorales Martinique, from the *Volpini Suite*
1889
Zincograph
6¹⁵⁄₁₆ × 8⅞ in. (17.7 × 22.5 cm)
Provenance: Robert Light, Boston; Yale University Art
Gallery, New Haven, Conn., University Purchase,
Everett V. Meeks, B.A. 1901, Fund, 1964.9.9.

Parau Parau (Whispered Words)
1892
Oil on canvas
30⅜ × 38 in. (77.1 × 96.5 cm)
Provenance: Vente Gauguin [sale organized by the artist],
Hotel Drouot, Paris, 1895; the artist; A. Vollard, Paris.
Galerie Tanner, Zurich. Marquis Maeda, Japan; New York
art market; John Hay Whitney, New York; Yale University
Art Gallery, New Haven, Conn., John Hay Whitney, B.A.
1926, HON. 1956, Collection, 1982.111.5.

Paul Gauguin's work expresses a withdrawal from European
civilization and the search for "pure" art, far away from
the Parisian art world, where the artist had encountered
meager success and would only receive a large retrospective
at the 1906 Salon d'Automne, three years after his death.[1]
He first retreated to Brittany, a region in western France
with strong local traditions and customs, before venturing
further afield, spending time in Panama and Martinique
in 1886 and 1887. After his return to Paris, Gauguin made
a series of eleven zincographs, known as the *Volpini Suite*,
inspired by these travels.[2] *Pastorales Martinique* attempts
to capture the lush, tropical landscape and local population,
using a fluidity of forms that Gauguin also employed in
his works from the artists' colony of Pont-Aven, in Brittany
(fig. 1). The undulating bodies of the women in *Pastorales
Martinique* are only differentiated from those of Breton
peasants through their darker skin, patterned dresses, and
headpieces. There are similarities in the natural elements
as well; the fields and foliage in the Martinique print are
reminiscent of details in his Brittany landscapes. A few
years later, in 1891, Paul Gauguin departed for his first trip
to Tahiti in a conscious break from Western civilization
and the Parisian artistic milieu, imposing on himself a
voluntary exile. Earlier, in 1890, when Gauguin began
making plans to go to Polynesia, he wrote in a letter to
fellow artist Odilon Redon: "Even Madagascar is too near
the civilized world; I shall go to Tahiti and I hope to end
my days there. I judge that my art . . . is only a seedling thus
far, and out there I hope to cultivate it for my own pleasure
in its primitive and savage state. In order to do that I must
have peace and quiet."[3]

Parau Parau (Whispered Words) was painted in 1892
in Tahiti. The canvas represents a seemingly idyllic scene
of a group of women in a tropical landscape. One woman
standing in the foreground looks at the viewer, and another
turns her back, while the seated women seem absorbed in
other activities. This scene is not a realistic depiction of
what Gauguin saw in Tahiti but rather a utopian vision of it.
Upon his arrival, Gauguin did not find the untouched paradise he had sought, with natives "uncorrupted" by European
colonialism and a pristine tropical landscape. Instead,
he noticed that the Polynesian island had largely been
invaded by Western civilization, first through the arrival
of missionaries, followed by more and more settlers—a
trend that hastened when Tahiti and the Marquesas Islands
were made a French protectorate in 1842, then annexed
by France in 1880. In the quest for his idealized paradise,
Gauguin relied on other sources for his Tahitian imagery:
like many artists of the French avant-garde, he was drawn
to images and artworks from the Far East, and he had
brought with him in a trunk photographs of artworks, Asian
artifacts, postcards, and other ephemera.[4] In *Parau Parau*
the standing figure holding a fruit or other offering might
derive from a fourteenth-century Buddhist relief from the
temple of Borobudur, in Java, Indonesia, of which Gauguin
owned a photographic reproduction (fig. 2).[5] The simplifica-
tion and masklike rendering of the figures' facial features
in the painting, as well as their static posture, also reflect
his interest in Polynesian sculpture and his own work with
wood, both in sculpture and in woodblock printmaking,
undertaken in Tahiti.[6] Despite the decidedly non-European

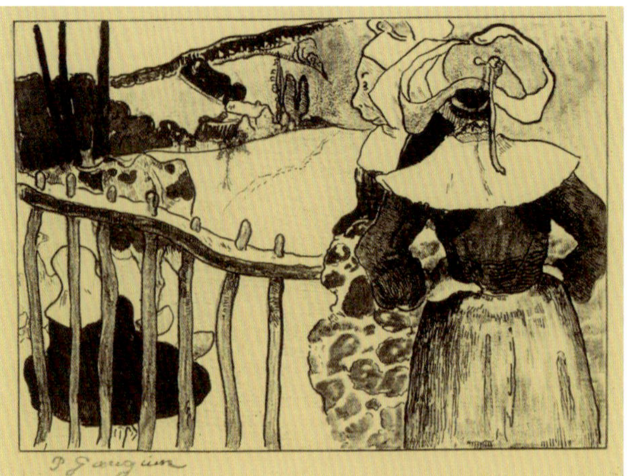

Fig. 1. Paul Gauguin, *Bretonnes à la barrière*, from the
Volpini Suite, 1889. Zincograph, 6⁵⁄₁₆ × 8⁷⁄₁₆ in. (16 × 21.4 cm).
Metropolitan Museum of Art, New York, Rogers Fund, 1922,
22.82.2(2)

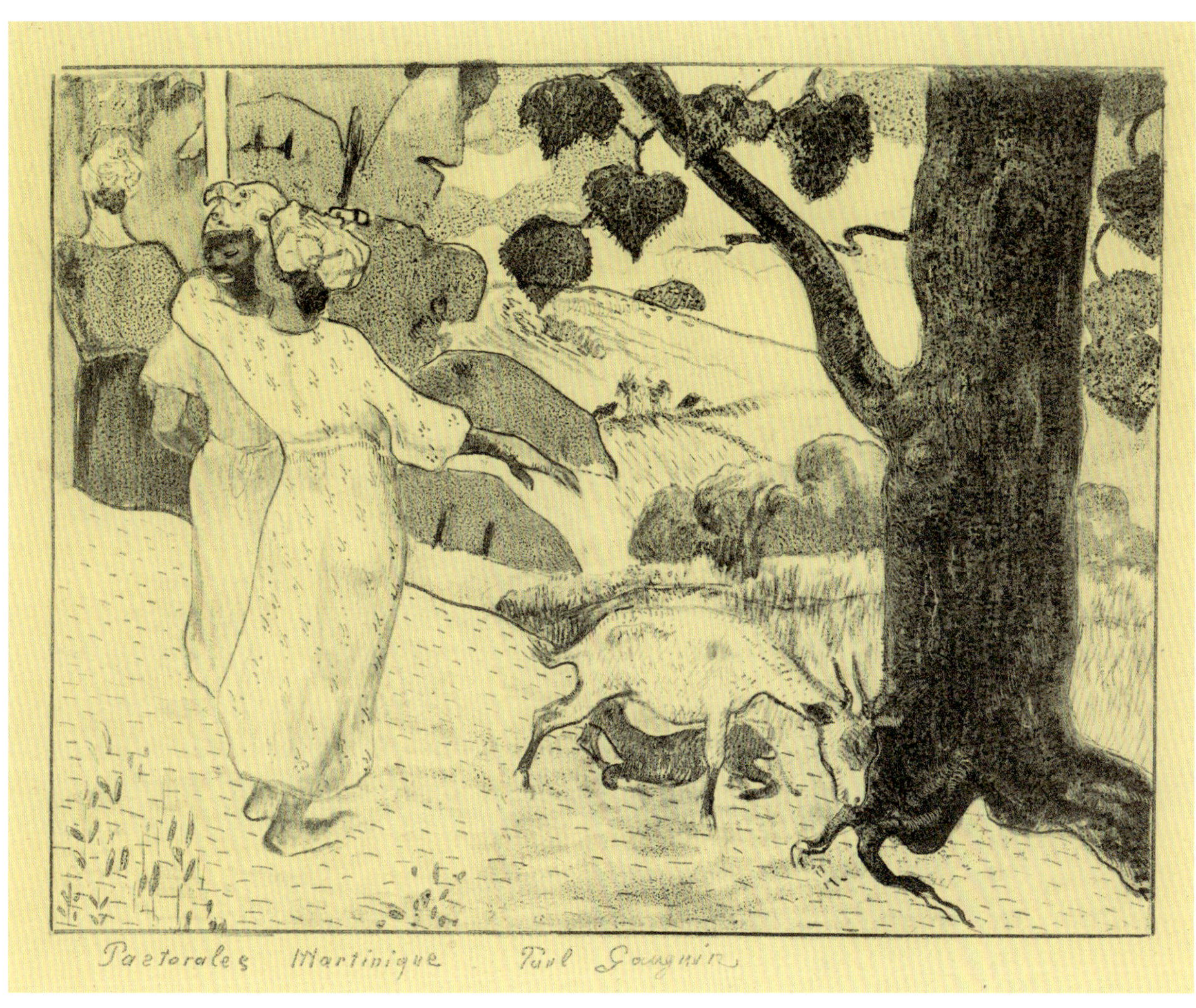

Pastorales Martinique

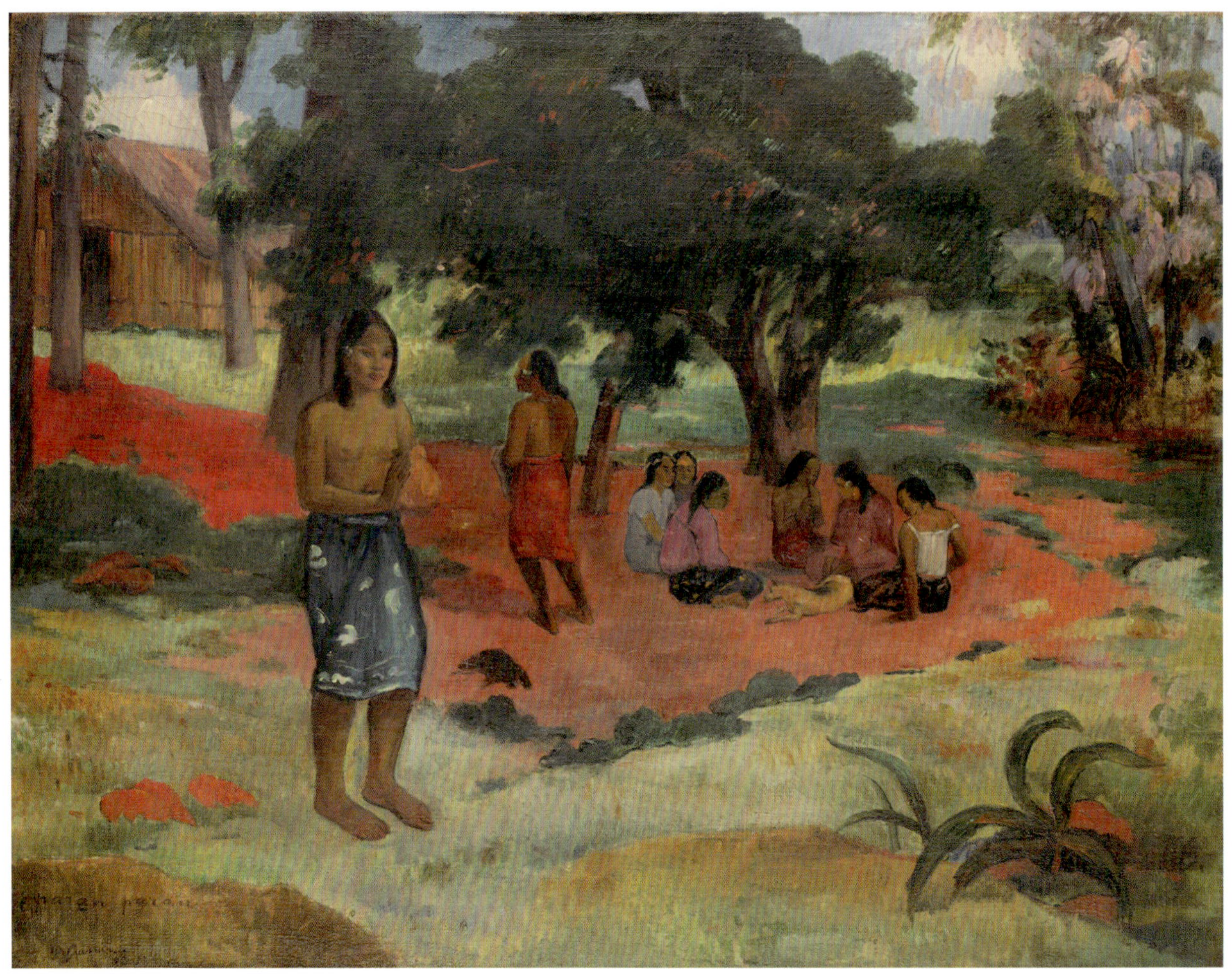

Parau Parau (Whispered Words)

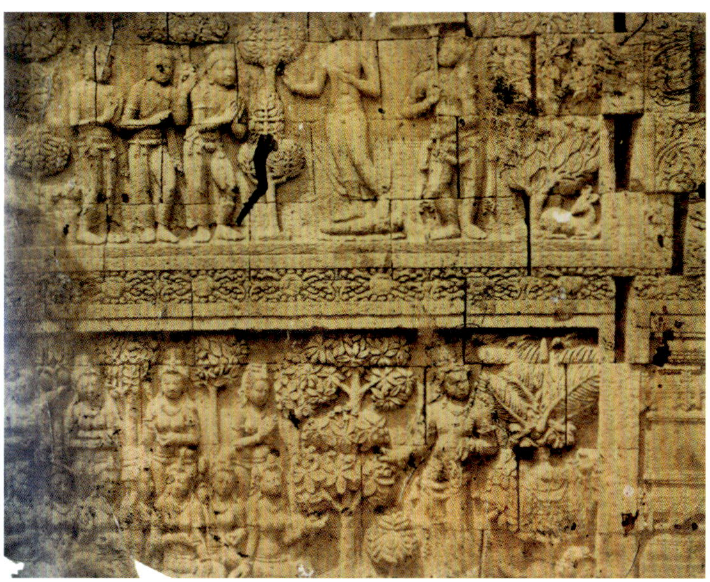

Fig. 2. Isidore van Kinsbergen, *Relief at the Temple of Borobudur*, 1874. Albumen photograph from a glass-plate negative, 10 × 11¹³⁄₁₆ in. (25.5 × 30 cm). Musée de Tahiti et des Îles, Punaauia, 22.82.2(2)

influences in *Parau Parau*, Gauguin still employed an Impressionist style, with visible, hatched brushstrokes and the juxtaposition of complementary colors such as red and green. Gauguin had used a similar palette, with red accents, in his earlier Impressionist works, but the extensive use of reds in this painting, especially in the plants and trees, reveals his symbolic use of unrealistic color in the depiction of nature.[7]

When Gauguin returned to France in 1893, he did not find the financial and critical success he was hoping for, and he felt misunderstood, no longer at home. As he wrote to his friend, and first biographer, Daniel de Monfreid, "I have definitely resolved to go live forever in Oceania. . . . Then I'll be able to spend the rest of my life free and easy— without worrying about tomorrow and without having to struggle all the time with imbeciles."[8] Gauguin left Europe permanently for his second and final exile to Tahiti in 1895.[9] This departure was followed by an even further retreat from Western civilization when he moved to the Marquesas Islands in 1901. —FVJ

1. Isabelle Cahn, "Belated Recognition: Gauguin and France in the Twentieth Century, 1903–1949," in *Gauguin Tahiti: The Studio of the South Seas*, ed. George T. M. Shackelford and Claire Frèches-Thory, exh. cat. (Boston: Museum of Fine Arts, 2004), 285–301, esp. 286–92.

2. Starr Figura, *Gauguin: Metamorphoses*, exh. cat. (New York: Museum of Modern Art, 2014), 76.

3. Paul Gauguin to Odilon Redon, September 1890, in Paul Gauguin, *The Writings of a Savage*, ed. Daniel Guérin, trans. Eleanor Levieux (New York: Viking, 1978), 42.

4. Alastair Wright, "Paradise Lost: Gauguin and the Melancholy Logic of Reproduction," in *Gauguin's Paradise Remembered: The Noa Noa Prints*, ed. Alastair Wright and Calvin Brown, exh. cat. (Princeton, N.J.: Princeton University Art Museum, 2010), 49–99, esp. 78.

5. Alan G. Wilkinson, *Gauguin to Moore: Primitivism in Modern Sculpture*, exh. cat. (Toronto: Art Gallery of Ontario, 1981), 50–52; Wright, "Paradise Lost," 79.

6. Anne Pingeot, "Sculpture of the First Voyage," in Shackelford and Frèches-Thory, *Gauguin Tahiti*, 67–78.

7. Colta Ives and Susan Alyson Stein, *The Lure of the Exotic: Gauguin in New York Collections*, exh. cat. (New York: Metropolitan Museum of Art, 2002), 192.

8. Paul Gauguin to Daniel de Monfreid, September 20, 1894, in Gauguin, *The Writings of a Savage*, 104.

9. Vincent Gille, "The Last Orientalist: Portrait of the Artist as Mohican," in *Gauguin: Maker of Myth*, ed. Belinda Thomson et al., exh. cat. (London: Tate Publishing, 2010), 48–55, esp. 54.

Spiel (Play)
ca. 1941–45
Watercolor on paper
7¾ × 6¾ in. (19.7 × 17.2 cm)
Provenance: Stiftung Seebüll Ada und Emil Nolde, Seebüll,
Germany; Knoedler and Co., New York; Philip H. Isles,
New York.

Sunset
ca. 1941–45
Watercolor on paper
8¾ × 10 in. (22.2 × 25.4 cm)
Provenance: Galerie Abels, Cologne, Germany;
Mrs. Bertram Smith, New York; Spencer A. Samuels &
Company, Ltd., New York; Philip H. Isles, New York.

Two Women in a Park
ca. 1941–45
Watercolor on paper
9¼ × 5⅝ in. (23.5 × 14.3 cm)
Provenance: Stiftung Seebüll Ada und Emil Nolde, Seebüll,
Germany; Knoedler and Co., New York; Philip H. Isles,
New York.

Das Flötenspiel (The Flute Playing)
ca. 1941–45
Watercolor on paper
9¾ × 7½ in. (24.8 × 19.1 cm)
Provenance: Stiftung Seebüll Ada und Emil Nolde, Seebüll,
Germany; Knoedler and Co., New York; Philip H. Isles,
New York.

After the Nazi regime labeled his work "degenerate,"
forbidding him from exhibiting or engaging in any kind of
professional artistic activity, and included nearly fifty of his
works in the *Entartete Kunst* (Degenerate Art) exhibition
in 1937 and 1938, Emil Nolde went into self-imposed exile
in the small town of Seebüll, Germany, from 1938 until
the end of World War II.[1] During this time of reclusion, he
continued to paint despite the ban and produced a corpus of
approximately 1,300 works in secret, mostly watercolors—
among them *Spiel* (Play), *Sunset, Two Women in a Park*,
and *Das Flötenspiel* (The Flute Playing)—which he called
Ungemalte Bilder (Unpainted Pictures). Nolde purposely
abstained from using oil paint in these works, fearing that
its distinct smell would lead to him being discovered.

    Nolde's ostracism followed years of being one of the
most successful artists in Germany, during the 1920s and
early 1930s, although he had always been on the outskirts
of artistic circles. He considered his work—largely
religious scenes, landscapes, and flowers expressively

painted with thick layers of paint and flamboyant
colors (fig. 1)—to be quintessentially German. Nolde's
nationalism was based on his deep attachment to the land
where he grew up, along the border between Germany
and Denmark, and the Nordic nature mysticism that he
subscribed to was close to the Nazis' Norse mythology;
like too many of his countrymen, he followed a party
whose racial discrimination he chose at best to ignore,
or in some instances even echoed.[2] Nolde never thought
of emigration after the Nazis took power, and he even
joined the National Socialist Working Association of North
Schleswig in the fall of 1934, a party that became part of
the North Schleswig (Danish) branch of the Nazi Party
the next year. His inclusion in the infamous propaganda
exhibition against modern art, where his work *The Life
of Christ* particularly aroused attacks (fig. 2), thus came
almost as a surprise to him as well as to critics and even

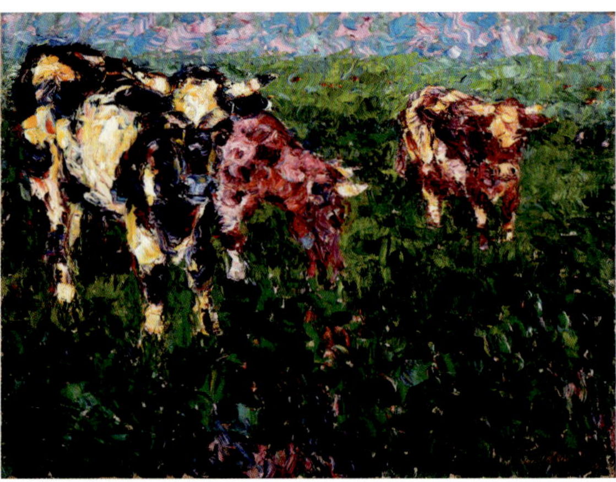

Fig. 1. Emil Nolde, *Cows in the Lowland*, 1909. Oil on canvas,
39 × 47 in. (99.1 × 119.4 cm). Los Angeles County Museum of
Art, Gift of Josef von Sternberg, 46.26.4

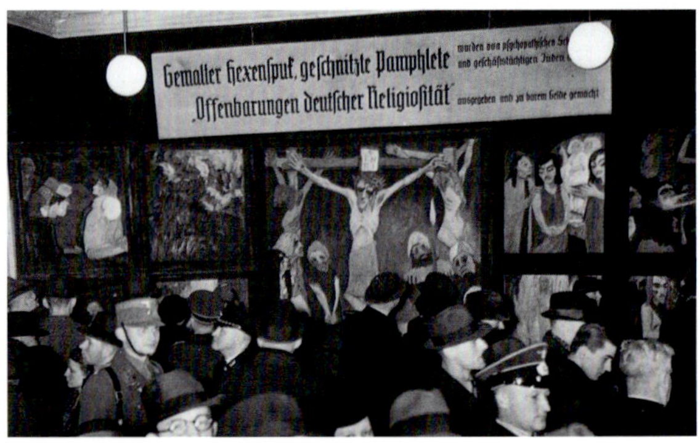

Fig. 2. Archival photograph of Emil Nolde's *The Life of Christ*
in the exhibition *Entartete Kunst* (Degenerate Art) in Berlin,
February 1938. Bildarchiv des Süddeutschen Verlags, Munich

52

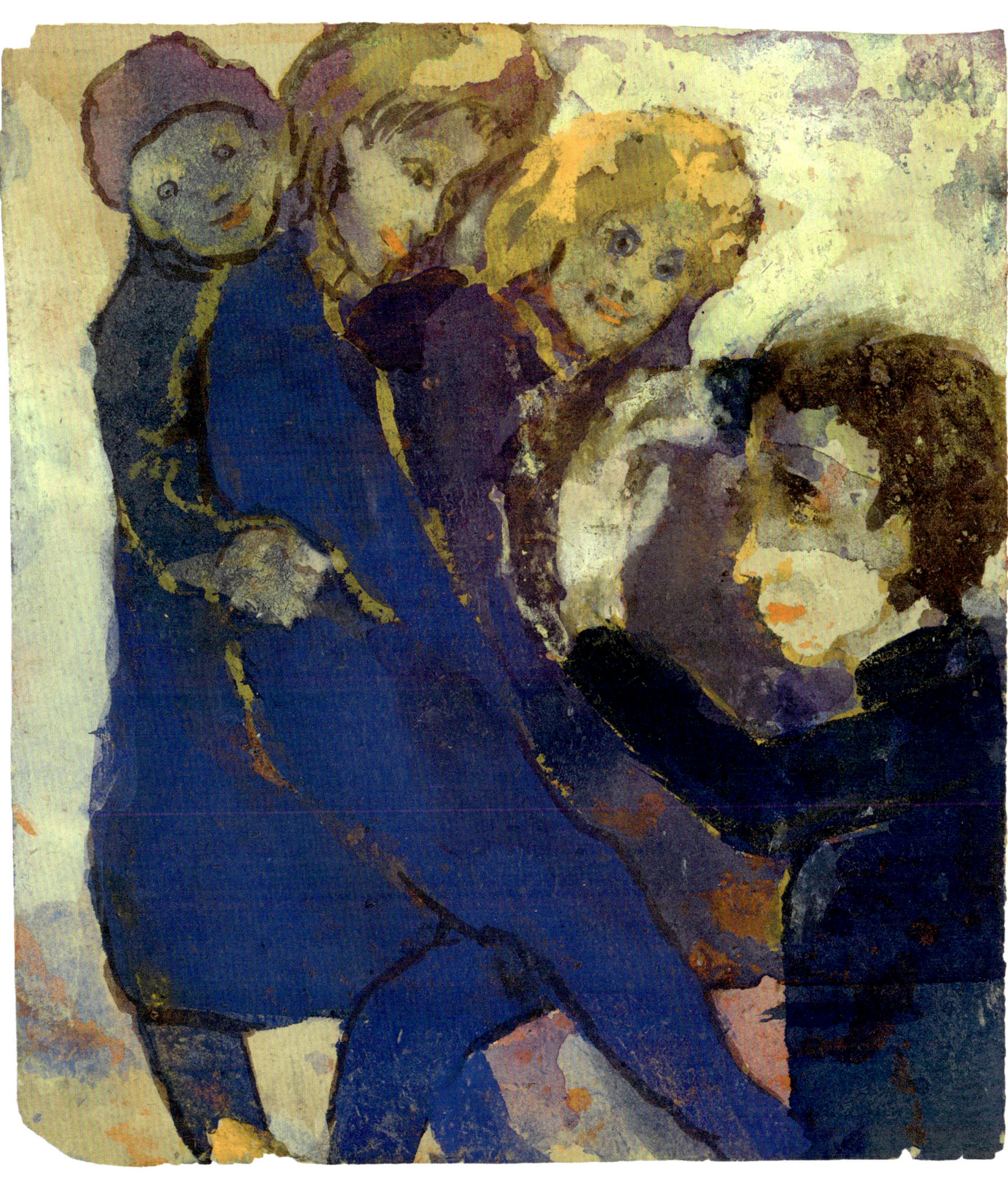

Spiel (Play)

53

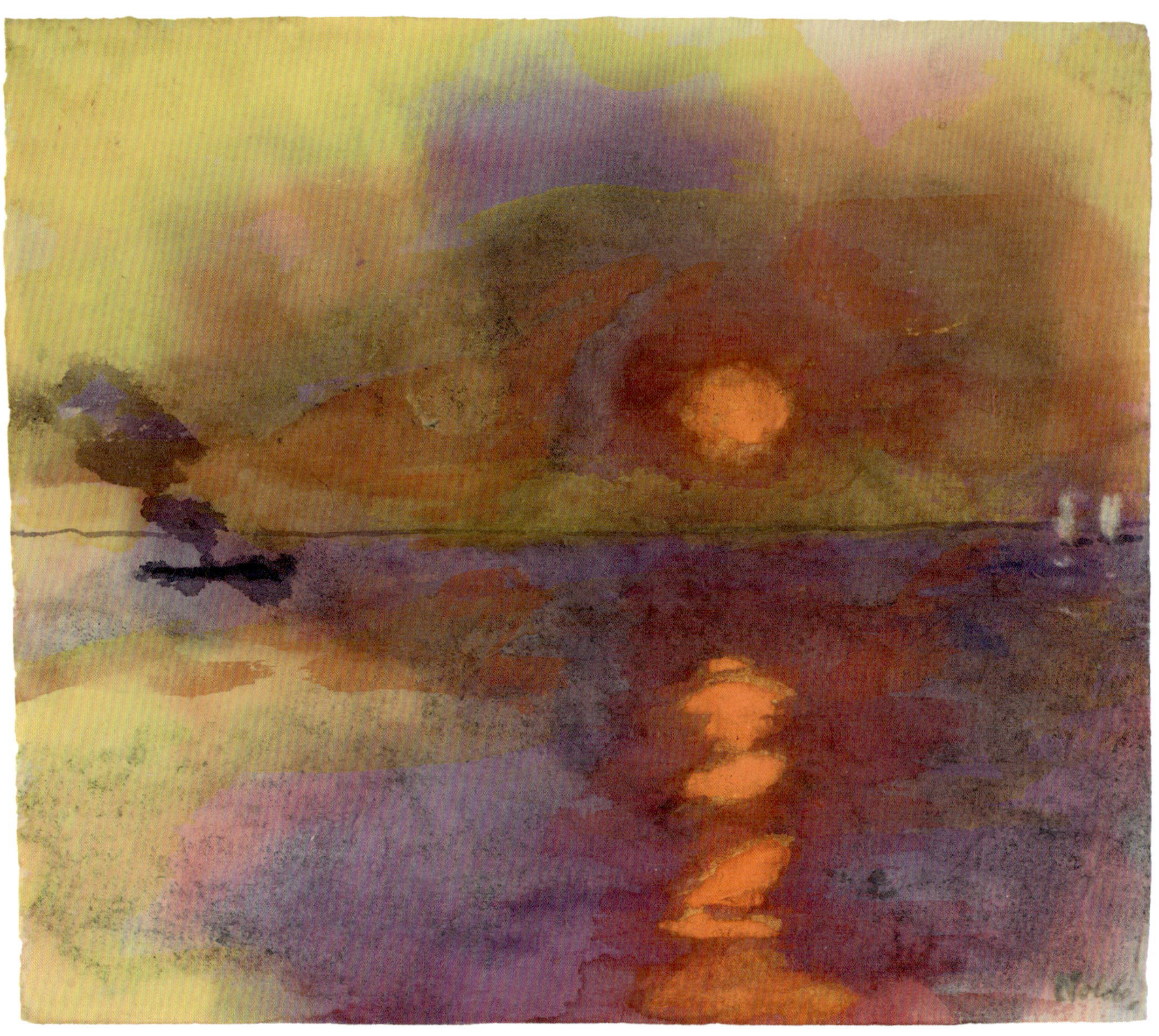

Sunset

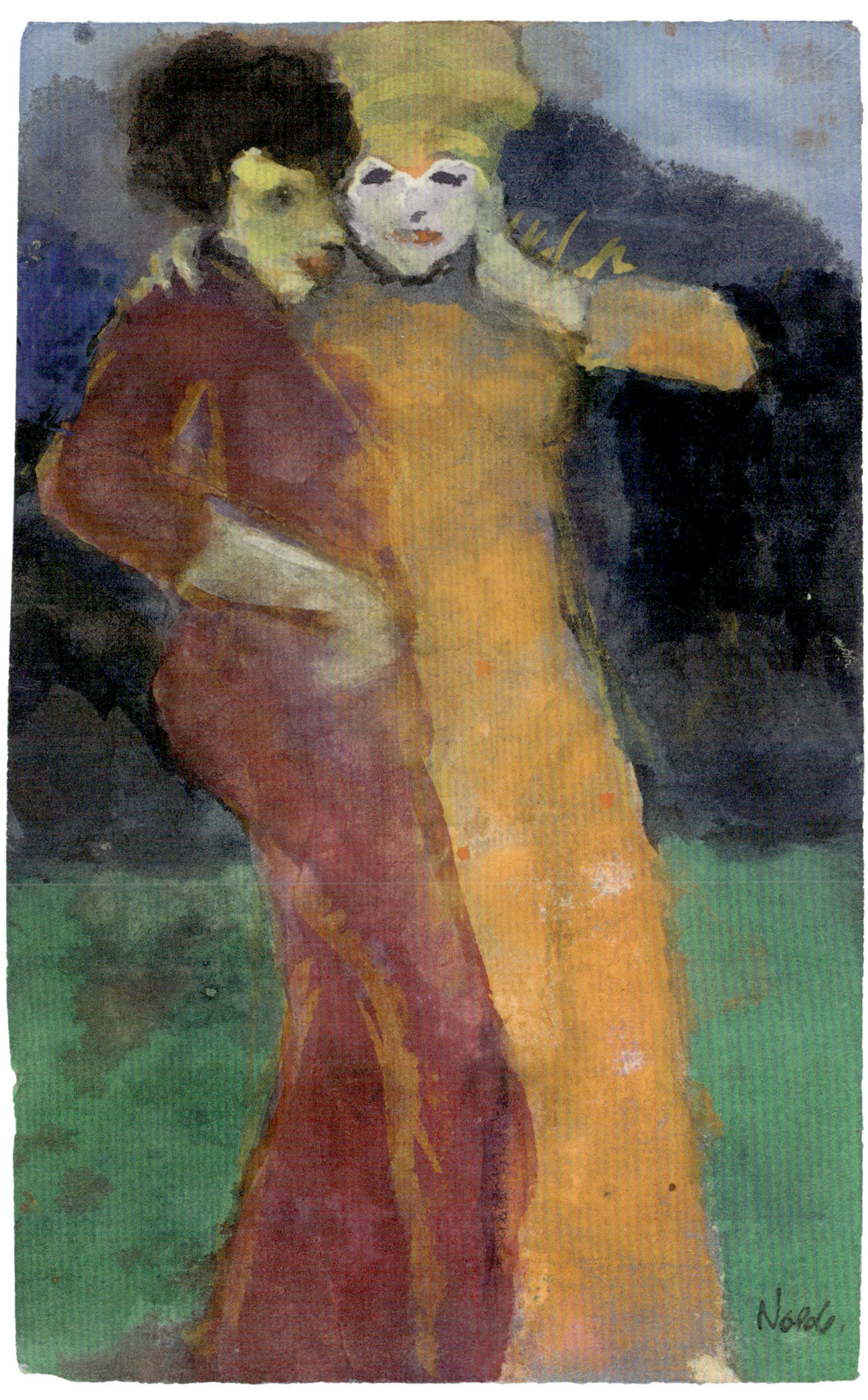

Two Women in a Park

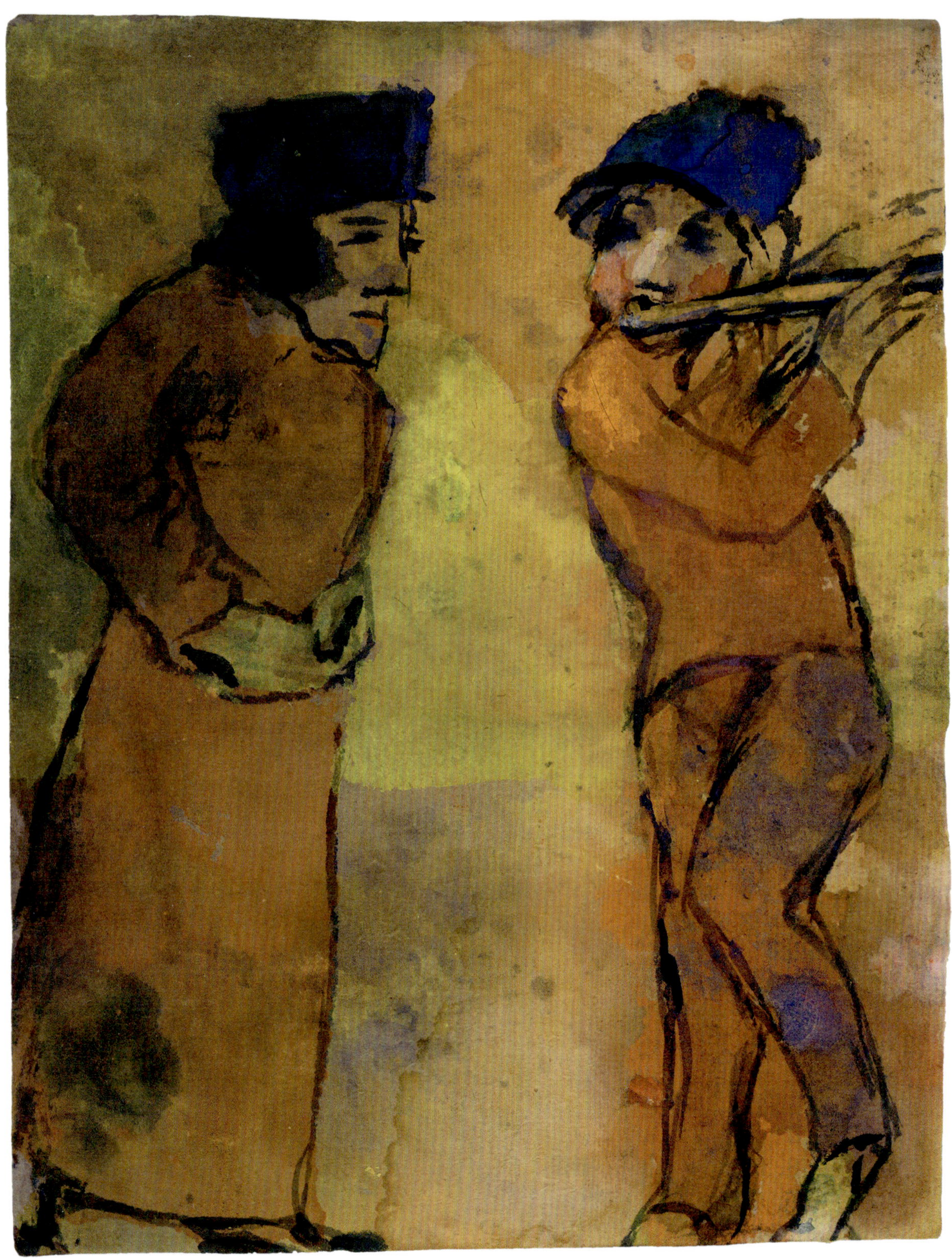

Das Flötenspiel (The Flute Playing)

to party officials.[3] Nevertheless, he was the artist with the most works confiscated from German museums.[4]

The artist chose exile in Seebüll because it was close to his birthplace, the town of Nolde. The physical retreat by Nolde was followed by a psychological and social one during these years; the artist withdrew even further, painting not in his spacious studio but only in a narrow room in his house.[5] He turned to an inner, invented world of the fantastic and the spiritual. "During the nocturnal hours I wandered off to a breathtaking landscape, a landscape full of wonder and splendors," he wrote in his journal *Worte am Rande* (Words in the Margin) on December 6, 1941.[6] The small, delicate watercolors shown here are characterized by vibrant, unrealistic colors, and by figures and landscapes inspired by fairy tales and legends. Each of them depicts an abstract, blurred background, a field of color from which shapes and figures emerge: women, men, and children playing, walking in a park, and playing the flute, as well as a sunset over the sea.

These works also testify to Nolde's further explorations of paper as a support and the medium of watercolor. Since he was not permitted to procure materials, Nolde was restricted to using whatever he could find—small-format paper, paper scraps, and the margins of larger watercolors.[7] He played with the absorbent qualities of Japan paper and employed a wet-on-wet technique, repeatedly painting layers of colors of varying density; he contoured some of the silhouettes with black outlines and highlighted some areas with opaque white. He also incorporated the element of chance into the artistic process, embracing pictorial "accidents," such as colors blending into one another, as part of the creation.[8]

These watercolors combine abstract and figurative elements in a deeply personal way, as conveyed through the technique and the small scale. They seem suspended in time, giving no indication about a specific place or period, and disconnected from reality, the outside world, and the horrors of war that Germany had caused. With their introspective character, they seem to exist only for themselves and mark a departure from Nolde's earlier works, which, although characterized by their subjective style and, in some cases, already populated by fantasy creatures, were mostly inspired by actual landscapes or objects observed by the artist.[9] The instinctive, liberated use of color in the works, without any compositional concern, appears to generate the forms that emerge rather than delineate them. Nolde's *Ungemalte Bilder* speak to his retreat from the turmoil of his time, and to his attempt to create in these works a world outside of time and space, an inner sanctum to which he could escape. —FVJ

1. On August 23, 1941, Nolde received a letter from Adolf Ziegler, president of the Reichskammer der bildenden Künste, outlining Nolde's expulsion from the organization and interdiction from painting professionally; see Thomas Knubben, "'My Suffering, My Torment, My Contempt': Emil Nolde in the Third Reich," in *Emil Nolde: Unpainted Pictures: Watercolours 1938–1945 from the Collection of the Nolde-Stiftung Seebüll*, ed. Tilman Osterwold and Thomas Knubben (Ostfildern, Germany: Hatje Cantz, 2000), 136–49, esp. 145.

2. Ibid., 137–41.

3. Aya Soika and Bernhard Fulda, "'German Down to the Deepest Mystery of His Origins': Emil Nolde and the National Socialist Dictatorship," in *Emil Nolde: Retrospective*, ed. Felix Krämer, exh. cat. (New York: Prestel, 2014), 45–55, esp. 47.

4. Dagmar Grimm, "Emil Nolde," in *"Degenerate Art": The Fate of the Avant-Garde in Nazi Germany*, ed. Stephanie Barron, exh. cat. (Los Angeles: Los Angeles County Museum of Art, 1991), 315–24.

5. Jörg Garbrecht, "With 'Tied Hands'—The 'Unpainted Pictures,'" in *Emil Nolde: Unpainted Pictures*, ed. Manfred Reuther, exh. cat. (Neukirchen, Germany: Nolde Stiftung Seebüll, 2009), 21–35, esp. 24–25.

6. Manfred Reuther, "When My Tied Hands Were Freed," in Osterwold and Knubben, *Emil Nolde*, 8–18, esp. 10.

7. Garbrecht, "With 'Tied Hands,'" 22–23.

8. Stephan Koja, "'A Notion Solely of Radiance and Color': Emil Nolde's *Unpainted Pictures*," in *Emil Nolde—In Radiance and Color*, ed. Agnes Husslein-Arco and Stephan Koja (Munich: Hirmer Verlag, 2013), 223–35, esp. 223.

9. Werner Haftmann, *Emil Nolde: Ungemalte Bilder* (Cologne, Germany: Verlag M. DuMont Schauberg, 1963), 10.

Allégorie de genre (Genre Allegory)
1944
Collage; offset lithographed die-cut paper over printed and embossed sheet
12½ × 9⁷⁄₁₆ in. (31.8 × 24 cm)
Provenance: Estate of Katherine S. Dreier [presumed gift of the artist]; Yale University Art Gallery, New Haven, Conn., Gift of the Estate of Katherine S. Dreier, 1953.6.350.

Allégorie de genre (Genre Allegory) is based on a collage of the same name (fig. 1) that Duchamp made in 1943 as a submission to a *Vogue* contest seeking a portrait of George Washington for the cover of the Independence Day issue of the magazine. The artist composed the initial collage out of medical gauze stained with bloody-looking iodine, cardboard, and gold stars—materials that he fashioned into a double image: a profile of Washington and, when turned 90 degrees counterclockwise, a map of the United States. When *Vogue* rejected the strange, macabre portrait, André Breton quickly purchased it and ran its reproduction (of which this lithograph is an uncut proof) on the cover of the Surrealist magazine *VVV*.

 Allégorie de genre—a title that suggests the work as a pictorial allegory of the "Star-Spangled Banner," with its references to warfare—reflects Duchamp's disdain for the "hypertrophic nationalism" of his day, which led to the two world wars that considerably shaped his life.[1] In 1941 the artist fled German-occupied Paris, staying with his sister, Suzanne Duchamp, and her husband, Jean Crotti, in the South of France.[2] He received a visa to travel to the United States from the Emergency Rescue Committee with the help of Varian Fry in 1942. This was the artist's second escape from a world war, though the first was a more voluntary departure; after the onset of World War I, the artist had dodged the patriotic militarism of France by going to New York, only to find himself leaving again (this time for neutral Buenos Aires) when parallel sentiments surged in the United States after it joined the war in 1917.[3]

 With its grotesque gauze darkened by bloody spills evoking violence, *Allégorie de genre* and its printed reproduction present a dark vision of the most cherished symbols of the United States. The work is related to another *VVV* cover that Duchamp had designed earlier that year (fig. 2), which reproduces an etching depicting an allegory of death. Carrying a scythe and bedecked with the American flag, Death rides astride a horse that gallops across the globe. By aligning symbols of patriotism and imperialism with morbid iconography, both of these cartographic images suggest Duchamp's estrangement from his new home. They speak more broadly to the violence of nationalism that

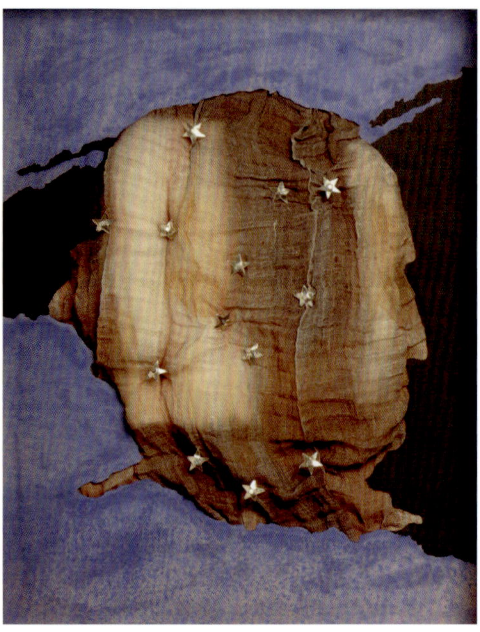

Fig. 1. Marcel Duchamp, *Allégorie de genre* (Genre Allegory), or *Allégorie de genre* (*George Washington*), 1943. Tinted gauze, cotton, gouache, torn and gold paper, nails, wood, and glass, 21⁹⁄₁₆ × 16⁹⁄₁₆ × 3⁵⁄₁₆ in. (54.8 × 42 × 8.4 cm). Centre Pompidou, Musée National d'Art Moderne, Paris, AM 1987-632

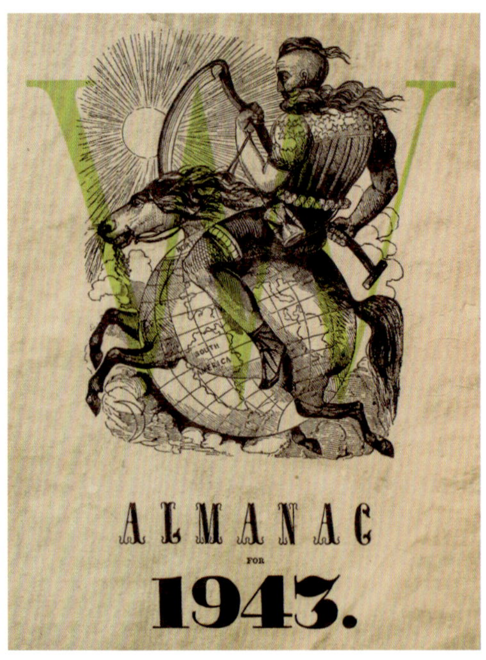

Fig. 2. Marcel Duchamp, cover of *VVV*, nos. 2–3 (March 1943)

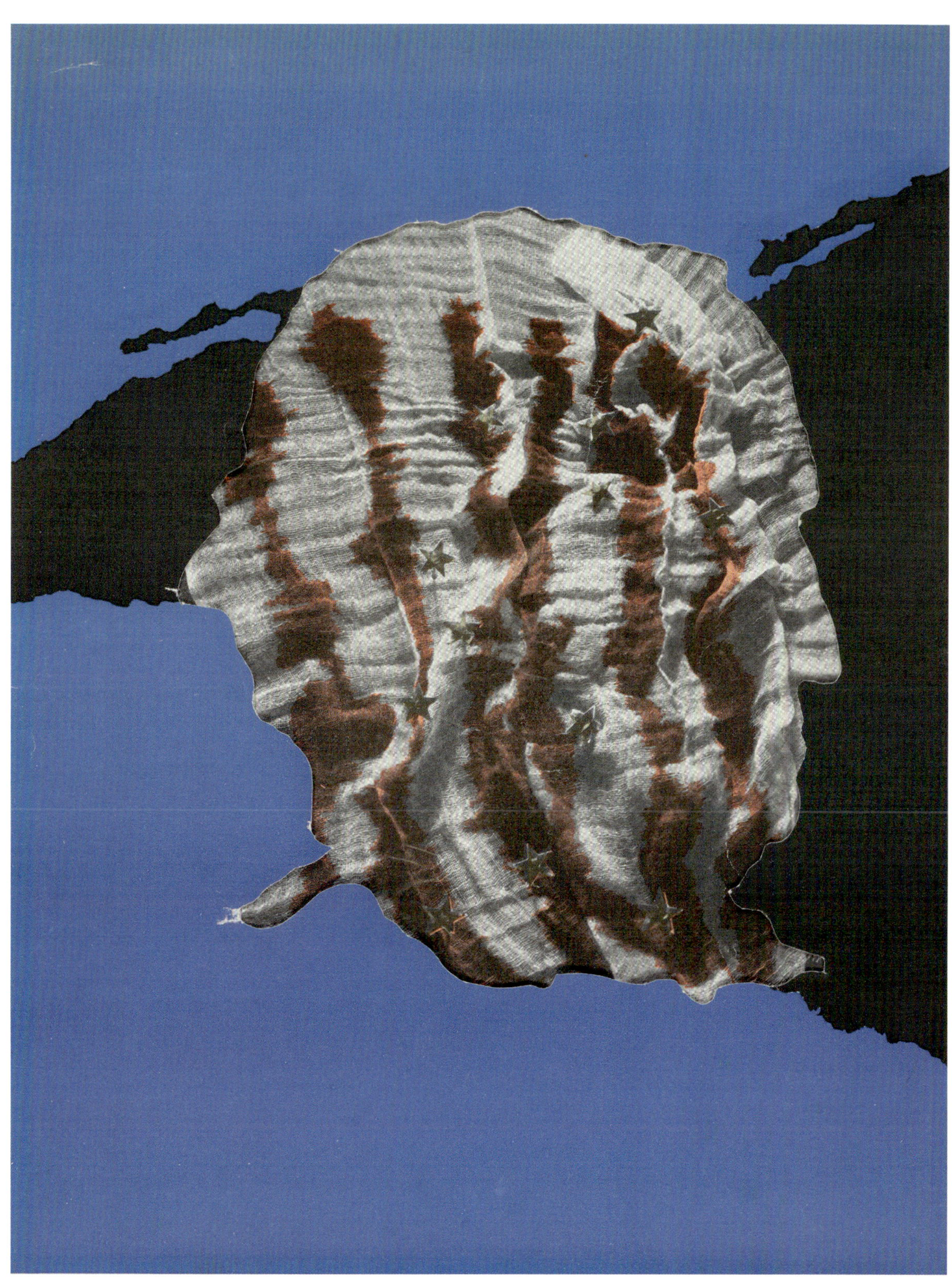

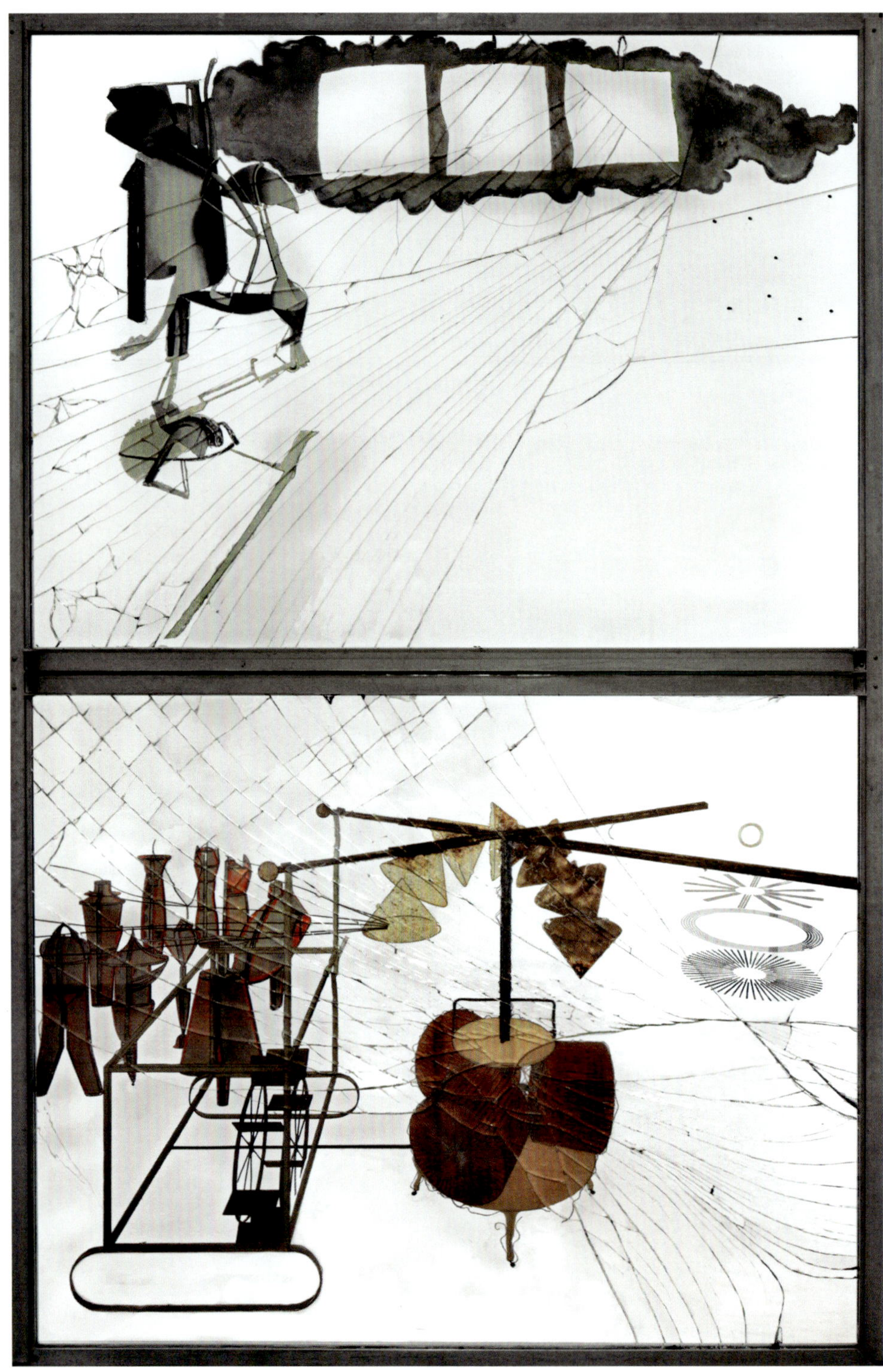

Fig. 3. Marcel Duchamp, *The Bride Stripped Bare by Her Bachelors, Even (The Large Glass)*, 1915–23. Oil, varnish, lead foil, lead wire, and dust on two glass panels, 9 ft. 1¼ in. × 5 ft. 10 in. × 3⅜ in. (277.5 × 177.8 × 8.6 cm). Philadelphia Museum of Art, Bequest of Katherine S. Dreier, 1952, 1952-98-1

compelled the itinerancy that became a central motif in Duchamp's work, as T. J. Demos argues in *The Exiles of Marcel Duchamp*.[4]

Allégorie de genre also stages a more complex meditation on nationalism through its relation with the symbolism of Duchamp's enigmatic *The Bride Stripped Bare by Her Bachelors, Even (The Large Glass)* (fig. 3). The use of gauze (*gaze*) in the former recalls the invisible illuminating gas (*gaz*) of *The Large Glass*, said to be produced by the "bachelors"—the vertical, cylinder-like figures clustered in the bottom left.[5] As indicated in Duchamp's writings, the bachelors used this gas to reach the "bride"—the irregular, sinewy figure in the upper left. Moreover, the stars affixed to the gauze in the collage are perhaps analogous with the "Milky Way," or cloudlike form, that the bride emits. The intricate iconography of *The Large Glass*, whose meaning is supplemented by Duchamp's extensive notes, is one of eternally unconsummated sexual desire: despite their efforts, the bachelors never manage to penetrate the realm of the bride.[6] By relating this elaborate dance with the visceral seepages in *Allégorie de genre*, Duchamp would seem to ironize nationalism by linking love of country with imperiled masculinity and failed conquest. Moreover, the double portrait in *Allégorie de genre* of the United States and President Washington evinces Duchamp's interest in the Wilson-Lincoln effect, an optical trick that he associates in his notes with the zone of attempted transgress between the lower and upper registers of *The Large Glass*. In this effect, a dual image painted on a slatted surface offers an image of President Abraham Lincoln from one vantage point and President Woodrow Wilson from another. Here, Duchamp conflates the images of Washington and the United States. Yet unlike cartographic precedents for such conflations, such as the map of Europe as the personified *Europa regina*, in this double image both entities are rendered somewhat elusive by the fusion. Duchamp turns two immediately recognizable icons into something strange and opaque, tempering these symbols of patriotic mythology and perhaps even melancholically conveying his own frustrated desires for homeland, made unattainable by the bloody realities of the state. —ND

1. Arturo Schwarz, *The Complete Works of Marcel Duchamp* (London: Thames and Hudson, 1970), 1:165.

2. Duchamp was forced to smuggle pieces of his *Boîte-en-valise* between the occupied and unoccupied territories by disguising himself as a cheese merchant carrying his wares.

3. Pierre Cabanne, *Dialogues with Marcel Duchamp*, trans. Ron Padgett (Boston: Da Capo, 1987), 59.

4. See T. J. Demos, *The Exiles of Marcel Duchamp* (Cambridge, Mass.: MIT Press, 2012).

5. Schwarz points out these connections, citing Ulf Linde. Schwarz, *The Complete Works of Marcel Duchamp*, 1:179.

6. Duchamp published these notes in 1934 in the form of a separate artwork, *The Green Box* (edition of 320). Michel Sanouillet and Elmer Peterson, eds., *The Writings of Marcel Duchamp* (Boston: Da Capo, 1989), 65.

Gracieuse figure
1955
Welded steel and wood
29 × 7½ × 6½ in. (73.7 × 19.1 × 16.5 cm)
Provenance: Poindexter Gallery, New York; Richard Brown Baker, 1955; Yale University Art Gallery, New Haven, Conn., Richard Brown Baker, B.A. 1935, Collection, 2008.19.66.

The sculptor Harold Cousins developed his mature style amid the vibrant artistic scene of postwar Paris. He was one of many African American artists—visual artists such as Barbara Chase-Riboud, Ed Clark, and Beauford Delaney, writers such as James Baldwin and Richard Wright, and musicians such as Sidney Bechet—who pursued careers in the French capital, where black Americans sought refuge from a United States still riven by Jim Crow laws.[1] Though Cousins initially worked figuratively, often in wood and terracotta, he began to move toward abstraction in metal in Paris in the early 1950s. Yet his abstract works maintained a figurative dimension, evoking flora and fauna, or human figures, as is frequently suggested by their titles.[2]

Cousins's welded forms were spurred toward abstraction in part by the form, composition, and materials of the African art that he encountered in Parisian museums. His interest in this art was also inspired by the writings of the philosopher Alain Locke, the chair of the philosophy department at Cousins's alma mater, Howard University, who argued for the importance of African art for contemporary black artists.[3] Cousins's largely formal engagement with the African masks and ritual objects at the ethnographic museum the Musée de l'Homme and with the ancient Egyptian art at the Musée du Louvre is also reminiscent of the borrowings of European Modernists such as Georges Braque and Pablo Picasso, whose encounters with non-Western objects in museums proved decisive for modern art in the twentieth century. Additionally, Cousins was heavily influenced by his discovery of the welded metal sculpture of the Catalonian artist Julio González (fig. 1), and by the Cubist-Expressionism of his teacher, Ossip Zadkine, both of whom were active in Paris. This melding of different influences attests not only to Cousins's cosmopolitanism as an expatriate American in Europe but also to the diasporic aesthetic of African American Modernism. The hybridization of aesthetic styles and forms that characterizes this Modernism is traceable to the violent rupture caused by the slave trade. African American artists frequently engage creatively with their lost homelands, as Cousins does in this work.

Gracieuse figure represents one of an extended series of sculptures composed of linear elements—"drawings in space" (a term borrowed from González) that Cousins began in the early 1950s using scrap metal that he purchased by the pound from the iron market along the river Seine. The negative spaces created by these conjoined metal rods are just as crucial to the sculpture; Cousins was impressed by the use of such negative spaces in Egyptian antiquities (fig. 2).[4] Here, the welded metal rods of the small sculpture cut crescents in space that evoke a standing figure. The two branching supports suggest an abstract bipedal form in con-trapposto. This complex arrangement of components takes on a radically different shape from each viewing angle. The comb that juts through the uppermost crescent is perhaps a ribcage in the disarticulated cavity of the torso, while the small parabolic forms at the upper extremities recall hands or the rounded contours of facial features.

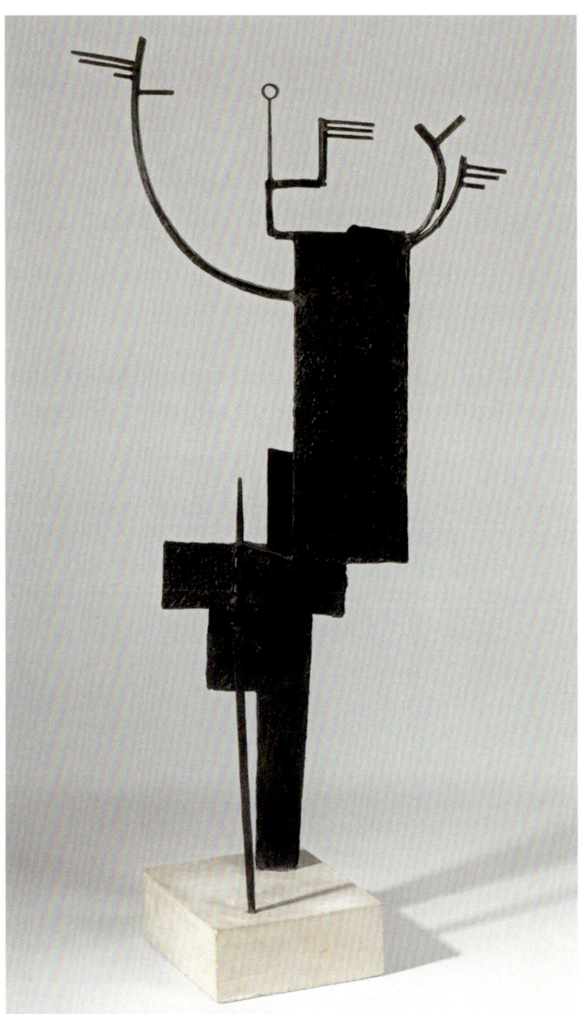

Fig. 1. Julio González, *Daphné*, 1937/66. Bronze, 55¹⁵⁄₁₆ × 27¹⁵⁄₁₆ × 20½ in. (142 × 71 × 52 cm). Centre Pompidou, Musée National d'Art Moderne, Paris, AM 1491 S

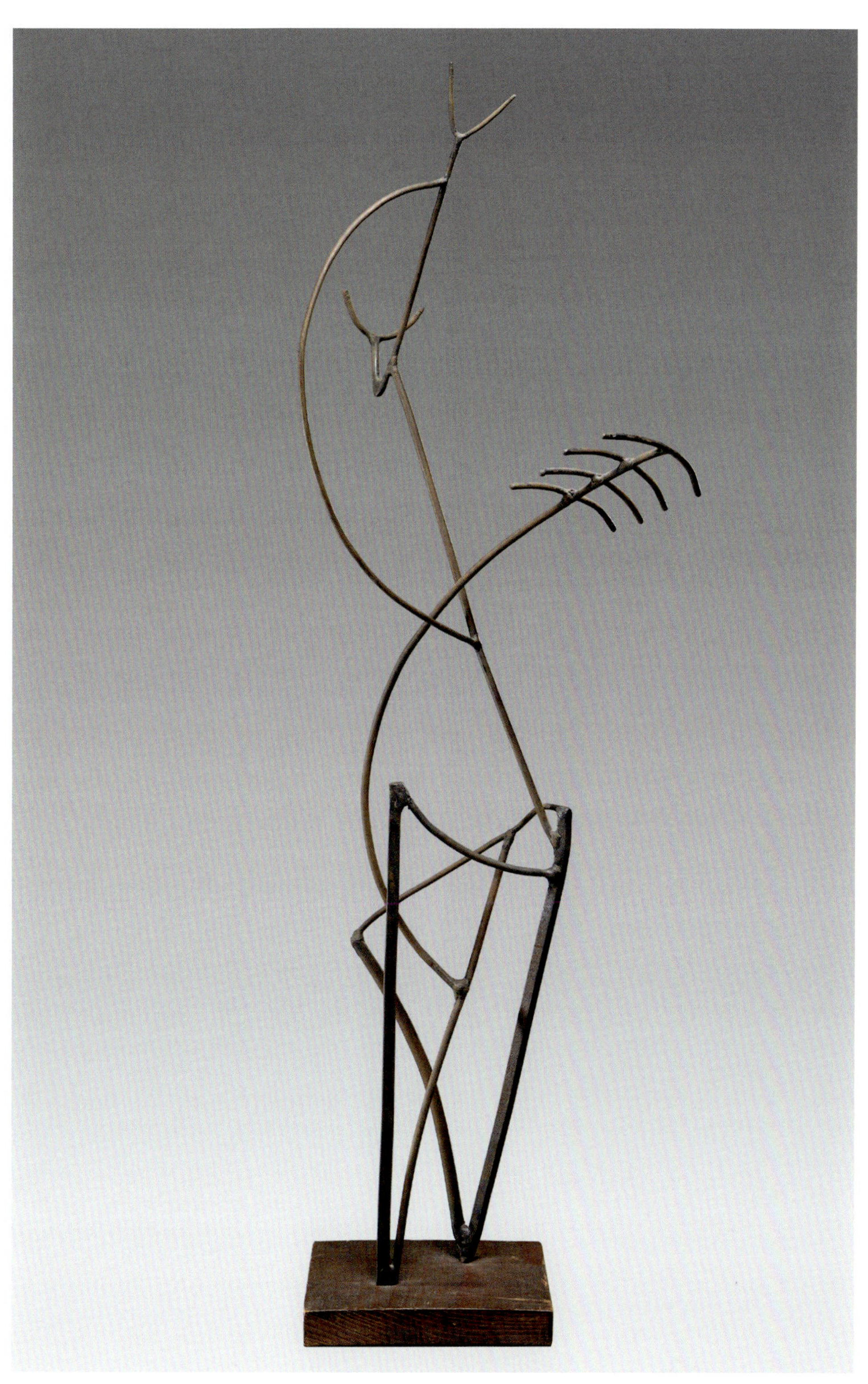

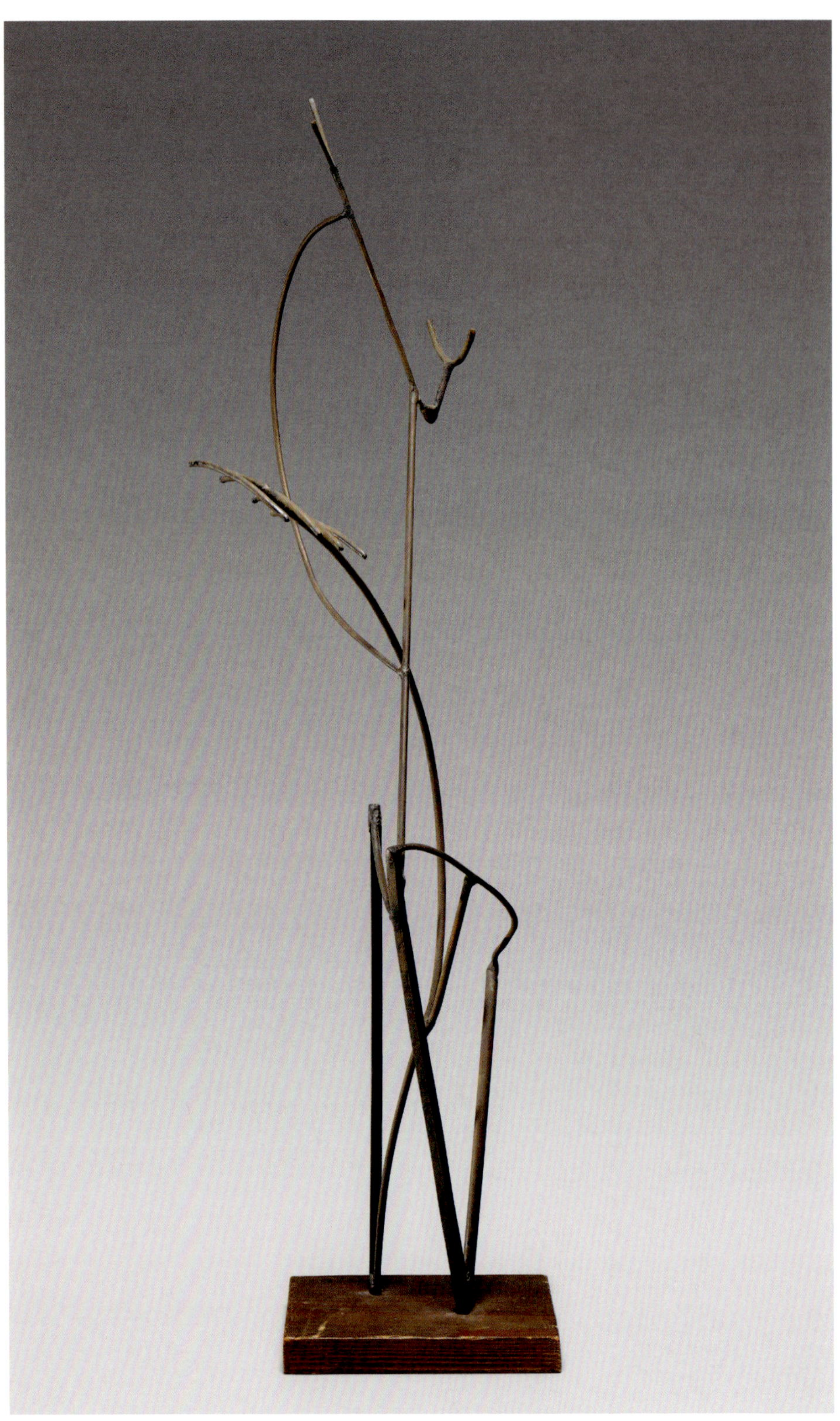

Alternate view of *Gracieuse figure*

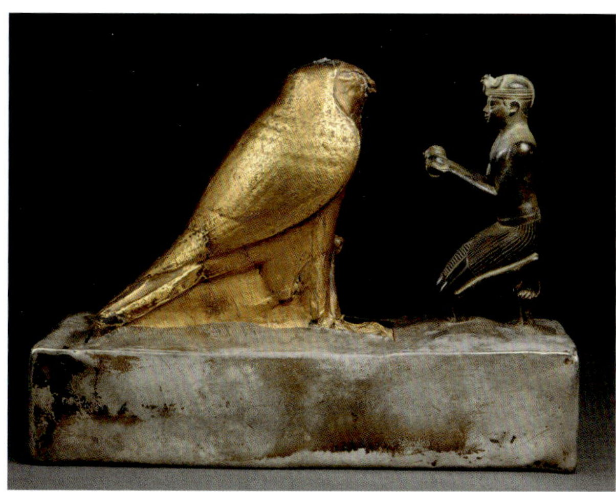

Fig. 2. *Statuette of Taharqa and the Falcon God*, 1069–404 B.C. Bronze and gold-plated graywacke on a silver-plated wood base, 7¾ × 10¼ × 4¹⁄₁₆ in. (19.7 × 26 × 10.3 cm). Musée du Louvre, Paris, E25276

Though the works he created using this distinctive style of abstraction are often marked by playfulness and humor, Cousins made a number of works during the heyday of the American civil rights movement about the plight of African American citizens in the United States. These sculptures, such as *Political Prisoner* (1954, location unknown), *Slave* (1963, location unknown), and *Figure debout* (Standing Figure, 1963, private collection), convey Cousins's ongoing connection to his home country, as well as his decrial of the segregated conditions that caused him to leave and to live out the rest of his days in Europe. The first large-scale exhibition in his native country to include his work was not mounted until 1996, four years after his death, at the Studio Museum in Harlem.[5] —ND

1. For an in-depth exploration of African American expatriates in Paris, see Asake Bomani and Belvie Rooks, eds., *Paris Connections: African American Artists in Paris* (San Francisco: Q.E.D. Press, 1992); and Audreen Buffalo, ed., *Explorations in the City of Light: African-American Artists in Paris, 1945–1965*, exh. cat. (New York: Studio Museum in Harlem, 1996).

2. For example, see *Le musicien* (1954), *Le matador* (1955), and *La forêt* (The Forest, ca. 1960) at Michael Rosenfeld Gallery, New York; see also "Harold Cousins (1916–1992)," Michael Rosenfeld Gallery, accessed December 7, 2016, http://www .michaelrosenfeldart.com/artists/harold-cousins-1916-1992.

3. Buffalo, *Explorations in the City of Light*, 62.

4. "The [Egyptian bird and tomb sculptures] gave one the visual impression of something existing that was not present in the forms of their material parts. I became convinced that this 'something' was the form of the empty space between the parts of a sculpture or around a solid." Harold Cousins, "'Plaiton' Sculpture: Its Origin and Development," *Leonardo* 4 (1971): 352.

5. "Harold Cousins (1916–1992)," Michael Rosenfeld Gallery. The exhibition, *Explorations in the City of Light: African-American Artists in Paris, 1945–1965*, was on view at the Studio Museum in Harlem from January 18 to June 2, 1996, before traveling to other venues.

10 prints from the series *Esculturas Rupestres*
(Rupestrian Sculptures)
> *Jaruco Caves (Cueva del Aguila)*
> Untitled
> *Guabancex (Goddess of the Wind)*
> *Iyare (Mother)*
> *Guanaroca (First Woman)*
> *Guacar (Our Menstruation)*
> *Guabancex (Goddess of the Wind)*
> *Atabey (Mother of the Waters)*
> *Guanaroca (First Woman)*
> *Itiba Cahubaba (Old Mother Blood)*
1982, printed 1983
Photoetching and chine collé
Ranging from 3⅝ × 5⁵⁄₁₆ in. (9.2 × 13.5 cm) to 5⁹⁄₁₆ × 3¹¹⁄₁₆ in.
(14.2 × 9.4 cm)
Provenance: Galerie Lelong, New York; Yale University Art
Gallery, New Haven, Conn., Leonard C. Hanna, Jr., Class of
1913, Fund, 2005.54.1–.10.

This series of photoetchings documents sculptures that Ana
Mendieta made when she returned to her native Cuba from
the United States, where her Catholic, counterrevolutionary
parents had sent her as a political refugee at the age of
twelve. She made these works during one of the multiple
trips to her homeland that she took in the period of greater
exchange between the two countries in the early 1980s.
The artist carved the *Esculturas Rupestres* (Rupestrian
Sculptures) into the soft limestone walls of the Jaruco caves
outside Havana and named each work after a goddess ven-
erated by the indigenous Taíno tribes.[1] The Taíno attached
great importance to caves: they represented their gods,
called *zemis*, in petroglyphs, and their mythology describes
the birthplace of the sun and the moon in caves.[2] Yet rather
than directly mimicking the representational practices
of indigenous religion, Mendieta drew creatively from
them in her ephemeral carvings, which evoke primordial
female forces while also referring to the artist's own body.
Eschewing notions of simple reunification and reclamation
that might be suggested by a wholesale appropriation of
native art or immutable alteration of the landscape, these
works convey a far more complex and open-ended meditation on homecoming.

Mendieta first visited Cuba on a trip organized by the
New York–based cultural organization Círculo de Cultura
Cubana, to which she belonged. On successive trips, she
befriended numerous Cuban artists, including José Bedia,
who also were interested in Prehispanic cultures. In the
summer of 1981 these artists helped her scout the Escaleras
de Jaruco (Stairs of Jaruco) site where she was to produce

the *Esculturas Rupestres*, eventually helping her secure
permission from the Cuban Ministry of Culture to do so.[3]
The Escaleras de Jaruco national park area has a long history
of inhabitation by indigenous peoples before and during
the colonial era. Mendieta's choice of this site reflects her
deep anthropological interest in the Taíno, as well as her
identification with their dispossession from their land.[4] (By
the eighteenth century, the Taíno had been largely decimated
by the Spaniards through enslavement and disease.)

Continuing ideas expressed in her earlier works—
such as her series *Silueta Works in Mexico* (see Josenhans,
"(Re)Defining the 'I' in Exile," fig. 13), in which the artist
created transient imprints and effigies of her body in different
locales—the *Esculturas Rupestres* evince Mendieta's process
of marking, shaping, and hollowing out the earth. Like the
Silueta series, the later works are partially self-referential;
while no longer corresponding mimetically to, or physically
incorporating, the artist's body, they still roughly corre-
spond to the size of Mendieta's petite frame. Though not
as impermanent as the works in the earlier series (whose
materials included sand, flowers, moss, branches, gunpowder,
and fire), the *Esculturas Rupestres* are provisional in that,
though Mendieta made an effort to shield them from the
elements, the exposed markings in the soft stone of the caves
would erode over time. Carved directly into the undulating
topography of the grottos, these works, with their zones of
relief and excision, confuse positive and negative form as well
as figure and ground. (In this manner, they recall the *Silueta*
images and a number of earlier works that mar the division
between form and landscape through camouflage, erosion,
and combustion.) Each thus stages a dynamic between
rupture and continuity, physical presence and dissolution.

Mendieta displayed large black-and-white
photographs of the *Esculturas Rupestres* that show their
wider geological context at A.I.R. Gallery, in New York, in
November 1981. For the related photoetchings, initially
prepared by the artist and author Luis Camnitzer with the
help of a grant from the New York State Council on the Arts
in 1983, Mendieta closely cropped the images, thereby making
the precise orientation of the *Esculturas Rupestres* in the
landscape unclear. Photodocumentation was an integral part
of Mendieta's practice due to the site-specific and ephemeral
nature of much of her work, but here the images seem to
underscore the formal properties of the carvings by omitting
their surrounding environs. Perhaps this accentuated
distance between the sculptures and their reproductions
marks the importance of site in these works. The elimination
of landscape preserves Mendieta's sculptures as in situ
transactions with the history and material reality of her
homeland. —ND

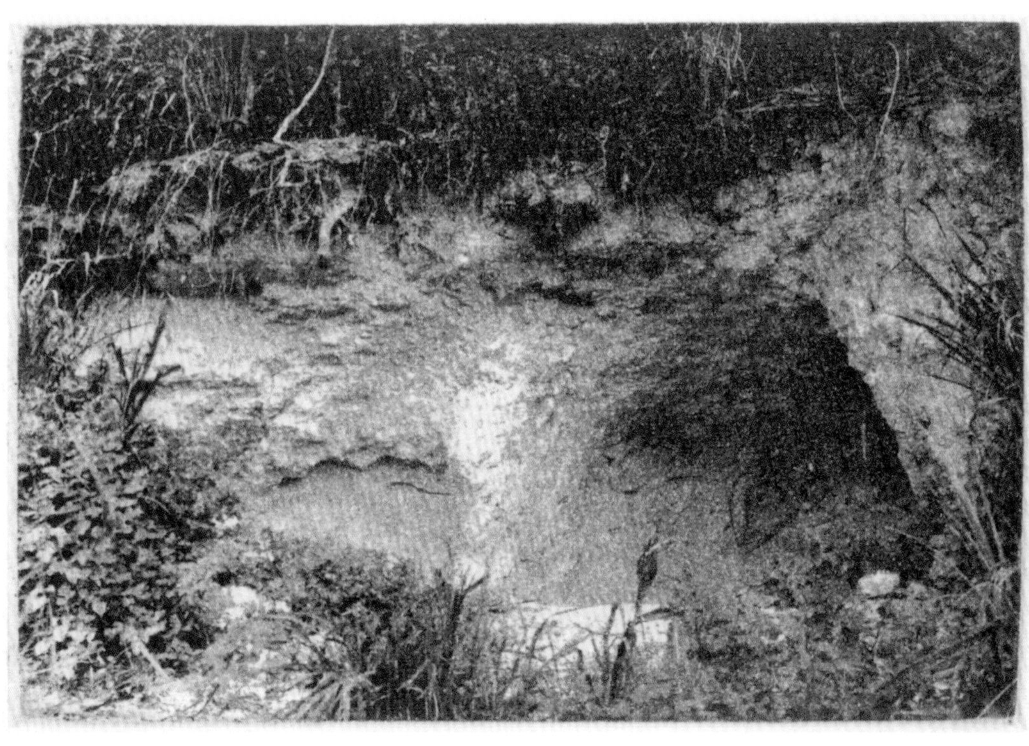

Jaruco Caves (Cueva del Aguila)

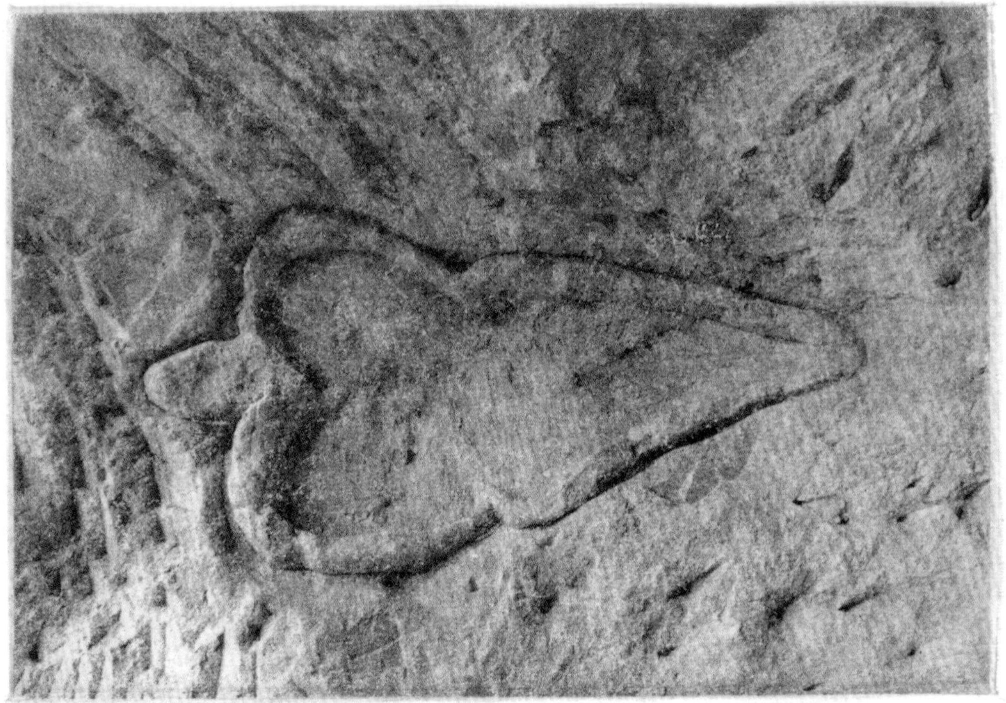

Untitled

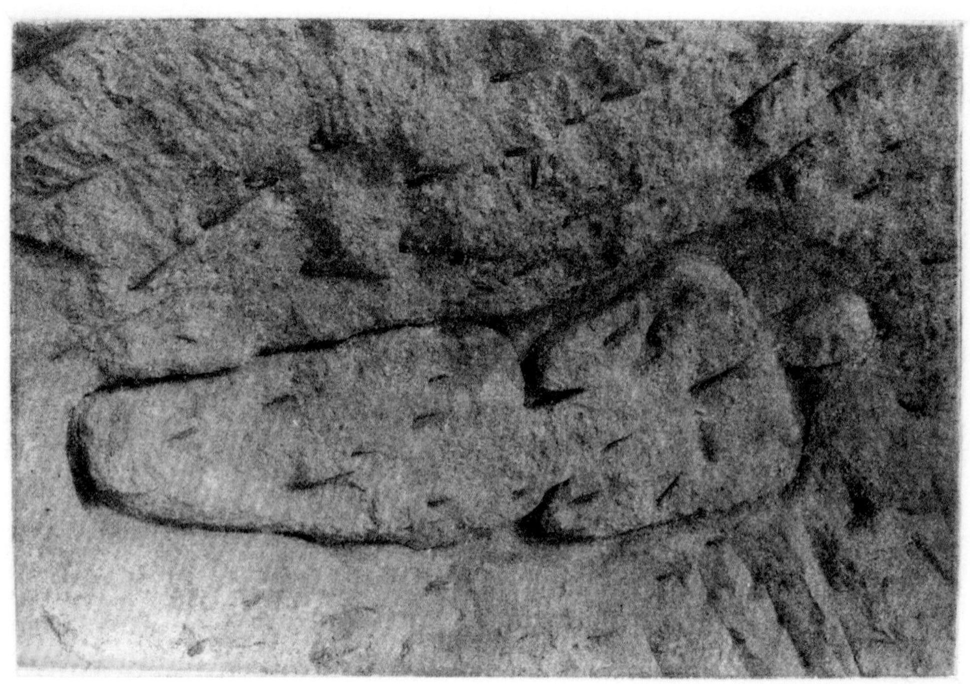

Guabancex (Goddess of the Wind)

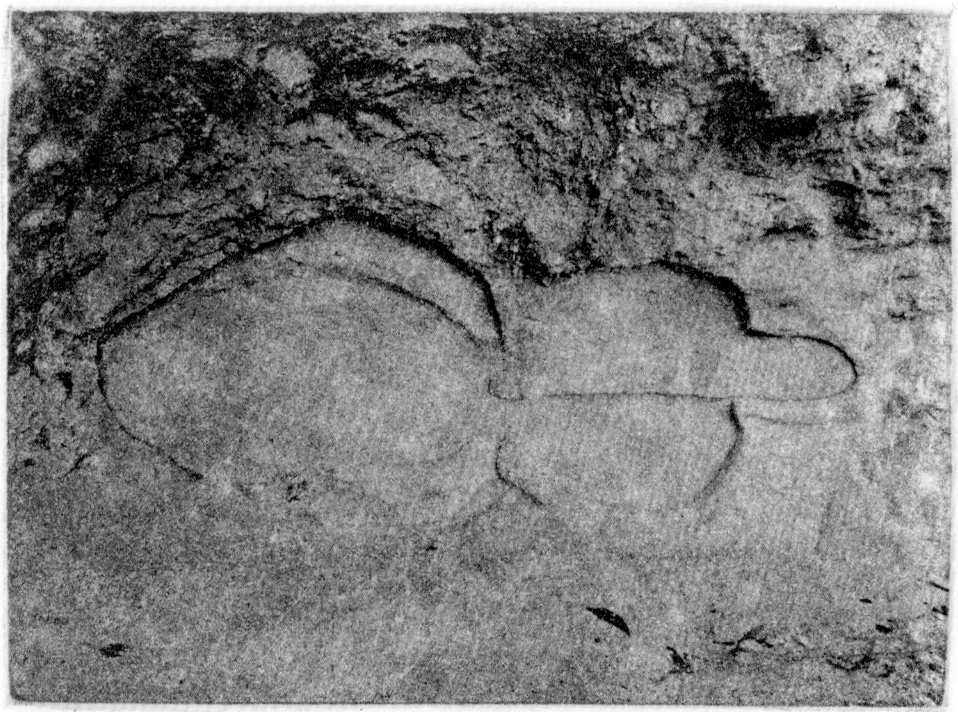

Iyare (Mother)

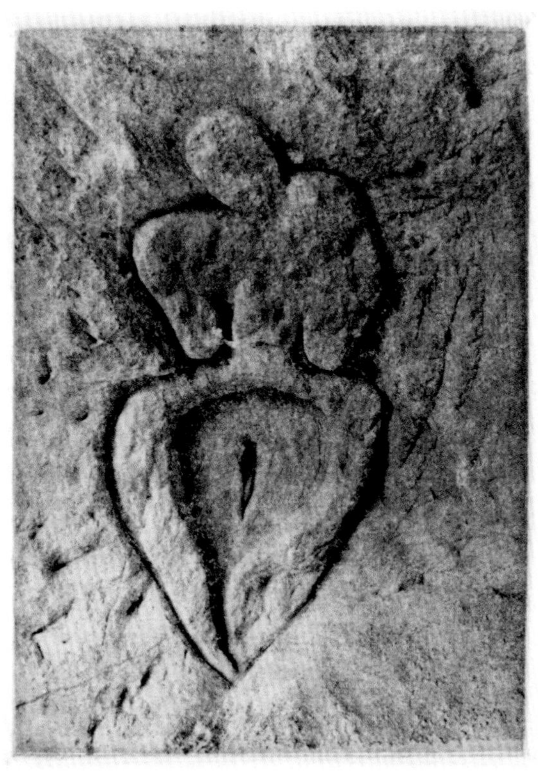

Guanaroca (First Woman)

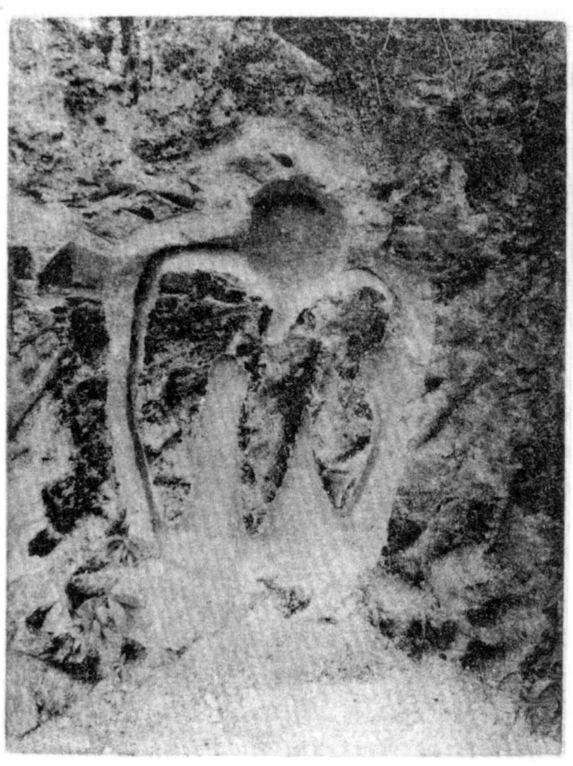

Guacar (Our Menstruation)

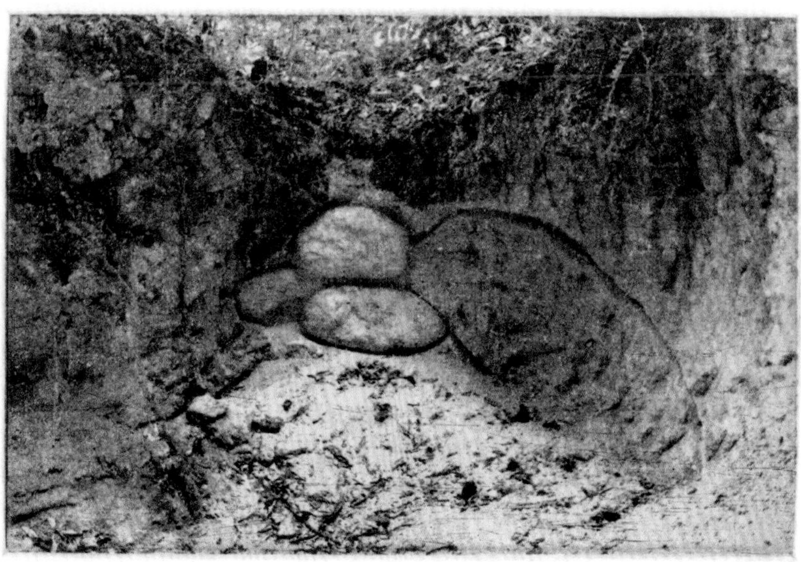

Guabancex (Goddess of the Wind)

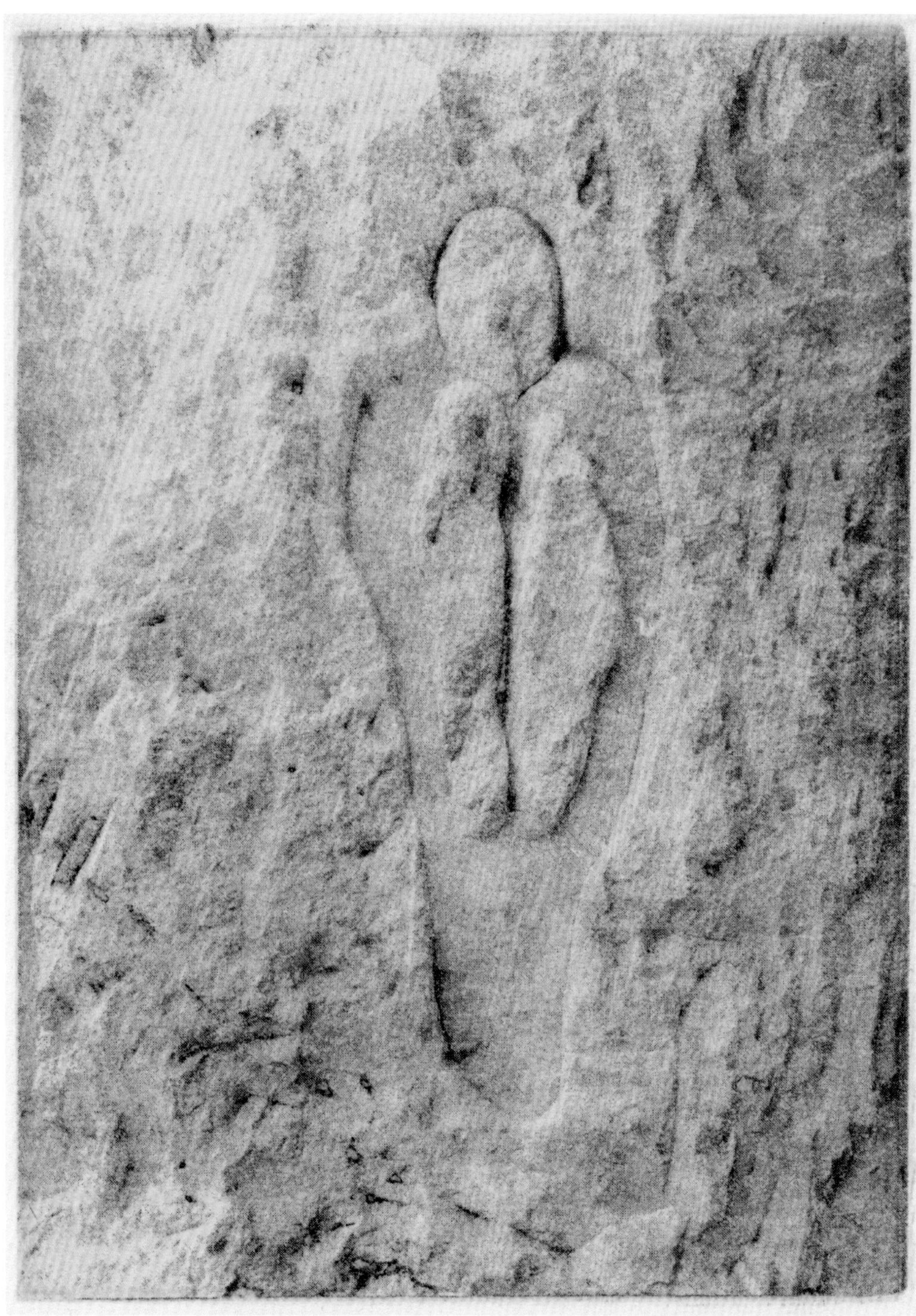

Atabey (Mother of the Waters)

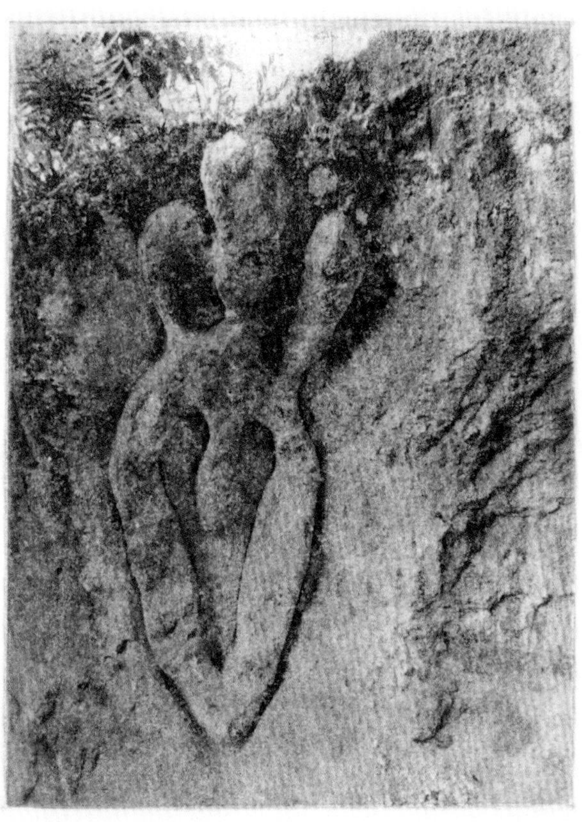 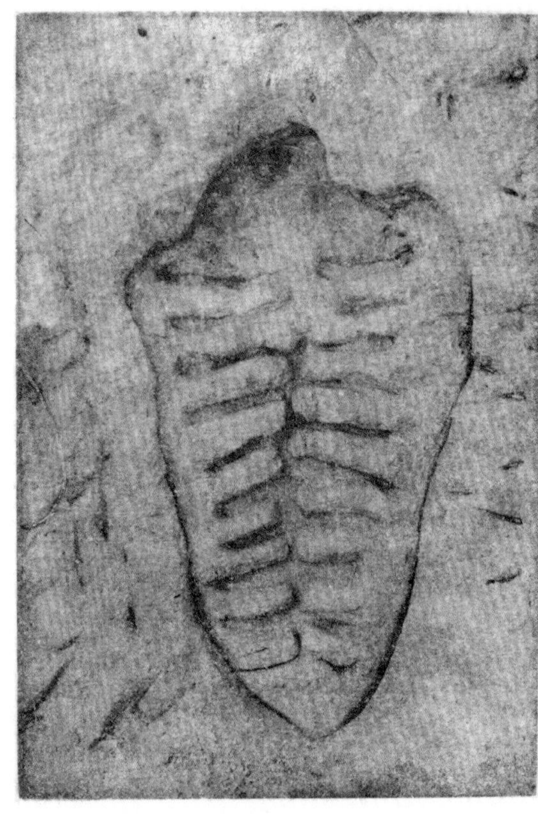

Guanaroca (First Woman)   *Itiba Cahubaba (Old Mother Blood)*

1. Meaning "good" or "noble," the name Taíno comes from the way the people described themselves in their encounter with Christopher Columbus (to differentiate their people from the aggressive Island Caribs). It refers to indigenous inhabitants of the Bahamas, the Greater Antilles, and some of the Lesser Antilles. See Irving Rouse, *The Taínos: Rise and Decline of the People Who Greeted Columbus* (New Haven, Conn.: Yale University Press, 1992).

2. See Antonio M. Stevens Arroyo, *Cave of the Jagua: The Mythological World of the Taínos* (Albuquerque: University of New Mexico Press, 1988).

3. Mendieta received a Guggenheim Foundation Fellowship that enabled her to return to Cuba to realize the works.

4. Bonnie Clearwater, *Ana Mendieta: A Book of Works* (Miami Beach, Fla.: Grassfield Press, 1993), cited by Laura Roulet, "Ana Mendieta as Cultural Connector with Cuba," *American Art* 26, no. 2 (Summer 2012): 21–27.

Amerika (Baseball)
1983–84
Oil on canvas
58 × 58 in. (147.3 × 147.3 cm)
Provenance: Charles B. Benenson Collection;
Yale University Art Gallery, New Haven, Conn.,
Charles B. Benenson, B.A. 1933, Collection, 2006.52.14.

R. B. Kitaj was a second-generation Russian-Jewish immigrant who grew up in Cleveland, Ohio, in the 1930s yet found a new home in the United Kingdom, moving there in 1958 to study art and remaining for most of his adult life.[1] As an American expatriate, Kitaj used the motif of baseball to convey a strong national sentiment mediated by a sense of distance or estrangement. In a short text about his painting *Amerika (Baseball)*, published in the catalogue for his 1994 retrospective at the Tate Gallery in London, he remarked, "From time to time I have to make a baseball painting to express a deep national love. By national I mean where you come from, grow up, get formed, national pride, etc. etc. What can it be if not a national feeling translated into painting?"[2] As underscored by the scholar Aaron Rosen, the stories of classic Jewish-American authors such as Chaim Potok and Philip Roth construe baseball as an important symbol of aspirational American belonging for young Jewish boys of Kitaj's generation and those that followed.[3]

This outsider status that Kitaj and his Jewish peers sought to overcome is captured in the isolated figure in the lower-right corner of the painting who gazes upon the scene of play from a distance, and whose features echo those of the artist. It is reflected as well in the title, which refers to Franz Kafka's story of a young European immigrant's trials in the United States, as told in his unfinished novel *Amerika: The Man Who Disappeared* (1927). Made while Kitaj was living in the United Kingdom, *Amerika (Baseball)* reflects not only the complexities of American immigrant identity but also a nuanced longing for home that suggests the artist's feelings of remove from his adopted land of residence. As such, the painting speaks to the condition of perpetual diaspora, a leitmotif in Kitaj's life and work that he theorized in his two *Diasporist Manifestos* (written in 1989 and 1992).

Amerika (Baseball) attests to this state of never being quite at home in any one place, not only through its depiction from overseas of the iconic American game but also in its embodiment of the omnivorous cultural consumption and multiple artistic quotations that frequently shape Kitaj's work; references to literature, music, and European art history often pepper his paintings and prints. In a follow-up to his *First Diasporist Manifesto*, he describes this heterogeneity as reflective of the diasporic condition, because artists in a diaspora must reconcile their own outsider aesthetic traditions and tendencies—what Kitaj calls a "pariah-art"—with those of the predominating "host-art"—in his case the established European canon.[4] In Kitaj's work, this reconciliation frequently manifests as a tendency to incorporate aspects of this canon into a more personal style. For instance, he based the composition of *Amerika (Baseball)* in part on the Spanish Baroque master Diego Velázquez's *Philip IV Hunting Wild Boar (La Tela Real)* (fig. 1), which he saw in the National Gallery, London.[5] The flat expanses of color and the centrifugal composition also recall the work of the European modern master Henri Matisse (fig. 2).[6] The manner in which Kitaj has distorted the bodies in athletic motion contains a hint of the violence of Francis Bacon's figures. In 1976 Kitaj included Bacon in *The Human Clay*, a landmark exhibition of the work of British artists that he curated for the Arts Council of Great Britain.

In his aforementioned text about the painting, Kitaj refers to the field upon which the seemingly directionless bodies engage in acts of sport as a "theater," an allusion to the end of Kafka's novel, in which the protagonist, Karl Rossmann, joins the Nature Theater of Oklahoma. It is there that Karl hopes to find "a profession, a stand-by, his freedom, even his old home and his parents, as if by some celestial witchery."[7] In the painting, the complex marriage of patriotic nostalgia and the outsider's quest for home is furthered by Kitaj's inclusion of the African American baseball star Satchel Paige in the foreground of the playing field. The word "Cleveland" is discernible on Paige's jersey, referencing the major-league team that finally recruited the much-loved forty-two-year-old pitcher from the Negro Leagues in 1947. By recalling the bittersweet legacy of African American integration in the United States in a painting that meditates on the artist's own sense of belonging and nonbelonging, *Amerika (Baseball)* speaks to the challenges and dreams of inclusion that characterize a broader experience of diaspora. —ND

72

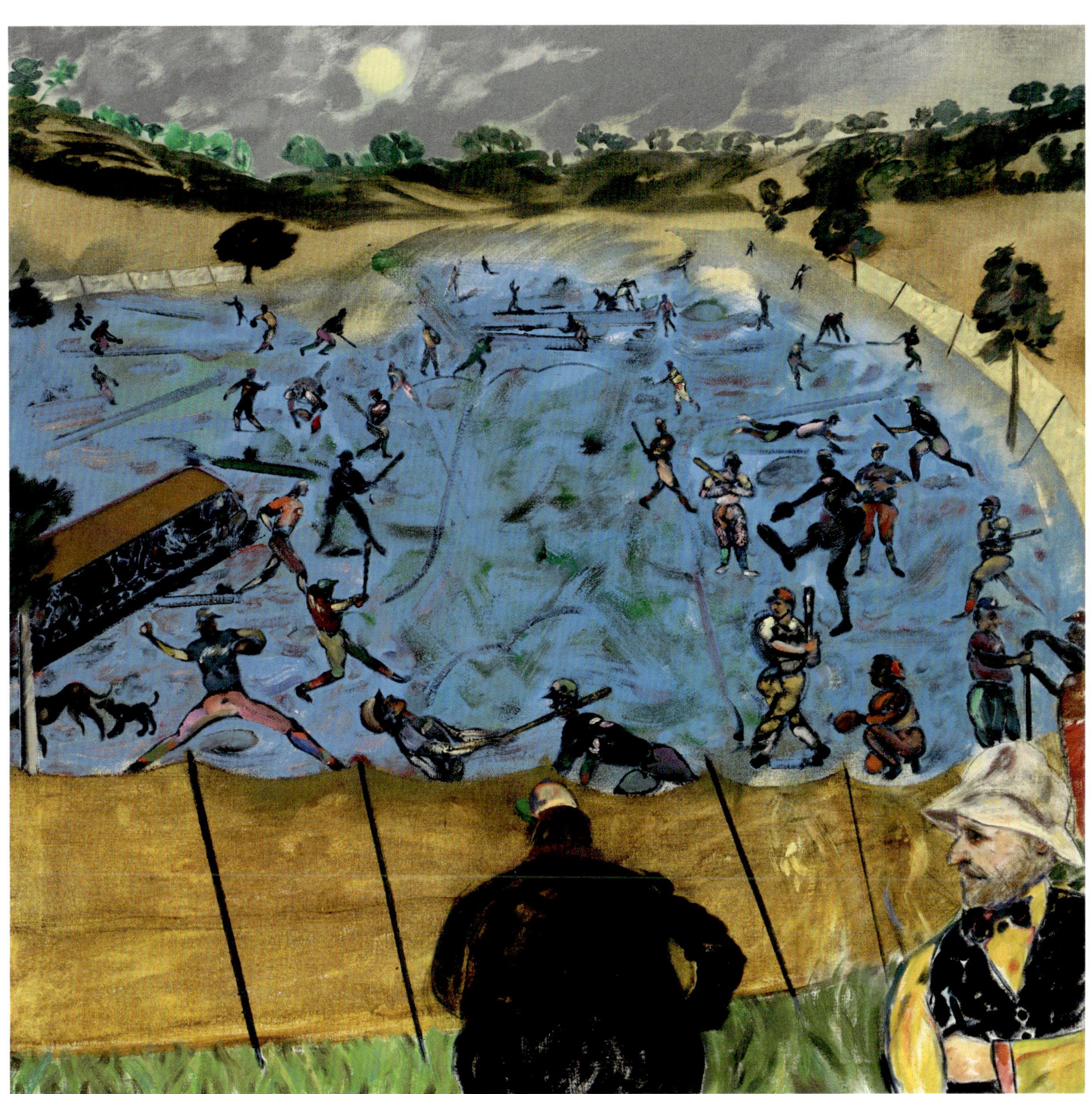

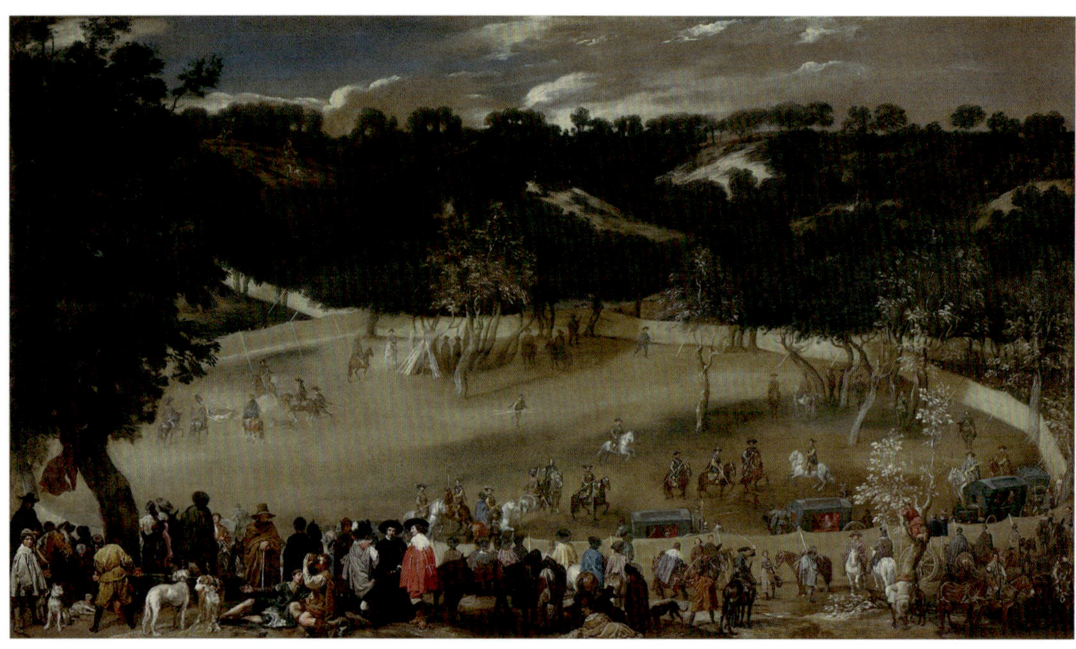

Fig. 1. Diego Velázquez, *Philip IV Hunting Wild Boar (La Tela Real)*, probably 1632–37. Oil on canvas, 5 ft. 11¹¹⁄₁₆ in. × 9 ft. 11 in. (182 × 302 cm). National Gallery, London, NG197

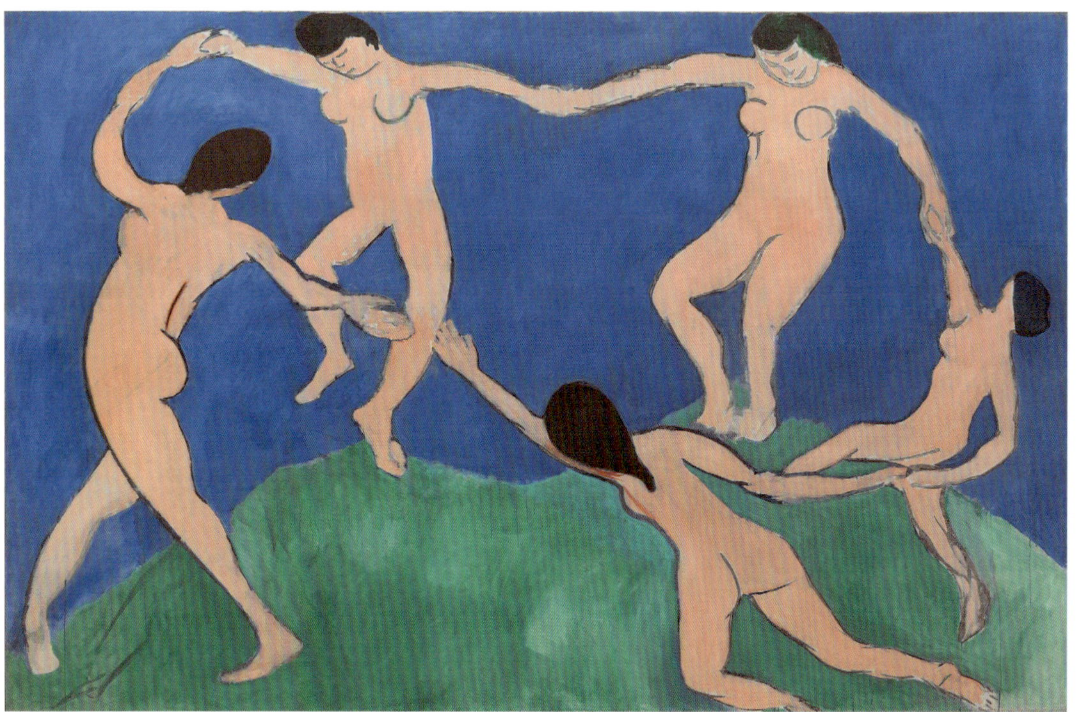

Fig. 2. Henri Matisse, *Danse (I)*, 1909. Oil on canvas, 8 ft. 6½ in. × 12 ft. 9½ in. (259.7 × 390.1 cm). Museum of Modern Art, New York, Gift of Nelson A. Rockefeller in honor of Alfred H. Barr, Jr., 201.1963

1. Kitaj was born Ronald Brooks but assumed the surname of his mother's second husband, a Viennese refugee and doctor named Walter Kitaj.

2. R. B. Kitaj, "Preface to *Baseball*, 1983–84," in *R. B. Kitaj: A Retrospective*, ed. Richard Morphet, exh. cat. (London: Tate Gallery Publications, 1994), 150.

3. Aaron Rosen, *Imagining Jewish Art: Encounters with the Masters in Chagall, Guston, and Kitaj* (London: Modern Humanities Research Association and W. S. Maney & Son, 2009), 112.

4. "What I think may be new and radical . . . are the energies I have found for my own painting at that crossroads, that very conjunction where pariah-art and host-art . . . meet in passionate embrace." R. B. Kitaj, "Diasporism," quoted by Marco Livingstone, *Kitaj* (London: Phaidon, 2014), 41.

5. Maria Taroutina, "R. B. Kitaj," in *Eye on a Century: Modern and Contemporary Art from the Charles B. Benenson Collection at the Yale University Art Gallery*, ed. Cathleen Chaffee (New Haven, Conn.: Yale University Art Gallery, 2012), 144, cat. 68.

6. For instance, see Henri Matisse, *La musique* (1910, State Hermitage Museum, Saint Petersburg) or *Le bonheur de vivre* (1905–6, Barnes Foundation, Philadelphia).

7. Max Brod recounting Kafka's statement; Kitaj, "Preface," 150.

Camera Obscura: Houses Across the Street in Our Living Room
1991
Gelatin silver print
17⅞ × 22½ in. (45.4 × 57.1 cm)
Provenance: Yale University Art Gallery, New Haven, Conn., The Allan Chasanoff, B.A. 1961, Photography Collection, 2004.130.84.

Abelardo Morell's *Camera Obscura: Houses Across the Street in Our Living Room* is one of a series of images that the artist made by transforming an interior space into a camera obscura, a prephotographic image-making device, and then photographing the result.[1] A camera obscura projects inverted images of the outside world onto the wall of a darkened box or space by filtering light through a convex lens or aperture. Knowledge of this technology dates back to ancient China and Greece, and it was adapted in the nineteenth century to make the first photographic camera. Rather than using neutral, featureless projection spaces, as was conventional in order to obtain a more unadulterated image, Morell often creates his camera obscura works within furnished domestic interiors (or, since 2010, on earthen or geological surfaces with the help of a self-fashioned tent).[2] Here, he morphs the living room in his family's home in Brookline, Massachusetts, into a strange and whimsical space.

In a speech he made upon receiving an honorary doctor of fine arts degree from Bowdoin College in 1997, Morell connected his photographic practice—in which he often defamiliarizes mundane objects (such as glassware, books, maps, and money) and spaces by capturing them in surprising ways—to the dreamlike nature of his own early experience of leaving Cuba at age fourteen as a political refugee. He noted, "It's interesting to me that in my ongoing artistic work I struggle with picturing the real within the aura of imaginary and seemingly irrational worlds."[3] As this photograph attests, Morell brings his

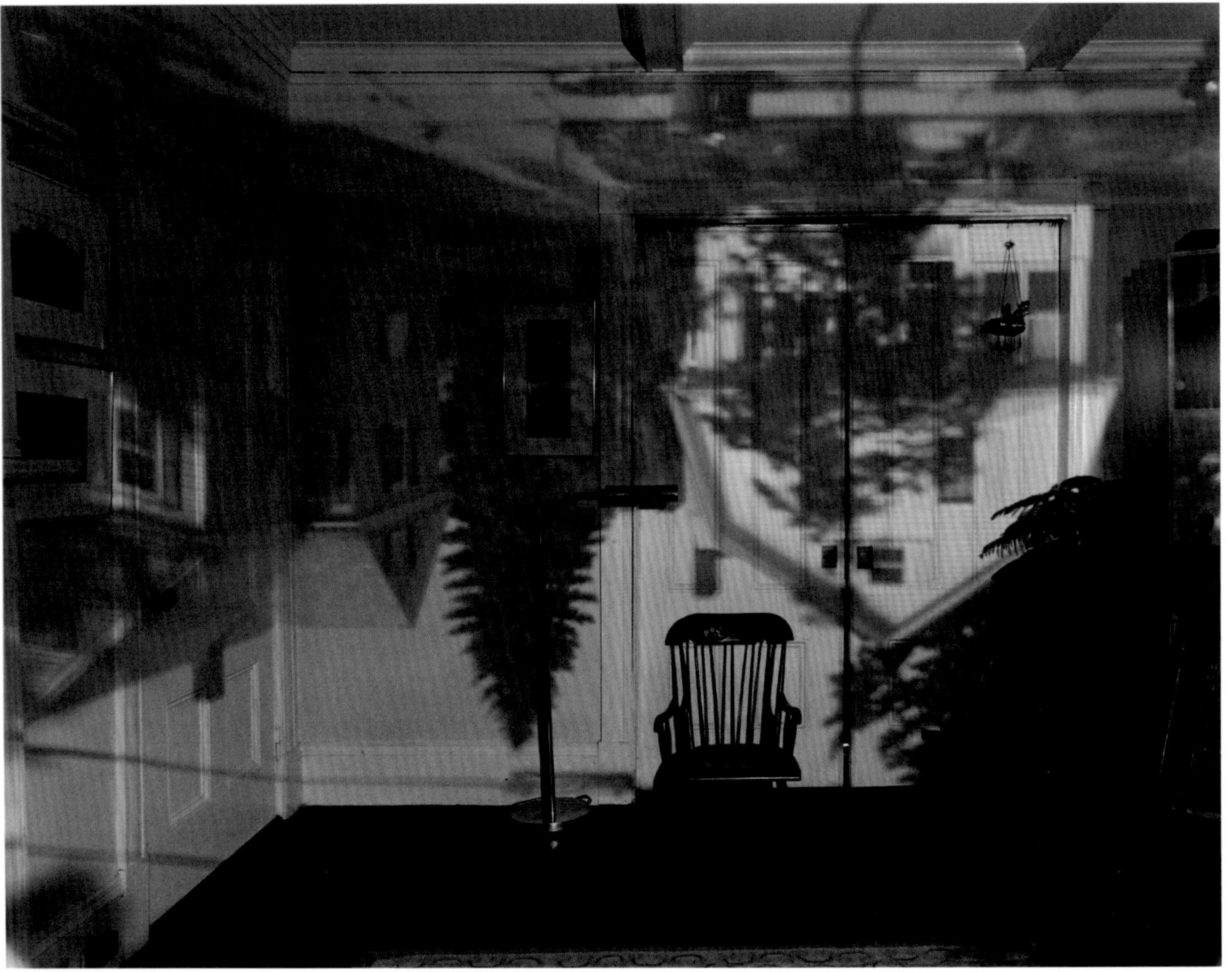

76

inclination to seek reality through the counterintuitive and the magical to bear on the motif of the home, which runs in various ways throughout his work.[4] Rather than a specific locale that serves as a stable, private refuge from the world, the home in Morell's oeuvre is a continually surprising and amorphous landscape, one constructed as much in the imagination as out of brick and mortar.[5]

Through photographic intervention, Morell transforms his family home by overlaying the living room with the spectral, upside-down image of the suburban street outside, rendering porous the borders between interior and exterior. The composition, which he captured in an exposure lasting over eight hours in order to register the dim projection, is highly deliberate. Its fusion of the domestic interior and the dark, somewhat unfocused image of houses and trees generates a formal resonance between their respective features: the outdoor foliage rhymes with the potted plant in the corner of the room; the wooden slats of the French doors recall the facades of the houses; and the double-hung windows echo the framed double-hung photos. The domestic space is unsettled through the projection of a foreign image, which mutates it into something uncanny.

The ongoing elusiveness of home for Morell is suggested biographically by the fact that, despite living in the United States since his teenage years, he did not become a U.S. citizen until 2002, when he did so in order to more safely return to Cuba for the first time to make a number of camera obscura photographs for Terry McCoy's book *Cuba on the Verge*, published in 2003 (fig. 1). For Morell, home is inherently unsettling; it is haunted by distant memories of migration, which in turn persistently destabilize notions of foundation or rootedness. —ND

1. The artist does so by covering the windows with black plastic, save for a hole three-eighths of an inch in diameter, in which he places a lens. Richard B. Woodward, *Abelardo Morell* (London and New York: Phaidon, 2005), 11.

2. "Conversation with Abelardo Morell and Peter Essick," *National Geographic*, April 22, 2014, accessed August 25, 2016, http://proof.nationalgeographic.com/2014/04/22/conversation-with-abelardo-morell-and-peter-essick.

3. As quoted by Elizabeth Siegel, "Wonderlands" in *Abelardo Morell: The Universe Next Door* (New Haven, Conn.: Yale University Press, 2013), 17.

4. Siegel notes the persistence of this motif; ibid., 15.

5. Morell's artistic interest in the home emerged in the late 1980s, after the birth of his son, Brady, compelled him to focus on simple objects within the space of the house in which he was suddenly more confined with something akin to the naive eye of a child; ibid., 14.

77

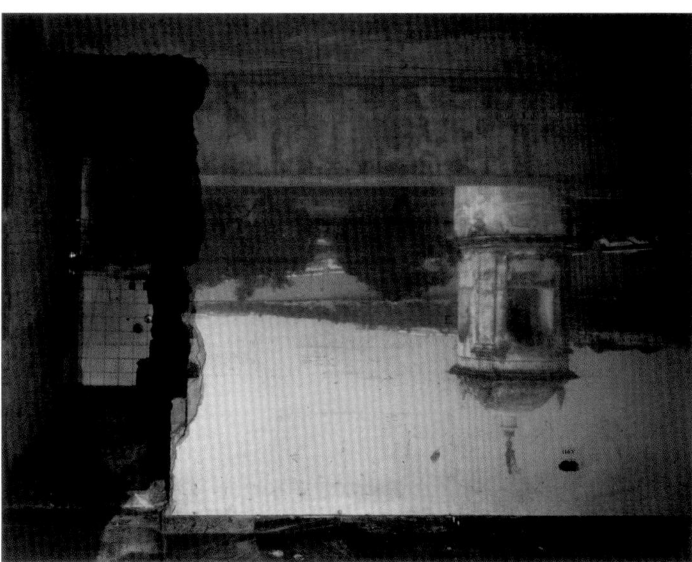

Fig. 1. Abelardo Morell, *Camera Obscura: La Giraldilla de la Habana in Room with Broken Wall*, 2002. Gelatin silver print, 18⅛ × 22⁷⁄₁₆ in. (46 × 57 cm). Yale University Art Gallery, New Haven, Conn., Gift of Robinson A. Grover, B.A. 1958, M.S.L. 1975, and Nancy D. Grover, 2016.26.23

Untitled [Ho Chi Minh City], from the series *Viêt Nam*
1998, printed 2006
Gelatin silver print
15 ⅞ × 22 ¹¹⁄₁₆ in. (40.3 × 57.7 cm)
Provenance: Yale University Art Gallery, New Haven, Conn.,
Gift of the artist in honor of Richard Benson, 2006.229.1.

In her photographs, An-My Lê combines motifs from her
childhood in Ho Chi Minh City (then called Saigon), and
from the Vietnam War, with more universal notions of
home and of the transformation of contemporary landscape
through social and economic changes. After fleeing Vietnam
for the United States as a teenager with her family in 1975,
she did not visit her native country until 1994. This trip
initiated the series *Viêt Nam* (1994–98), in which Lê depicts
landscapes and cityscapes of the war-torn country. Drawn to
landscapes in South Vietnam that she remembered from her
youth, as well as places in the North described to her by her
mother, whose family was from there, Lê documented rural
and urban scenes with people engaged in everyday activities.[1]

This large-format, black-and-white photograph
shows people gathered in an open field in Ho Chi Minh
City; they appear split up into smaller groups, busy riding
their bicycles, talking to each other, or flying kites, in what
seems like a peaceful scene. The image is dominated by
an almost cloudless sky, the white disrupted only by black
kites. The fuzziness of the kites creates a certain ambiguity:
are they simply toys, meant to delight the people below,
or are they falling bombs, reminiscent of those that
battered the city during the Vietnam War? The blurred
motion of the kites and the people in the foreground—the
result of an intentionally long exposure time—evokes
nineteenth-century photographs, which were not yet able
to capture rapid movements.[2] The large format and the
small figures under the immense sky convey a feeling of
distance, as if the photographer, although in close proximity to the people and of the same ancestry, is separated from
them, making it impossible for her to ever fully return to
her native country. Lê's American life separates her from
the others, and she is constrained to the role of an observer.
As she explained in an interview in 2015, "After my whole
Viêt Nam (1994–98) project, I actually felt much more
American. But the colors, the air remains. You reconnect to
the land in spite of the changes."[3]

The *Viêt Nam* series, like Lê's broader oeuvre, is
defined by a tension between her documentary approach

78

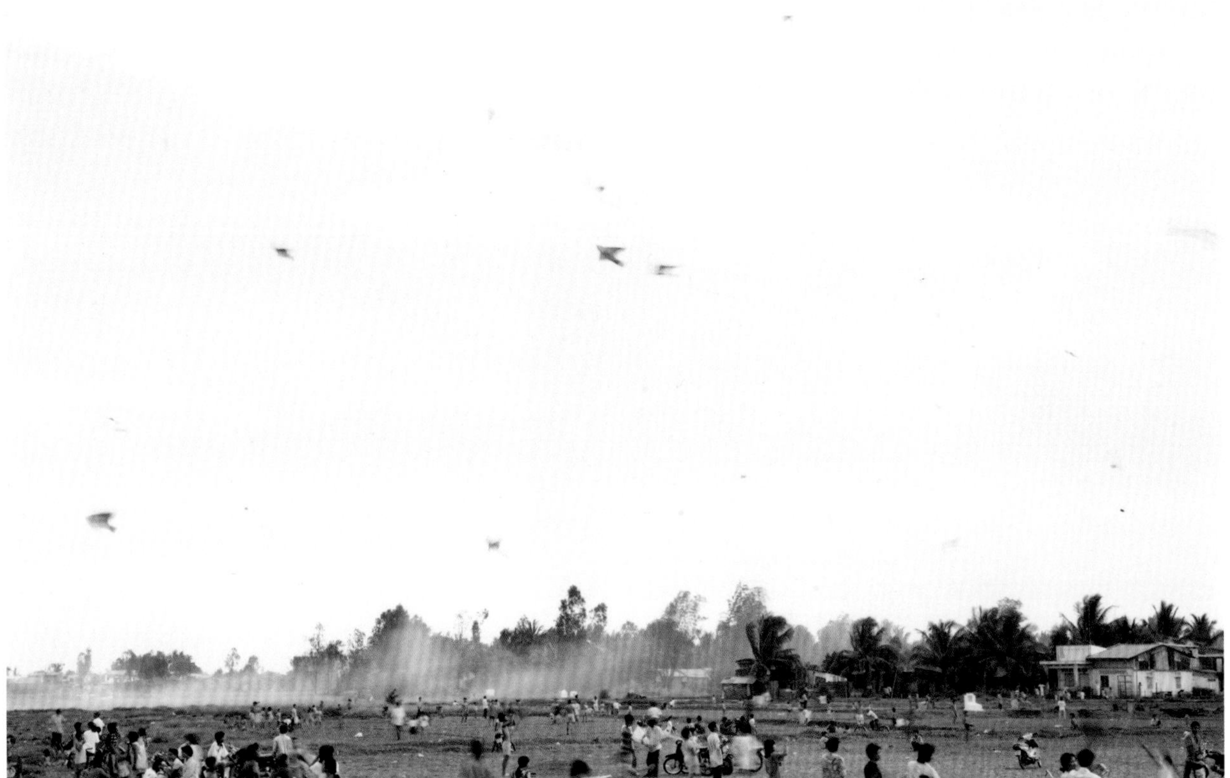

to sites and people and her reliance on personal memory. This persistent oscillation between real life and memory is expressed most strongly in photographs like this one. During the years between her departure from and return to Vietnam, Lê had only a few family pictures, and her impression of her native land was based mostly on her own recollection. Upon returning, she was drawn to making photographs "that use the real to ground the imaginary," instead of merely documenting contemporary Vietnam.[4] Focusing on landscape was a way for her to re-enter a world that had become foreign to her, to visit actual places but to reimagine them through the folktales, legends, and other stories told by her mother and grandmother.[5] The landscape she photographs thus foregrounds the idea of home for Lê, and it stands equally for the traditional agricultural society of Vietnam, where families used to live on and from the land.[6] In the artist's mind, the Vietnamese people and land are irrevocably linked.

Lê has cited photographers Robert Adams and Eugène Atget as inspirations, explaining that their work has infused her own with a lyrical, timeless approach.[7] Adams documented the landscape of his native Colorado throughout the mid-twentieth century as it underwent urbanization and industrial growth (fig. 1), capturing a sense of ephemeral beauty. Atget, decades earlier, took photographs of Paris at a time when the city faced radical

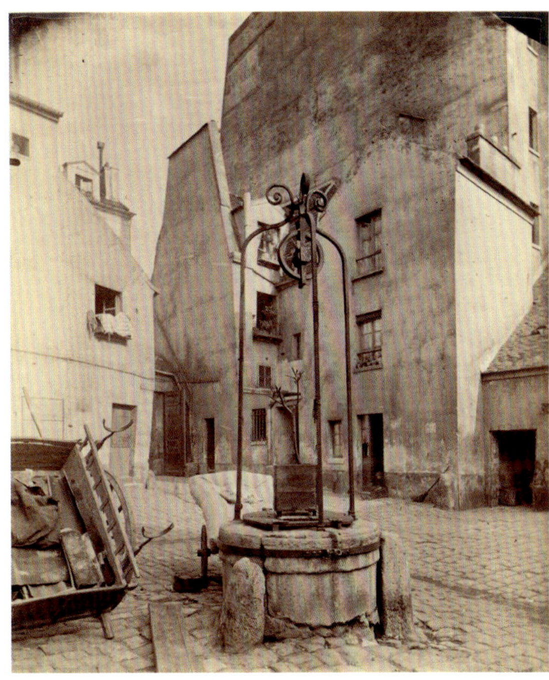

Fig. 2. Eugène Atget, *Rue Saint-Jacques*, 1899. Vintage albumen print, 8⅜ × 6¹³⁄₁₆ in. (21.2 × 17.3 cm). Yale University Art Gallery, New Haven, Conn., Everett V. Meeks, B.A. 1901, Fund, 2002.61.4

urban and social changes; he focused on aspects of the city—street vendors, shop windows, narrow alleyways, courtyards (fig. 2), and buildings that were about to be demolished—that seemed to belong to the past. Lê, in a similar way, documents, observes, and captures the fleeting facets of Vietnam—a country and society foreign and yet familiar to her, where the echoes of the former war are still omnipresent. —FVJ

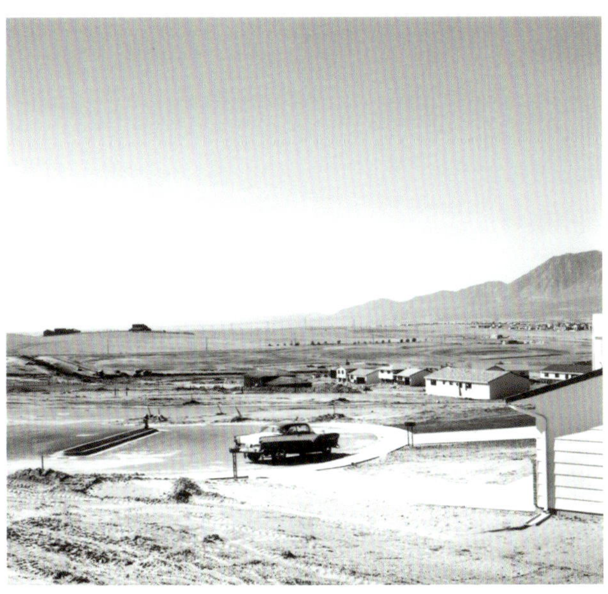

Fig. 1. Robert Adams, *Colorado Springs, Colorado*, 1968. Gelatin silver print mounted on board, 5¹⁵⁄₁₆ × 6⅛ in. (15.1 × 15.6 cm). Yale University Art Gallery, New Haven, Conn., Purchased with a gift from Saundra B. Lane, a grant from the Trellis Fund, and the Janet and Simeon Braguin Fund, 2008.52.6.14

1. Richard B. Woodward, "Essay," in An-My Lê, *Small Wars* (New York: Aperture, 2005), 109–17, esp. 112–13.

2. Ibid., 111.

3. An-My Lê, interview by Sarah Christoph, *The Brooklyn Rail*, February 5, 2015, http://www.brooklynrail.org/2015/02/art/ an-my-l-with-sara-christoph.

4. An-My Lê, interview by Hilton Als, in Lê, *Small Wars*, 119–25, esp. 119.

5. Ibid.

6. Ibid.

7. An-My Lê, interview by *Art21*, accessed December 12, 2016, http://www.art21.org/read/an-my-lê-vietnam.

Nature morte aux grenades
2006–7
Crystal, mild steel, and rubber
37⅜ × 81⅞ × 27⁹⁄₁₆ in. (95 × 208 × 70 cm)
Provenance: Yale University Art Gallery, New Haven,
Conn., The Heinz Family Fund and Katharine Ordway Fund,
2010.150.1.

Mona Hatoum's life and art have been largely shaped by
the violence in the Middle East, notably the civil war in
Lebanon (1975–90), where she grew up. She addresses this
topic in her work along with themes of exile, war, alienation, and personal space. Her sculptures and installations
in various media transform familiar themes and objects
into something strange and discomforting for the viewer.
Nature morte aux grenades is an intriguing work that
deliberately plays with the viewer's perception. At first
glance, the work represents a steel table on wheels with

colorful objects on top. This sculpture takes its title from a
still life that Henri Matisse painted in 1947 in Vence, in the
South of France (fig. 1). Hatoum's sculpture borrows from
Matisse's canvas the vivid colors and the motif of objects
displayed on a table. However, whereas Matisse painted a
"traditional" still life, in which fruits become decorative
patterns, Hatoum adopts the title and motif but completely
reverses both to create a politically charged sculpture. She
plays with the homophone of *grenade* (French for both
"pomegranate" and "grenade"); thus, what sounds like a
bucolic topic inspired by Matisse's still life with colorful
"grenades" is in fact a representation of the deadly tools. The
image of the grenade recalls its fatal use in combat, such
as during the Lebanese Civil War. In addition, the brightly
colored glass hints at the conflation of toys and weapons
that pervades mass and social media. *Nature morte aux grenades* thus speaks to the glorification and aestheticization of
weapons in popular culture. Yet the play of associations and

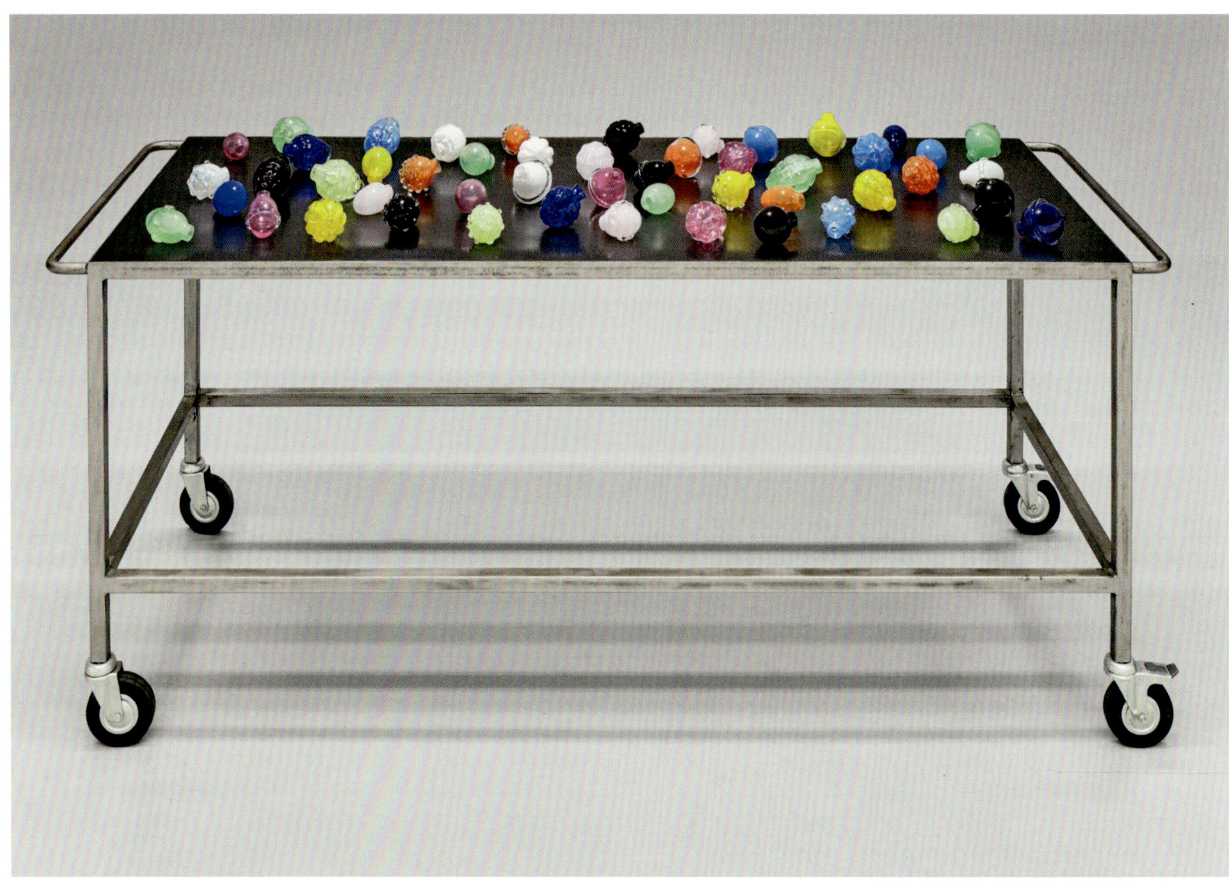

meanings goes even further in this work: the pomegranate was also an attribute of Aphrodite, the goddess of beauty in Greek mythology, and is mentioned in the Bible as a symbol of fertility. Hence the symbolic character of the fruit and its "lethal" homophone here stand in radical opposition—one evoking the idea of life, while the other conjures death. Moreover, the stainless-steel table holding the grenades resembles a surgical or embalming table, further stressing the association with violence and death.

Nature morte aux grenades also emphasizes the tension between the fatal use of grenades and the fragility and beauty of the crystal material Hatoum uses to render them (fig. 2). The crystal objects, unlike the weapons, which are typically made in specialized factories, were hand-blown and created through Hatoum's collaboration with craftspeople in Colle di Val d'Elsa, Tuscany, a town that specializes in crystal production.[1] The artist has transformed these deadly objects into something beautiful, with

seductive power.[2] Hatoum also partnered with glassmakers from Murano, an Italian city famous for its glassworks, to produce other delicate hand-blown glass variations on these grenades, as well as *A Bigger Splash* (fig. 3)—perhaps a nod to David Hockney's famous 1967 painting of the same name (Tate, London)—which evokes splashes of blood. Mirroring contemporary global culture, Hatoum's sculpture intertwines beauty and violence, and it challenges the perception of both notions. In addition to its symbolic use, glass also exemplifies Hatoum's interest in diverse materials and reflects her own nomadic lifestyle, which led to encounters with local craftspeople and resources in other countries, such as Italy.[3] These various components and readings of *Nature morte aux grenades* illustrate how Hatoum transferred the trauma of exile into a productive and integral part of her work. —FVJ

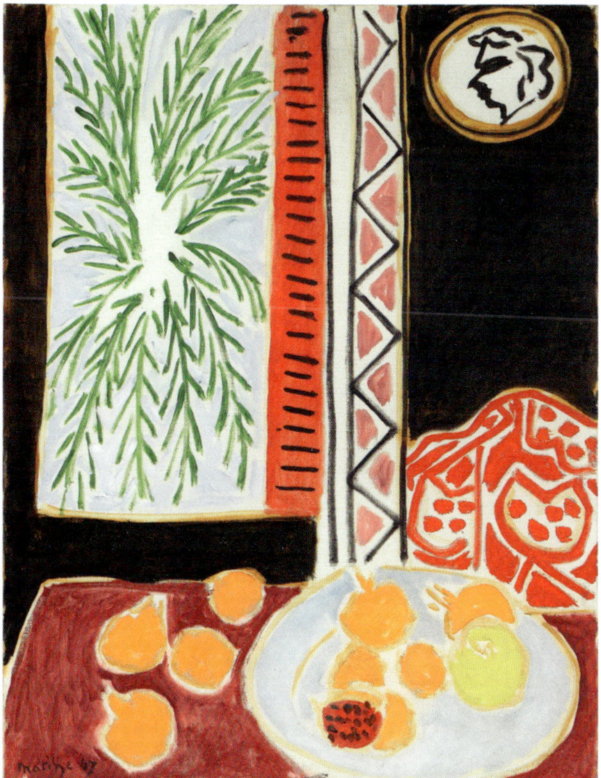

Fig. 1. Henri Matisse, *Nature morte aux grenades*, 1947. Oil on canvas, 31¹¹⁄₁₆ × 23⅝ in. (80.5 × 60 cm). Musée Matisse, Nice, France, Gift of Henri Matisse, 1953, Inv. 63.1.1

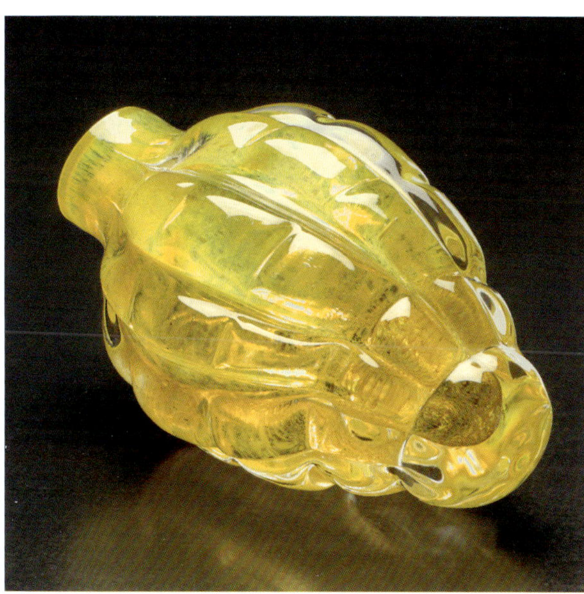

Fig. 2. Detail of Mona Hatoum's *Nature morte aux grenades*

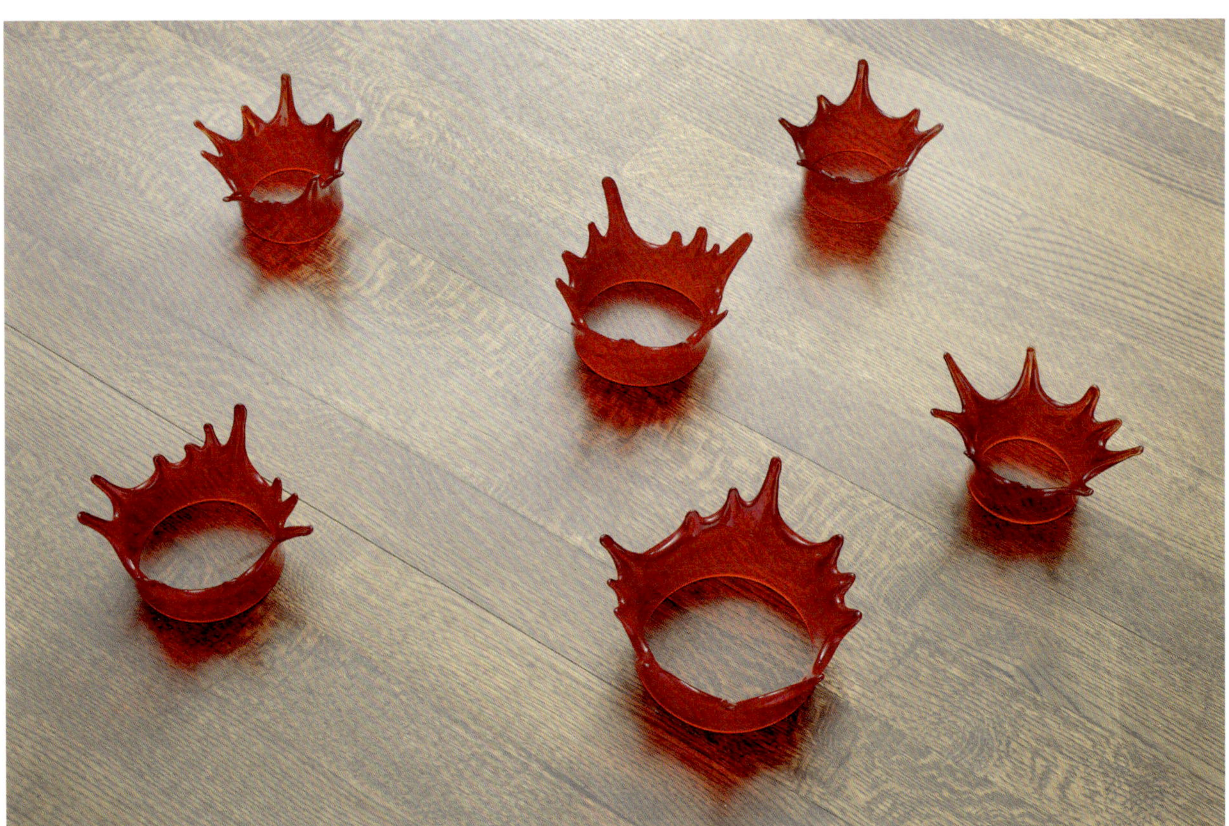

Fig. 3. Mona Hatoum, *A Bigger Splash*, 2009. Glass, dimensions variable. Museum of Fine Arts, Houston, Museum purchase funded by contemporary@mfah, the Caroline Wiess Law Accessions Endowment Fund, and Rosanette and Harry H. Cullen, 2015.418

1. The author thanks Mona Hatoum Studio for providing this information.
2. Mona Hatoum and Kirsty Bell, *Mona Hatoum: Unhomely*, exh. cat. (Berlin: Galerie Max Hetzler, 2008), 69.
3. Clarrie Wallis, "Matériaux et fabrication," trans. Jean-François Cornu, in *Mona Hatoum*, ed. Christine Van Assche (Paris: Centre Pompidou, 2015), 118–36, esp. 119.

Nostalgia

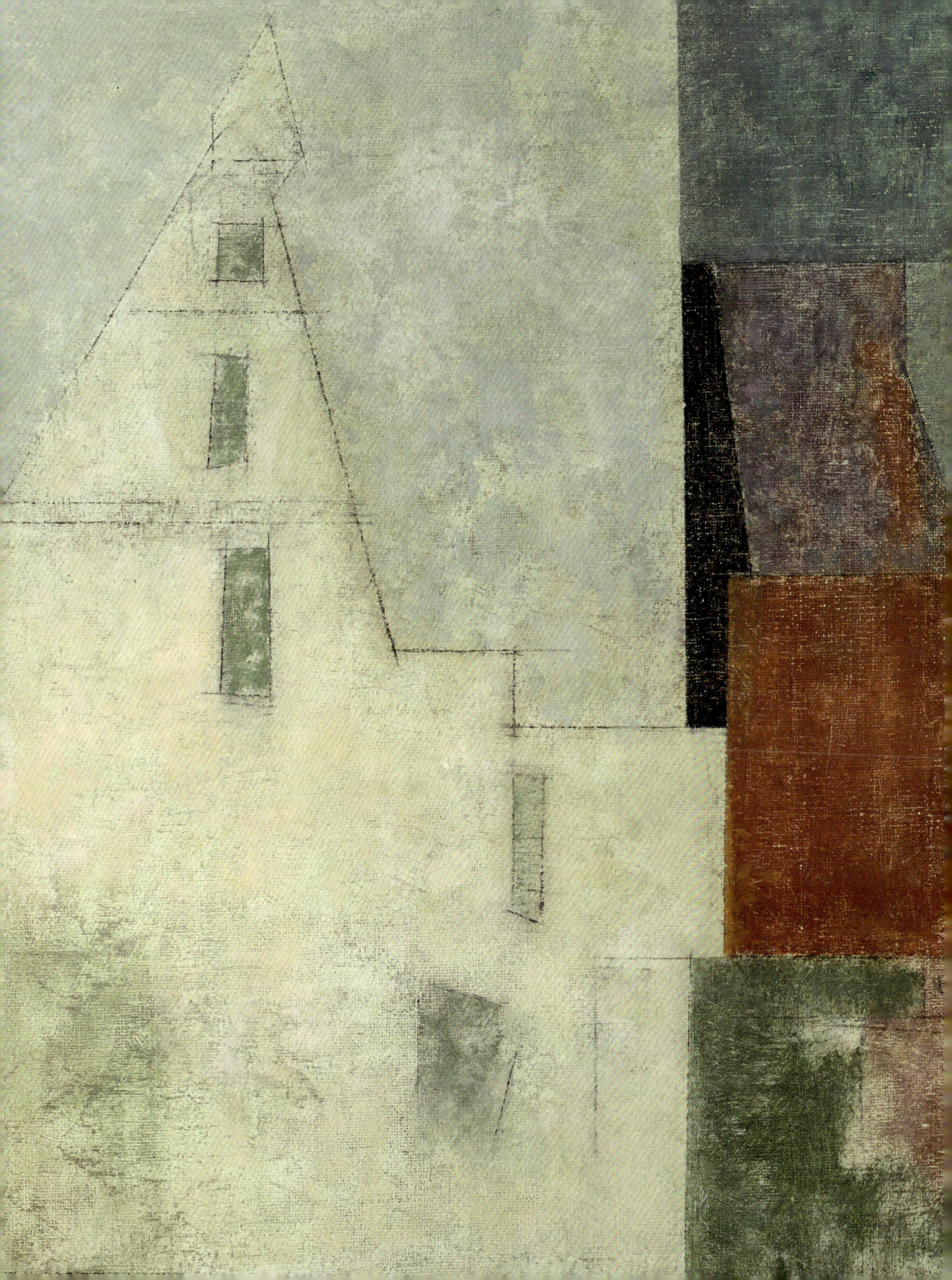

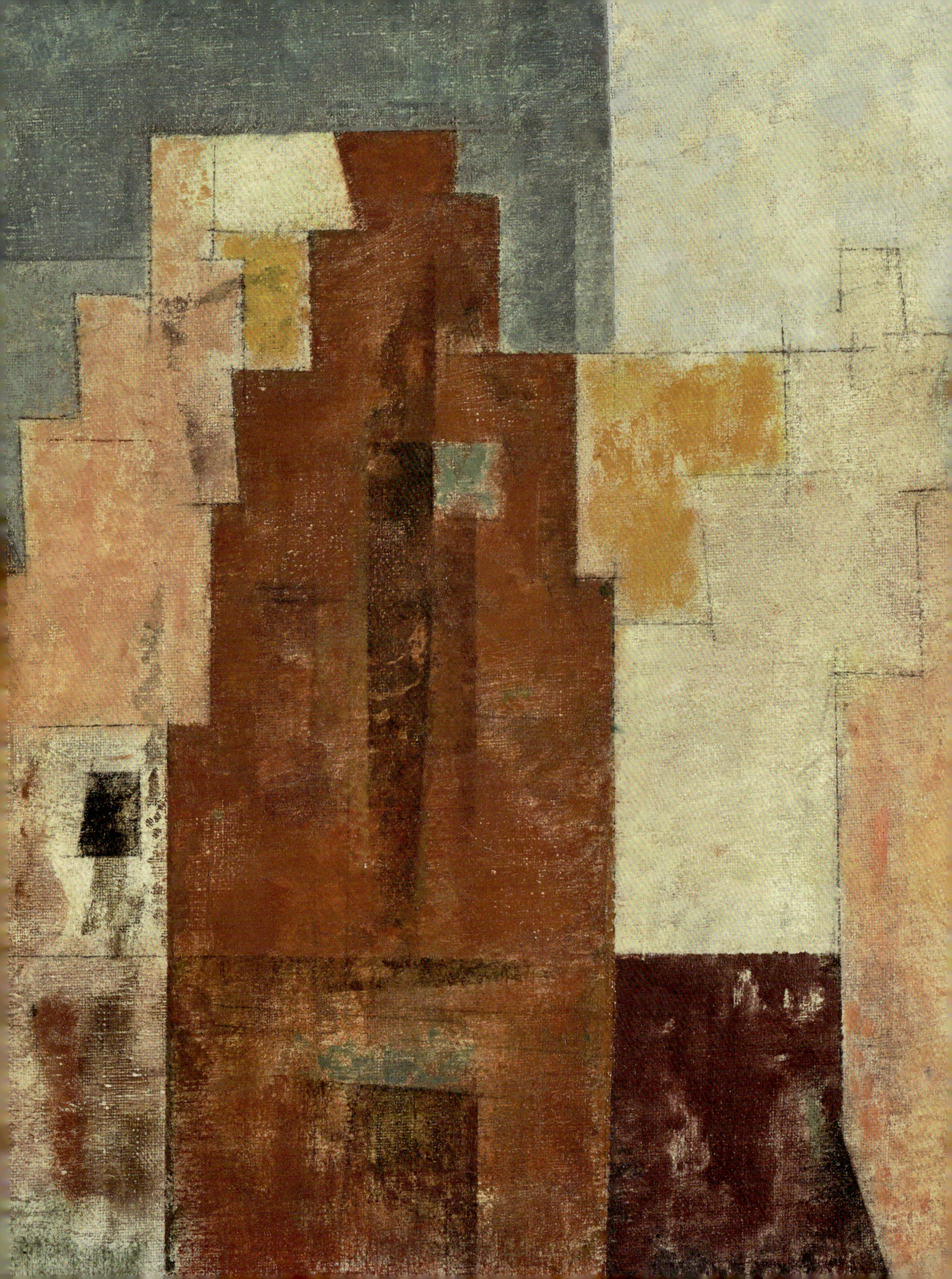

RUSSIA IN EXILE: NOSTALGIA FOR OTHER SHORES

Marijeta Bozovic

I: Nostalgia

> The twentieth century began with utopia and ended with nostalgia. Optimistic belief in the future became outmoded, while nostalgia, for better or worse, never went out of fashion, remaining uncannily contemporary. The word "nostalgia" comes from two Greek roots, *nostos* meaning "return home" and *algia* "longing." I would define it as a longing for a home that no longer exists or has never existed. . . . A cinematic image of nostalgia is a double exposure, or a superimposition of two images—of home and abroad, of past and present, of dream and everyday life. The moment we try to force it into a single image, it breaks the frame or burns the surface.
> —Svetlana Boym, "Nostalgia and Its Discontents," 2007[1]

The late scholar, writer, and—in her last metamorphosis—visual artist Svetlana Boym was no stranger to nostalgia. A third-wave Russian Jewish émigré from the Soviet Union herself, as well as a scholar of Vladimir Nabokov, Joseph Brodsky, and many misplaced others, Boym theorized the malady turned modern condition in her 2001 book *The Future of Nostalgia*. Locating home-longing (*nostos-algia*) as a central trope of Romantic nationalism, she posits, "'I long, therefore I am' was the Romantic motto."[2] Although so many intellectuals and poets across cultural traditions claimed that their national languages contained radically untranslatable words for homesicknesses, "all of those untranslatable words of national uniqueness proved to be synonyms of the same historical emotion."[3] So, too, the notorious Russian *toska*.

Boym distinguishes between two types of nostalgia, restorative and reflective:

> Restorative nostalgia stresses *nostos* (home) and attempts a transhistorical reconstruction of the lost home. Reflective nostalgia thrives on *algia* (the longing itself) and delays the homecoming—wistfully, ironically, desperately. . . . Restorative nostalgia does not think of itself as nostalgia, but rather as truth and tradition. Reflective nostalgia dwells on the ambivalences of

human longing and belonging and does not shy away from the contradictions of modernity. Restorative nostalgia protects the absolute truth, while reflective nostalgia calls it into doubt.[4]

The latter of these nostalgic tendencies finds favor with the cosmopolitan intellectual; the former conjures associations with nationalism and the myths of ethnic and local purity that helped fuel the last century's lived nightmares.

Nostalgia and *exile* are marked words in the cultural discourse of the twentieth century. On the American and Western European side of the Cold War, exile carried ethical, aesthetic, and political weight. The names of celebrated exiles like writers Nabokov and Brodsky, artists Wassily Kandinsky and Marc Chagall, composer Igor Stravinsky, choreographer George Balanchine, ballet dancer Mikhail Baryshnikov, and many others came to stand for individual liberty, creative freedom, and modern humanism—against an implied backdrop of corresponding and opposed Soviet values of collectivism, politically motivated cultural production, and socialism. In the global struggle between Socialist Realism and what might be termed "Capitalist Modernism," twentieth-century Russian exiles (with "Russian" loosely, culturally understood) came to dominate a number of creative fields, across media and decades of experimentation, setting the standard for a cosmopolitan Modernist style. So strong is the cultural weight of their stories and cumulative mythology that it threatens not only to define the present but also to obfuscate the more complicated legacies of the past.

88

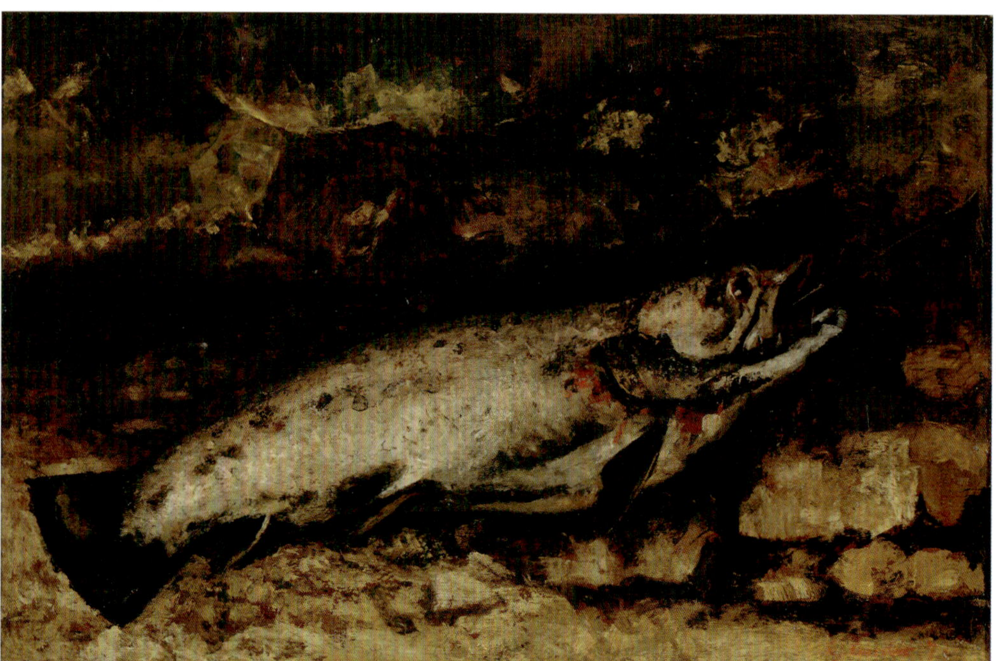

Fig. 1. Gustave Courbet, *La truite* (The Trout), 1873. Oil on canvas, 25¹³⁄₁₆ × 38¹³⁄₁₆ in. (65.5 × 98.5 cm). Musée d'Orsay, Paris, RF 1978-15

If we turn to the century prior, we find a dramatically different—if intimately related—tradition of Russian political exile. The difference is readily understandable: the radical dissident figures of the nineteenth century, such as Aleksandr Herzen and Mikhail Bakunin, fled the repressive climate of imperial Russia for the more permissive and chaotic urban centers of Europe. Their political heirs arguably helped to bring about the Russian revolution(s), which in turn forced even greater numbers into flight from the Soviet Union. The exiles of both centuries feared the censors and the secret police—but the repressive regime for earlier generations was a backward and belated empire, not the unprecedented experiment of state socialism.

My essay attempts to set two centuries of Russian exiles against one another, with the hope of imagining resolution in a third. One story describes a political shift from the radical left to the center right, albeit with hordes of exceptions and uncategorizable political stances along the way. Another sketches a move across media, from political philosophical writing to abstraction and (on the surface) depoliticized art. Both dichotomies falter in the text- and theory-heavy practices of contemporary art. I return to my late mentor Boym's characteristic themes: from the great nineteenth-century thought of Herzen to the contemporary challenges of the art collective Chto Delat (which takes its name from the Russian for "What is to be done?"), I attempt to practice as well as ponder reflective nostalgia, setting past and present into superimposition.

II: Revolutionary Exiles

> We do not build, we destroy; we do not proclaim a new revelation, we eliminate
> the old lie. Modern man, that melancholy *Pontifex Maximus*, only builds a
> bridge—it will be for the unknown man of the future to pass over it. You may
> be there to see him. . . . But do not, I beg, remain on *this shore*. . . . Better to
> perish with the revolution than to seek refuge in the almshouse of reaction.
> —Aleksandr Herzen, *From the Other Shore*, 1850 [5]

Tom Stoppard's *The Coast of Utopia*, a 2002 trilogy of plays about the nineteenth-century Russian writers living in Europe in exile, stages an imagined dialogue among Aleksandr Herzen, Mikhail Bakunin, Ivan Turgenev, and Vissarion Belinsky in the Paris of 1847. Stoppard gives the following lines to the critic Belinsky:

> At home [in Russia] the public look to writers as their real leaders. The title of
> poet or novelist really counts with us. My articles get cut by the censor, but
> a week before the *Contemporary* comes out students hang around Smirdin's
> bookshop asking if it's arrived yet . . . and then they discuss it half the night
> and pass copies around. . . . Writers here, they think they're enjoying success.
> They don't know what success is. You have to be a writer in Russia.[6]

Stoppard's play, covering a period from 1833 to 1868, imagines the rise and fall of the Russian intelligentsia who first inspired that term, who helped to shape the European left of the nineteenth century, and whose ideas set the stage for the Russian Revolution.

These Russian exiles have prompted as many interpretations as there are fictional and nonfictional accounts of their colorful lives and times. The titles alone of a handful of iconic histories speak volumes: Woodford McClellan's *Revolutionary Exiles: The Russians in the First International and the Paris Commune* focuses on the Russian presence in the European revolutions of the nineteenth century.[7] E. H. Carr's *The Romantic Exiles* and *Michael Bakunin* cast Herzen and Bakunin as Romantics with oversize personalities and more thrilling personal lives than political philosophies.[8] Avrahm Yarmolinsky's *Road to Revolution* contextualizes the exiled intelligentsia within several centuries of Russian radicalism; the chapter "The Coasts of Utopia" inspired Stoppard's title.

Many studies by British and American historians were written prior to World War II or after the 1970s. Even to write about Herzen and Bakunin's circles in the context of the Cold War was a fraught political choice. While hagiographies of some, but not all, of the nineteenth-century exiles proliferated in Soviet historiography, liberal cultural historians "were not disposed to concede merit or insight" to thinkers they saw as precursors to Bolshevism.[9] The intellectual historian Isaiah Berlin phrased it thus:

> In the eyes of many Western liberals, the Soviet tyranny was the inescapable outcome of the ideas and actions of Dostoevsky's "possessed": the Russian

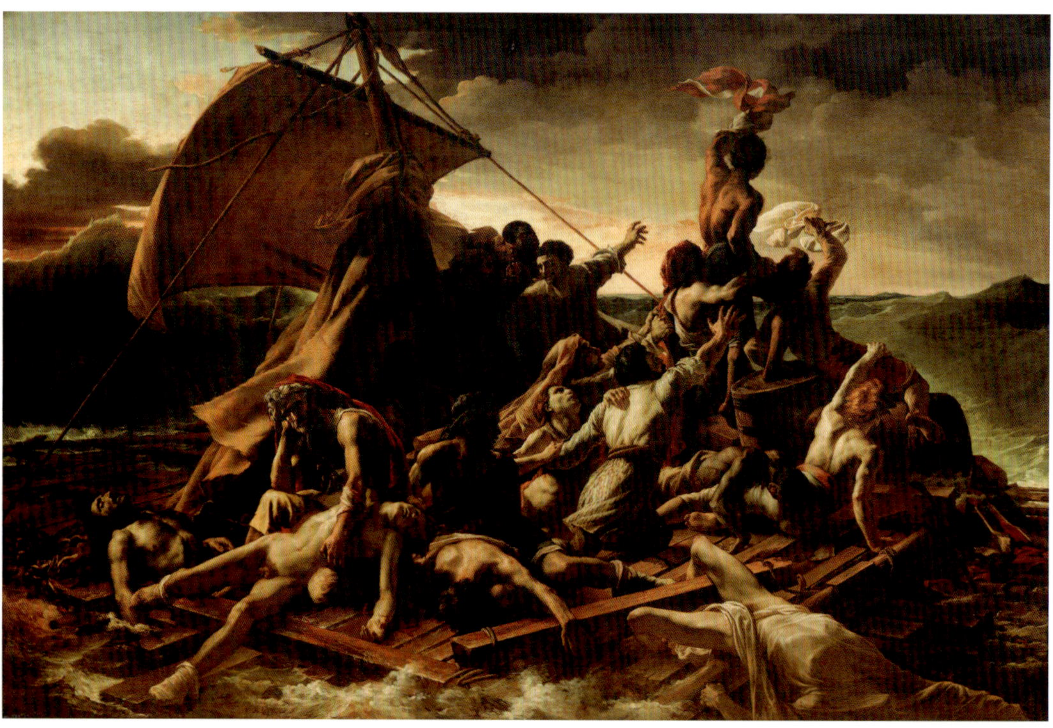

Fig. 2. Théodore Géricault, *Le Radeau de la Méduse* (The Raft of the Medusa), 1818–19. Oil on canvas, 16 ft. 15⁄16 in. × 23 ft. 5⁄8 in. (491 × 716 cm). Musée du Louvre, Paris, INV 4884

radical intelligentsia. In the degree of their alienation from their society and of their impact on it, the Russian intelligentsia of the nineteenth century were a phenomenon almost *sui generis* . . . But they are too often treated by English and American historians with a mixture of condescension and moral revulsion . . . because in their fanatical passion for extreme ideologies they are held to have rushed, like Dostoevsky's devils, to blind self-destruction, dragging their country, and then much of the rest of the world, after them.[10]

The French travel writer Marquis de Custine described his impressions of 1839 Russia as "a cauldron of boiling water, tightly closed and placed on a fire which is becoming hotter and hotter; I fear an explosion."[11] The outstanding figures among a new generation of politically-minded students were the young Herzen, Bakunin, and Belinsky. In the essay "A Remarkable Decade," Pavel Annenkov describes the nascent intelligentsia as a movement of young men, fresh from the university or in the midst of study. Berlin describes the term "intelligentsia" and its consequences as "the largest single Russian contribution to social change in the world."[12] More than an intellectual elite, the Russian intelligentsia saw themselves as an order endowed with a political and ethical mission.

At the center was Herzen: the author of *From the Other Shore*, reflections on European socialism after the revolutions of 1848, as well as of the monumental autobiography *My Past and Thoughts*; and the editor of *Kolokol* (The Bell, 1857–67). *Kolokol*, a Russian-language opposition paper published in London and Geneva and widely read (though banned) in Russia, took on the status of a Russian *Uncle Tom's Cabin* vis-à-vis the emancipation reforms of 1861 and the abolition of serfdom. Even the tsar was said to be a reader. Herzen seemed a natural heir to the failed Decembrist revolt of 1825: forged in the student circles of the metropolitan universities, and arrested at the age of twenty-two for his presence at a reading of anti-imperial verses. Herzen returned to Moscow in 1840 after internal banishment only to emigrate permanently seven years later.

It was Herzen's lines, inspired by Georg Wilhelm Friedrich Hegel in turn, that offered the metaphor of the longed-for "other shore" of freedom and reason. As prescient as any of his contemporaries,

In 1849, just one year after the Communist Manifesto had proclaimed the coming of a revolution which would end "exploitation, oppression, and enmity among nations," Herzen wrote that nobody should expect that the victory of socialism would provide a conclusive solution to the problems of society. Socialism would generate its own inner contradictions and absurdities, until "a mortal struggle will begin, in which socialism will play the role of contemporary conservatism, and be overwhelmed in the subsequent revolution, as of yet unknown to us."[13]

Bakunin, founding father of socialist anarchism, proved a perpetual thorn in Herzen's side—as in Marx's. He was the revolutionary to Herzen's gradual reforms, the anarchist to Marx's organized party control. Making his way to Berlin in 1840, Bakunin moved ever further from academic pursuits to active revolutionary agitation. Ordered to cease and return to Russia several times, Bakunin chose instead to keep moving. While his property was confiscated, it was not until 1849 that he was arrested for participating in the Dresden May uprising and turned over to Russian authorities. After three years in the Peter and Paul Fortress and many more in Siberian exile, Bakunin managed a daring escape in 1861 through Japan and the United States to return to Europe. He immediately traveled to London to see Herzen.

Around these two figures swirled a host of Russians in exile: comrades, rivals, lovers, and friends. Among them were Turgenev, Herman Lopatin, Nikolai Ogarev, Elizabeth Tomanovskaya (known as Madame Dmitrieff on the barricades of the Paris Commune), and the sinister Sergei Nechaev, whose strategic murder of a coconspirator helped inspire Fyodor Dostoevsky's 1872 novel *Demons*.[14] A Russian émigré newspaper described Geneva circa 1869 as a hotbed of revolutionary activity: "The pioneers of socialism held meetings; the international union of socialists came into being; the awakening working class was seething with activity which in time took on truly grandiose dimensions."[15] When it came, the inevitable rift between Herzen and Bakunin marked a turning point in Russian and European political thought. According to Carr, Bakunin was "not merely, like Herzen, a Romantic by conviction; he was a Romantic by temperament," and optimism and faith in human nature "were of the marrow of his bones."[16] Yet it was Bakunin's challenge that succeeded in rattling Marx, prompting him to end the First International rather than see it fall into anarchist hands.[17]

Nikolai Chernyshevsky, Russia's most famous internal exile of the period, stands in marked contrast to both Herzen and Bakunin. Much had changed between the 1840s and the 1860s in Europe and in Russia, as Turgenev's 1862 novel *Fathers and Sons* pointedly illustrated. A generation of Russian liberal intellectuals dispersed, grew old, and gave up; embittered and radicalized youth moved to take their place:

> Such men as these found the plodding genius of Chernyshevsky—his attempts to work out specific solutions to specific problems in terms of concrete statistical data; his constant appeals to facts; his patient efforts to indicate attainable, practical, immediate ends ... more serious and ultimately more inspiring than the noble flights of the romantic idealists of the 1840s.[18]

In July 1862, despite lack of evidence, Chernyshevsky was arrested for subversion and sentenced to seven years of penal servitude followed by lifetime exile to Siberia. He had neither the erudition of Herzen nor the charisma of Bakunin, but his integrity, lifelong struggle against injustice, and early departure from the stage made him a hero of the new times. Throughout his writings, but above all in the novel *What Is to Be Done?*, Chernyshevsky formulated an intellectual structure and worldview upon which a new way of life might be based. Remarkably, it rested on radical reconsiderations of gender, sexuality, and family structures that proved ahead of their time by more than a century.

What Is to Be Done? took on the status of a revolutionary manual, though neither Chernyshevsky's contemporaries nor later literary historians could explain its reach or excuse its apparent lack of sophistication. Berlin summarizes the novel as "a social *Utopia*, which, grotesque as a work of art, had a literally epoch-making effect on Russian opinion."[19] Banned from shortly after its publication until 1905, the novel found its readers through émigré editions smuggled into Russia.[20] Chernyshevsky himself was permitted to return to European Russia only after the terrorist organization *Narodnaia volia* (People's Will) negotiated his release in 1882, in exchange for peace during the coronation of Alexander III after the assassination of Alexander II on March 1, 1881.

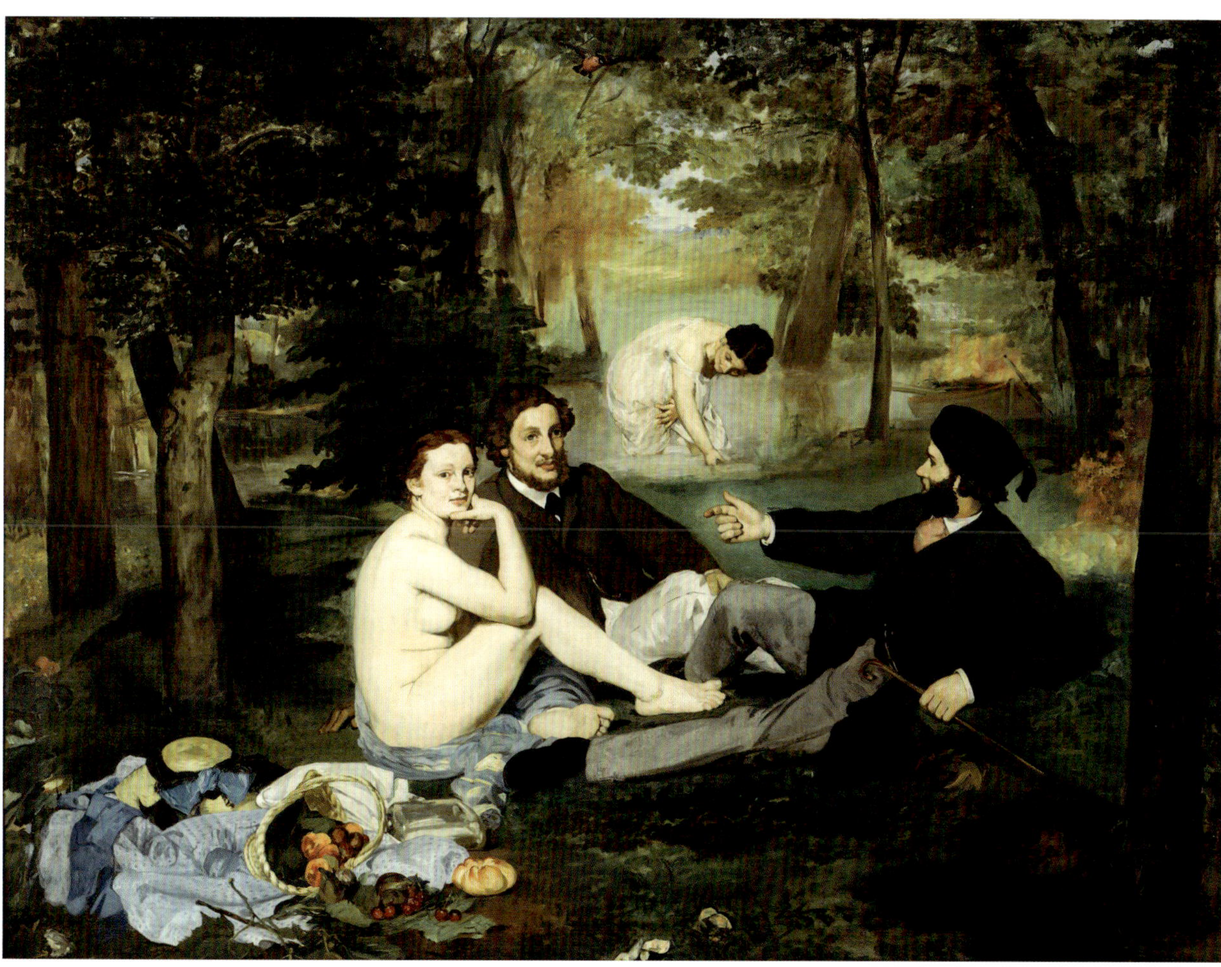

Fig. 3. Édouard Manet, *Le déjeuner sur l'herbe* (The Luncheon on the Grass), 1863. Oil on canvas, 6 ft. 9½ in. × 8 ft. 8⁵⁄₁₆ in. (207 × 265 cm). Musée d'Orsay, Paris, RF 1668

Six years later, on March 1, 1887, a group of conspirators attempted a copycat assassination of Alexander III. Among the five hanged for it was Alexander Ulyanov, older brother to Lenin. The young Lenin—born Vladimir Ulyanov—discovered Chernyshevsky and *What Is to Be Done?*, his brother's favorite book, after the execution:

> He read and reread every line of Chernyshevsky's articles in the *Contemporary* . . . but it was *What Is to Be Done?* that overturned (in Lenin's words "plowed over") his whole life. . . . Chernyshevsky's greatest service, claimed Lenin, was that his novel showed the particular type of man that a revolutionary should be, and specified the methods and means for attaining this ideal.[21]

One narrative of Russian exile ends, if not here, with Lenin reading Chernyshevsky, then with Lenin's own return to then-Petrograd in 1917: from the salon coasts of utopia to days that shook the world.

III: From Exile to Émigré

> The censorship permitted [Chernyshevsky's novel] to be published in *The Contemporary*, reckoning on the fact that a novel which was "something in the highest degree anti-artistic" would be certain to overthrow Chernyshevski's authority, that he would simply be laughed at for it. . . . But nobody laughed. Not even the great Russian writers laughed. Even Herzen, who found it "vilely written," immediately qualified this with: "On the other hand there is much that is good and healthy." . . . Instead of the expected sneers, an atmosphere of general, pious worship was created around *What to Do?* It was read the way liturgical books are read—not a single work by Turgenev or Tolstoy produced such a mighty impression. The inspired Russian reader understood the good that the talentless novelist had vainly tried to express.
> —Vladimir Nabokov, *The Gift*, 1938 [22]

Vladimir Nabokov's fictional essay on Chernyshevsky remains a bizarre episode in the work of the best-known Russian émigré of the twentieth century. As the fourth chapter of his most ambitious Russian-language novel on the Russian emigration in Berlin, Nabokov unexpectedly felt compelled to insert a satirical treatise on a thinker from whom he could not be further, politically or stylistically. It is as if, one hundred years later, Nabokov looked to the radical exiles for the origins of his own experience. He even titled the Russian-language version of his autobiography *Drugie berega* (Other Shores, 1954) in a suggestive echo of Herzen.

The waves of Russian exiles increased in intensity after 1917. "Russia abroad" became a mass phenomenon stretching from New York to China, with celebrated stops in Berlin,

Paris, Belgrade, and Prague. Two cultural histories share the name: Marc Raeff's *Russia Abroad: A Cultural History of the Russian Emigration, 1919–1939* and John Glad's *Russia Abroad: Writers, History, Politics*.[23] Glad's overview covers what are commonly known as the three "waves" of Soviet-era Russian emigration—in keeping with the imagery of other shores. The first-wave émigrés, hopeful that they would return as soon as the Bolshevik revolution blew over, did not attempt to adapt to the countries and cultures of their new home but instead clung stubbornly to native roots. Even the second-wave writers, who left after World War II, and the primarily Jewish third wave of the 1970s and 1980s, who had no such illusions, followed suit.

For many who fled the Bolshevik revolution, exile entailed a mission "to preserve the values and traditions of Russian culture and to continue in creative efforts for the benefit and ongoing spiritual progress of the homeland."[24] Determined to go on living a culturally Russian life despite their surroundings, the twentieth-century émigrés set about re-creating and reimaging both the forums and content they needed to do so. Russia abroad implicitly pledged to be the "truest and culturally most creative of the two Russias that political circumstances had brought into being."[25] Nabokov claimed:

> As I look back at those years of exile, I see myself, and thousands of other Russians, leading an odd but by no means unpleasant existence, in material indigence and intellectual luxury, among perfectly unimportant strangers, spectral Germans and Frenchmen in whose more or less illusory cities we émigrés happened to dwell. These aborigines were to the mind's eye as flat and transparent as figures cut out of cellophane, and although we used their gadgets, applauded their clowns, picked their roadside plums and apples, no real communication, of the rich human sort so widespread in our own midst, existed between us and them.[26]

If Nabokov—who was equally fluent in several languages and soon to be recognized as a paradigmatic world writer—could make such a statement, the breach between émigré and host cultures must have seemed insurmountable to other Russian refugees. If anything, many of Nabokov's émigré contemporaries found him to be not Russian enough: Ivan Bunin prophesied that Nabokov would "die in dreadful pain and complete isolation."[27]

While the politics of the twentieth-century exiles were more diverse than those of their prerevolutionary precursors, the cultural figures most celebrated in the West were those artists and writers whose work or lives challenged the Soviet narrative of progress and emancipation: Nabokov, Bunin, and Vladislav Khodasevich; Wassily Kandinsky and Marc Chagall; Igor Stravinsky; George Balanchine; and Joseph Brodsky, winner of the last Nobel Prize to go to a Soviet dissident (although the 2015 Belarusian winner, Svetlana Alexievich, arguably belongs as much to this tradition as to the post-Soviet present).[28]

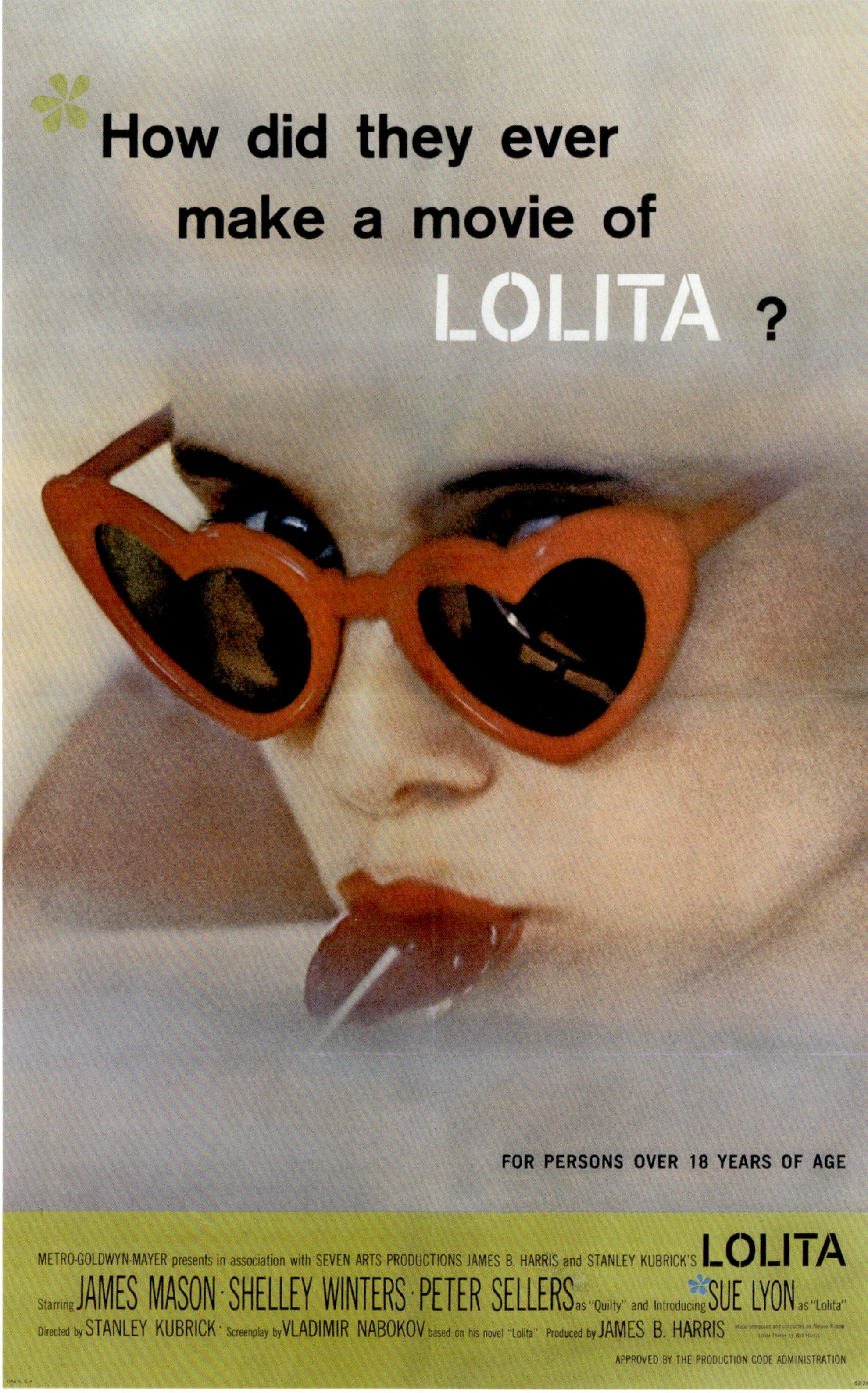

Fig. 4. Poster for the U.S. release of Stanley Kubrick's film adaptation of Vladimir Nabokov's *Lolita*, 1962

The Russian—and in subsequent decades, Eastern European—exiles of the twentieth century who rose to greatest international prominence shared common characteristics across genres, languages, and media. Many of them were towering figures of Modernism: nearly inevitably male, individualistic to the point of eccentricity, cosmopolitan virtuosos whose exotic roots, exilic melancholy, and escape stories made them human emblems of individual liberty and creative freedom. Even complicated figures like Kandinsky (or Kazimir Malevich, who remained in the Soviet Union) took on special significance in the global culture wars, as abstraction itself became highly politically charged during the Cold War. The United States and the Soviet Union each had their aesthetic: Capitalist Modernism evolved as the counterpart and challenge to Socialist Realism. It is hard today to imagine comparable government defense funding for the arts—or the rapid appropriation of Russian avant-gardes for ubiquitous decorative corporate prints.[29]

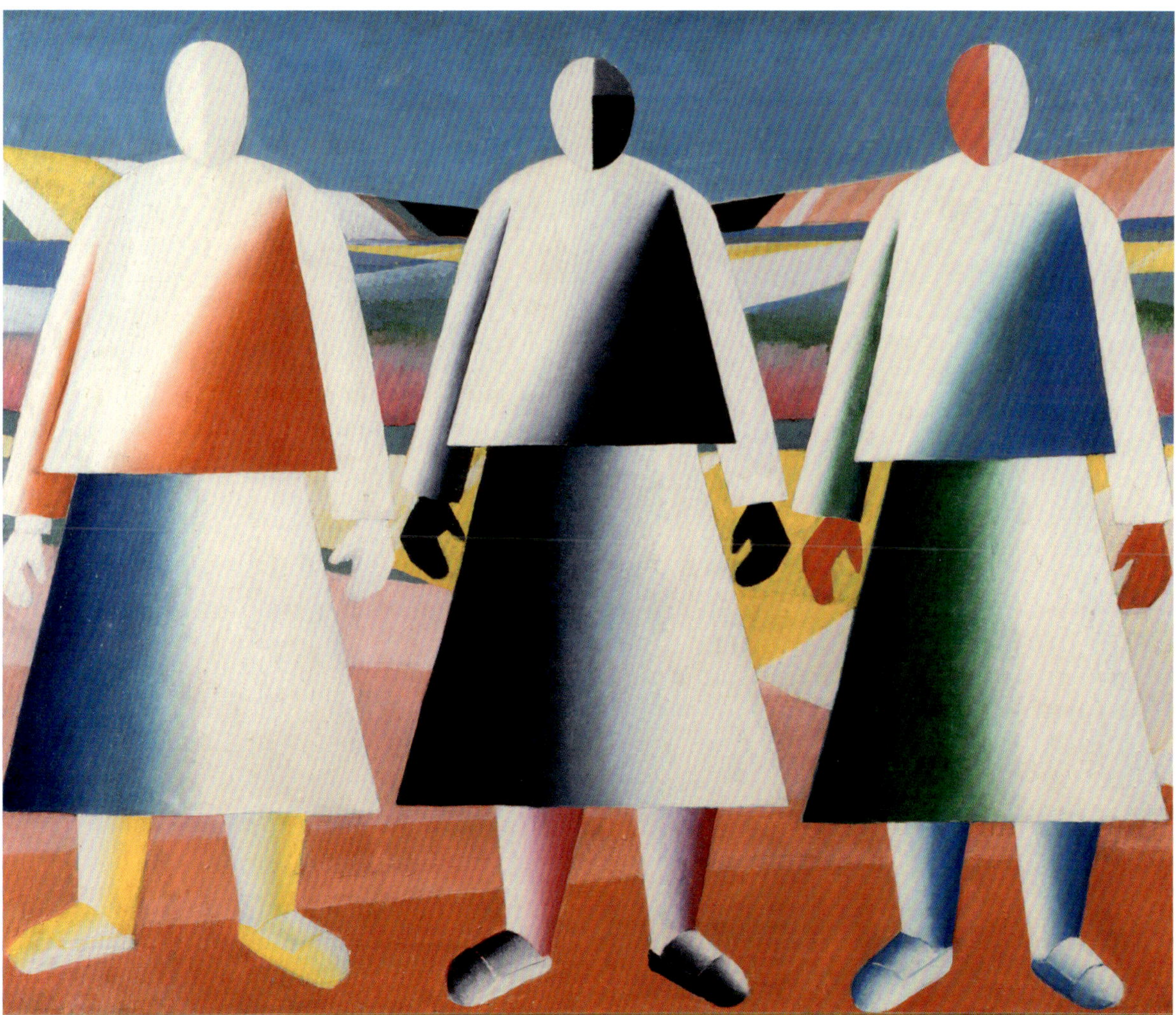

Fig. 5. Kazimir Malevich, *Girls in a Field*, 1928–32. Oil on canvas, 41¾ × 49¼ in. (106 × 125 cm). State Russian Museum, St. Petersburg, Ж-9433

Another narrative of Russian exile and twentieth-century émigré literature and culture ends then with Brodsky, recipient of the Nobel Prize in 1987. Glad writes that the stubborn, rebellious autodidact "who as a 23-year-old responded to the Soviet judge about to sentence him for 'parasitism' that his poetic gift was 'from God' . . . maintained a love-disdain (actually, more disdain than love) relationship with his fellow Russian émigré writers."[30] Bunin's Nobel Prize had been seen as a victory for the Russian émigré community; Nabokov was pointedly ignored by Stockholm; but Brodsky's win sparked mixed feelings in his contemporaries before becoming the stuff of legend for subsequent generations. Comparing the latter two legendary Russian-American writers, Svetlana Boym writes,

> Unlike Nabokov, Brodsky has little nostalgia for his own childhood, which is understandable, since it took place during the war and the poverty-stricken postwar years at the end of the Stalinist era. . . . . Brodsky's figure for exile is not a cryptically disguised spy or a double with a great propensity for mimicry, but rather someone who is "less than one," a part of speech, a fragment, a ruin, a crying monster.[31]

And yet for both—as for so many exiles without their linguistic possibilities for expression—home and abroad appear as mirror images and double exposures.

The figure who most complicates the émigré narrative of escape into freedom and triumphant self-fashioning, however, is a woman: the failed émigré Marina Tsvetaeva. One of the most original voices of the twentieth century, Tsvetaeva never found acceptance among her compatriots abroad, though her poetry and prose were widely published. Her stylistic vitality, formal experimentation, and organic merging of folklore and Modernism, as well as the ambition and intensity of her themes and self-expression, made her unlike any other living Russian-language writer, but critics and fellow members of Russia abroad like Georgy Adamovich "saw no way that other poets could profit from her example." In the Soviet Union, in turn, Maxim Gorky deemed her "hysterical" and in poor command of the Russian language. In 1939, feeling alienated from fellow exiles, Tsvetaeva followed her politically compromised family back to the Soviet Union. After two years of indigence and psychological torment, having determined that there was no place (u-topia) for her at home or abroad, Tsvetaeva hanged herself.

IV: What Is to Be Done?

> At this reactionary historical moment, when elementary demands for the possible are presented as a romantic impossibility, we remain realists and insist on certain simple, intelligible things. We have to move away from the frustrations occasioned by the historical failures to advance leftist ideas and discover anew their emancipatory potential. . . . The first thing that

motivates us is the rejection of all forms of oppression, the artificial alienation of people, and exploitation. That is why we stand for a distribution of
the wealth produced by human labor and all natural resources that is just
and directed towards the welfare of everyone. We are internationalists: we
demand the recognition of the equality of all people, no matter where they
live or where they come from. We are feminists: we are against all forms of
patriarchy, homophobia, and gender inequality.
　　—Chto Delat, "A Declaration on Politics, Knowledge, and Art," 2008 [32]

The art collective Chto Delat was founded in early 2003 in St. Petersburg by a group
of Russian artists, theorists, and activists. The group derives its name from the title
of Chernyshevsky's novel, as well as Lenin's own 1902 publication *What Is to Be Done?*
Chto Delat defines itself as a "self-organized platform . . . intent on politicizing knowledge production through redefinitions of an engaged autonomy for cultural practice
today."[33] Recalling via its very name and central activities (e.g., the publication of an
international leftist newspaper) the first collectively organized socialist projects in
Russia, Chto Delat embodies the paradoxes and possibilities of the present. Dialectically
borrowing from the nineteenth and twentieth centuries, Chto Delat reimagines the

99

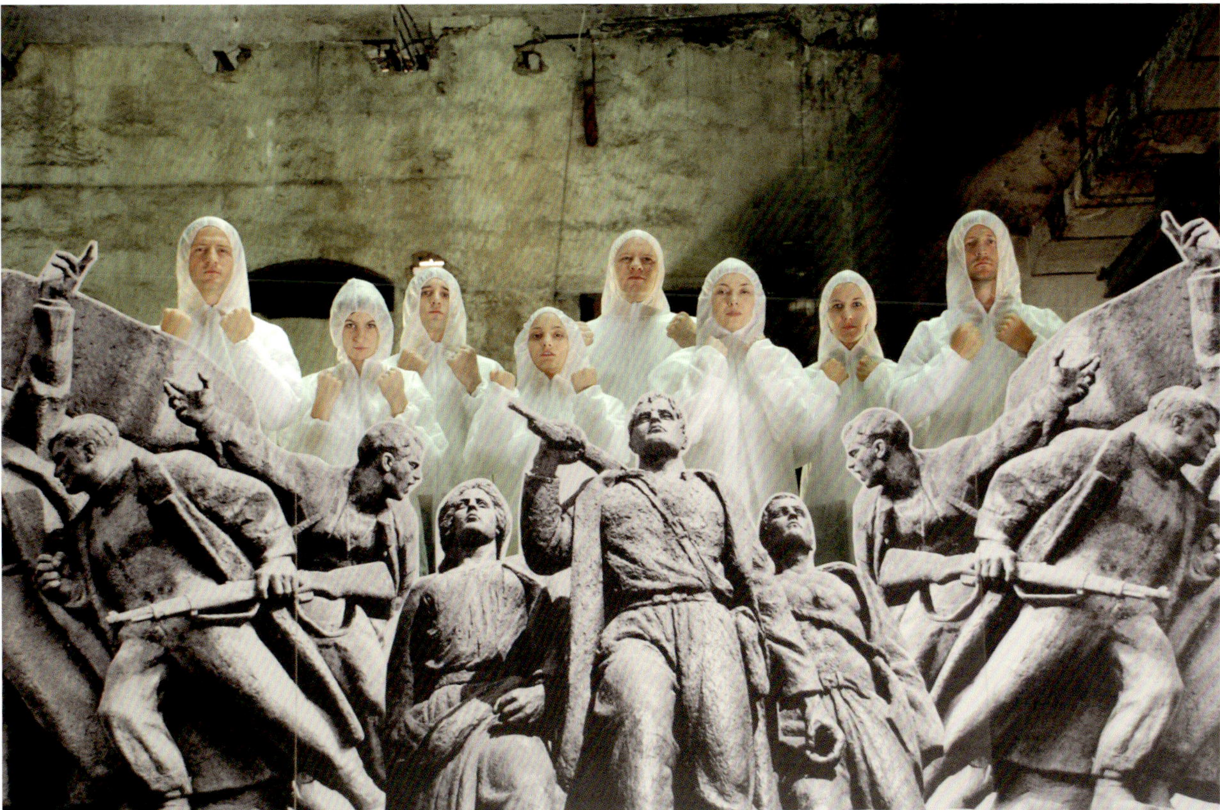

Fig. 6. Chto Delat, still from *Partisan Songspiel, a Belgrade Story*, 2009. Digital film, 15 mins.

legacies of both for a contemporary left: their performances and productions turn to narratives of exile beyond Modernism (for example, the experience of Central Asian guest workers in today's Moscow) and to the centrality of gender as a lasting social challenge.

Unprecedented millions have been displaced during the twentieth century and the first decades of the twenty-first—by war, by economic hardship, by ethnic, religious, and political persecution—and in the coming years, more will be displaced by climate change. In the face of such an unimaginable change of scale, Edward W. Said urged us to set aside Modernist maestros and Romantic exile to see instead the voiceless, uncountable masses of United Nations databases.[34] The legacies of the Cold War have left behind not only lingering worldviews but also narratives of torch-passing: the preservation of sacred symbolic temples from barbarians by a handful of masters. No small part of this mythology was the doing of émigré elites themselves, and their defiant recasting of their fate as misplaced aristocrats rather than an impoverished and marginalized precariat. But Russia in exile has been more than that.

A quarter of a century after the fall of the Berlin Wall signaled the beginning of the end of the Cold War and World War II alike, new walls are rising in Europe. The powerful writers of the past have given us language to imagine the possibilities and deprivations of exile; now we must move beyond elite imaginaries to eulogize less singularity and exception than kinship and shared experience. As Boym wrote, "Nostalgia can be a poetic creation, an individual mechanism of survival, a countercultural practice, a poison, or a cure."[35] Across complicated waters, the other shores of freedom and reason remain an open challenge.

This essay is in memory of
Svetlana Boym.

1. Svetlana Boym, "Nostalgia and Its Discontents," *The Hedgehog Review* 9, no. 2 (Summer 2007): 7. Essay adapted from Svetlana Boym, *The Future of Nostalgia* (New York: Basic, 2001).

2. Boym, "Nostalgia and Its Discontents," 11–12.

3. Ibid.

4. Ibid., 13.

5. Herzen presented his fifteen-year-old son with a dedication of the Russian edition of his book, *From the Other Shore*, at a New Year's Eve party in 1855: "He told the boy that the only religion he was bequeathing to him was that of revolution, enjoined him to go and preach it in good time to their people at home, and added his blessing, in the name of human reason, personal liberty, and brotherly love." Avrahm Yarmolinsky, *Road to Revolution* (New York: MacMillan, 1959), 90.

6. Tom Stoppard, *The Coast of Utopia: Shipwreck* (New York: Grove, 2007), 155.

7. Woodford McClellan, *Revolutionary Exiles: The Russians in the First International and the Paris Commune* (New York: Routledge, 1979).

8. E. H. Carr, *The Romantic Exiles* (London: Penguin, 1933); and E. H. Carr, *Michael Bakunin* (New York: MacMillan, 1937).

9. Aileen Kelly, *Toward Another Shore: Russian Thinkers between Necessity and Chaos* (New Haven, Conn.: Yale University Press, 1998), 3.

10. Isaiah Berlin, *Russian Thinkers* (New York: Viking, 1978), xxiv.

11. Yarmolinsky, *Road to Revolution*, 66.

12. Berlin borrows the title of Annenkov's 1870s essay; Berlin, *Russian Thinkers*, 133.

13. Kelly, *Toward Another Shore*, 346.

14. McClellan, *Revolutionary Exiles*, 47–48.

15. Carr, *The Romantic Exiles*, 74.

16. Ibid., 196–97.

17. On the whole, the characterizations of Bakunin remain more ambivalent than those of Herzen. See Kelly, *Toward Another Shore*, 245.

18. Berlin, *Russian Thinkers*, 257–58.

19. Ibid., 261.

20. Irina Paperno, *Chernyshevsky and the Age of Realism: A Study in the Semiotics of Behavior* (Palo Alto, Calif.: Stanford University Press, 1988), 28.

21. Ibid., 30–31.

22. Vladimir Nabokov, *The Gift*, trans. Michael Scammell (New York: Vintage, 1991), 276–77.

23. Marc Raeff, *Russia Abroad: A Cultural History of the Russian Emigration, 1919–1939* (Oxford: Oxford University Press, 1990); and John Glad, *Russia Abroad: Writers, History, Politics* (Tenafly, N.J.: Hermitage and Birchbark Press, 1999).

24. Raeff, *Russia Abroad*, 4.

25. Ibid., 5.

26. Quoted in Glad, *Russia Abroad*, 30–31.

27. Ibid., 282.

28. Brodsky's Nobel Prize in literature in 1987 was the second to go to Russia abroad, after Bunin's in 1933, and the fifth to go to a Russian-language author, after Boris Pasternak in 1958, Mikhail Sholokhov in 1965, and Aleksandr Solzhenitsyn in 1970. Andrei Sakharov won the Nobel Peace Prize in 1975.

29. For stories of CIA-backed funding for Abstract Expressionism, avant-garde art, international circulation for Boris Pasternak's novel *Dr. Zhivago*, or creative writing programs across the United States, see Frances Stonor Saunders, *The Cultural Cold War: The CIA and the World of Arts and Letters* (New York: New Press, 2000), and Eric Bennett, *Workshops of Empire: Stegner, Engle, and American Creative Writing during the Cold War* (Iowa City: University of Iowa Press, 2015), among others.

30. Glad, *Russia Abroad*, 465.

31. Boym, *The Future of Nostalgia*, 289.

32. Chto Delat, "A Declaration on Politics, Knowledge, and Art," last modified December 2008, https://chtodelat.org/b5-announcements/a-6/a-declaration-on-politics-knowledge-and-art-4/; previously published in Chto Delat, *When Artists Struggle Together* (November 2008): 15.

33. Ibid.

34. Edward W. Said, *Reflections on Exile: And Other Literary and Cultural Essays* (New York: Granta, 2001), 139.

35. Boym, "Nostalgia and Its Discontents," 18.

*Portrait of Comte Henri-Amédée-Mercure de
Turenne d'Aynac*
1816
Oil on canvas
28¼ × 22⅛ in. (71.8 × 56.2 cm)
Provenance: Henri-Amédée-Mercure de Turenne
d'Aynac, until 1852; Comte, later Marquis, Sosthène-Paul
de Turenne-d'Aynac (his grandson), Paris, by 1878, until
at least 1880; de Turenne family, by descent, until 1999;
Blondeau et Cie, Paris, 1999; Sterling and Francine Clark
Art Institute, Williamstown, Mass., Acquired by the
Clark, 1999, 1999.2.

Portrait of François-Antoine Rasse de Gavre
1816
Oil on canvas
28¾ × 24 in. (73 × 61 cm)
Provenance: François-Antoine Rasse de Gavre or his
father Charles-Alexandre de Gavre; Marie-Aloïse Egger
(sister-in-law); Baron Jules Houtart; Édouard Houtart;
Baron Maurice Houtart; Madame Yves Pierpont Surmont
de Volsberghe; private collection, Belgium; private
collection, United States.

Jacques-Louis David became famous for his portraits
of Napoléon and his family, which became emblematic
symbols of the French Empire.[1] Because David voted for
the death of Louis XVI and supported Napoléon during
the Hundred Days—the emperor's last, brief period of
rule in 1815 before he was defeated and exiled—the artist
was banished by the Bourbon government in January 1816
and chose to settle in Belgium. When he started his new
life in Brussels, he was already sixty-eight years old, yet
he was a sought-after painter and even received an offer
from the king of Prussia to become *premier peintre* (first
painter)—an offer he declined, however.[2]

David focused on portraits in particular during
the first year of his exile.[3] He was highly in demand
among other French exiles, especially those who had
been close to Napoléon, such as the Comte Henri-
Amédée-Mercure de Turenne d'Aynac. The imperial
officer had held several important court appointments
during Napoléon's reign, followed by a promotion to
colonel in 1814.[4] He supported Napoléon again during his
return in 1815 and received the title of *maréchal de camp* (a
military title equivalent to major general) as recompense.
The Second Bourbon Restoration was thus skeptical of
Turenne, who, although not banished, realized that he
would never regain the status that he had held under
Napoléon and chose to settle in Belgium, to wait for more

clement circumstances. Given their joint opposition to
the Bourbon monarchy and their exile in Brussels, David
and Turenne were naturally drawn to each other. David's
portrait, with its close-cropped bust format, evinces
Turenne's high military rank gained under the Empire
through his uniform, saber, and medals. Four crosses
in the middle of the composition, placed strategically
under Turenne's gaze, are among the elements that
capture the eye. Painted in great detail, they represent
the medal of the Legion of Honor (the five-branch cross);
the Malta cross, with its black ribbon; the medal of the
military order of Saint Louis; and the medal of the order
of Maximilian I of Bavaria, a former ally of Napoléon.[5]
The portrait of Turenne is ostensibly an image of a
general loyal to Napoléon and the Empire, and nothing
in the picture reveals the emperor's downfall and exile.
The portrait that David painted in 1816 was followed
by another one (fig. 1), in which the count was depicted
not in military attire but in civilian clothes, yet with an
equally proud and confident allure.

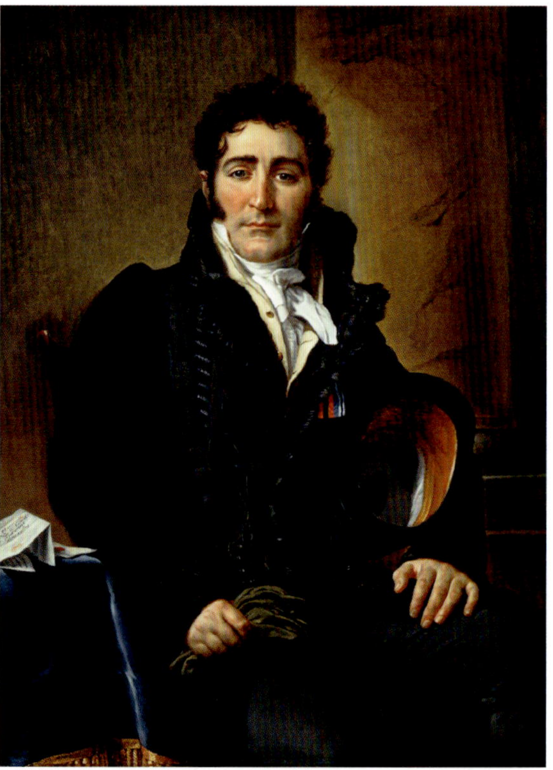

Fig. 1. Jacques-Louis David, *Comte Henri-Amédée-Mercure de
Turenne d'Aynac*, 1816. Oil on panel, 44⅛ × 31⅞ in. (112 × 81 cm).
Ny Carlsberg Glyptotek, Copenhagen, I.N. 1900

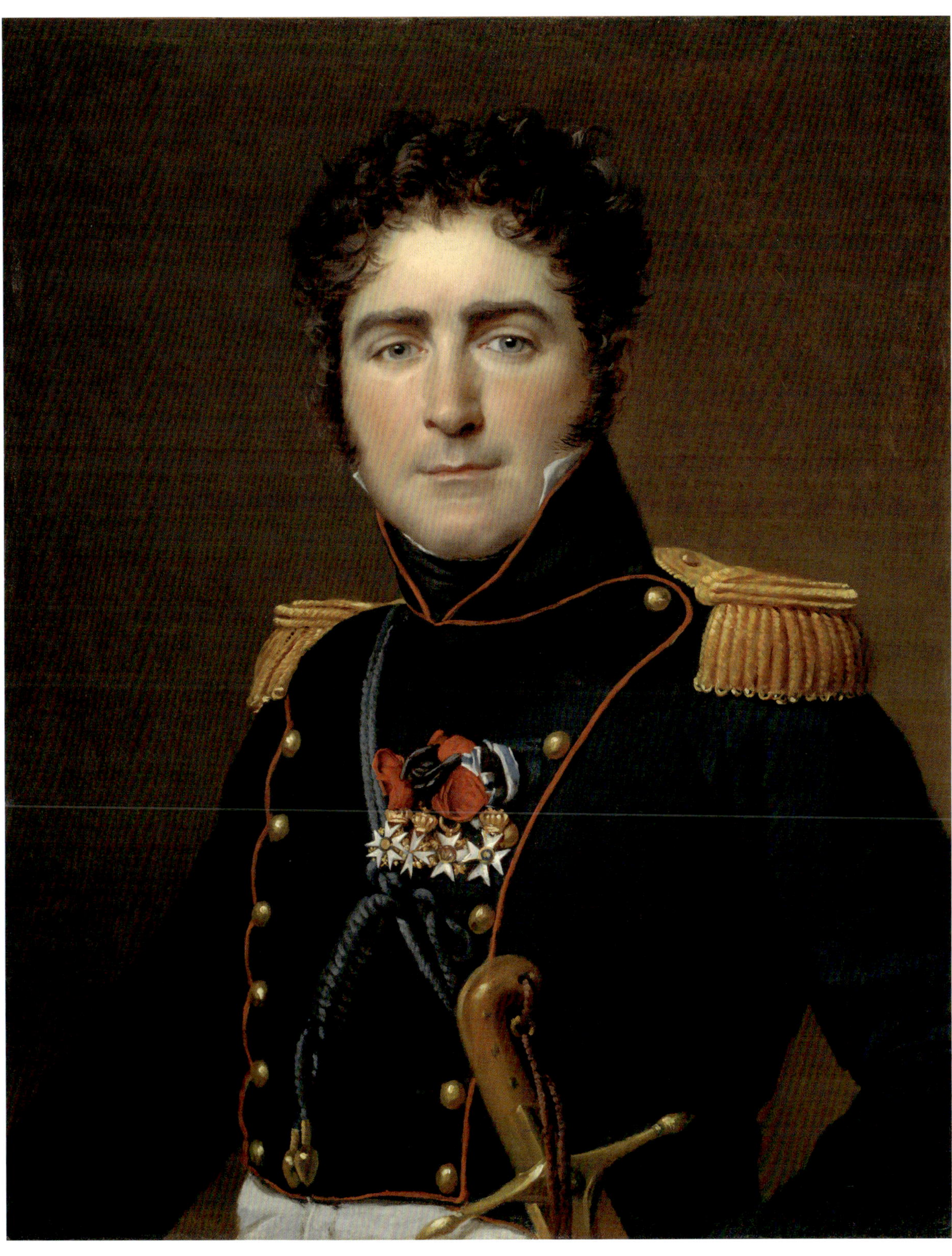

Portrait of Comte Henri-Amédée-Mercure de Turenne d'Aynac

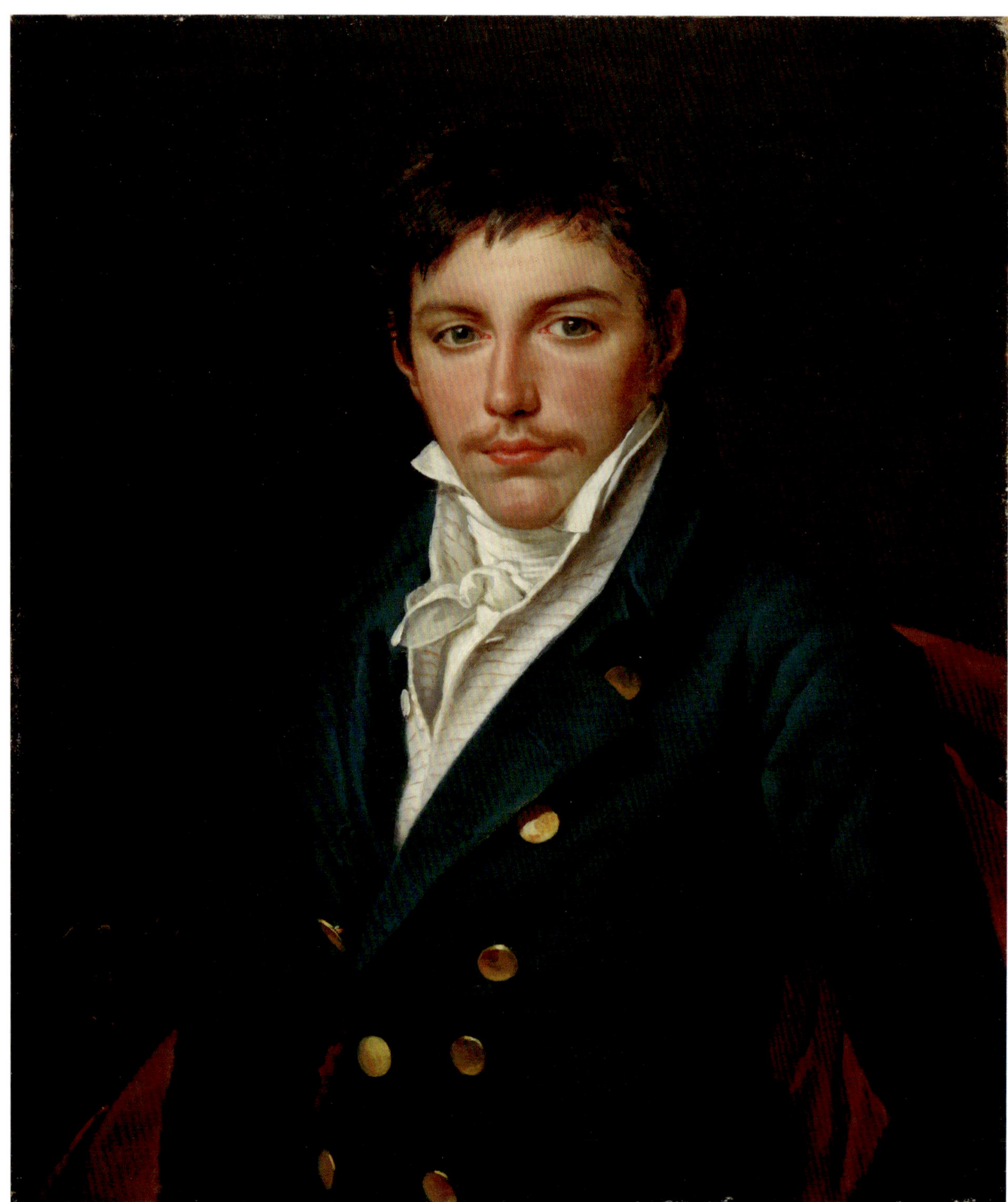

Portrait of François-Antoine Rasse de Gavre

David was also sought after by local aristocracy in Belgium, and one of the first commissions that he received in 1816, after having painted Turenne's portrait, was from Comte Vilain XIIII for a portrait of his wife.[6] The same year, he was commissioned by Prince Charles-Alexandre de Gavre to paint a portrait of his son, François-Antoine Rasse de Gavre. The half-length portrait shows the young man sitting on a covered stool in front of a dark wall. The rosy cheeks and tousled hair, as well as the loose golden button on the blue jacket, are discreet signs of youth. François-Antoine was only sixteen years old when this portrait was painted, yet David depicts him as a confident young man, with only small details such as the thin moustache and unbuttoned shirt indicating his real age. Although it was a commission, the painting also conveys David's ongoing attachment to the Empire and to Napoléon. Indeed, the Prince de Gavre had close ties to Napoléon, serving as a chamberlain to the sovereign's first wife, Joséphine, and then to the emperor.[7]

The portraits of both men are characterized by a realistic depiction of the facial features. During his exile, David became more committed to injecting a dose of realism into his portraits as well as into his historical compositions, certainly owing to the influence of Old Masters from the Dutch and Flemish schools.[8] This realism is also due to the painter's typical method of working; he had the men and women that he painted sit for several hours, and he spent extensive time on the facial features.[9] The hair decorations and garments, on the other hand, were in some cases inventions. The great detail given to the physiognomy of the sitters speaks to David's attempt to maintain his reputation and contradict those who considered him too old and his style repetitive.[10] These portraits, however, also convey an image of the past, of the bygone Empire, and express David's desire to remain close to his former persona by depicting figures with strong ties, be they direct or indirect, to Napoléon.[11] Both paintings were listed on an inventory, divided by the different stages of his career and locations where David lived and worked (such as Paris and Rome), that specifies these portraits as being painted not in Brussels but "dans mon exil" (during my exile).[12] —FVJ

1. For example, see *Bonaparte franchissant les Alpes au Grand-Saint-Bernard* (Bonaparte Crossing the Alps at the Saint-Bernard Pass; ca. 1801, Musée National des Châteaux de Malmaison & Bois-Préau, Rueil-Malmaison, France); *Sacre de l'empereur Napoléon Ier et couronnement de l'impératrice Joséphine dans la cathédrale Notre-Dame de Paris, le 2 décembre 1804* (The Coronation of the Emperor Napoléon I and the Crowning of the Empress Joséphine in Notre-Dame Cathedral on December 2, 1804; 1806–7, Musée du Louvre, Paris); and *Portrait de Napoléon dans son cabinet de travail* (The Emperor Napoleon in His Study at the Tuileries; 1812, National Gallery of Art, Washington, D.C.).

2. Philippe Bordes, *Jacques-Louis David: Empire to Exile*, exh. cat. (Williamstown, Mass.: Sterling and Francine Clark Art Institute, 2005), 295.

3. Ibid, 293–97.

4. Philippe Bordes, "David's Portrait of the Comte de Turenne at Williamstown," *The Burlington Magazine* 142, no. 1166 (May 2000): 276–80, esp. 277.

5. Bordes, *Jacques-Louis David*, 302–4, cat. 48.

6. See *Portrait of the Comtesse Vilain XIIII and Her Daughter* (1816, National Gallery, London); see also Bordes, *Jacques-Louis David*, 298–300, cat. 47.

7. Ibid., 312, cat. 51.

8. Jean-Claude Lebensztejn, "Histoires belges," in *David contre David*, ed. Régis Michel, conference proceedings (Paris: Musée du Louvre and La Documentation française, 1993), 2:1011–23, esp. 1016.

9. Sue Jones and Kathryn Calley Galitz, "Jacques-Louis David's Portrait of Comtesse Vilain XIIII and Her Daughter," *The Burlington Magazine* 142, no. 1166 (May 2000): 301–3.

10. Etienne-Jean Delécluze, *Louis David, son école et son temps* (Paris: Didier, 1855; reprint Paris: Macula, 1983), 367–68; Lebensztejn, "Histoires belges," 2:1014.

11. See also Josenhans, "(Re)Defining the 'I' in Exile," in this volume, 186–89.

12. This inventory list is published in Antoine Schnapper and Arlette Sérullaz, *Jacques-Louis David: 1748–1825*, exh. cat. (Paris: Musée du Louvre and Réunion des musées nationaux, 1989), 20–21.

Composition with Three Figures
ca. 1816–20
Black chalk on paper
5³⁄₁₆ × 7⁷⁄₁₆ in. (13.1 × 18.9 cm)
Provenance: Private collection; Christie's, London, July 4, 2000, lot 185; with W. M. Brady, New York; Yale University Art Gallery, New Haven, Conn., Everett V. Meeks, B.A. 1901, Fund, 2013.80.1.

Although the paintings that Jacques-Louis David made during his exile in Brussels continued the genres for which he had been renowned in France—history painting and his extraordinary portraiture (cat. 10), both powerful and perceptive—in the medium of drawing he began to create images unlike any of his previous works. When David was at the Académie de France in Rome from 1775 to 1780, he made hundreds of drawings, recording both antiquities and paintings by Renaissance and Baroque masters, such as Raphael and Nicolas Poussin. Aside from these works with their educational and mnemonic function, and some landscapes made in Switzerland in the summer of 1815—a period that could perhaps be considered his first exile—virtually all of the drawings that David made before his move to Brussels were preparatory for his paintings.[1] In Brussels, however, David created a group of drawings that stand as independent works of art, rather than as part of a preparatory process.

Some thirty of them are similar to this intriguing one, and about the same size, and almost all of them have the same horizontal format, with two to five bust-length figures. In most of these drawings, the figures, like those in the present work, are tantalizingly suggestive of an interrelationship but ultimately seem to have none; the figures are psychologically isolated, as indeed the artist must have felt at least to some extent, beginning life in a foreign place at close to seventy years of age.

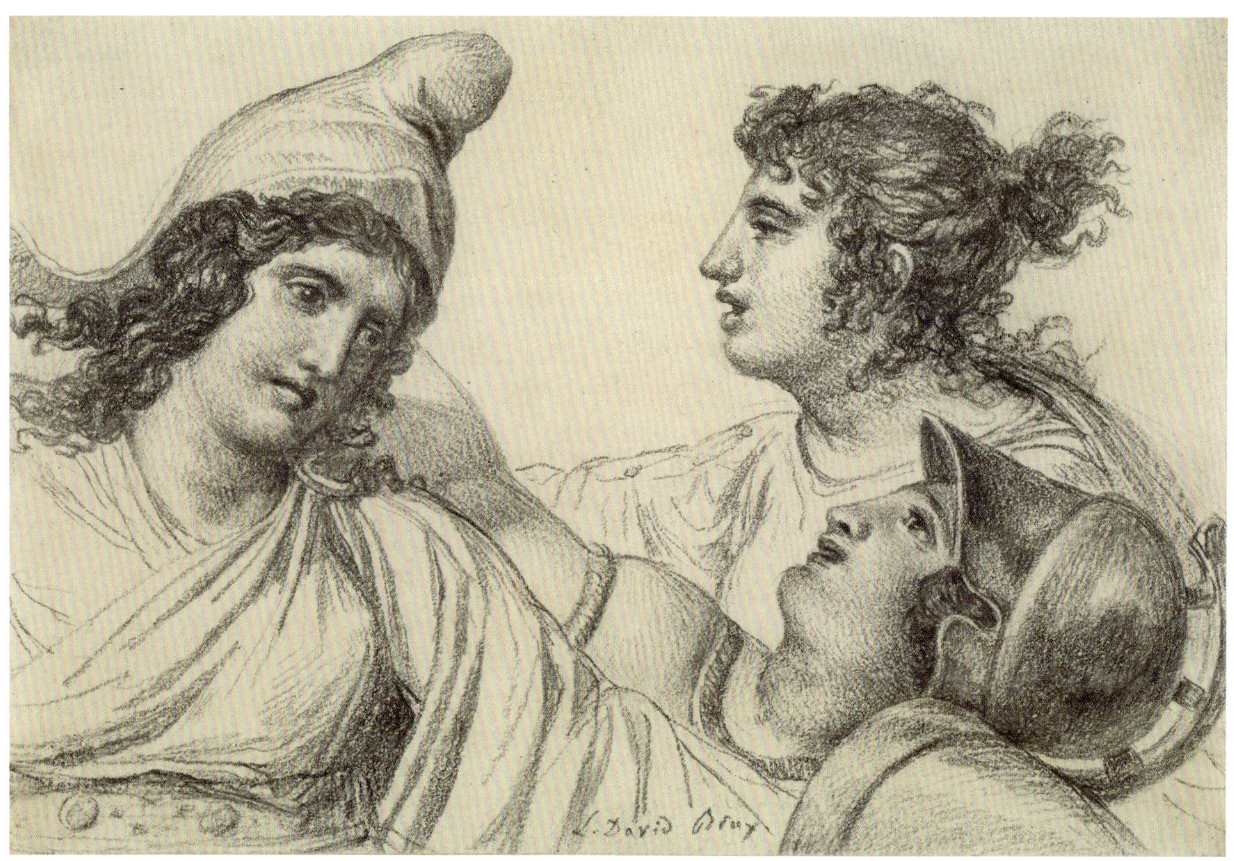

In a letter of January 1818 to his former student Joseph-Denis Odevaere, David described these drawings as *croquis, caprices* (sketches, caprices), writing that after having "tossed onto the paper the follies that passed through my head," his "self-respect then became involved and I really made drawings." He went on to state his conviction that this group would hold its own among his works.[2] David's grandson Jules asserted that the artist made these drawings at night if the opera and the theater were closed.[3]

The drawing in the Gallery's collection includes three figures.[4] The one at left, in three-quarter view, wears a Phrygian cap, a soft conical hat with the top pulled forward, which originated in antiquity and was adopted during the French Revolution as a symbol of liberty. The figure at lower right, in nearly pure profile, leaning backward, wears a helmet, and the one at upper right, in pure profile, is bareheaded with hair pulled back in a chignon. The three figures are so close that they seem to be touching, and yet they do not interact; their gazes do not meet. The group of drawings has been characterized as "demonstrably dramatic," and this image has even been read as part of a specific drama, the Judgment of Paris, known from multiple antique Greek sources. The figure in the Phrygian cap would be Paris, the one in the helmet Athena, and the other Hera: the two goddesses would be evincing their dismay and anger after Paris chose Aphrodite as the most beautiful of the three.[5]

Paris conventionally is shown in a Phrygian cap, and he wears one in David's painted renditions of Paris and Helen (1788, Musée du Louvre, Paris; 1789, Musée des Arts Décoratifs, Paris). But few other Phrygian caps are found in the artist's oeuvre, and it is thus all the more noteworthy that two of the men on the Roman side in David's *Les Sabines* (The Intervention of the Sabine Women) of 1799 (fig. 1) do wear Phrygian caps. Furthermore, the figure at left in the drawing bears a striking resemblance to the most prominent one in a Phrygian cap in the painting, the young man near the right

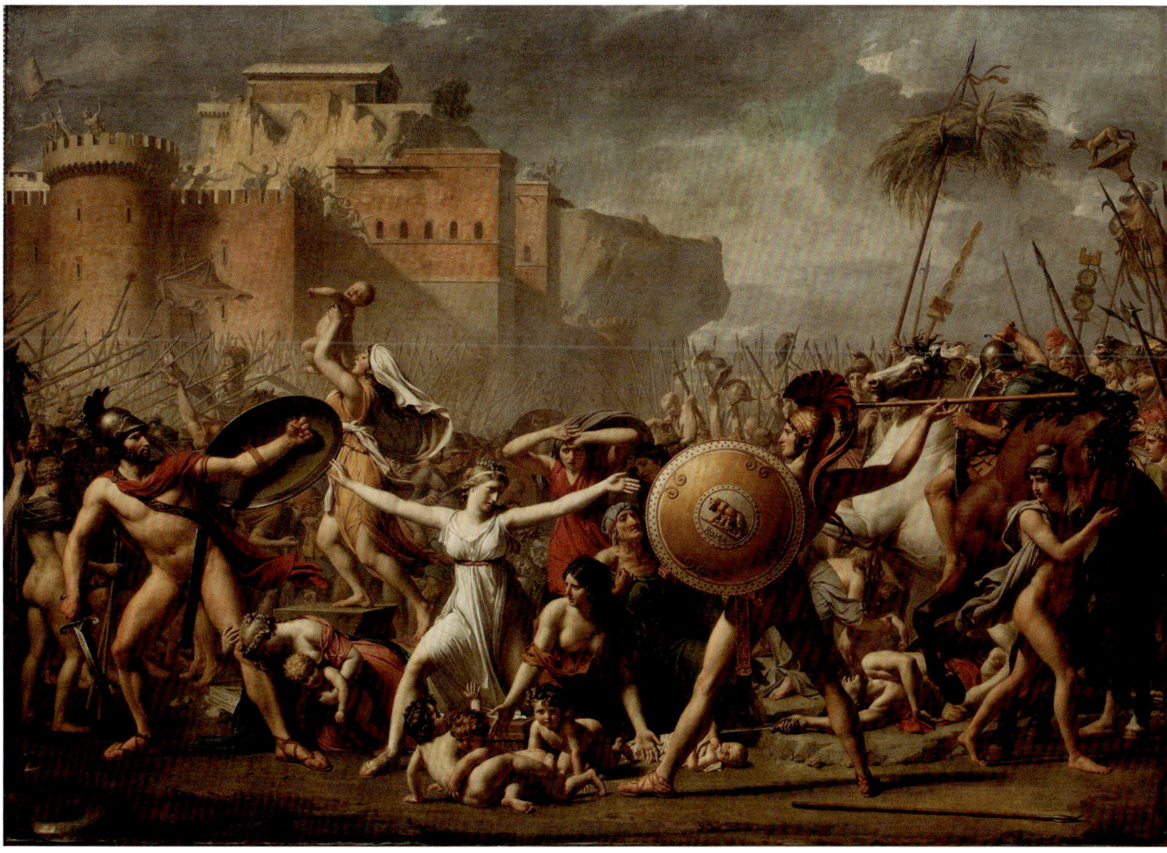

Fig. 1. Jacques-Louis David, *Les Sabines* (The Intervention of the Sabine Women), 1799. Oil on canvas, 12 ft. 7⁹⁄₁₆ in. × 17 ft. 1½ in. (385 × 522 cm). Musée du Louvre, Paris, 3691

edge, calming a frightened horse, whose body is turned to the right but whose head looks back toward the central action.

At least two of the group of thirty or so drawings have figures that David reprised from his well-known paintings *Les Sabines* and *Léonidas aux Thermopyles* (Leonidas at Thermopylae, 1814, Musée du Louvre, Paris), which originally was meant as a pendant to *Les Sabines*.[6] These drawings (see fig. 2) are called "variations" on those paintings, although their drastic reduction of the number of figures and elimination of context or setting result in compositions of a character utterly different from the paintings; additionally, some of the faces, such as that of the Sabine heroine Hersilia, are of a different type. In addition to the resemblance between the head with a Phrygian cap in the present drawing and those in *Les Sabines*, there is a remarkable resemblance between the head shown in profile in the upper right and the frontally depicted head of Hersilia in the drawn variation—a head that, as mentioned, differs considerably from that in the painting. The third figure in the Gallery's drawing may also have a connection with the Sabine composition—in David's first sketch of the subject, made in 1794, when he was in prison, a female figure is just to the left of Hersilia, on her knees, with her head thrown back and right arm up in a defensive gesture (this figure was later replaced by a woman standing on a block, holding her baby high).[7] Thus the Gallery's drawing may well be another variation on *Les Sabines*. Philippe Bordes observed that *Les Sabines*, for David, was "the source of many of his later preoccupations"; indeed it seems more than likely that this painting, first conceived when David was in prison, and the subject of which was a group of women forcibly taken from their home, was one that David's thoughts would have returned to repeatedly while he was in exile.[8] —SB

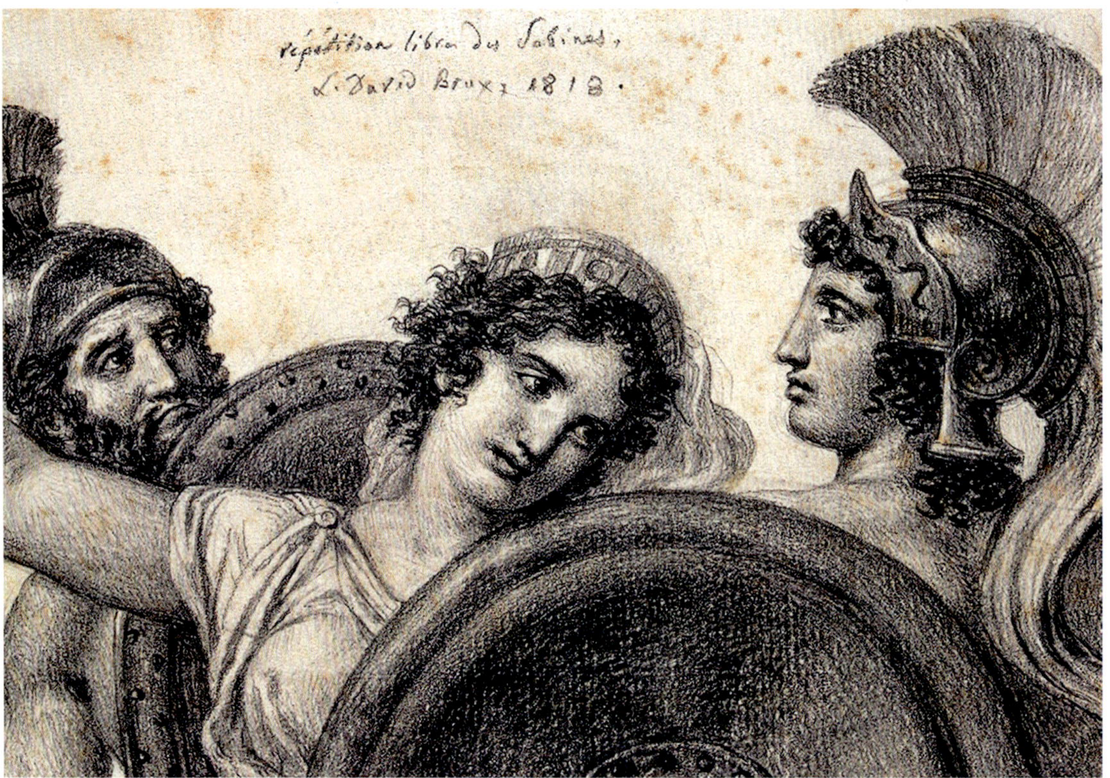

Fig. 2. Jacques-Louis David, *Variation on "The Intervention of the Sabine Women,"* 1818. Charcoal and black chalk, 5¼ × 7⅞ in. (13.4 × 20 cm). The Peabody Collection, Maryland Commission on Artistic Property of the Maryland State Archives, on loan to the Baltimore Museum of Art, MSA SC 4680-13-0000, R.11826.352

1. For David's itinerary in Switzerland, see Antoine Schnapper and Arlette Sérullaz, *Jacques-Louis David, 1748–1825*, exh. cat. (Paris: Musée du Louvre, 1989), 620–21. For his drawings, see Pierre Rosenberg and Louis-Antoine Prat, *Jacques-Louis David, 1748–1825: Catalogue raisonné des dessins*, 2 vols. (Milan: Leonardo arte, 2002).

2. "Ce sont des croquis, des caprices j'ai commencé d'abord sans prétension, je jetois sur le papier les folies qui me passoient par la tête . . . ensuite l'amour propre s'en est mêlé et j'ai fait des dessins réellement. . . . Je crois cependant pouvoir dire sincèrement que cette collection tiendra son rang parmi mes ouvrages." This letter, at that time recently discovered by Mark Ledbury, was quoted in Ledbury, "Introduction," in *David after David: Essays on the Later Work*, ed. Mark Ledbury (Williamstown, Mass.: Sterling and Francine Clark Art Institute, 2007), xiv, xvi n26.

3. See J. L. Jules David, *Le peintre Louis David, 1748–1825: Souvenirs & documents inédits* (Paris: Havard, 1880–82), 1:566.

4. Rosenberg and Prat, *Jacques-Louis David, 1748–1825*, cat. 363.

5. See Philippe Bordes, *Jacques-Louis David: Empire to Exile*, exh. cat. (Williamstown, Mass.: Sterling and Francine Clark Art Institute, 2005), 266, 282. The identification of the figures as Paris, Athena, and Hera was made in an auction catalogue at Christie's, London (see provenance for sale date and lot number).

6. Rosenberg and Prat, *Jacques-Louis David, 1748–1825*, cats. 332, 340; Bordes, *Jacques-Louis David*, cats. 33–34. In yet another drawing, four of its five figures are quotations from *The Burial of Saint Denis* (1533[?], Musée de l'Art Wallon, Liège, Belgium) by the Renaissance master Lambert Lombard. Rosenberg and Prat, *Jacques-Louis David, 1748–1825*, cat. 344; Bordes, *Jacques-Louis David*, cat. 39. See Pierre-Yves Kairis, "Jacques-Louis David et Lambert Lombard," *Cahiers d'histoire de l'art 3* (2005): 91–96. It seems likely that other sources for some of the figures in these drawings will be identified.

7. This sketch is in the collection of the Musée du Louvre, Paris; Rosenberg and Prat, *Jacques-Louis David, 1748–1825*, cat. 146.

8. Bordes, *Jacques-Louis David*, 242.

Le Château de Chillon
ca. 1874–77
Oil on canvas
28¾ × 36¼ in. (73 × 92 cm)
Provenance: Collection Eugène Cusenier d'Ornans (friend of Courbet); Collection Mme Goulu (his niece); Mme Rigaud (daughter of Mme Goulu); private collection, Aubagne, France; private collection, United States.

After a brief imprisonment due to his involvement in the revolutionary government of the Paris Commune, Gustave Courbet left France in July 1873 to avoid another pending prison sentence and mandated reparation payments that he could not afford. Forced to abandon his native country, family, and friends, Courbet went into exile in Switzerland, which damaged the painter's reputation permanently.[1] He settled in the town of La-Tour-de-Peilz, on the border of Lake Geneva (Lac Léman) near France. He remained there until his death, and these years in exile were marked by financial worries and illness caused by his drinking. However, he continued to paint and, in order to make a living, set up a studio where assistants helped him produce paintings.[2] Because of the uneven quality of work from Courbet's time in Switzerland, the authenticity of many of his paintings from this period has been in doubt.[3] Scholars seemed almost reluctant to study the motifs that Courbet turned to most frequently during his exile—which were seen as tainted by the artist's political activities—or to compare them to the enthralling paintings he had done in the 1840s and 1850s, such as *L'atelier du peintre* (The Artist's Studio, 1854–55, Musée d'Orsay, Paris) and *Les casseurs de pierre* (The Stonebreakers, 1849, formerly Dresden, Germany, now destroyed), which had shocked both critics and the public and instated Courbet as one of the leading voices of Realism.

Nevertheless, Courbet created some stunning alpine and forest landscapes, seascapes, and still lifes during his exile in Switzerland—including this version of *Le Château de Chillon*—that equal in intensity the mesmerizing canvases for which he is best known. The Château de Chillon (Chillon Castle) is located on the shore of Lake Geneva, not far from the town where Courbet settled. The site had been used as a Roman outpost to guard the strategic route through the Alps, and the castle was built during the Middle Ages and became a famous prison during the sixteenth century. Lord Byron contributed to the romanticization of the castle with his poem "The Prisoner of Chillon" (1816), which was inspired by the story of François Bonivard, a prisoner there from 1530 to 1536. The isolated castle on the edge of the lake, surrounded by water and mountains, appealed to writers, tourists, and painters alike, and reproductions and postcards of this scene circulated widely in the second half of the nineteenth century.[4] Courbet, aware of the popularity of this view, painted several versions of the scene.[5] In this version, the gloomy presence of the massive castle, with its compact military architecture, high-reaching watchtower, and high walls, dominates more than half of the painted surface. The rest of the composition is occupied by the water of the lake, the Alps, and the overcast sky, with gray clouds signaling an approaching storm. The castle is reflected in the water, its walls and shadowed corners echoed in the murky surface at left, near the rocky shore. Heavy raindrops, depicted as dark splatters, fall on the lake. Courbet was known for his unconventional painting methods; he would often use a palette knife not only for its traditional function, mixing paints on a palette, but also to apply pigment directly to the canvas, then scrape away parts of the wet paint with the knife.[6] This technique gave his paintings an "unfinished" appearance, with brushstrokes and even palette-knife marks clearly visible in some areas, as seen here in the lake and the mountains. He embraced this intentional unfinished look, and he even used the technique to indicate light and shadow by applying unmixed dots of color, lighter or darker, to indicate reflections, such as the areas of lighter blue on the surface of the lake and the orange spots on the peak of the mountain.

This depiction of the Château de Chillon is certainly one of the darker versions of the castle that Courbet painted between 1874 and 1877. The almost melancholy mood of this composition stems from the narrowed view, centered on the castle encircled by mountains, which creates a confined space. This view is quite different from the panoramic depictions of the castle and surrounding landscape meant for tourists, which Courbet also painted, such as a more famous version that belongs to the Musée Courbet in Ornans (fig. 1). Many of these representations, and especially the Ornans version, were based on a famous photograph taken by Adolphe Braun in the 1860s (fig. 2), which included the earthen dam in front of the castle that was removed to make space for railroad tracks in the 1870s.[7] In contrast to other versions, in which Courbet depicted a boat on the lake, this painting does not suggest a human presence.[8] Part of the castle lies in shadow, alluding to its somber past as a prison and conveying a sense of isolation; this feeling is reinforced by the mountains and castle that block the horizon, creating an almost enclosed space within the painting. This grim

110

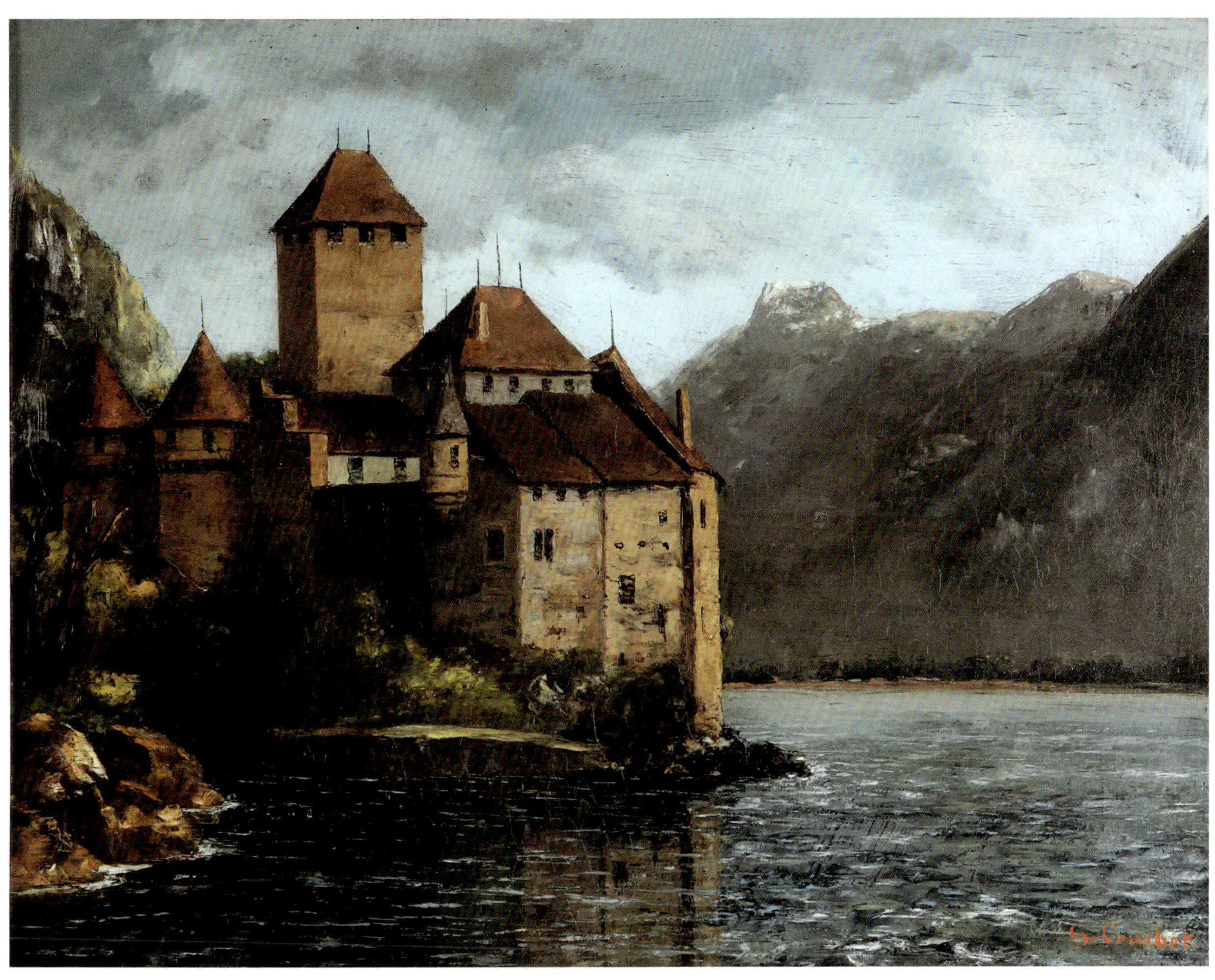

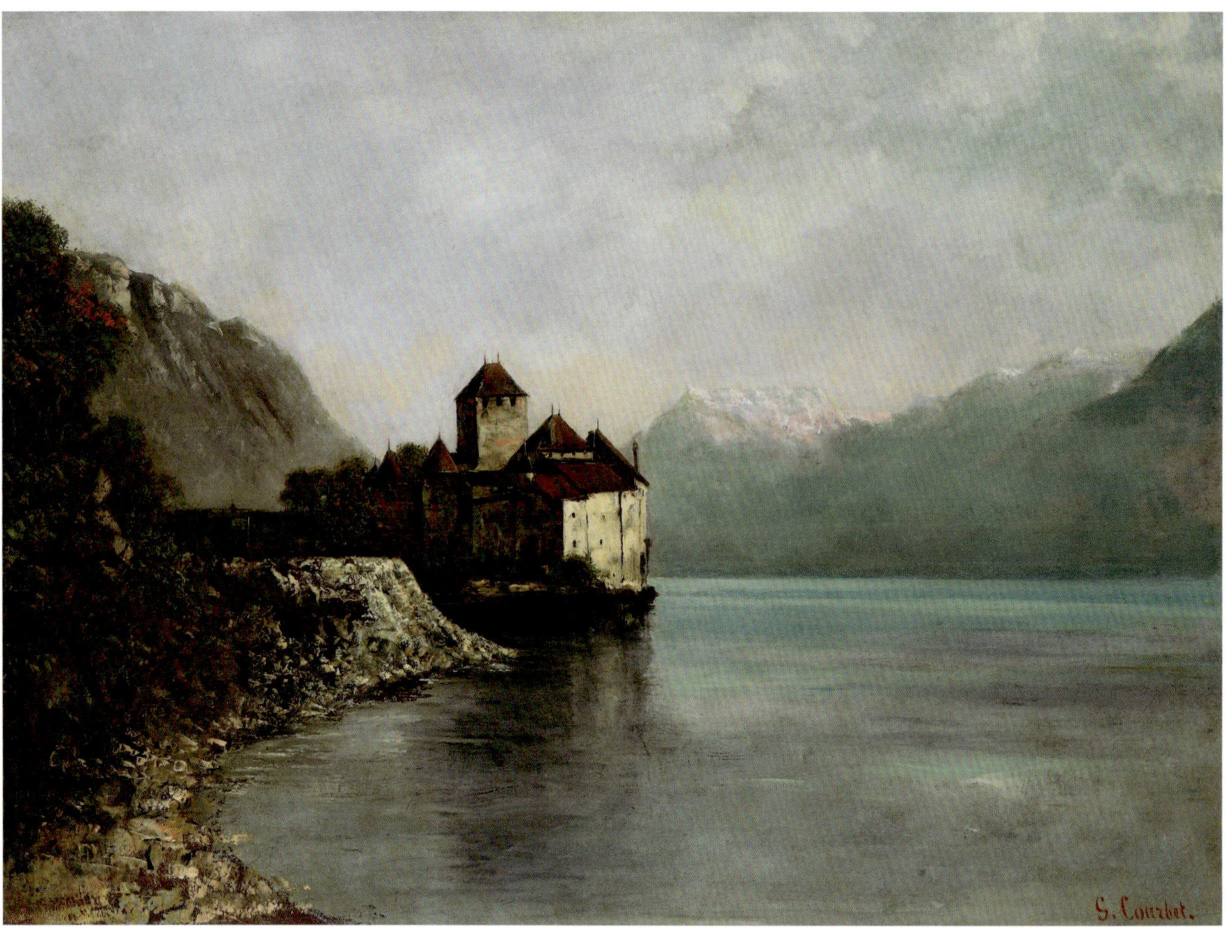

Fig. I. Gustave Courbet, *Château de Chillon*, 1874. Oil on canvas, 33⅞ × 39⅜ in. (86 × 100 cm). Musée Courbet, Ornans, France, D.1976.1.3

depiction of the otherwise idyllic scene of a castle on a lake also foregrounds Courbet's recent experience of imprisonment and resonates with his status as an exile, or a prisoner without walls, separated from his native France. Still, the top of the mountain shimmers slightly with gold and pink, as if the sun were about to break through the clouds and chase away the rain. —FVJ

1. Mary Morton, "To Create a Living Art," in Mary Morton and Charlotte Eyerman, *Courbet and the Modern Landscape*, exh. cat. (Los Angeles: J. Paul Getty Museum, 2006), 14; Laurence des Cars, "The Experience of History: Courbet and the Commune," in Dominique de Font-Réaulx et al., *Gustave Courbet*, exh. cat. (New York: Metropolitan Museum of Art, 2008), 409–11.

2. Klaus Herding, *Courbet: To Venture Independence*, trans. John William Gabriel (New Haven, Conn.: Yale University Press, 1991), 142–46.

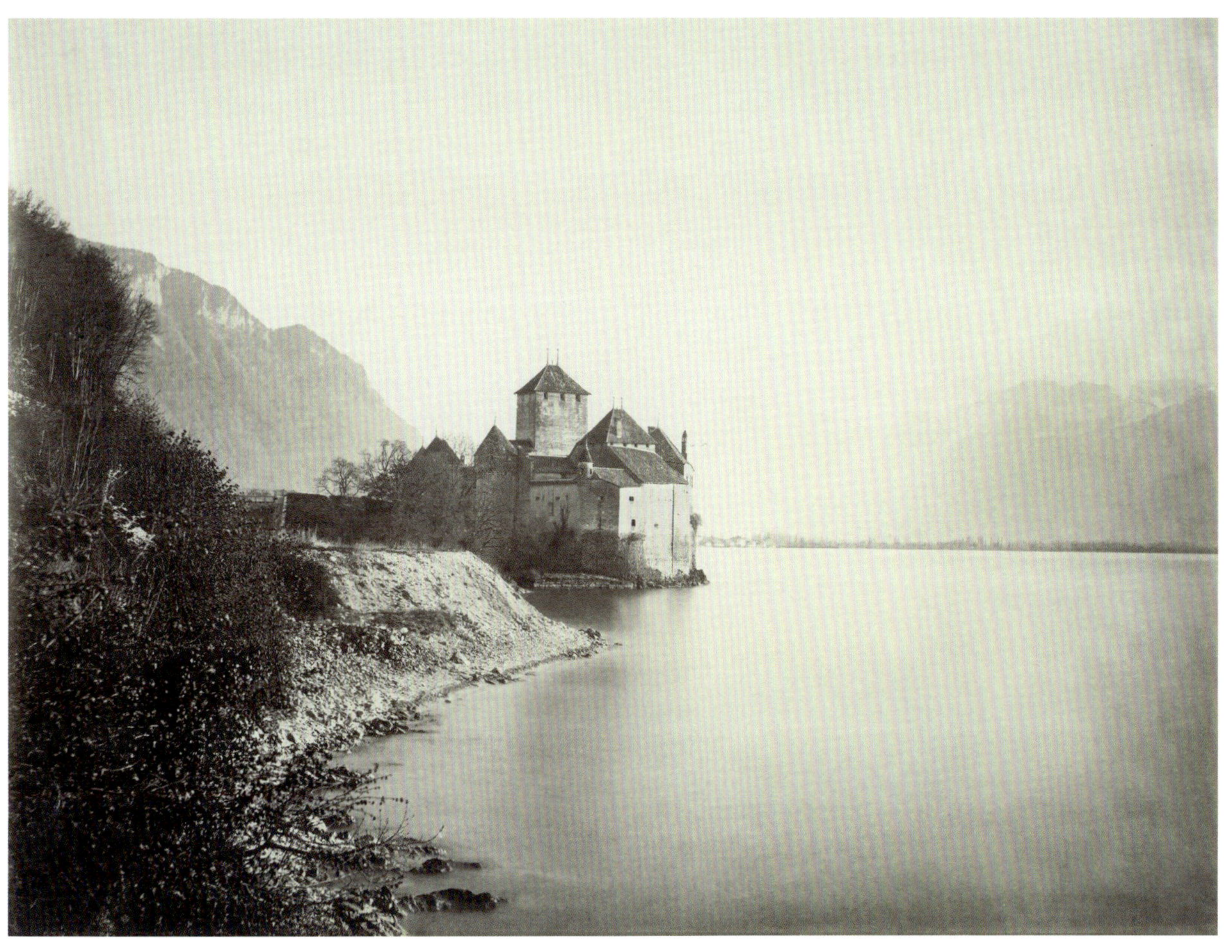

Fig. 2. Adolphe Braun, *The Castle of Chillon*, ca. 1867. Albumen print, 14⁵⁄₁₆ × 18¹¹⁄₁₆ in. (36.4 × 47.5 cm). Museum of Fine Arts, Boston, Lucy Dalbiac Luard Fund, 1982.322

3. Laurence des Cars, "L'impossible œuvre tardif de M. Courbet," in *Gustave Courbet: Les années suisses*, ed. Laurence Madeline, exh. cat. (Paris: Éditions Artlys, 2014), 55–57.

4. Petra ten-Doesschate Chu, "Le 'marketing' du château de Chillon," in Madeline, *Gustave Courbet*, 187–93.

5. Robert Fernier counted twenty-one versions of this motif; Robert Fernier, *La vie et l'œuvre de Gustave Courbet: Catalogue raisonné* (Geneva and Lausanne: Fondation Wildenstein, 1977–78), 2:192–96, 214, 232, cats. 931–45, 989–90, 992–93, 1043, 1046.

6. Morton, "To Create a Living Art," 6–8.

7. Mary Morton, "Switzerland," in Morton and Eyerman, *Courbet and the Modern Landscape*, 121–23; Pierre Chessex, *Courbet et la Suisse* (La Tour-de-Peilz, Switzerland: Château de La Tour-de-Peilz, 1982), 62.

8. See, for instance, Fernier, *La vie et l'œuvre de Gustave Courbet*, 2:cats. 935, 943, 992.

Sunset, from the portfolio *A Hungarian Memory*
1917, printed 1980
Gelatin silver print
7¹⁄₁₆ × 9¾ in. (18 × 24.7 cm)

Heavy Burden, from the portfolio *A Hungarian Memory*
1916, printed 1980
Gelatin silver print
7⅜ × 9¾ in. (18.8 × 24.8 cm)

Forced March to the Front between Lonie and Mitulen, from the portfolio *A Hungarian Memory*
1915, printed 1980
Gelatin silver print
6¾ × 9¾ in. (17.1 × 24.8 cm)

Budafok, from the portfolio *A Hungarian Memory*
1919, printed 1980
Gelatin silver print
7¹⁄₁₆ × 9¹³⁄₁₆ in. (17.9 × 24.9 cm)

Provenance: Gerald Levine; Yale University Art Gallery, New Haven, Conn., Gift of Gerald Levine, B.A. 1960, 1992.78.1.5, .7–.9.

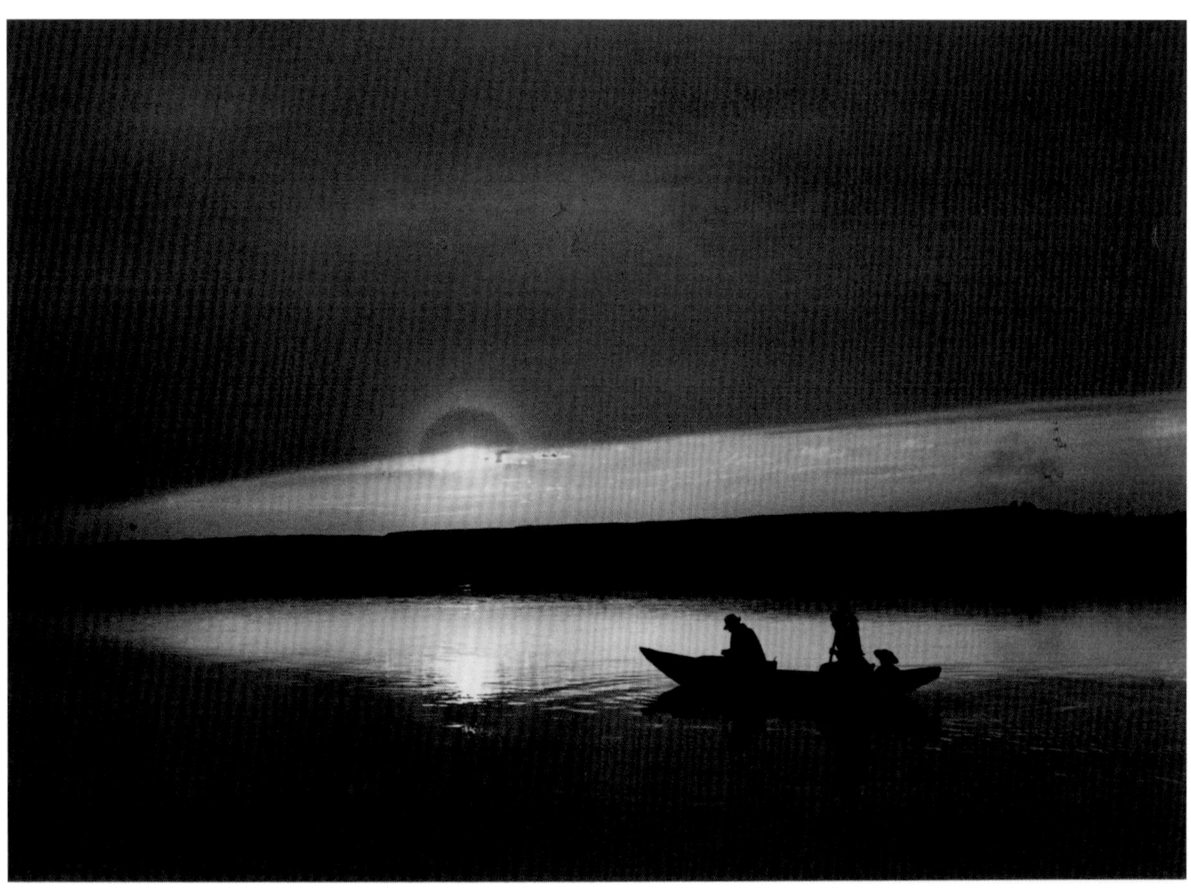

Sunset

André Kertész is best remembered for his photographs documenting life in Paris and New York, many of which, like those of the Jardin du Luxembourg and Montmartre, have entered the collective memory, thanks to gracefully structured compositions based on form and geometry, innovative perspectives such as high or very close vantage points, and the artist's ability to capture fleeting moments. However, toward the end of his life, he returned to motifs from his youth and from the very beginning of his career as a photographer. Kertész was born in 1894 in what was then the Austro-Hungarian Empire, which ceased to exist after World War I. He fought in the imperial army during the war, and as a soldier he started to take amateur photographs of what he witnessed at the front. While convalescing, after having been wounded in battle, he took photographs of soldiers and nurses at their daily occupations.[1] With the end of the war, and the fall of the Austro-Hungarian Empire and the establishment of a republic in Hungary, Kertész continued his practice of photography while making a living from day jobs. The photographs that he took during that time foreground his interest in rural and folkloric motifs, as well as in urban scenes. Despite the critical success of these early images, he experienced increasing anti-Semitism in his country.[2] He immigrated to France in 1925, and

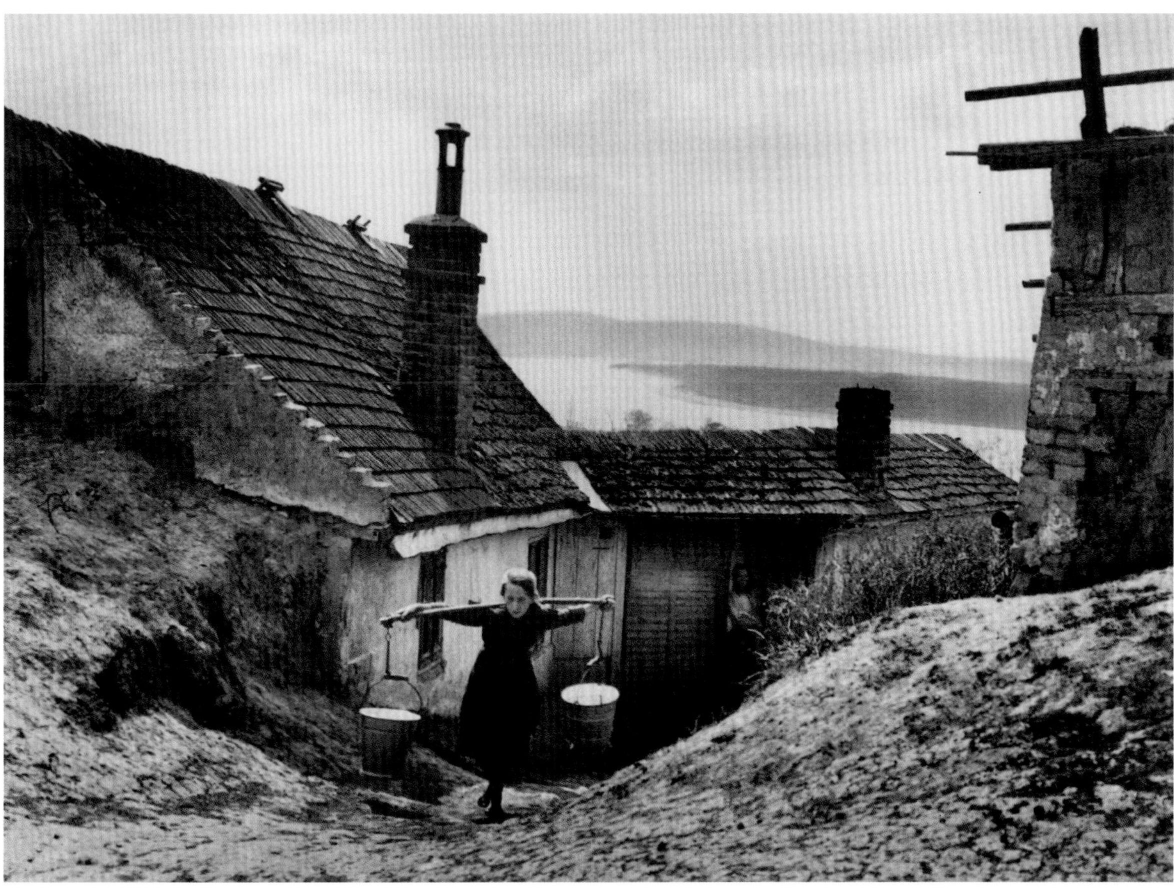

Heavy Burden

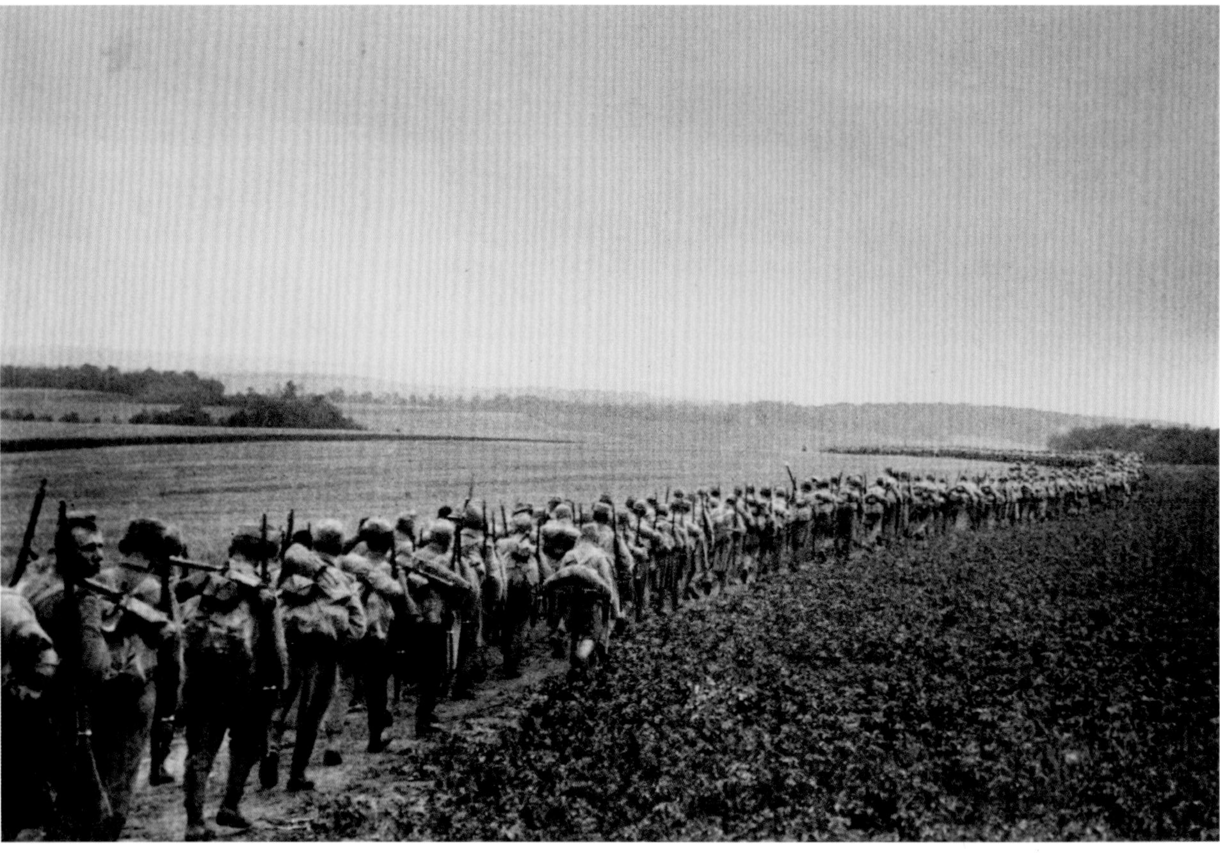

Forced March to the Front between Lonie and Mitulen

only after his arrival there did he became a professional photographer, making a name for himself with his views documenting Parisian street life, which were published in photographic magazines.[3] Kertész then moved from France to the United States in 1938, on an invitation to work for the Keystone Photographic Company in New York. In his early years there, he captured American cityscapes with skyscrapers and people in the streets.[4]

In the 1980s, after a successful international career and shortly before his death, Kertész turned back to the early years of his life in Hungary, in the former Austro-Hungarian Empire, and his memories of it. The photographs he had taken in the 1910s were printed and published as a portfolio under the title *A Hungarian Memory*. In addition, in 1982 he published the book *Hungarian Memories*, which compiled a larger selection of photographs from his youth in Budapest and further

emphasized his deep attachment to his Hungarian roots.[5] Most of the photographs in *A Hungarian Memory* show peaceful and banal scenes, which give the impression of being remote from the war. The poetic scene of a lake at sunset seems like a moment out of time; images of a village with houses nestled against each other and a girl carrying buckets evoke a tranquil life in the countryside. Adopting a bird's-eye view, Kertész also features the structural lines of the farm buildings and surrounding fields. In another image, a line of marching soldiers winding through the fields toward the front seems to become part of the surrounding landscape. Even at this early stage of his career, the artist demonstrated his capacity to observe and wait to seize a meaningful moment, while still being mindful of the overall pictorial structure.[6] Kertész's choice of motifs and his compositional sense, which emphasizes

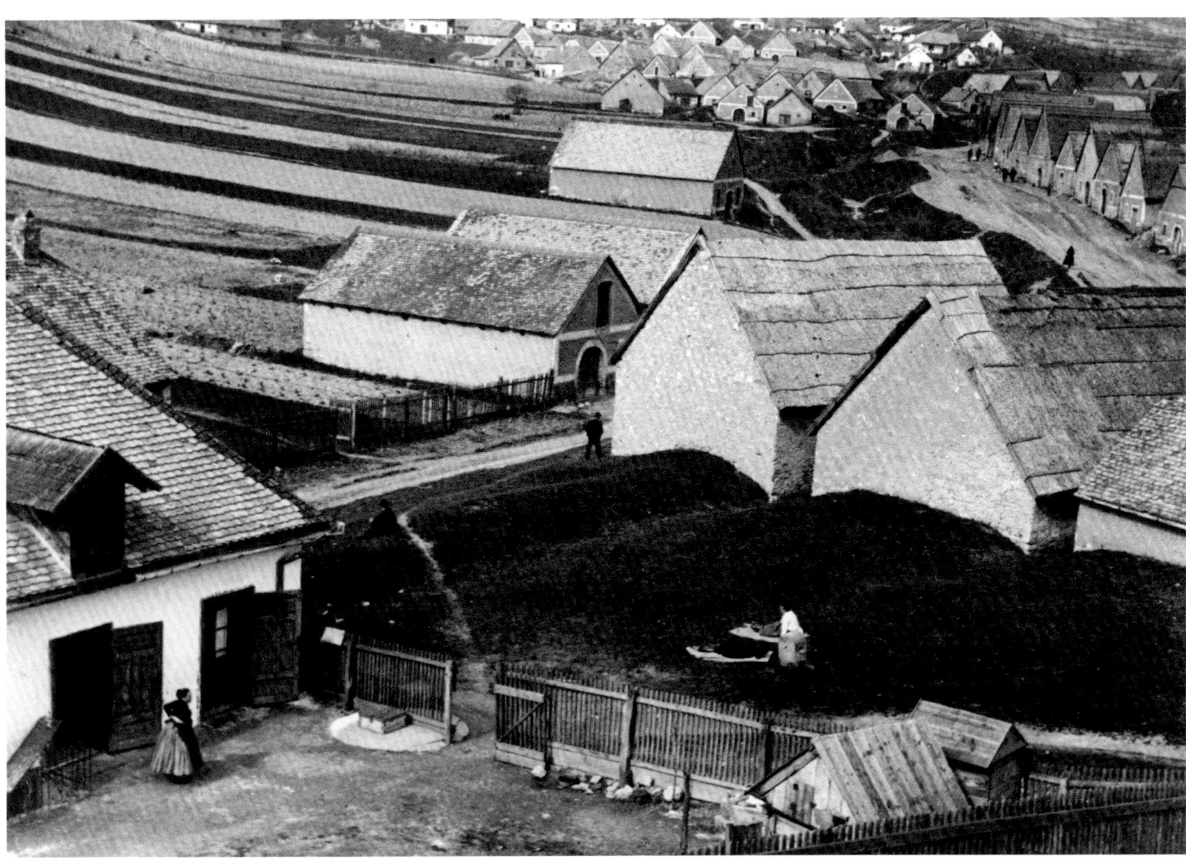

Budafok

the lyrical aspect of these works, also reveal his emotional attachment to the Hungarian soil. By including the word *memory* in the title of this portfolio, Kertész draws the viewer's attention to the personal, subjective nature of the photographs and invokes his reminiscences of a long-gone past. For a modern viewer looking at these works with a knowledge of history, it is not the documentary character of the images that captures the attention; rather, it is their nostalgic aspect that prevails, as they seem to predict the end of an era. —FVJ

1. Michel Frizot and Annie-Laure Wanaverbecq, *André Kertész* (Paris: Editions du Jeu de Paume, 2010), 48.

2. László Beke, "The Hungarian Period (1894–1925): A Photographer from Birth," in Pierre Borhan, *André Kertész: His Life and Work* (Boston: Bulfinch, 1994), 36–45, esp. 39, 45n13.

3. Frizot and Wanaverbecq, *André Kertész*, 183–85.

4. Deborah Irmas, "Experiencing the New World: Andreas Feininger, André Kertész," in *Exiles and Emigrés: The Flight of European Artists from Hitler*, ed. Stephanie Barron, exh. cat. (Los Angeles: Los Angeles County Museum of Art, 1997), 195–207, esp. 203–4.

5. André Kertész, *Hungarian Memories* (Boston: New York Graphic Society, 1982); Richard Teleky, *Hungarian Rhapsodies: Essays on Ethnicity, Identity, and Culture* (Seattle: University of Washington Press, 1997), 30.

6. Beke, "The Hungarian Period," 36–45, esp. 37.

Untitled (Head)
1932–34
Oil on canvas
38½ × 30½ in. (97.8 × 77.5 cm)
Provenance: Frederick Muschenheim; William Muschenheim; Sidney Janis Gallery, New York, 1962; Carroll and Donna Janis; Yale University Art Gallery, New Haven, Conn., Gift of Carroll and Donna Janis, 2013.142.1.

Arshile Gorky played a crucial role in the emergence of American Modernism, particularly by introducing elements of European Surrealism through a highly personal style that spanned from representation to abstraction. His art reflects the repercussions of the Armenian genocide of 1915–23, when the Ottoman government authorized the arrest, deportation, and killing of more than one million Armenians. This event had an impact on his own family's fate—Gorky's mother died of starvation during their flight from the Van province where they lived, a tragedy that echoed throughout his work both visually and thematically.[1] His paintings reveal a nostalgic quest for identity: motifs reminiscent of his Armenian heritage, memories from his childhood, and cultural artifacts

that he had seen as a child reappear in the paintings and drawings that he executed after moving to the United States, and he recomposed these various influences over and over again.

Untitled (Head) is a transitional work that mixes European Modernism with Gorky's Armenian culture at a time when the artist was concealing his origins, notably through taking a pseudonym.[2] This canvas is situated at a crossroads of Gorky's career, between works such as *Nighttime, Enigma, and Nostalgia* (fig. 1)—which, with its undulating biomorphic forms and cryptic title, was indebted to Surrealism and its emphasis on the subconscious—and the colorfully abstract works of his later period. The present painting shows a female face, albeit in a way that draws toward abstraction, with the overall composition treated without any illusion of depth.[3] The head does not seem to be attached to a physical body but instead appears to float on a sphere. Other corporeal features are absent or only suggested, such as the elongated shape above the head, which resembles an arm with a three-fingered hand. The form of the head, shown in profile, is simplified to the extreme, with the prominent forehead and nose unified and a dent suggesting an open mouth. An almond-shaped

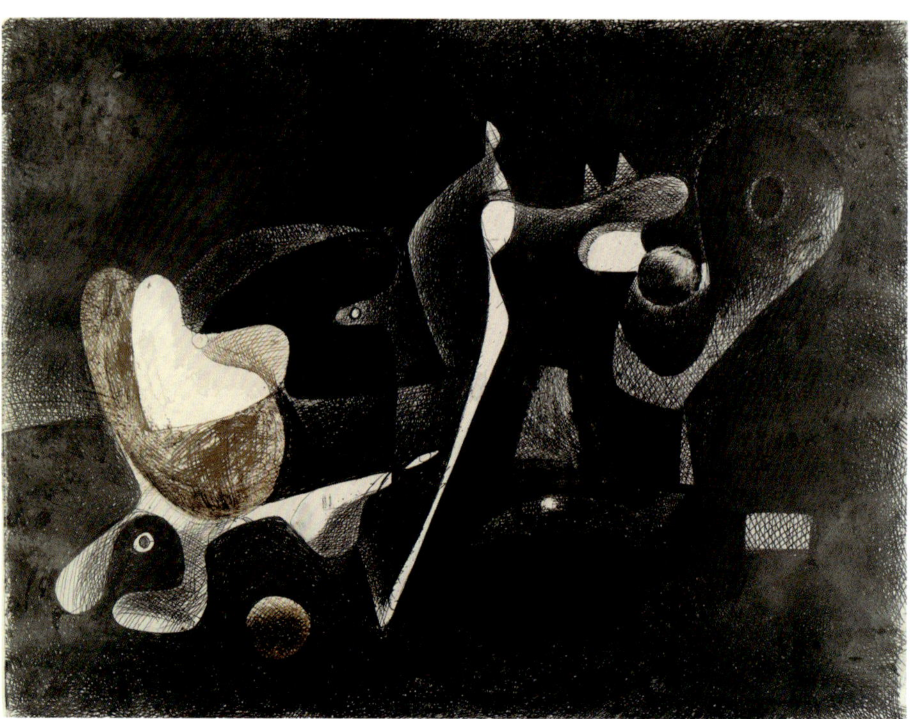

Fig. 1. Arshile Gorky, *Nighttime, Enigma, and Nostalgia*, 1931–32. Black and brown ink on paper, 22¹¹⁄₁₆ × 28⅞ in. (57.7 × 73.3 cm). Yale University Art Gallery, New Haven, Conn., Gift of Collection Société Anonyme, 1941.487

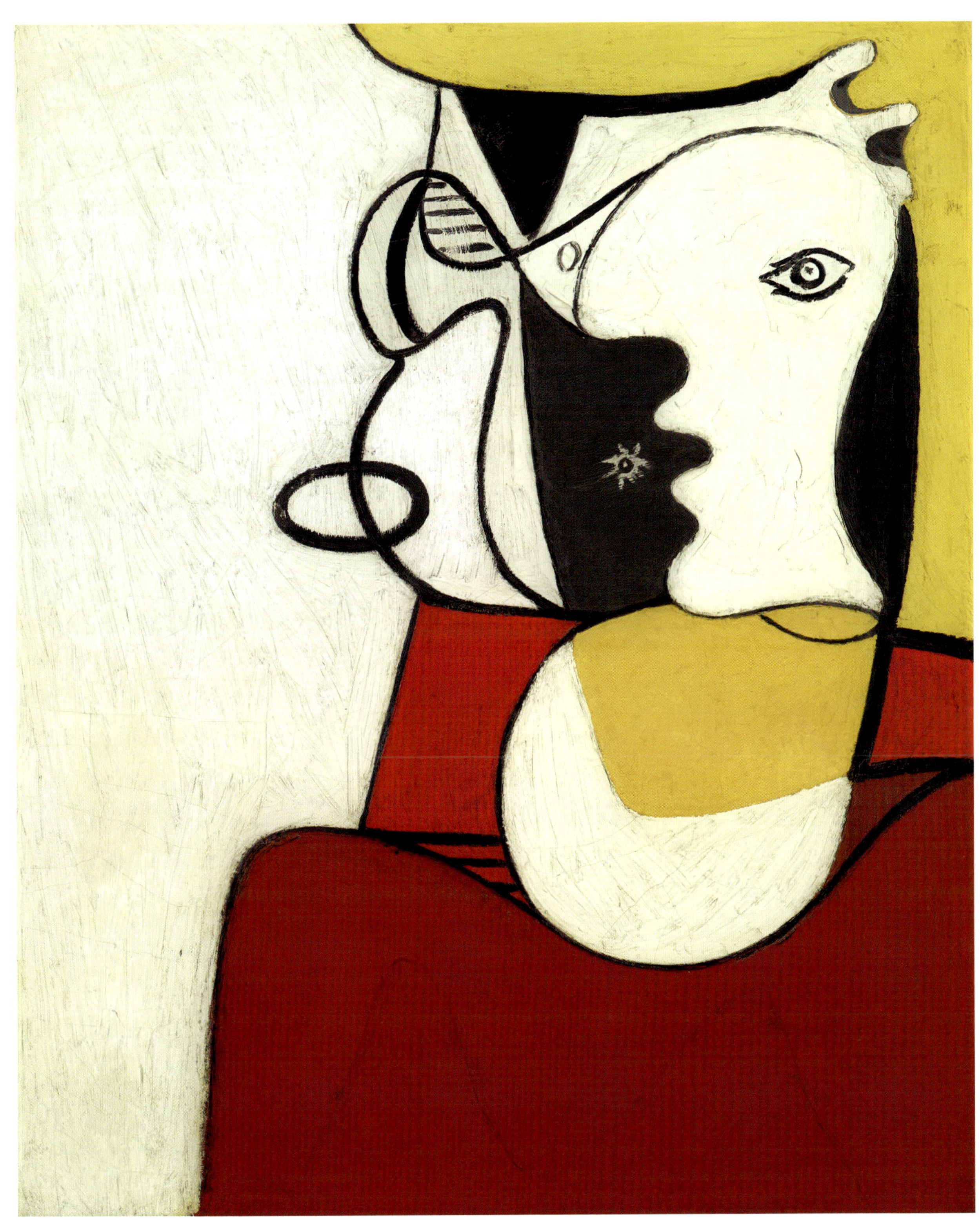

eye gives these organic shapes a human character. Similar to how the head and the arabesques in the middle of the canvas are delineated with only a few lines, the palette of the composition is very restrained: white, black, some bright yellow, vivid red, and darker red. An enigmatic starlike form is painted in white on the black surface surrounding the woman's head and is situated right in front of her mouth. The red base features a zigzag line incised into the paint. The artist applied thick layers of paint to the canvas, especially in some areas such as the head, where the white coats of pigment seem to almost form a relief. This manipulation of the paint echoes the attempts of other American artists, such as John Graham and Jackson Pollock, to alter the medium of oil paint though the addition of other materials or of multiple layers of paint applied directly to the canvas.

The formal appearance of this work, however, illustrates how, in the 1930s, Gorky turned to Pablo Picasso as a source of inspiration.[4] Many of its features are reminiscent of Picasso's deconstructed renditions of the human body (fig. 2), and the organization of flat, overlapping shapes on the picture plane is taken from Cubism. But *Untitled (Head)* also points back to other sources, notably to Gorky's Armenian heritage. The head in this painting evokes the ornamental stylization of facial features, depicted without any realism, that characterizes medieval Armenian wall paintings, manuscripts (fig. 3), and sculptures, notably the bas-reliefs of the Church of the Holy Cross, on Aghtamar Island, Lake Van (today eastern Turkey).[5] The artist could have seen these religious works as a child, given that his mother, Shushanig (Shushan) der Marderosian, was a

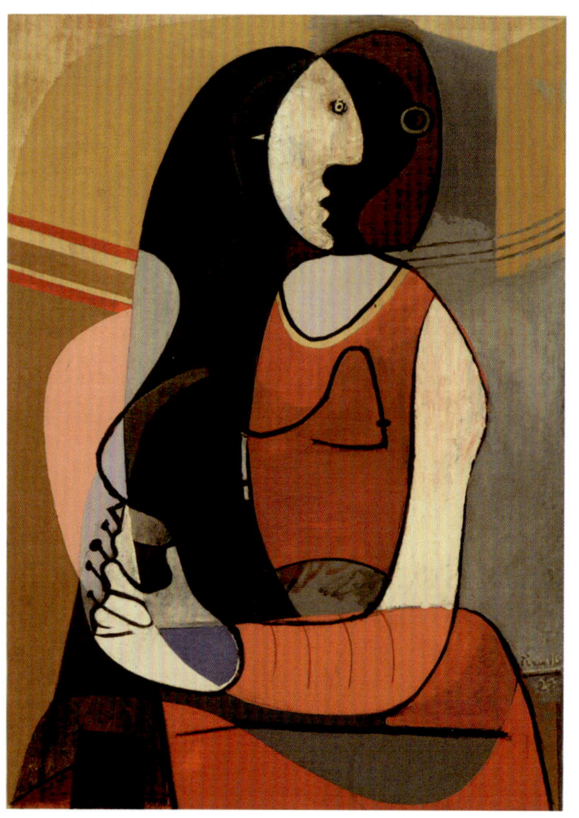

Fig. 2. Pablo Picasso, *Seated Woman*, 1927. Oil on wood, 51⅛ × 38 ¼ in. (129.9 × 96.8 cm). Museum of Modern Art, New York, Gift of James Thrall Soby, 516.1961

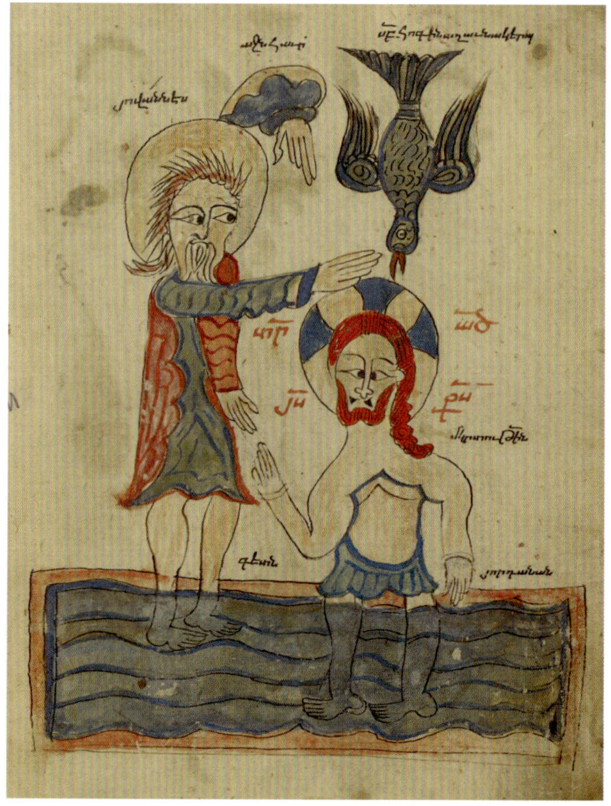

Fig. 3. Unknown artist, *The Baptism of Christ*, from an Armenian Gospel book, 1386. Ink and watercolor on paper, 9⁷⁄₁₆ × 6½ in. (24 × 16.5 cm). J. Paul Getty Museum, Los Angeles, Ms. Ludwig II 6, fol. 7, 83.MB.70.7

descendant of priests of the Armenian Apostolic Church.[6] Although the haunting presence of Gorky's mother is more explicit in other works, such as *The Artist and His Mother* (fig. 4), here the stylized female figure might be an abstract memory of his mother, transformed into a symbol of his lost culture. Indeed, behind the Modernist surface appears the image of an exile expressing his own displacement and his estrangement from the Armenian culture to which he still felt connected.[7] —FVJ

1. His mother died at the age of thirty-nine in 1919, after having fled the Armenian genocide with her children.
2. Barbara Rose, "Arshile Gorky and John Graham: Eastern Exiles in a Western World," *Arts Magazine* 50, no. 7 (March 1976): 62–69. See also Josenhans, "(Re)Defining the 'I' in Exile" in this volume, 193–94.
3. Gorky executed a very similar version of this motif in gouache; Diane Waldman, *Arshile Gorky: 1904–1947, A Retrospective*, exh. cat. (New York: Abrams, in collaboration with the Solomon R. Guggenheim Museum, 1981), pl. 27.
4. Ibid., 41–42.
5. Hayden Herrera, *Arshile Gorky: His Life and Work* (New York: Farrar, Straus and Giroux, 2003), 40–42.
6. Melissa Kerr, "Chronology," in *Arshile Gorky: A Retrospective*, ed. Michael R. Taylor (Philadelphia: Philadelphia Museum of Art, 2009), 353.
7. Kim Servart Theriault, "Exile, Trauma, and Arshile Gorky's *The Artist and His Mother*," in ibid., 40–55, esp. 47.

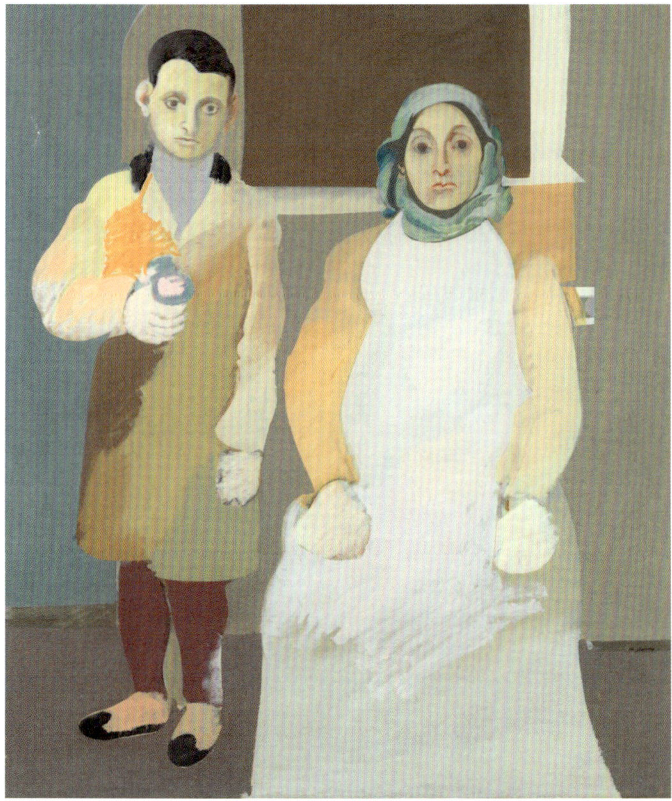

Fig. 4. Arshile Gorky, *The Artist and His Mother*, 1926–ca. 1936. Oil on canvas, 60 × 50¼ in. (152.4 × 127.6 cm). Whitney Museum of American Art, New York, Gift of Julien Levy for Maro and Natasha Gorky in memory of their father, 50.17

Old Gables V
1943
Oil on canvas
18 × 29 in. (45.7 × 73.7 cm)
Provenance: Philip L. Goodwin, New York; Yale University
Art Gallery, New Haven, Conn., Gift of Philip L. Goodwin,
B.A. 1907, 1947.423.

Lyonel Feininger developed his singular style during his
time as a teacher at the Bauhaus, blending formal elements
drawn from German Gothic architecture (fig. 1) with the
flat, fractured picture planes of Cubism and the chromatic
abstraction of Robert Delaunay. Although Feininger was
never a political artist and became famous for his cityscapes,
seascapes, and architectural depictions, he was one of the
artists targeted by the Nazis and labeled "degenerate" in 1937.
This effectively ruined his career in Germany, where he had
spent his entire professional life and had established himself
as an important artist of the Weimar Republic. Feininger
left Germany shortly thereafter and returned to his native
country, the United States. After having lived abroad for fifty
years, he was suddenly forced to adapt to a culture that had
become foreign to him and to rebuild his career in a place
where he was nearly unknown, with almost no financial
resources.[1] When he settled permanently in New York, he
became increasingly interested in depicting the Manhattan
skyline, especially in regard to the effect of light on spatial
relationships.[2] In subsequent years, some of Feininger's
works also grew more abstract, as he created dynamic
compositions of diverging lines that evoke the forces of water
and wind (fig. 2) and testify to his perpetual interest in the
sea and in coastal scenes. However, during the same period,
motifs reminiscent of Germany resurfaced in his American
works, such as *Old Gables V*.

    Indeed, in the United States, Feininger turned
again to a subject that had fascinated him in the 1920s: the
buildings of Lüneburg, a town in northern Germany.[3] He
was drawn to Lüneburg's distinctive *Backsteingotik* or "Brick
Gothic" architecture, a medieval style common in cities in
northern Europe, especially around the Baltic Sea. Brick
Gothic buildings are constructed with red bricks and often
possess stepped gables and grid patterns on the facades.
Old Gables V shows several of these typical buildings in
Lüneburg; the houses are represented aligned as flat, shallow
planes, without any spatial depth. The forms and color
planes overlap, and a few doors and windows, either opaque
or translucent, dot the facades, revealing the underlying
colors. A stepped gable in red dominates the middle of the
composition. To its left and right, other buildings are painted
in lighter hues and seem to dissolve into the background. The
canvas is organized horizontally by the stacked gables, and
vertically by bands of bright and darker blue, emphasizing
the abstract qualities of the painting.

    Feininger had first visited Lüneburg in August 1921
with his wife Julia, during a vacation from his teaching at the
Bauhaus, and he visited again one year later for the second,
and last, time.[4] During both trips, he made numerous drawings of the buildings, which served as the basis for a series of
prints and paintings (figs. 3–4) that he created within a few
years of those visits. *Old Gables V* shows how, twenty years
after his final trip to Lüneburg and thousands of miles away
from it, Feininger was again drawn to the quintessential
architectural style of the medieval town. He made approximately ten different versions of this German motif while in
the United States, creating a visual memory of a culture and
country that were by then lost to him.[5] —FVJ

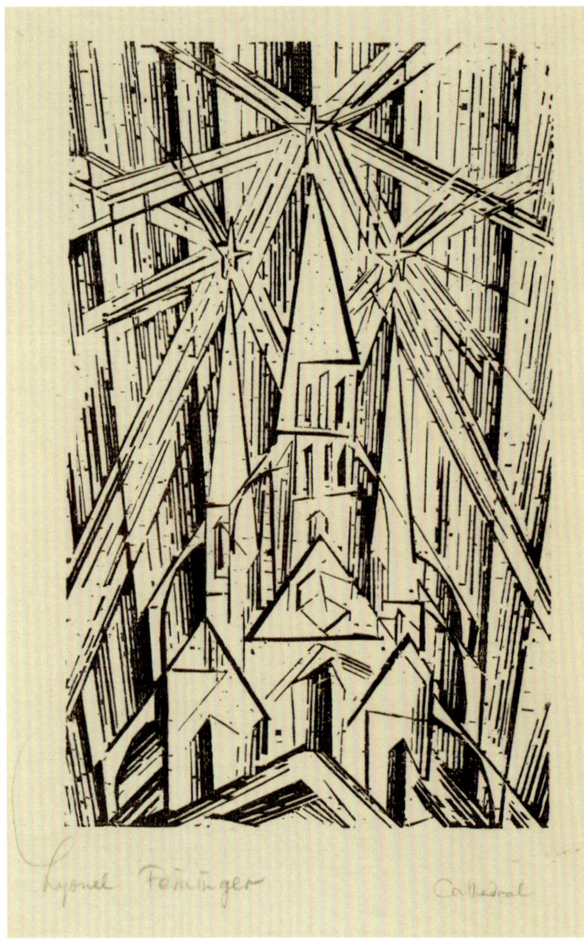

Fig. 1. Lyonel Feininger, *Kathedrale* (Cathedral), 1919. Woodcut,
16⅛ × 12³⁄₁₆ in. (41 × 31 cm). Museum of Modern Art, New York,
Gift of Abby Aldrich Rockefeller, 156.1945

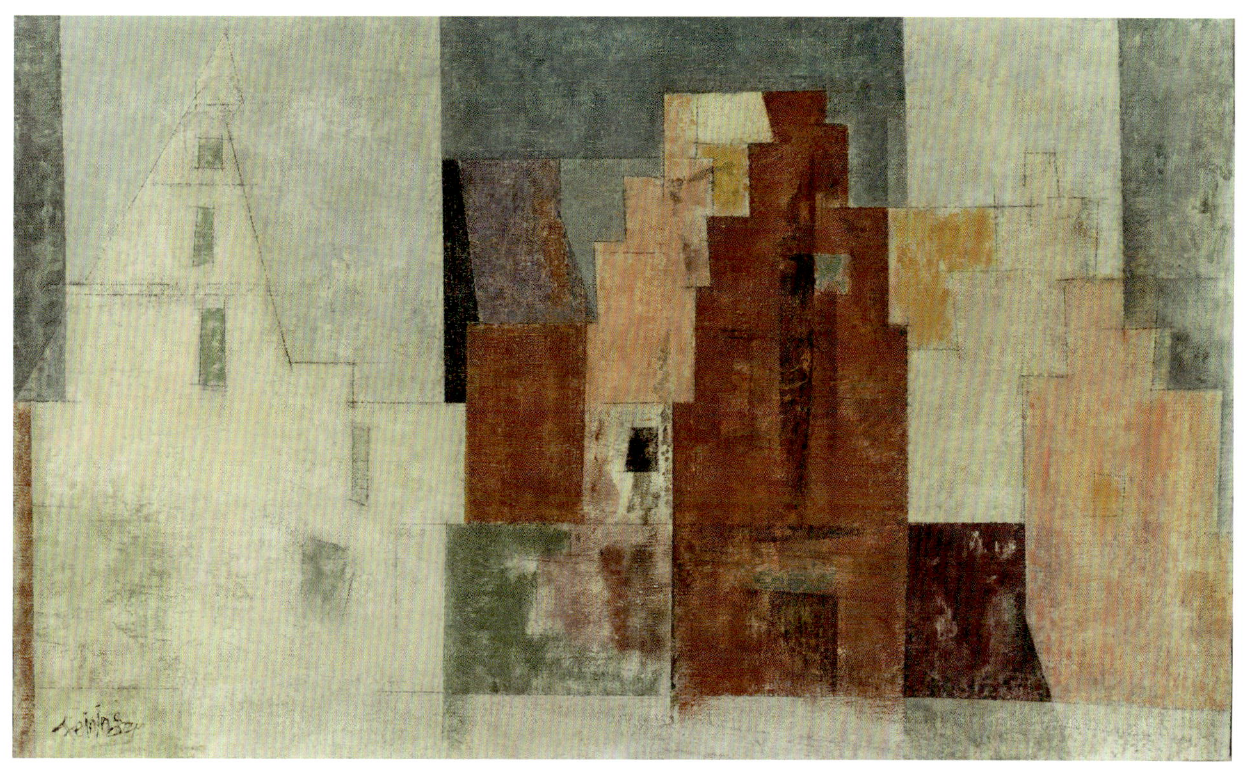

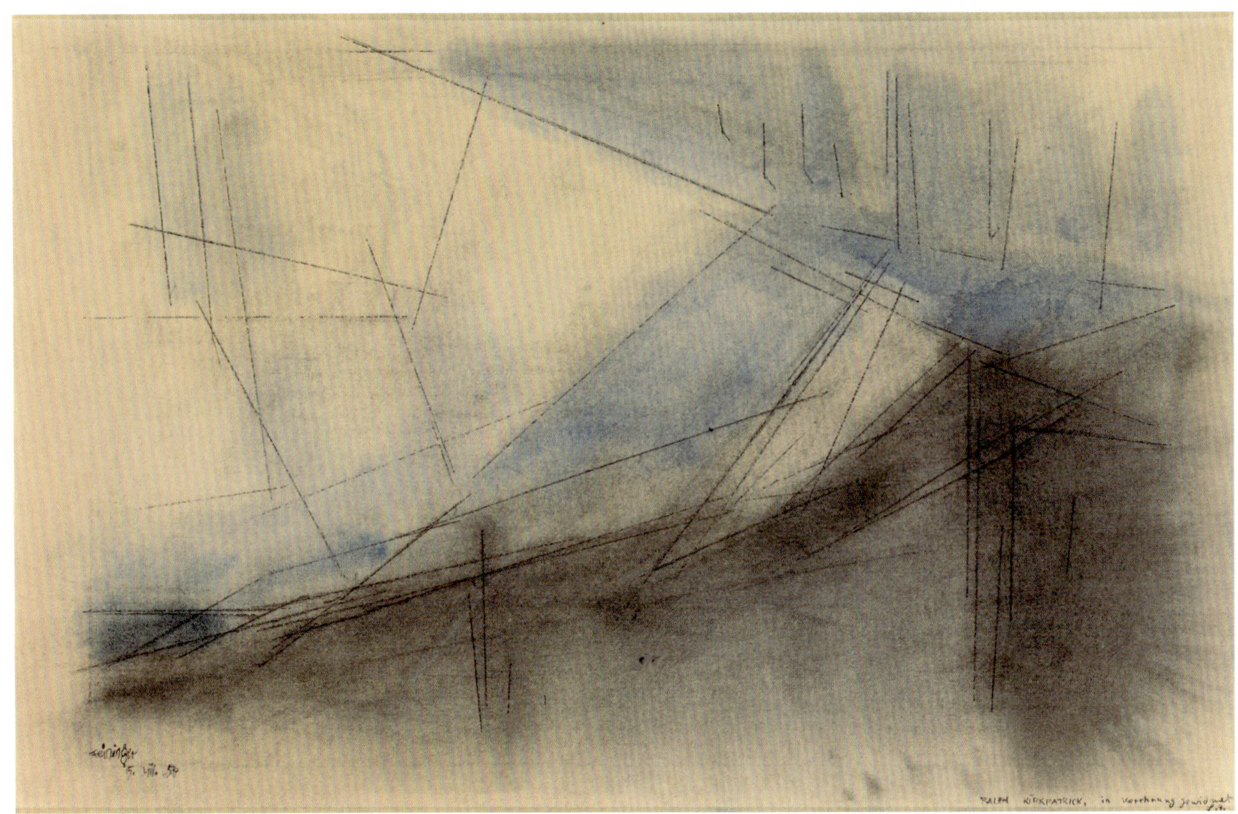

124 Fig. 2. Lyonel Feininger, *Untitled (15.VIII.54)*, 1954. Charcoal, ink, and watercolor on paper, 11^{15}/$_{16}$ × 18½ in. (30.3 × 47 cm). Yale University Art Gallery, New Haven, Conn., Bequest of Ralph Kirkpatrick, HON. 1965, 1984.54.84

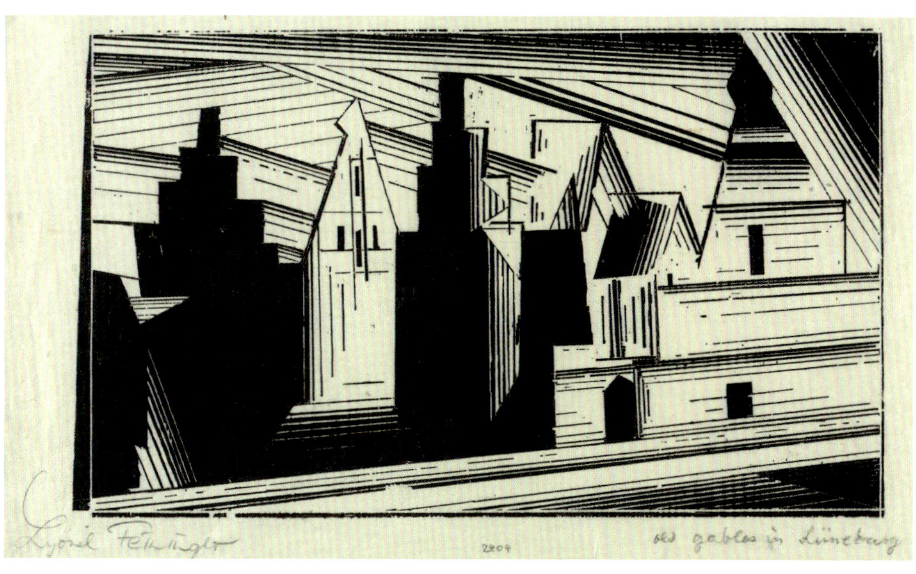

Fig. 3. Lyonel Feininger, *Old Gables in Lüneburg*, 1924. Woodcut, 9¾ × 16 ¹⁄₁₆ in. (24.7 × 40.7 cm). Cleveland Museum of Art, Gift of The Print Club of Cleveland, 1952.30

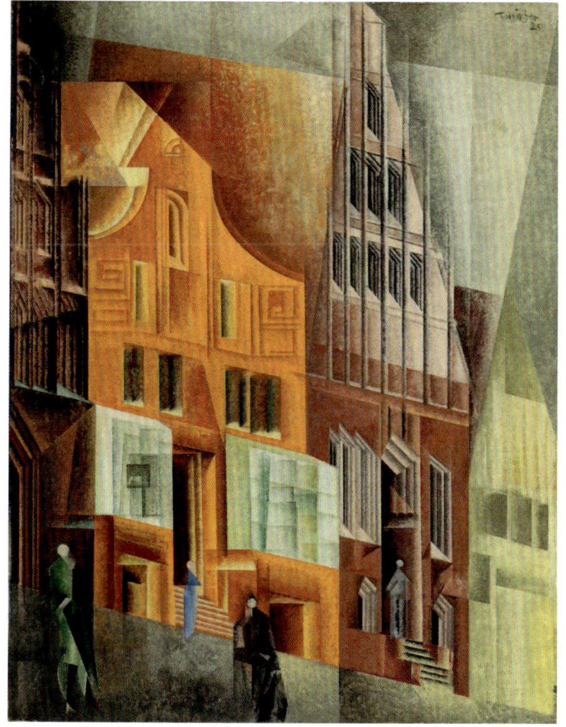

Fig. 4. Lyonel Feininger, *Gables I, Lüneburg*, 1925. Oil on canvas, 37¾ × 28½ in. (95.9 × 72.4 cm). Smith College Museum of Art, Northampton, Mass., Gift of Nanette Harrison Meech (Mrs. Charles B. Meech), class of 1938, in honor of Julia Meech, class of 1963, SC 1985:20

1. Barbara Haskell, "Redeeming the Sacred: The Romantic Modernism of Lyonel Feininger," in *Lyonel Feininger: At the Edge of the World*, ed. Barbara Haskell, exh. cat. (New York: Whitney Museum of American Art, 2011), 1–197, esp. 154–55.

2. Ibid., 156–57.

3. Sabine Dylla, *Lyonel Feininger: Begegnung und Erinnerung: Lüneburger Motive, 1921–1954* (Lüneburg, Germany: Kulturforum Lüneburg, 1991), 11–13.

4. Ibid., 12.

5. Wolfgang Büche, ed., *Lyonel Feininger: Zurück in Amerika, 1937–1956* (Munich: Hirmer, 2009), 31.

Transfer / Adjustment

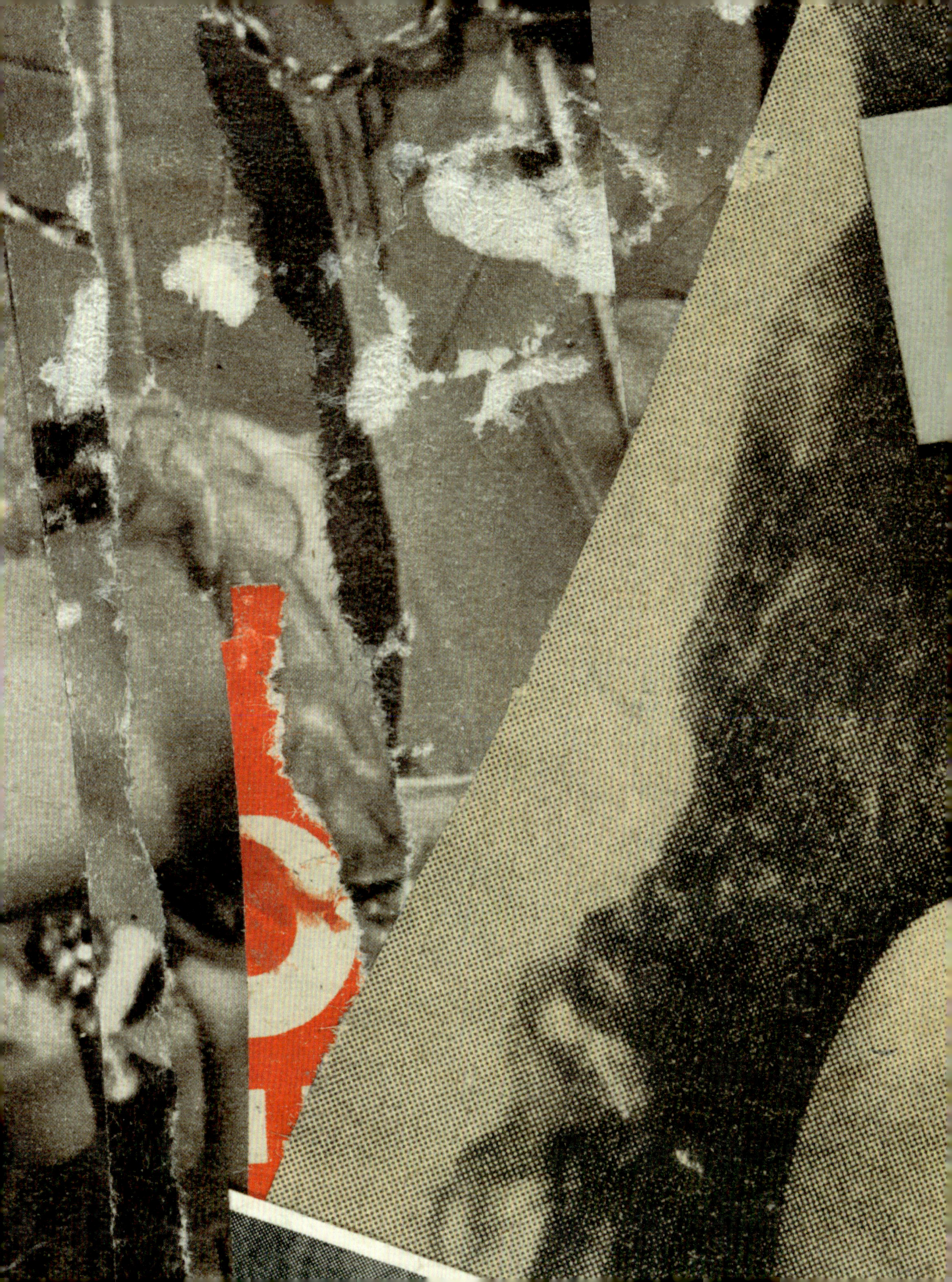

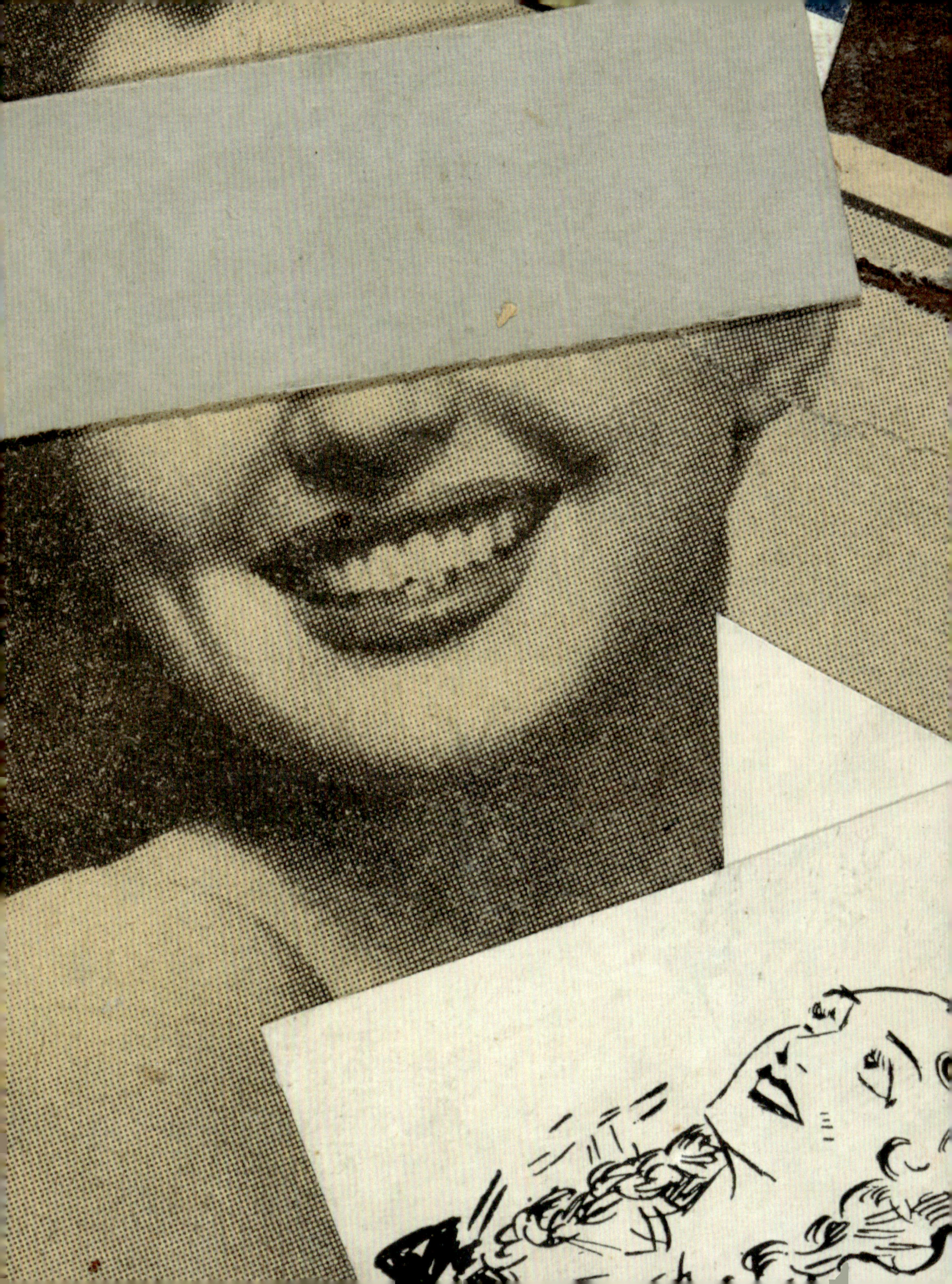

In an interview from March 1965, the artist and teacher Josef Albers (1888–1976, HON. 1950, HON. 1962) recalled how he transferred his pedagogical approach from the Bauhaus, the German art school where he had taught for nearly a decade, to Black Mountain College, where he was hired to establish the art education program. The experimental college in North Carolina had been founded just months before he, together with his wife, the master weaver Anni Albers, arrived in the United States on November 24, 1933. He described how, despite speaking almost no English, he presented one of the very first exercises in visual observation he had developed for his new students:

> One of the first classes I [told them] to write your signature, what you put underneath your check, and then write it in the air. And I wrote my name in the air. But so that *they* could read it—not for my reading. I did it backwards, and then they didn't know what I am doing, so I went to the blackboard and wrote it. Who got it? Who didn't get it? Be honest. Who got it now? Let's admit that wc arc visually underdeveloped. Now write *your* name into the air. Now try whether you can do it backwards. *Ja?* Now you see you must know that the motor sense helps us do this. You can also do this visually.[1]

Albers went on to recount that he repeated the exercise, this time writing his name upside down, and once again, writing it upside down and backward (fig. 1). This lesson, part of what he called "drawing in air," was intended to teach students how to coordinate their vision with the movement of their bodies, to see motion or visualize the trace of a contour in their minds and execute it accurately through gesture.[2] For Albers, this process of reflecting on vision through the body was deeply empathetic—"a matter of *feeling*, not of seeing."[3] And it was a process that had to be repeated again and again. His task as a teacher was to "present the same problem a thousand times" until the feeling for space, for orientation, and for form became a reflex—something his pupils could carry with them into any situation by "getting it into the bones."[4] As one of his students at Black Mountain later reflected, "It was a teaching in sensitivity and awareness and in making yourself tremendously ready, concentrated, poised, ready to catch it, ready to see."[5]

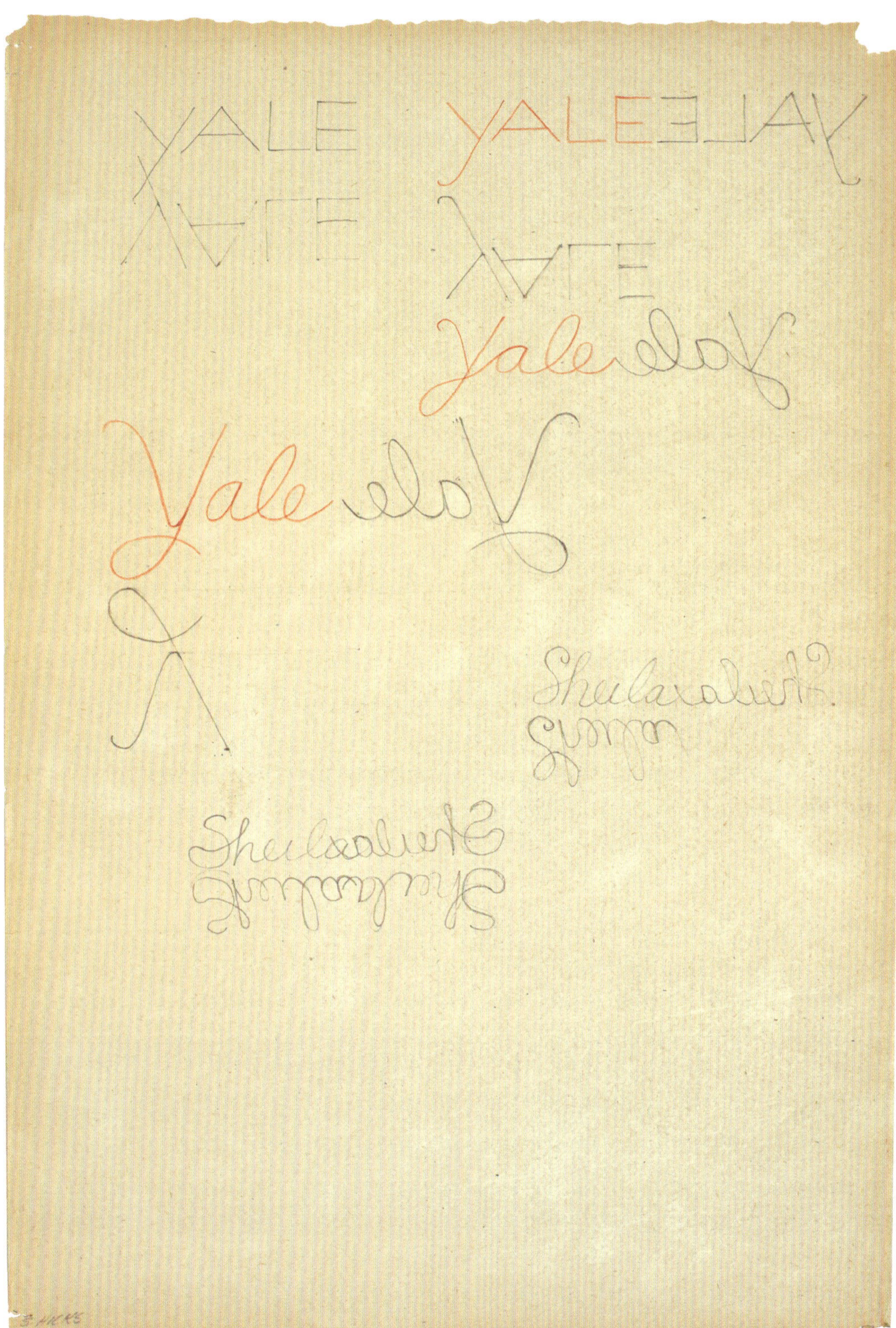

Fig. 1. Sheila Hicks, *"Mirror Writing," Basic Drawing Course, Yale University,* 1954–56. Blue and red pencil and graphite on newsprint, 17¾ × 11¾ in. (45.1 × 29.9 cm). Josef and Anni Albers Foundation, Bethany, Conn., 1976.26.775

Departing from traditional academic methods for teaching art, such as life drawing from nude models, Albers was after a more basic, flexible, and ultimately portable kind of knowledge, one that, as he put it, would make you "really learn to observe visually—in order to transfer anything we see outside in lines."[6] This knowledge was internalized in the body, which served to mediate the external world into an image. Line was, in effect, the trace of this transfer from an image seen to an image made. For Albers's students, his efforts to cultivate new instincts made them "tremendously ready" for any future encounter, yet his methods also demanded that they break down habits ingrained in the past. As such, we may consider how these attempts to foster a perceptual and material transfer unburdened by one's personal history or academic tradition were themselves a product of Albers's own migration.[7] Indeed, in the same 1965 interview, he explicitly asserted that his performance of his "mirror writing" exercise and his newfound emphasis on training proprioception—a felt sense of the position of one's body as it moves in space—were innovations born of his life as an émigré in the United States. As he recalled, these lessons were "not done at the Bauhaus—not even by myself. Here, in this new part of the world, I felt obliged to start a new life on my own, and a new life that was related to the mentalities here, and so I developed drawing." He summarized the difference he confronted between the Old World and the New World, highlighting how, in Europe, one shoots a gun by aiming with the eye, but in America, "the shooting is with the arm moving through the air without aiming."[8]

In his anecdote about his lesson in drawing in space at Black Mountain, Albers did not choose just any line to transfer into an image for his students but, specifically, his *signature*. The signature is a graphic trace of identity, one that, through iteration, validates the individual within legal and economic systems (as Albers said, it is "what you put underneath your check"). Yet its specific powers of signification function only through the singularity of its form—that is, its resistance to forgery. As Albers wrote his name in the air, he authenticated his presence in the classroom. This was surely no small matter for a man still deeply embroiled with setting the record straight about his activities at the Bauhaus with bureaucrats of the Nazi government in Dessau, who had, with their forcible termination of the faculty and all courses of instruction on October 1, 1932, charged him with fostering "a germ-cell of Bolshevism" that threatened the integrity of the state.[9] By drawing his name in reverse, he oriented his movements to others—to the American students with whom he now sought to communicate and to the ideologues back in Germany who had stripped him of his livelihood and, inevitably, his home. "I am here, still teaching," the gesture seems to say. As the lesson goes on and signatures flip and spin along multiple axes, the imperative for legibility cedes to a masterful execution of form and orientation that becomes less contingent upon an imagined perceiver—at least, that is, upon a perceiver imagined to be fixed in space, rooted to the ground.

Standing before his students, scribbling his name into the void, Albers enacted a process much like printing without paper. The central aim of the lesson, after all, was to foster his students' manual and mental dexterity so they could inscribe a line accurately in reverse. He carved into the air much as he might the matrix of a woodblock, anticipating the transfer of the image and directing his gesture to a beholder who met him face-to-face. Albers frequently made the irruption of difference in the act of this transfer the very subject of the woodcut prints he made in his final months in Germany after the closure of the Bauhaus and in his first year at Black Mountain.[10] When we compare *Weisser Kreis* (White Circle, fig. 2) and *Schwarzer Kreis* (Black Circle, fig. 3)—both printed in 1933 at Ullstein press in Berlin—for instance, one appears to be the "positive" to the other's "negative," almost as if each had been pulled from a block that, on its surface, would have looked much like its partner. Yet, for all the temptation to read one print as the inverse of the other—one as cause, the other as copy—we cannot help but notice the subtle variations in his rendering of the irregular frame around the central circle in each. In the transfer from one image to another, form is not reproduced but altered, and it is impossible to give chronological priority to either print in the pair. The different densities of wood grain captured in *Schwarzer Kreis* contrast with the bold regularity of the field of horizontal lines in *Weisser Kreis*. However, this field in *Weisser Kreis* is not the product of an indexical transfer of the grain of the block used to print it, but of Albers's own manual transfer of his visual perception of texture into depicted form. "Instead of imitation, we need translation," he would tell his students.[11]

As he settled into the life of an émigré, Albers consistently worked to cast doubt on the relative stability of relationships between self and environment, making this the principal aim of his art and teaching in the United States. He encouraged experimentation with the instability of color perception, the reversibility of figure and ground, and the unpredictable interaction of found materials in exercises that he developed for his students. By privileging the dynamism of contingent relationships above all else, students learned to challenge the expectation that a form, material, or even a person ought to have a secure and proper place.[12] If the basic elements of artistic creation could be *seen* in different ways, then it was possible to imagine that they could also *be* different, and, as an educator reinventing his pedagogy and practice in a foreign country, Albers understood that this insight had powerful social implications, too. Origins and outcomes were less important than the unstable, intermediary state of transfer. Living as a refugee in New York, the German-born philosopher Ernst Bloch understood that this state of transfer was especially difficult—if not impossible—to maintain, particularly among intellectuals who felt at a loss for words as they confronted an alien culture in America and looked back at a degraded one in Germany. Yet, as Bloch saw it, their alternatives were too grim to entertain, whether they sought to alienate themselves from their new environment entirely, leaving Americans "justifiably astonished at such willful isolation, and at the transfer of a currency which cannot and should not be exchanged," or to assimilate fully through "a hectic I'd-like-so-much-to-please Americanism, almost all of which is escapism and mimicry"—what the political theorist and fellow émigré Hannah Arendt, writing at the height of the war, later called an "insane optimism which is next door to despair."[13]

Working through this conundrum for himself, Albers developed another exercise at Black Mountain that he called "figure-ground." He would point to a checkerboard pattern

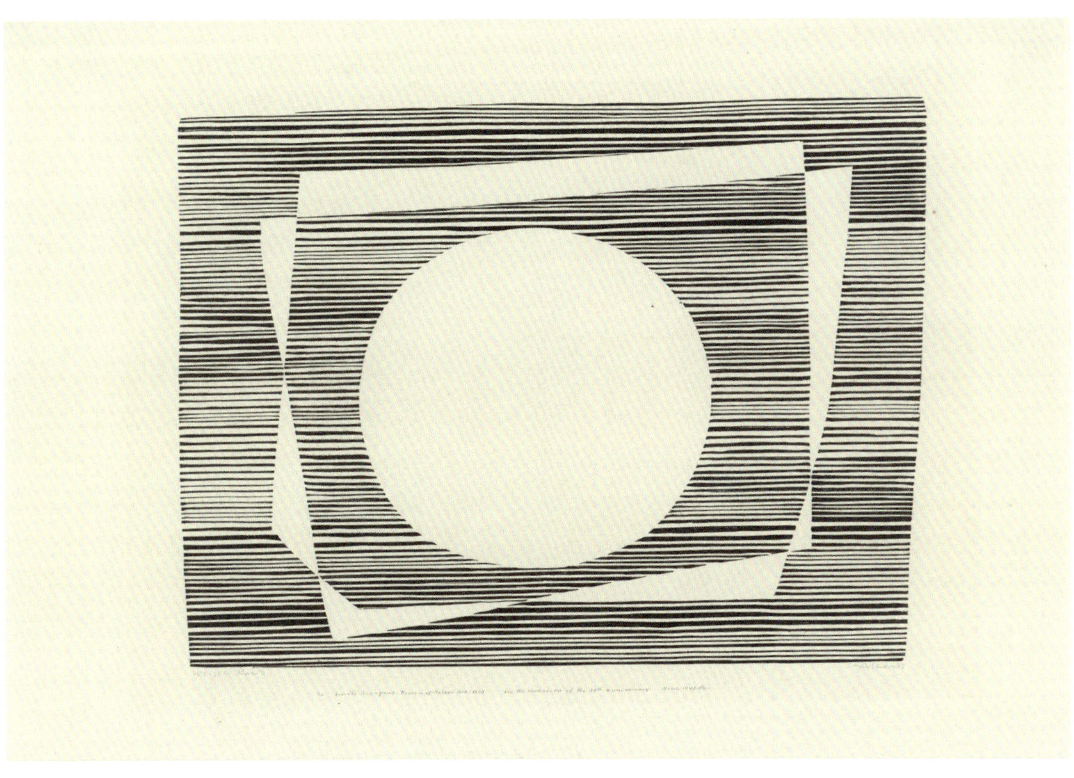

Fig. 2. Josef Albers, *Weisser Kreis* (White Circle), 1933. Woodcut, 10⁹⁄₁₆ × 13⁷⁄₈ in. (26.9 × 35.3 cm). Yale University Art Gallery, New Haven, Conn., Gift of Collection Société Anonyme, 1941.327

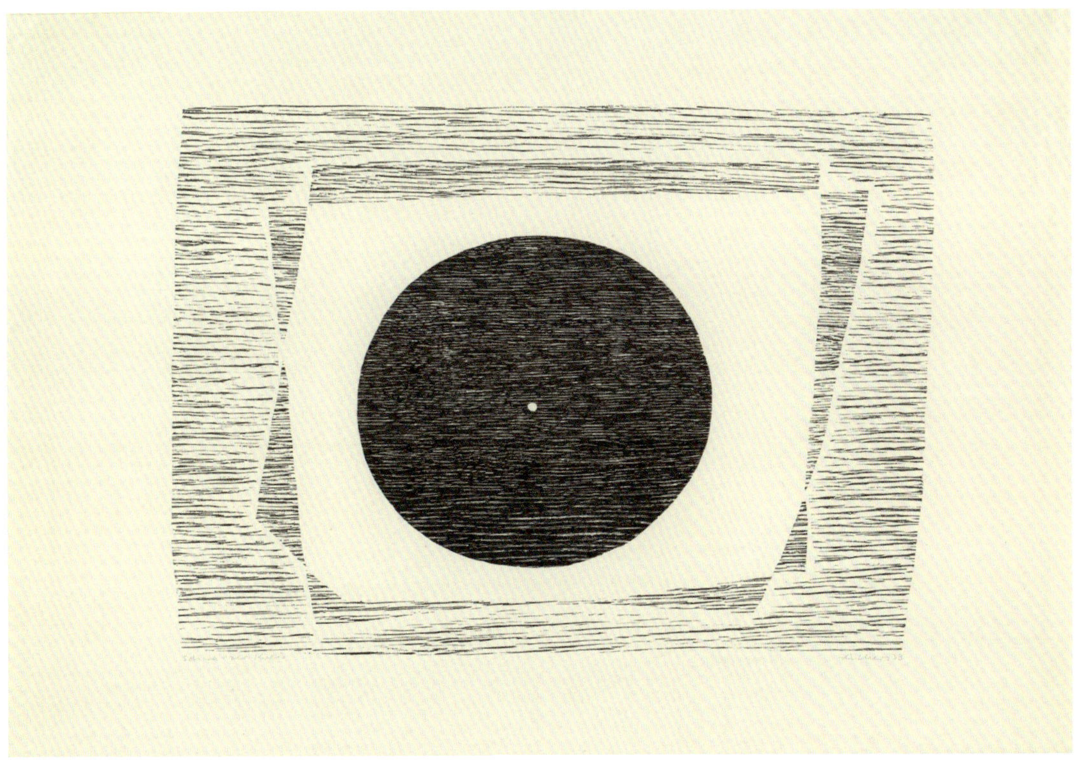

Fig. 3. Josef Albers, *Schwarzer Kreis* (Black Circle), 1933. Woodcut, 10³⁄₁₆ × 13¹⁵⁄₁₆ in. (25.8 × 35.4 cm). Yale University Art Gallery, New Haven, Conn., Gift of Anni Albers and The Josef Albers Foundation, Inc., 1978.11.2

and ask, "Is it white on black, or black on white . . . ? Which is the 'figure' and which the 'ground'?" The ability to read the same form in two mutually opposing ways opened students' eyes to the fact that "whatever is figure or whatever is ground is interchangeable."[14] This lesson had the consequence of destabilizing perception and, by extension, identity. The task of the artist, he believed, was "to deal with the discrepancy between physical fact and psychic effect."[15] In his view, this lack of fixity—both in terms of what something was and how it was seen—was not a loss to be mourned; rather, it promised a kind of bountiful, almost irrational, excess. As he often liked to remind his students, to see the negative space separating two forms as an "in-between figure" meant that suddenly "1 + 1 = 3."[16] If Bloch saw in America "the limitless transformation of all life into price and merchandise," Albers cannily understood that artists were in a position to take this calculating tendency for exchange to an absurd extreme and thereby reverse its effects. The artist "is expected to cheat us," he wrote, "but in a positive way, to our advantage. And so, only the artist is selling more than we pay for. This leads us to see that we, that men, carry Janus heads with a front and a back face looking in two opposite directions."[17]

The idea that vision depended on the context in which it transpired lay at the core of Albers's study of the interaction of color, which he elaborated in his later series of *Homage to the Square* paintings and in the courses he developed while on the faculty at Yale University in the 1950s. For instance, he frequently assigned exercises in simultaneous contrast, which

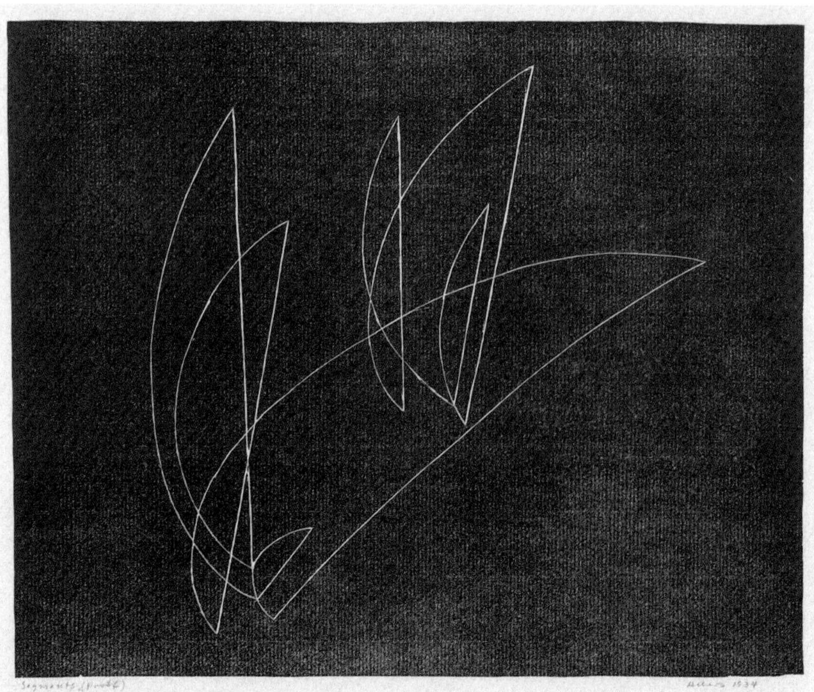

Fig. 4. Josef Albers, *Segments*, 1934. Woodcut, 9½ × 11⁷⁄₁₆ in. (24.1 × 29 cm). Yale University Art Gallery, New Haven, Conn., Gift of the artist, 1941.326

demonstrated how the same color could appear radically different against backgrounds of different colors. Likewise, the ceaseless circuit of exchange between articulated form and ambient space structured his various series of complex, ambiguous images, where lines divide the picture plane to support multiple points of view simultaneously. His later *Structural Constellations* extend these preoccupations, which he first worked out in prints from his years at Black Mountain, as seen in *Segments* (fig. 4), with its scriptlike tracery, and *Multiplex B* (fig. 5), whose projecting transparent form against a wood-grain ground can be seen convincingly as if from above and below. For Albers, the relativity of color and the flipping of form in space were never purely formal matters but also social and ethical ones.[18] The ability to see a color or a form in different, even contradictory, ways had the power to redefine human relationships in an age of mass migration and exile, when, as the émigré philosopher Theodor Adorno reflected, "the compulsion to fit in was worse than in earlier emigrations."[19] In the "mirror writing" exercise at Black Mountain, Albers had enlisted the motif of the signature to stress the performative constitution of identity and the process of printmaking to visualize difference in repetition. Yet there was also a third lesson in his demonstration, namely his demand that his audience take his place, first by recognizing what it was that he was doing and then by performing their own drawings in space—not for his benefit, but for their own. With this final transfer, he asked his students: What are the consequences of adopting another's gesture as your own (fig. 6), of alienating yourself so as to internalize the other?

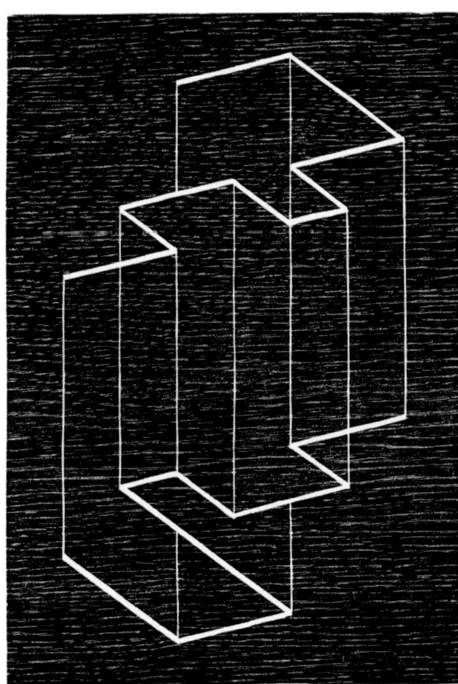

Fig. 5. Josef Albers, *Multiplex B*, 1948. Woodcut, 12 × 8¹⁄₁₆ in. (30.5 × 20.5 cm). Metropolitan Museum of Art, New York, Gift of the Josef Albers Foundation, Inc., 1971, 1971.636.33

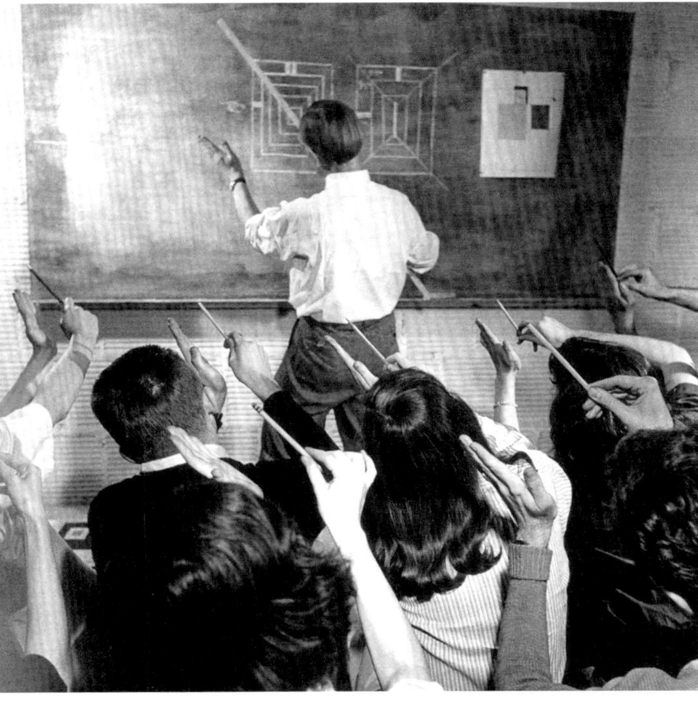

Fig. 6. Genevieve Naylor, *Josef Albers and Students at Black Mountain College Holding Out Their Pencils to Study Angles*, 1946. Photograph from a Black Mountain College brochure, Josef Albers Papers (MS 32), box 3, folder 34, Manuscripts and Archives, Yale University Library, New Haven, Conn.

In another print from 1934, titled *i* (fig. 7), Albers offered one possible response. Exploiting the white-black binary that had structured his "figure-ground" exercise, he transformed the physical support of the paper to make it appear like two torn horizontal strips laid over a black ink ground peeking out at the top and bottom margins of the image. Here the paper distinguishes itself visibly from the white margins of the print to bracket a central field of alternating horizontal black and white lines. A white rectangle interrupts and frames an excerpt of this field as the paper assumes yet another identity, one that mimics, in miniature, the operations of the entire work. Whether this rectangle is embedded within or affixed on top of the striped field is, however, impossible to determine. Frame and field are both figure and ground. Optically, we sense a collagelike stacking of discrete planes, but without the literal overlap of collage or a single cut to disturb the smooth surface of the support, the relative proximity of these planes to the beholder is perceptually unstable. The paper is not a mere surface to be worked or a neutral surround, and only the uppermost element in this assembly appears unambiguously "on top"—the massive lowercase *i*, written in *Sütterlinschrift*, the particular cursive script introduced in German schools in the first decades of the twentieth century that came to characterize the handwriting of Albers's generation.

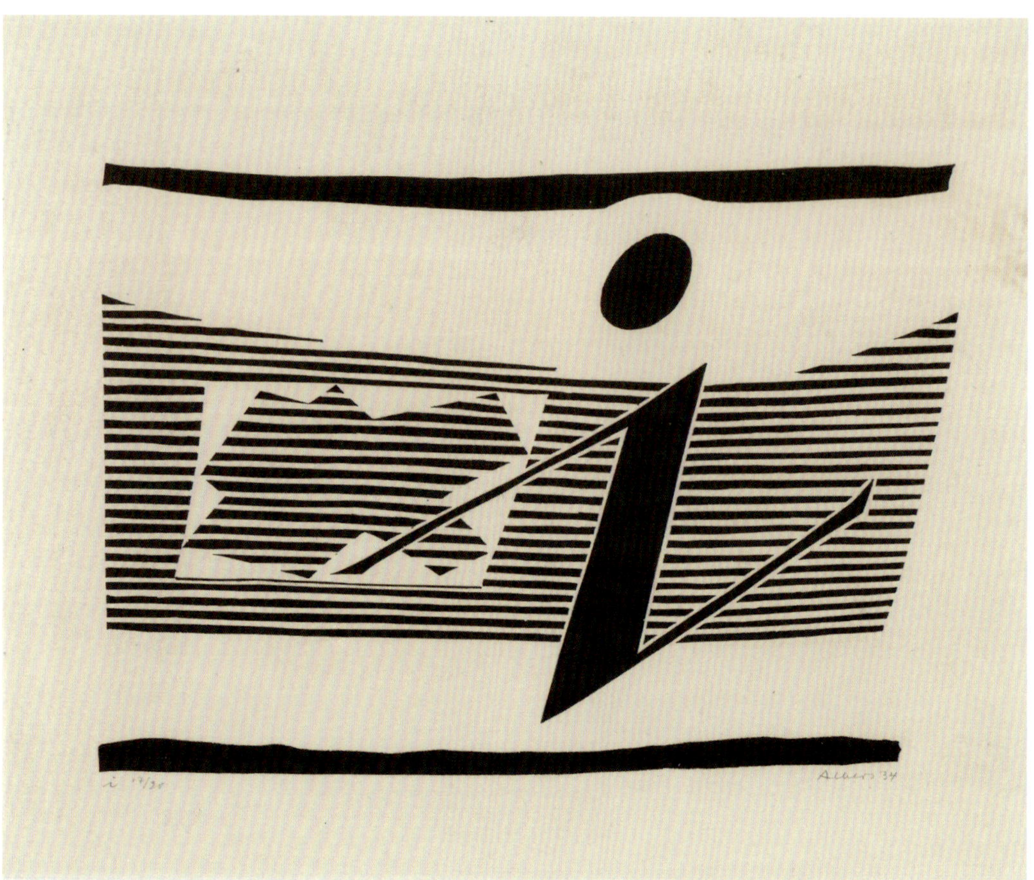

Fig. 7. Josef Albers, *i*, 1934. Linocut, 8¹⁄₁₆ × 11¼ in. (20.4 × 28.5 cm). Yale University Art Gallery, New Haven, Conn., Gift of Anni Albers and The Josef Albers Foundation, Inc., 1978.11.7

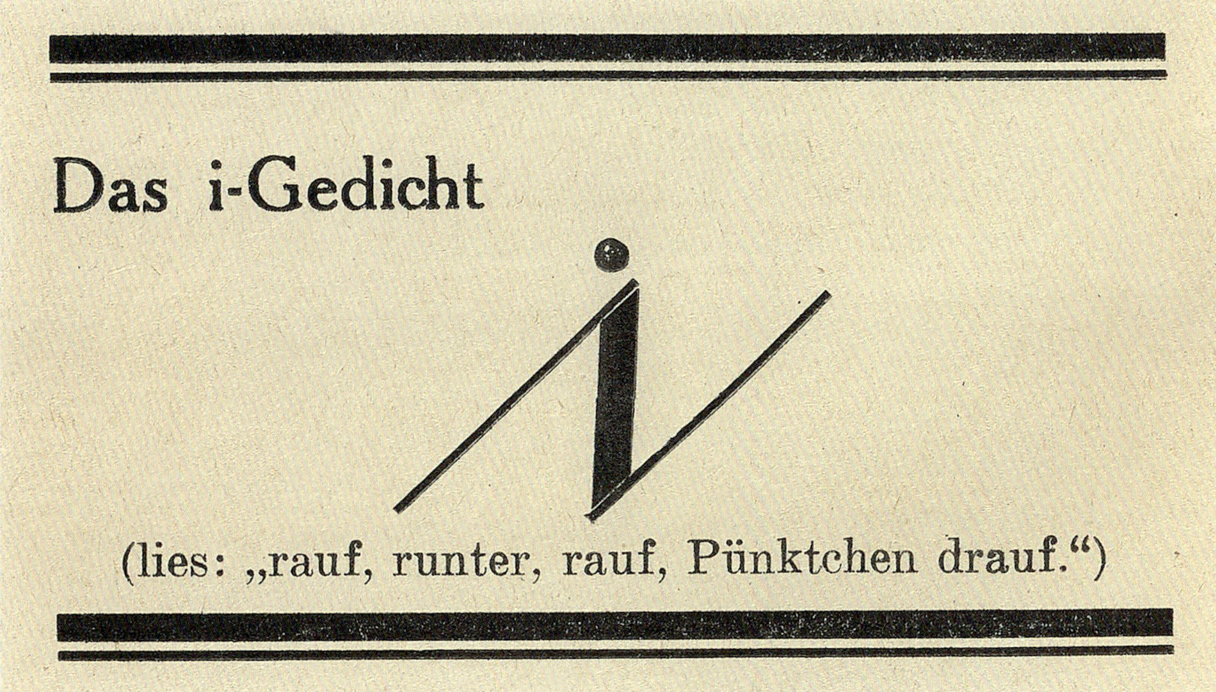

Fig. 8. Kurt Schwitters, "Das i-Gedicht." From Schwitters, *Elementar: Die Blume Anna; Die neue Anna Blume* (Berlin: Verlag der Sturm, 1922), 30

With this *i*, Albers recalled and appropriated a poem by Kurt Schwitters (fig. 8), published in 1922, which consisted solely of this graphic sign, supplemented by a pithy, juvenile rhyme: "lies: 'rauf, runter, rauf, Pünktchen drauf'" (read: up, down, up, little dot on top).[20] Although children might sing this rhyme as they learned how to write this letter, Schwitters included it as an instruction for how a Dada performer ought to "read" a poem of a single letter aloud, playing with the dual identity of language as something both spoken and seen. Throughout the 1920s, Schwitters used this letter *i* as a kind of logo to refer to a distinct method of making images with found materials. Whereas he synthesized paper fragments from various sources into new compositions to make his famous *Merz* collages, such as *Zeichnung I 9 Hebel 2* (1920, Yale University Art Gallery, inv. no. 1953.6.70; see also cat. 16, fig. 3), his series of "i-drawings" (fig. 9) were simply signed and dated fragments excised from larger sheets of printer's errors, which he likely collected from the printer A. Molling in Hanover. These drawings, he claimed, were made by "recognizing art in the work of others."[21] By adopting this *i* and reintegrating it into an optical collage of his own design, Albers demonstrated that what he learned from Schwitters was that recognition was itself a creative act. It was not enough for an artist to aim for invention and self-expression—a conceit for which he repeatedly voiced little patience. Rather, one had to give form to the fact that expression always happened with and through others.

Sometime in 1936, well after he made this homage to an artist he deeply admired, Albers invited Schwitters to join him as a visiting professor at Black Mountain. This

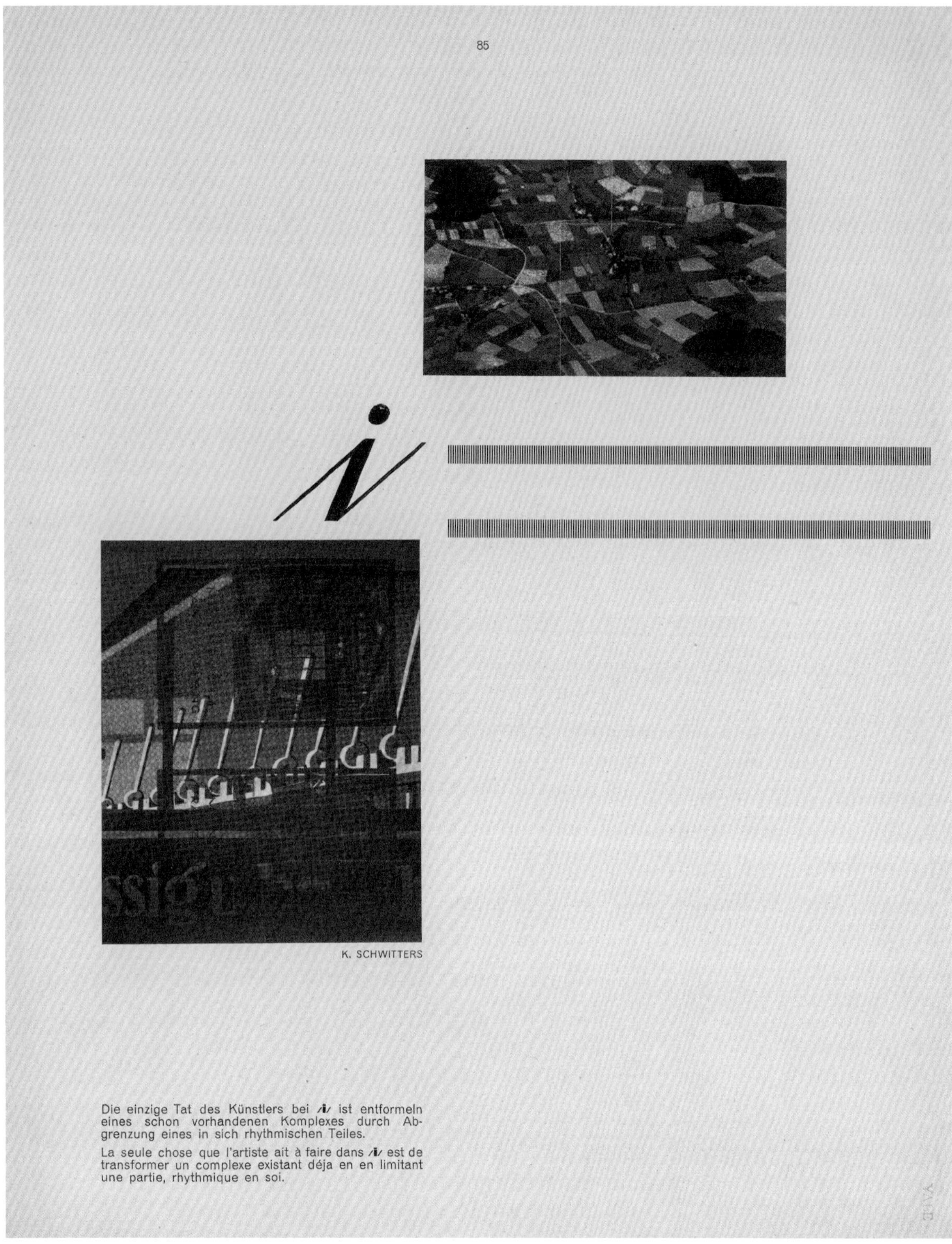

Fig. 9. Page reproducing Kurt Schwitters's *Untitled (I 9 Hebel 2?)* (1920, location unknown). From El Lissitzky and Kurt Schwitters, *Merz 8/9, Nasci* (April–July 1924): 85

invitation was likely motivated by his mounting concern for the artist, who could no longer publicly exhibit his work in Germany and whose attempts to immigrate to the Netherlands had come to nothing. Schwitters responded with a thorough report on the development of his art and expressed his desire to continue the conversation in America.[22] Yet just a few weeks later, while helping to relocate his son to Norway to escape prosecution for anti-Nazi organizing, Schwitters learned that the Gestapo was looking for him, too. He found himself living in exile—forced to remain in Norway to avoid interrogation and certain imprisonment, cut off from his wife and mother whom he had left behind in Germany. Suddenly, Albers's offer to teach in the United States appeared out of the question. For Albers, as for so many émigré and exiled artists of his generation, the recognition of oneself in another, and the constitution of the work of art in the trace of that transfer, would have to take place through memory. And for Albers's students, it was a lesson he could not have them repeat often enough.

139

1. Josef Albers, "Josef Albers: March 1965 Interview," in *Black Mountain College: Sprouted Seeds: An Anthology of Personal Accounts*, ed. Mervin Lane (Knoxville: University of Tennessee Press, 1990), 36. Anni Albers worked as his translator upon the couple's arrival to the United States, and it may have been through her (or other colleagues) that Josef initially articulated this lesson; ibid., 44–46.

2. Frederick A. Horowitz and Brenda Danilowitz, *Josef Albers: To Open Eyes* (London: Phaidon, 2006), 161.

3. "Josef Albers: March 1965 Interview," 35.

4. Ibid., 36; Horowitz and Danilowitz, *Josef Albers*, 174.

5. Mary Phelan Bowles, interview by Mary Emma Harris, December 21, 1971; cited in Horowitz and Danilowitz, *Josef Albers*, 152.

6. "Josef Albers: March 1965 Interview," 35.

7. See Sheri Bernstein, "Josef Albers," in *Exiles and Émigrés: The Flight of European Artists from Hitler*, ed. Stephanie Barron, exh. cat. (Los Angeles: Los Angeles County Museum of Art, 1997), 257.

8. "Josef Albers: March 1965 Interview," 35, 37. In another interview, Albers insisted that when he arrived in the United States, "all I knew was Buster Keaton and Henry Ford." See Neil Welliver, "Albers on Albers," *Art News* 64, no. 9 (January 1966): 51.

9. The vote to close the school in Dessau by the Nazi-controlled municipal legislature (20 to 5) took place on August 22, 1932, and Albers's contract was officially terminated a week later. He was among the faculty who joined director Mies van der Rohe when the school reopened in Berlin in October. Albers's correspondence with Dessau officials from July 3, 1933—mere weeks before he, together with the rest of the Bauhaus faculty, voted to dissolve the school in the wake of further closures by the Berlin police—shows that he continued to resist the charge and contest the financial terms of his termination. In an undated letter written as late as October of that year, just before he was set to depart for the United States, he was still seeking to remove the charge of Bolshevism, so as "not to be politically burdened abroad." Dossier of correspondence relating to the closure of the Bauhaus in the Josef Albers Papers (MS 32), box 3, folders 30 and 31, Manuscripts and Archives, Yale University Library, New Haven, Conn. See also Hans Maria Wingler, *The Bauhaus: Weimar, Dessau, Berlin, Chicago* (Cambridge, Mass.: MIT Press, 1976), 188.

10. See Brenda Danilowitz, *The Prints of Josef Albers: A Catalogue Raisonné 1915–1976*, rev. ed. (Manchester, Vt.: Hudson Hills Press, 2010), 16–19.

11. Josef Albers, "'Abstract Art.' Speech made in Asheville, NC," Albers Papers, box 22, folder 193. Regarding *Weisser Kreis*, he recounted that "the woodblock was glued together with appropriate and selected wood strips . . . the white horizontal white lines were not [cut], but were actually soft grain pushed down with a bookbinder's bone folder" (cited in Danilowitz, *Prints of Josef Albers*, 18).

12. See Werner Spies, *Josef Albers* (New York: Abrams, 1970), 32; and Helen Molesworth, ed., *Leap Before You Look: Black Mountain College, 1933–1957*, exh. cat. (Boston: Institute of Contemporary Art, 2015), 33–41.

13. Ernst Bloch, "Disrupted Language, Disrupted Culture," *Direction* 2, no. 8 (December 1939): 17, 36; Hannah Arendt, "We Refugees," in *Altogether Elsewhere: Writers on Exile*, ed. Marc Robinson (London: Faber and Faber, 1994), 113; this text was originally published in *Menorah Journal* 31, no. 1 (1943): 69–77.

14. Martin Duberman, *Black Mountain: An Exploration in Community* (New York: Dutton, 1972), 55.

15. Josef Albers, "One Plus One Equals Three and More," in *Search Versus Re-Search: Three Lectures by Josef Albers at Trinity College, April 1965* (Hartford, Conn.: Trinity College Press, 1969), 18.

16. Ibid., 17–18.

17. Bloch, "Disrupted Language," 17; Albers, "One Plus One," 18.

18. Quoting Ludwig Wittgenstein, he declared, "I consider ethics and aesthetics as one"; Josef Albers, interview by Katherine Kuh, in *The Artist's Voice: Talks with Seventeen Artists* (New York: Harper and Row, 1960), 12.

19. Theodor Adorno, "The Curious Realist: On Siegfried Kracauer," trans. Shierry Weber Nicholsen, *New German Critique* 54 (Autumn 1991): 173.

20. Kurt Schwitters, "Das i-Gedicht," in *Elementar: Die Blume Anna; Die neue Anna Blume* (Berlin: Verlag der Sturm, 1922), 30. Albers owned a copy of this book (Danilowitz, *Prints of Josef Albers*, 69).

21. Kurt Schwitters, "i," *Merz* 2, Nummer i (April 1923): 17. On Schwitters's scavenging at Molling, see Kate T. Steinitz, *Kurt Schwitters: Erinnerungen aus den Jahren 1918–1930* (Zurich: Arche, 1963), 71–72. For an extended discussion of the importance of the i concept for Schwitters's work and ideas about artistic subjectivity, see Megan R. Luke, *Kurt Schwitters: Space, Image, Exile* (Chicago: University of Chicago Press, 2014), 23–31.

22. "Und nun habe ich mich mit Ihnen auch etwas ausgesprochen. Hoffentlich mehr in Amerika, wenn ich als ausserordentlicher Hilfsprofessor an der schwarzen Gebirgsschule angestellt bin."

(And now I have talked some things out with you. Hopefully more in America when I am installed as a visiting professor at the Black Mountain school.); Kurt Schwitters to Josef Albers, November 23, 1936, Albers Papers, box 2, folder 24. On February 8, 1937, Schwitters wrote from Norway, turning down the offer to teach.

Merzbild mit Regenbogen (*Merz* Picture with Rainbow)
1920–39
Mixed media on plywood
61⅝ × 47¾ × 10½ in. (156.5 × 121.3 × 26.7 cm)
Provenance: Given by the artist to Teodor Hoel, Hjertøya, Norway, 1939–63; Lord's Gallery, London, 1963; Ernst Schwitters, Lysaker, Norway, and Marlborough Fine Art, London, 1963–67; Marlborough-Gerson Gallery, New York, 1963–67; Charles B. Benenson, New York, 1967; Yale University Art Gallery, New Haven, Conn., Charles B. Benenson, B.A. 1933, Collection, 2006.52.4.

47 20 Carnival
1947
Collage; newspaper and magazine clippings, painted paper, wove paper, and journal cover on cardstock
6⅛ × 4⅞ in. (15.6 × 12.4 cm)
Provenance: Presumably given by the artist to Katherine S. Dreier, West Redding, Conn., 1947; Yale University Art Gallery, New Haven, Conn., Gift of the estate of Katherine S. Dreier, 1953.6.76.

Although Kurt Schwitters's art was not political per se, his unconventional use of materials and his abstract visual language did not conform to the Nazis' aesthetic dogma of Social Realism. By 1933, after Hitler's takeover of Germany, the artist quickly felt restricted by the new regulations that the Nazi regime had imposed on art exhibitions, publications, and teaching. His collage *Ohne Titel* (*Der Wunsch des Künstlers*) (Untitled [The Artist's Wish]) from 1934 (fig. 1) shows his own name written in prominent letters on an envelope, which seems to be an affirmation of his identity during a time when his status as an artist was questioned.[1] From the early 1930s onward, Schwitters had been thinking about and planning his flight from the country, as his position in Germany grew increasingly fragile.[2] However, he was forced to leave the country even sooner than he had expected, in January 1937, following his son Ernst, who had left Germany in December 1936 because of his affiliation with a socialist resistance group. Schwitters and his son settled in Norway, a country that he had been regularly visiting since 1929. He took up residence in Lysaker, near Oslo, and spent the summer months in the town of Molde.

Merzbild mit Regenbogen (*Merz* Picture with Rainbow) was begun in Germany in 1920 but finished in Norway. Schwitters's wife, who had remained in Hanover, shipped this assemblage and other works to him in 1938.[3] The work consists of assembled pieces of found and prefabricated materials that Schwitters arranged on a flat surface. The artist introduced fake shadows to create a trompe l'oeil effect, as with the painted shadow of the broken wheel. The colors in the background, as well as the rainbow, seem to be a reference to the natural or rural environment that Schwitters experienced in Norway, as opposed to the urban one of his hometown of Hanover. The gray-green and cool blue in particular evoke the glaciers, mountains, and forests that he painted during excursions in the countryside—such as in *Isbræ under sne* (Isbreen under Snow, fig. 2). He sold landscapes like this one, as well as portraits, to locals and tourists; this constituted his major source of income while in exile.[4]

Schwitters saw an inherent link between the laws of nature and abstraction, and thus he did not consider his landscape painting to be opposed to his abstract *Merz* works.[5] His new surroundings inspired a tangible interest in organic forms and natural materials, as well as a relaxation of his earlier geometric structures.[6] The whole composition of *Merzbild mit Regenbogen* seems less visually agitated than his earlier assemblages

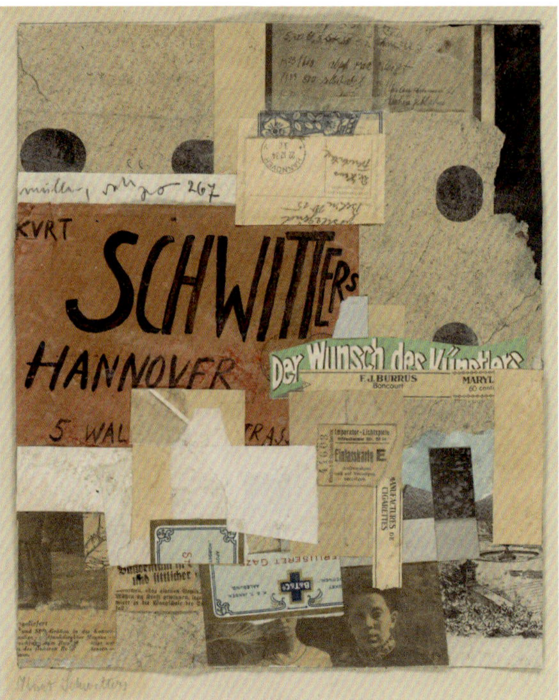

Fig. 1. Kurt Schwitters, *Ohne Titel* (*Der Wunsch des Künstlers*) (Untitled [The Artist's Wish]), 1934. Collage; newspaper clippings, wrappers, tickets, and mailing labels on paper, mounted on board, 12¾ × 10¼ in. (32.4 × 26 cm). Yale University Art Gallery, New Haven, Conn., Charles B. Benenson, B.A. 1933, Collection, 2006.52.5

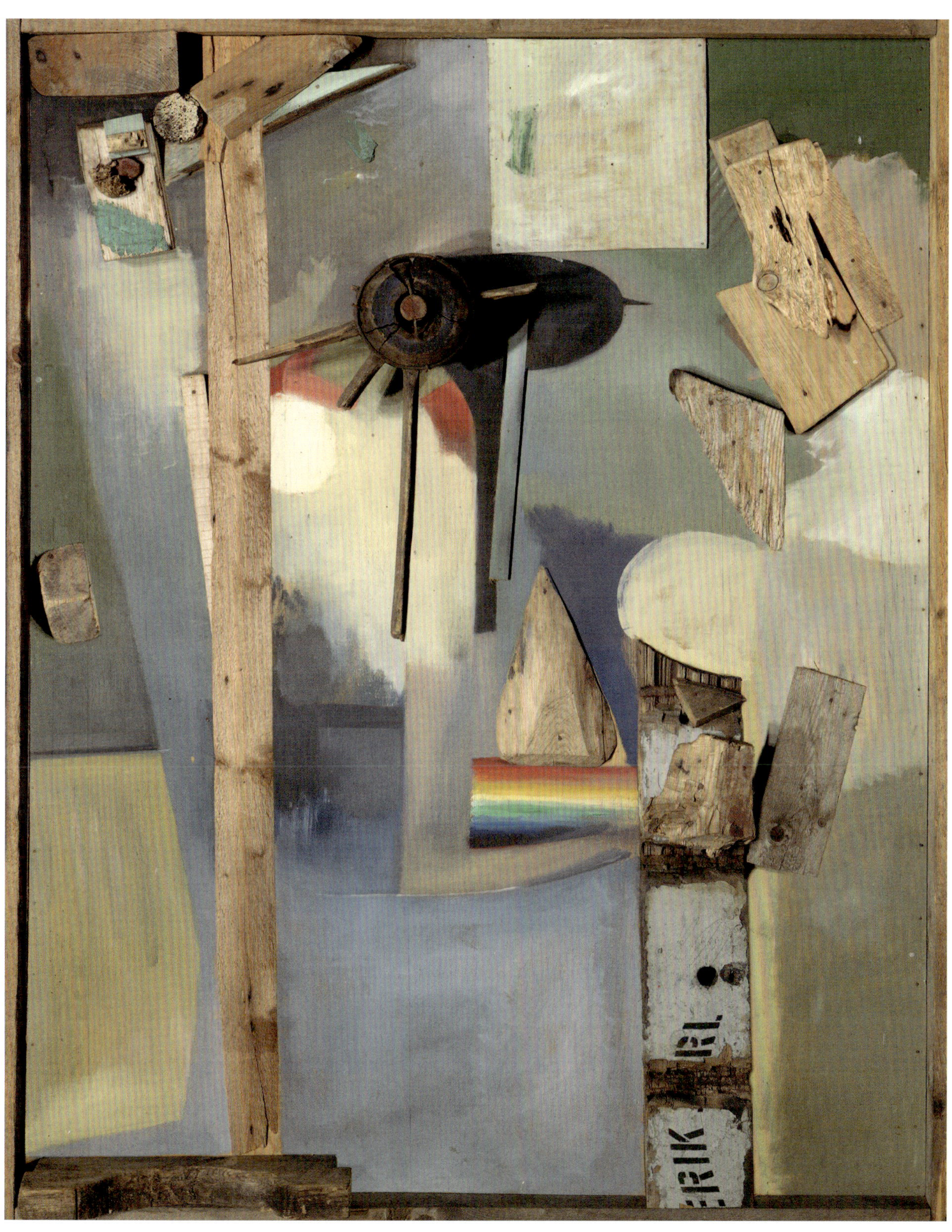

Merzbild mit Regenbogen (Merz Picture with Rainbow)

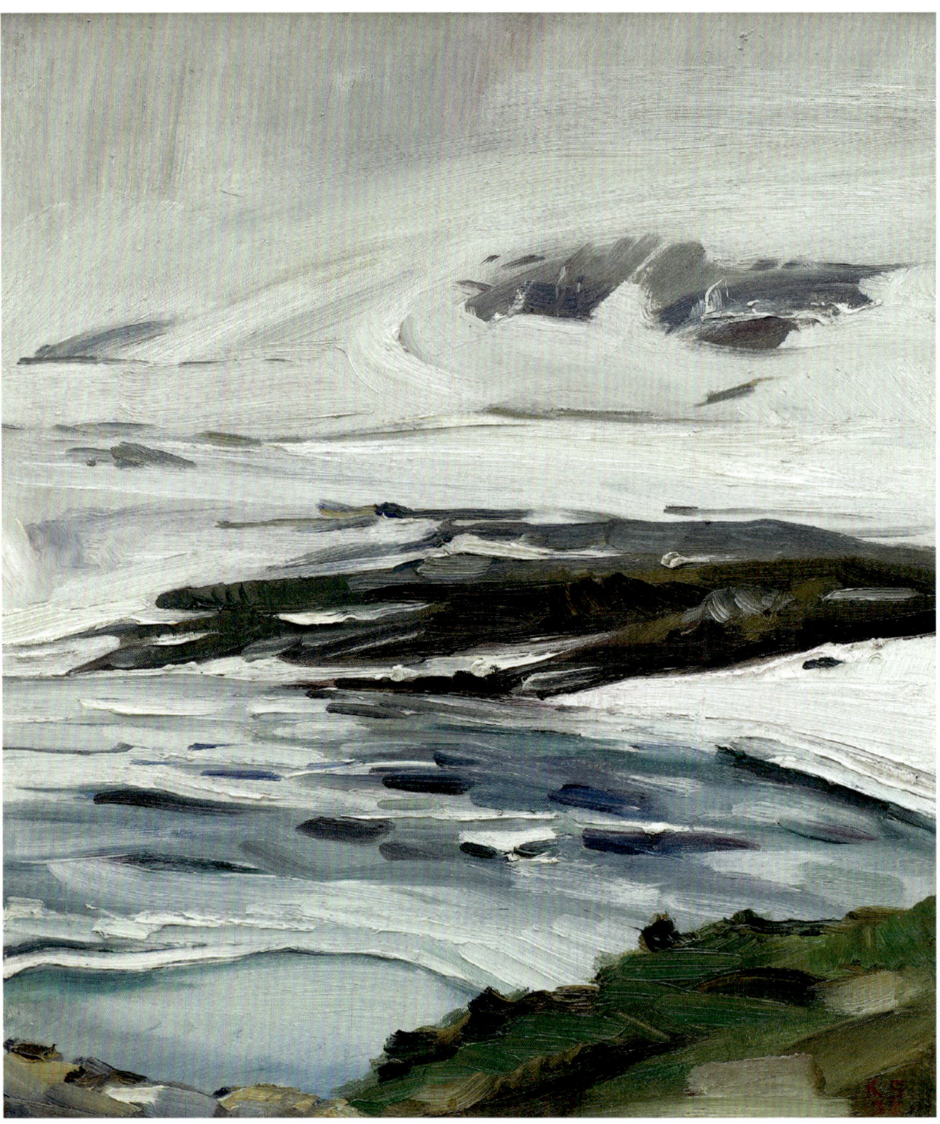

Fig. 2. Kurt Schwitters, *Isbræ under sne* (Isbreen under Snow), 1937. Oil on wood, 26 ⅜ × 22 1/16 in. (67 × 56 cm). Sprengel Museum Hannover, on loan from the Kurt und Ernst Schwitters Stiftung, Hanover, Germany

from the 1920s, and it gives each of the formal elements, including the painted parts, more pictorial weight. The physical substance of materials, such as the raw, unpainted pieces of wood, is suddenly no longer subordinate to the overall composition, but rather seems to dictate it.[7]

In 1940, after the German invasion of Norway, Schwitters fled to the United Kingdom and was first interned as an "enemy alien" on the Isle of Man. During his time in the internment camp, he painted landscapes and accepted portrait commissions.[8] Still, he continued his abstract collage works, again using everyday objects such as newspaper clippings, envelopes, and wrapping paper.[9] Although he was restricted in his own movements, his abstract works circulated outside of Europe.[10] He sent many of these collages to the renowned art patron Katherine S. Dreier in the United States, asking her to sell them.[11] The collage *47 20 Carnival*, which he may have sent to her as a gift, is one of his more figurative pieces, as opposed to the more abstract and gridlike, organized *Merz* collages that he had made earlier in Germany (fig. 3). Whereas Schwitters

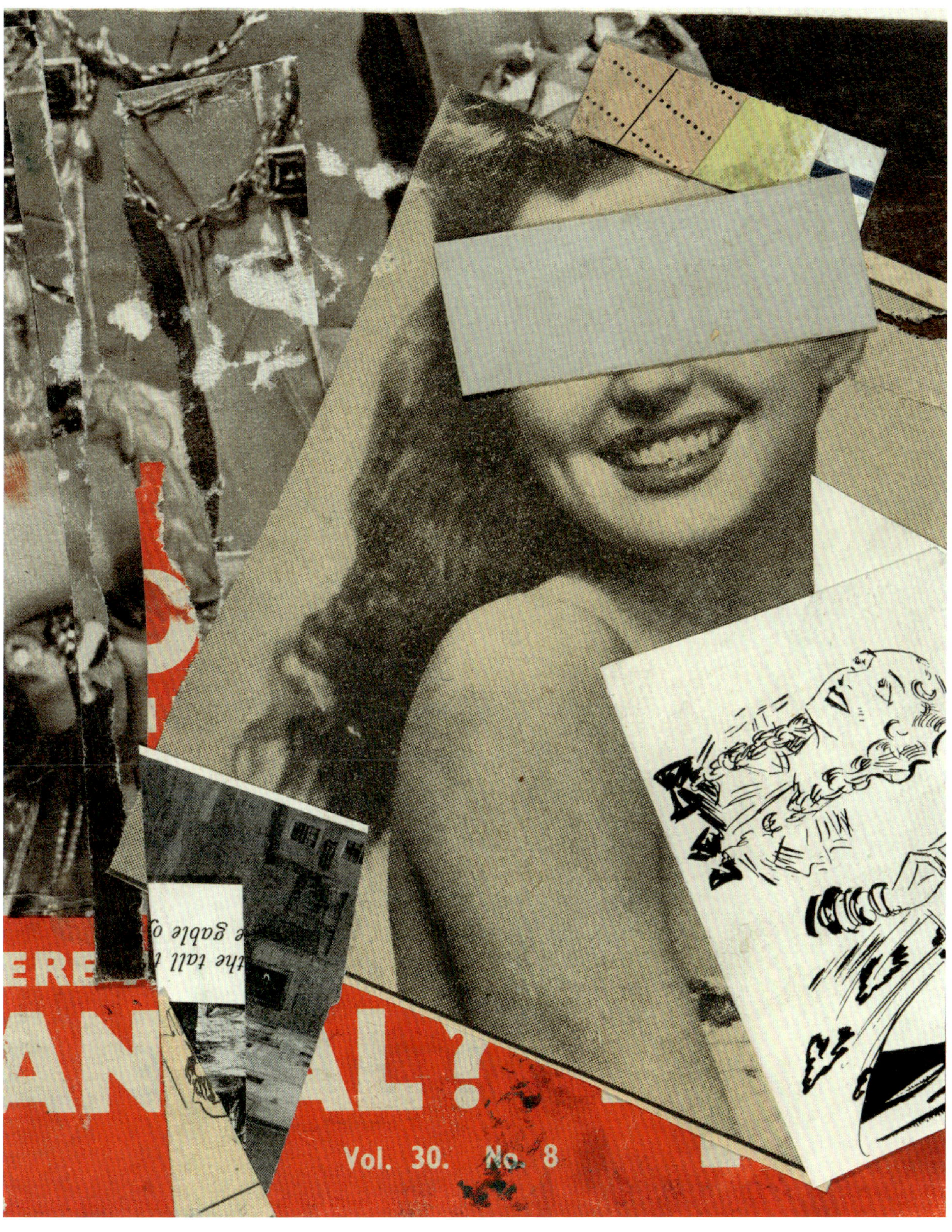

47 20 Carnival

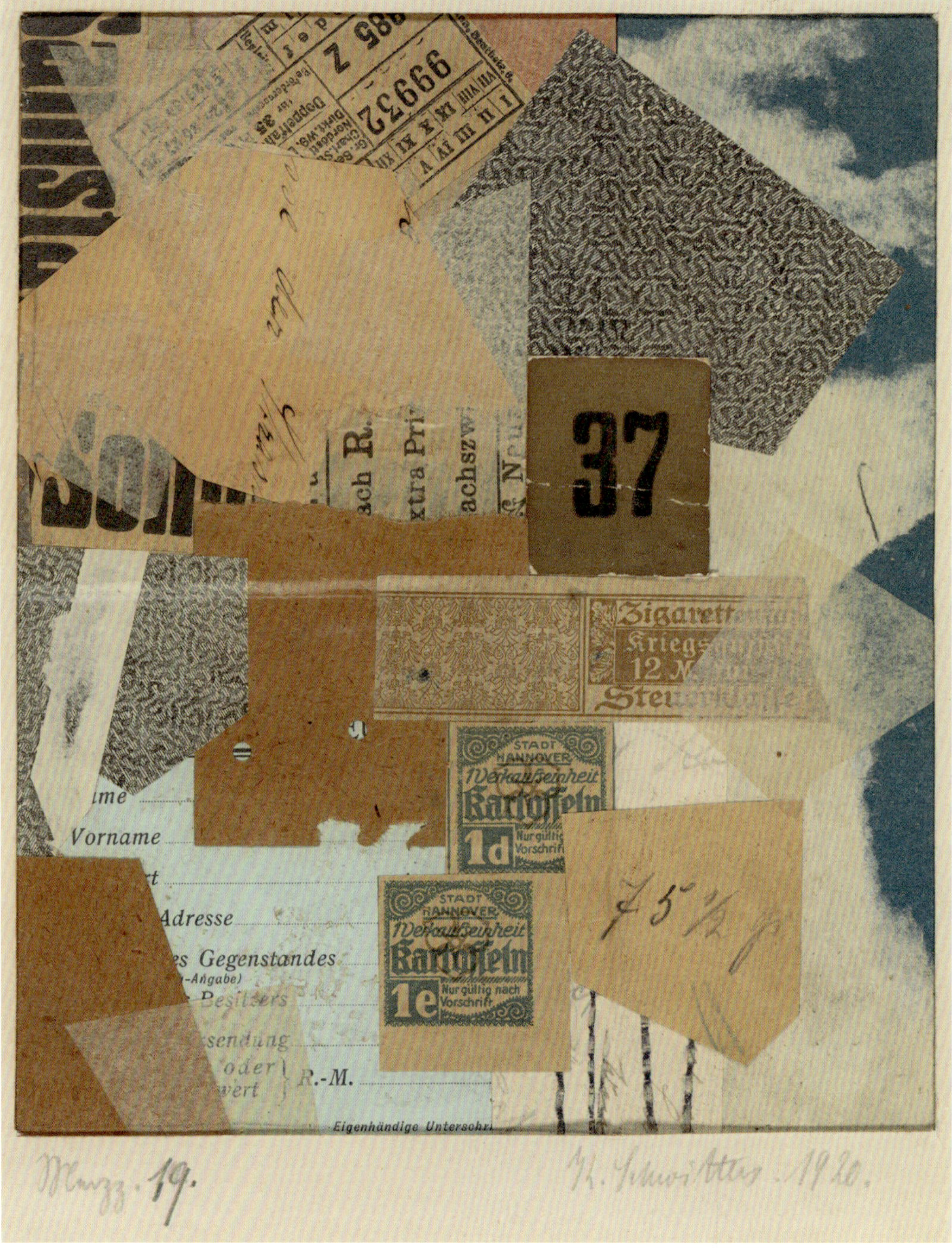

Fig. 3. Kurt Schwitters, *Merzz. 19*, 1920. Collage; mixed media on paper, 7⁵⁄₁₆ × 5⁷⁄₈ in. (18.5 × 15 cm).
Yale University Art Gallery, New Haven, Conn., Gift of Collection Société Anonyme, 1941.681

focused primarily on the colors and shapes of the materials that he used in his collages from the 1920s, during his exile years in the United Kingdom he deliberately engaged with representational images and text from graphic materials, using them as a way to incorporate the British culture and language that he subsequently embraced. In *47 20 Carnival*, he used a large image of a woman, probably taken from an advertisement, as well as a drawing of a female head, possibly a magazine illustration, which appears to turn toward the other woman. The woman with the stripe hiding her eyes seems enigmatic, almost disturbing, given the postwar context. The levity conveyed by her beaming smile, shiny hair, and attire (perhaps a bathing suit) stands in sharp contrast to the gravity of Schwitters's personal life, with the death of his wife in 1944 in Hanover as well as his own internment and several severe health problems. However, the overall image certainly alludes to his new environment, and to mass media and popular culture, in a more tangible way than before. His efforts to steep himself in his new life also became obvious in his request to obtain British citizenship, and in his frequent refusal to use the German language, even when writing to his former Dadaist friends such as Raoul Hausmann.[12] —FVJ

1. Megan R. Luke, "Kurt Schwitters," in *Eye on a Century: Modern and Contemporary Art from the Charles B. Benenson Collection at the Yale University Art Gallery*, ed. Cathleen Chaffee (New Haven, Conn.: Yale University Art Gallery, 2012), 46–48.

2. John Elderfield, *Kurt Schwitters* (New York: Thames and Hudson, 1985), 197–98.

3. Kurt Schwitters to Sophie Taeuber-Arp, Lysaker, Norway, May 10, 1938, reproduced in Kurt Schwitters, *Wir spielen, bis uns der Tod abholt: Briefe aus fünf Jahrzehnten*, ed. Ernst Nüdel (Frankfurt: Ullstein, 1974), 144–45.

4. Karin Orchard, "'It's namely someone else painting, it's not me': Kurt Schwitters's Paintings in Norway," in *Schwitters in Norway* (Hovikodden, Norway: Henie Onstad Art Centre, 2009), 100–107.

5. Megan R. Luke, *Kurt Schwitters: Space, Image, Exile* (Chicago: University of Chicago Press, 2014), 207.

6. Elderfield, *Kurt Schwitters*, 198–99.

7. Ibid., 202–3; Luke, *Kurt Schwitters*, 226.

8. Shulamith Behr and Marian Malet, eds., *Arts in Exile in Britain 1933–1945: Politics and Cultural Identity* (Amsterdam: Rodopi, 2005), 20–22.

9. Nicholas Wadley distinguishes three different types of collages during Schwitters's exile years, one of which evolves from a single ready-made image, such as *47 20 Carnival*. See Wadley, "The Late Work of Kurt Schwitters," in *Kurt Schwitters in Exile: The Late Work 1937–1948* (London: Marlborough Fine Art, 1981), 63–74, esp. 67.

10. Robert L. Herbert, Eleanor S. Apter, and Elise K. Kenney, *The Société Anonyme and the Dreier Bequest at Yale University: A Catalogue Raisonné* (New Haven, Conn.: Yale University Art Gallery, 1984), 596.

11. Katherine S. Dreier to Kurt Schwitters, March 16, 1947, Société Anonyme Papers, YCAL MSS 101, box 31, folder 925, Beinecke Rare Book and Manuscript Library, New Haven, Conn.

12. Kurt Schwitters to Raoul Hausmann, Ambleside, England, June 18, 1946, Raoul Hausmann Series I: Correspondence 1901–1971, 850994, Correspondence with Kurt Schwitters 1946–1947, box 1, folder 16, Getty Research Library, Los Angeles.

Albert Einstein, Physicist, Princeton, New Jersey
1938, printed later
Palladium print
13³⁄₈ × 10¹⁄₁₆ in. (33.9 × 25.6 cm)

Marc Chagall, Artist, New York
1942, printed later
Palladium print
9¹³⁄₁₆ × 7³⁄₁₆ in. (24.9 × 18.3 cm)

Untitled (Inv. #12)
ca. 1950
Gelatin silver print
10⁵⁄₁₆ × 13⁷⁄₈ in. (27.8 × 35.2 cm)

Photogenic
1946–55
Gelatin silver print
6¹⁵⁄₁₆ × 9⁵⁄₈ in. (17.6 × 24.4 cm)

Photogenic
1946–55
Gelatin silver print
9⁵⁄₈ × 12¹³⁄₁₆ in. (24.5 × 32.5 cm)

Provenance: Doris Bry Collection; Yale University Art Gallery, New Haven, Conn., Gift of the Doris Bry Trust, Inadvertent Collection, 2016.101.89, .97, .102, .104, .450.

Lotte Jacobi's oeuvre straddles prewar Europe and the United States, where the photographer restarted her career in 1935 after Hitler's rise to power and the subsequent persecution of modern artists and fellow Jews forced her to flee Germany. A fourth-generation photographer who had inherited her family's business in Berlin before the war forced her to abandon it, she reestablished her practice in New York with the help of her European connections and acquaintances who had already emigrated.[1] In her new home, Jacobi both registered and resisted contemporary debates about the aesthetics of photography. She continued her longstanding focus on studio portraiture; before the war, she had photographed many leading figures of the Weimar Republic in the thriving world of arts and culture, such as Käthe Kollwitz, Lotte Lenya, and Kurt Weill. Despite the waning status of portraiture in a new world of mass media and the rise of new aesthetic dogmas, such as the straight photography of Alfred Stieglitz and the Constructivism of László Moholy-Nagy, Jacobi remained devoted to studio portraiture because she found artistic inspiration in the singularity

of her subjects and in the immediacy of her exchanges with them.[2] Yet she also experimented with abstraction in a series of works that would come to be known as the *Photogenics.*

Her 1938 portrait of Albert Einstein clad in a leather jacket in his office in Princeton, New Jersey, suggests the connections that Jacobi sustained with other Jewish refugees in the United States (she had photographed Einstein twice in Europe, and again in Huntington on Long Island, New York, in 1936), as well as the challenges that she faced as a female émigré photographer whose style put her at odds with the slick, journalistic photography that was becoming popular in America.[3] Though the Einstein portrait would become one of the most widely known in Jacobi's oeuvre, it was never published by its commissioner, *Life* magazine, because its unstaged quality and nuanced, slightly melancholic tenor were deemed unsuited to the publication's popular aesthetic. Jacobi's portrait is intimate, capturing Einstein in a casual moment from a high vantage point while he looks into the distance, most likely out a window. The grave expression of the physicist's features suggests a mind preoccupied less with equations than with contemporary world events.[4] The initial rejection of the photograph indicates the difficulty that Jacobi had in winning magazine and newspaper commissions—a major source of income for photographers at the time.[5]

However, Jacobi did find a number of important American supporters, including eminent photographers such as Berenice Abbott, Barbara Morgan, and Stieglitz. Well-known sitters also supported Jacobi by having their portraits taken by her. In addition to Einstein, who specifically requested Jacobi for the *Life* shoot, fellow émigré Marc Chagall voiced an appreciation for her work after getting his portrait taken by her. When the painter ordered multiple prints of the photographs that Jacobi had taken of him and his daughter, Ida (ca. 1945, Lotte Jacobi Collection, University of New Hampshire), he claimed that the images helped him realize that photography, too, was an art form.[6] In contrast to the jovially smiling father-daughter pair, this closely cropped palladium print from 1942 shows a solitary Chagall gazing with fierce intensity.

Though Jacobi found it challenging to simultaneously gratify her aesthetic interests and meet the demands of sustaining an economically viable atelier in New York, she engaged in some emphatically modern experiments with form with her abstract, cameraless series of images begun in the late 1940s, which the painter and art historian Leo Katz referred to as

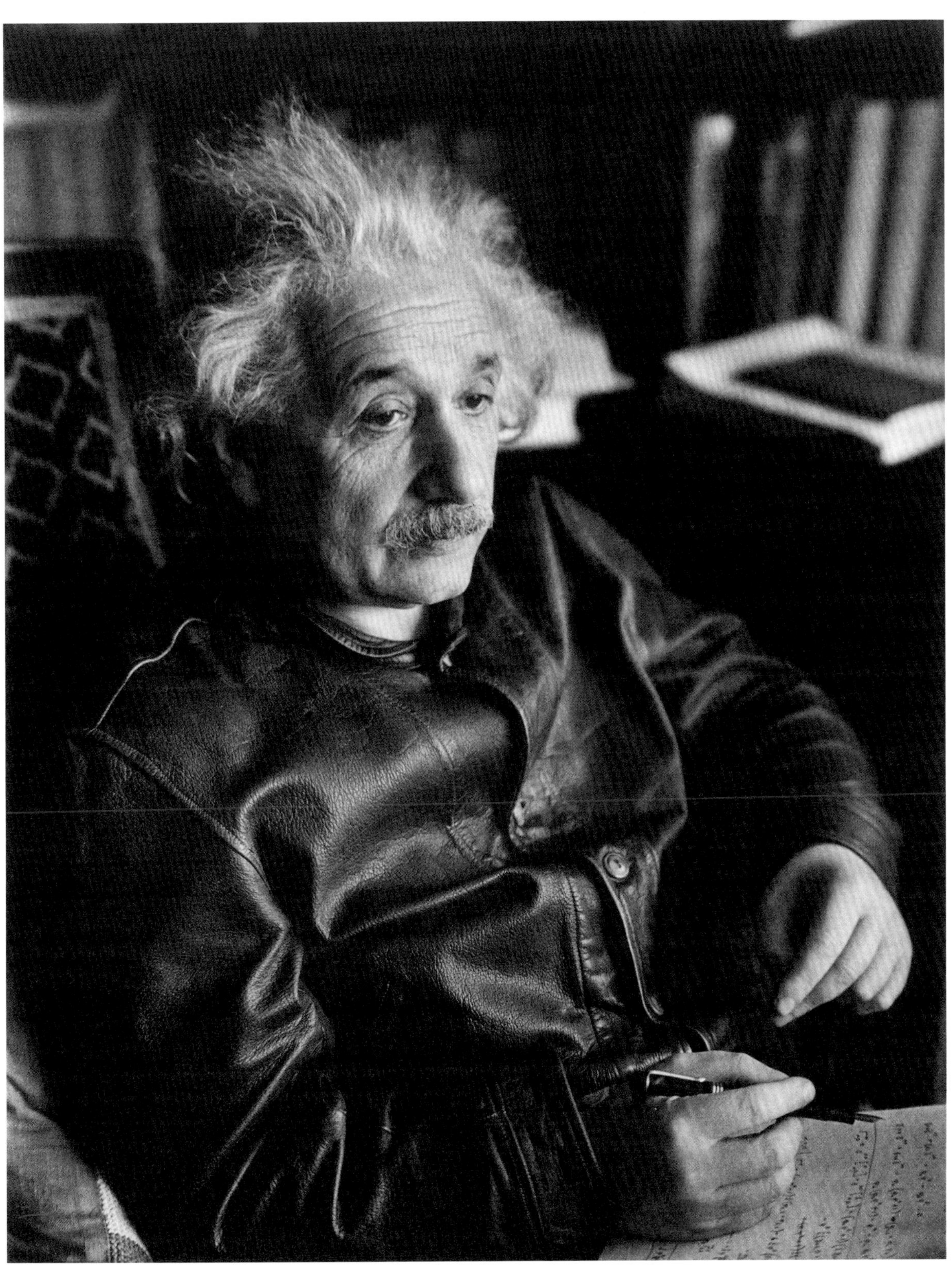

Albert Einstein, Physicist, Princeton, New Jersey

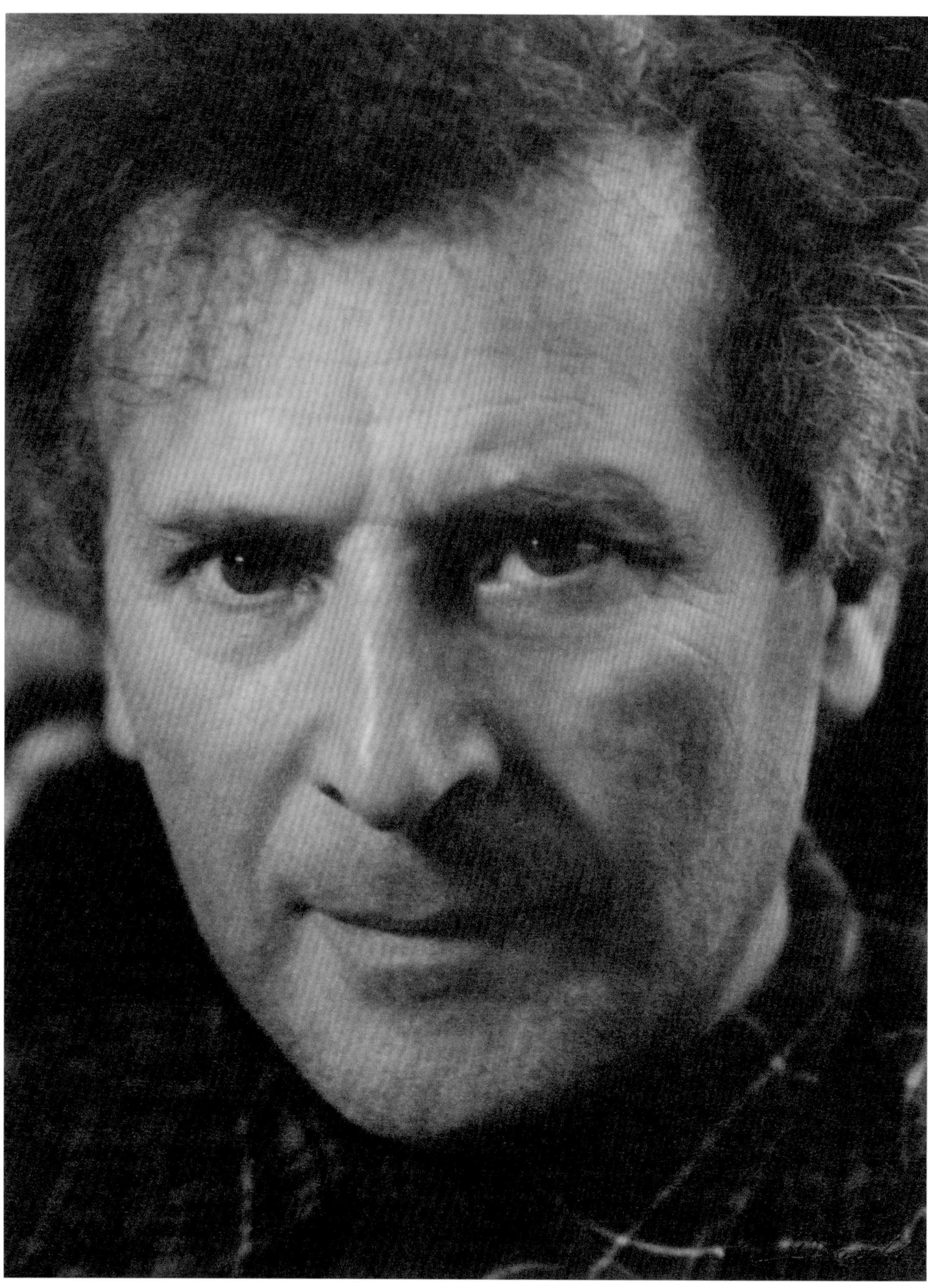

Marc Chagall, Artist, New York

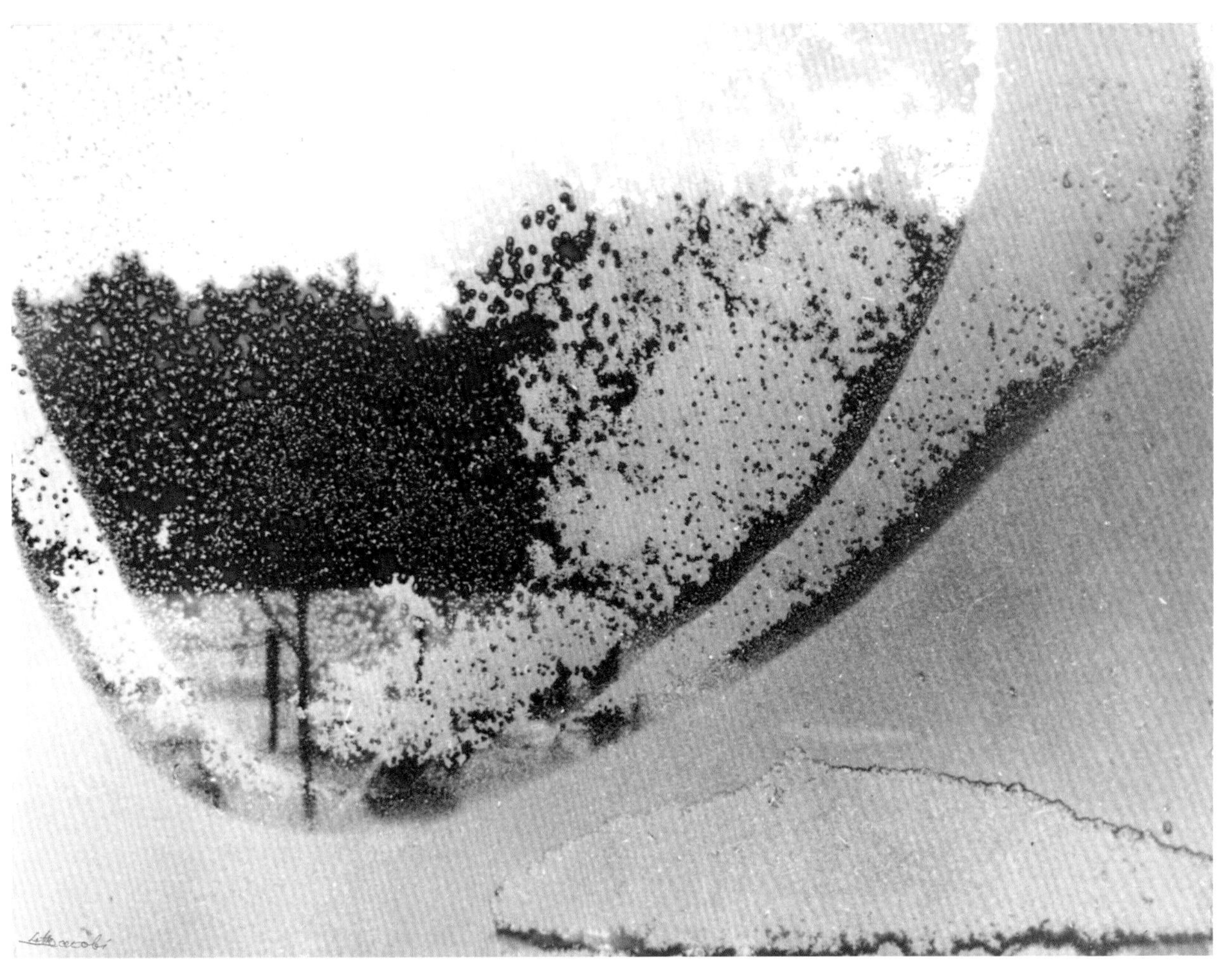

Untitled (Inv. #12)

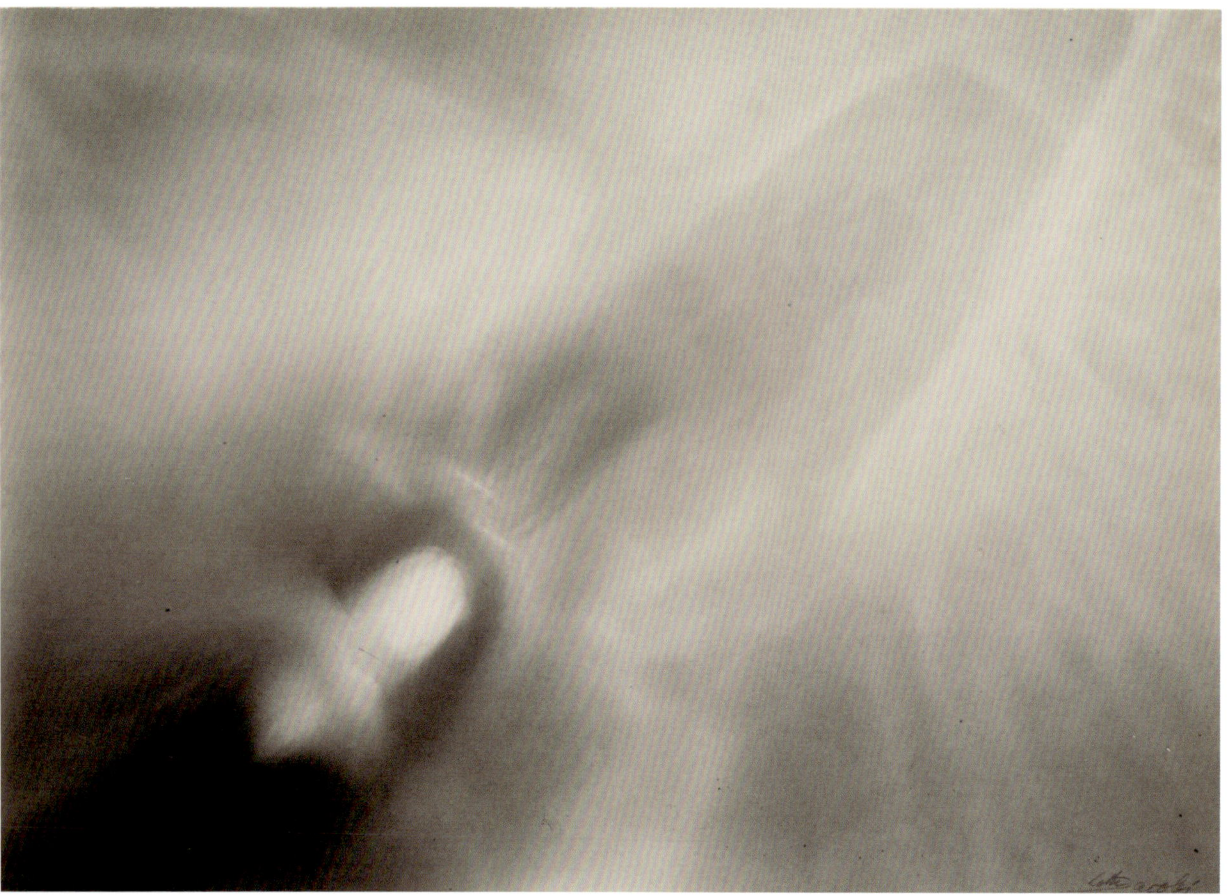

Photogenic

"photogenics."[7] In 1947 Jacobi started making abstract works in the darkroom by filtering light onto photosensitive paper through transparent materials such as cellophane. The *Photogenics* represented a realm of uninhibited formal experimentation for the photographer, one that sent her into an "altered state of joyful excitement."[8] They manifest her interest in scientific theories about multidimensionality, such as Einstein's, as well as her desire to explore the purely expressive dimensions of photography. Unlike Jacobi's portraits, the *Photogenics* accorded with movements toward abstraction in photography—as can be seen in the contemporary works of Moholy-Nagy, Man Ray, and Edward Weston. Her *Photogenics* found favorable reception, even among those skeptical of Jacobi's portraiture, such as the photographer Edward Steichen. As the head of the photography department at the Museum of Modern Art, New York, Steichen displayed five of the *Photogenics* at a 1948 show at the museum titled *In and Out of Focus*. Still, Jacobi continued her more figurative work during and after pursuing these "adventures in light."[9] The aesthetic inspiration that she found in her new home in the United States supplemented, rather than supplanted, the iconic approach to photography with which she had made a name for herself in Berlin. —ND

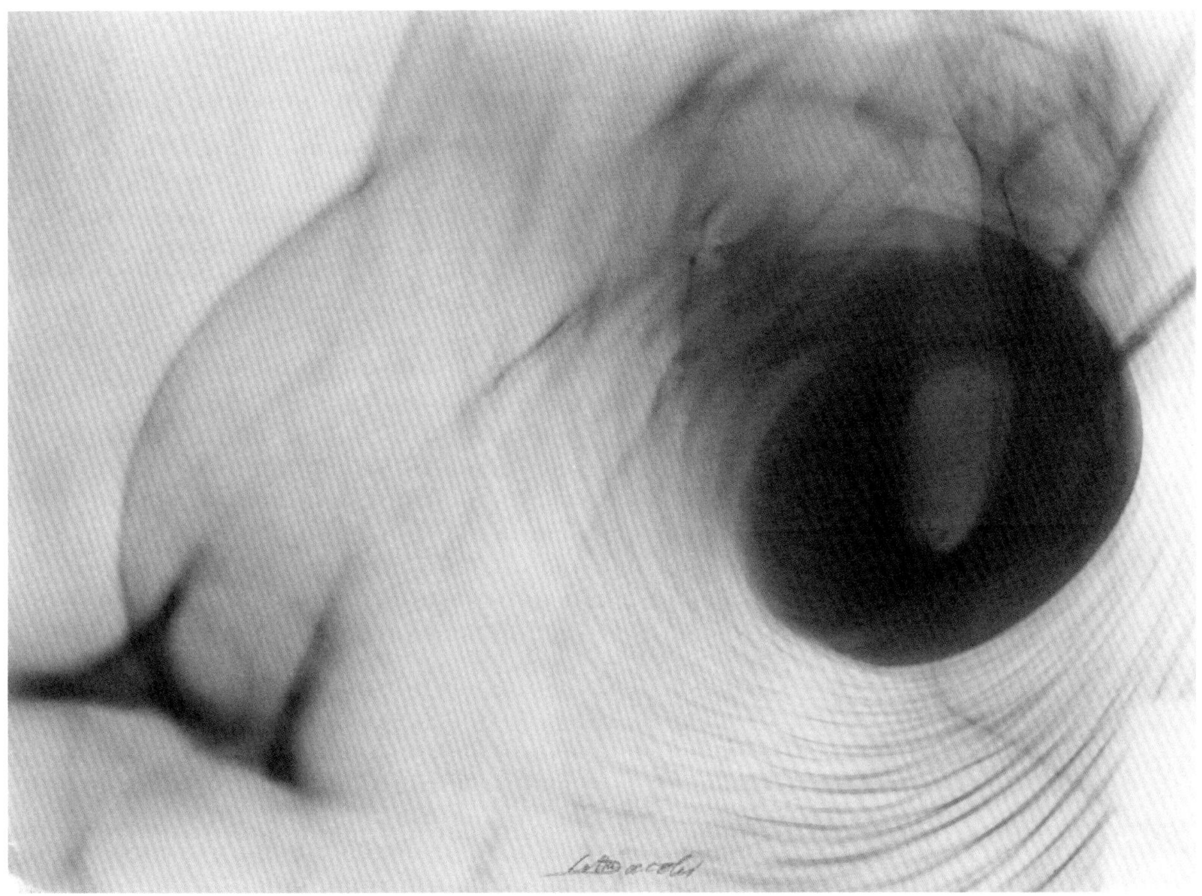

Photogenic

1. Save for a handful of negatives that she transported with her to the United States, much of Jacobi's work of the 1920s and 1930s was lost in the war.

2. Toward the end of her life, Jacobi described her approach: "My style is the style of the people I photograph." Marilyn Myers Slade, "Lotte Jacobi," *New Hampshire Profiles* 36, no. 1 (1987): 38.

3. Marion Beckers and Elisabeth Moortgat, *Atelier Lotte Jacobi: Berlin/New York* (Berlin: Das Verborgene Museum Nicolai, 1998), 156.

4. A substantial feature of Einstein and Jacobi's camaraderie was their anti-Nazi sentiment and their hopes that America would stop Hitler's regime; in another photo shoot in Princeton with Einstein and Thomas Mann, Jacobi would prod the scientist to use his influence to resist Nazi participation in the New York World's Fair. Ibid., 162.

5. Edward Steichen would eventually publish the image in 1942 in *U.S. Camera*.

6. Lotte Jacobi, interview by Peter Moriarty, November 22, 1976, transcript, Rochester Institute of Technology Library, N.Y.

7. Beckers and Moortgat, *Atelier Lotte Jacobi*, 183.

8. Lotte Jacobi, "Über Photogenics" (unpublished notes), Lotte Jacobi Archives, University of New Hampshire, cited by Beckers and Moortgat, *Atelier Lotte Jacobi*, 183.

9. Ibid.

Plusieurs ont vécu (Many Have Lived)
1939
Oil on canvas
27⅝ × 21¾ in. (70.2 × 55.2 cm)
Provenance: Acquired from the artist by Pierre Matisse
Gallery, New York, 1940; sold to Thomas Howard,
New York, 1944; Yale University Art Gallery, New Haven,
Conn., Gift of Thomas F. Howard, 1956.46.1.

Plusieurs ont vécu (Many Have Lived) was painted in
1939, the year Yves Tanguy left France and immigrated
to the United States. The canvas was probably executed
while the artist was still in France, and he might have
taken it with him or had it shipped separately to the
United States. Tanguy had thought of leaving France
earlier due to "fascist symptoms" that he had recognized
as early as 1934.[1] The dark palette of Tanguy's canvases
of the 1930s is perhaps a visual echo of his urge to leave
France amid a sense of mounting danger. *Plusieurs ont
vécu* in particular might be seen as a reflection on contemporary events, most notably the German invasion of
Poland in September 1939 and the subsequent declarations of war from the United Kingdom and France.[2]

The canvas depicts a deserted landscape. The
lower part is painted in darker tones, mostly variations
of gray, suggesting an undefined terrain, and the upper
part is executed in lighter shades of brown and gray,
evoking a muddy sky that obscures the view of the
horizon. Several colorful biomorphic forms populate the
scene, connected by a few white lines that are incised
into the paint. These shapes are deliberately devoid of
any representational elements and bear no resemblance
to actual creatures or objects. The Surrealist André
Breton wrote of Tanguy's works, "He saw them as landscapes of the inner world, revealing the elusive beings,
the wraiths, that lurk behind the scenes of life."[3] These
"elusive beings" seem disconnected from their environment, and only their shadows connect them to the
ground. The surrounding landscape induces a sentiment
of isolation and melancholy, reinforced by the lack of
horizon and the monotony of the background—except
for several dark, horizontal shadows that menacingly
transgress the lower half of the canvas.

Once Tanguy settled in New York, he reunited with
the American painter Kay Sage, with whom he had started
a relationship in France; they married in 1940. Tanguy's
adaptation to the American art scene was a relatively
smooth one, due not only to his wife's contacts but also
to his own connections, notably the art dealer Pierre
Matisse, his former schoolmate at the Lycée Montaigne

in Paris.[4] One month after his arrival, in December 1939,
he had his first solo exhibition at Matisse's gallery in
New York, in which *Plusieurs ont vécu* was shown.[5] His
new surroundings also affected his compositions and
sense of color; Tanguy admitted that his palette changed
after his arrival in the United States. Due to the light
and to the expansiveness of the American landscape, he
began to experiment with more intense colors and with
the openness of space, where earth and sky seem to merge
into one another (fig. 1).[6]

Nonetheless, during the subsequent years,
marked by the escalation of World War II and the
declaration of war by the United States on Japan and
Germany in 1941, Tanguy's Surrealist, almost playful
biomorphic shapes of the 1930s evolved into metallic
forms, culminating in the skeletal towers in his paintings of the early 1950s, such as *De mains pâles aux cieux
lasses* (From Pale Hands to Weary Skies, fig. 2). The fluid,
colorful forms have morphed here into amalgamated
shapes conveying an aura of menace, emphasized
through their cold gray color, the sharp bleached
points inserted between them, and the cropping of

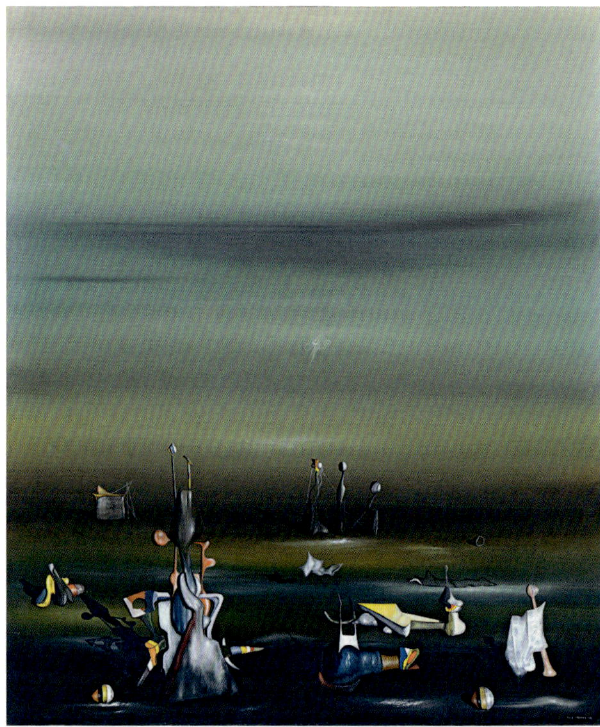

Fig. 1. Yves Tanguy, *Encore et toujours* (Time and Again), 1942.
Oil on canvas, 39⅜ × 31⅞ in. (100 × 81 cm). Museo Thyssen-
Bornemisza, Madrid, 770 (1975.46)

154

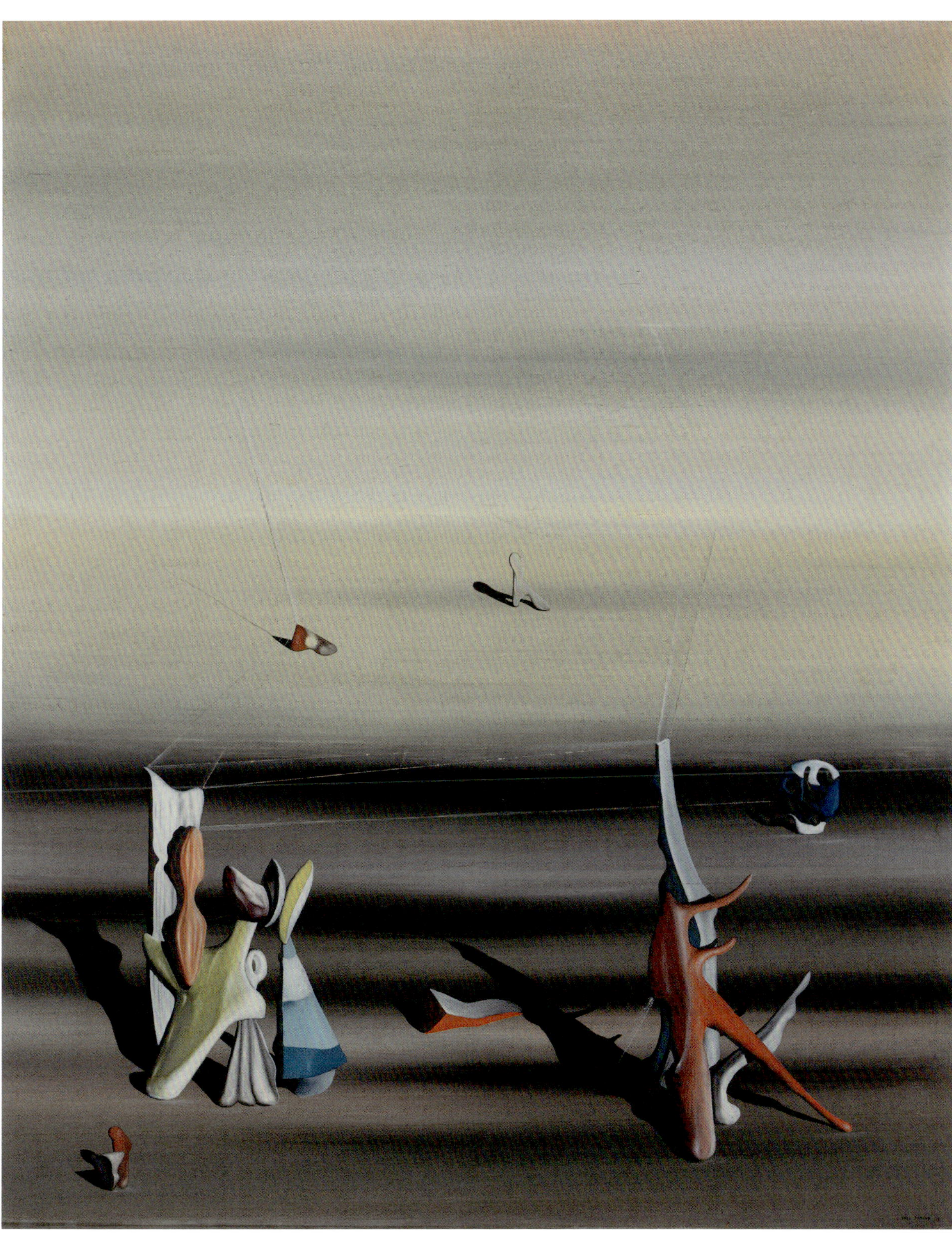

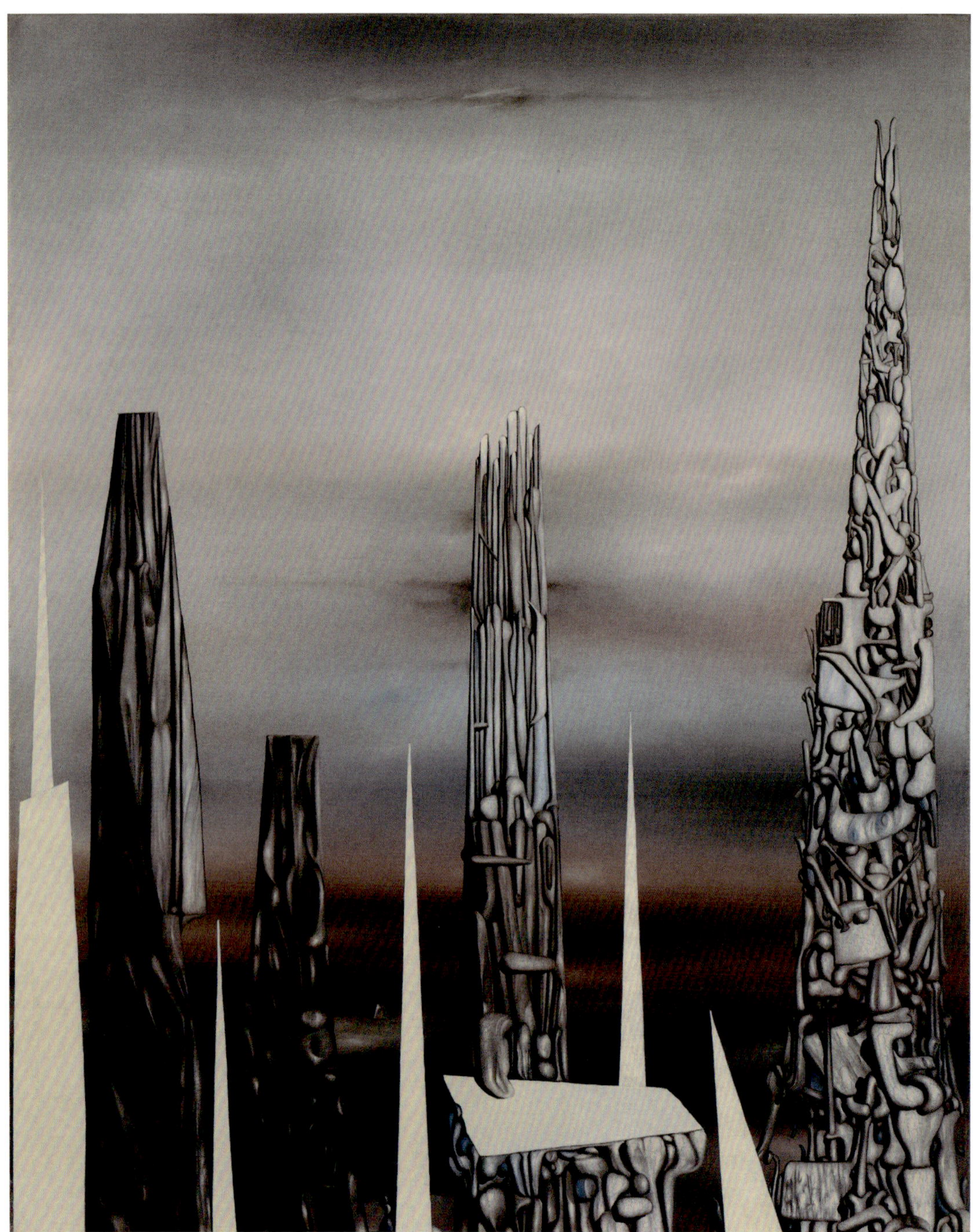

Fig. 2. Yves Tanguy, *De mains pâles aux cieux lasses* (From Pale Hands to Weary Skies), 1950. Oil on canvas, 35⅝ × 28⅛ in. (90.5 × 71.4 cm). Yale University Art Gallery, New Haven, Conn., Bequest of Kay Sage Tanguy, 1963.43.4

the foreground that implies a sense of threatening
monumentality. Clearly, in exceedingly subtle ways,
Tanguy translated the zeitgeist of this era into enigmatic
compositions that seem to organically respond to his exile
and the geopolitical situation. —FVJ

1. "Dès le début même de 1934, j'avais commencé à reconnaître
    certains symptômes fascistes en France, une éruption ici,
    une dispute là, j'ai failli partir pour l'Amérique avec Paalen";
    André Cariou, "Premières reconnaissances, 1930–1939,"
    in *Yves Tanguy: L'univers surréaliste*, exh. cat. (Quimper,
    France: Musée des Beaux-Arts de Quimper, 2007), 124–35,
    esp. 124.
2. Karin von Maur, "Yves Tanguy or 'The Certainty of the
    Never-Seen,'" in *Yves Tanguy and Surrealism*, exh. cat.
    (Ostfildern, Germany: Hatje Cantz, 2001), 11–133, esp.
    83–88.
3. André Breton, "What Tanguy Veils and Reveals," *View* 2,
    no. 2 (May 1942): 4–7.
4. Agnès Angliviel de La Beaumelle and Florence Chauveau,
    Yves Tanguy: Rétrospective, 1925–1955, exh. cat. (Paris:
    Centre Georges Pompidou, 1982), 212.
5. Information provided by the Pierre and Tana Matisse
    Foundation, New York, from its database for a forthcoming
    revised catalogue raisonné of Tanguy's oils, gouaches, and
    objects.
6. Sabine Eckmann, "Yves Tanguy in Connecticut, 1939–45,"
    in *Exiles and Emigrés: The Flight of European Artists from
    Hitler*, ed. Stephanie Barron, exh. cat. (Los Angeles: Los
    Angeles County Museum of Art, 1997), 170–75, esp. 174;
    and André Cariou, "'L'exil américain,' 1940–1946," in
    Yves Tanguy: L'univers surréaliste, 170–75, esp. 175: "Il y a
    plus de liberté, plus d'espace dans ce pays, c'est pourquoi
    je suis venu ici . . . Ici, aux USA, le seul changement que
    je puisse discerner dans mon œuvre concerne peut-être
    ma palette. Quelle est la raison de cette intensification de
    la couleur? Je ne saurais le dire. Mais je reconnais qu'il y
    a eu un changement considérable. Peut-être est-ce dû à la
    lumière, j'ai aussi une impression de plus grand espace ici,
    plus de 'champ'."

Composition No. 126
1941
Oil on canvas
23¾ × 23¾ in. (60.3 × 60.3 cm)
Provenance: Purchased from the artist by William S. Huff, Pittsburgh, 1954; Yale University Art Gallery, New Haven, Conn., Gift of William S. Huff, B.A. 1949, M.ARCH. 1952, 2014.123.2.

Friedrich Vordemberge-Gildewart was one of the leading abstract painters in Germany during the 1920s and 1930s, and he was part of several avant-garde groups, such as Gruppe K and Die abstrakten hannover in Germany as well as the Abstraction-Création group in Paris. Theo van Doesburg, one of the founders of the Dutch artists' group De Stijl, visited Vordemberge-Gildewart's studio in 1925 with Kurt Schwitters. Impressed by the abstract works he saw in the young artist's studio, van Doesburg invited him to join De Stijl.[1] These artists around van Doesburg and Piet Mondrian were advocates of Neoplasticism, an idealized art style that used the most basic visual elements (color, form, and line) in their purest states: vertical and horizontal lines, and no colors other than black, white, gray, and the three primary hues. While associated with De Stijl, Vordemberge-Gildewart resorted to a similar restrained language of colors and elementary geometric forms to create nonrepresentational works of art.

He and his Jewish wife, Ilse, left Germany in 1937 because of the Nazis' anti-Semitic agenda and their persecution of abstract artists. They fled first to Switzerland and eventually settled in the Netherlands. Although Vordemberge-Gildewart and his family lived in fear of persecution during the German occupation of the Netherlands, he continued to paint and was acquainted with other exiles, notably Max Beckmann, who represented him in the canvas *Les Artistes mit Gemüse* (The Artists with Vegetable, fig. 1), an image that conveys the isolation and constraints to which these artists were subjected.[2] *Composition No. 126* was painted during this period; it exemplifies how, during his time in the Netherlands, the artist focused on the interplay of lines, surface areas, and color. Whereas in earlier years Vordemberge-Gildewart had also utilized three-dimensional elements mounted to the surface of his canvases (fig. 2), after his emigration he preferred to work solely with the two-dimensional picture plane.[3] The canvas is painted a mustard yellow; triangles, lines, and rectangles interrupt the monotony of the color and create a playful overlapping of forms. *Composition No. 126* is part of a group of similar paintings that experiment with free-floating shapes.[4] These works seem to represent not only a stylistic evolution but also a reaction against the rigid formal principles of Neoplasticism.[5] The interwoven triangles generate new shapes, guiding the eye from one point to the next and creating movement. The top corner of the large triangle on the left of the composition appears cropped by the edge of the painting, creating the illusion that the lines continue beyond the canvas and thus giving the impression of infinity. A coarse-textured area in pale pink, where the triangle overlaps with the adjacent diamond outline, disrupts the smooth surface of the yellow paint and attracts the eye.

After the German invasion of the Netherlands in 1940, Vordemberge-Gildewart was no longer able to exhibit his paintings and showed only his typographic work.[6] A year before painting *Composition No. 126*, he published *millimeter und geraden* (Millimeter and Lines), a book of poetry accompanied by illustrations that prefigure the motif he later replicated in color in this and other paintings.[7] Evidently, the same motif appears

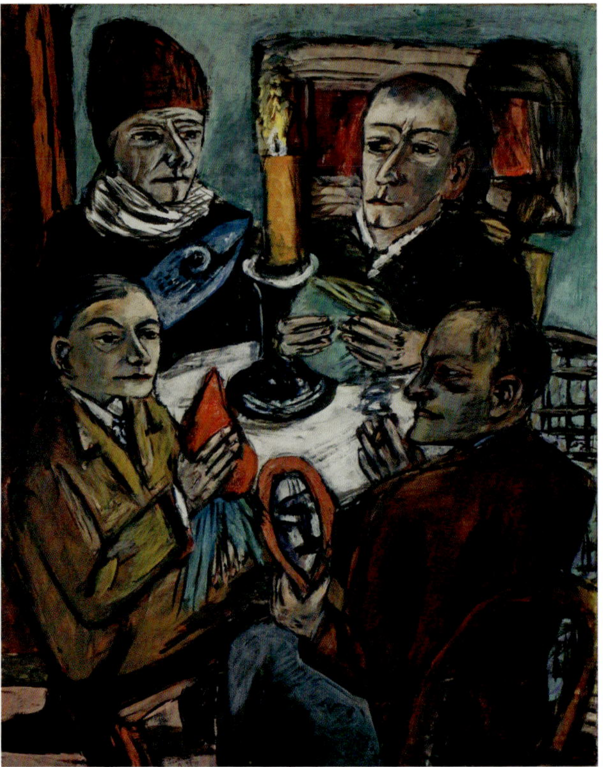

Fig. 1. Max Beckmann, *Les Artistes mit Gemüse* (The Artists with Vegetable), 1943. Oil on canvas, 59 × 45⅜ in. (149.9 × 115.3 cm). Washington University in Saint Louis, Mildred Lane Kemper Art Museum, University purchase, Kende Sale Fund, 1946, WU 3789

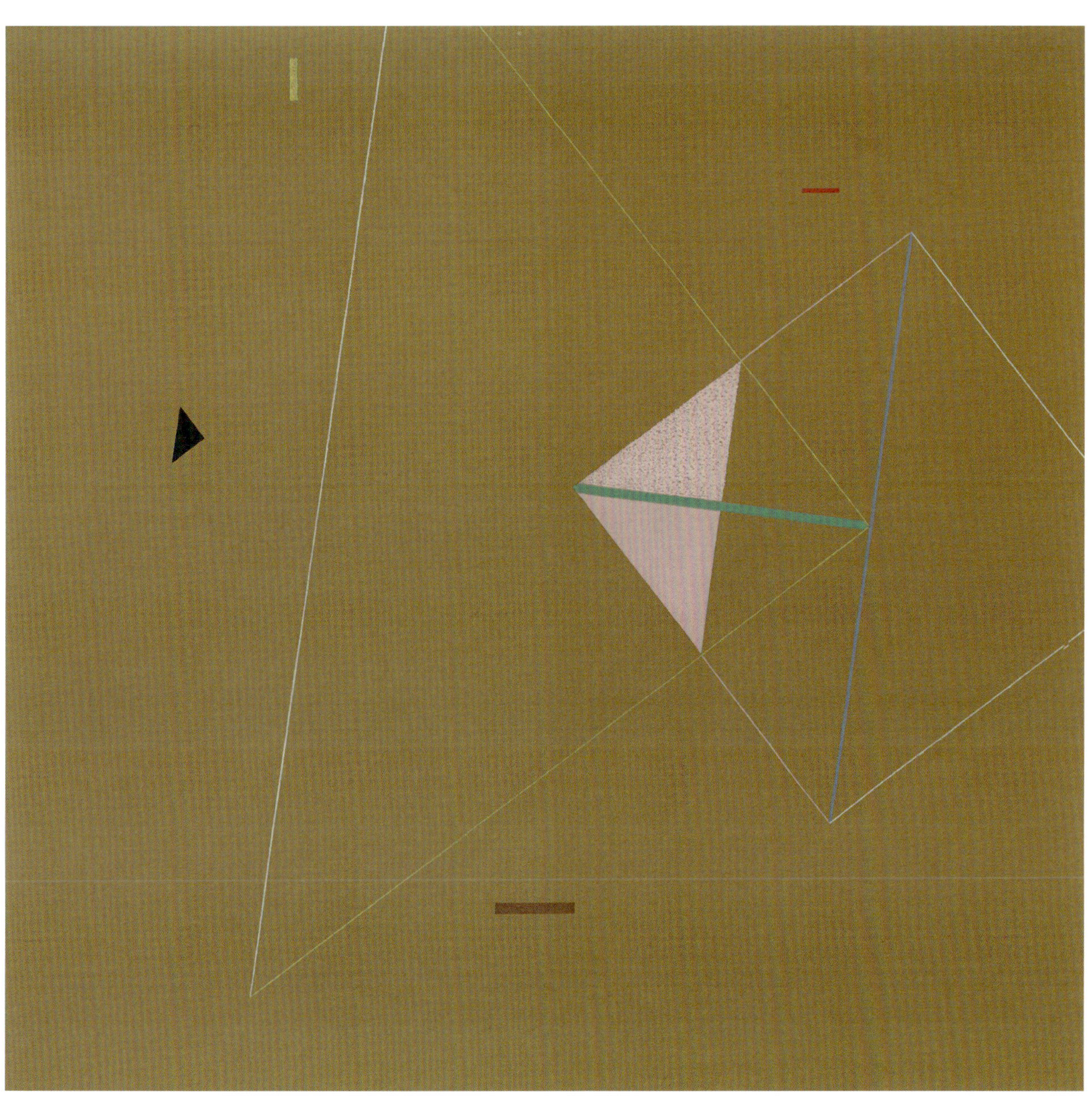

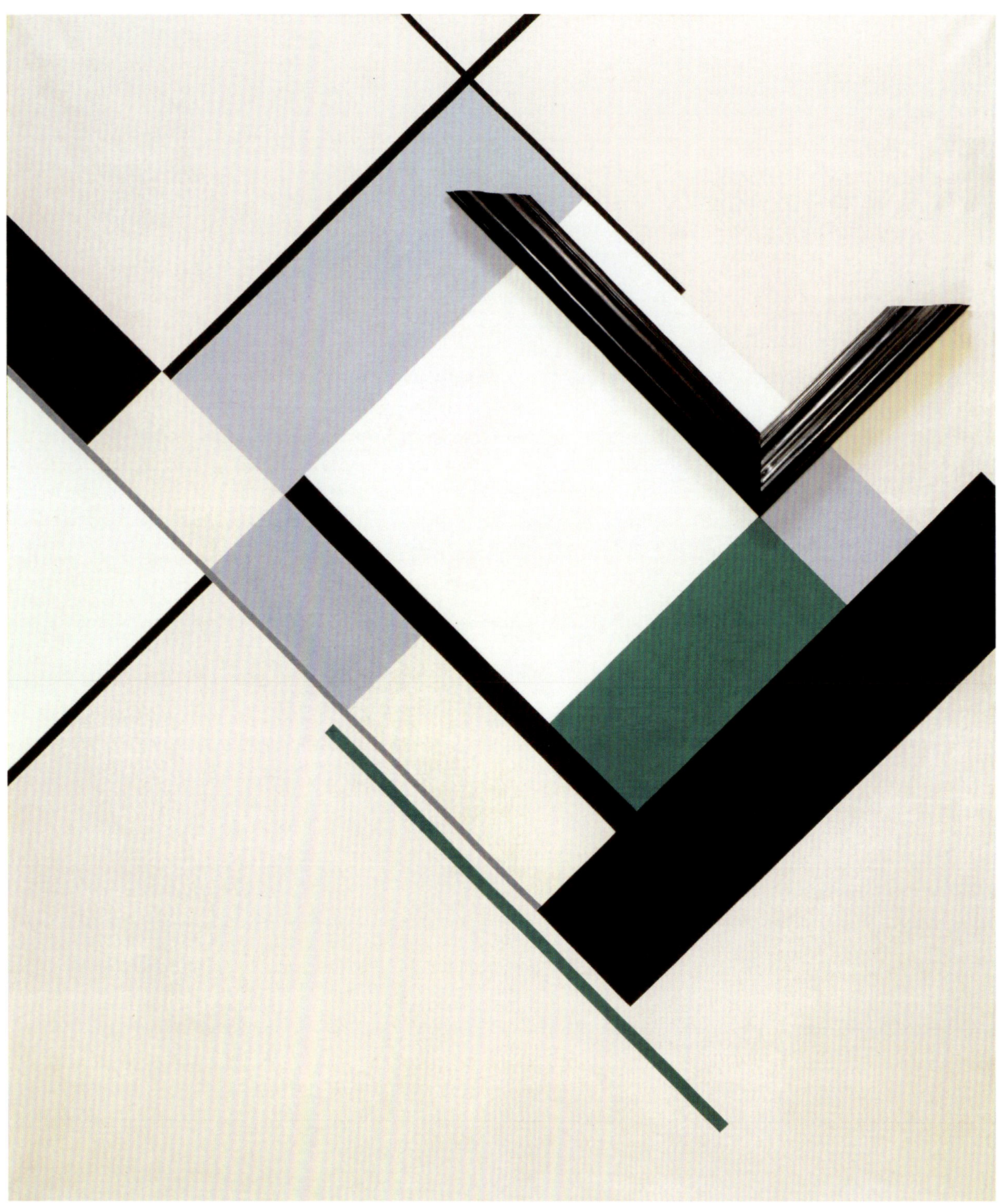

Fig. 2. Friedrich Vordemberge-Gildewart, *Composition No. 23*, 1926. Oil on canvas with wood frame section,
7 ft. 10¾ in. × 6 ft. 6⅜ in. (240.4 × 199 cm). Museum of Modern Art, New York, The Riklis Collection of McCrory
Corporation, 1082.1983

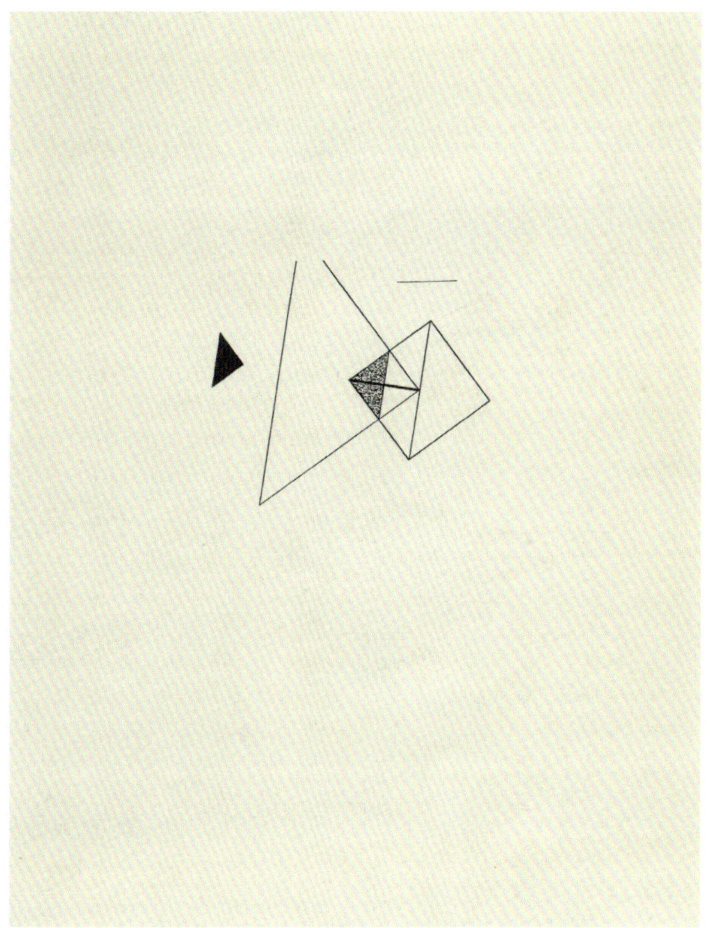

Fig. 3. Friedrich Vordemberge-Gildewart, cover of *millimeter und geraden* (Millimeter and Lines), 1940. Letterpress, 13⅜ × 10¼ in. (34 × 26 cm). Special Collections, Getty Research Institute, Los Angeles, 91-B24434

on the cover (fig. 3) and then again as a drawing inside the booklet, opposite a poem, emphasizing the importance of this interplay of forms for Vordemberge-Gildewart in the early 1940s. It also stresses how the artist experimented with the same forms in different media—drawing and painting—and veered away from the plane of the canvas and strict geometric interactions to playfully investigate color and texture. —FVJ

1. Michael White, *De Stijl and Dutch Modernism* (Manchester and New York: Manchester University Press, 2003), 91–92.

2. Barbara Copeland Buenger, "Max Beckmann in Paris, Amsterdam, and the United States, 1937–50," in *Exiles and Emigrés: The Flight of European Artists from Hitler*, ed. Stephanie Barron, exh. cat. (Los Angeles: Los Angeles County Museum of Art, 1997), 58–67, esp. 61–62.

3. Arta Valstar-Verhoff, "Playful Lightness: Continuity and a New Beginning during Vordemberge-Gildewart's Years in Holland," in Volker Rattemeyer et al., *Friedrich Vordemberge-Gildewart: Retrospektive*, exh. cat. (Wiesbaden, Germany: Museum Wiesbaden and IVAM Centre Julio González, 1996), 129–35, esp. 129, 132.

4. See, for instance, *Composition No. 135* (1942, Yale University Art Gallery, inv. no. 2010.139.1) and *Composition No. 131* (1942, Solomon R. Guggenheim Museum, New York).

5. Dietrich Helms, ed., *Vordemberge-Gildewart: The Complete Works* (Munich: Prestel-Verlag, 1990), 238–39, 292–300.

6. Ibid., 163.

7. Friedrich Vordemberge-Gildewart, *millimeter und geraden* (Amsterdam: N. V. Drukkerij en Uitgeverij J. F. Duwaer & Zonen, 1940), n.p.; Helms, *Vordemberge-Gildewart*, 356, cat. D52.

Provincetown
1942
Ink on paper
14 × 16¹⁵⁄₁₆ in. (35.6 × 43.1 cm)
Provenance: Yale University Art Gallery, New Haven, Conn., Richard Brown Baker, B.A. 1935, Collection, 2008.19.148.

Carafe
1946–54
Oil on panel
16 × 13 in. (40.6 × 33 cm)
Provenance: Given by the artist to Samuel M. Kootz Gallery, New York, 1955; Richard Brown Baker, 1955; Yale University Art Gallery, New Haven, Conn., Richard Brown Baker, B.A. 1935, Collection, 2008.19.22.

The Pond
1958
Oil on canvas
40 × 50 in. (101.6 × 127 cm)
Provenance: Given by the artist to Samuel M. Kootz Gallery, New York, 1959; Richard Brown Baker, 1959; Yale University Art Gallery, New Haven, Conn., Gift of Richard Brown Baker, B.A. 1935, 1995.32.5.

The singular painting and teaching career of Hans Hofmann transcended the divide between Europe and the United States both geographically and aesthetically. As a teacher, Hofmann ran an eponymous school in Munich before moving to the United States—first temporarily in 1932, then permanently with the onset of World War II—where he instructed many important artists of a younger generation in the schools that he eventually opened in New York and Provincetown, Massachusetts. While in the United States, Hofmann cultivated an original mode of painting, one that influenced younger artists as much as his teaching did. At the same time, his work sustained a dialogue with the earlier European styles and aesthetic philosophies with which he had become familiar as a young artist in Germany and in Paris. While the Abstract Expressionists with whom the painter was affiliated tended to distance their work from European Modernism in order to proclaim a new American art, Hofmann remained more openly indebted to artists such as Paul Cézanne, Robert Delaunay, Henri Matisse, and Piet Mondrian.

With its geometricized features, the 1942 drawing of the New England town where Hofmann taught his renowned classes evokes the proto-Cubist landscapes of Pablo Picasso and Georges Braque (fig. 1), as well as the angular forms depicted by Expressionists such as Lyonel Feininger (see cat. 15). Yet *Provincetown* also speaks to the unique inspiration that Hofmann found in American natural environments—first in California, where he taught at the University of California, Berkeley, then on Cape Cod.

Even before creating his most abstract works, Hofmann emphasized the structural role of figurative elements in the picture plane, often creating rhythmic arrays of forms such as those that comprise the *Provincetown* landscape. This tendency is also evident in a later work, *Carafe*; though the painting depicts the kind of vessel Hofmann might have included in the still lifes that he constructed for his students to paint at his Provincetown school, the most striking aspect of the work is the dynamic relationships between warm and cool colors, and between flat zones of paint and graphic lines. The sense of volume of the bulbous pitcher is generated through the "push and pull" of the advancing red, the receding sky blue, and the teal ground plane that seems to hover in the middle ground.[1]

Hofmann closed his Provincetown school in 1958, when he was seventy-eight years old and finally making enough income from his painting to retire from teaching and focus solely on his own artwork. That year, the artist

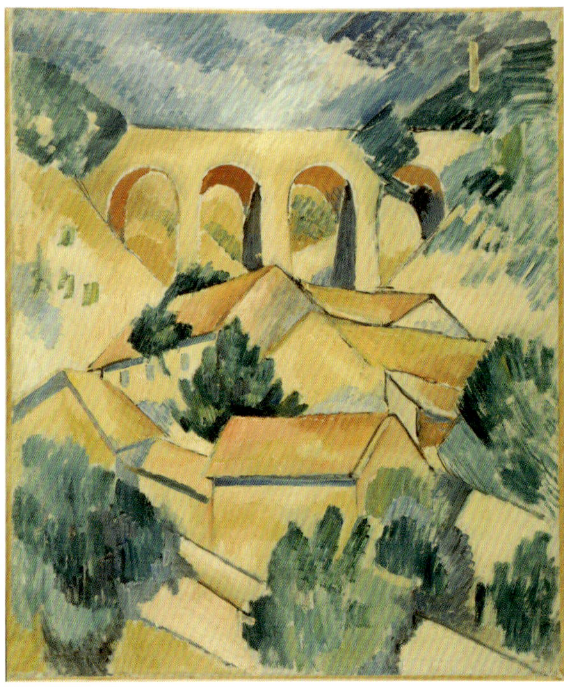

Fig. 1. Georges Braque, *Le viaduc à L'Estaque* (The Viaduct at L'Estaque), 1908. Oil on canvas, 28⁹⁄₁₆ × 23¼ in. (72.5 × 59 cm). Centre Pompidou, Musée National d'Art Moderne, Paris, AM 1984-353

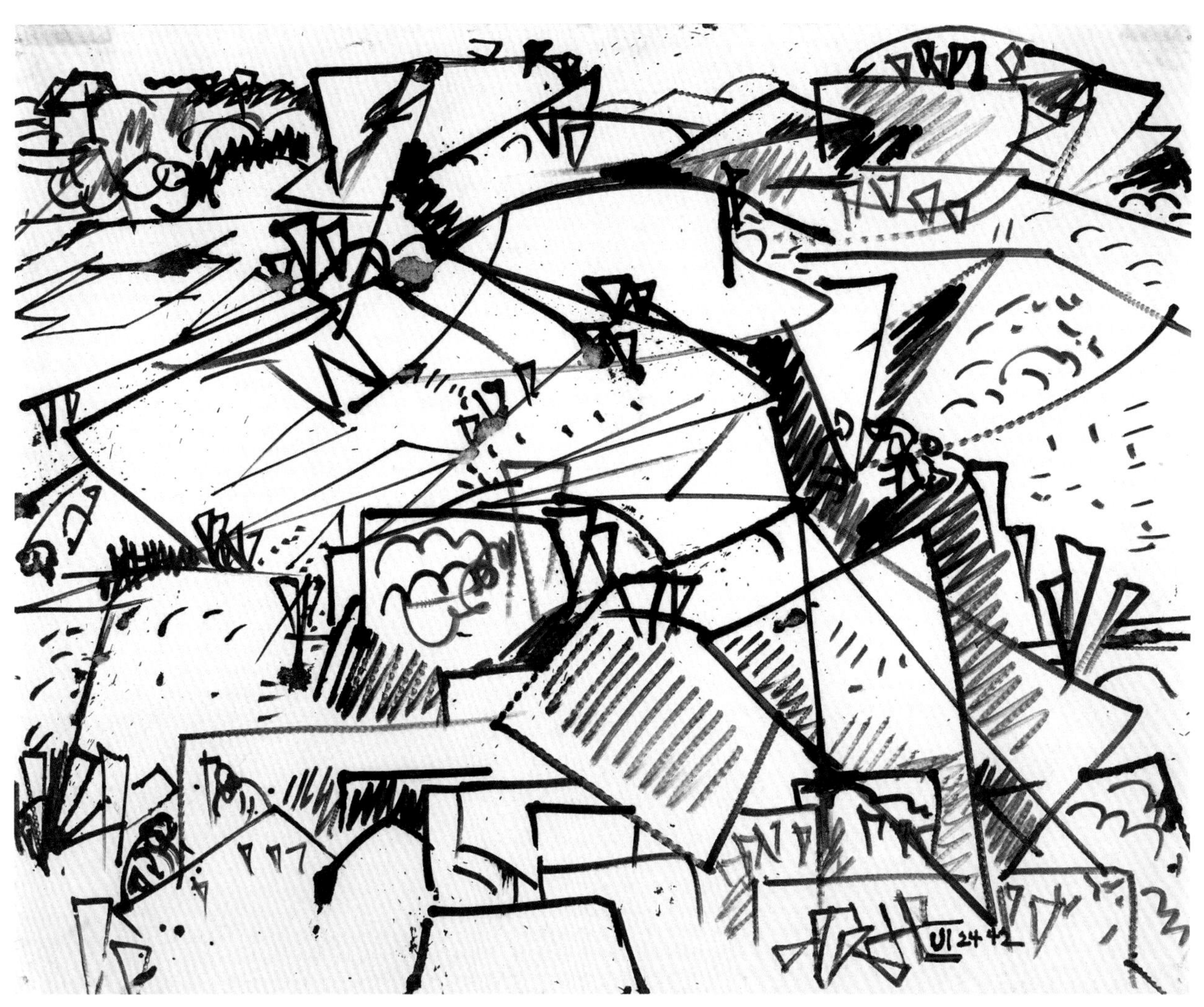

Provincetown

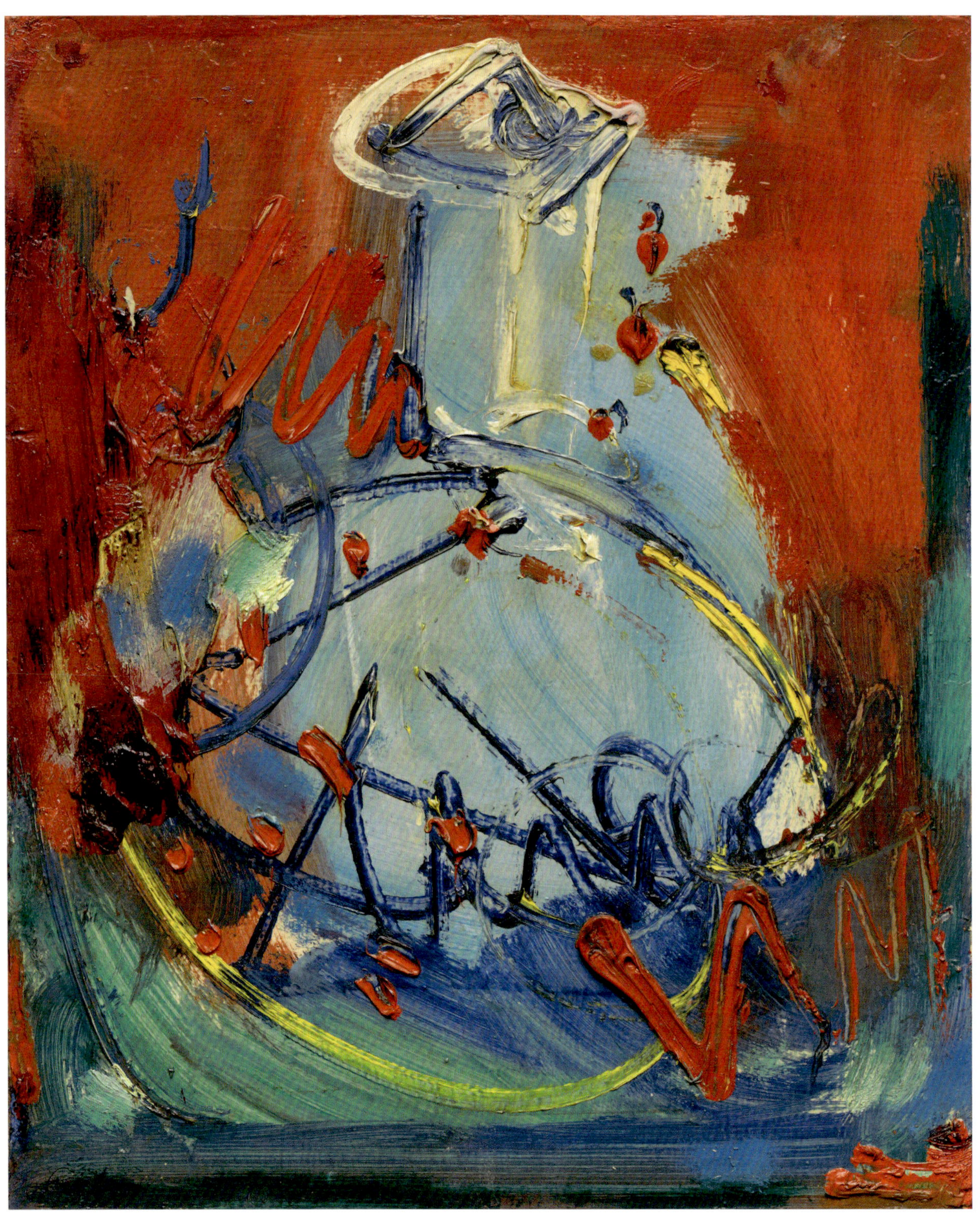

Carafe

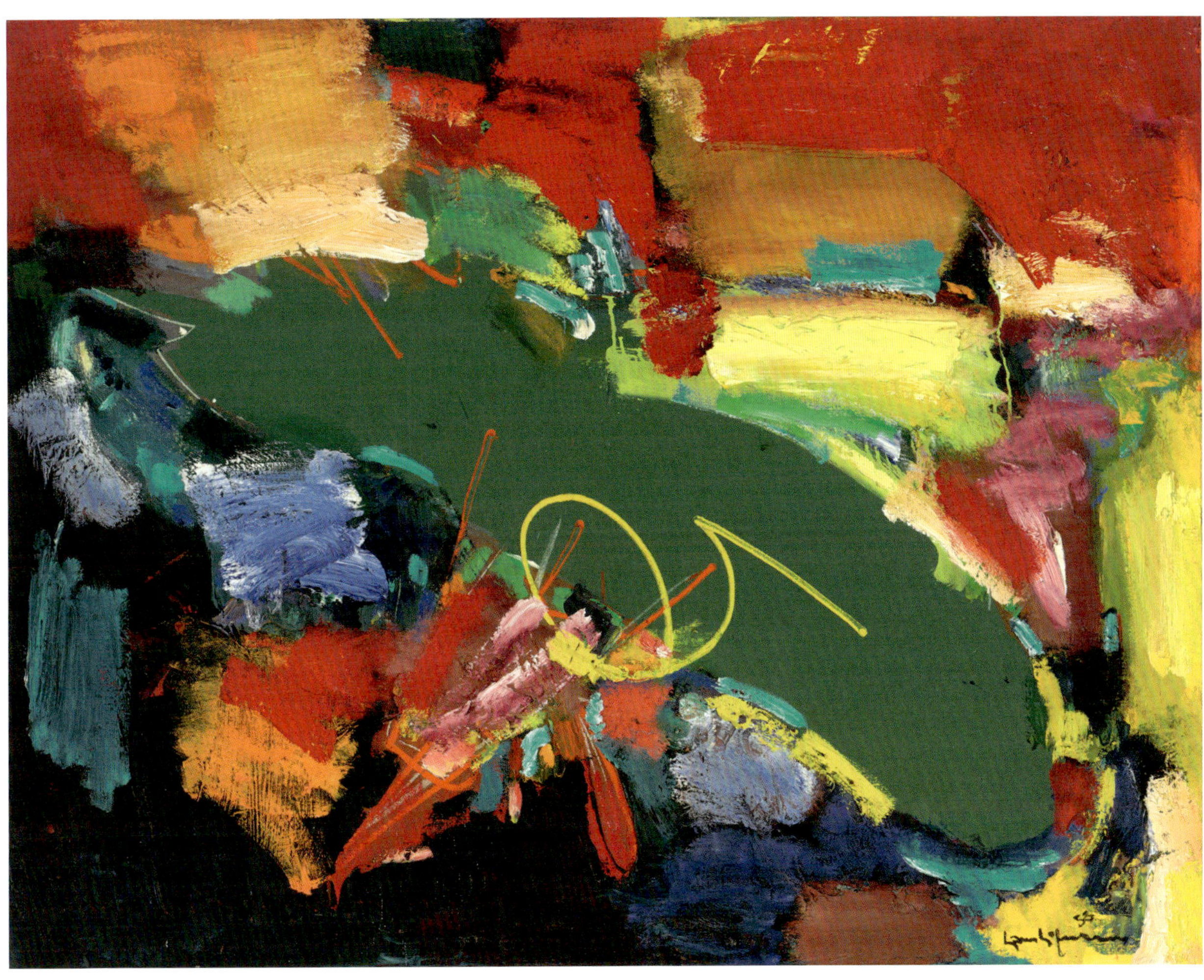

The Pond

165

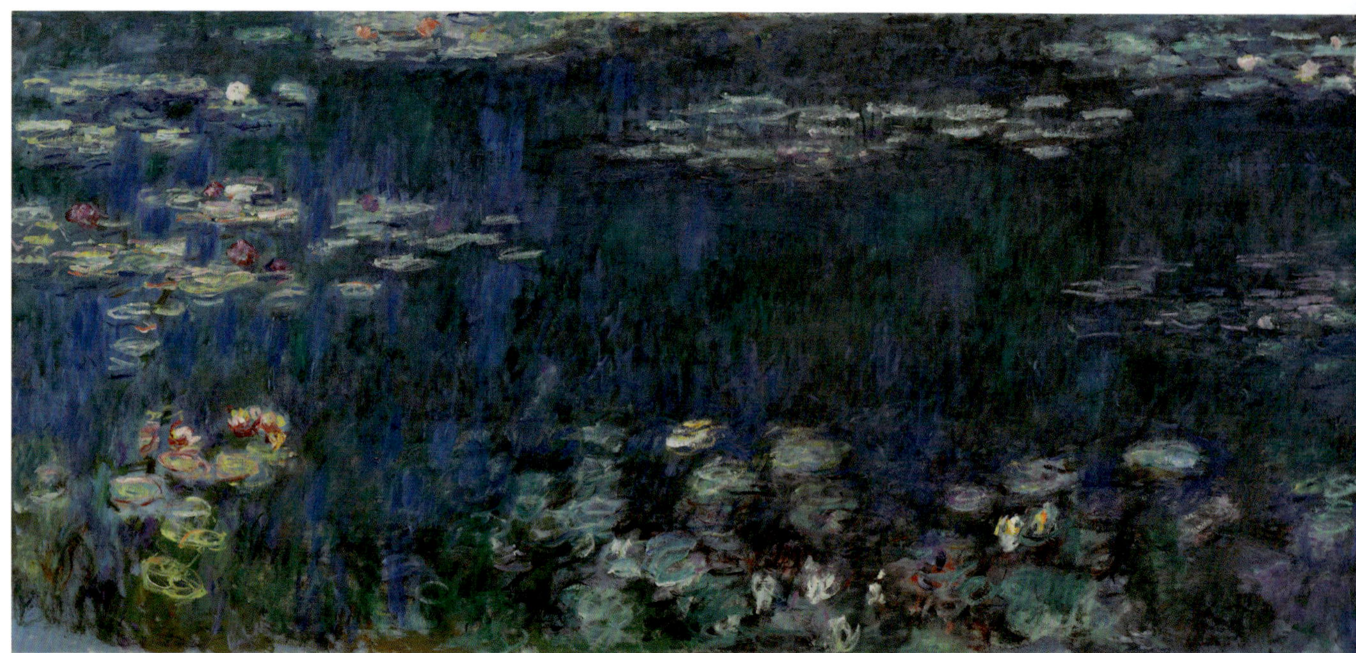

Fig. 2. Claude Monet, *Les Nymphéas: Reflets verts* (The Water Lilies: Green Reflections), ca. 1915–26. Oil on canvas, 6 ft. 6¾ in. × 27 ft. 10⅝ in. (200 × 850 cm). Musée de l'Orangerie, Paris, INV 20102

166

made *The Pond*, which demonstrates his advancement to the abstract, architectonic compositions that characterized the last decade of his career. It also suggests how this advancement was a matter of bringing new innovations to bear on subjects and formal considerations with which he had long been engaged. As Cynthia Goodman explains, despite the veer toward total abstraction by the mid-1950s, "how to capture nature with paint while remaining respectful to the inherent differences between pictorial experiences and those of the natural world endured as one of Hofmann's main preoccupations."[2]

The flat, warm, matte-green pool that dominates the center of the painting conveys the calm stillness of the pond indicated in the title. Here, color comes to fruition as a spatial element, recalling Hofmann's debt to Matisse,

yet also, with the thick physicality of the color application, to Claude Monet's paintings of water lilies on the pond at his home in Giverny (fig. 2)—both references suggested by an ardent supporter of Hofmann, the American critic Clement Greenberg. Yet, as Greenberg argues in relation to other works, the "open, pulsating" surface of Hofmann's painting that results from his "prodding and pushing, scoring and marking, rather than . . . simply inscribing or covering" establishes the painter's affinity with Abstract Expressionists, such as Franz Kline, Willem de Kooning, and Jackson Pollock, many of whom were inspired either directly or indirectly by both Hofmann's instruction and his work.[3] Hofmann's dynamically "breathing" surfaces had a profound influence on the iconically American style these artists would forge.[4] —ND

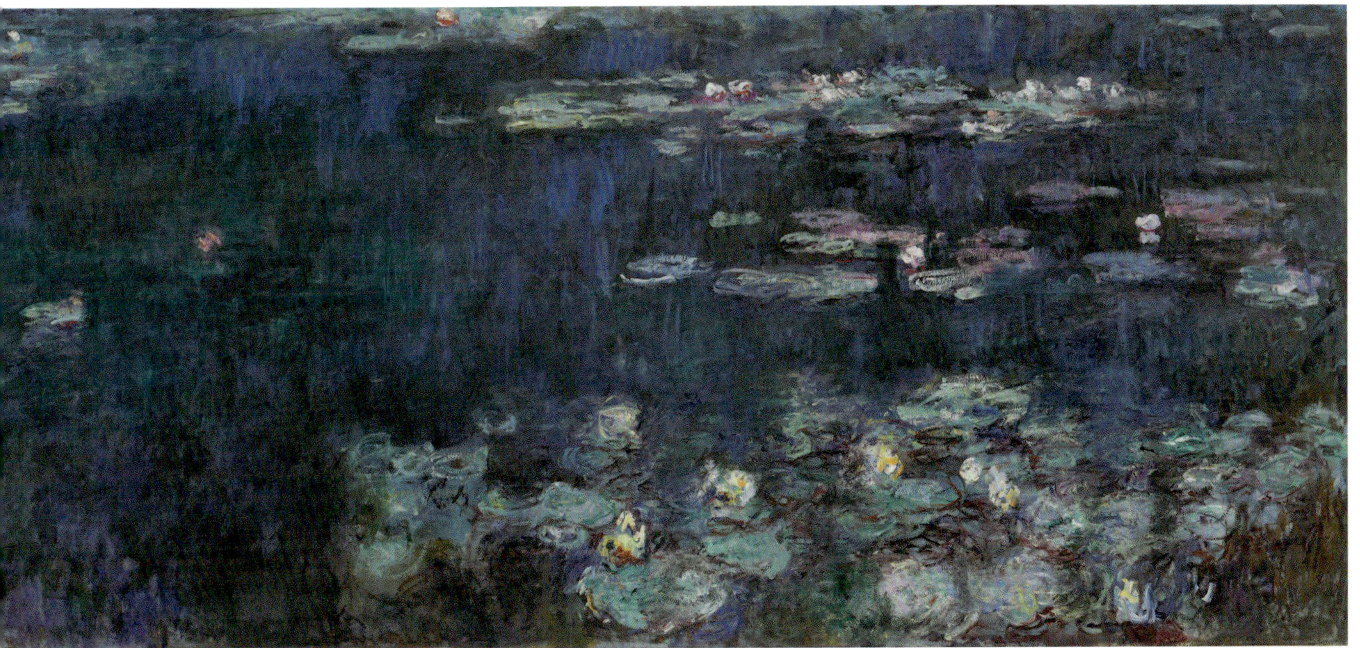

1. Cynthia Goodman, *Hans Hofmann* (New York: Abbeville, 1986), 41. As Goodman explains, "push and pull" was a favorite phrase Hofmann used while teaching to describe the counterbalancing movement required by the introduction of any painterly form in order to achieve compositional balance.

2. Ibid., 80.

3. Clement Greenberg, "Hofmann," in *Art and Culture: Critical Essays* (Boston: Beacon Press, 1965), 193. The painter Lee Krasner, Pollock's wife, was a student of Hofmann's. Pollock in particular is reputed to have been inspired upon seeing the calligraphic drips Hofmann was then deploying on a visit to the elder artist's Provincetown studio in the early 1940s; Goodman, *Hans Hofmann*, 49.

4. Greenberg, "Hofmann," 195.

Untitled
1943–44
Graphite and colored crayon on paper
15⁵⁄₁₆ × 19 in. (39 × 48.3 cm)
Provenance: Thomas T. Solley; Yale University Art Gallery,
New Haven, Conn., Gift of Thomas T. Solley, B.A. 1950,
2002.15.24.

Before he eventually settled in Paris, Matta had initially
trained as an architect in his hometown of Santiago,
Chile. In the French capital he abandoned architecture
for painting and in 1937 joined the Surrealist group led
by André Breton.[1] Two years later, in October 1939, Matta
emigrated from Paris to New York. Although he left before
the Fall of France and Germany's ensuing invasion, the
political climate in Europe had already shifted, with
the German occupation of Poland, and with the United
Kingdom's and France's subsequent declarations of war
against Nazi Germany in September 1939. Matta explained
to American journalists that he had to leave because he had
signed "too many anti-Hitler and anti-Stalin papers not to
be persecuted by the SS."[2]

He remained close to fellow European Surrealists
who were also exiled in New York, and he contributed
illustrations to Breton's 1942 publication *Prolegomena to
a Third Manifesto of Surrealism or Else*.[3] However, little
by little, his substantial differences with the Surrealist
doctrine became more obvious. From the psychological
base of Surrealism, Matta tried to expand his practice to
include themes relating to the physical world. He strived to
create an art that revealed the constantly shifting forms of
human existence and depicted the process of change itself.
As an artist from South America, he was influenced by Latin
American culture, which only increased his outsider status
and set him apart from the circles of European exiles and
North American artists.

In his early years in the United States, Matta
continued in the style he developed while in Europe,
painting biomorphic landscapes—scenes populated with
shapes vaguely resembling amoebas or organisms—such as
*Fabulous Race Track of Death (Instrument Very Dangerous
to the Eye)* (fig. 1). Although the untitled drawing in the Yale
University Art Gallery's collection was executed only a few
years later, it exemplifies the striking way in which Matta's
art evolved in the United States, and how he responded
to the geopolitical climate. As Matta later recalled in an
interview, "My early years in America were ones of hope
in being part of something new. I had hoped to combine
the Surrealism of Europe with the dynamics of America.
But I soon became disillusioned."[4] In this drawing Matta

168

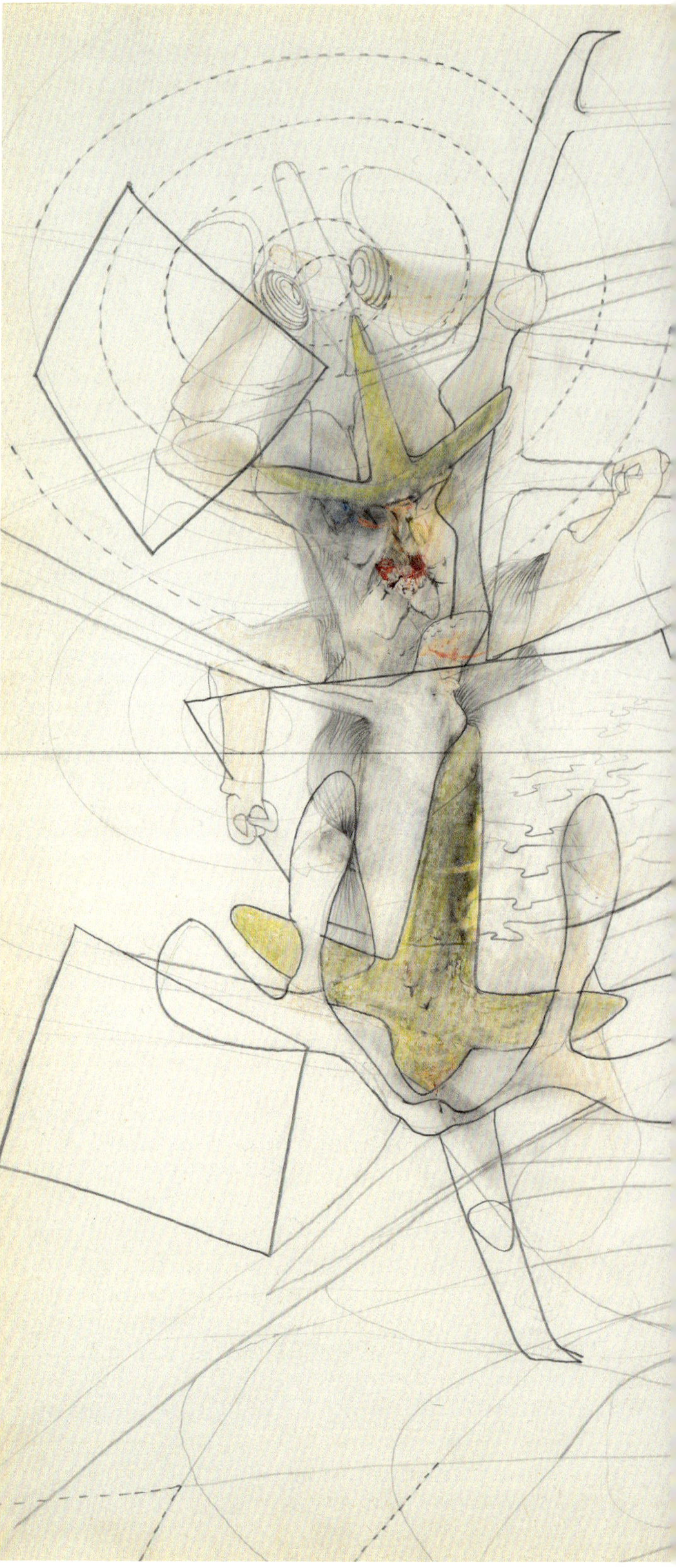

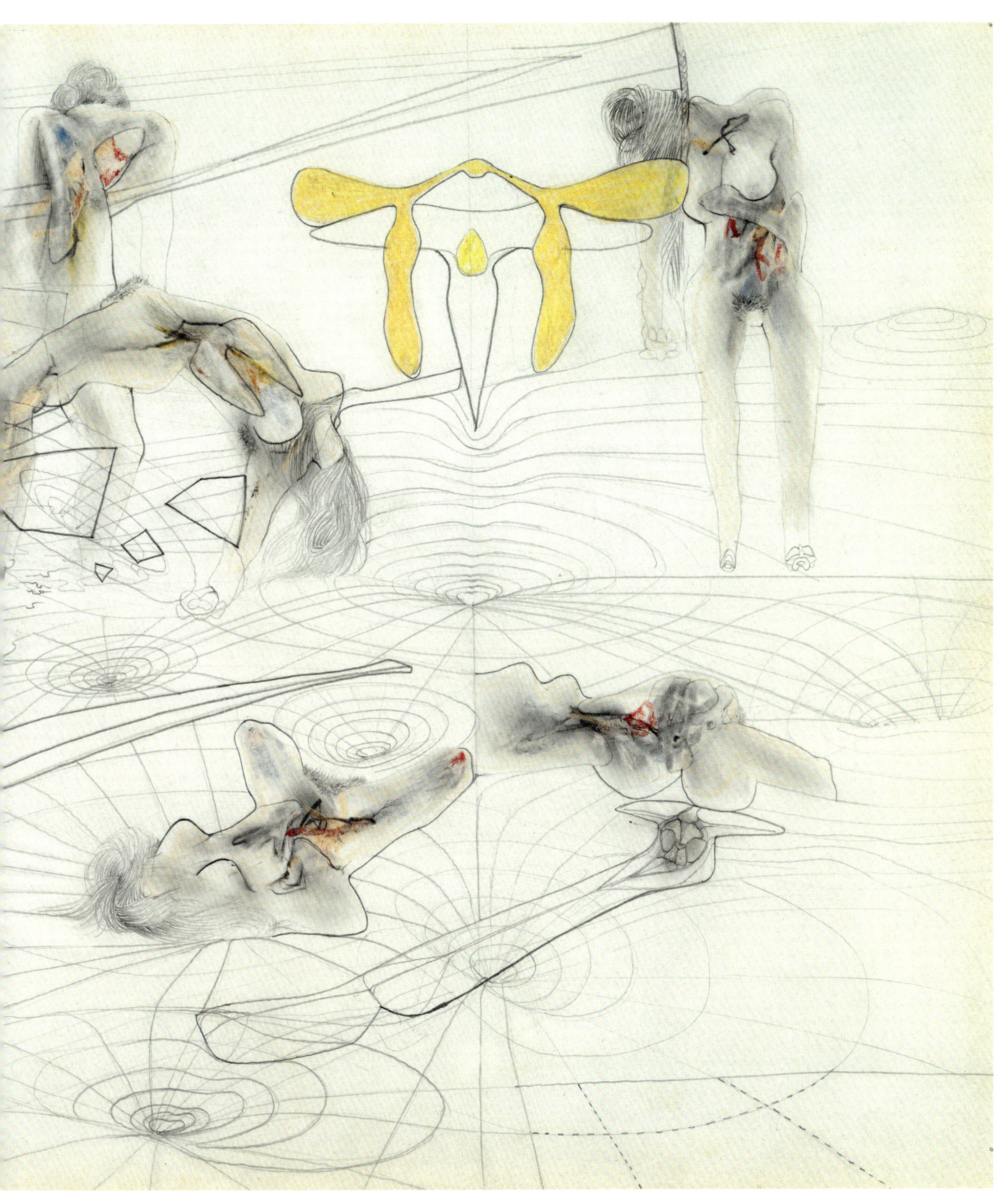

depicts an undefined surface, interrupted by craters and populated by amorphous forms. Matta most certainly used the technique of automatism in the biomorphic figures, relying on spontaneous and uncontrolled lines, guided by his subconscious mind. Although at first glance the shapes seem completely abstract, a closer look reveals female bodies. Some of the forms seem to be melting, while others are easier to identify. In the upper-right corner, a naked woman dangles from a cord, as if hanged. Her body is completely limp, her face covered by her long hair. Other female bodies seem to float in space, speckled with red pencil strokes that evoke blood and insinuate a violent death. The forms in the foreground only represent parts of bodies, as if torn apart, with some darker areas perhaps representing genitalia and the red scribbles resembling open wounds and flesh. On the left side of the composition, the lines seem to form a monstrous insect, with two compound eyes and several legs.

The drawing also testifies to Matta's admiration for Marcel Duchamp. Indeed, Matta developed much of his personal style based on the morphology and spatial techniques of the elder artist's seminal work *The Bride Stripped Bare by Her Bachelors, Even (The Large Glass)* (see cat. 3, fig. 3).[5] The cracks in the glass of Duchamp's work, caused by accident but embraced by the French artist as part of the work, were often imitated by Matta in his own works.[6] The 1942 *First Papers of Surrealism* show in New York, the first major Surrealist exhibition in the United States, included a weblike twine installation conceived by Duchamp (fig. 2) that disrupted the space of the gallery with hundreds of lines going in different directions. Intertwined lines, forming a net, also appear in Matta's drawing, dividing the space and connecting the various forms. At the same time, the concentric circles with intersecting lines converging in the middle refer to black holes and, more specifically,

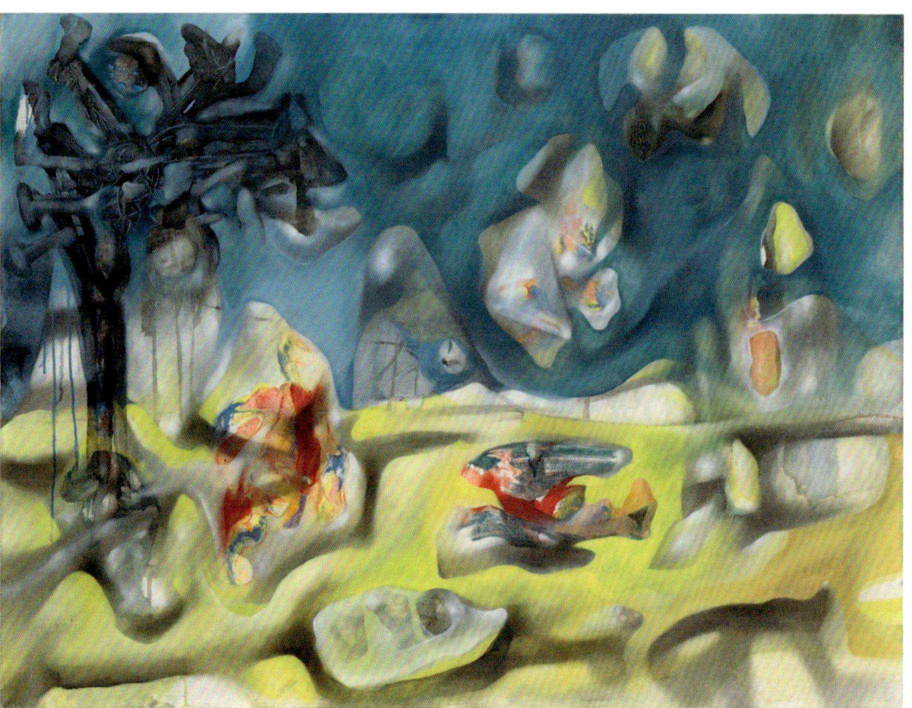

Fig. 1. Matta, *Fabulous Race Track of Death (Instrument Very Dangerous to the Eye)*, ca. 1941. Oil on canvas, 28 × 36 in. (71.1 × 91.4 cm). Yale University Art Gallery, New Haven, Conn., Gift of Collection Société Anonyme, 1941.559

to diagrams of the Schwarzschild radius (the radius of the spherical boundary within which a mass, such as a star, must collapse to become a black hole).[7] This drawing is an example of a new, semiabstract Surrealism that Matta developed as he became increasingly disillusioned by events in the world and in his own life; however, based on scientific theories about space-time and layers of reality, his vision points toward the future. —FVJ

1. Dominique Bozo, ed., *Matta*, exh. cat. (Paris: Éditions du Centre Pompidou, 1985), 266–67.

2. Sabine Eckmann, "Roberto Sebastián Matta Echaurren in New York, 1939–45," in *Exiles and Emigrés: The Flight of European Artists from Hitler*, ed. Stephanie Barron, exh. cat. (Los Angeles: Los Angeles County Museum of Art, 1997), 176–82, esp. 176, 182n2; and Sidney Simon, "An Interview with Peter Busa and Matta," *Art International* 12 (Summer 1967): 17–20.

3. Bozo, *Matta*, 273.

4. Nancy Miller, "Interview with Matta," in *Matta: The First Decade* (Waltham, Mass.: Rose Art Museum, Brandeis University, 1982), 14.

5. Robert L. Herbert, Eleanor S. Apter, and Elise K. Kenney, *The Société Anonyme and the Dreier Bequest at Yale University: A Catalogue Raisonné* (New Haven, Conn.: Yale University Art Gallery, 1984), 446–47, cat. 455.

6. Elizabeth A. T. Smith and Colette Dartnall, "'Crushed Jewels, Air, Even Laughter': Matta in the 1940s," in *Matta in America: Paintings and Drawings of the 1940s*, exh. cat. (Chicago: Museum of Contemporary Art, Chicago, 2001), 22–23.

7. *Merriam-Webster Online*, s.v. "Schwarzschild radius," accessed January 12, 2017, https://www.merriam-webster.com/dictionary/Schwarzschild radius; Fabrice Flahutez, *Nouveau monde et nouveau mythe: Mutations du surréalisme, de l'exil américain à l' "Écart absolu" (1941–1965)* (Dijon, France: Les presses du réel, 2007), 166–70.

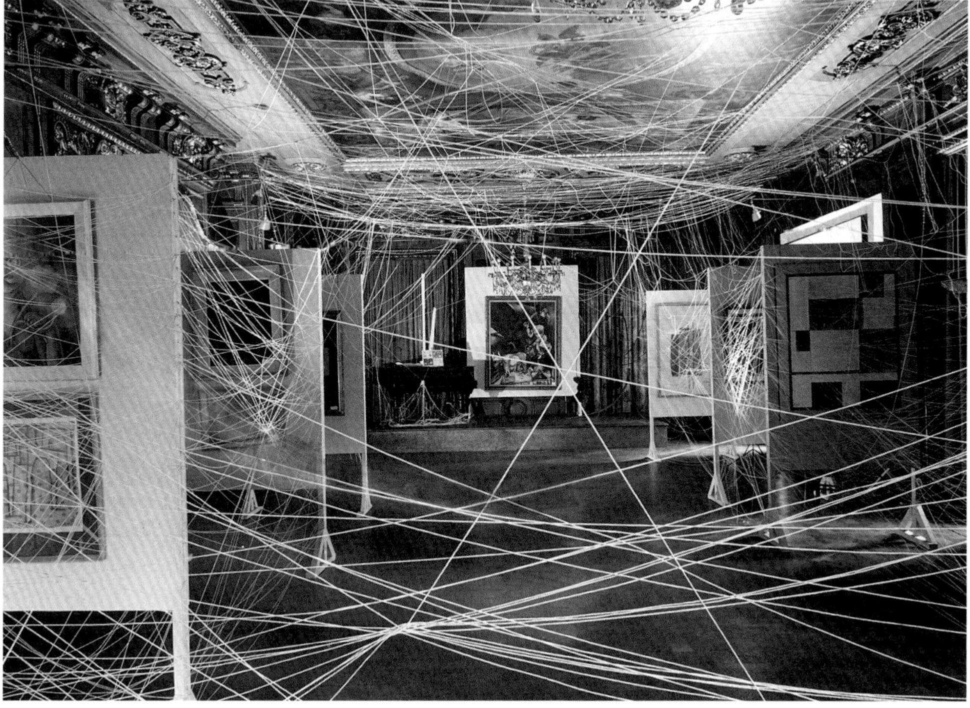

Fig. 2. John D. Schiff, view of the *First Papers of Surrealism* exhibition, showing Marcel Duchamp's twine installation, 1942. Gelatin silver print, 7⅝ × 10 in. (19.4 × 25.4 cm). Philadelphia Museum of Art, Gift of Jacqueline, Paul, and Peter Matisse in memory of their mother, Alexina Duchamp

6 prints from the portfolio *The Myth of Oedipus*
    The Childhood of Oedipus
    The Slaying of Laius
    The Sphinx
    The Riddle
    The Marriage
    Oedipus at Colonus
1944
Etchings
Ranging from 17⅝ × 11¹¹⁄₁₆ in. (44.7 × 29.7 cm) to 17¹³⁄₁₆ × 11¹³⁄₁₆ in. (45.3 × 30 cm)
Provenance: Mr. and Mrs. R. Kirk Askew, Jr.; Yale University Art Gallery, New Haven, Conn., Gift of Mr. and Mrs. R. Kirk Askew, Jr., 1970.32a–f.

The Swiss-born artist Kurt Seligmann came to New York from Paris in 1939 and was one of the first Surrealist artists to immigrate to the United States. Though his departure was prompted by the German invasion of Poland and the outbreak of World War II, he had been planning to leave Europe for a while, and he had already shipped some of his works to America. Shortly after Seligmann's arrival, the art dealer Karl Nierendorf organized the exhibition *Specters 1939 A.D.—13 Variations on a Macabre Theme* at his New York gallery to introduce the artist's Surrealist works to an American audience.[1] The artist conveyed in his works the violent political climate through complex imagery that alluded to medieval sorcery and alchemy, classical myths, and European history (fig. 1). Seligmann explained that "around 1937, . . . [my] paintings became crowded with agitated distorted human forms, expressing probably the general political and social unrest."[2]

    In the United States, Seligmann learned how to print his own works and set up a printing press in his studio.[3] He met the American art historian Meyer Schapiro, who taught at Columbia University and shared his interest in magic and the occult. In 1944 the two men collaborated on *The Myth of Oedipus*, a print portfolio that became an early example of Surrealist illustration in the United States.[4] This publication was also one of the first *livres de peintre* (a type of book in which text and image are equally prominent) to be produced in America.[5] It narrates a saga from Greek mythology: the life of Oedipus. In the myth, Oedipus's father, Laius, the King of Thebes, had been warned by an oracle that his son would slay him, and after the boy's birth, Laius and his wife, Jocasta, left him in the mountains to die. A shepherd took the child in, and Oedipus was subsequently adopted by the king of Corinth and his wife and raised as their son (shown in *The Childhood of Oedipus*). Years later, as a young man, Oedipus visited the oracle in Delphi and learned that he was to kill his father and marry his mother. He resolved not to return to Corinth, fearing for the safety of his supposed parents, and he traveled to Thebes instead. On the way, he encountered his real father, Laius, and killed him in a quarrel (*The Slaying of Laius*). He then found the city of Thebes plagued by the Sphinx, who asked every traveler a riddle and killed those who could not answer it (*The Sphinx*). Oedipus solved the riddle (*The Riddle*), causing the Sphinx to kill herself in dismay, and as a reward for this feat, Oedipus received the throne of Thebes and the recently widowed Jocasta's hand in marriage (*The Marriage*). Once the truth about Oedipus's parentage became known, Jocasta committed suicide, and the stricken Oedipus went into exile in Colonus, near Athens, where—according to some versions of the tale—he was swallowed into the earth (*Oedipus at Colonus*).

    Seligmann kept only the very essence of this classical myth, representing the main protagonists in an indefinite, abstract space. The figures are depicted as almost fluid, organic forms, with their corporeal features disguised under robes and bands, barely visible, and their faces covered by veils. Some of the figures, such as the Sphinx and Laius, seem to dissolve into the ground beneath them. The agitated shapes are inspired by the "wrapped and cyclonic landscapes" that the artist started

172

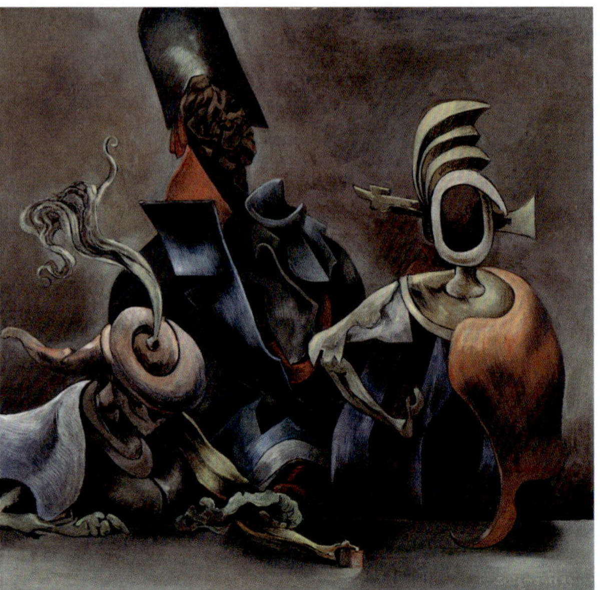

Fig. 1. Kurt Seligmann, *Game of Chance*, 1949. Oil on canvas, 22 × 22 in. (55.9 × 55.9 cm). Yale University Art Gallery, New Haven, Conn., Gift of Thomas F. Howard, 1959.34.2

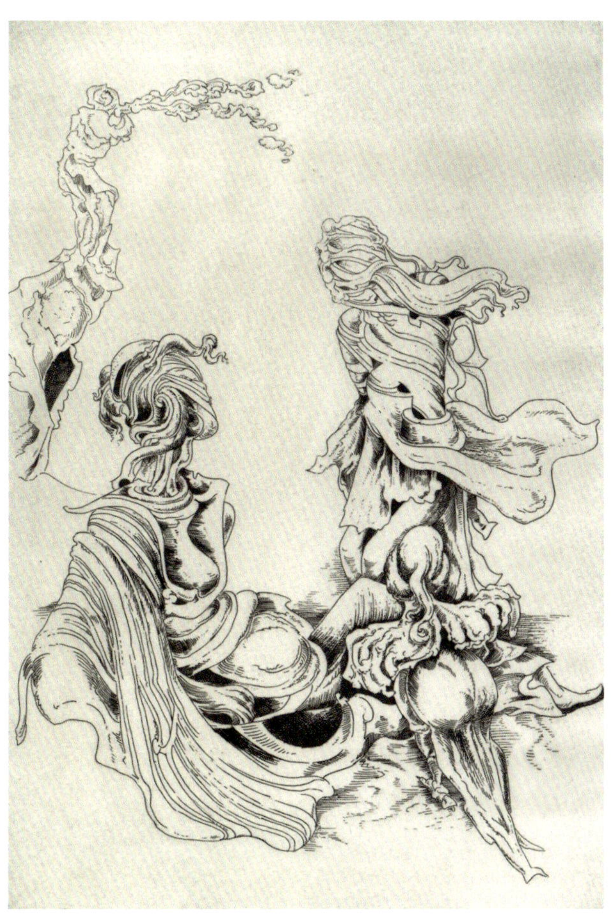

The Childhood of Oedipus

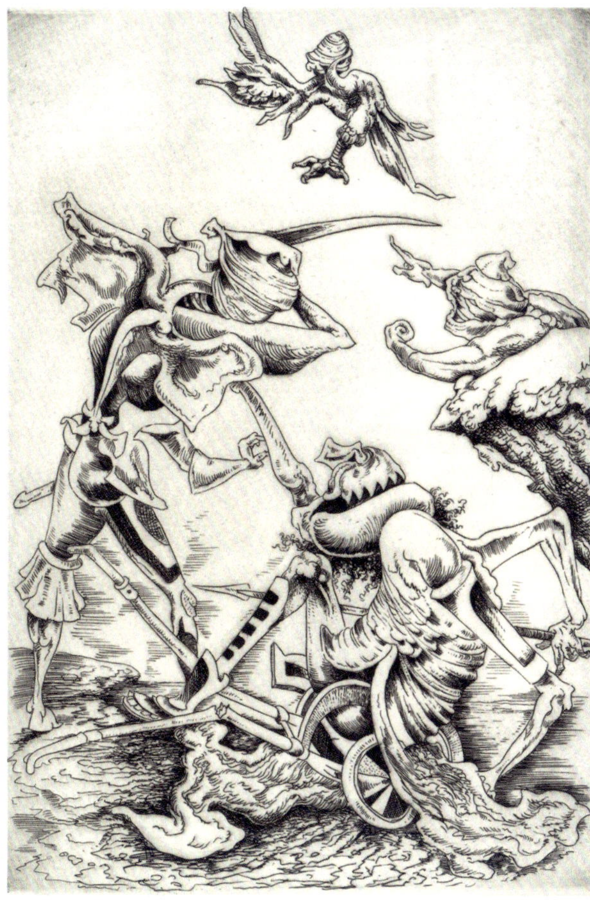

The Slaying of Laius

173

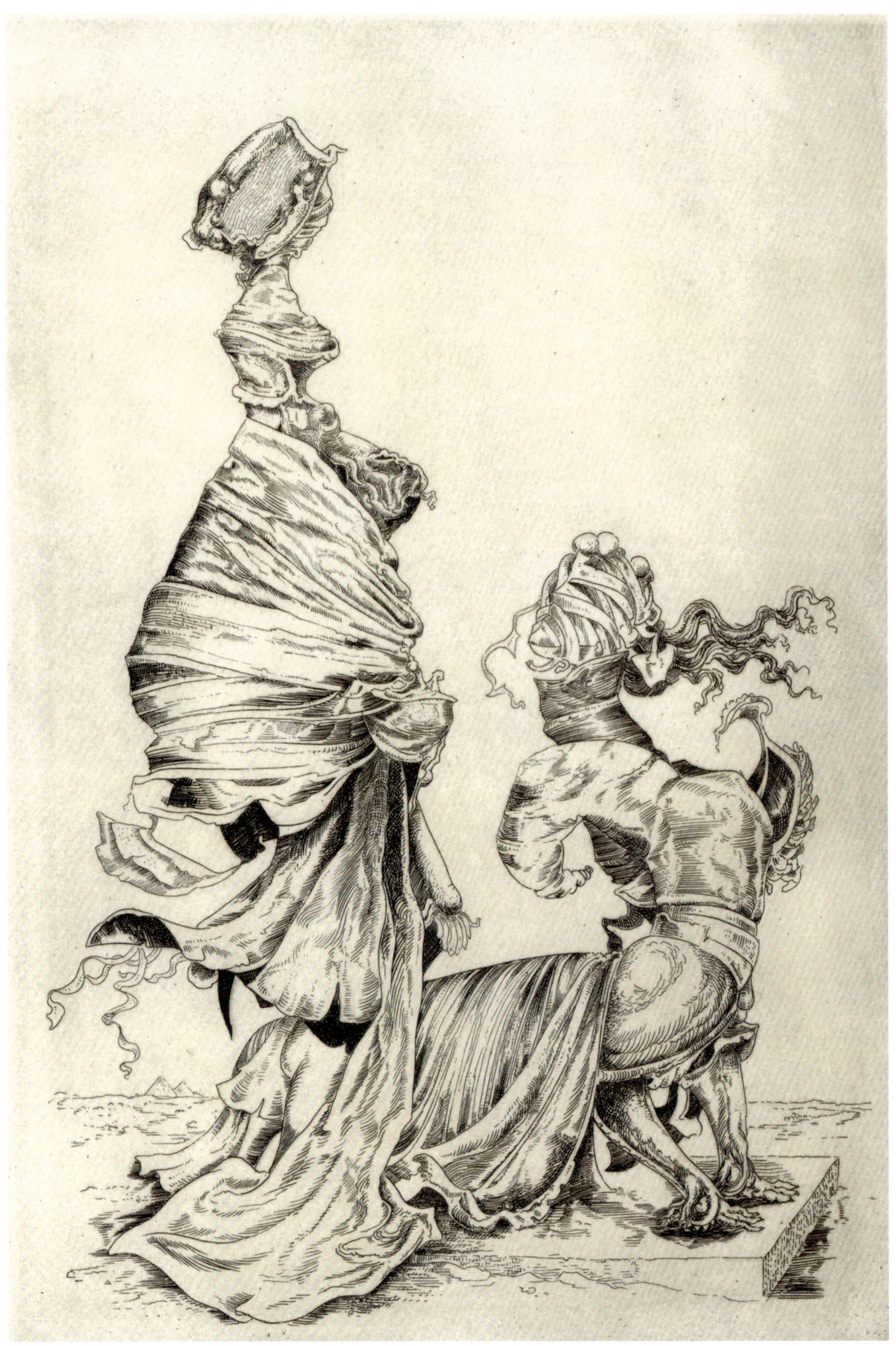

The Sphinx

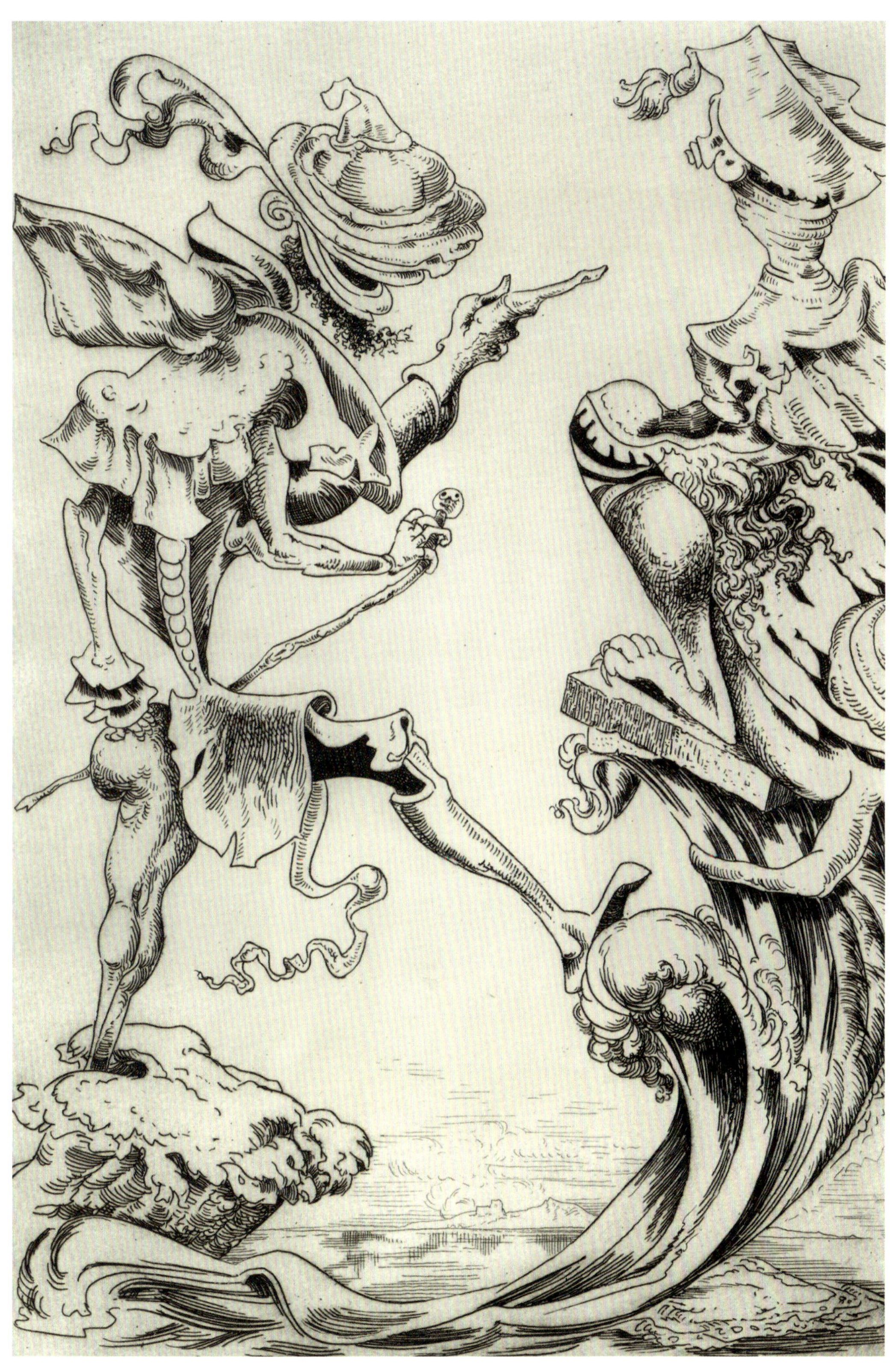

The Riddle

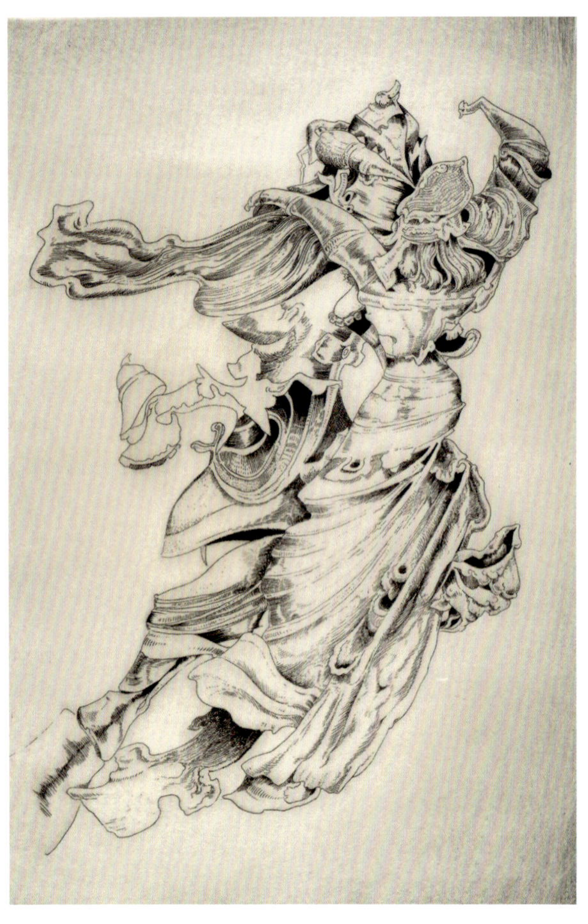

The Marriage

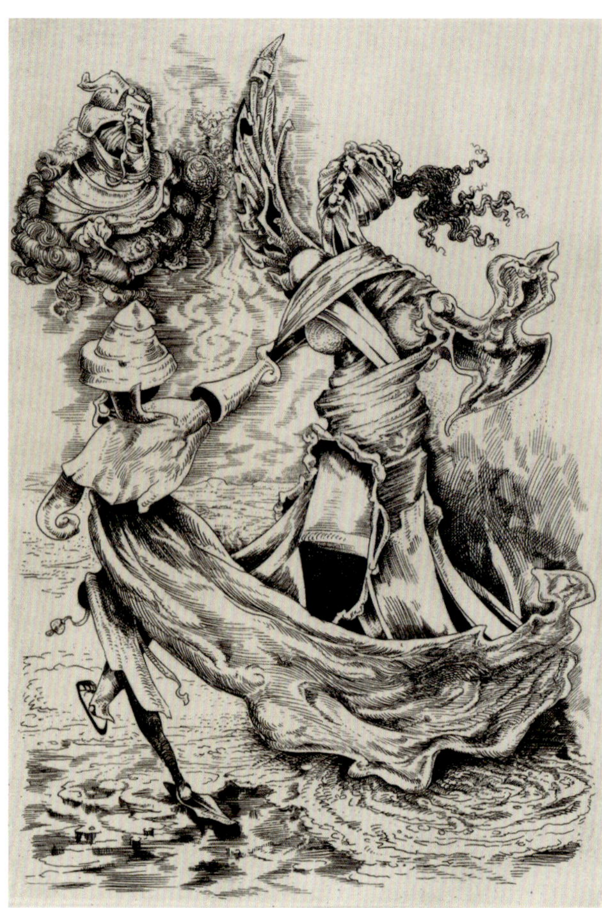

Oedipus at Colonus

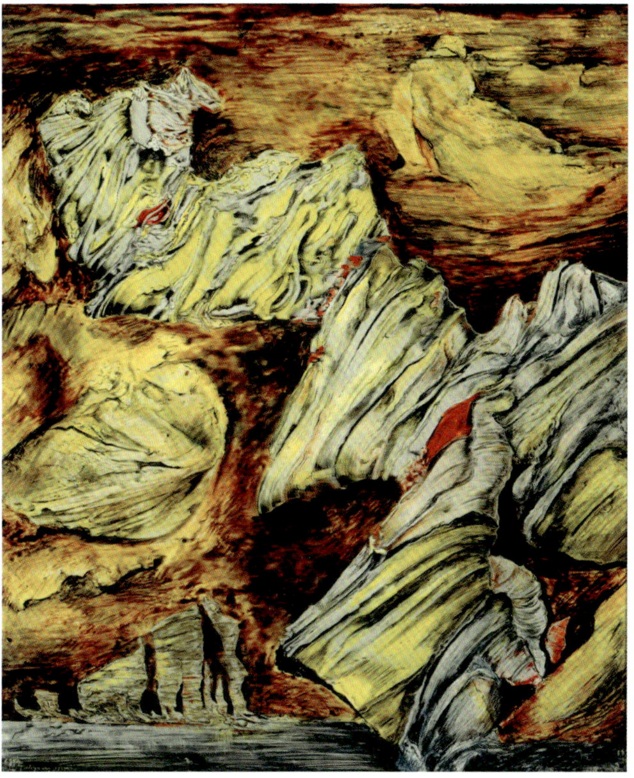

Fig. 2. Kurt Seligmann, *The Environs of the Château d'Argol*,
1943 (restored by the artist 1953). Oil on glass, 33½ × 27½ in.
(85.1 × 69.9 cm). Art Institute of Chicago, Mary and Earle Ludgin
Collection, 1981.265

to produce in the early 1940s, dominated by tornado-like forms (fig. 2).[6] These shapes were created through a semi-automatist process of manipulating the surface of glass until it cracked or formed small craters, and then using a projector to trace the cracks and fissures onto paper.[7] By pairing the element of chance in his artistic process with depictions of Oedipus's certain fate, Seligmann evokes the tension between the conscious and the subconscious mind, as well as the inescapable consequences of human behavior. His choice of subject, the tale of a famous exile, was certainly no coincidence, and the artist might have personally identified with the protagonist, forced to leave his home and wander a new realm. This tale also allowed Seligmann to merge his figurative work with his newly developed technique of working with glass, creating images that are grounded in Surrealist principles but also embrace new technical experiments. —FVJ

1. Stephan E. Hauser, *Kurt Seligmann 1900–1962: Leben und Werk* (Basel, Switzerland: Schwabe and Co., 1997), 164, 166.

2. Addison Gallery of American Art, *European Artists Teaching in America*, exh. brochure (Andover, Mass.: Addison Gallery of American Art, 1941), 45–47, esp. 47.

3. Martica Sawin, *Surrealism in Exile and the Beginning of the New York School* (Cambridge, Mass.: MIT Press, 1995), 178–80.

4. Published with Durlacher Bros. Gallery, New York, with a renarration of the Oedipus myth by Meyer Schapiro and six illustrations by the artist, in a boxed, numbered set of approximately fifty copies. Philip Hofer and Eleanor M. Garvey, *The Artist and the Book, 1860–1960, in Western Europe and the United States*, exh. cat. (Boston: Museum of Fine Arts, 1972), 192, cat. 283.

5. Hauser, *Kurt Seligmann*, 250.

6. Addison Gallery of American Art, *European Artists Teaching in America*, 47; Sawin, *Surrealism in Exile*, 181.

7. Ibid.; Hauser, *Kurt Seligmann*, 189–91.

Untitled (Knife and Rolling Pin)
1965
Mixed media on board
15¾ × 11¾ × 1⅛ in. (40 × 29.9 × 2.9 cm)
Provenance: Charles B. Benenson, B.A. 1933;
Yale University Art Gallery, New Haven, Conn., Charles B.
Benenson, B.A. 1933, Collection, 2006.52.77.

Jiří Kolář was a prominent poet, visual artist, and translator whose avant-garde artistic practice and radical political stance made him a dissident under the Stalinist Czechoslovakian government that assumed power in 1948. Though he began his artistic career writing poetry, in the late 1950s and early 1960s Kolář moved his practice into the realm of the visual; he innovated many different forms of collage by recombining magazine images, newspapers, mundane objects, and reproductions of works of art in new ways. By dissolving the relationships between word and image that structure conventional language and representation, his works resisted the bureaucratic apparatus of state socialism that relied on propagandistic communication with the masses, as is evident in the academic and Socialist Realist artwork favored by the communist regime of Czechoslovakia.

Kolář made *Untitled (Knife and Rolling Pin)* while in a state of exile within his own country—he had been imprisoned for several months a decade earlier for writing poetry deemed critical of state communism, leading the Communist Party of Czechoslovakia to issue a ban on publishing his work. Kolář had begun to lose faith in the expressive capacity of the word and to escalate his concrete approach to language and materials in the aftermath of World War II, with the mass destruction of cities and villages and the revelation of the horrors of the concentration camps. In an interview, he cited Claude Lévi-Strauss's assertion in his 1955 memoir *Tristes Tropiques* that the appearance of writing in a society is always accompanied by the enslavement of human beings.[1] He also described being compelled toward assemblage by a visit to the Auschwitz-Birkenau Museum, where the displayed piles of remaining personal effects from Holocaust victims overwhelmed him.[2] Yet it was his 1953 detention that ultimately pushed Kolář's deconstruction of language and signs into the realm of visual art. As he wrote, alluding to the experience, "When a person encounters something decisive in his life he usually has to communicate quite differently than with more words. He reacts with silence, wordlessly, with a gesture."[3]

Untitled (Knife and Rolling Pin) is an example of what the artist called *chiasmages*, one of the many neologisms denominating the collage techniques that he developed after his books were no longer being published (others include *confrantages*, *rollages*, and *crumplages*). Chiasmages are composed of evenly sized units of printed matter arranged in an orderly fashion to create an overall compositional field.[4] These compositions often include three-dimensional objects camouflaged by an overlay of the same collage treatment as the two-dimensional surfaces onto which they are affixed (fig. 1).[5] The use of magazine fragments suggests an estrangement of language from its expressive function. The way in which the three-dimensional objects are visually diminished by the cacophony of text that overruns them further unsettles the normative operation of language, suspending any preconceived relationships between object and signifier, as evident in this work.

In *Untitled (Knife and Rolling Pin)*, objects fuse with text in a surprising combination of bold, modern, dynamically oriented typography and humble kitchen utensils. The collage has stripped the fragmented and brightly colored words of their meaning, reducing them to a graphic image. Moreover, the vertical orientation of the utensils accentuates their loose affinity with male and female forms, evoking the Surrealist embrace of ambiguous anthropomorphism by artists such as Alberto Giacometti, and adding to the multifarious layers of meaning in the work. By dissolving the original identities of its components through playful juxtaposition and suspending them in a new, suggestive configuration, *Untitled (Knife and Rolling Pin)* achieves a dual purpose: it demonstrates how Kolář used visual art to trouble the efficacy of language and communicative media for authoritarian metanarratives, and, at the same time, it reenchants the materials of everyday life as a means of opposing the forces that constrain and standardize expression. This work strives for sensory plenitude that can express the full extent of human "suffering, humiliation, and the desire to live," as necessitated by Kolář's historical moment and personal experiences.[6] —ND

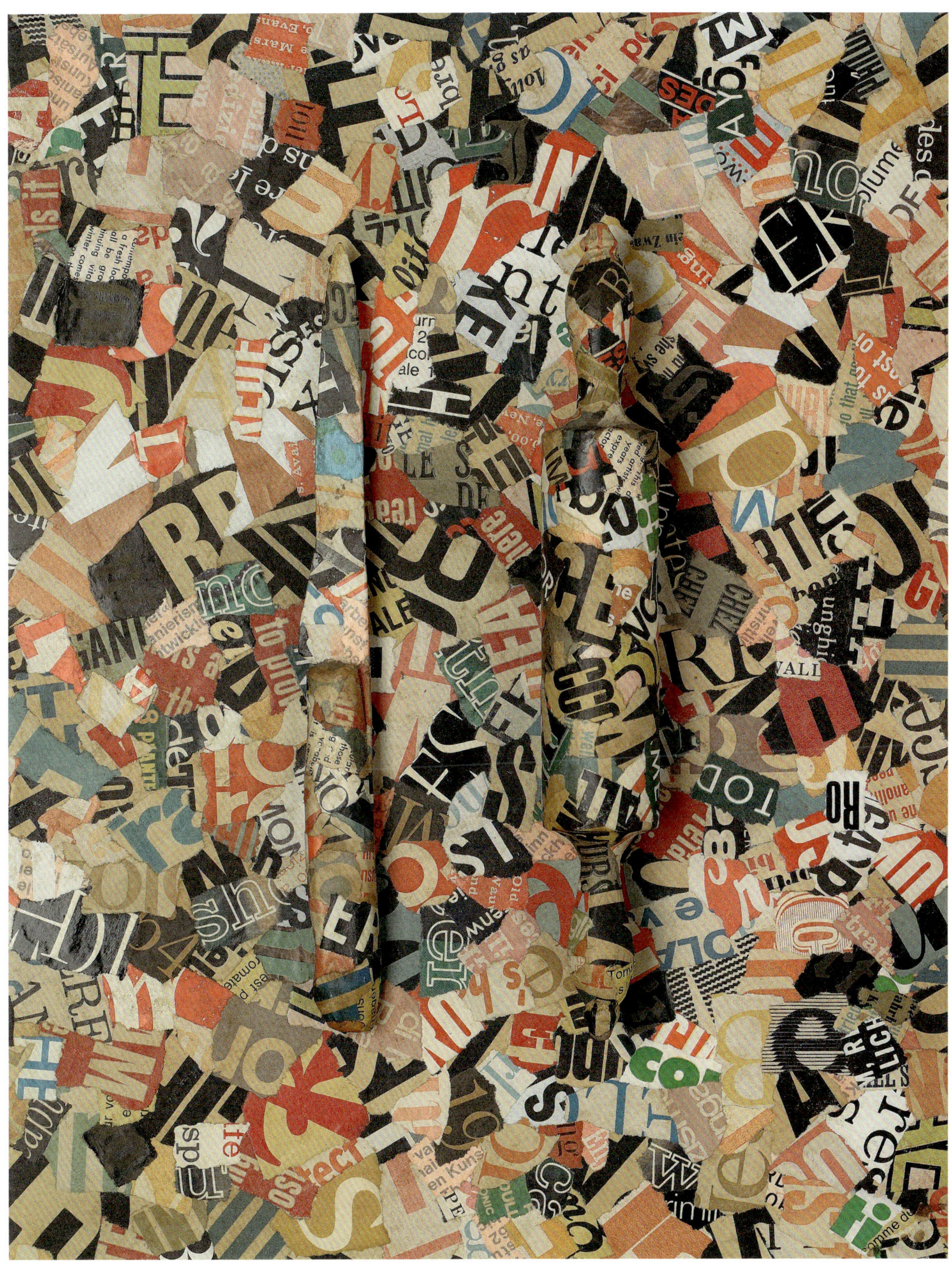

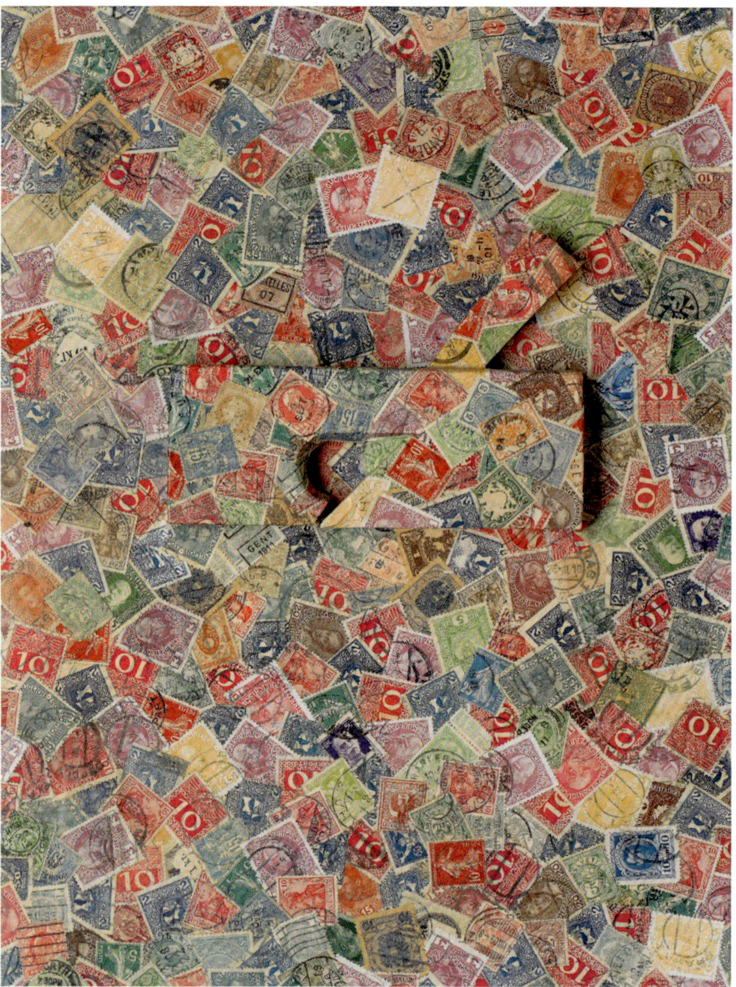

Fig. 1. Jiří Kolář, *Untitled (Stamps)*, 1965. Mixed media on board, 15^{15}/$_{16}$ ×
11¾ × 1³/₁₆ in. (40.5 × 29.9 × 3 cm). Yale University Art Gallery, New Haven,
Conn., Charles B. Benenson, B.A. 1933, Collection, 2006.52.76

1. Francesca Pola, *Jiří Kolář*, exh. cat. (Prato, Italy: Museo di Pittura Murale, 2015), 80.

2. Ibid., 50.

3. Jiří Kolář, unpublished manuscript, n.d., trans. Paul Wilson, 23; quoted in Charlotta Kotik, *Jiří Kolář: Transformations*, exh. cat. (Buffalo: Albright-Knox Gallery, 1978), 10.

4. In his essay in the catalogue from Kolář's 1975 Guggenheim retrospective, Thomas Messer lists the following as sources for the artist's chiasmages: "old handwriting, letters, dictionaries, woodcut illustrations, writing samples in Arabic, Hebrew, Chinese, Persian, Latin, Gothic, Cyrillic, and Greek, as well as maps, music scores, chessboard charts, and magazine photos." Thomas M. Messer, *Jiří Kolář*, exh. cat. (New York: Solomon R. Guggenheim Museum, 1975), 14.

5. See Cathleen Chaffee, "Jiří Kolář," in *Eye on a Century: Modern and Contemporary Art from the Charles B. Benenson Collection at the Yale University Art Gallery*, ed. Cathleen Chaffee (New Haven, Conn.: Yale University Art Gallery, 2012), 92–95, cats. 39–40. Kolář first covered low reliefs in printed matter in his chiasmages in 1964, and created freestanding chiasmages in the late 1960s; Kotik, *Jiří Kolář*, 16.

6. Kolář, quoted in Pola, *Jiří Kolář*, 76.

Identity

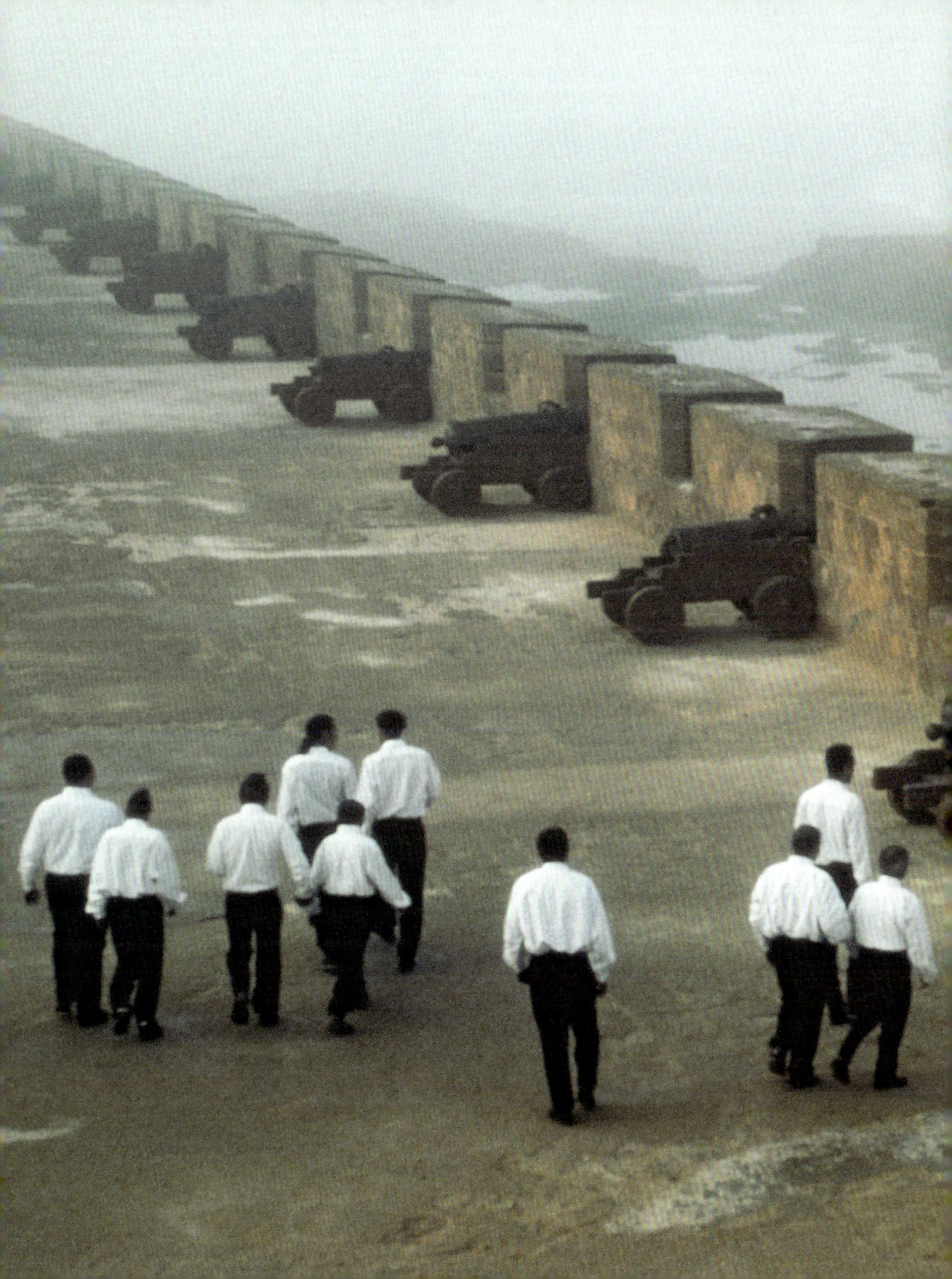

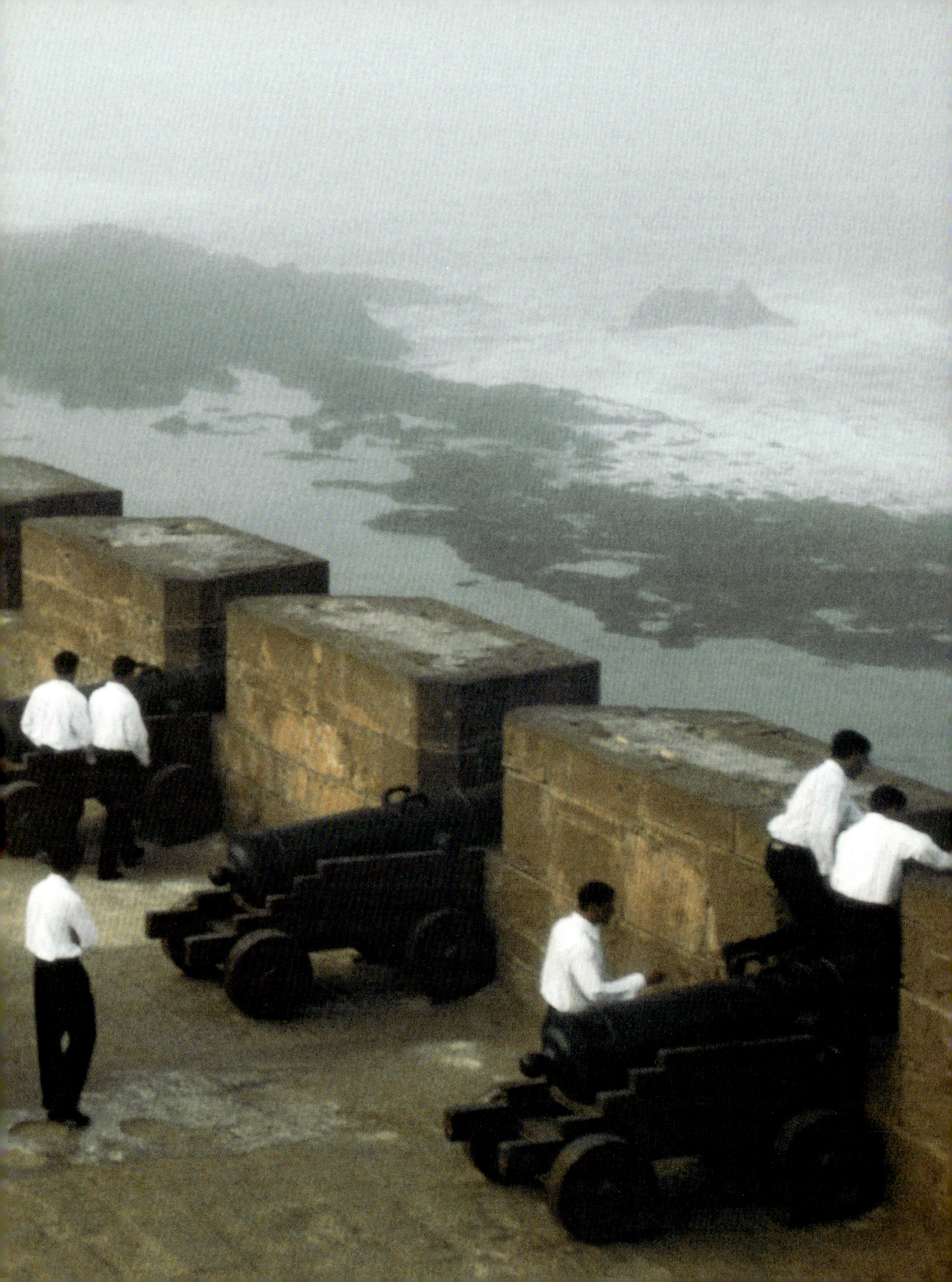

(RE)DEFINING THE "I" IN EXILE

Frauke V. Josenhans

"Sometimes we feel that we straddle two cultures; at other times,
that we fall between two stools."
—Salman Rushdie, *Imaginary Homelands: Essays and Criticism 1981–1991*[1]

Identity is what makes each person different from others; it is defined by affiliations, be they national, religious, or other, as well as by physical and psychological characteristics. It is affected by outside factors and by the emotional and intellectual growth of an individual. For an artist, identity refers to characteristics of style, techniques and materials, or subject matter specific to the author. The experience of exile enriches but also complicates the evolution or construction of one's identity; in most cases, it puts individuals outside of their social and cultural references and may even cause the loss of their mother tongue. Different from authors and poets, whose writings are often inseparable from their native language, visual artists do not lose their ability to create in a new environment, nor do they need to learn a new visual language or to translate from one language into another.[2] However, being uprooted from one's home, either physically or psychologically, by force or by choice, challenges not only one's vision of the world, but also the perception of one's self. The German-Jewish philosopher Ernst Bloch, who immigrated to the United States after the Nazis came to power, distinguished between two kinds of immigrants: those who reject completely the culture and language of their former home and search to adapt by all means, and those who wish to retain their "old existence and consciousness."[3] Differences of language, customs, and culture can create insurmountable barriers due to the fact that artists have to define their new identity while, in many cases, simultaneously facing external pressure to assimilate quickly and enthusiastically to their new home.[4] Works created in exile by artists who have experienced this loss and subsequent adaptation or rejection offer a crucial way of understanding how their authors expressed identity through either visual or material means.

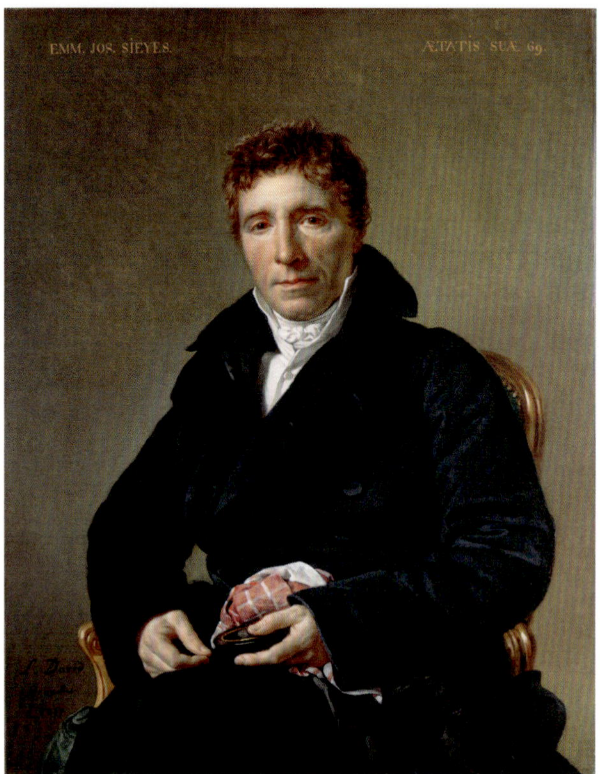

Fig. 1. Jacques-Louis David, *Emmanuel-Joseph Sieyès (1748–1836)*,
1817. Oil on canvas, 38½ × 29⅛ in. (97.8 × 74 cm). Harvard
Art Museums/Fogg Museum, Cambridge, Mass., Bequest of
Grenville L. Winthrop, 1943.229

186

Identity through Representation

For artists who clung to their "former" identity or social role even in their displacement,
visual representation—through content or style—served as a powerful tool to sustain
their self-image. Portraits, and especially self-portraits, have provided the most obvious
vehicle for explorations of identity. In such works, artists scrutinize a subject's exterior
appearance (or their own), often employing specific cultural signifiers, such as posture,
gesture, and physical or material attributes. The famous exile Jacques-Louis David is one
example of an artist who used his craft to reaffirm identity. During his exile in Brussels
from 1816 until his death in 1825, David created almost a myth around his persona,
painting portraits, mostly of fellow French exiles, local aristocrats, and supporters of
the republic, and thus maintaining his association with the bygone French Empire
and his status as *premier peintre* under Napoléon. He excelled in the art of depicting an
individual's physiognomy and social status, but at the same time he expressed a more
personal involvement in the act of painting, revealing his own affinities.[5] For instance,
in Brussels he painted portraits of regicides like himself, French citizens who had voted
for the execution of Louis XVI—among them Emmanuel-Joseph Sieyès (fig. 1) and
Dominique-Vincent Ramel de Nogaret (fig. 2).[6] David and his fellow countrymen did not

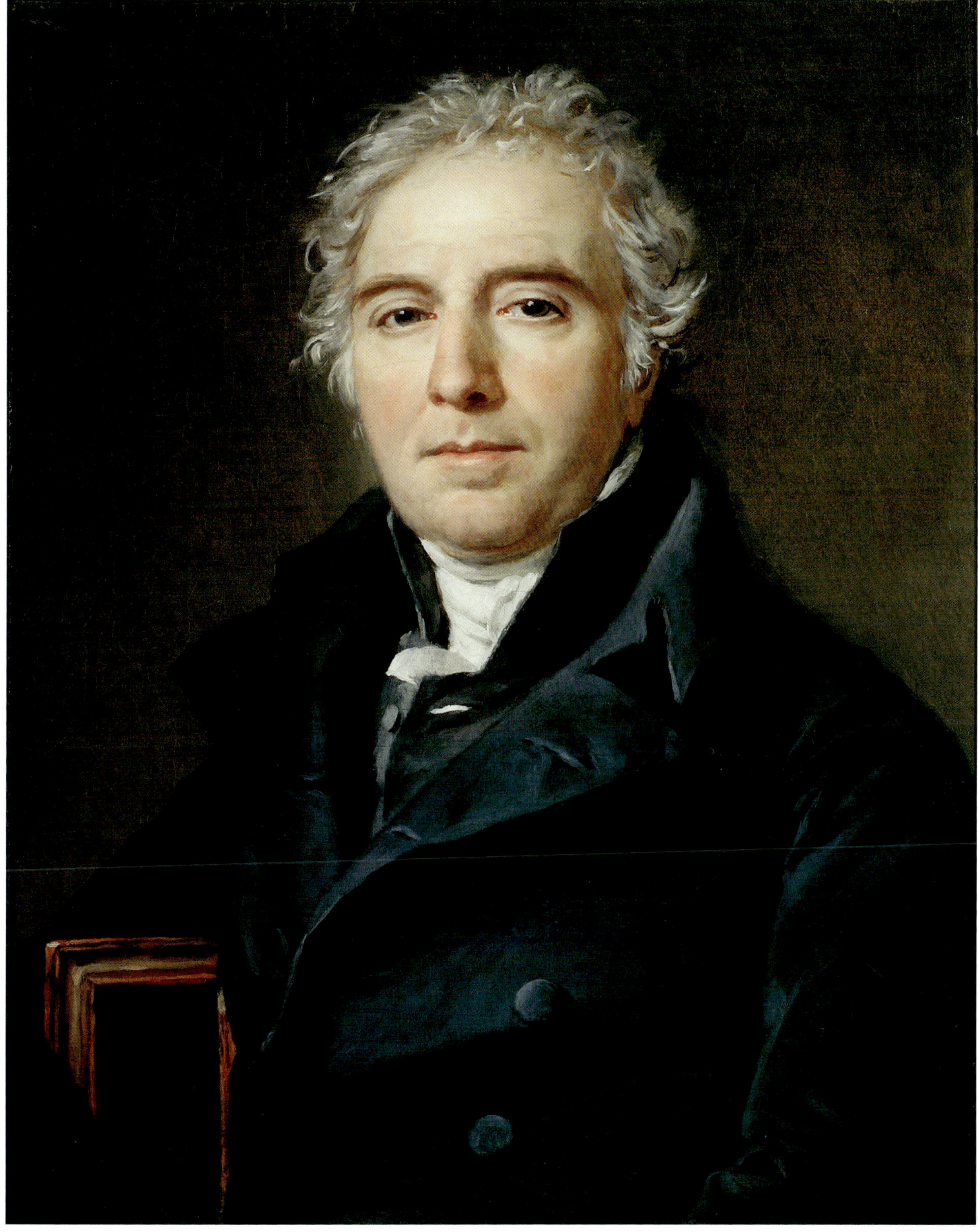

Fig. 2. Jacques-Louis David, *Portrait of Dominique-Vincent Ramel de Nogaret*, 1820. Oil on canvas, 23¾ × 18¾ in. (60.5 × 47.5 cm). Private collection

IDENTITY

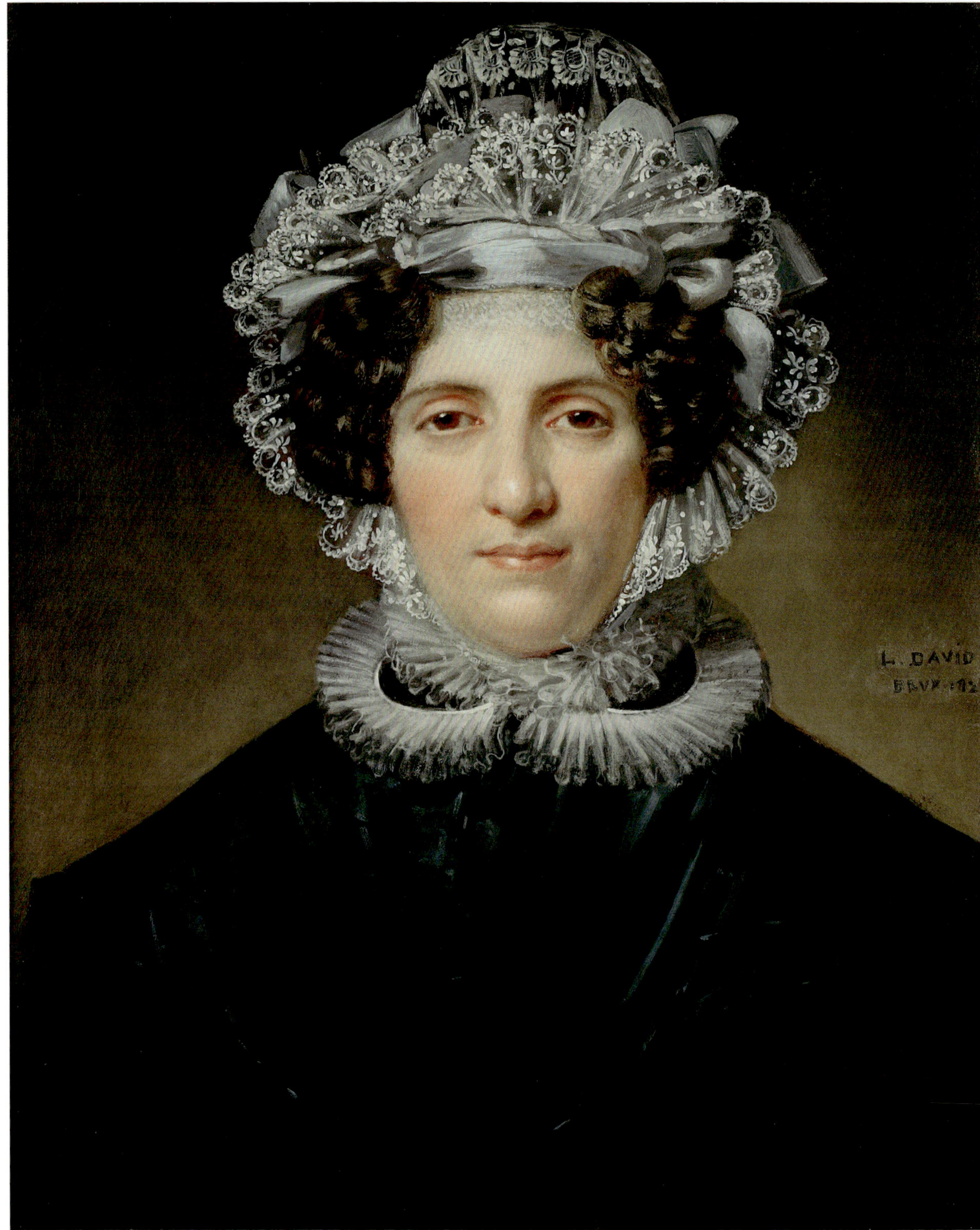

Fig. 3. Jacques-Louis David, *Portrait of Ange-Pauline-Charlotte Ramel de Nogaret, née Panckoucke*, 1820. Oil on canvas, 23⅜ × 18¾ in. (59 × 47.5 cm). Private collection

deny their involvement, and under the Bourbon Restoration they proudly assumed responsibility for it.[7]

Ramel de Nogaret was a minister of finance from 1796 to 1799, during the Directory, the provisionary government set up after the French Revolution, and he had rallied with Napoléon during the emperor's last period of rule, the Hundred Days. He was exiled in January 1816, at the same time as David, and also settled in Brussels.[8] The two men knew each other well, and Ramel de Nogaret later delivered the artist's funeral oration in Brussels. In his portrait, David represented Ramel de Nogaret slightly turned toward the viewer, in an informal attitude with an arm wrapped around the back of the chair in which he sits. Although he lived comfortably and possessed several shops and factories in Brussels, Ramel de Nogaret is not portrayed with any explicit signs of his wealth. His wife, Ange-Pauline-Charlotte (fig. 3), on the other hand, directly faces the viewer in a more official attitude, with an elaborate lace headpiece and collar that convey her status and wealth. The lace is depicted with great delicacy to indicate the transparency of the fabric. These details allude not only to the prosperity of the couple but also to their place of residence, since Belgium was famous for its lace manufacturing, and they might also be an allusion to the family's trade.

Yet David depicts both men, Ramel de Nogaret and Sieyès, in sober, unassuming *redingotes* (riding coats), sitting in nonchalant, tranquil poses and looking at the viewer. Neither their postures nor their expressions convey the fact that they are in perpetual exile, stripped of their titles and possessions.[9] Rather, their portraits emanate a self-confidence that seems to contradict the idea of banishment, and their physical appearances convey health, as visible in Ramel de Nogaret's slightly reddish cheeks.[10] Here, neither the sitter nor the depiction of him is innocuous; David represents important men of the French exile community in Brussels in a way that stresses their individuality and pride. By painting the portraits of these men during his own exile, David ostensibly stated his republican beliefs and his affiliation with men such as Ramel de Nogaret and Sieyès and, by extension, with the former emperor Napoléon.

After the triumph of individuality during the nineteenth century, with artworks and especially portraits stressing the self-consciousness of their authors, the twentieth century witnessed, on one hand, the rise of abstraction and the rejection of figuration and all mimesis, and, on the other, the employment of naturalistic, hyperrealist, and Surrealist imagery.[11] The dramatic changes both in the visual arts and in the sociopolitical domain forced artists to explore the question of identity through new avenues. The most striking instance of this occurred when Germany's Third Reich labeled Modernist, abstract, leftist, and Jewish artists *entartet* (degenerate) or *undeutsch* (un-German), and thus not only rejected these artists from their native country but also, in many cases, persecuted them, revoked their citizenship, and even murdered them. George Grosz was one of those who left Germany and immigrated to the United States, settling in New York in 1933. The art that he produced in exile foregrounds the discrepancy between the cultural identity assigned to him and the one he tried to invent for himself. Indeed, Grosz refused to be considered an exile, and instead he pursued assimilation and sought to be recognized as an American painter.[12] In a letter that he wrote to the German writer Max Herrmann-Neisse a few months after his arrival in New York, Grosz insisted that he came to the United States in pursuit of better opportunities, rather than as a political refugee.[13]

In his quest to assimilate, and in his enthusiasm for American culture, Grosz depicted the city of New York and its inhabitants in numerous drawings and watercolors, one of them being *The American Scene* (fig. 4), which he painted in 1939, a few years after he had immigrated. The scene shows a group of people of varying ages, from a young boy to an elderly woman. The men and women in the foreground are depicted in

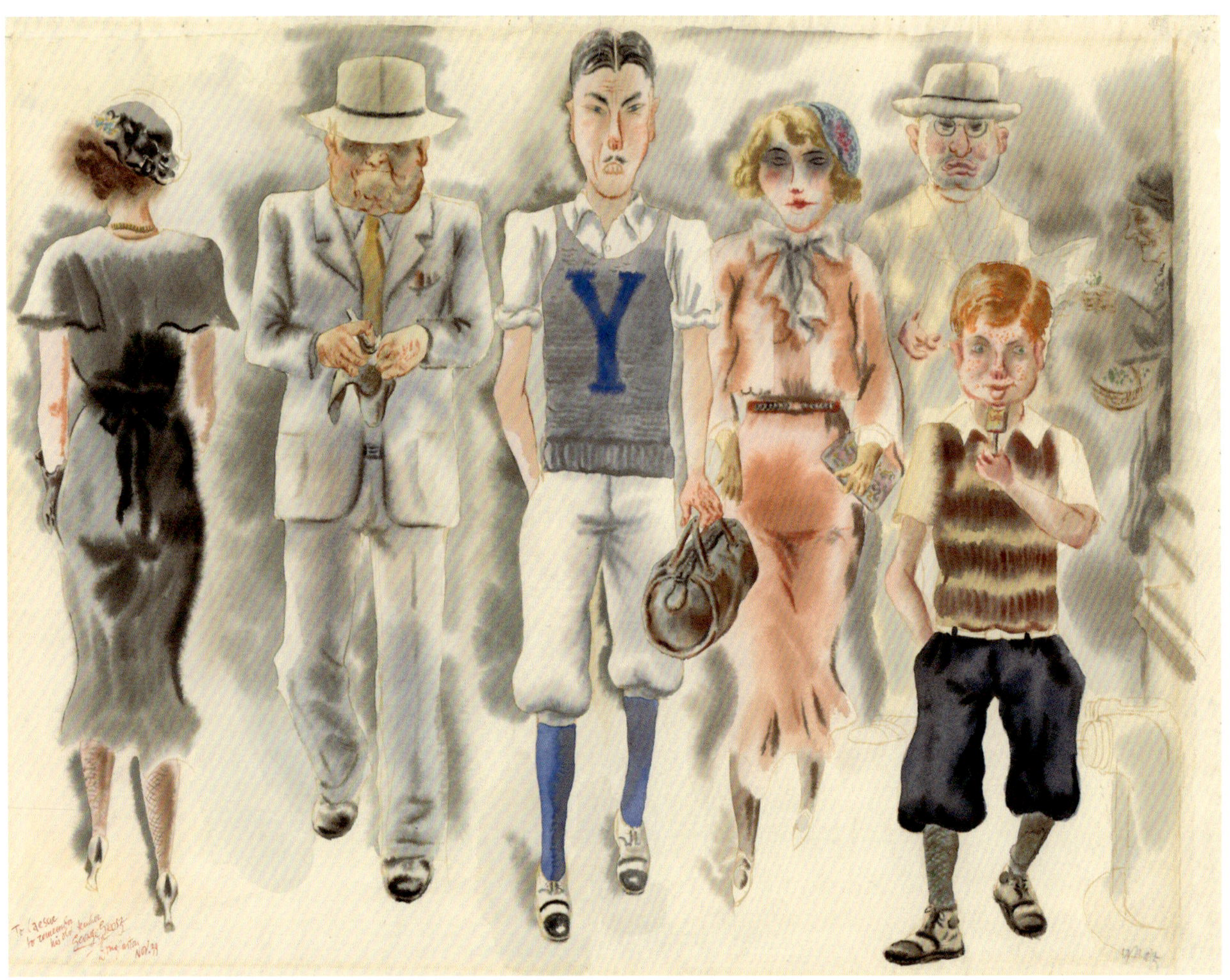

Fig. 4. George Grosz, *The American Scene*, 1939. Watercolor on paper, image: 18¼ × 22¹³⁄₁₆ in. (46.4 × 58 cm). Yale University Art Gallery, New Haven, Conn., Gift of George Hopper Fitch, B.A. 1932, 1953.29.1

dynamic postures, with most of them directly facing the viewer. Only the figure of the old woman in the background is shown in profile, distanced from the others, almost like an outcast. In the middle of the composition is the artist Yasuo Kuniyoshi, who taught with Grosz at the Art Students League. Despite the different types of people represented in this work, the rendering of the faces and bodies seems less satirical than those in Grosz's works from the Weimar Republic, such as *Drinnen und Draussen* (cat. 24, fig. 1). *The American Scene* appears to have more in common with the style and subject matter of the Ashcan School, which focused on urban reality, and of painters such as Reginald Marsh and Isabel Bishop.[14] Works like this one illustrate how Grosz sought to observe and capture the American spirit and manner. In an article titled "Amerikanische Umgangsformen" (American Manners) that he wrote for the German periodical *Querschnitt*, Grosz pondered the different models of behavior, courtesy, and even dress in the United States and in Germany, stressing the liberty that he found in his new home.[15] He noted, for instance, that the American "appears on first look more ill-bred, more casual, but also fresher . . . shortly (if an ominous word is permitted, which in Europe is so detested): more democratic."[16]

Grosz changed his subject matter as well as his technique while in the United States, turning primarily toward watercolor and oil paint, but even after all these efforts he was still seen as an exiled German artist, and his art was perceived through the lens of his Dada past and his earlier criticism of fascism and the military. In 1934 the gallery An American Place in New York organized an exhibition of Grosz's watercolors; on this occasion, the American artist Marsden Hartley wrote a short text for the accompanying brochure. In it, Hartley described Grosz as "a willing exile because of his hatred of present régimes," and emphasized the latter's antireligious and antifascist stance, adding that "Grosz would certainly have been shot against the wall—if he had remained [in Germany]."[17] Hartley also noted that Grosz's American works differed from his famous satirical illustrations, explaining this discrepancy as follows:

> The foreign eye is bound to see another place, another people with almost unerring vision and it is for our amusement that we are to see ourselves as others see us without too much of compromise. If Grosz is perhaps kinder in these American satires than he was in his scalpel-like incisions into the coarse flesh-crust of obtuse and vulgar humanity as he knew it in Berlin . . . there is doubtless a reason, for Grosz likes us, he entertains the hope of being one of us and all of our droll behaviour is to him fresh with vital energy.[18]

Despite the relative success that Grosz encountered in the United States, he became disenchanted with the American art scene, where other European artists were

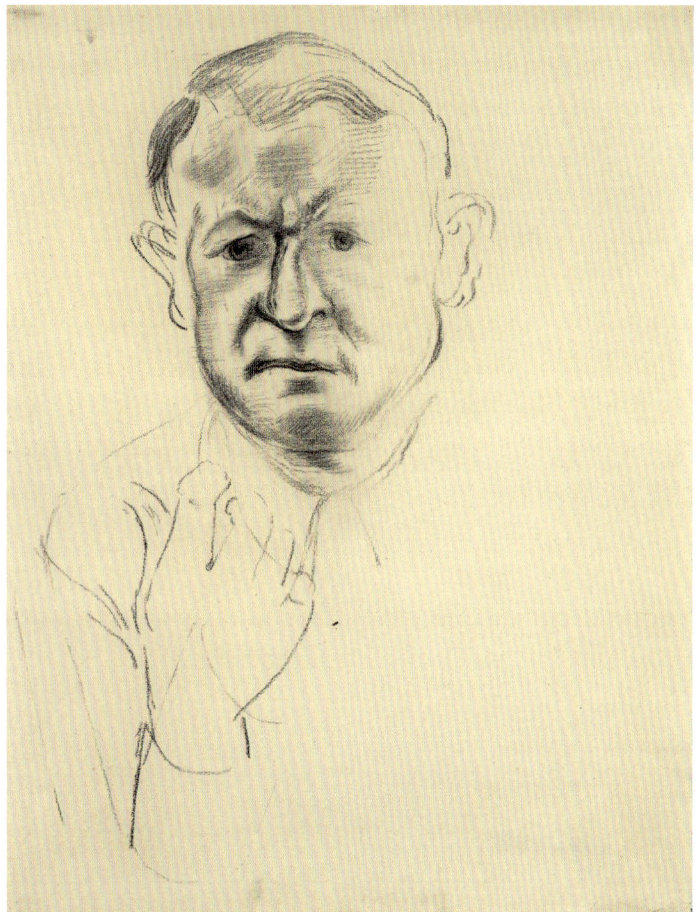

Fig. 5. George Grosz, *Self-Portrait*, 1938. Charcoal on paper, 24⅞ × 18¾ in. (63.2 × 47.6 cm). Private collection

en vogue.[19] He was obligated to continue teaching at the Art Students League in order to make a living. He also felt misunderstood by critics and the public, and he became increasingly isolated, a situation that was aggravated by his problems with alcohol.[20] A seemingly spontaneously drawn self-portrait (fig. 5) seems to give a glimpse into the divided soul of the artist.

Grosz's disillusionment began to manifest in his work through a return to the past and to an iconography reminiscent of famous old German masters, as visible in works such as *An Old Tree* (cat. 24). In 1943 Grosz painted *The Wanderer* (fig. 6), a self-portrait disguised as an allegory that shows a lonely figure traversing a watery landscape, with crows as his only companions and fire in the background. The painting conveys a sense of isolation and homelessness, perhaps reflecting Grosz's own state of mind.[21] The figure of the wanderer, a popular motif in German literature and the visual arts, reached its culmination in Caspar David Friedrich's *Wanderer über dem Nebelmeer* (Wanderer above the Sea of Fog, ca. 1817, Hamburger Kunsthalle) and *Mönch am Meer* (Monk by the Sea; see Koerner, "Home and the World," fig. 8), works that express the quest for something unreachable and that place the isolated human figure in an environment dominated by the elements. Similarly, other artists exiled from Germany turned to themes from the Northern Renaissance or Romanticism, searching for humanist values to express in their works and constructing a new identity. The American artist Lyonel Feininger, who had lived for fifty years in Germany, repeatedly depicted German motifs, architecture, and port scenes when he returned to the United States (cat. 15). Max Beckmann, during his exile in the Netherlands, also created highly allegorical paintings with references to a past German culture (cat. 25).[22]

Other immigrants to the United States followed a similar trajectory to that of Grosz, adopting certain new, more "American" ways to identify themselves, while at the same time searching for artistic inspiration in their upbringing as they began to feel progressively more alienated from American society. Arshile Gorky, John Graham, and Jack Tworkov were forcibly deracinated from the places where they spent the early years of their lives, places that were torn apart by subsequent wars. These artists spent the majority of their careers in the United States, becoming part of the emerging Abstract Expressionists, yet were constantly reminded of the past. All three changed their names in ways that distanced them from their origins; whereas Graham and Tworkov chose a first name or surname that sounded more American, Gorky chose as his pseudonym the surname of the famous Russian writer Maxim Gorky,

193

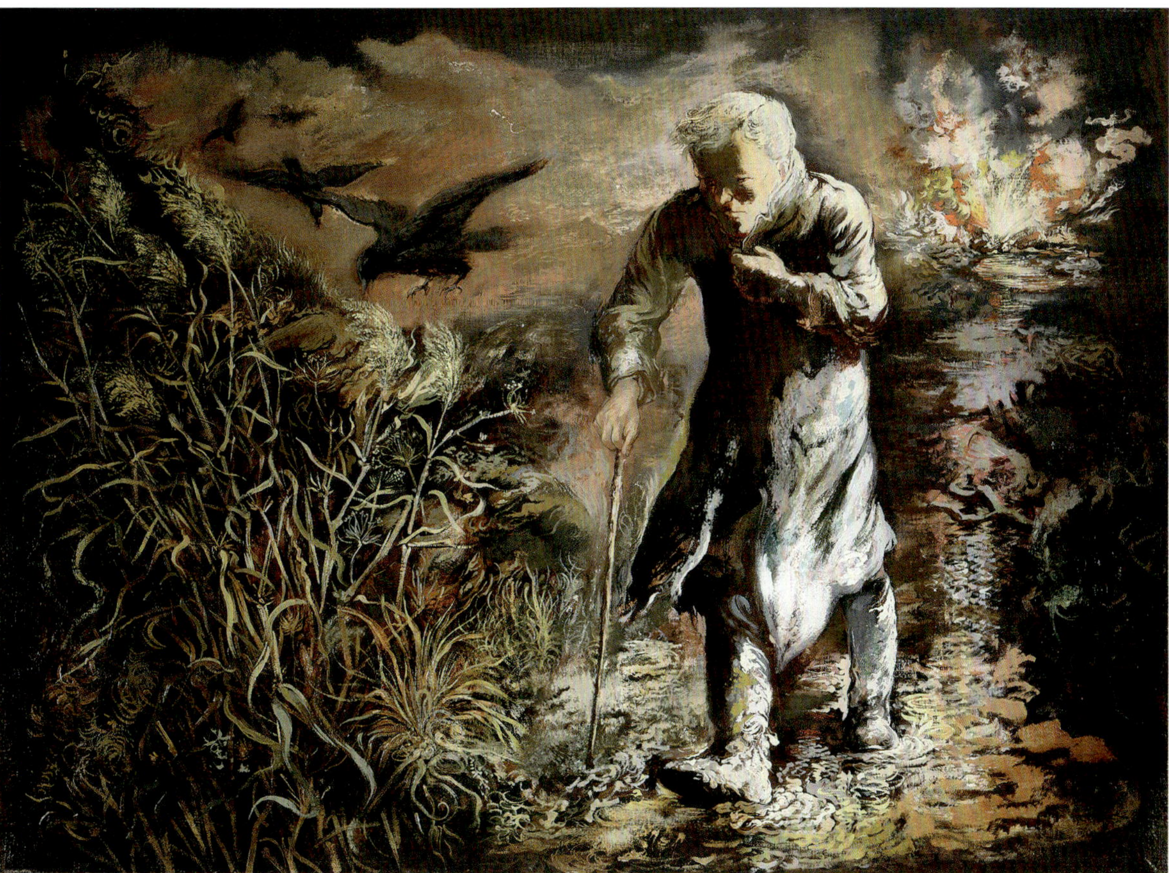

Fig. 6. George Grosz, *The Wanderer*, 1943. Oil on canvas, 30 × 40 in. (76.2 × 101.6 cm). Memorial Art Gallery, University of Rochester, N.Y., Marion Stratton Gould Fund, 51.6

sometimes even telling people that he was a relative. Both Gorky and Graham consciously chose to tell various false stories about their origins and upbringings, which gave them a mysterious aura and enhanced their alienation.[23] This crossing of fictionalized biographies and invented alter egos especially nourished Graham's work, which encompassed still lifes, self-portraits, and figure paintings, notably his cross-eyed women (such as *Two Sisters*, 1944, Museum of Modern Art, New York). One of his untitled drawings (fig. 7), for instance, features fractured planes drawn from Cubism and biomorphic forms inspired by Surrealism, a stylistic synthesis that transmits, in a sense, Graham's own status as an outsider.[24]

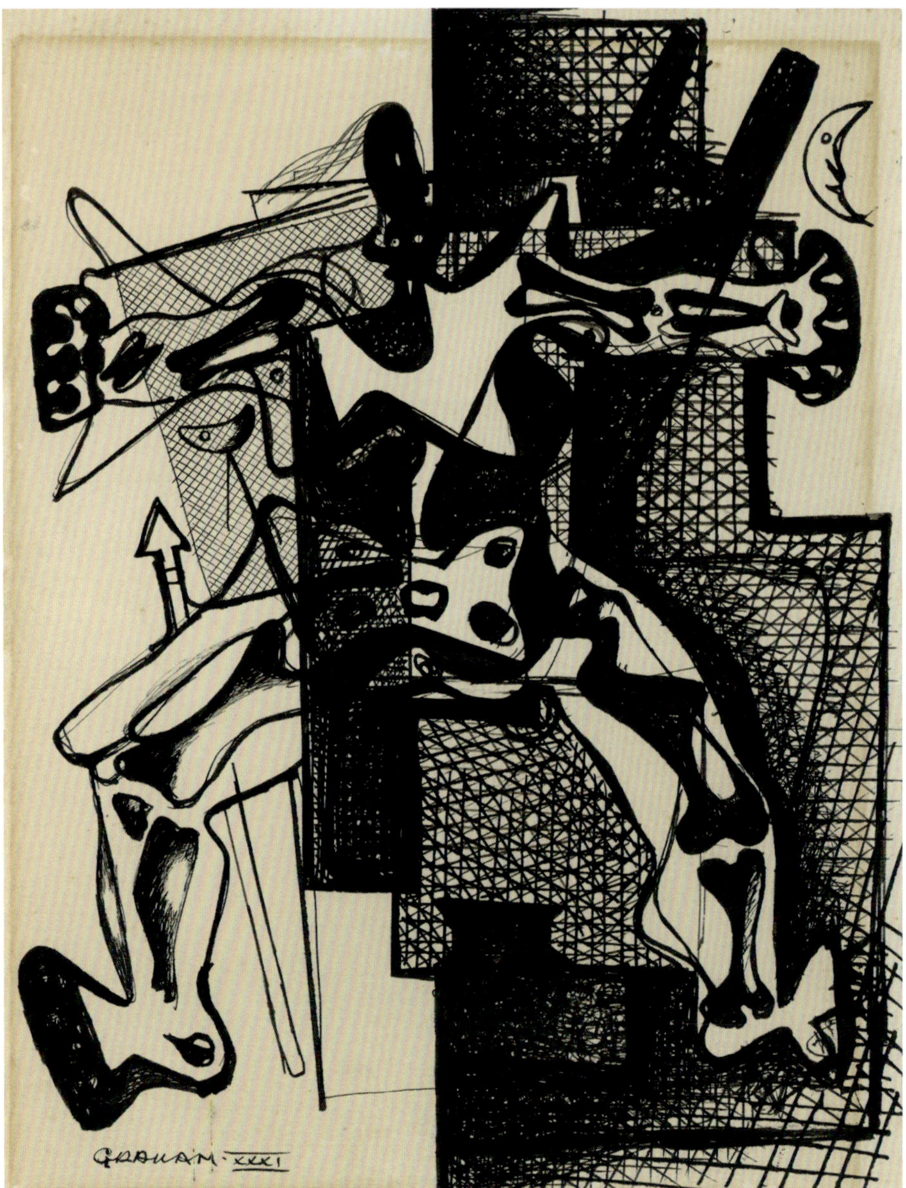

Fig. 7. John Graham, Untitled, 1931. Ink on paper, 12¹⁄₁₆ × 9 in. (30.6 × 22.9 cm). Yale University Art Gallery, New Haven, Conn., Everett V. Meeks, B.A. 1901, Fund, 2000.99.1

Tworkov, despite being part of the New York avant-garde circles, felt isolated, as he expressed in his writings: "Nevertheless, the feeling that I have been an alien in the world persists with me to this day."[25] He was torn between the country and culture that he had left behind and his need to adapt to his new world. Born Yakov Tworkovsky, he became Jacob Bernstein when he came to the United States, adopting the surname of a relative who was already living there. He then changed his name again when he applied for citizenship, a choice he came to regret, as he never felt comfortable with the name Jack.[26] An untitled, numbered drawing (fig. 8), perhaps made when he was teaching

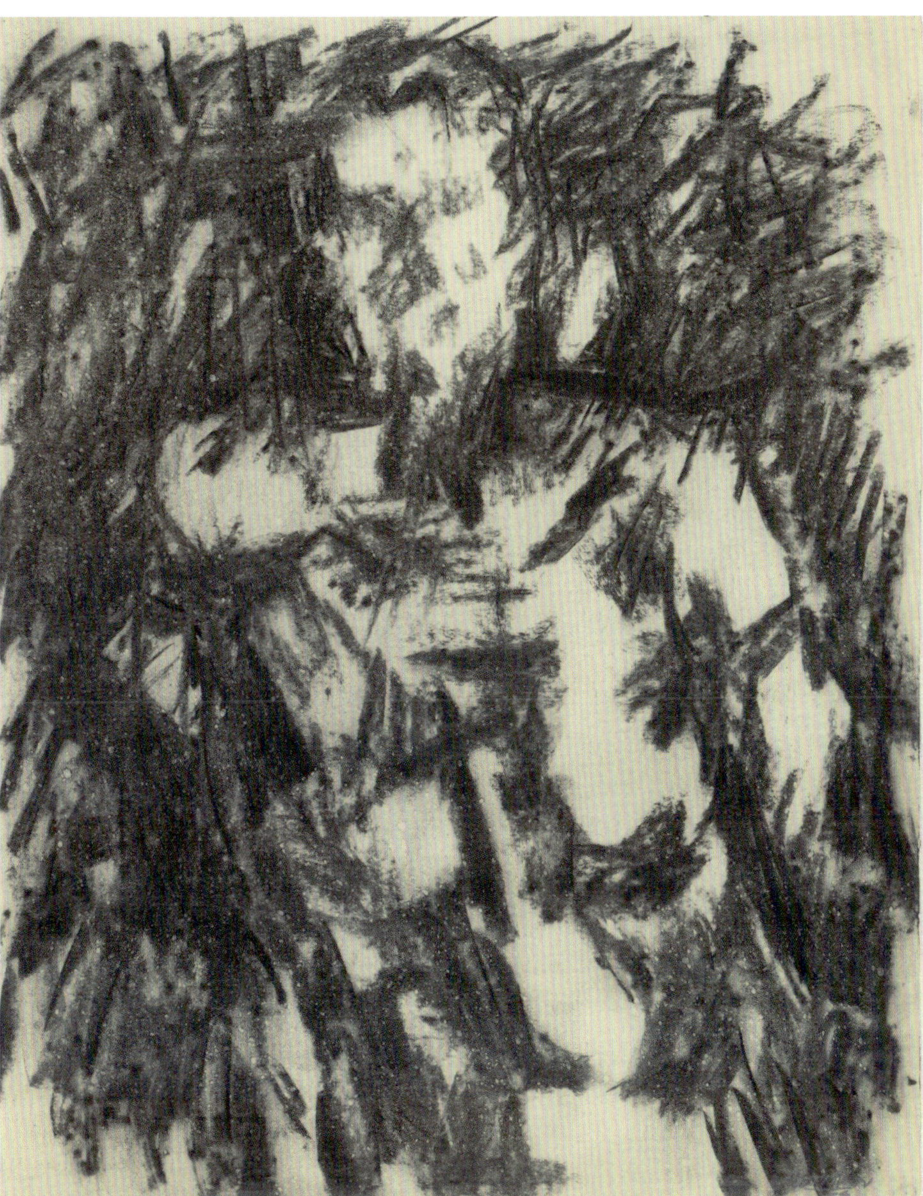

Fig. 8. Jack Tworkov, *Drawing No. 3958*, 1954. Charcoal on paper, 26⅛ × 19⅞ in. (66.3 × 50.5 cm). Yale University Art Gallery, New Haven, Conn., Richard Brown Baker, B.A. 1935, Collection, 2008.19.81

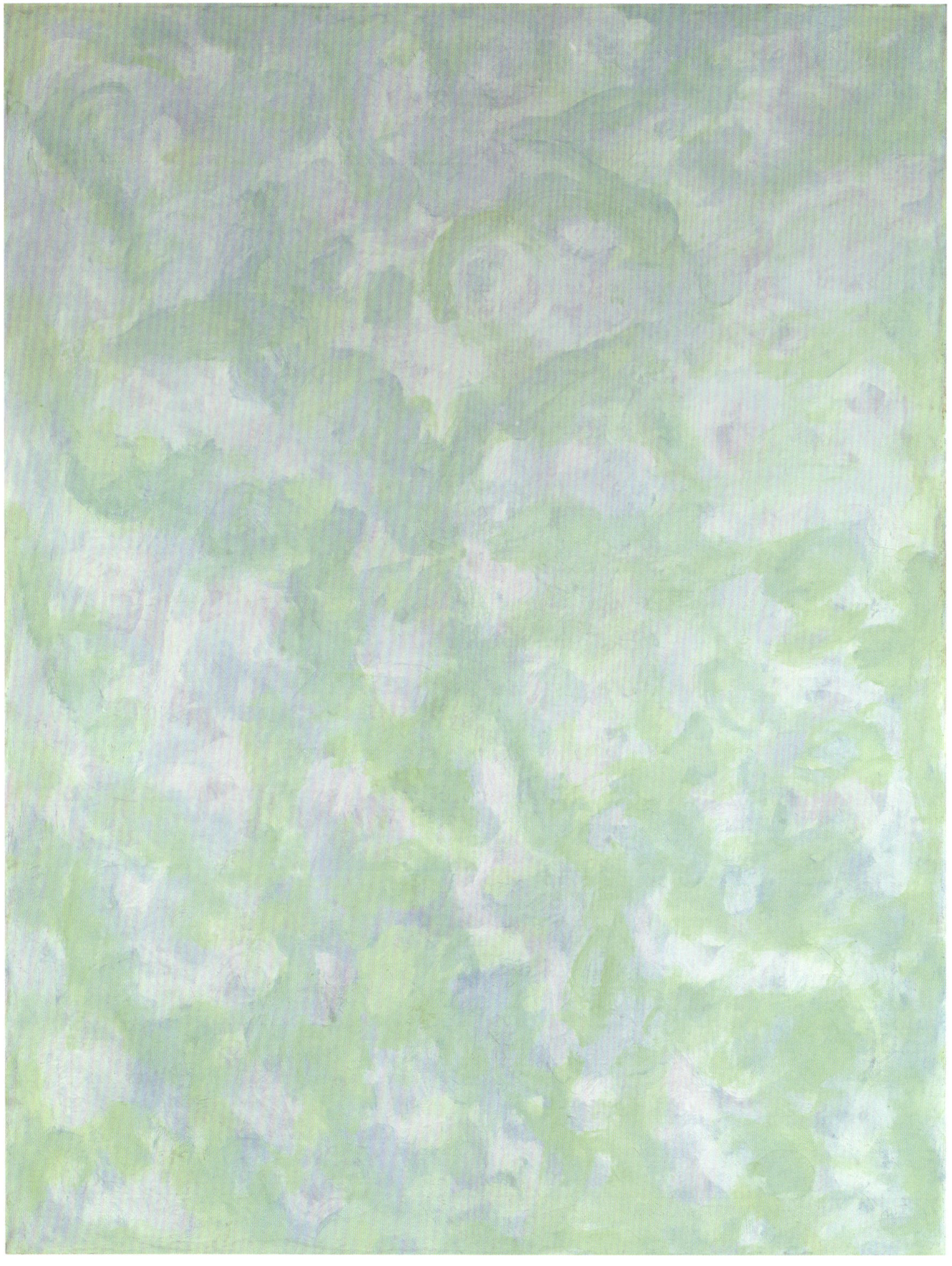

Fig. 9. Beauford Delaney, Untitled, 1960. Oil on canvas, 51¼ × 38⅜ in. (130.2 × 97.5 cm). Bowdoin College Museum of Art, Brunswick, Maine, Gift of halley k harrisburg, Class of 1990, and Michael Rosenfeld, 2004.25

either at Indiana University or at the University of Mississippi, shows a vaguely human form without any facial features emerging from a misty web of lines—a nameless, isolated silhouette. This haunting figure seems to embody his feeling of being "alien" and disappearing behind a fictitious identity.

Even in the postwar period, some artists chose to leave their homes and sought countries and cities where they would not be stigmatized because of their race, religion, or sexual orientation. The African American artist Beauford Delaney, although one of the precursors of Abstract Expressionism, remains curiously neglected in writings about modern art. His style and personality made him an outsider in American avant-garde circles; his homosexuality seemed contrary to the "virile" image of the New York School, and his art was not as politically charged as that of other African American artists.[27] Yet he was able to adapt to each new milieu, every time showing a different side of his persona. He chose to settle in Paris in 1953 to pursue personal freedom, not only artistic but also sexual, and he further developed his abstract style through contact with works by artists such as Vincent van Gogh, Claude Monet, and Henri Matisse.[28] In an untitled painting from 1960 (fig. 9), Delaney created a completely abstract composition from which light seems to emanate, conveying a sense of freedom from any social or cultural restraints. The vibrant colors seem to exist only for themselves, no longer subject to any artistic doctrine. This newfound liberty of brushwork and color was a style that he developed only once he had settled in Paris. As his friend the African American writer James Baldwin wrote in 1965, "From Tennessee, he eventually came to Paris . . . and for a while lived in a suburb of Paris, Clamart. It was at this time that I began to see Beauford's painting in a new way, and it was also at this time that Beauford's paintings underwent a most striking metamorphosis into freedom."[29] Nevertheless, Delaney's work remained an art-historical anomaly, as critics had a hard time reconciling his identity as a gay male painter from the American South with his abstract and figurative aesthetics.[30]

Identity through Making

A work of art is defined not only by its formal qualities but also by the act of creation itself, which is as intentional as what is represented. Artists found new ways of affirming their identities by employing certain techniques, tools, or materials, either because they had a personal resonance, or because of physical or social circumstances, reflecting a particular zeitgeist.[31] In the nineteenth century, various artists, notably from the Symbolist movement, acted against the mimetic aspect of painting and instead emphasized the emotional and symbolic aspects of colors, forms, and even materials.

For one, Paul Gauguin, in search of his true self—the "*sauvage*" (savage) in him— abandoned European civilization altogether. The works that he made in the various places to which he escaped—first Pont-Aven in Brittany, then Martinique, followed by Tahiti and the Marquesas Islands—encapsulate his desire to depict himself as an outcast from the Western art world. Returning to Paris in 1893 from his first voyage to

Tahiti, Gauguin began to work on a book accompanied by woodcuts, titled *Noa Noa*, to contextualize his Polynesian experience, and showed ten of these works at the Galerie Durand-Ruel.[32] The richly textured woodcuts reconfigured, in some cases, motifs from his paintings to evoke what Gauguin saw as the erotic and mysterious nature of Tahiti. Woodcut was a new technique for Gauguin, and it stemmed from his previous preoccupation with wood carving.[33] These prints are intentionally crude, with forms left unfinished and the grain of the wood apparent. Compared to previous works such as *Pastorales Martinique* (cat. 1), the forms are rough-textured and more angular, and the figures are barely defined. The prints are highly symbolic and stylized illustrations of the utopian paradise and culture that Gauguin had set out to find, evoking Tahitian pantheism, as illustrated in *Maruru* (Offering of Gratitude, fig. 10), in which natives venerate a statue of one of the Tahitian gods. Gauguin also sought to capture a life in harmony with nature, as seen in *Noa Noa* (Fragrant Scent, fig. 11). The female figure on the left, carrying fruit, is taken from the painting *I Raro te Oviri* (Under the Pandanus, 1891, Dallas Museum of Art), which Gauguin had painted during his first sojourn in Tahiti. In the woodcut, the composition is more restrained. The second female figure seems almost to disappear into the landscape, or maybe to emerge from the water

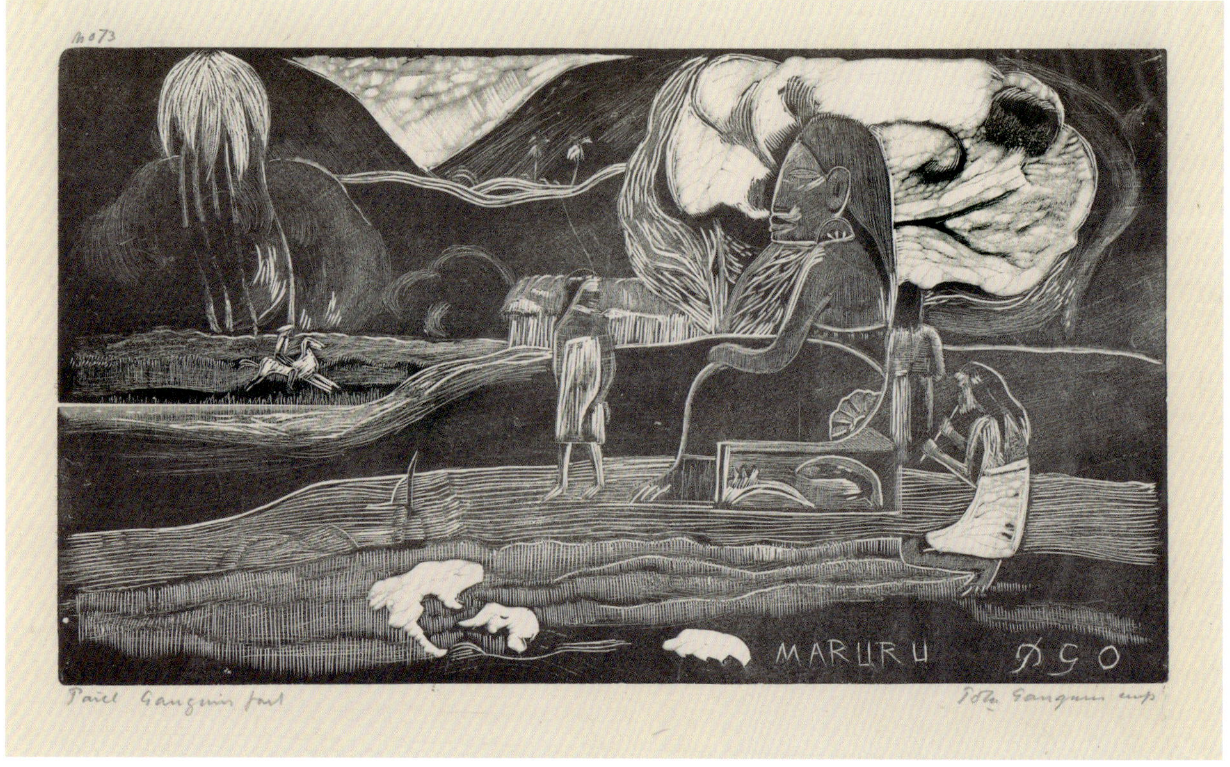

Fig. 10. Paul Gauguin, *Maruru* (Offering of Gratitude), ca. 1898. Woodcut, 8¹⁄₁₆ × 14 in. (20.5 × 35.5 cm). Yale University Art Gallery, New Haven, Conn., Everett V. Meeks, B.A. 1901, Fund, 1981.40

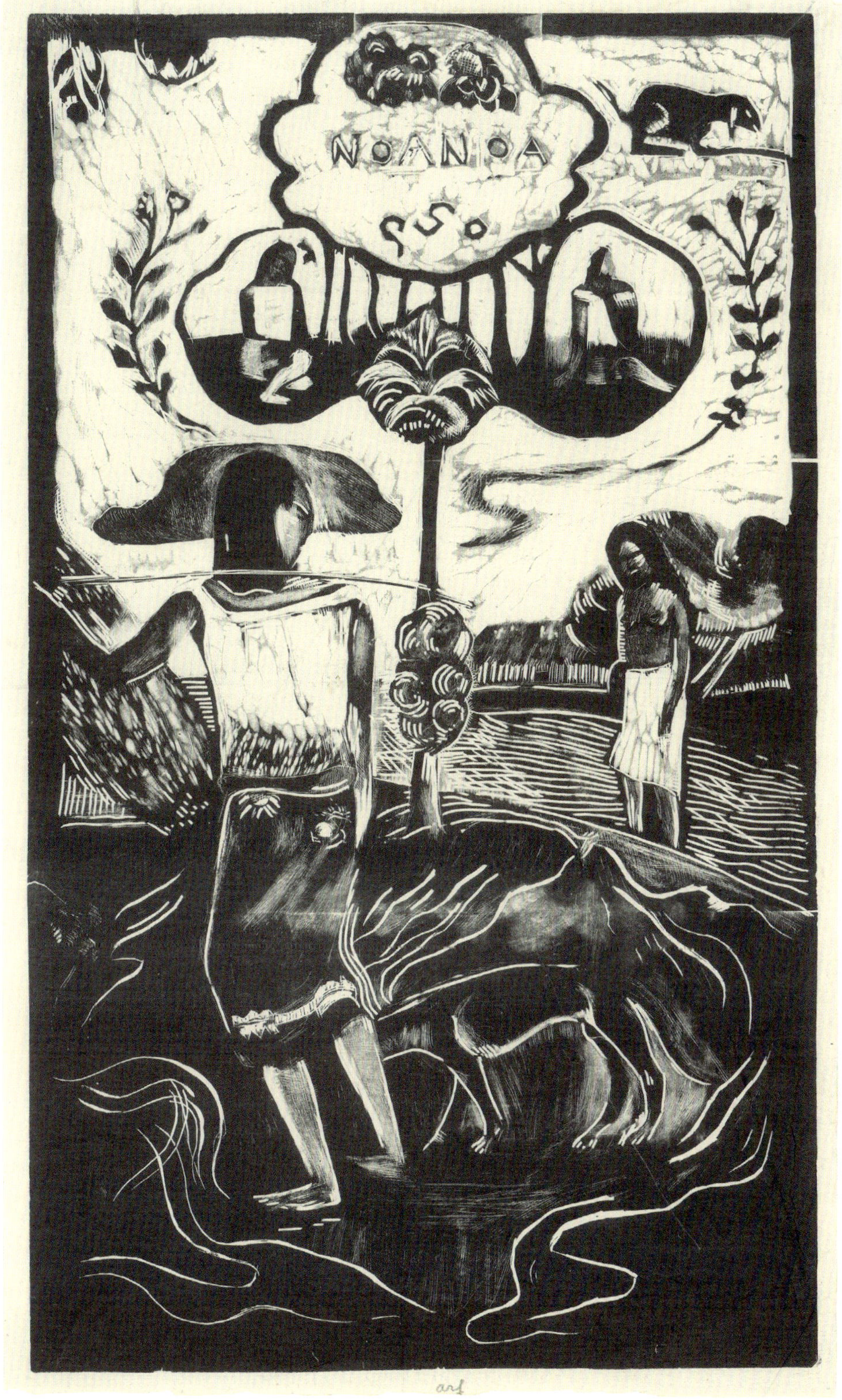

Fig. 11. Paul Gauguin, *Noa Noa* (Fragrant Scent), 1893–94. Woodcut, 14 × 8¹/₁₆ in. (35.5 × 20.4 cm).
Yale University Art Gallery, New Haven, Conn., Bequest of Ralph Kirkpatrick, HON. 1965, 1984.54.91

IDENTITY

around her. The grain of the wood is visible in the sky and in the costume of the figure in the foreground. Gauguin carved boxwood blocks, meant for wood engravings, for each of the ten woodcuts; he employed a range of techniques, as well as different tools, that draw from wood engraving, woodcut, and sculpture, and he also experimented with incorporating color in a way that was opposed to academic standards that prevailed in France at the time.[34]

With the advent of Modernism, artists were increasingly drawn to experiment with unconventional materials and go beyond the limits of traditional painting or sculpture. Expressionism, Fauvism, Cubism, Futurism, and Dada were all movements that broke with the academic dogma and challenged artistic conventions. This exploration of new creative avenues continued after World War II as a way to capture the rapidly changing postwar society and culture, with numerous displaced artists seeking to establish their identity. The Greek-born artist Lucas Samaras started to create his pin-covered boxes in the 1960s; these objects combine qualities of painting with sculpture, and play with the relationship between interior and exterior.[35] Undertaking far more than the mere conceptual exercise of transforming a utilitarian object into an artwork, Samaras decorates these objects with various found materials, including pins and razor blades, creating a tension between the appealing sensuality and tactility of some of the elements and their hidden danger. The boxes have a physical and psychological connection to his childhood. During World War II, Samaras's hometown of Kastoria, Greece, and even his family home were occupied by Italian and German forces. The Greek Civil War followed from 1946 to 1949, during which time he and his family had to seek shelter in basements. He witnessed the dropping of mortar shells on their house, which killed his grandmother. Samaras also remembers seeing boxes of bones dug up from the churchyard at a nearby chapel, to make space for new burials.[36] His art integrates these traumatic events of his childhood into his identity, acknowledging and transforming them. Donald Kuspit, in his essay "The Aesthetics of Trauma," outlines the artist's noncompliance and capacity for converting his wartime experience into a driver of creativity that takes the self as its base.[37] He further explains Samaras's affinity for small, portable objects as the artist's wish to protect himself from a hostile world and to create a "womblike and reclusive" space similar to the cave or basement where he hid with his mother during the bombing.[38] In an untitled box from 1963 (fig. 12), Samaras used wool strings pierced by needles; the overall effect is ornamental, and the needles, when viewed from above, resemble part of a colorful wall decoration. The work is reminiscent of Byzantine mosaics with representations of saints, which Samaras would have seen as a child, with schematized figures painted in bold colors on a golden background. The bright colors of the wool thread treacherously invite the viewer to touch and thus be hurt by the needles. Rather than being merely a nostalgic expression of Samaras's upbringing, his box works are grounded in the making, the transformation of materials into something both beautiful and deceptive.

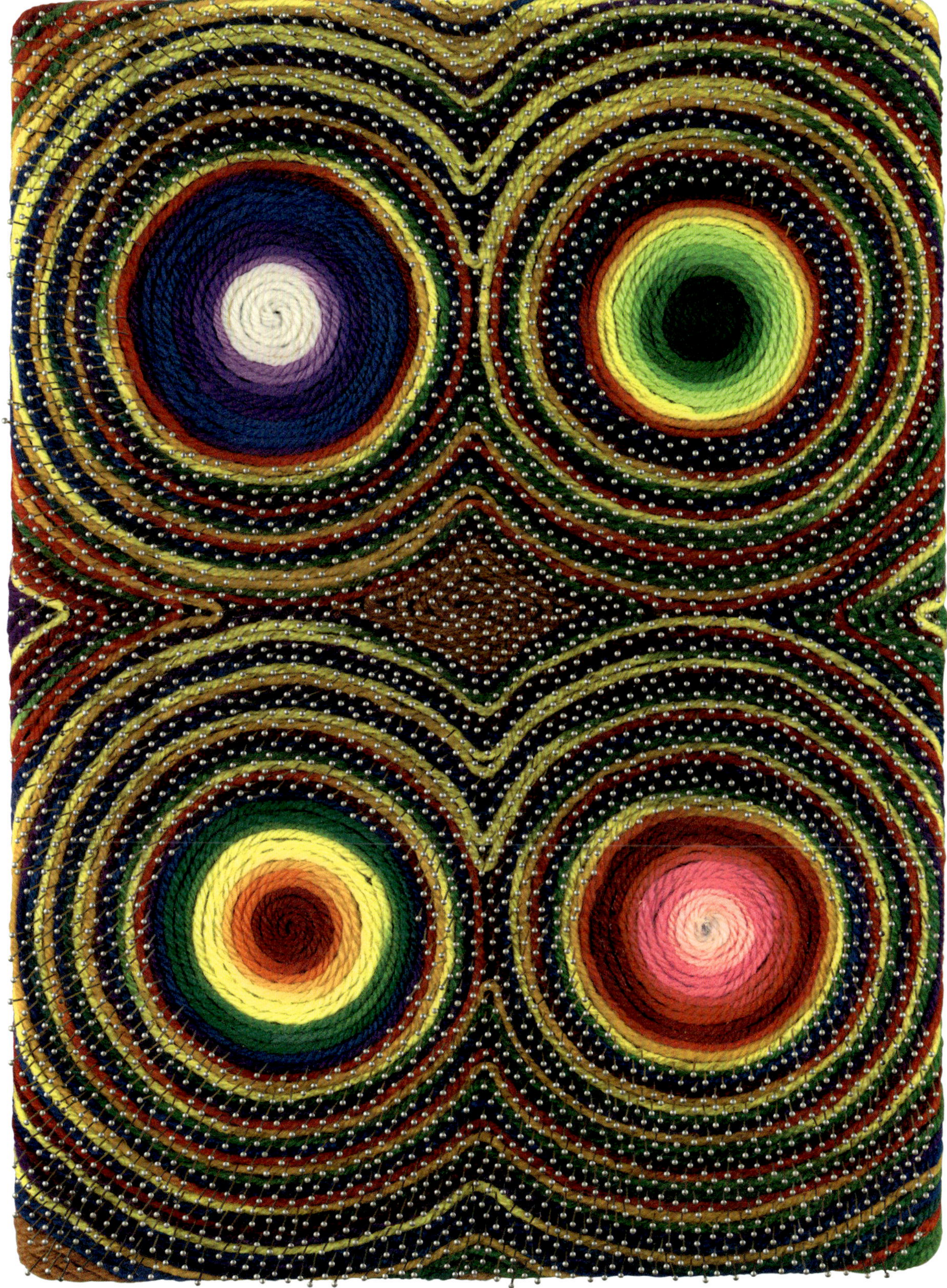

Fig. 12. Lucas Samaras, Untitled, 1963. Mixed media on board, 15¾ × 11½ × 2⅝ in. (40 × 29.2 × 6.7 cm). Yale University Art Gallery, New Haven, Conn., Richard Brown Baker, B.A. 1935, Collection, 2008.19.250

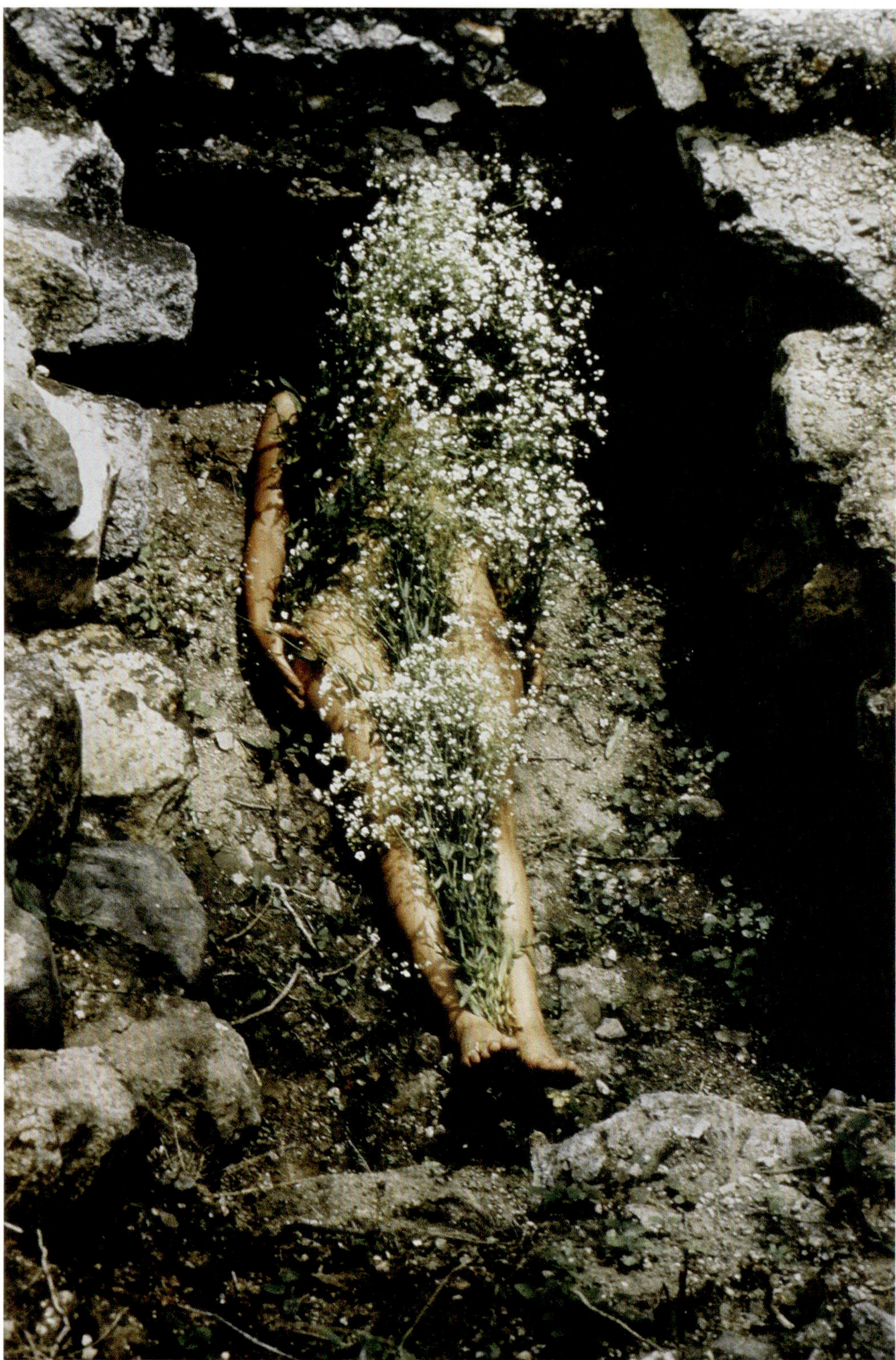

Fig. 13. Ana Mendieta, *Untitled: Silueta Series, Mexico,* from the series *Silueta Works in Mexico,* 1973, printed 1991. C-print on Kodak Professional paper, 20 × 13¼ in. (50.8 × 33.7 cm). Smith College Museum of Art, Northampton, Mass., Purchased with the Janice Carlson Oresman, class of 1955, Fund and the Josephine A. Stein, class of 1927, Fund in honor of the class of 1927, SC 2001:22-7

Other artists who suffered a traumatic displacement from their country of birth during childhood have explored similar avenues in searching for lost or new identities. The Cuban-born artist Ana Mendieta repeatedly used her own body not only to interrogate her role as a female artist but also to reaffirm her cultural roots and connect to the land of her native country. She created body- and identity-oriented art that crossed media and cultures, and she resisted categorization as either Hispanic or merely feminist.[39] In her series *Silueta Works in Mexico*, Mendieta expressed her emotional ties to the earth through the imprint or re-creation of her corporeal form on the soil. Uprooted from Cuba at the age of twelve, she was separated from her parents and her culture, living in foster homes in the midwestern United States. Mendieta initiated a search for her origins in her work, which initially manifested in her interest in the Prehispanic history of Mexico and Cuba.[40] By reconnecting with ancient civilizations, she created a sense of belonging that had been taken from her:

> I have been carrying on a dialogue between the landscape and the female body (based on my own silhouette). I believe this has been a direct result of my having been torn from my homeland (Cuba) during my adolescence. I am overwhelmed by the feeling of having been cast from the womb (nature). My art is the way I re-establish the bonds that unite me to the universe. It is a return to the maternal source. Through my earth/body sculptures I become one with the earth.[41]

In her *Silueta* series, she combined performance art and Land art with the making of an object, stressing the use of her own body as a tool, which she traced in photography and film, as if to ground herself to her origins in yet another way and to document her presence. Using her own physical features as a base for any composition, covering or tracing her body's contour with flowers (fig. 13), gunpowder, stones, or fire, she created a universal connection to the earth. Although she employed strategies inspired by Minimalism, producing self-contained works with only the most essential elements, she also drifted back to the actual making of objects in her *Silueta* series and later in her *Esculturas Rupestres* (Rupestrian Sculptures) series, in which she carved humanoid forms in limestone (cat. 5).[42]

In a similar approach, the American sculptor Ursula von Rydingsvard creates monumental wooden sculptures that recall her own origins. The artist's family came from Eastern Europe, and she grew up in labor camps under the Nazis, and then in refugee camps in postwar Germany. Von Rydingsvard's painstakingly hewn sculptures in wood testify to her craftsmanship and familiarity with the material. Descending from a long line of Polish farmers who worked and lived from the land, von Rydingsvard imbues her art with a feeling of sturdiness, with an emphasis on wood and woodwork. At the same time, her sculptures indicate a search for a new formal vocabulary, a language that is raw and elemental, and that shivers between Minimalism and Abstract Expressionism.[43] Her work, although composed of modular units whose symmetry is indebted to Minimalism, is highly individual and personal, sourced from her own cultural heritage. *Three Bowls* (fig. 14) illustrates how the artist cut each beam, then stacked them and rubbed them with graphite to achieve a weathered texture, thus altering the inherent qualities of the wood. The material guides her work, as she does not make any preparatory drawings.[44] Sculptures such as this one have a massive, almost monolithic presence, and their austere and darkened aspect gives them an aura of mystery. Through their monumentality, they evoke rustic houses, perhaps cabins in the woods or barracks, like those in which the artist spent the first years of her life.[45] The bowl is a recurring motif in von Rydingsvard's oeuvre, reminiscent of her peasant ancestors. The artist's quest to connect with her family heritage and cultural roots clearly links her art to her own life, a fact that she noted during a trip to Poland in 1990: "I am almost afraid that what I'm looking for is the human equivalent to my bowls, shovels—that is peasant, earth working types much like my parents but kinder. The object version of what I want I have considerably near figured out; the human version is not as clear."[46] Works such as *Three Bowls* emphasize the transformation of a utilitarian object into a metaphor for the past and for rural life.

All of these artworks from the nineteenth century to the present demonstrate how, for centuries, artists have found ways to ponder and express their identity and sense of belonging, through style, technique, subject, or material. This dynamic continues even today, and despite—or perhaps because of—the current ease of moving and communicating around the globe, artists who have left their home countries still seek to answer questions of who they are

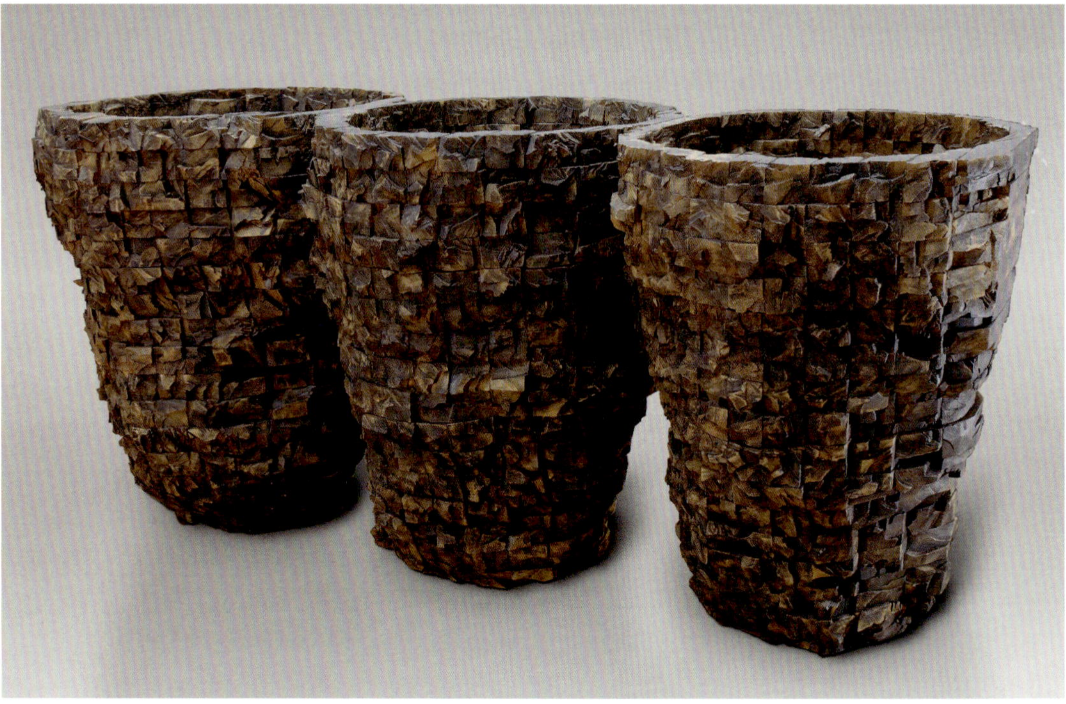

Fig. 14. Ursula von Rydingsvard, *Three Bowls*, 1989. Cedar and graphite, 56¾ × 116 × 60 in. (144.1 × 294.6 × 152.4 cm). Yale University Art Gallery, New Haven, Conn., Charles B. Benenson, B.A. 1933, Collection, 2006.52.58

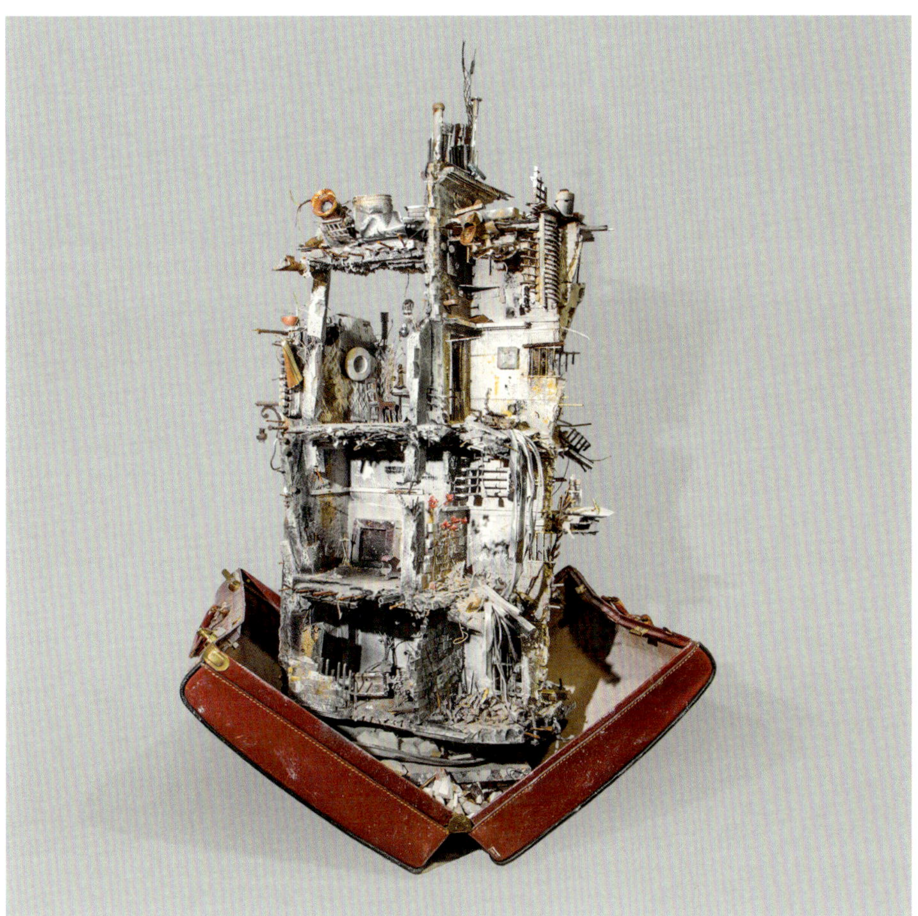

Fig. 15. Mohamad Hafez, *Baggage Series #4*, 2016. Plaster, paint, antique suitcase, found objects, and foam, 30 × 30 × 48 in. (76.2 × 76.2 × 121.9 cm). Collection of the artist

and how they define their place in the world. For instance, artists affected by the current and ongoing political crisis in the Middle East have been driven to respond to the destruction of social and cultural structures that are vital to their sense of self. One such artist, Syrian-born Mohamad Hafez, makes intricate sculptural works that painstakingly re-create the bombed facades of houses and apartments that people fled, leaving belongings and loved ones behind.[47] In *Baggage Series #4* (fig. 15) a suitcase, housing a destroyed structure, serves as more than a vessel for personal possessions—it stands for the emotional baggage that everyone forced to leave their home carries with them. This work also symbolizes the identity that most of the world now assigns to Syria, as its once-vibrant, eclectic culture that is thousands of years old is superseded by the image of a war-torn nation.[48]

Examples such as those discussed in this essay foreground how the loss of one's culture and identity, and the ensuing construction of new affiliations and a new self, can prompt a creative return to traditional roots, or a radical break with them, leading to complex visual responses. It is ultimately the artwork that bears testimony to the peregrinations, struggles, and quests of its maker and is the direct reflection of the exiled identity.

1. Salman Rushdie, *Imaginary Homelands: Essays and Criticism 1981–1991* (London: Granta, 1992), 15.

2. Eva Hoffman, *Lost in Translation: A Life in a New Language* (New York: Penguin, 1989), 107–8.

3. Ernst Bloch, "Disrupted Language, Disrupted Culture," *Direction* 2, no. 8 (December 1939): 16–17, 36.

4. Hannah Arendt, "We Refugees," in *Altogether Elsewhere: Writers on Exile*, ed. Marc Robinson (London: Faber and Faber, 1994), 110–19.

5. Joanna Woodall, "Introduction: Facing the Subject," in *Portraiture: Facing the Subject*, ed. Joanna Woodall (Manchester, England: Manchester University Press, 1997), 1–25, esp. 5–7.

6. The three regicides were Charles-Jean-Marie Alquier, Dominique-Vincent Ramel de Nogaret, and Emmanuel-Joseph Sieyès. Sieyès was one of the most famous figures of the French Revolution and the author of the political pamphlet *Qu'est-ce que le Tiers-État* (What Is the Third State, 1789). See Ewa Lajer-Burcharth, "The Self in Exile: David's Portrait of Sieyès," in *David after David: Essays on the Later Work*, ed. Mark Ledbury, conference proceedings (New Haven, Conn.: Yale University Press, 2007), 232–51, esp. 234.

7. Ibid., 244.

8. Philippe Bordes, *Jacques-Louis David: Empire to Exile*, exh. cat. (Williamstown, Mass.: Sterling and Francine Clark Art Institute, 2005), 314–18, cats. 52–53.

9. Lajer-Burcharth, "The Self in Exile," 244.

10. Although at the time the portrait was made, Sieyès was sixty-nine years old (as per the inscription in the upper-right corner, AETATIS SUAE 69), David painted him in his prime, giving him the face and body of a much younger man. Dorothy Johnson, "L'expérience de l'exil: l'art de David à Bruxelles," in *David contre David*, ed. Régis Michel, conference proceedings (Paris: Musée du Louvre and La Documentation française, 1993), 1025–45, esp. 1028.

11. Woodall, "Introduction," 7–8.

12. Barbara McCloskey, "Cartographies of Exile," in *Exile and Otherness: New Approaches to the Experience of the Nazi Refugees*, ed. Alexander Stephan (New York: Peter Lang, 2005), 135–52, esp. 138.

13. George Grosz to Max Herrmann-Neisse, May 5, 1933, George Grosz Papers (MS Ger 206), Series II, folder 640, Houghton Library, Harvard University, Cambridge, Mass.: "so ging ich nicht als 'politischer' Flüchtling fort . . . sondern, weil ich hier mich wohler fühlte und meine bessere Chance sah."

14. Birgit Möckel, "'A Little Yes and a Big No': George Grosz in Amerika," in *George Grosz: Berlin–New York*, ed. Peter-Klaus Schuster, exh. cat. (Berlin: Nationalgalerie, 1994), 283–97, esp. 286.

15. George Grosz, "Amerikanische Umgangsformen," *Querschnitt* 13, no. 1 (1933): 16–19; Möckel, "A Little Yes and a Big No," 285.

16. Grosz, "Amerikanische Umgangsformen," 16: "Er erscheint auf den ersten Blick unerzogener, salopper, aber auch frischer . . . kurz (wenn ein ominöses Wort gestattet ist, das in Europa so verhaßt ist): demokratischer."

17. Marsden Hartley, "George Grosz at An American Place," in *George Grosz: Exhibition of Water Colors (1933–1934)*, exh. brochure (New York: An American Place, 1935), n.p.

18. Ibid.

19. Möckel, "A Little Yes and a Big No," 292.

20. Birgit Möckel, *George Grosz in Amerika 1932–1959* (Frankfurt: Peter Lang, 1997), 187.

21. Birgit Möckel, "Die Gemälde der amerikanischen Jahre von 1934 bis 1959," in Schuster, *George Grosz: Berlin–New York*, 378, no. IX.62.

22. Beatrice von Bormann, "Traces of Exile in Art: Max Beckmann and Herbert Fiedler in the Netherlands, 1939–1945," in Stephan, *Exile and Otherness*, 153–75, esp. 157–58.

23. Barbara Rose, "Arshile Gorky and John Graham: Eastern Exiles in a Western World," *Arts Magazine* 50, no. 7 (March 1976): 62–69, esp. 64–65. For instance, Gorky sometimes falsely claimed that he was Russian and that he had studied with Kandinsky in Russia. Graham deliberately maintained doubts about his origins and his supposedly aristocratic upbringings.

24. James Kalm, "John Graham," *Brooklyn Rail*, December 2005, http://www.brooklynrail .org/2005/12/artseen/ john-graham.

25. Mira Schor, ed., *The Extreme of the Middle: Writings of Jack Tworkov* (New Haven, Conn.: Yale University Press, 2009), 9.

26. Ibid., 3–4.

27. Eloise Johnson, "Out of the Ashes: Cultural Identity and Marginalization in the Art of Beauford Delaney," in *Notes in the History of Art* 24, no. 4 (Summer 2005): 46–55.

28. David Leeming, *Amazing Grace: A Life of Beauford Delaney* (New York: Oxford University Press, 1998), 29–30, 112.

29. James Baldwin, "On the Painter Beauford Delaney," in *Art in America: 1945–1970, Writings from the Age of Abstract Expressionism, Pop Art, and Minimalism*, ed. Jed Perl (New York: Library of America, 2014), 545–47, esp. 547.

30. Johnson, "Out of the Ashes," 53.

31. For instance, Kobena Mercer argued, in his essay on Romare Bearden, that collage may be a form of *Kunstwollen*—a German term for an aesthetic form that is nearly inseparable from the social dynamism of its

age—whose development echoed the intermingled character of diaspora identities, shaped by both African and European elements. See Kobena Mercer, "Romare Bearden, 1964 Collage as 'Kunstwollen,'" in *Cosmopolitan Modernisms*, ed. Kobena Mercer (Cambridge, Mass.: MIT Press, 2005), 124–45, esp. 126.

32. Alastair Wright and Calvin Brown, eds. *Gauguin's Paradise Remembered: The Noa Noa Prints*, exh. cat. (Princeton, N.J.: Princeton University Art Museum, 2010), 9.

33. Calvin Brown, "Paradise Remembered: The Noa Noa Woodcuts," in Wright and Brown, *Gauguin's Paradise Remembered*, 101–26, esp. 101–2.

34. Erika Mosier, "Gauguin's Technical Experiments in Woodcut and Oil Transfer Drawing," in *Gauguin: Metamorphoses*, ed. Starr Figura, exh. cat. (New York: Museum of Modern Art, 2014), 60–71, esp. 62.

35. Thomas McEvilley, "Intimate but Lethal Things: The Art of Lucas Samaras," in *Lucas Samaras: Objects and Subjects, 1969–1986*, exh. cat. (Denver: Denver Art Museum, 1988), 11–30, esp. 18 19.

36. Marla Prather, "Chronology," in *Unrepentant Ego: The Self-Portraits of Lucas Samaras*, ed. Marla Prather, exh. cat. (New York: Whitney Museum of American Art, 2003), 15–16.

37. Donald Kuspit, "The Aesthetics of Trauma," in Prather, *Unrepentant Ego*, 44–61, esp. 47.

38. Ibid., 46–47.

39. Olga Viso, *Unseen Mendieta: The Unpublished Works of Ana Mendieta* (New York: Prestel, 2008), 7–8.

40. Ibid., 109.

41. Ana Mendieta, quoted in Petra Barreras del Rio and John Perreault, *Ana Mendieta: A Retrospective*, exh. cat. (New York: New Museum of Contemporary Art, 1988), 10.

42. Ibid., 13–14.

43. Marek Bartelik, "Reclaiming Spaces," in *The Sculpture of Ursula von Rydingsvard* (New York: Hudson Hills, 1996), 73–93, esp. 77–78. Von Rydingsvard said, "I feel like a child of the minimalists. The regularity, the repetitive regularity . . . There's a whole myth of perfection. My work is not sanitized and pure in terms of the kind of layering they did. . . . In some ways, I combine Abstract Expressionism and Minimalism. . . . I got my mixture using some of the tools of both of these styles"; ibid., 77, 90n17.

44. Amy Canonico, "Ursula von Rydingsvard," in *Eye on a Century: Modern and Contemporary Art from the Charles B. Benenson Collection at the Yale University Art Gallery*, ed. Cathleen Chaffee (New Haven, Conn.: Yale University Art Gallery, 2012), 162.

45. Bartelik, "Reclaiming Spaces," 73.

46. Ibid., 89, 93n66.

47. Jake Halpern, "An Artist's Obsession with the Ruins of His Homeland," *The New Yorker*, April 4, 2017, http://www.newyorker.com/culture/culture-desk/an-artists-obsession-with-the-ruins-of-his-homeland.

48. Mohamad Hafez, email correspondence with author, April 19–20, 2017.

The Filling Station
1934
Watercolor on paper
Image: 24¹⁵⁄₁₆ × 17⅝ in. (63.3 × 44.8 cm)
Provenance: George Hopper Fitch, New York; Yale University Art Gallery, New Haven, Conn., Gift of George Hopper Fitch, B.A. 1932, 1968.80.16.

An Old Tree
1943
Watercolor on paper
Image: 18½ × 13½ in. (47 × 34.3 cm)
Provenance: William Block, Pittsburgh; by inheritance to his wife, Maxine Block, Pittsburgh; Yale University Art Gallery, New Haven, Conn., Gift of Maxine and William Block, 2007.102.4.

The Filling Station was executed in 1934, the year after George Grosz and his family settled permanently in the United States. Grosz's departure was triggered by an increasingly hostile and fascist climate in Germany: he was targeted by the Nazis because of his antimilitary stance and his former membership in the Communist Party, and he hoped for better opportunities abroad. When he arrived in the United States, Grosz abandoned the politically engaged satiric caricature for which he had become famous during the Weimar Republic (fig. 1) and turned toward landscapes, cityscapes, nudes, and allegories. *The Filling Station* illustrates the shock that Grosz experienced vis-à-vis American culture, which he had become captivated by years earlier in Germany.[1] In this watercolor, he depicts an American cityscape, a metropolis filled with signs, letters, and billboards,

which captures the overwhelming visual excitement that he encountered there. As Grosz later described it, "The city was charged with stimuli for me and I was filled with inner fire and receptivity. . . . There was light, color and joy inside me! I filled numerous little books with thousands of sketches that I subsequently included in my paintings. I loved the buses that rumbled along the streets. I loved the store windows . . . The displays here were like real fairy palaces."[2] *The Filling Station* renders his fascination with the big city, and the life within it, in strong symbols.[3] The middle of the composition is dominated by a streetlight. Houses, water towers, and skyscrapers are stacked atop each other in the back, and they cover almost the entire top of the sheet but for a few dabs of blue serving as the sky. Grosz filled the foreground with signs of American mass culture and materialism: advertisements and shop signs, as well as images of the automobile industry, such as the car on the right side, a gas pump advertising the price, and the back of a mechanic clad in blue overalls.

A few years later, Grosz's work in the United States, particularly his landscapes, became more introspective.[4] In the 1930s and 1940s, Grosz spent the summer months in Cape Cod, Massachusetts, and traveled to Garnet Lake, in upstate New York. *An Old Tree*, which he painted at Garnet Lake, is an example of pure landscape: Grosz depicts an idyllic scene with a tree on the bank of a lake and mountains in the background, with no human presence. Yet some elements disrupt the peaceful character of the scene; the vivid colors, for instance, give it a surreal character. The tree, although occupying nearly the whole length of the sheet, seems almost forlorn, without any needles or leaves, and disturbs the otherwise peaceful scenery. This work bears similarities to a number of apocalyptic landscapes Grosz painted during the war years that were inspired by Northern Renaissance art—notably paintings by Albrecht Altdorfer (fig. 2), Hieronymus Bosch, and Pieter Bruegel, and botanical drawings by Albrecht Dürer (fig. 3).[5] At the same time, this work draws parallels to landscapes by contemporary American artists, particularly Charles Burchfield, who also painted numerous watercolors of nature scenes without signs of civilization. Burchfield's depiction of flowers, trees, and fields morphed in a similar way in the 1950s to become more unrealistic, characterized by a fluidity of forms and vivid colors (fig. 4). The works by both of these artists exemplify how, even at a time when Abstract Expressionism emerged as a new, fiercely American style, Grosz and others turned to artistic tradition, figuration, and narrative as a way to cope with the realities of their time.

208

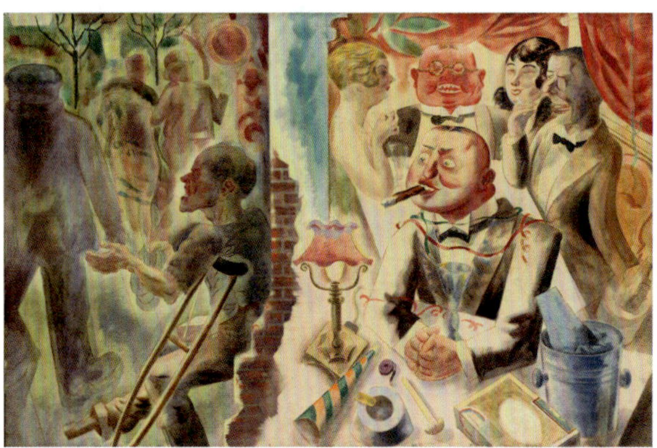

Fig. 1. George Grosz, *Drinnen und Draussen* (Inside and Outside), 1926. Oil on canvas, 31½ × 46¾ in. (80 × 118.7 cm). Yale University Art Gallery, New Haven, Conn., Promised gift of Dr. and Mrs. Herbert Schaefer

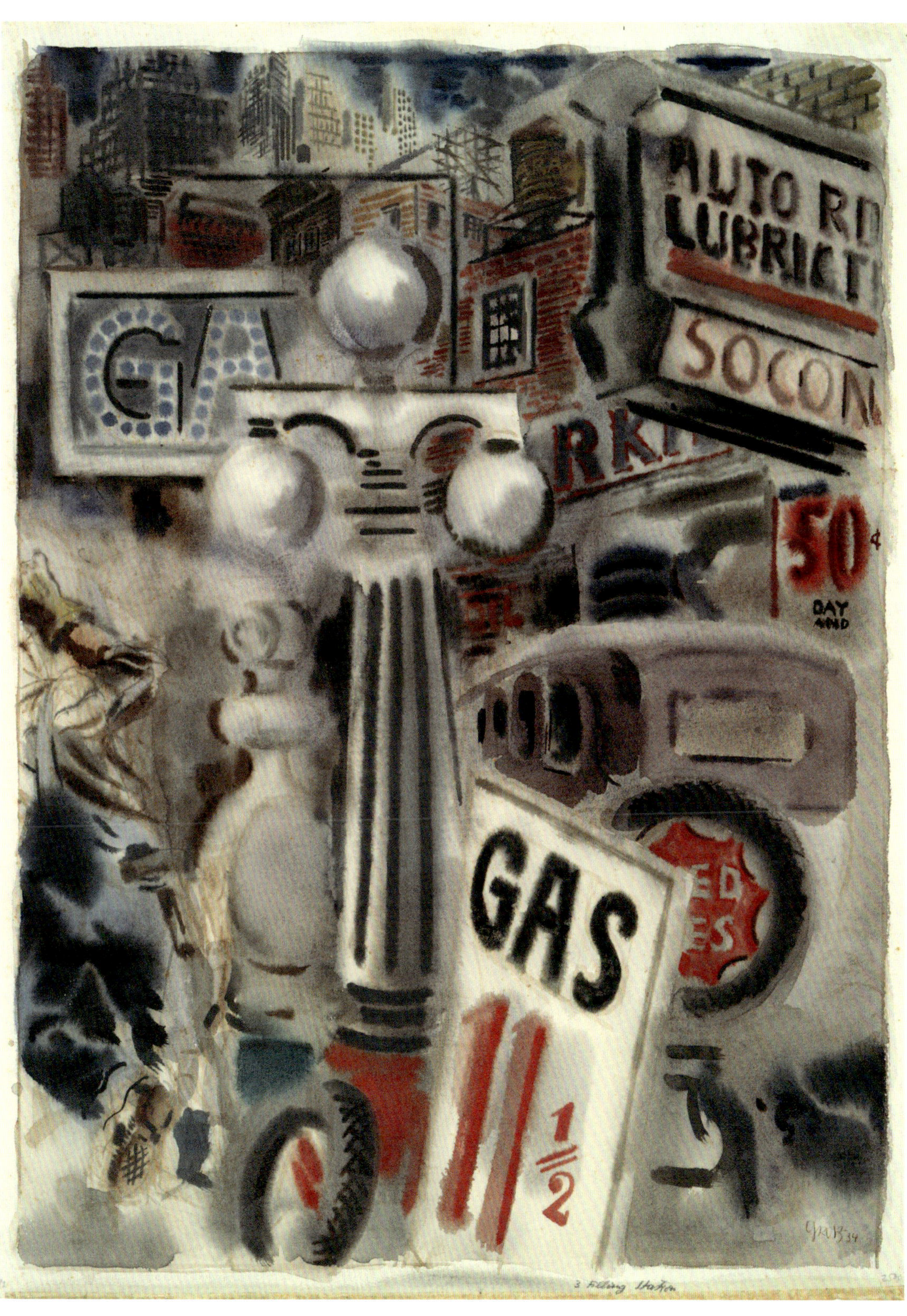

The Filling Station

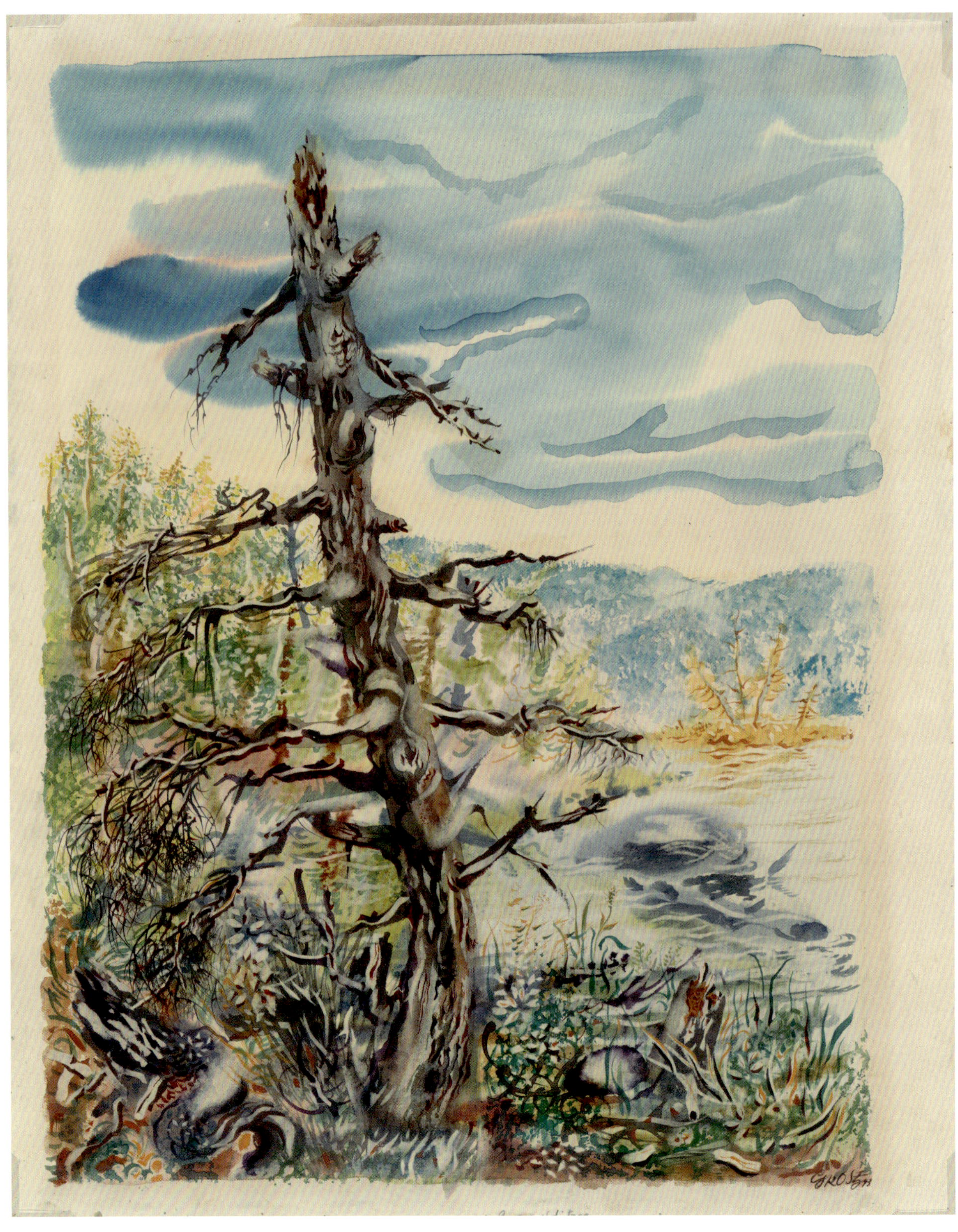

An Old Tree

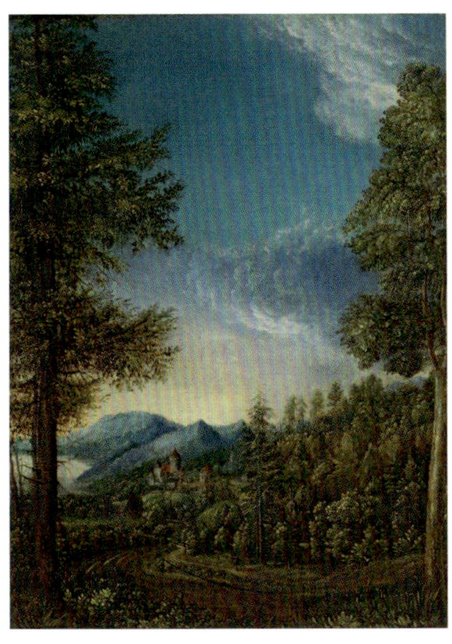

Fig. 2. Albrecht Altdorfer, *Donaulandschaft mit Schloss Wörth* (Danube Landscape with Wörth Castle), 1520–25. Oil on parchment on wood, 11¹³⁄₁₆ × 8⅝ in. (30 × 22 cm). Alte Pinakothek, Munich, WAF 30

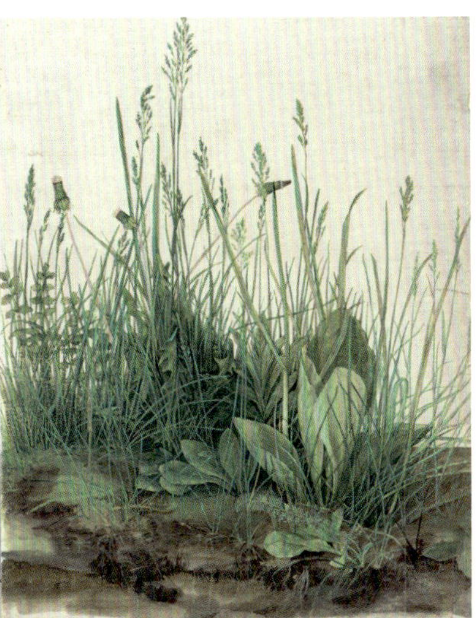

Fig. 3. Albrecht Dürer, *Das große Rasenstück* (The Great Piece of Turf), 1503. Watercolor and gouache heightened with white, mounted on cardboard, 16 × 12⅜ in. (40.8 × 31.5 cm). Albertina, Vienna, 3075

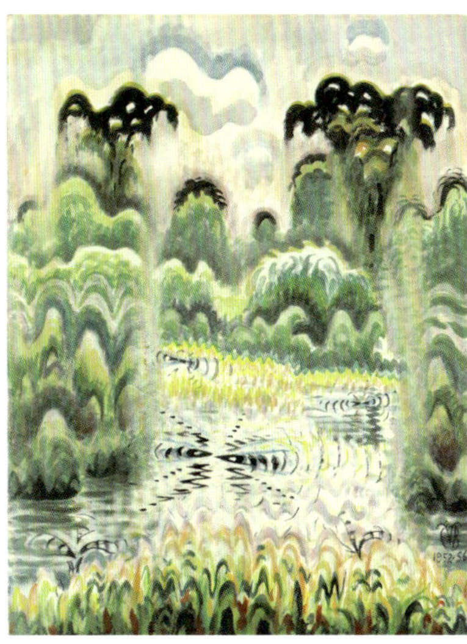

Fig. 4. Charles Burchfield, *Marsh in June*, 1952–56. Watercolor, 34¹³⁄₁₆ × 25¹³⁄₁₆ in. (88.4 × 65.6 cm). Yale University Art Gallery, New Haven, Conn., Katharine Ordway Collection, 1980.13.65

These kinds of seemingly traditional works irritated many of Grosz's supporters. His longtime friend and patron Felix Weil wrote to Grosz in 1941, "Du bist also wieder bei der 'Kunst' angelangt" (You have thus gone back to "art"), an explicit reproach of the artist's choice to focus on landscapes and other genres instead of on socially critical works.[6] Grosz's American work expresses not only his fascination with his new country but also his desire for assimilation. Whereas many of his fellow exiles considered their time in America an intermission with the hope of returning to their respective countries, Grosz embraced his new home and tried to establish himself as an American artist, abandoning his activist past.[7] However, the American audience was more interested in his earlier dissident, satirical art than in his landscapes and allegories. Grosz was put in the role of a famed exile from Nazi persecution by critics and the public alike, although the artist was opposed to having his work used for propaganda purposes.[8] For decades after Grosz's death, critics and art historians dismissed his seemingly anti-Modernist style as a manifestation of personal and artistic decline.[9] Yet for Grosz, this return to nature was a sign of a new beginning that he so desperately wanted to have in the United States.[10] —FVJ

1. George Grosz, *A Little Yes and a Big No*, trans. Lola Sachs Dorin (New York: Dial Press, 1946), 261–64.

2. Ibid., 270.

3. Hans Hess, *George Grosz* (New Haven, Conn.: Yale University Press, 1985), 201.

4. Grosz had drawn and painted landscapes throughout his career, and he made several works of the Baltic Coast and Southern France. Roland März, "Die Gemälde der Berliner Jahre von 1915 bis 1931," in *George Grosz: Berlin—New York*, ed. Peter-Klaus Schuster, exh. cat. (Berlin: Staatliche Museen zu Berlin, 1994), 351, cat. IX.35; Birgit Möckel, *George Grosz in Amerika: 1932–1959* (Frankfurt: Peter Lang, 1997), 136.

5. Barbara McCloskey, *The Exile of George Grosz: Modernism, America, and the One World Order* (Oakland: University of California Press, 2015), 22; Möckel, *George Grosz in Amerika*, 138–39.

6. Felix Weil to George Grosz, October 29, 1941, George Grosz Papers (MS Ger 206), Series I, 451, Houghton Library, Harvard University, Cambridge, Mass.

7. McCloskey, *The Exile of George Grosz*, 2–3.

8. See Josenhans, "(Re)Defining the 'I' in Exile," in this volume, 189–92.

9. McCloskey, *The Exile of George Grosz*, 5.

10. Grosz, *A Little Yes and a Big No*, 275.

Birds' Hell (Hölle der Vögel)
1938
Oil on canvas
47¼ × 63³⁄₁₆ in. (120 × 160.5 cm)
Provenance: Studio Max Beckmann, Paris; Käthe von Porada, Paris and Venice; Buchholz Gallery–Curt Valentin, New York; Stephen Radlich, New York; Fine Arts Associates, New York; Morton D. May, Saint Louis; private collection; Christie's, London, June 27, 2017, lot 11; private collection.

While *Birds' Hell (Hölle der Vögel)* can be seen as an allegorical depiction of hell, the painting also explicitly refers to Max Beckmann's exile during the Third Reich and conveys his vivid criticism of Nazism.[1] By the time he left Germany in 1937, Beckmann was a well-known, successful artist, although he had never formally joined any of the art movements that were popular during his time, such as Expressionism, Dada, or Neue Sachlichkeit (New Objectivity). Instead he established a highly personal, figurative style, drawing from different sources. Many of his works are allegories, portraiture, still lifes, and landscapes that seem disconnected from reality, are highly symbolic, and express a larger reflection on history and humankind. They also express the artist's ambition to capture "the magic of reality and to transfer this reality into painting—to make the invisible visible through reality."[2]

Beckmann made this painting shortly after he had left Germany for the Netherlands, due to his dismissal from his teaching position in Frankfurt, the removal of his works from public collections by the Nazi government, and the inclusion of several of his paintings in the *Entartete Kunst* (Degenerate Art) exhibition.[3] He painted *Birds' Hell* in Amsterdam and in Paris, where he spent some time in 1938 and 1939.[4] The work depicts a scene of torture in a confined space filled with gigantesque birds and a crowd of people. A man with bound hands and feet is stretched out on a table in the center of the composition, and one of the birds slices his back open with a knife. Although the iconography is exceedingly complex, several signs refer specifically to the Third Reich's ideology. For instance, a female figure with several breasts, emerging from a cracked egg, stands next to the torture scene with her arm raised in the Nazi salute. This creature, with additional nude women lined up behind her, expresses the cult of motherhood, a trope of Nazi propaganda that reduced women to fertility objects.[5] Below her outstretched arm is a Prussian eagle, which derived from the black eagle of the Holy Roman Empire and had been used on coats of arms since the Middle Ages, and which was subsequently embraced by the Nazis. Beckmann depicts this historically charged symbol here hoarding golden coins, alluding to the hidden connection between German capitalism and the Nazi party.[6] Even the other birds, with their colorful feathers, seem to be a direct reference to Nazi party officials, who wore brown and red uniforms with gold insignia and were referred to as *Goldfasanen* (gold pheasants).[7] On the floor, a newspaper, with the German word *Zeitung* (newspaper) partially visible, might refer to the censorship of the press. The crowd in the back consists of unidentified figures, all raising their arms in the Nazi salute, threateningly watched over by another bird. The birds' flamboyant plumage contradicts the atrocity of the scene and stands in stark contrast to the crowd in the back, depicted in muddy colors. The space does not give any clear indications of location, although the large red openings in the back might be meant to evoke ovens, which would further emphasize the idea of "hell." The overpopulated composition creates a terrifying atmosphere, with no visible escape.

The torture scene derives from a much older German work, Stefan Lochner's *Martyrdom of Saint Bartholomew* (fig. 1), a scene from the *Martyrdoms of the Apostles* altarpiece, in which the saint is tortured

212

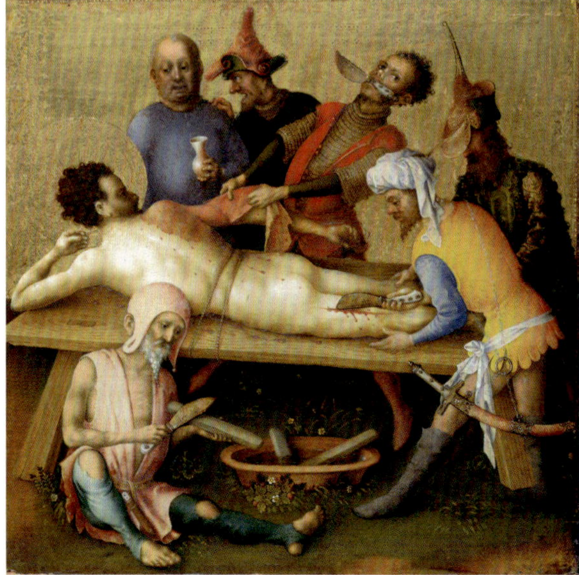

Fig. 1. Stefan Lochner, *Martyrdom of Saint Bartholomew*, detail of *The Martyrdoms of the Apostles*, ca. 1435. Mixed media on walnut, overall 49¹⁵⁄₁₆ × 69⅛ in. (126.8 × 175.6 cm). Städel Museum, Frankfurt, 821

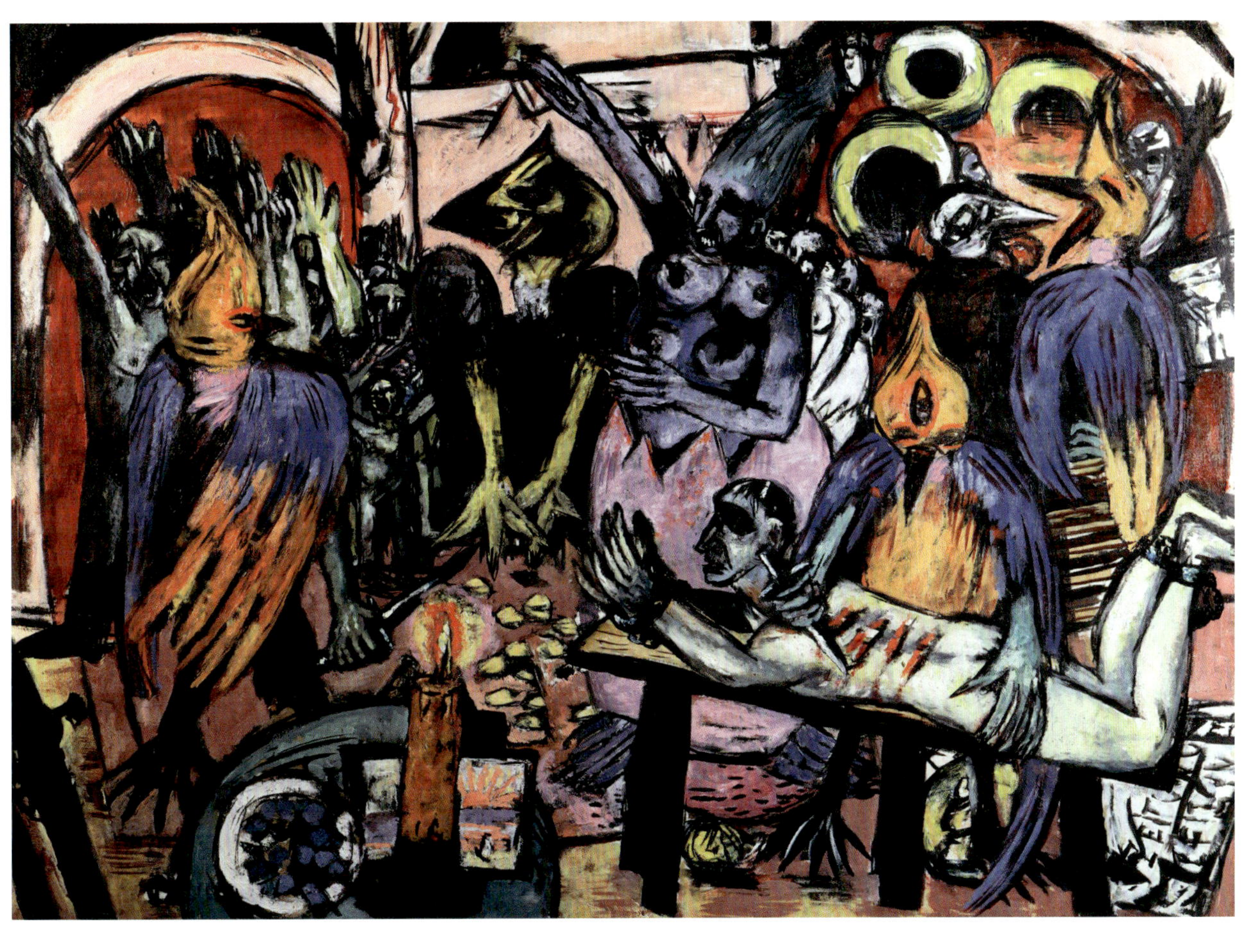

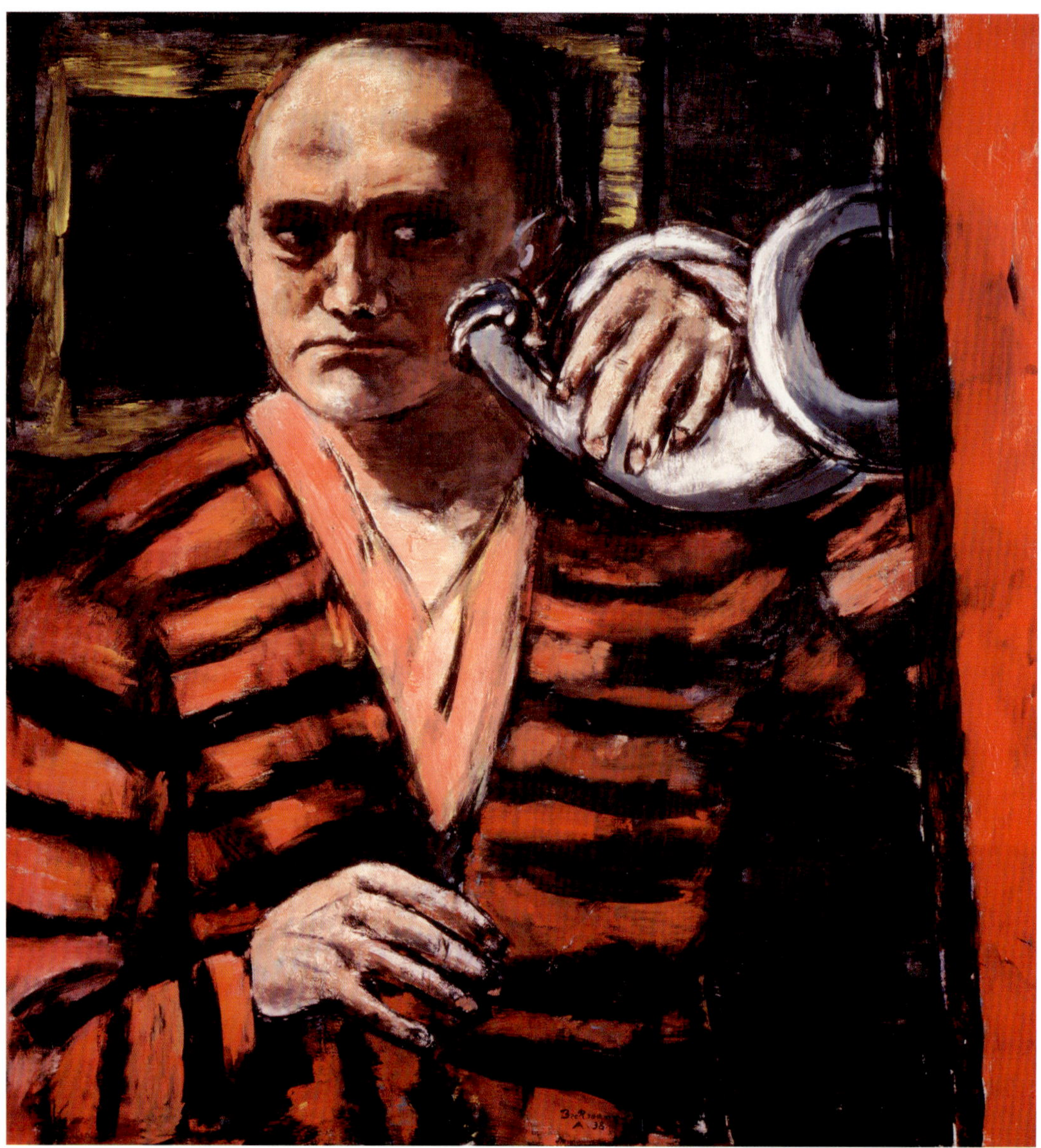

Fig. 2. Max Beckmann, *Selbstbildnis mit Horn* (Self-Portrait with Horn), 1938. Oil on canvas, 43⁵⁄₁₆ × 39¾ in. (110 × 101 cm). Neue Galerie, New York, and private collection

by several figures pulling flesh from his bones.[8] The martyrized man in Beckmann's work might be seen as a disguised image of the artist himself, or rather a figure emblematic of the fate of the many artists and intellectuals in Germany whose work was banned, whose lives were threatened, and who were disconnected from their culture, either physically or emotionally, and declared "un-German."

During his exile, Beckmann painted several enigmatic self-portraits that show him isolated and withdrawn from the world, such as *Selbstbildnis mit Horn* (Self-Portrait with Horn, fig. 2), in which the artist stands partially in shadow in a confined space, warily looking at a horn, his sole companion. *Birds' Hell*, though painted at around the same time as *Selbstbildnis mit Horn*, is much more blatant in its illustration of the misery Beckmann had felt as an artist in Nazi Germany; he depicts a human figure, here symbolizing the fate of millions as well as that of the artist himself, helpless in the face of others who blindly follow a totalitarian ideology. And yet the artist makes the allegory even more complex by introducing an element that seems to contradict this living hell. The small table in the foreground of *Birds' Hell* has several objects on its top: a burning candle, a plate of grapes, and a picture of the sun over the sea—a small still life in a scene of atrocity. In the midst of this inferno created by mankind, the candle is a sign of hope, a light in the dark.[9] —FVJ

1. Carla Schulz-Hoffmann, *Max Beckmann: Retrospektive*, exh. cat. (Munich: Haus der Kunst and Prestel-Verlag, 1984), 270–71, cat. 84.

2. Max Beckmann, "On My Painting," speech at the *Exhibition of Twentieth-Century German Art*, London, New Burlington Galleries, 1938, reproduced in Barbara Stehlé-Akhtar, Stephan Lackner, and Reinhard Spieler, *Max Beckmann in Exile*, exh. cat. (New York: Solomon R. Guggenheim Museum, 1996), 119–23, esp. 119.

3. Uwe M. Schneede, *Max Beckmann: Der Maler seiner Zeit* (Munich: C. H. Beck, 2009), 177–80; Lynette Roth, *Max Beckmann at the Saint Louis Art Museum: The Paintings*, exh. cat. (Saint Louis: Saint Louis Art Museum, 2015), 128–31.

4. Erhard Göpel and Barbara Göpel, *Max Beckmann: Katalog der Gemälde* (Bern, Switzerland: Verlag Kornfeld und Cie, 1976), 1:320–21, cat. 506; Barbara Copeland Buenger, "Max Beckmann in Paris, Amsterdam, and the United States, 1937–50," in *Exiles and Emigrés: The Flight of European Artists from Hitler*, ed. Stephanie Barron, exh. cat. (Los Angeles: Los Angeles County Museum of Art, 1997), 58–67, esp. 59–60.

5. Stephan Lackner, *Max Beckmann* (New York: Abrams, 1977), 130.

6. While the Nazi government was supposedly anticapitalist, it in fact benefited from capitalism and worked closely with many major companies; ibid.

7. Ibid.

8. Buenger, "Max Beckmann in Paris, Amsterdam, and the United States," 60–61.

9. A burning candle can be found in other paintings that Beckmann made during his exile years: *Les Artistes mit Gemüse* (The Artists with Vegetable, 1943; see cat. 19, fig. 1), and *Birth* (1937) and *Death* (1938), both in the collection of the Staatliche Museen zu Berlin, Neue Nationalgalerie.

215

Sharecropper
1945
Linocut
4¼ × 6 in. (10.8 × 15.2 cm)
Provenance: Sragow Gallery, New York; Yale University
Art Gallery, New Haven, Conn., Leonard C. Hanna, Jr.,
Class of 1913, Fund, 1995.5.1.

My right is a future of equality with other Americans,
from the series *The Negro Woman*
1947
Two-color linocut
9¹⁄₁₆ × 6 in. (23 × 15.2 cm)
Provenance: Sragow Gallery, New York; Yale University
Art Gallery, New Haven, Conn., Leonard C. Hanna, Jr.,
Class of 1913, Fund, 1995.5.3.

*My reward has been bars between me and the rest of the
land,* from the series *The Negro Woman*
1947
Linocut
4½ × 5¹³⁄₁₆ in. (11.5 × 14.8 cm)
Provenance: Monroe E. Price and Aimée Brown Price;
Yale University Art Gallery, New Haven, Conn., Gift of
Monroe E. Price, B.A. 1960, LL.B. 1964, and Aimée Brown
Price, M.A. 1963, PH.D. 1972, 2011.203.8.

Elizabeth Catlett's art addresses issues of race, gender, segregation, and civil rights. Yet, her work cannot simply be
reduced to Social Realism or activism and indeed relates
to all human experience.[1] A granddaughter of freed slaves
who grew up in a middle-class African American family
in Washington, D.C., Catlett was always conscious of the
suffering and exploitation of African American citizens
in the United States. However, it was not until she moved
to New York in 1942 and began teaching adult-education
classes at the George Washington Carver School—which
served working-class Harlem residents—that she came
to gain a better understanding of the lives of the working
poor.[2] During this time, Catlett explored labor and
oppression in her own prints, of which *Sharecropper* is an
early example. The motif of the sharecropper reappeared
in her oeuvre, notably in her famous later version of a
female laborer (fig. 1).

Drawing on her time in Harlem and her own
background, Catlett began to focus on the subjugation
and revolt of black women in particular. She was awarded
a fellowship from the Rosenwald Fund, which supported
African American artists and intellectuals, and used
the funds to go to Mexico in 1946 to study the socially

216

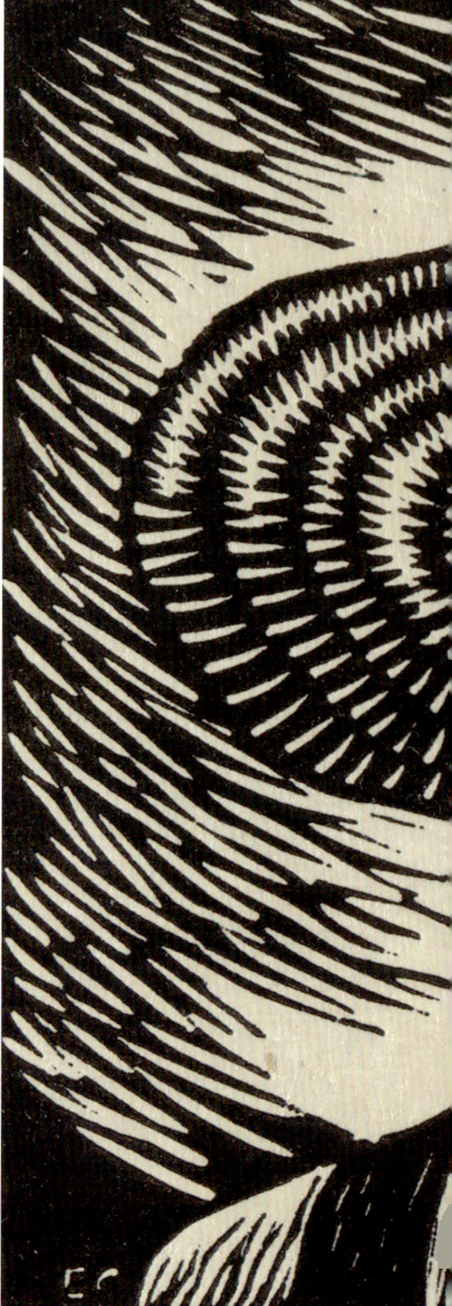

Sharecropper

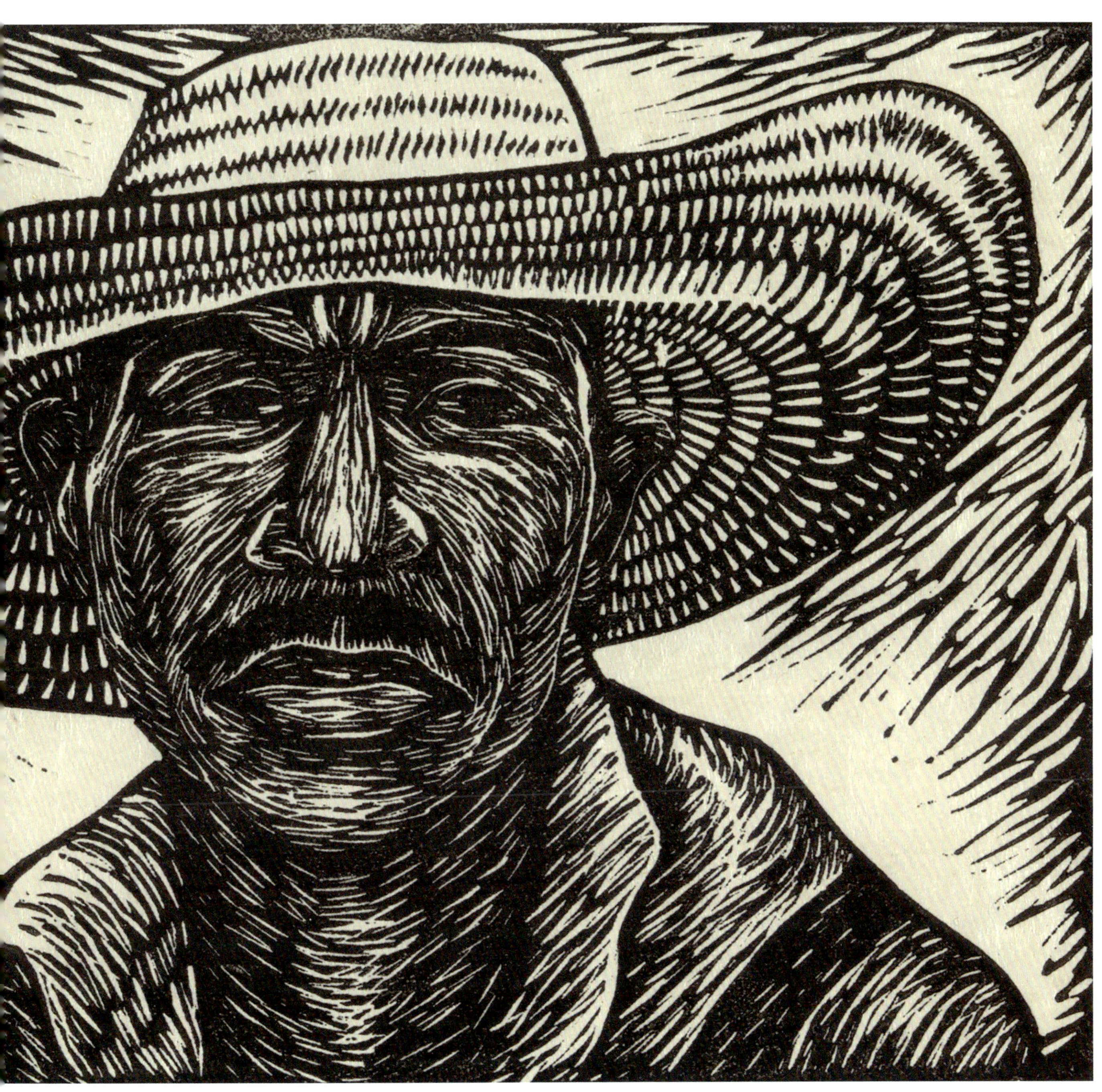

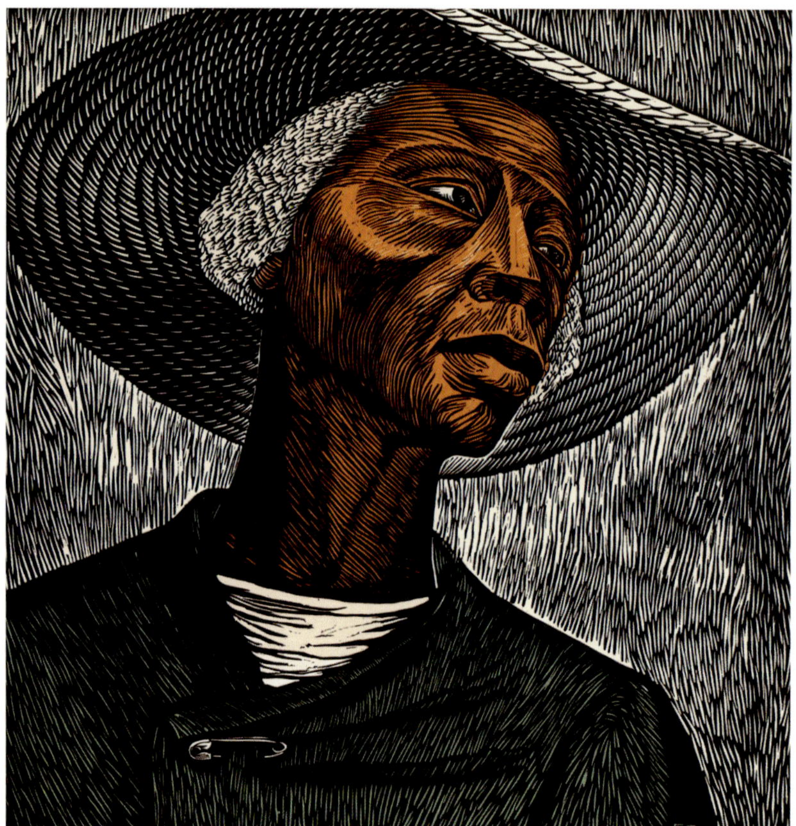

Fig. 1. Elizabeth Catlett, *Sharecropper*, 1952, printed 1970. Color linocut on cream Japanese paper, 17¹¹⁄₁₆ × 17 in. (45 × 43.1 cm). Art Institute of Chicago, Restricted gift of Mr. and Mrs. Robert S. Hartman, 1992.182

engaged art of Mexican muralists.[3] In Mexico she found a new home and a politically involved artistic community. She joined the Taller de Gráfica Popular (TGP), a renowned workshop and artists' collective that created didactic artworks on sociopolitical topics, inspired by the idealism of the muralists who supported the Mexican Revolution of 1910–20. Catlett's decision to leave the United States for Mexico was also partly due to the climate of repression and suspicion during the Cold War and McCarthy era. Socially engaged artists were presumed "communist" and thus subject to harassment, which for Catlett continued even after she moved to Mexico and throughout the 1950s.[4]

At the TGP, Catlett began to work increasingly in linocut, a technique that produces inexpensive prints and can accommodate large editions. In 1946 and 1947, Catlett created a series of fifteen prints titled *The Negro Woman*, which honors African American women—both historical figures and ordinary people. The prints are relatively small, but the close-up framing of the faces, which in each case occupy almost the entire sheet, lends them a monumental quality. By titling each print in the first person, in the voice of the subject, Catlett paired these visually powerful and expressive images with a narrative and implied that she identified personally with these women. The titles allude to the struggles and achievements of her heroines, giving her subjects an individual, as well as a collective, voice.[5] In *My right is a future of equality with other Americans*, the foreshortened head of a woman, with her eyes turned toward the sky, is simple yet captivating, and her upward gaze expresses hope and dignity. *My reward has been bars between me and the rest of the land* shows a woman behind a barbed wire that creates distance between her and the

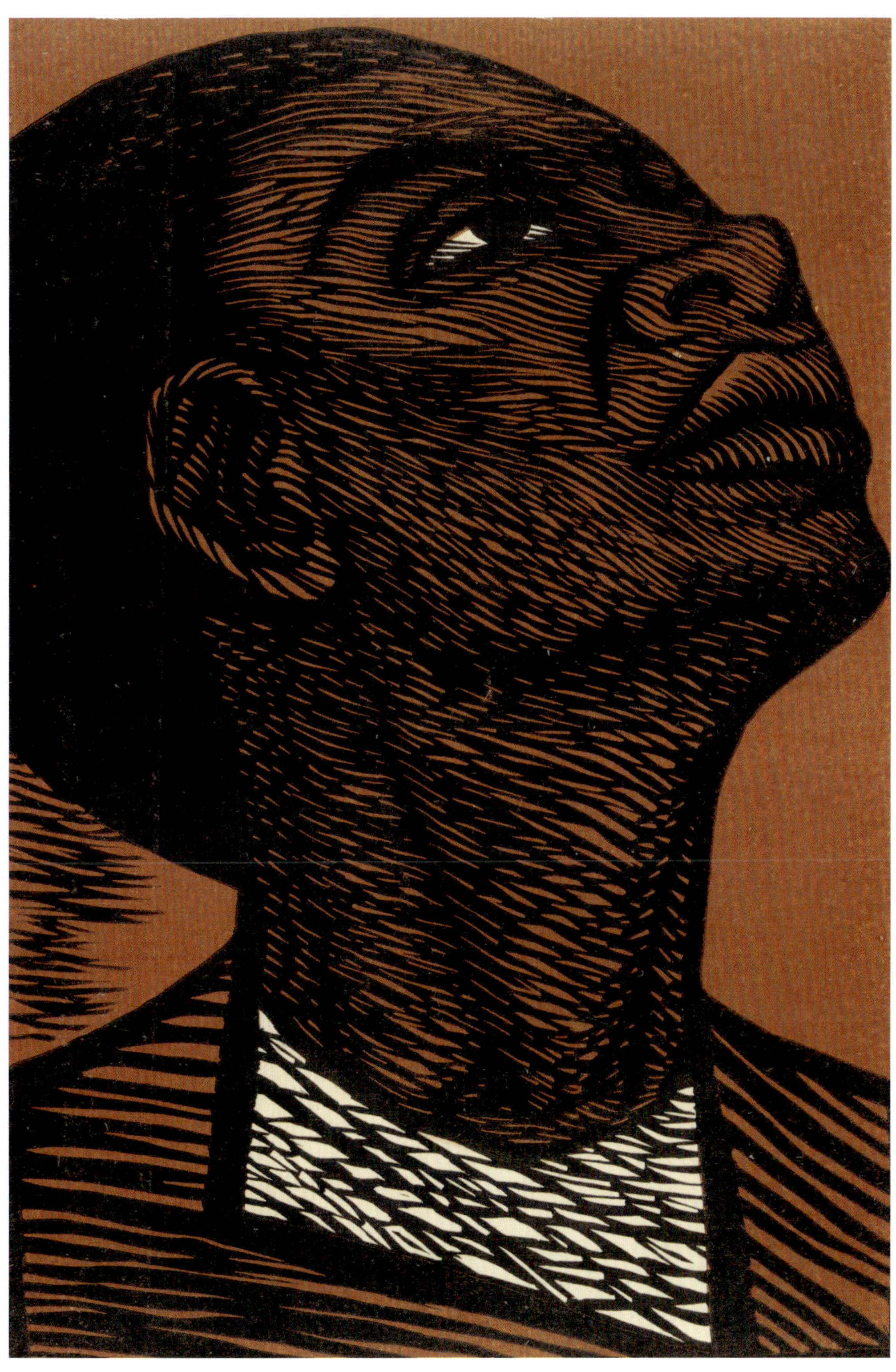

My right is a future of equality with other Americans

viewer. Despite the confining composition, the figure's posture is upright, and she looks beyond the obstacle.

All three portraits illustrate the essence of Catlett's art. Each print focuses on a face that reflects a life of hardship. Even though these men and women must withstand harsh social conditions, they convey strength and dignity, as visible in their serene postures and their unflinching, direct gazes. These subjects also reflect the artist's own unwavering beliefs. After she became a Mexican citizen, Catlett was denied access to her native country, but she remained involved with social issues in the United States and supported the Black Arts Movement during the 1960s.[6] After Malcolm X was killed in 1965, Catlett created a print (fig. 2) to emphasize his importance for African American women and to make this symbolic figure accessible to everyone, combining yet again her activism with empathy.[7] —FVJ

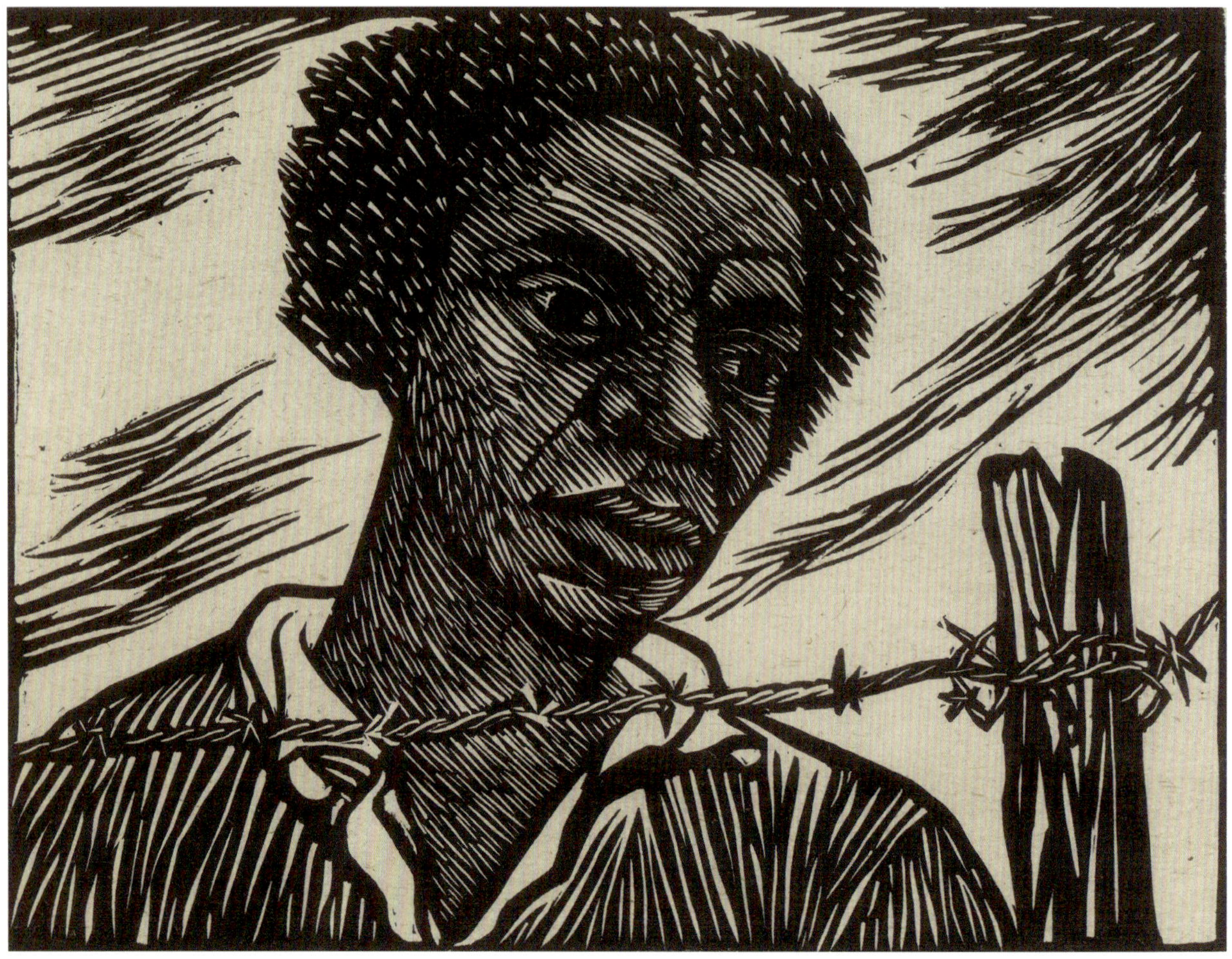

My reward has been bars between me and the rest of the land

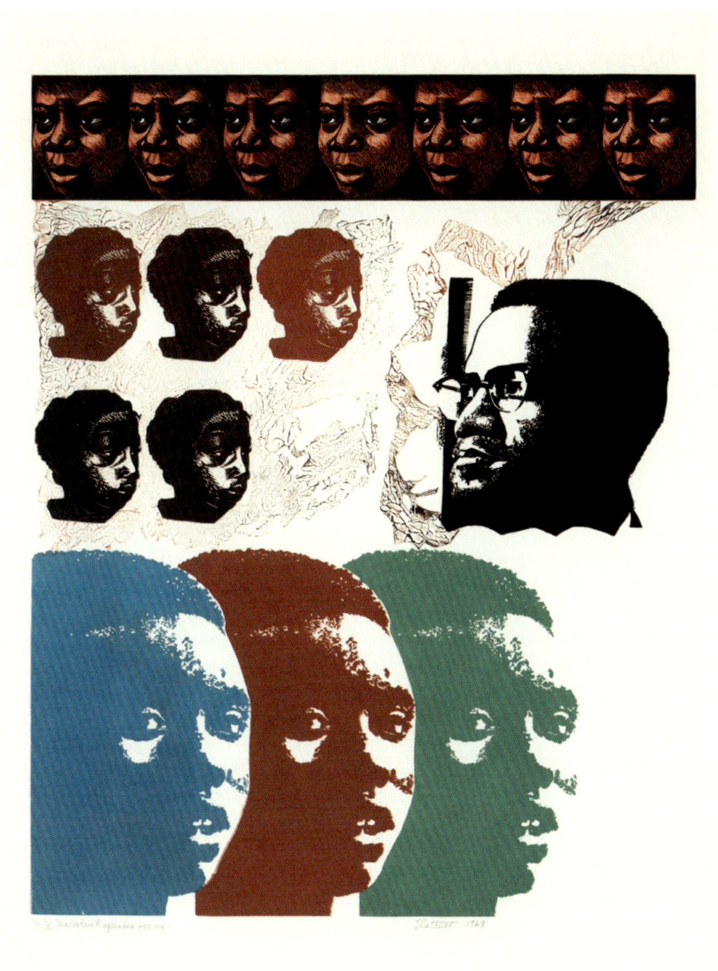

Fig. 2. Elizabeth Catlett, *Malcolm X Speaks for Us*, 1969. Linocut,
34¹³⁄₁₆ × 27³⁄₁₆ in. (88.4 × 69.1 cm). Museum of Modern Art, New York,
Gift of the artist, 332.1988

1. Richard J. Powell, "Face to Face: Elizabeth Catlett's Graphic Work," in *Elizabeth Catlett: Works on Paper, 1944–1992*, ed. Jeanne Zeidler, exh. cat. (Hampton, Va.: Hampton University Museum, 1993), 49–53, esp. 51.

2. Melanie Anne Herzog, *Elizabeth Catlett: In the Image of the People*, exh. cat. (Chicago: Art Institute of Chicago, 2005), 6; Melanie Anne Herzog, "Elizabeth Catlett (1915–2012)," *American Art* 26, no. 3 (Fall 2012): 105–9, esp. 106.

3. Herzog, *Elizabeth Catlett: In the Image of the People*, 7.

4. Melanie Anne Herzog, *Elizabeth Catlett: An American Artist in Mexico* (Seattle: University of Washington Press, 2000), 75–78.

5. Ibid., 56–66; Herzog, *Elizabeth Catlett: In the Image of the People*, 9–10.

6. Herzog, *Elizabeth Catlett: An American Artist in Mexico*, 133–35.

7. Deborah Wye, ed., *Artists and Prints: Masterworks from the Museum of Modern Art* (New York: Museum of Modern Art, 2004), 218.

Photo-Transformation
1974
Color instant print (Polaroid) with hand additions
3⅛ × 3⅛ in. (7.9 × 7.9 cm)
Provenance: Given by the artist to Pace Gallery,
New York; purchased by Richard Brown Baker, 1974;
Yale University Art Gallery, New Haven, Conn.,
Richard Brown Baker, B.A. 1935, Collection, 2008.19.638.

Lucas Samaras made this altered self-portrait using
a Polaroid SX-70 camera. It is part of the artist's
Photo-Transformations (1973–76), an extensive series
of manipulated photographs that he created by placing
colored sheets of plastic over the camera lens and over
spotlights, as well as by working variously into the
dye of the film by hand before it set. These works are a
continuation of Samaras's materially experimental and
insistently self-referential practice. Enacting alterations
on his own body that are at once violent, beautiful,
and uncanny, the artist conveys simultaneous themes
of narcissism and the instability or dissolution of the
self. These motifs can be traced back to Samaras's early
experiences as a child growing up amid the violence and
destruction of war-torn Greece, which he fled when he
immigrated to New Jersey with his mother in 1948.

222

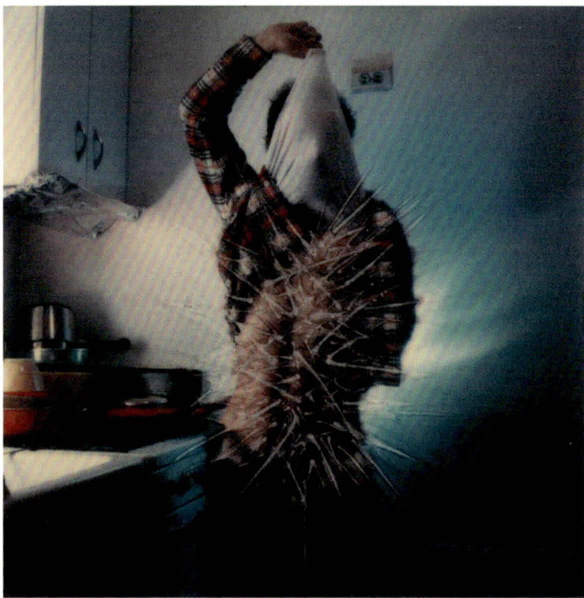

Fig. 1. Lucas Samaras, *Photo-Transformation*, 1974. Color instant
print (Polaroid SX-70), 3⅛ × 3⅛ in. (7.9 × 7.9 cm). Museum of
Modern Art, New York, Gift of Robert and Gayle Greenhill, 67.1992

By enabling the immediate reproduction of his
own image, the rapid, automatic development of Polaroid
film seems to have abetted an inherent narcissistic
impulse in Samaras. This inclination is evident in his
earlier works, as in his small pastel self-portraits dating
back to the beginning of his career as a student at
Rutgers University in the late 1950s, and in the images
of himself that he included in his sculptural boxes of
the 1960s.[1] Yet the often simultaneously irreverent,
violent, and playful nature of Samaras's many different
auto-representations seems to loosen, rather than to
fortify, the strictures of the self.[2] Here, instead of pre-
serving the capacities of the photograph to mimetically
capture the whole likeness of a person, he alters the form
of his figure by smudging, incising, and swirling the ink
of the wet negative (fig. 1).

In this *Photo-Transformation*, Samaras appears
to be caught in a state of ecstatic emotion, an impression
accentuated by the red and green hues that distort his
skin and suggest extreme rage, envy, or passion. His
head is tilted back and to the left to reveal the inside of
his open, screaming mouth. His body is positioned close
to the camera yet contorts away from view. This tension
between presence and distance is further evident in
the manner in which the artist has scrawled his first
name across the dark background of the negative.
Writing one's name is both an assertion and a formalized
abstraction of identity. Samaras makes his letters nearly
incomprehensible, heightening this paradox between
expression and alienation.

According to the art critic Donald Kuspit,
Samaras's compulsive repetition of his own likeness
serves as a kind of totem against the chaos and death
that he witnessed at a young age; his family home was
damaged and his grandmother was killed during the
Greek Civil War.[3] Yet the vigorous experimentation that
characterizes this repetition also suggests a sense of self
that is expanded, perhaps pathologically, by early experiences of devastation and migration.[4] As a child, Samaras
made toys out of scraps of material that he found in the
rubble-strewn landscape of his hometown, Kastoria, and
he continues this connection between creativity and
destruction in the *Photo-Transformations* by creating
images that are made beautiful through defacement.
Instead of being closed off and rigidified by trauma, the
self in this art is the malleable center of an expansive and
tumultuous practice of self-expression. —ND

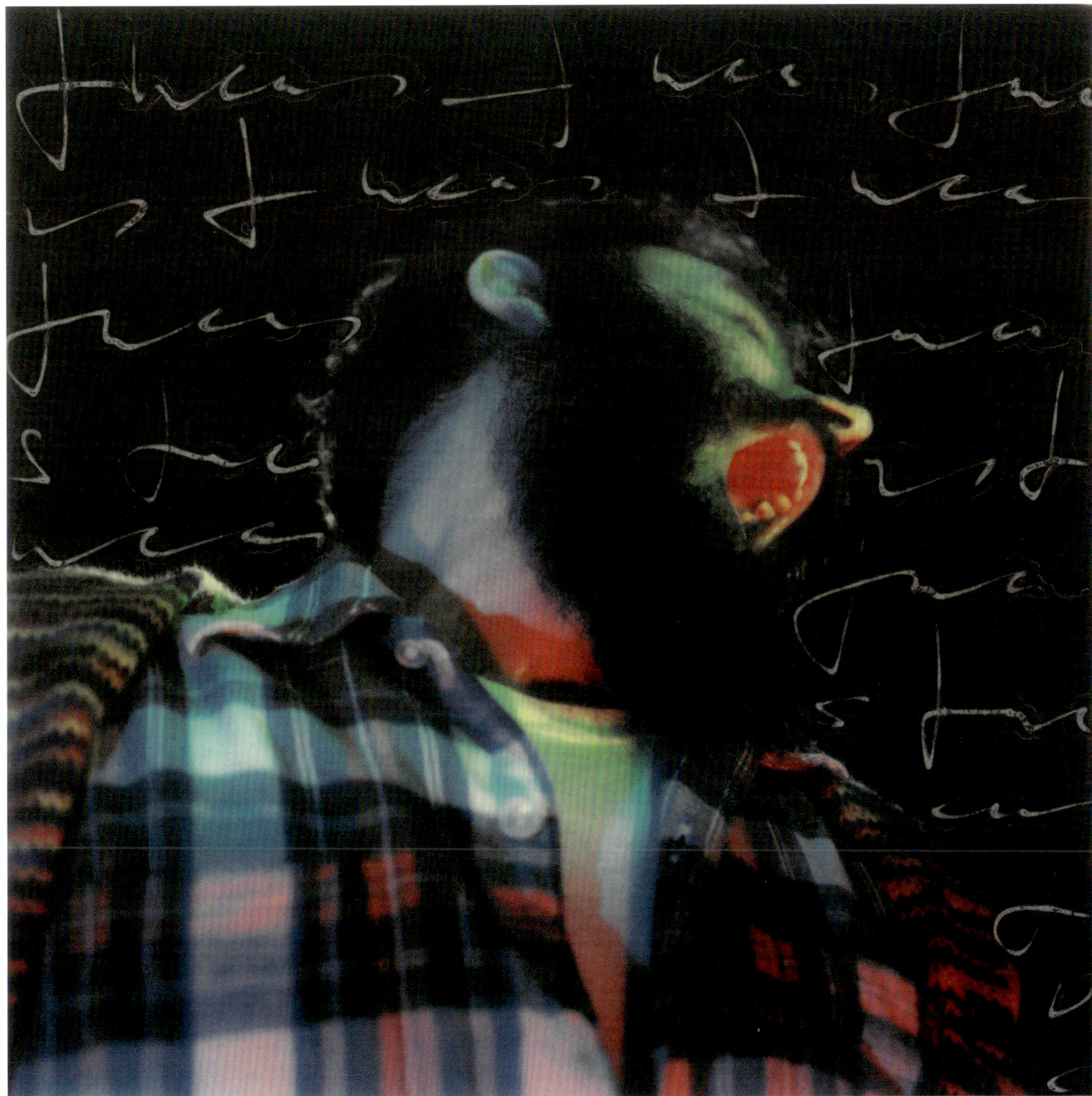

1. See, for instance, Untitled (1963, Los Angeles County Museum of Art) or *Box #10* (1963, collection of the artist).

2. Rosalind Krauss, "Video: The Aesthetics of Narcissism," *October* 1 (1976): 55.

3. Donald Kuspit, "The Aesthetics of Trauma," in *Unrepentant Ego*, ed. Marla Prather, exh. cat. (New York: Whitney Museum of American Art, 2003), 46. This repetition is not only pictorial but extends to the autobiographical significance of the materials that Samaras deploys. See also Josenhans, "(Re)Defining the 'I' in Exile," in this volume, 200.

4. "Creativity is his way of capitulating to inner and outer chaos. Creativity is his way of finding pleasure in painful experiences, assimilating the otherwise horrendously unassimilable." Kuspit, "The Aesthetics of Trauma," 47. Kuspit also describes Samaras's boxes, as well as his use of the small interior of his Upper West Side apartment in his work, as symptomatic of the artist's creation of a womblike space "in which his creativity could grow and develop undisturbed"; ibid., 46.

Dawn Mood at Bohai
1977–79
Ink and gouache on paper
6⁹⁄₁₆ × 13 in. (16.7 × 33 cm)

Pure Mind amid Colored Clouds
1977–79
Ink and gouache on paper
5½ × 12⅞ in. (14 × 32.7 cm)

Noon Thunder in the Shade of a Banyan Tree
1977–79
Ink and gouache on paper
8¼ × 13 in. (21 × 33 cm)

In Lonely Leisure, Seeking Beautiful Scenery
1977–79
Ink and gouache on paper
8⅛ × 13 in. (20.7 × 33 cm)

Autumn Colors at Jinling
1977–79
Ink and gouache on paper
12⅞ × 7⅞ in. (32.7 × 20 cm)

224

Provenance: The Rosenkranz Charitable Foundation, New York [acquired directly from the artist]; Yale University Art Gallery, New Haven, Conn., Gift of the Rosenkranz Charitable Foundation at the request of Alexandra Munroe and Robert Rosenkranz, B.A. 1962, 2010.84.6–.7, .10, .13, .30.

In 1977, while under house arrest, Mu Xin began to paint a suite of small landscape paintings to mark his fiftieth birthday that year. His intention had been to create fifty pictures, but by 1979, painting only at night, he had completed just thirty-three of them. Subsequently, when an exhibition of his work was proposed nearly two decades later, the paintings were grouped with notes that he had written in 1971 and 1972 during China's Cultural Revolution (1966–76).[1] At that time, he had been imprisoned by Red Guards (student soldiers mobilized by Mao Zedong) for "dangerous and decadent thoughts" in an underground former air-raid shelter, a "people's prison."[2] He collectively titled these two bodies of work *Tower within a Tower* and explained, "The tower on the inside is the ivory tower, a metaphor with ironic connotations. The tower that contains this tower is the Tower of London, a trope for a specific situation. So the title means 'An ivory tower inside London Tower.' . . . All I am saying is that I made an ivory tower when I was, so to speak,

a prisoner in the Tower of London."[3] The paintings come from the period after the close of the Cultural Revolution, and after the death of Mao Zedong and the fall of the Gang of Four, when the artist retreated into a mental world, an ivory tower, separate from the world around him.

These paintings by Mu Xin defy easy categorization; they appear both Chinese and non-Chinese, both Eastern and Western, and seem to transcend historical circumstance. Mu Xin was adamant about not wanting to be seen as a dissident artist. He was wont to quote Gustave Flaubert: "Reveal art; conceal the artist."[4]

Dawn Mood at Bohai is a horizontal seascape with shapes evoking cumulus clouds above a stable horizon with what appear to be distant boats. The foreground is defined by dunelike shapes and spits of land with gulls gliding over the water. The tonalities are bluish and black; the forms have been created by daubing and smearing, creating spongelike effects, and then were articulated with the use of a brush. Similar effects are achieved in *Pure Mind amid Colored Clouds*: the effects of blotting and smearing along with bleeding of areas of wash, one into another, create a cloudscape that is also an image of the mind. There is very little, if any, use of a brush. A third horizontal landscape, *Noon Thunder in the Shade of a Banyan Tree*, is somber: a giant banyan tree, appearing like a small grove of trees on an islet, is set against a darkening sky. Once again, blotted and dabbed shapes are articulated by the brush, creating an immediate entry into the foreground leading to the tree. As in *Dawn Mood at Bohai* and *Pure Mind amid Colored Clouds*, this work gives a clear sense of the horizon.

In the work *In Lonely Leisure, Seeking Beautiful Scenery* the brush has been employed to depict trees in a scene brought close to the viewer. On the right, a path in the foreground leads to a cave, which appears like the entry to a Daoist underground utopia, a cavern-heaven; on the left, another path winds back toward mountains in the near distance. The composition is anchored by the paths in the foreground, and the mountains seem foreshortened. It is like a passage from a traditional Chinese handscroll.

Autumn Colors at Jinling departs from the somberness of the suite of paintings as a whole; the use of a russet color creates a warmer feeling. In this vertical composition Mu Xin has turned the dabbed shapes into superimposed mountains rising up the picture plane. A stone staircase is indicated, along with a pagoda surmounting a distant peak. Compared with the horizontal compositions with their horizon lines, which suggest Western painting, this picture appears more like a traditional Chinese composition—a hanging scroll. The dichotomy between

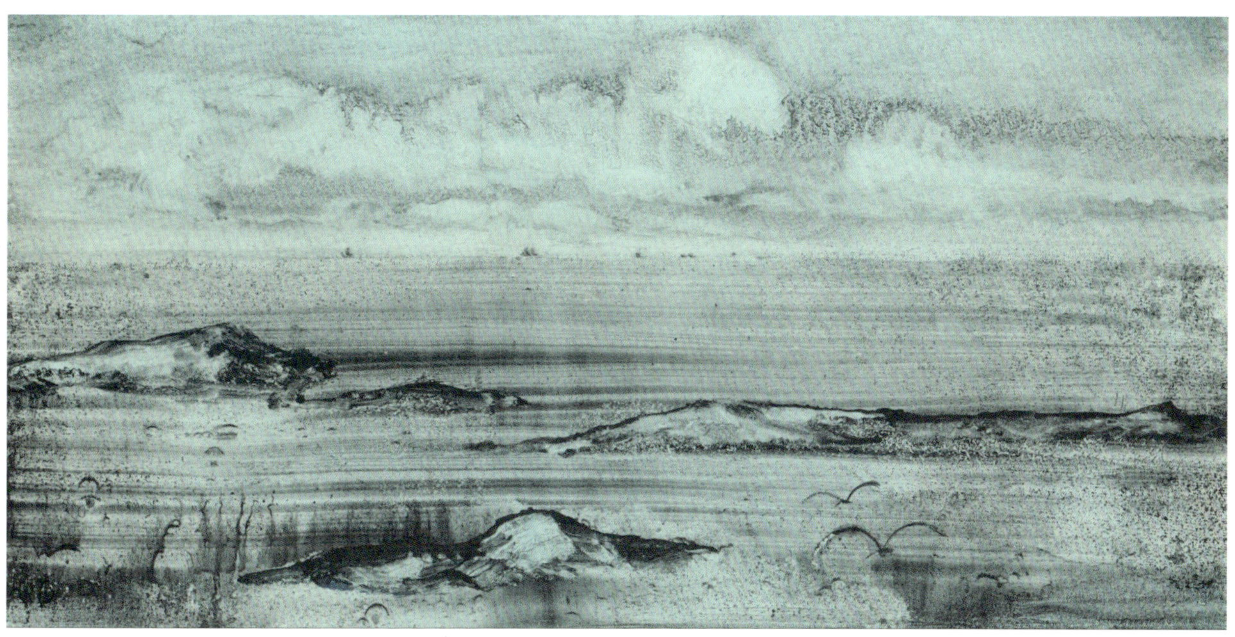

Dawn Mood at Bohai

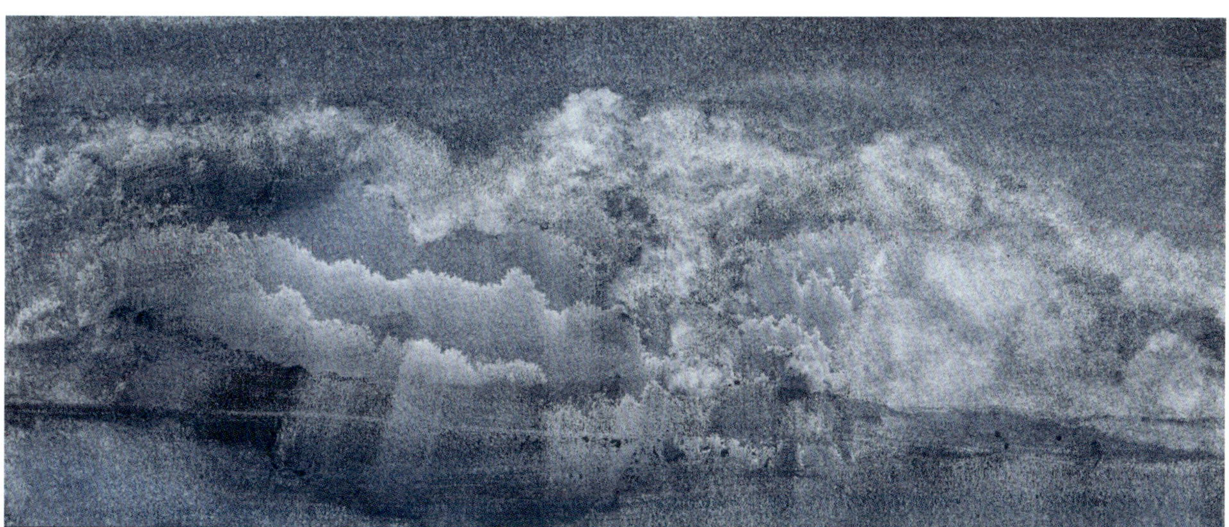

Pure Mind amid Colored Clouds

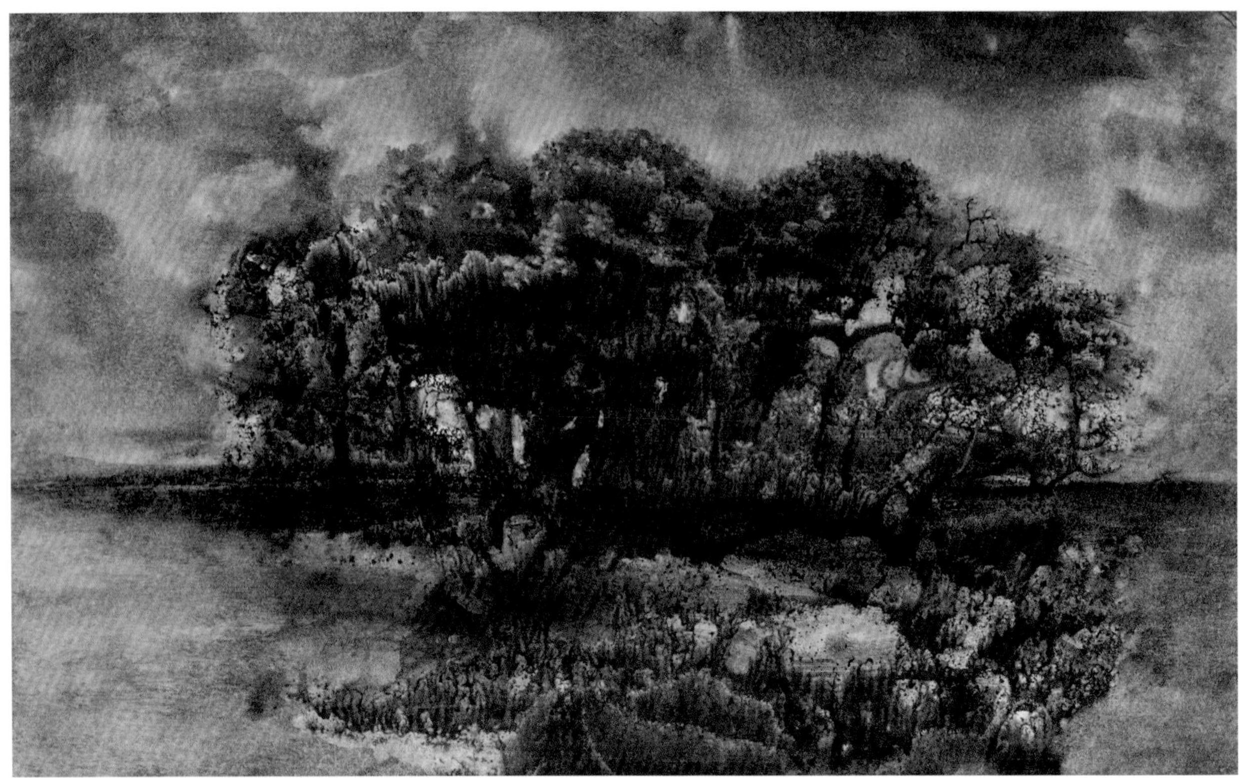

 Noon Thunder in the Shade of a Banyan Tree

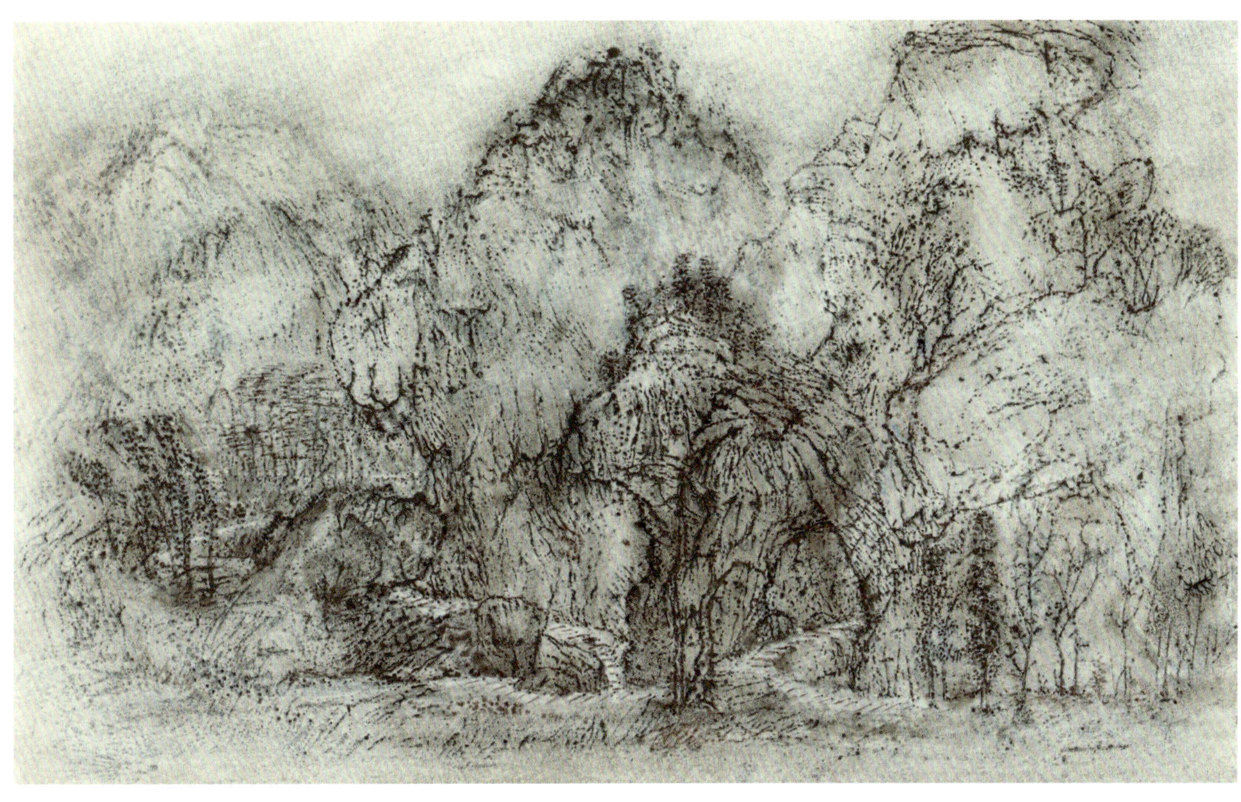

In Lonely Leisure, Seeking Beautiful Scenery

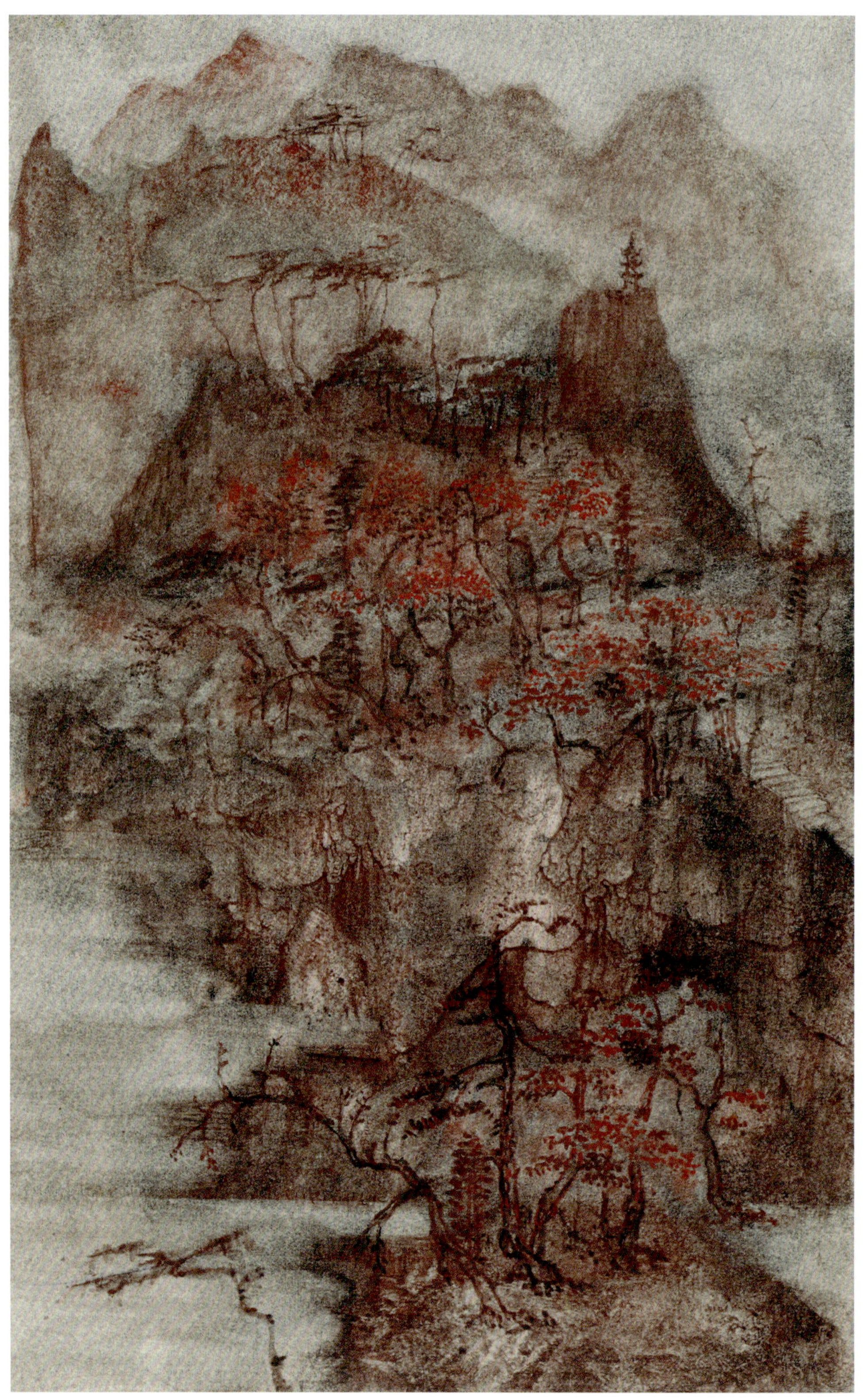

Autumn Colors at Jinling

Western and Eastern, between the horizontal paintings with stable horizon lines and the Chinese compositions, both horizontal and vertical, runs throughout the suite of paintings. All of the paintings exhibit a concern with surface textures.

Mu Xin calls his process of creating an image "controlled coincidence." In this process, a first level of color and form is applied to the surface by techniques that are reminiscent, as pointed out by Alexandra Munroe, of monoprints, frottage, and decalcomania—techniques employed by Surrealists such as Oscar Dominguez and Max Ernst.[5] It is difficult to know how Mu Xin might have been exposed to such techniques, or if he arrived at them on his own. He was clearly exposed to Western oil painting through his teachers and contemporaries, some of whom had studied in Europe or in Japan before World War II. Lin Fengmian, who had studied in France, was one of his teachers in Hangzhou in the late 1940s. After 1945 Mu Xin could also have seen Western magazines and publications. One thing is known: somehow, after the establishment of the People's Republic of China in 1949, he was able to obtain a copy of Ludwig Goldscheider's study of Leonardo da Vinci.[6] According to his interviews, Mu Xin had been attracted to Leonardo since childhood and considered Leonardo his early teacher.[7] With this book in hand, he studied the reproductions carefully. The Italian Renaissance, especially Leonardo's sfumato technique, became an important component of his art. His surface textures may even relate to the photogravures that he saw in the Leonardo publication.

These paintings bear witness to a remarkable mind. They stand apart in Mu Xin's oeuvre. Almost all of his early writings and paintings were destroyed during the Cultural Revolution, and although in his later paintings he continued to explore some of the techniques seen in the *Tower within a Tower* suite, those works do not have the intensity of the suite of thirty-three paintings. From 1977 to 1979, his paintings were his way to stay alive.[8] —DAS

1. The exhibition *The Art of Mu Xin: Landscape Paintings and Prison Notes* was on view at the Yale University Art Gallery, the David and Alfred Smart Museum at the University of Chicago, the Honolulu Academy of Arts, and the Asia Society, New York, in 2001 through 2003. It was accompanied by a catalogue: Alexandra Munroe et al., *The Art of Mu Xin: Landscape Paintings and Prison Notes*, exh. cat. (New Haven, Conn.: Yale University Art Gallery, 2001).

2. Toming Jun Liu, introduction to "Notes from Underground," in Mu Xin, *An Empty Room* (New York: New Directions Publishing Corporation, 2011), 52.

3. Toming Jun Liu, "A Dialogue with Mu Xin," in Munroe et al., *The Art of Mu Xin*, 142.

4. Ibid., 137. In one of the dialogues, Mu Xin says, "The value of art lies in the work of art itself. How or why the work of art was created is less than important." See ibid., 140. See also the discussion by Wu Hung, "Reading Mu Xin: An Exile without a Past," in Munroe et al., *The Art of Mu Xin*, 40–45.

5. Alexandra Munroe, "Palimpsest: Nearby Mu Xin," in Munroe et al., *The Art of Mu Xin*, 15–16.

6. Ludwig Goldscheider's *Leonardo da Vinci* (London: Phaidon Press) was first published in 1943, with a second edition in 1944. Alexandra Munroe cites a 1954 copy; Munroe, "Palimpsest," 12.

7. Ibid., 12–14. Munroe recounts that Mu Xin remembered being given a book on Renaissance painting when he was a boy.

8. Mu Xin remarked to Toming Jun Liu about the notes written during the Cultural Revolution, "It was my way to stay alive." See Liu's introduction to "Notes from Underground," in *An Empty Room*, 53.

Untitled, from the series *Rapture*
1999
Iris print
15⅛ × 23 in. (38.4 × 58.4 cm)
Provenance: Artists Space, New York; Susan and Arthur
Fleischer; Yale University Art Gallery, New Haven, Conn.,
Gift of Susan and Arthur Fleischer, Jr., B.A. 1953, LL.B. 1958,
2012.137.25.

Untitled, from the series *Rapture*
1999
Gelatin silver print
42½ × 67¹¹⁄₁₆ in. (108 × 172 cm)
Provenance: D'Amelio Terras Gallery, New York; Susan and
Arthur Fleischer; Yale University Art Gallery, New Haven,
Conn., Gift of Susan and Arthur Fleischer, Jr., B.A. 1953,
LL.B. 1958, 2012.137.26.

Shirin Neshat came to the United States from Iran in 1975 to
complete high school and attend college, but the outbreak of
the Iranian Revolution of 1978–79, followed by the Iran-Iraq
War from 1980 to 1988, prevented her from returning home.
Only in the 1990s was she able to visit her native country
again, an experience that had a deep impact on her artistic
practice and on her use and manipulation of photographic
images. As an Iranian exile in New York, she turned to art as
a way of reflecting on the political and social conditions in
her home country; in particular, she has explored the condition of women in Islamic societies and at the same time
has tried to break Western stereotypes of them. The artist
has become known for her preoccupation with topics that
are directly related to her own experiences as a woman born
into an Islamic society and as an exile, which, although
broadly applicable, also make her art deeply personal.[1]

Rapture was first conceived as an installation of two
black-and-white video projections. One of the projections
features a group of men, all dressed alike in black trousers
and white shirts, in an unidentified architectural environment. A photograph taken from this sequence shows the
men standing on a fortification wall overlooking the sea,
facing away from the viewer. The other dominant element
in this view is the row of cannons that are aligned and positioned in the embrasures. Although the video installation
was initially black-and-white, this photograph was printed
in color. The brown stone walls and the blue-gray water
make the white shirts of the men even more prominent.
The composition also emphasizes the misty ambience, with
the fog coming off the sea and slowly creeping up the wall,
blurring the contours of the fortress. The other projection
shows women, all wearing chadors (full-length cloaks), in

various natural settings, first in a desert, then near the sea.
The black-and-white photograph shows the female figures
on a beach, walking toward the water. The black chadors
clearly stand out from the surroundings and create a sort of
zigzag in sharp contrast to the flat sand and sea.

Rapture can be seen as a study of gendered group
dynamics and a reflection on freedom and repression. These
works also ponder the role of women in modern Islamic
societies, as observed by the artist from the outside. The
fortress symbolizes a masculine space, implying the idea
of military and defense, yet within it the male figures are
constrained by the walls. The men's clothing, which is
more suited for an office, contrasts sharply with the robust
stones.[2] In comparison, the women on the beach move
in an unlimited space with the sea as a way of escape, a
promise of freedom.[3] Yet the open sea and the seashore are
devoid of any spatial indications and convey the idea of
a rootless existence, with no end of the journey in sight,
hence mirroring Neshat's own experience as an expatriate.
Although it addresses sociopolitical topics and explores
postrevolutionary Iranian culture, Neshat's art does not
simply document the life of women in Islamic societies;
instead, the artist opts for a poetic and philosophical
approach that transforms questions of gender and religion
into wider issues of belonging and freedom. In *Rapture*,
Neshat does not give any indication of a specific time or
place, which adds to the timeless and mystical character
of the work, and the women become a symbol of courage
and self-determination, appealing to Western and Eastern
audiences alike.[4] Although the artist certainly identifies
with her female protagonists and their bravery, she also
assumes the role of an outside observer, separated from the
cultural and ethnic group into which she was born. —FVJ

1. Melissa Chiu, "Poetic History: An Interview with Shirin
    Neshat," in *Shirin Neshat: Facing History*, ed. Melissa Chiu and
    Melissa Ho, exh. cat. (Washington, D.C.: Hirshhorn Museum
    and Sculpture Garden, 2015), 34.

2. Shirin Neshat, "*Rapture* (Estasi), 1999," in Giorgio Verzotti,
    Shirin Neshat, exh. cat. (Milan: Edizioni Charta, 2002), 106.

3. Shirin Neshat, commentary on *Rapture*, in Chiu and Ho,
    Shirin Neshat, 113.

4. Neshat, "*Rapture* (Estasi), 1999," 106.

230

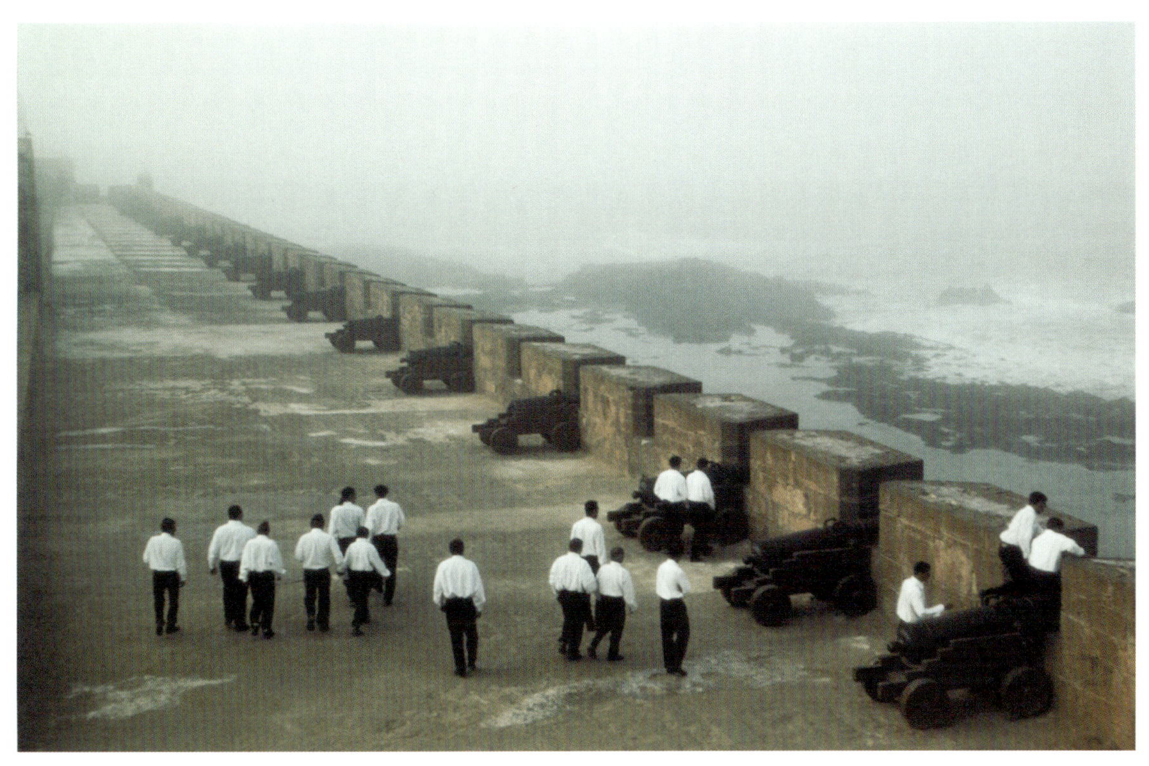

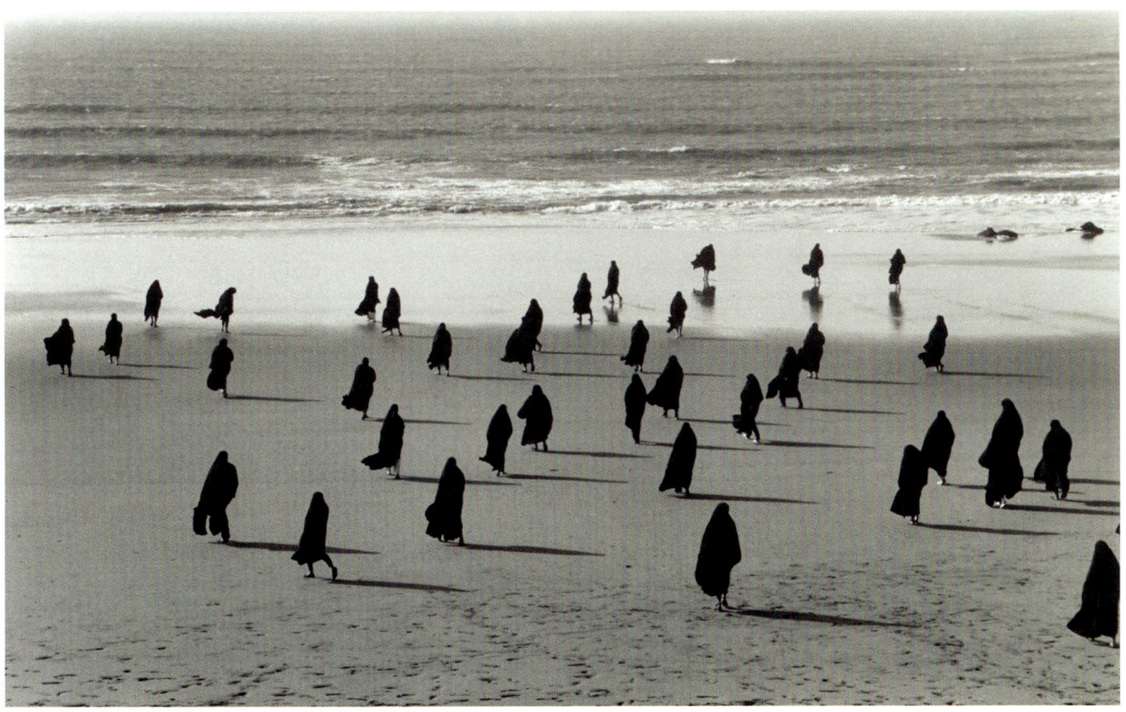

Untitled
2008
Hardground etching, aquatint, spit bite, and drypoint
24 × 24¹⁄₁₆ in. (60.9 × 61.1 cm)
Provenance: Wingate Studio, Hinsdale, N.H., 2012;
Yale University Art Gallery, New Haven, Conn.,
Purchased with a gift from the Arthur and Constance
Zeckendorf Foundation, 2012.112.1.

The haunting works made by the painter Ahmed Alsoudani are born out of extreme states of violence. The artist grew up in Baghdad, Iraq, during the Iran-Iraq War and the First Gulf War, but he was forced to leave the country as a teenager after vandalizing a mural depicting Saddam Hussein. His paintings, drawings, and prints are laden with elements that evoke specific places and memories from his life in Iraq. The macabre scenes and visceral forms also suggest violence in a more general sense, a universality accentuated by the lack of titles in much of Alsoudani's oeuvre.

His ghoulish figures loosely formed from exploded fragments seem to speak to the many forms of war, repression, dispossession, and disenfranchisement transpiring around the world.

The unstable bust in this print is a collection of parts sutured with snaking bands and secured with metal bolts. These components appear to float against a dark, amorphous background. Alsoudani used multiple printmaking techniques (including hardground etching, spit bite, aquatint, and drypoint) and five copper plates to create the different strata of colors and the complex interplay between figure and ground. Thinly etched lines roughly delineate the features of the face, which is overwhelmed by prosthetic protrusions and pestilent growths. These lines recall the charcoal underdrawings of Alsoudani's paintings. The murky, featureless background of the print is also consistent with much of the artist's work (such as *We Die Out of Hand*, 2007, Barjeel Art Foundation, Sharjah, United Arab Emirates). It seems to suspend the figures in a state of half dream, half memory. Yet rather than conveying some spectral fantasy, the artist's forms appear fleshy and concrete, evocative of what he calls a "living memory," something that strongly shapes current experience rather than being confined to the distant past.[1]

In an interview, Alsoudani suggested that each of his paintings has an iconography that can be read like a book, much of it referring to the painter's biographical experiences.[2] Here, the circulatory system of pipes and veins in this figure recalls the exposed and jutting infrastructure of a devastated cityscape, perhaps similar to those in Iraq during the Iran-Iraq conflict and during subsequent invasions led by the United States. The tectonics of the face evoke geographic entities; the blue and red shapes in its lower half might seem to represent Iran and Iraq, along with a bright pool of blood. Yet, with its lack of explicit references and its seeming embodiment of pure horror, the figure could also represent a nameless everyman who manifests a dark vision of the human condition.

Alsoudani's work evinces diverse stylistic influences: Otto Dix's representations of the disarticulated bodies of German soldiers after World War I (fig. 1); the nightmarish scenes depicted by the Spanish artist Francisco Goya in his *Los caprichos* and *Los desastres de la guerra* (The Disasters of War) series; and the menacing distortions of Francis Bacon's portraits (fig. 2). Yet the artist has metabolized these various influences into a highly personal idiom, shaped by his

232

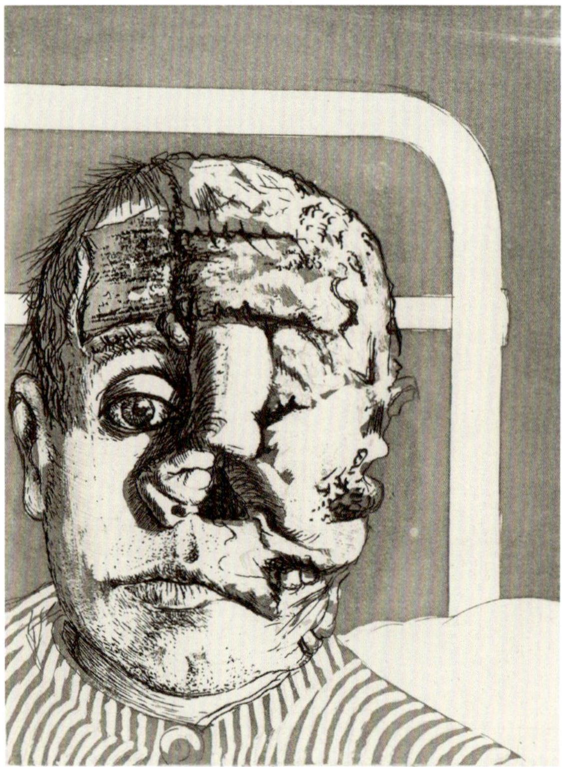

Fig. 1. Otto Dix, *Skin Graft*, 1924. Etching with aquatint on copperplate paper, 7¹³⁄₁₆ × 5⁷⁄₈ in. (19.8 × 14.9 cm). Los Angeles County Museum of Art, The Robert Gore Rifkind Center for German Expressionist Studies, M.82.288.54j

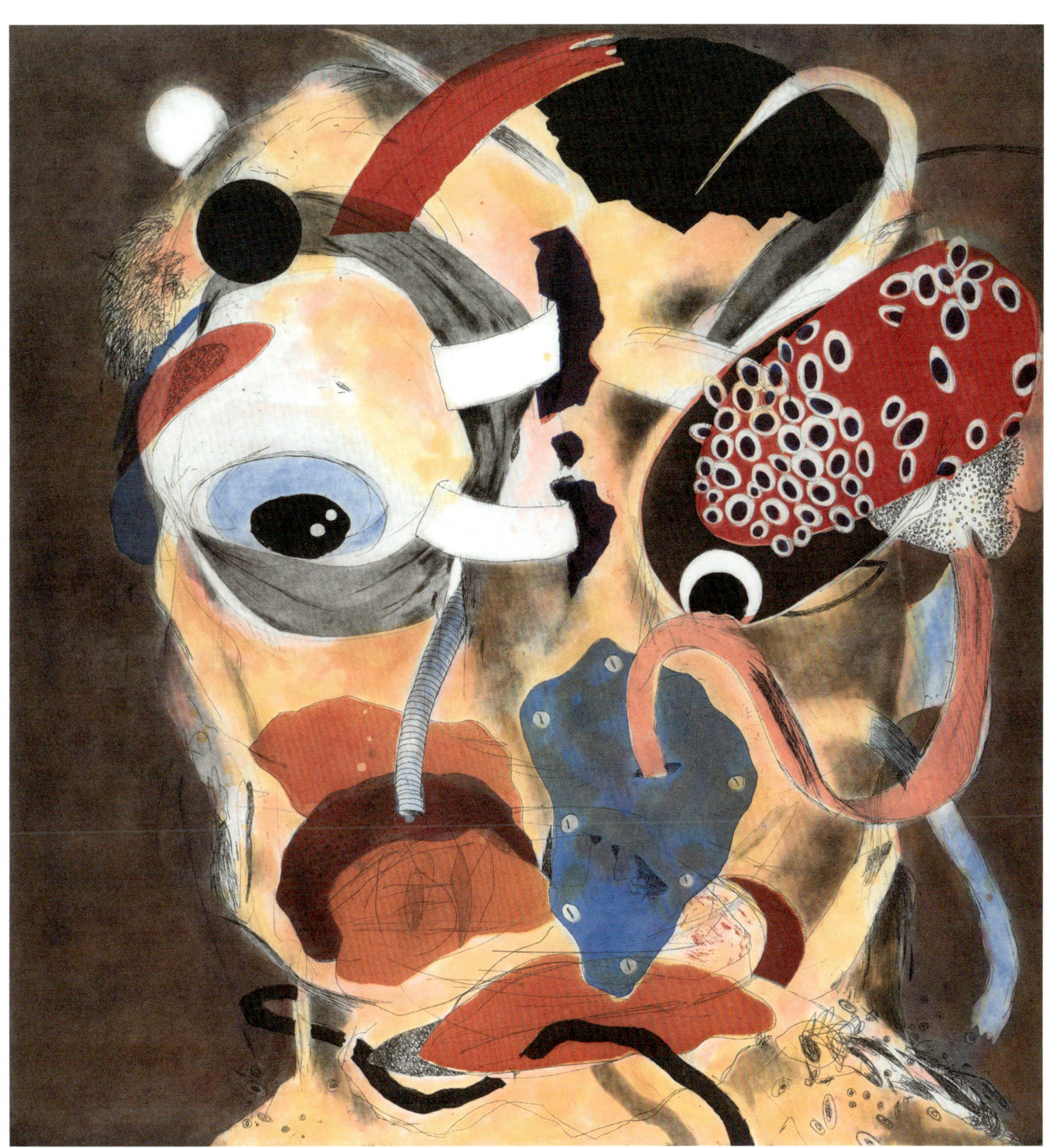

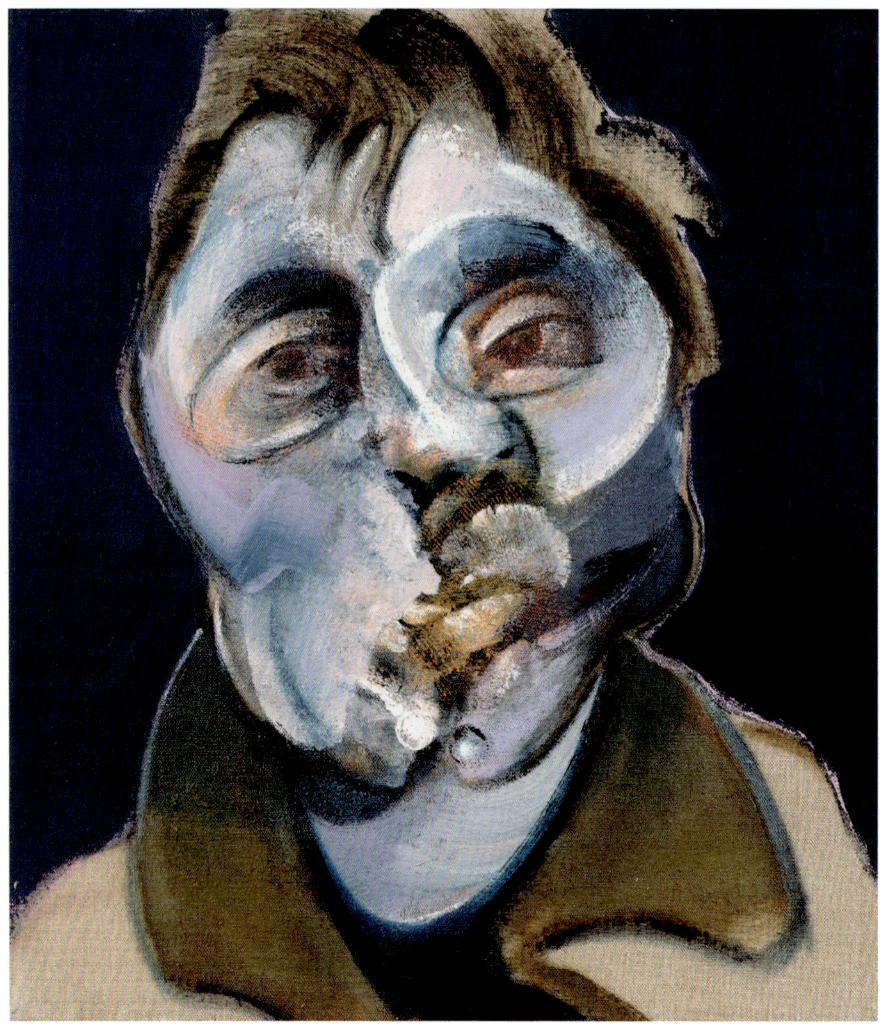

Fig. 2. Francis Bacon, *Self-Portrait*, 1969. Oil on canvas, 14 × 12 in. (35.5 × 30.5 cm). Private collection

strong connection to the homeland where much of his family still resides, and to which he has not returned since leaving more than twenty years ago. Alsoudani's art reflects his complex, liminal experience of diaspora. Referring to the hybrid nature of his work, he has explained, "I came from one culture and was educated in another place, in [a] different culture. There was a conflict and we met, and I saw myself as two people, we met in the middle and came up with a solution."[3] —ND

1. Ahmed Alsoudani, interview by Samuel Rowlett, "On Painting, the Melting Pot, and Making Soup: An Interview with Iraqi Artist Ahmed Alsoudani," *Hyperallergic*, November 28, 2012, http://hyperallergic.com/61032/painting-the-melting-pot-and-making-soup-an-interview-with-iraqi-artist-ahmed-alsoudani.
2. "Ahmed Alsoudani on Split Screen with Shannon Moss," YouTube video, 8:53, posted by Split Screen with Shannon Moss, October 21, 2013, https://www.youtube.com/watch?v=KTwdGJviM5s.
3. Alsoudani, "On Painting, the Melting Pot, and Making Soup."

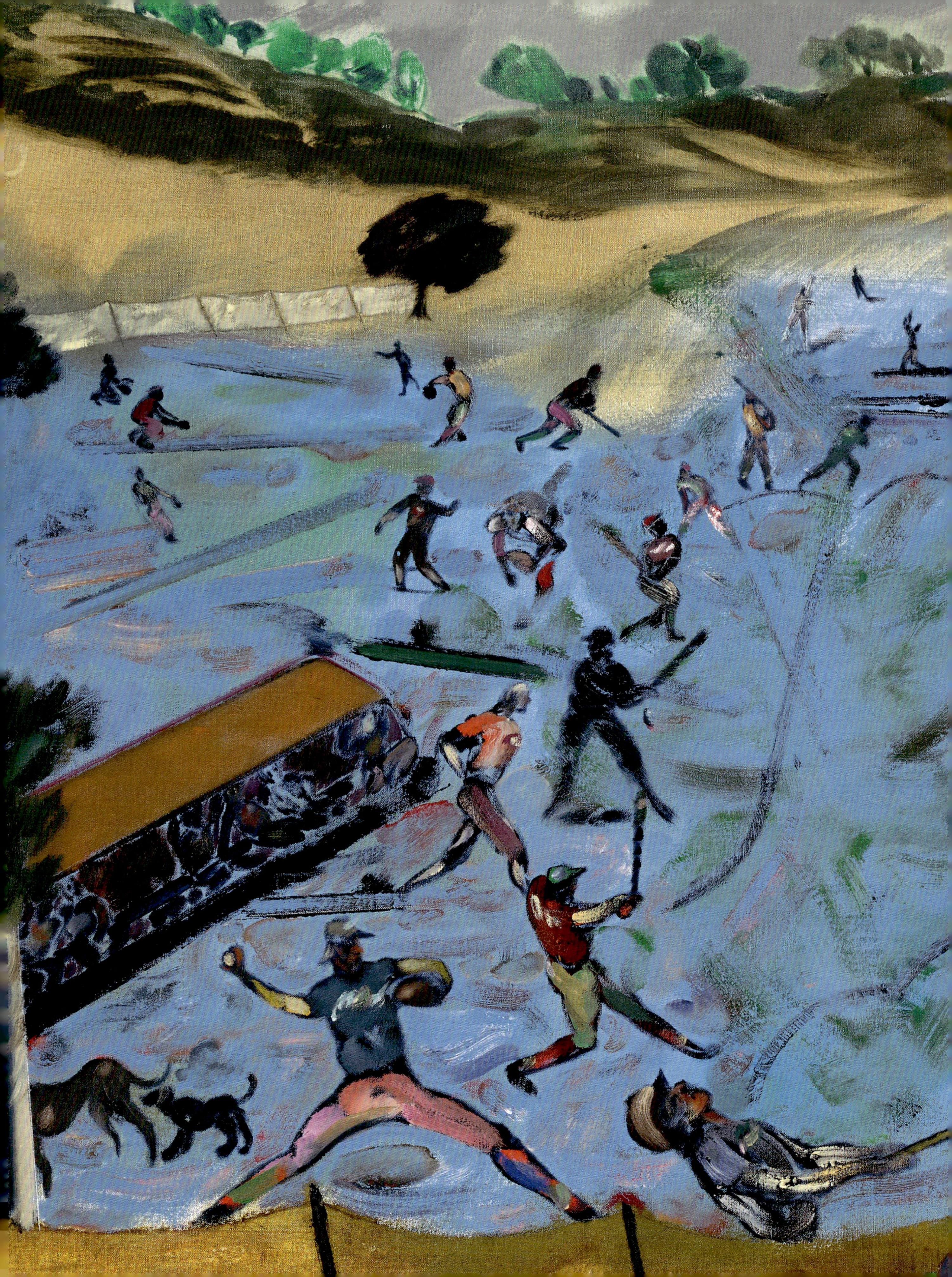

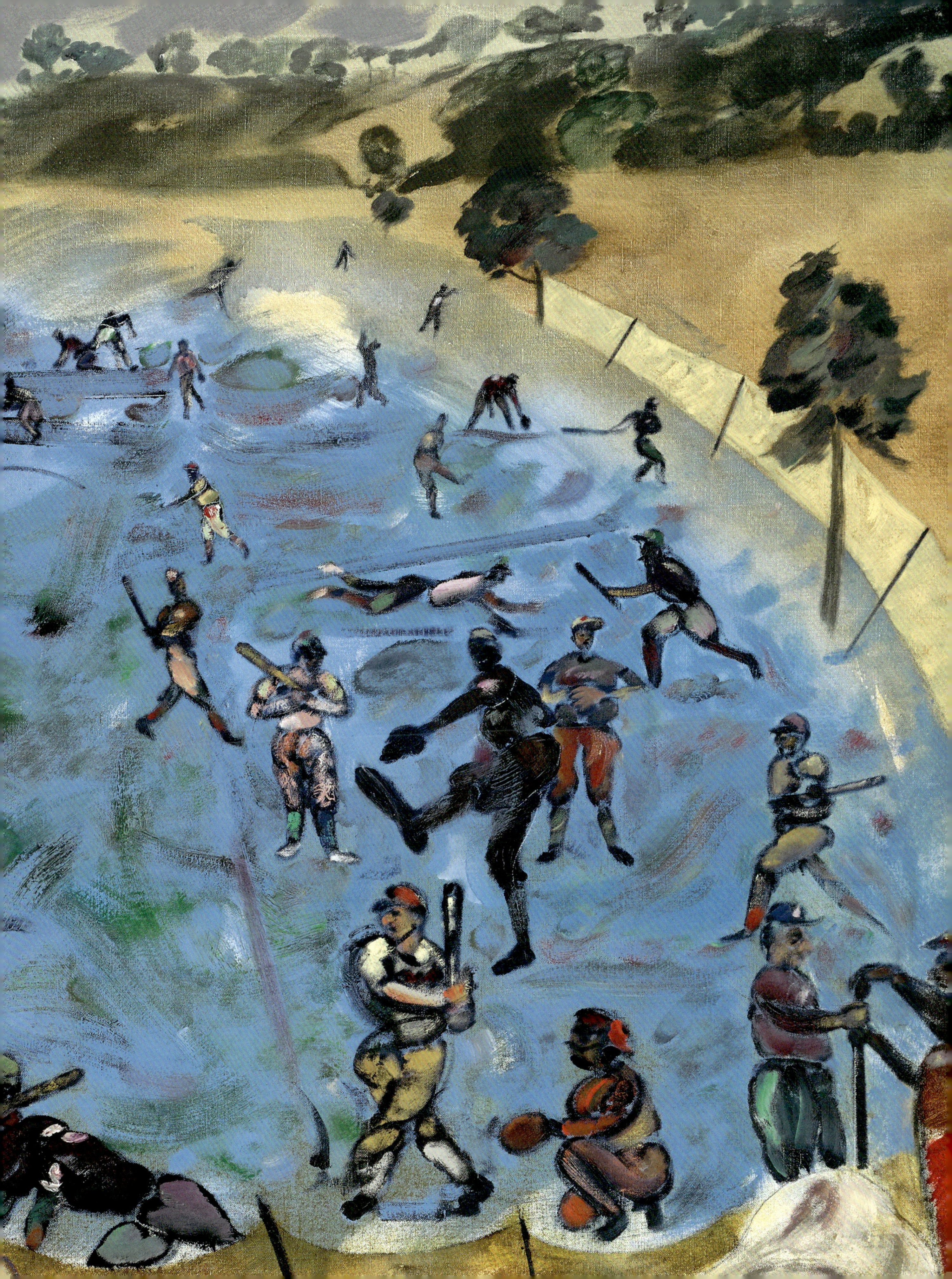

These biographies and this checklist represent all artists and artworks included in the exhibition *Artists in Exile: Expressions of Loss and Hope*. The artists are listed alphabetically, and works by each artist are ordered chronologically, then alphabetically by title. Unless otherwise noted, dimensions for prints and photographs are those of the image, and for drawings, the sheet.

JOSEF ALBERS
Painter and printmaker
German and American, born Bottrop, Germany, 1888, died New Haven, Connecticut, 1976

Josef Albers first trained and worked as a schoolteacher before studying at the Königliche Kunstschule in Berlin from 1913 to 1915. He attended the newly founded Staatliches Bauhaus in Weimar in 1920. In 1923 he began teaching the *Vorkurs* (preliminary course) about material and design, and he was appointed a Bauhaus master in 1925. During his years at the Bauhaus, he also created sandblasted glass paintings, designed furniture, and lectured on educational methods. In 1933, when the Bauhaus was shut down due to pressure from the Nazi government, Albers returned to printmaking, which he had pursued earlier in his career. The same year, he and his wife, Anni, a textile artist, were invited to teach at the newly opened Black Mountain College in North Carolina. In the United States, Albers started to paint in oil, exhibiting his graphics and paintings in American museums and galleries, and he and his wife made several trips to Latin America, travels that affected both of their work considerably. In 1939 he and Anni became American citizens. In 1950, the same year that Albers began his famous *Homage to the Square* series, he was appointed chair of the Department of Design at the Yale School of Art. After Albers retired from Yale in 1958, he was awarded an honorary doctorate in fine arts by the school, in 1962. He continued his teaching at various American universities. Albers's seminal treatise *Interaction of Color*, based on his color course, was published by Yale University Press in 1963. In 1971 Albers became the first living artist to have a retrospective at the Metropolitan Museum of Art, New York.

Schwarzer Kreis (Black Circle), 1933
Woodcut, 10³⁄₁₆ × 13¹⁵⁄₁₆ in. (25.8 × 35.4 cm)
Yale University Art Gallery, Gift of Anni Albers and The Josef Albers Foundation, Inc., 1978.11.2
Luke, fig. 3

Weisser Kreis (White Circle), 1933
Woodcut, 10⁹⁄₁₆ × 13⁷⁄₈ in. (26.9 × 35.3 cm)
Yale University Art Gallery, Gift of Collection Société Anonyme, 1941.327
Luke, fig. 2

i, 1934
Linocut, 8¹⁄₁₆ × 11¼ in. (20.4 × 28.5 cm)
Yale University Art Gallery, Gift of Anni Albers and The Josef Albers Foundation, Inc., 1978.11.7
Luke, fig. 7

Segments, 1934
Woodcut, 9½ × 11⁷⁄₁₆ in. (24.1 × 29 cm)
Yale University Art Gallery, Gift of the artist, 1941.326
Luke, fig. 4

Gate, 1936
Oil on Masonite, 19½ × 20³⁄₁₆ in. (49.5 × 51.3 cm)
Yale University Art Gallery, Gift of Collection Société Anonyme, 1941.325

AHMED ALSOUDANI
Painter and printmaker
Iraqi and American, born Baghdad, Iraq, 1975, active in New York

Fearing arrest, Ahmed Alsoudani fled Baghdad at age nineteen after defacing a public mural of Saddam Hussein with graffiti; he lived in Syria for several years before ultimately seeking political asylum in the United States in 1999. He studied painting at the Maine College of Art and received an M.F.A. from the Yale School of Art in 2008. Alsoudani works in painting and printmaking, with his paintings frequently combining charcoal drawing and acrylic. He has had solo exhibitions at the

238

Phoenix Art Museum and the Portland Museum of Art in Maine. He represented Iraq in 2007 at the Gwangju Biennale, in South Korea, and again in 2011 at the Venice Biennale. He lives and works in New York.

Untitled, 2008
Hardground etching, aquatint, spit bite, and drypoint, 24 × 24¹⁄₁₆ in. (60.9 × 61.1 cm)
Yale University Art Gallery, Purchased with a gift from the Arthur and Constance Zeckendorf Foundation, 2012.112.1
Cat. 30

MAX BECKMANN
Painter and printmaker
German, born Leipzig, Germany, 1884,
died New York, 1950

Max Beckmann demonstrated artistic promise from a young age and enrolled at the Grossherzoglich-Sächsische Kunstschule in Weimar, Germany, at age sixteen. In 1903 he moved to Paris to study the French avant-garde before settling in Berlin the following year, where he showed his work in exhibitions organized by the Berliner Secession, an artistic association, and in galleries. During World War I, he served as a volunteer nurse but suffered a nervous breakdown in 1915 and was discharged from service in 1917. The war experience profoundly affected his work, and he turned toward contemporary allegories and symbolic portraits, which made him one of the leading artists in the 1920s, loosely associated with the Neue Sachlichkeit (New Objectivity) movement. Starting in 1925, he taught at the Städelschule in Frankfurt and was represented in various exhibitions in Europe and in the United States. Soon after Hitler became head of the government in 1933, Beckmann lost his teaching position, his works were pulled from museums, and the gallery at the Kronprinzenpalais in Berlin dedicated to his work was closed. Beckmann stayed in Germany until 1937 but, due to the removal of hundreds of his works from museums and his inclusion in the *Entartete Kunst* (Degenerate Art) exhibition, he and his second wife, Quappi, departed Germany for Amsterdam, never to return. During the

next couple of years, he spent time in Paris and traveled to London, where he had an important place in the *Exhibition of Twentieth-Century German Art* at the New Burlington Galleries in 1938, which was a direct response to the Nazi-organized *Entartete Kunst* exhibition. The outbreak of World War II, however, hindered further travels, and Beckmann remained in Amsterdam during the war years, where he continued to paint, albeit in relative isolation. Although Beckmann was offered a teaching position at the School of the Art Institute of Chicago in 1940, he could not accept it—his visa application was refused by the U.S. consulate in The Hague because of the imminent American entry into the war. In 1947 he finally departed for the United States to teach at the Washington University School of Fine Arts in Saint Louis, and in 1949 he moved to New York after obtaining a professorship at the Brooklyn Museum Art School.

Birds' Hell (Hölle der Vögel), 1938
Oil on canvas, 47¼ × 63³⁄₁₆ in. (120 × 160.5 cm)
Private collection
Cat. 25

DAVID BURLIUK
Painter and writer
American, born Kharkov, Russia (now Ukraine), 1882,
died Southampton, New York, 1967

David Burliuk studied at various art schools between 1898 and 1904, notably in Kazan, Russia; Odessa, now in Ukraine; Munich; and Paris. In 1911 he returned to Russia to study sculpture and architecture at the Moscow School of Painting and participated in the Blaue Reiter (Blue Rider) exhibition in Munich. He became interested in poetry and published the manifesto *A Slap in the Face of Public Taste* in 1912, which signified the beginning of Russian Futurism. In 1916 his brother was drafted and killed during World War I; Burliuk left the following year when the Russian Revolution broke out, traveling to Siberia, Japan, and the South Pacific before settling in New York in 1922. There, Burliuk continued to paint, inspired most notably by Vincent van Gogh and Magic Realism, and kept close ties to the Russian community.

He became an American citizen in 1930. Burliuk also worked as a proofreader and art editor for *Russky Golos*, a newspaper for Russian immigrants living in the United States, and published with his wife the periodical *Color and Rhyme* from 1937 to 1966. In 1940 he asked for permission to visit Russia, which was denied by the Soviet regime, and he was able to visit his native country only years later, in 1956 and 1965.

South Sea Fishermen, 1921
Oil on burlap, 19 5/16 × 68½ in. (49 × 174 cm)
Yale University Art Gallery, Gift of Collection
Société Anonyme, 1941.379

HEINRICH CAMPENDONK
Painter, printmaker, and stained-glass designer
German and Dutch, born Krefeld, Germany, 1889,
died Amsterdam, 1957

Heinrich Campendonk went against his father's wishes that he become a textile designer and instead studied at the Kunstgewerbeschule in Krefeld. In the following years, his struggles to earn an income as an artist led him to participate in mural projects, notably in the cathedral in the city of Osnabrück. He became acquainted with the Expressionist painter August Macke, who encouraged him to move to Bavaria; there he was invited to join the Blaue Reiter (Blue Rider) group around Wassily Kandinsky in Munich. Campendonk exhibited his lyrical paintings and prints with the group in the following years, before he was drafted into the army in 1915. He was soon discharged and retreated to the Bavarian countryside, where he worked on stained glass and decorative murals. In 1926 he started to teach at the Kunstakademie Düsseldorf but was forced to resign by the Nazi administration in 1933, and his works were confiscated from public collections. Campendonk left Germany in 1934 and settled first in Belgium, and then the following year in Amsterdam, where he taught at the Rijksakademie van beeldende kunsten, but he suffered from persecution from the Gestapo during the German occupation of the Netherlands. He remained in the Netherlands during and after the war and became a naturalized Dutch citizen in 1951.

Barnyard, 1934
Watercolor with graphite, image: 21⅞ × 16⅝ in.
(55.5 × 42.2 cm)
Yale University Art Gallery, Gift of the Estate of
Katherine S. Dreier, 1953.6.20

ELIZABETH CATLETT
Sculptor and printmaker
American and Mexican, born Washington, D.C., 1915,
died Cuernavaca, Mexico, 2012

Elizabeth Catlett was the daughter of a professor who had taught at Tuskegee University and at public schools in Washington, D.C., and the granddaughter of enslaved African Americans. Refused admission to the Carnegie Institute of Technology, she obtained a B.S. in art from Howard University in 1935, and subsequently earned an M.F.A. in sculpture from the University of Iowa in 1940. Catlett taught at Dillard University in New Orleans; in 1942 she moved to New York, where she worked in the studio of the Modernist sculptor Ossip Zadkine, who had fled France during World War II, and she taught at the George Washington Carver School in Harlem. In 1946 Catlett obtained a Rosenwald fellowship, a grant that supported black intellectuals and cultural figures; she used the funds to travel to Mexico, where, finding a more welcoming environment for a female and socially engaged artist, she decided to settle. In Mexico City, she joined the artists' collective Taller de Gráfica Popular, and she produced a series of linocuts titled *The Negro Woman* in 1946 and 1947. She married the Mexican artist Francisco Mora in 1947 and gained citizenship in 1962. Because of her political affiliations, she was denied entry to the United States throughout the 1960s and until 1971, when she was granted a visa to attend her solo show at the Studio Museum in Harlem. Catlett taught at the National School of Fine Arts in Mexico City until 1976, and continued to produce politically and emotionally charged graphics and sculptures.

Sharecropper, 1945
Linocut, 4¼ × 6 in. (10.8 × 15.2 cm)
Yale University Art Gallery,
Leonard C. Hanna, Jr., Class of 1913,
Fund, 1995.5.1
Cat. 26

My reward has been bars between me and the rest of the land, from the series *The Negro Woman*, 1947
Linocut, 4½ × 5 13/16 in. (11.5 × 14.8 cm)
Yale University Art Gallery, Gift of
Monroe E. Price, B.A. 1960, LL.B. 1964, and
Aimée Brown Price, M.A. 1963, PH.D. 1972,
2011.203.8
Cat. 26

*My right is a future of equality with other
Americans*, from the series *The Negro Woman*,
1947
Two-color linocut, 9¹⁄₁₆ × 6 in. (23 × 15.2 cm)
Yale University Art Gallery,
Leonard C. Hanna, Jr., Class of 1913,
Fund, 1995.5.3
Cat. 26

GUSTAVE COURBET

Painter
French, born Ornans, France, 1819,
died La Tour-de-Peilz, Switzerland, 1877

After first training as an artist in his hometown of
Ornans, Gustave Courbet moved to the nearby city of
Besançon and studied with a follower of Jacques-Louis
David. He came to Paris in 1839 to study law but
committed entirely to painting when he discovered
the work of Old Masters at the Musée du Louvre and
that of contemporary Romantic artists such as Eugène
Delacroix. Courbet became a principal proponent of
the Realist movement, often turning his attention to
scenes of rural life. Despite early successes, including
a gold medal at the Paris Salon, Courbet largely
shocked the artistic community because he depicted
his mundane subjects on large canvases normally used
for history paintings. When the jury of the Exposition
Universelle of 1855 rejected some of the paintings he
had submitted, he defiantly hung the works in his
own gallery next door, called the Pavillon du Réalisme
(Pavilion of Realism). Courbet also became an active
member of the Paris Commune, a revolutionary
government that took hold after the defeat of France
in the Franco-Prussian War in 1870 and the fall of
the Second Empire. He advocated the removal of the
column in the Place Vendôme, a monument to the
French Army that had been erected by Napoléon; the
column was torn down in 1871, without Courbet's
active involvement. Shortly thereafter the Commune
was defeated and replaced by a new French republican
government. The new government charged Courbet
with the destruction of the column, and he was sent
to jail for six months. After finishing his sentence,
he was ordered to pay the costs of reconstructing the
column; unable to pay, Courbet chose to exile himself
to Switzerland in 1873, fearing further imprisonment
if he remained in France. He settled in the Swiss town
of La Tour-de-Peilz, while the French government
seized his belongings and surveilled his family and
friends. He remained in Switzerland for the rest of
his life and continued to produce numerous canvases
with the help of assistants.

Le Château de Chillon, ca. 1874–77
Oil on canvas, 28¾ × 36¼ in. (73 × 92 cm)
Private collection
Cat. 12

HAROLD COUSINS

Sculptor
American, active in France and Belgium,
born Washington, D.C., 1916,
died Brussels, 1992

Harold Cousins grew up in the neighborhood of
Washington, D.C., known as "Black Broadway" for its
African American artistic community. He attended
Howard University—interrupted by his service in
the Coast Guard as a sonar operator during World
War II—and completed his associate's degree in 1947.
Cousins was rejected from American University in
Washington, D.C., where he applied in an attempt to
continue his studies with a focus on art, and in 1948 he
moved to New York and took classes at the Art Students
League with the painter Reginald Marsh, the sculptor
William Zorach, and the engraver Will Barnett. Using
the G.I. Bill, he then relocated to Paris in 1949 to study
with the sculptor Ossip Zadkine at the Académie de la
Grande Chaumière, joining a vibrant community of
fellow African American expatriates who found a more
tolerant environment in Paris. There he also befriended
European artists such as Karel Appel and Sonia
Delaunay. In the early 1950s, Cousins began to develop
his abstract style of metalwork, first using scrap metal
to create linear, welded sculptures, which he called
"forests" due to their repetition of vertical elements.
Around 1954 he began integrating hammered metal
plates into his sculpture, referring to these as *plaitons*, a
combination of the English word "plate" and the French
word *laiton*, meaning brass. In 1967 Cousins moved to
Belgium, where he worked for the remainder of his life.

Gracieuse figure, 1955
Welded steel and wood, 29 × 7½ × 6½ in.
(73.7 × 19.1 × 16.5 cm)
Yale University Art Gallery, Richard Brown
Baker, B.A. 1935, Collection, 2008.19.66
Cat. 4

SALVADOR DALÍ

Painter and printmaker
Spanish, born Figueres, Spain, 1904,
died Figueres, 1989

Salvador Dalí was born into a wealthy family and began drawing at the age of three. He was only sixteen when his mother died, an event that profoundly affected his future work. After taking art classes in his hometown, he started studying at the Real Academia de Bellas Artes in Madrid in 1920. During the early 1920s, Dalí found inspiration in Sigmund Freud's psychoanalytic writings and began to experiment with psychoanalysis and paranoia in his paintings as well as in the film *Un chien andalou* (An Andalusian Dog) that he codirected with his friend Luis Buñuel in 1929. The same year, Dalí sojourned in Paris and was introduced by his friend Joan Miró to the Surrealists, notably André Breton and Paul Éluard. He also met Éluard's wife, Gala, and the two became inseparable; they got married a few years later, and Gala became his muse. However, Dalí's commercial success and celebrity, as well as his political opinions, led to a rupture with Breton's Surrealist circle in the late 1930s. With the outbreak of World War II and the German occupation of France in 1940, Dalí fled with Gala to New York, where his work was already well known, making him one of the most sought-after European artists in exile. Dalí and Gala returned to Europe in 1948, settling in the artist's hometown, Figueres, where he lived mostly as a recluse, although he still made public appearances and continued to exhibit his works successfully.

Saint George and the Dragon, 1942
Etching, 17⅝ × 11¼ in. (44.8 × 28.6 cm)
Yale University Art Gallery, Gift of
Mrs. Paul Moore, 1959.24.17
Josenhans, "Exiles in Art," fig. 3

JACQUES-LOUIS DAVID

Painter and draftsman
French, born Paris, 1748,
died Brussels, 1825

Jacques-Louis David first trained in the studio of the history painter Joseph-Marie Vien in Paris before enrolling in the Académie Royale de Peinture et de Sculpture in 1766. In 1774 he obtained the Prix de Rome, a government scholarship for a stay at the Académie de France in Rome for four years. David returned to Paris in 1780 and was elected to the Académie Royale in 1784. His canvas *Oath of the Horatii* (Musée du Louvre), which the painter presented at the Paris Salon in 1785, was

a phenomenal success and was considered the first masterpiece of the new Neoclassical style, breaking entirely with the Rococo style and making its author an internationally acclaimed artist. In Paris, David opened his own studio, which was frequented by artists from all over Europe, many of them becoming part of the "school of David." During the French Revolution, David was a member of the extremist, left-wing Jacobin group led by Maximilien de Robespierre; he was elected to the Convention Nationale in 1792 and voted for the execution of Louis XVI. He was briefly imprisoned after the fall of Robespierre, but subsequently gained the favors of Napoléon under the Consulate. When Napoléon became emperor in 1804, David painted the monumental *Consecration of the Emperor* (Musée du Louvre), as well as several portraits of the emperor and his family. After the defeat of Napoléon in 1815 by the Allied forces and the restoration of the Bourbon monarchy, David left France and in 1816 settled in Brussels, where he lived for the remainder of his life, painting portraits and mythological scenes. After his death, David was denied a funeral in France for having been a regicide of Louis XVI, and he was buried in Brussels.

Portrait of Comte Henri-Amédée-Mercure de Turenne d'Aynac, 1816
Oil on canvas, 28¼ × 22⅛ in. (71.8 × 56.2 cm)
Sterling and Francine Clark Art Institute,
Williamstown, Mass., Acquired by the Clark,
1999, 1999.2
Cat. 10

Portrait of François-Antoine Rasse de Gavre, 1816
Oil on canvas, 28¾ × 24 in. (73 × 61 cm)
Private collection
Cat. 10

Composition with Three Figures, ca. 1816–20
Black chalk on paper, 5³⁄₁₆ × 7⁷⁄₁₆ in. (13.1 × 18.9 cm)
Yale University Art Gallery, Everett V. Meeks,
B.A. 1901, Fund, 2013.80.1
Cat. 11

Portrait of Ange-Pauline-Charlotte Ramel de Nogaret, née Panckoucke, 1820
Oil on canvas, 23⅜ × 18¾ in. (59 × 47.5 cm)
Private collection
Josenhans, "(Re)Defining," fig. 3

Portrait of Dominique-Vincent Ramel de Nogaret,
1820
Oil on canvas, 23¾ × 18¾ in. (60.5 × 47.5 cm)
Private collection
Josenhans, "(Re)Defining," fig. 2

BEAUFORD DELANEY
Painter
American, born Knoxville, Tennessee, 1901,
died Paris, 1979

Beauford Delaney was born the eighth of ten children,
to a mother born into slavery and to a father who was
a Methodist minister. He initially received informal
art training from the Knoxville-based painter Lloyd
Branson before leaving for Boston in 1923 to study at
the Massachusetts Normal School, followed by studies
at the Copley Society and the South Boston School of
Art. In 1929 he moved to New York, where he studied
briefly at the Art Students League and participated in
mural projects around the city, notably at the Harlem
Hospital Center. He was a member of the Harlem Artists
Guild, and he also stayed connected to the Greenwich
Village circles and was inspired by poetry and jazz.
Despite his involvement with New York artistic circles,
Delaney felt marginalized as a gay African American
artist from a modest background. In 1950 he received
a two-month fellowship at the artists' colony Yaddo in
Saratoga Springs, New York, which had opened its doors
to African American writers and artists a few years
earlier. In 1953 Delaney departed for Paris, supposedly
for a short visit, leaving his paintings in his New York
studio, but he settled permanently in the French capital,
first in Montparnasse, and then in the suburbs. Living
in a less segregated country, and being less subject to
racial and sexual prejudices, Delaney painted portraits
of fellow artists and American expatriates, but he also
experimented increasingly with chromatic abstraction,
influenced most notably by Claude Monet's late
Impressionist canvases. Yet Delaney struggled to find
an audience for his art, and he began to suffer from
paranoia and depression, caused by heavy drinking, and
could not afford treatment. After a trip to Greece in 1961,
he had a breakdown and had to be repatriated to Paris.
He was hospitalized for mental illness periodically in
the following years and eventually died at a hospital.
One year before his death, the Studio Museum in
Harlem organized his first major retrospective.

Untitled, 1960
Oil on canvas, 51¼ × 38⅜ in. (130.2 × 97.5 cm)
Bowdoin College Museum of Art, Brunswick,
Maine, Gift of halley k harrisburg, Class of 1990,
and Michael Rosenfeld, 2004.25
Josenhans, "(Re)Defining," fig. 9

MARCEL DUCHAMP
Painter, sculptor, and writer
French and American, born Blainville-Crevon,
France, 1887,
died Neuilly-sur-Seine, France, 1968

Marcel Duchamp spent most of his life between France
and the United States. His international career was
sparked by the controversy surrounding his painting
Nude Descending a Staircase, No. 2 (Philadelphia Museum
of Art) at the Armory Show in New York in 1913. In
1915, during World War I, Duchamp moved to New
York, where he joined the avant-garde circle around the
modern art collectors Walter and Louise Arensberg and
met like-minded artists such as Man Ray and Katherine
S. Dreier. Duchamp began to create and exhibit his
"readymades," in which he transformed commercial
objects into art, causing a scandal at the 1917 Society
of Independent Artists exhibition when his *Fountain*
was rejected. In 1920 Duchamp, together with Dreier
and Man Ray, founded the Société Anonyme, Inc., an
art association that collected modern art and organized
related exhibitions and lectures. After returning to Paris
in 1923, Duchamp continued to push boundaries through
his eclectic activities—notably as his gender-norm-
challenging female alter ego, Rrose Sélavy—as well as
through his interest in optics, expressed in his work
Rotary Glass Plates (1920) and in his film *Anémic Cinéma*
(1926). He was close to many avant-garde movements,
such as Dada and Surrealism, without ever adhering to
any one artistic doctrine. After the German invasion of
France, Duchamp fled to New York in 1941, smuggling
some of his works out of the country. In New York, he
established himself among other exiled European artists,
and co-organized, with André Breton, the *First Papers
of Surrealism* exhibition at the Whitelaw Reid Mansion.
In the last twenty years of his life, Duchamp remained
largely out of the public eye, focusing on his passion for
chess, collaborating with other artists, and organizing a
Dada exhibition at Sidney Janis Gallery in New York in
1953. He became an American citizen in 1955.

Allégorie de genre (Genre Allegory), 1944
Collage; offset lithographed die-cut paper over
printed and embossed sheet, 12½ × 9⁷⁄₁₆ in.
(31.8 × 24 cm)
Yale University Art Gallery, Gift of the Estate of
Katherine S. Dreier, 1953.6.350
Cat. 3

LYONEL FEININGER
Painter and illustrator
American, active in Germany, born New York, 1871,
died New York, 1956

Lyonel Feininger, born Léonell Charles Feininger, left
the United States for Europe in 1887 in order to pursue
artistic opportunities. Initially trained as a musician,
Feininger decided to study fine arts instead, first in
Hamburg and then in Berlin. He traveled to Paris,
Rome, and London, and made caricatures for German
magazines and the *Chicago Sunday Tribune*. In 1907 he
turned to painting and was invited in 1913 to exhibit
with the Blaue Reiter (Blue Rider) group; he had his first
solo exhibition at the Galerie Der Sturm in Berlin in
1917. Walter Gropius appointed him master of form in
the printing workshop at the newly founded Staatliches
Bauhaus in Weimar, and his woodcut *Cathedral* was the
cover of the *Bauhaus Manifesto* (1919). In 1924 he formed,
together with Alexej Jawlensky, Wassily Kandinsky, and
Paul Klee, the exhibition collective Die Blauen Vier (The
Blue Four). Under the Third Reich, Feininger's art was
considered "degenerate," forcing him to return with his
family to the United States permanently in 1937. He first
taught at Mills College in Oakland, California, and then
settled in New York, where he had a major retrospective
at the Museum of Modern Art in 1944. He was elected
to the American Academy of Arts and Letters in 1955.
His sons, Andreas and T. Lux Feininger, became noted
artists in the United States.

Old Gables V, 1943
Oil on canvas, 18 × 29 in. (45.7 × 73.7 cm)
Yale University Art Gallery, Gift of Philip L.
Goodwin, B.A. 1907, 1947.423
Cat. 15

Untitled (15.VIII.54), 1954
Charcoal, ink, and watercolor on paper,
11¹⁵⁄₁₆ × 18½ in. (30.3 × 47 cm)
Yale University Art Gallery, Bequest of Ralph
Kirkpatrick, HON. 1965, 1984.54.84
Cat. 15, fig. 2

PAUL GAUGUIN
Painter and printmaker
French, born Paris, 1848,
died Atuona, French Polynesia, 1903

Although he initially worked as a merchant marine and
stockbroker, Paul Gauguin eventually decided to pursue
a career as a painter after he became involved with the
avant-garde in Paris and was invited by Camille Pissarro
to participate in the fourth Impressionist exhibition in
1879. Distancing himself from urban life and hoping
to find societies uncorrupted by Western civilization,
Gauguin started to spend time in Brittany, France, and
traveled to Panama and Martinique between 1886 and
1887. In 1888 he moved to the South of France, where he
briefly worked alongside Vincent van Gogh. Following
his sojourns in Pont-Aven and Le Pouldu, Brittany,
and together with fellow painter Émile Bernard, he
developed Synthetism, a method of painting that
emphasized two-dimensional flat patterns, areas of pure
color, and the symbolic aspect of painting, thus breaking
with the Impressionist focus on perception. Gauguin
left in 1891 for Tahiti, where he painted highly symbolic
paintings of Polynesian nature and people. He returned
to Paris in 1893 with sixty-six paintings and several
sculptures, which he hoped to exhibit and sell in France.
He started to work on an autobiographical text about
his experiences in Tahiti, titled *Noa Noa*, accompanied
by woodcuts. Gauguin departed again in 1895, leaving
France permanently and settling in Tahiti. However,
his disillusionment with the Westernization of Tahiti
deepened, and, struggling with poverty and poor health,
Gauguin set off for the isolated Marquesas island of
Hiva Oa in 1901 and died there a few years later.

Pastorales Martinique, from the *Volpini Suite*,
1889
Zincograph, 6¹⁵⁄₁₆ × 8⁷⁄₈ in. (17.7 × 22.5 cm)
Yale University Art Gallery, University
Purchase, Everett V. Meeks, B.A. 1901, Fund,
1964.9.9
Cat. 1

Parau Parau (Whispered Words), 1892
Oil on canvas, 30³⁄₈ × 38 in. (77.1 × 96.5 cm),
Yale University Art Gallery, John Hay Whitney,
B.A. 1926, HON. 1956, Collection, 1982.111.5
Cat. 1

Noa Noa (Fragrant Scent), 1893–94
Woodcut, 14 × 8¹⁄₁₆ in. (35.5 × 20.4 cm)
Yale University Art Gallery, Bequest of Ralph
Kirkpatrick, HON. 1965, 1984.54.91
Josenhans, "(Re)Defining," fig. 11

Maruru (Offering of Gratitude), ca. 1898
Woodcut, 8 1/16 × 14 in. (20.5 × 35.5 cm)
Yale University Art Gallery, Everett V. Meeks,
B.A. 1901, Fund, 1981.40
Josenhans, "(Re)Defining," fig. 10

ARSHILE GORKY
Painter
American, born Khorkom, Armenia, 1904,
died Sherman, Connecticut, 1948

In 1915 Arshile Gorky, born Vosdanig Adoian, and his
family fled their home in Van, Armenia, during the
genocide committed by the Ottoman Army. During
the following years, they found refuge in the capital
city, Yerevan, and in Tbilisi, Georgia, but the stresses
and strains of their flight led to his mother dying of
starvation in 1919. In 1920 Gorky arrived in the United
States, joining his father, who had previously settled
there. In 1922 he enrolled in the New School of Design
in Boston. In 1924 Gorky moved to New York, where
he experienced European Modernism and started to
teach at the Grand Central School of Art. He published
and exhibited his work under different pseudonyms,
eventually settling on the name Arshile Gorky. In 1930
three of his still lifes were included in a show at the
Museum of Modern Art. In 1934 he had a solo exhibition
at the Mellon Galleries in Philadelphia, and his work
was selected for a show at the Whitney Museum of
American Art the following year. In 1933 Gorky joined
the government-sponsored Public Works of Art Project
(PWAP), which provided him with a salary, and in 1935, as
part of the Federal Art Project (FAP), he was assigned to
a mural project for the airport in Newark, New Jersey. In
the 1940s, he was close to some of the exiled Surrealists
in New York, notably André Breton and Matta. He entered
into an agreement with the Julien Levy Gallery that led
to several exhibitions in the early 1940s. In 1946 a fire in
Gorky's studio destroyed many of his paintings. In 1948
he suffered from severe injuries and depression as the
result of a car accident, and he ended his own life a few
weeks after his release from the hospital.

Nighttime, Enigma, and Nostalgia, 1931–32
Black and brown ink on paper, 22 11/16 × 28 7/8 in.
(57.7 × 73.3 cm)
Yale University Art Gallery, Gift of Collection
Société Anonyme, 1941.487
Cat. 14, fig. 1

Untitled (Head), 1932–34
Oil on canvas, 38 1/2 × 30 1/2 in. (97.8 × 77.5 cm)
Yale University Art Gallery, Gift of Carroll and
Donna Janis, 2013.142.1
Cat. 14

JOHN GRAHAM
Painter, printmaker, and theorist
American, born Kiev, Russia (now Ukraine), 1881,
died London, 1961

John Graham was born Ivan Gratianovich Dombrowsky
to Polish nobility. He began a career as a law student, and
then fought as a cavalry officer in World War I. During
the Russian Revolution, Graham was imprisoned by
Bolsheviks as a supporter of the White Army, associated
with the tsar. After being released, Graham fled to
Poland, spent time in Paris, and eventually moved to
New York with his family in 1920. There he began to
use the Americanized first name John. He studied with
the Ashcan painter John Sloan and befriended and
championed younger artists such as Willem de Kooning,
Arshile Gorky, and Jackson Pollock; he also made frequent
trips to France. In 1937 he published his influential book
System and Dialectics of Art on Modernism and the
avant-garde. However, Graham's personal reputation as
an artist was in decline in the 1940s as he returned from
abstraction to realism. He withdrew from the art world,
moved to Europe in 1959, and eventually died of poor
health while on a trip to London.

Untitled, 1931
Ink on paper, 12 1/16 × 9 in. (30.6 × 22.9 cm)
Yale University Art Gallery, Everett V. Meeks,
B.A. 1901, Fund, 2000.99.1
Josenhans, "(Re)Defining," fig. 7

Russian Still Life, 1941
Oil on canvas, 25 × 30 1/16 in. (63.5 × 76.4 cm)
Yale University Art Gallery, Gift of
Katherine S. Dreier to the Collection Société
Anonyme, 1942.216

GEORGE GROSZ
Painter, draftsman, and illustrator
German and American, born Berlin, 1893,
died West Berlin, 1959

George Grosz, born Georg Ehrenfried Gross, studied
first at the Königlich Sächsische Akademie der
Bildenden Künste in Dresden, Germany, followed by the
Kunstgewerbemuseum in Berlin, and spent some time in

Paris, where he attended the Académie Colarossi in 1913.
He enlisted in the military in 1914 but was permanently
discharged in 1917 for medical reasons; however, the
horrors of war had a profound impact on him. Around
this time, the artist anglicized and slavicized his name
to George Grosz to express his rejection of German
nationalism. He started to be part of radical artist circles
in Berlin, such as the Novembergruppe, and became close
friends with John Heartfield and his brother, Wieland
Herzfelde, who shared Grosz's criticisms of the German
government and became his artistic and editorial
collaborators. When Dada spread to Germany, he became
part of the Dada group in Berlin, along with Heartfield
and others, and participated in the International Dada
Fair in 1920. He also joined the German Communist
Party, and he published blasphemous, antimilitaristic,
antigovernment drawings that caused him to be arrested.
Grosz spent time in the United States, first in 1932 as a
summer-semester instructor at the Art Students League
of New York, and then he permanently settled there with
his family in 1933 when he was offered a regular teaching
position. Shortly after his departure, Nazi paramilitary
troops stormed his Berlin apartment, and subsequently
Grosz was deprived of his German citizenship. In New
York, he and the painter Maurice Sterne opened an art
school, where he taught until 1936. Though his work was
exhibited to acclaim at American institutions—including
the Addison Gallery of American Art, the Cleveland
Museum of Art, and the Museum of Modern Art, New
York—in Germany it was included in the *Entartete Kunst*
(Degenerate Art) exhibition and hundreds of his works
were confiscated from public collections. Grosz became
an American citizen in 1938. During World War II, his
mother and aunt were killed in an air raid in Berlin. In
1946 he published his abridged autobiography in English,
followed by a German unabridged version in 1955. He
traveled to Europe again in 1951, including to Germany,
a trip that was followed by longer stays in subsequent
years. Grosz was elected to the American Academy of
Arts and Letters in 1954, and he was an artist in residence
and lecturer at the Des Moines Art Center in 1957. He
was made a distinguished member of the Akademie der
Künste in Berlin, and in 1959, shortly before his death,
Grosz and his wife returned to Germany permanently.

The Filling Station, 1934
Watercolor on paper, image: 24¹⁵⁄₁₆ × 17⅝ in.
(63.3 × 44.8 cm)
Yale University Art Gallery, Gift of George
Hopper Fitch, B.A. 1932, 1968.80.16
Cat. 24

Self-Portrait, 1938
Charcoal on paper, 24⅞ × 18¾ in. (63.2 × 47.6 cm)
Private collection
Josenhans, "(Re)Defining," fig. 5

The American Scene, 1939
Watercolor on paper, image: 18¼ × 22¹³⁄₁₆ in.
(46.4 × 58 cm)
Yale University Art Gallery, Gift of George
Hopper Fitch, B.A. 1932, 1953.29.1
Josenhans, "(Re)Defining," fig. 4

An Old Tree, 1943
Watercolor on paper, image: 18½ × 13½ in.
(47 × 34.3 cm)
Yale University Art Gallery, Gift of Maxine and
William Block, 2007.102.4
Cat. 24

MOHAMAD HAFEZ
Sculptor and architect
Syrian, born Damascus, Syria, 1984,
active in New Haven, Connecticut

After spending the first years of his childhood in Saudi
Arabia, Mohamad Hafez returned to his home country of
Syria in 1999. Beginning in 2002, he studied electronics
and communication engineering at Damascus University.
In 2003 he came to the United States on a student visa and
enrolled at Northern Illinois University, followed by Iowa
State University, where he obtained a bachelor's degree
in architecture in 2009. In the aftermath of the terrorist
attacks of September 11, 2001, Hafez—being a Syrian
Muslim student—was unable to return home because of his
visa status and the possibility that he would not be able to
reenter the United States, which would jeopardize the com-
pletion of his degree. Hafez began to create Middle Eastern
streetscapes as a way to cope with his nostalgia, using his
architectural background to painstakingly re-create facades
of houses in Damascus. Hafez returned to Syria for the last
time in 2011, and on this trip he made photographs, videos,
and recordings of everyday sounds. With the outbreak of
the Syrian civil war, Hafez's sculptures became more and
more politically charged; depicting decimated cities, homes,
and apartments, they responded to the turmoil and violence
in his native country, and to the destruction of places once
so familiar to him. He began to show his work in group
exhibitions in 2006 and had several solo exhibitions in
Connecticut as well as in Vermont and Massachusetts. His
work has been profiled by NPR and in *The New Yorker*, and
he has given numerous talks on his practice and personal
experience. In 2015 he became a member of the American
Institute of Architects.

246

Baggage Series #4, 2016
Plaster, paint, antique suitcase, found objects, and foam,
30 × 30 × 48 in. (76.2 × 76.2 × 121.9 cm)
Collection of the artist
Josenhans, "(Re)Defining," fig. 15

MONA HATOUM
Sculptor, video artist, and installation artist
Palestinian, born Beirut, Lebanon, 1952,
active in London

Mona Hatoum was born to Palestinian parents living
in exile in Beirut. She studied graphic design at Beirut
University College from 1970 to 1972. While Hatoum
was visiting London in 1975, civil war broke out in
Lebanon, forcing her to stay in the United Kingdom.
There, she attended Byam Shaw School of Art from 1975
to 1979 and then the Slade School of Art from 1979 to
1981. Throughout the 1980s, she explored the human
body in video and performance work, often including
materials from her own life, such as letters and images
of her mother in Beirut that appear in her landmark
video work *Measures of Distance* (1988). In the 1990s, she
began to focus on larger installations that transformed
everyday objects, such as chairs and kitchen tools, into
disturbing and threatening creations that allude to
her personal experiences of exile, war, discrimination,
and loss. Hatoum began to teach in 1986 and held a
number of visiting professorships in London; Cardiff,
Wales; Maastricht, the Netherlands; and Paris. She was
awarded the Joan Miró Prize in 2011, an award given
by the Fundació Joan Miró to recognize contemporary
artists committed to innovation and freedom. A major
survey of her work was inaugurated at the Centre
Pompidou, Paris (2015), and toured to Tate Modern,
London (2016), and Kiasma, Helsinki (2016–17).

Nature morte aux grenades, 2006–7
Crystal, mild steel, and rubber, 37³⁄₈ × 81⁷⁄₈ ×
27⁹⁄₁₆ in. (95 × 208 × 70 cm)
Yale University Art Gallery, The Heinz Family
Fund and Katharine Ordway Fund, 2010.150.1
Cat. 9

HANS HOFMANN
Painter
German and American, born Weissenberg,
Germany, 1880,
died New York, 1966

After a short career as an administrator, Hans Hofmann
turned to art and took classes in Munich. In 1904, with

the support of his wealthy patron Philipp Freudenberg,
he moved to Paris and studied at the Académie de
la Grande Chaumière followed by the Académie
Colarossi. During a brief return to Germany in 1914,
war broke out between France and Germany, rendering
it impossible for Hofmann to go back to Paris. He
opened an art school in Munich in 1915, which became
very successful. In 1930 Hofmann was invited to
teach summer courses at the University of California,
Berkeley, and he continued to give these classes over
the next three years. To avoid rising political tensions
in Germany, Hofmann left Europe to settle in New
York in 1933, and first taught at the Art Students
League before founding the Hans Hofmann School of
Fine Arts the following year. In 1935 he also opened
a summer school in Provincetown, Massachusetts.
Among his students was the painter Lee Krasner, who
introduced him to the art critic Clement Greenberg;
the latter was instrumental in drawing wide public
recognition to Hofmann's art, leading to its inclusion
in several exhibitions in the 1940s and 1950s. During
this time, Hofmann also became an American citizen.
In 1960 his work represented the United States at the
Venice Biennale. In 1963, to acknowledge the role of
the University of California, Berkeley, in bringing him
to the United States, he gave forty-five of his paintings
and substantial funds to the university to help build a
museum on its campus.

Provincetown, 1942
Ink on paper, 14 × 16¹⁵⁄₁₆ in. (35.6 × 43.1 cm)
Yale University Art Gallery, Richard Brown
Baker, B.A. 1935, Collection, 2008.19.148
Cat. 20

Carafe, 1946–54
Oil on panel, 16 × 13 in. (40.6 × 33 cm)
Yale University Art Gallery, Richard Brown
Baker, B.A. 1935, Collection, 2008.19.22
Cat. 20

The Pond, 1958
Oil on canvas, 40 × 50 in. (101.6 × 127 cm)
Yale University Art Gallery, Gift of Richard
Brown Baker, B.A. 1935, 1995.32.5
Cat. 20

LOTTE JACOBI

Photographer
German and American, born Thorn, Germany
(now Poland), 1896,
died Concord, New Hampshire, 1990

Coming from a family of photographers, Johanna
Alexandra "Lotte" Jacobi was trained in her family's
studio; she studied literature and art history at the
Academy of Posen from 1912 to 1916, and then enrolled
at the Bayerische Staatslehranstalt für Lichtbildwesen
in Munich. She took over the family's business in Berlin
in 1927 and specialized in portraits of intellectuals and
artists such as Lotte Lenya, László Moholy-Nagy, and
Kurt Weill. She also made documentary photographs,
notably during a stay of several months in the Soviet
Union, where she traveled as far as Tajikistan and
Uzbekistan. With the rise of the Nazi regime, Jacobi
concealed her Jewish identity by adopting different
pseudonyms and finally fled Germany in 1935 and
settled in the United States, becoming a citizen in 1940.
In New York, she opened a studio and took portraits of
prominent sitters—often fellow exiles such as Marc
Chagall, Albert Einstein, and Thomas Mann. In 1940
Jacobi married the German publisher Erich Reiss, who
had escaped Germany after having been imprisoned
in a concentration camp. She was included in the
Museum of Modern Art's 1942 exhibition *Twentieth
Century Portraits*. After closing her studio in 1955,
Jacobi moved to Deering, New Hampshire, where she
maintained a studio and gallery from 1963 to 1970
and created her so-called *Photogenics*—abstract,
cameraless photographs. She was made honorary
curator of photography at the Currier Museum of Art in
Manchester, New Hampshire, in 1971.

Albert Einstein, Physicist, Princeton, New Jersey,
1938, printed later
Palladium print, 13⅜ × 10¹⁄₁₆ in. (33.9 × 25.6 cm)
Yale University Art Gallery, Gift of the Doris
Bry Trust, Inadvertent Collection, 2016.101.89
Cat. 17

Marc Chagall, Artist, New York,
1942, printed later
Palladium print, 9¹³⁄₁₆ × 7³⁄₁₆ in. (24.9 × 18.3 cm)
Yale University Art Gallery, Gift of the Doris
Bry Trust, Inadvertent Collection, 2016.101.97
Cat. 17

Photogenic, 1946–55
Gelatin silver print, 6¹⁵⁄₁₆ × 9⅝ in.
(17.6 × 24.4 cm)
Yale University Art Gallery, Gift of the Doris Bry
Trust, Inadvertent Collection, 2016.101.104
Cat. 17

Photogenic, 1946–55
Gelatin silver print, 9⅝ × 12¹³⁄₁₆ in.
(24.5 × 32.5 cm)
Yale University Art Gallery, Gift of the Doris Bry
Trust, Inadvertent Collection, 2016.101.450
Cat. 17

Untitled (Inv. #12), ca. 1950
Gelatin silver print, 10¹⁵⁄₁₆ × 13⅞ in.
(27.8 × 35.2 cm)
Yale University Art Gallery, Gift of the Doris Bry
Trust, Inadvertent Collection, 2016.101.102
Cat. 17

ANDRÉ KERTÉSZ

Photographer
American, active in France and the United States,
born Budapest, 1894,
died New York, 1985

André Kertész, born Kertész Andor, began photographing
in 1912 while working as a stock-exchange clerk in
Budapest. He served in the Austro-Hungarian Army during
World War I and took pictures on the Eastern Front, and
he continued his photographic practice in Budapest in
the following years. Kertész moved to Paris in 1925 and
began working professionally as a photographer. In 1928
he participated in the Premier Salon Indépendant de la
Photographie and became famous for his images of Parisian
scenery and street life. From 1928 to 1936, Kertész was the
lead photographer for the French pictorial magazine *Vu*
before leaving for New York, where he worked for Keystone
Press. Although he was dissatisfied with his life and work
in the United States, the onset of World War II and the
persecution of Jewish citizens in Germany and other
countries prevented his return to Europe. Between 1936
and 1947, Kertész worked as a freelance photographer for
various magazines, and in 1944 he became an American
citizen. In 1947 he signed an exclusive contract with
Condé Nast publications, quitting in 1962. In the following
decades, he focused again on more personal subjects and
published several books that were met with international
acclaim. His work was shown in various retrospectives
around the world, and he received several awards, including
a Guggenheim Fellowship, and was appointed Chevalier de
la Légion d'honneur by the French government.

Forced March to the Front between Lonie and Mitulen, from the portfolio *A Hungarian Memory*, 1915, printed 1980
Gelatin silver print, 6¾ × 9¾ in. (17.1 × 24.8 cm)
Yale University Art Gallery, Gift of Gerald Levine, B.A. 1960, 1992.78.1.8
Cat. 13

Heavy Burden, from the portfolio *A Hungarian Memory*, 1916, printed 1980
Gelatin silver print, 7⅜ × 9¾ in. (18.8 × 24.8 cm)
Yale University Art Gallery, Gift of Gerald Levine, B.A. 1960, 1992.78.1.7
Cat. 13

Sunset, from the portfolio *A Hungarian Memory*, 1917, printed 1980
Gelatin silver print, 7¹⁄₁₆ × 9¾ in. (18 × 24.7 cm)
Yale University Art Gallery, Gift of Gerald Levine, B.A. 1960, 1992.78.1.5
Cat. 13

Budafok, from the portfolio *A Hungarian Memory*, 1919, printed 1980
Gelatin silver print, 7¹⁄₁₆ × 9¹³⁄₁₆ in. (17.9 × 24.9 cm)
Yale University Art Gallery, Gift of Gerald Levine, B.A. 1960, 1992.78.1.9
Cat. 13

R. B. KITAJ
Painter and printmaker
American, active in the United Kingdom, born Chagrin Falls, Ohio, 1932, died Los Angeles, 2007

Born Ronald Brooks to the daughter of Russian-Jewish immigrants, R. B. Kitaj spent the majority of his career in the United Kingdom. After working as a merchant seaman and spending time in Europe, he attended the Akademie der bildenden Künste in Vienna and the Cooper Union in New York. He served two years in the U.S. Army, later using the G.I. Bill to study at the Ruskin School of Fine Art and Drawing in Oxford, and eventually at the Royal College of Art in London, where he became friends with the painter David Hockney. Kitaj gained critical acclaim through his first solo show at the Marlborough Gallery in 1963. In 1967 he organized the exhibition *The Human Clay* for the Arts Council of Britain, which included Frank Auerbach, Francis Bacon, Lucien Freud, Hockney, and other important British artists, called the School of London. In 1989 he published the *First Diasporist Manifesto*, which drew on his experience as a Jew to propose a

notion of diasporic aesthetics. He was elected to the American Academy of Arts and Letters in 1982 and to the Royal Academy in 1985. After the death of his second wife in 1997, he moved back to the United States and settled in Los Angeles.

Amerika (Baseball), 1983–84
Oil on canvas, 58 × 58 in. (147.3 × 147.3 cm)
Yale University Art Gallery, Charles B. Benenson, B.A. 1933, Collection, 2006.52.14
Cat. 6

HENRY KOERNER
Painter and graphic designer
American, born Vienna, 1915, died Vienna, 1991

Henry Koerner, born to Austrian Jewish parents, studied at the Graphische Lehr- und Versuchsanstalt in Vienna and started to work with the graphic designer Viktor Theodor Slama. After Germany invaded Austria in 1938, Koerner left for Milan and eventually immigrated to the United States in 1939. In New York, he designed jackets for detective and mystery books at Maxwell Bauer Studios. Koerner also created posters for and won prizes from the American Society for the Control of Cancer in 1940 and the Museum of Modern Art's National War Poster Competition in 1942. In 1943 he started to make posters for the Office of War Information and the Office of Strategic Services, became an American citizen, and transferred to the Office of Strategic Services in Washington, D.C. In 1944 he was sent to the United Kingdom to produce sketches documenting life during wartime, and in 1945 he was reassigned to Germany to sketch at the Nuremberg trials. Upon his return to Vienna, he learned that his parents and brother had been murdered in concentration camps. Back in the United States, exhibitions of his paintings garnered critical acclaim. In 1952 Koerner moved to Pittsburgh to teach at what is now Chatham University and at the Art Institute of Pittsburgh. In the following years, he also worked as a cover artist for *Time* magazine and received commissions for portraits. He started to travel to Austria frequently, where he died when he was hit by a car while riding his bicycle.

My Parents I, 1944
Oil on Masonite, 24½ × 25½ in. (62.2 × 64.8 cm)
Private collection
Koerner, fig. 1

My Parents IV, 1984
Triptych of watercolors on paper mounted on
cardboard, 18¹⁵⁄₁₆ × 39 in. (48 × 99 cm)
Private collection
Koerner, fig. 10

JIŘÍ KOLÁŘ

Poet, painter, and collagist
Czech, born Protivín, Czechoslovakia
(now Czech Republic), 1914,
died Prague, 2002

Born to working-class parents, Jiří Kolář became a
full-time writer in the early 1940s after apprenticing
as a carpenter and working a number of odd jobs. He
became associated with Skupina 42 (Group 42), a group
of avant-garde artists and theoreticians. Deemed a
subversive critical of the Communist Party, Kolář
spent nine months in prison in 1953, after which the
Communist regime banned him from publishing
until 1964. Though he began making collages in the
late 1930s, it was in the early 1960s that his practice
expanded fully into the realm of visual art. Kolář
exhibited in Prague in 1968, as democracy gained
strength in Czechoslovakia during the brief period
known as the Prague Spring. The next year, he won
first prize at the São Paulo Biennial. In 1975 he had his
first major exhibition in the United States, a landmark
show at the Guggenheim Museum in New York. While
on a scholarship in West Berlin in 1977, Kolář signed
the *Charta 77* along with other prominent writers
and artists, which demanded that Czechoslovakia
implement human rights and civil-liberties legislation;
this led the Czech government to banish him from
the country. In 1980 the artist settled in Paris, though
he returned to Prague after the Velvet Revolution of
1989—which ended Stalinist rule in the country. In
1991 Kolář was granted honorary citizenship and the
country's most prestigious award, the Seifert Prize.

Untitled (Knife and Rolling Pin), 1965
Mixed media on board, 15¾ × 11¾ × 1⅛ in.
(40 × 29.9 × 2.9 cm)
Yale University Art Gallery, Charles B.
Benenson, B.A. 1933, Collection, 2006.52.77
Cat. 23

Untitled (Stamps), 1965
Mixed media on board, 15¹⁵⁄₁₆ × 11¾ × 1³⁄₁₆ in.
(40.5 × 29.9 × 3 cm)
Yale University Art Gallery, Charles B.
Benenson, B.A. 1933, Collection, 2006.52.76
Cat. 23, fig. 1

Untitled (Woman), 1965
Mixed media on board, 15⅞ × 11⅞ in.
(40.4 × 30.1 cm)
Yale University Art Gallery, Charles B.
Benenson, B.A. 1933, Collection, 2006.52.39

AN-MY LÊ

Photographer
American, born Saigon (now Ho Chi Minh City),
Vietnam, 1960,
active in New York

Born in Saigon, An-My Lê grew up in a family of
Francophiles and spent five years with her mother
and brothers in Paris before returning to Vietnam in
1973. She fled with her family in 1975, when Saigon
was taken over by the North Vietnamese army and
the Viet Cong, and settled in the United States as
a political refugee. She graduated with a degree in
biology from Stanford University and later enrolled
in the photography program at the Yale School of Art,
from which she received her M.F.A. in 1993. In her
work as a photographer, she addresses the theme of
war—especially the preparation and aftermath of
the U.S. military's activities—even accompanying
soldiers during their training and visiting military
bases abroad. Lê returned to Vietnam several times
between 1994 and 1998, an experience she documented
in the series *Việt Nam*. In 1999 she started to work on
the series *Small Wars* (1999–2002), which documents
restaged battles of the Vietnam War in South Carolina.
She followed this with the series *29 Palms* (2003–4),
focusing on a military base in California where
soldiers are trained before being sent to Iraq. Lê has
been honored with numerous awards, most notably
a MacArthur Foundation fellowship in 2012. She is a
professor of photography at Bard College.

Untitled [Ho Chi Minh City], from the series
Việt Nam, 1998, printed 2006
Gelatin silver print, 15⅞ × 22¹¹⁄₁₆ in.
(40.3 × 57.7 cm)
Yale University Art Gallery, Gift of the artist in
honor of Richard Benson, 2006.229.1
Cat. 8

FERNAND LÉGER

Painter
French, born Argentan, France, 1881,
died Gif-sur-Yvette, France, 1955

Fernand Léger undertook an apprenticeship with an architect in his native Normandy before moving to Paris in 1903. He worked as an architectural draftsman and took classes at the École des Beaux-Arts and at the Académie Julian. Léger started painting, and in 1907 he moved to the artists' settlement La Ruche (The Beehive) in Montparnasse, where he became close with avant-garde artists such as Marc Chagall and Robert Delaunay. Subsequently, Léger started to work with a Cubist vocabulary. He participated in the Salon des Indépendants in 1910 and in following years. World War I disrupted his growing success; Léger served in the military from 1914 to 1917, depicting scenes from the front. After the war, he started to experiment with machine-inspired forms and designed sets and costumes. In 1924 he made, together with Dudley Murphy, his first film, *Ballet mécanique*, one of the earliest experimental films. Beginning in 1931 Léger began to travel to the United States frequently. He had his inaugural major American retrospective at the Museum of Modern Art, New York, in 1935 and gave a series of lectures in 1938 at the Yale School of Art. During World War II, he fled to the United States, and he spent the war years traveling and teaching across the country, notably at Mills College, in California. Léger returned to France in 1945 and joined the Communist Party. In the last years of his life, he created monumental paintings and murals as well as sculptures, stained-glass windows, and book illustrations. He won the Grand Prize at the São Paulo Biennial and ultimately settled in the South of France.

Masque nègre (Black Mask or Great Mask), 1942
Oil on canvas, 29 × 36½ in. (73.7 × 92.7 cm)
Yale University Art Gallery, Charles B.
Benenson, B.A. 1933, Collection, 2006.52.25

JACQUES LIPCHITZ

Sculptor
French and American, born Druskininkai, Russia
(now Lithuania), 1891,
died Capri, Italy, 1973

Jacques Lipchitz, born Chaim Jacob Lipchitz, first studied engineering in Vilnius, Lithuania, and moved in 1909 to Paris, where he began to take classes at the École des Beaux-Arts and at the Académie Julian. He became friends with avant-garde artists such as

Alexander Archipenko, Pablo Picasso, and Diego Rivera, and started to make sculpture. He created his first major Cubist sculptures, such as *Homme à la guitare* (Man with a Guitar), in 1915 and had his first one-man exhibition at the gallery of Léonce Rosenberg. In 1924 he gained French citizenship. Following the German occupation of France (which put Lipchitz in danger because of his Jewish faith and his antifascist views), the artist escaped to Toulouse, and he immigrated to New York in 1941 with the help of the American Emergency Rescue Committee. He began to focus increasingly on allegorical and mythological subjects. He returned to France for the first time since the war in 1946, when he was made Chevalier de la Légion d'honneur, but returned permanently to the United States after seven months. In 1954 a major retrospective of his work was shown at the Museum of Modern Art, New York, followed by the Walker Art Center in Minneapolis and the Cleveland Museum of Art, and he became an American citizen in 1958. For the last decade of his life, he spent summers in Italy and received important public commissions in Israel and in the United States, such as the monumental outdoor sculpture *Bellerophon Taming Pegasus* commissioned by Columbia Law School (installed in 1977).

Theseus and the Minotaur, ca. 1945
Etching, 13⅞ × 11¼ in. (35.2 × 28.5 cm)
Yale University Art Gallery, Everett V. Meeks,
B.A. 1901, Fund, 2006.169.2
Josenhans, "Exiles in Art," fig. 4

MATTA

Painter, architect, printmaker, and sculptor
Chilean, born Santiago, Chile, 1911,
died Civitavecchia, Italy, 2002

Roberto Matta Echaurren, known as Matta, left his native Chile in 1933 and moved to France to work for the Modernist architect Le Corbusier. In Paris, after meeting André Breton and Salvador Dalí, Matta abandoned architecture in favor of painting, joining the Surrealists. He began to focus on what he called "inscapes," explorations of the mind through landscape imagery, using automatism, an art-making process that abandons conscious control of the result and relies instead on the subconscious mind. With the outbreak of war in 1939, Matta relocated to New York. He had his first solo exhibition at Pierre Matisse Gallery in 1942 and participated the following year in the *First Papers of Surrealism* show, conceived by Breton and Marcel Duchamp. He became close to young American artists such as Arshile Gorky and Robert Motherwell, whom he encouraged to experiment with automatism. In 1948 he was expelled from the Surrealist group, partially because he had an affair with Gorky's wife, and he returned to Europe, spending time in Rome and Paris. Matta was blacklisted as a communist in the United States in the 1950s, making his visits more difficult. He returned to his native Chile and had the first major exhibition of his work there in 1954. He also started to make sculpture in the late 1950s. Matta rejoined the Surrealist group in 1959. Following the 1973 coup d'état that overthrew Salvador Allende in 1973, Matta, who had been a supporter of Allende's socialist government, left Chile permanently, and over the following decades he lived intermittently in the United Kingdom, France, and Italy while experimenting with various media.

Fabulous Race Track of Death (Instrument Very Dangerous to the Eye), ca. 1941
Oil on canvas, 28 × 36 in. (71.1 × 91.4 cm)
Yale University Art Gallery, Gift of Collection Société Anonyme, 1941.559
Cat. 21, fig. 1

Untitled, 1943–44
Graphite and colored crayon on paper, 15⁵⁄₁₆ × 19 in. (39 × 48.3 cm)
Yale University Art Gallery, Gift of Thomas T. Solley, B.A. 1950, 2002.15.24
Cat. 21

ANA MENDIETA
Sculptor and performance artist
Cuban and American, born Havana, 1948, died New York, 1985

Ana Mendieta grew up in Cuba, but when Fidel Castro and his communist regime seized power in 1959, her father, an opponent of Castro, decided to send her and her older sister to the United States in 1961 as part of Operation Pedro Pan, a program that allowed unaccompanied Cuban minors to seek political asylum. Both girls were placed in a series of foster homes in Iowa until their mother was able to join them in 1966. These years proved difficult for Mendieta as she adjusted to life in America without her parents, but they also fueled Mendieta's artistic exploration. In 1967 Mendieta began to attend the University of Iowa to study indigenous cultures, and afterward she pursued graduate studies in painting under the professor Hans Breder, whose art and support inspired her. She received an M.F.A. in 1972 and started to make frequent trips to Mexico with Breder. In 1973 she executed her first work in the *Silueta* series, in which the artist created dialogues between her own body and natural sites. Then she relocated to New York in 1978, taught at the

College of Old Westbury on Long Island, and joined A.I.R. Gallery (Artists in Residence, Inc.), the first gallery for women established in the United States. In 1979 Mendieta reunited with her father for the first time since leaving Cuba; the following year, she made her initial trip back to Cuba as part of a new program of cultural exchange with the United States. Mendieta received the Rome Prize in 1983, which gave her a one-year studio residency at the American Academy in Rome; during that time, she also visited ancient and prehistoric sites in Italy and Ireland. In 1985 she married the Minimalist sculptor Carl Andre in Rome, and both artists returned to New York. Mendieta died later that year when she fell thirty-four stories from the window of their apartment. (Andre was later tried and acquitted for her murder.)

Esculturas Rupestres (Rupestrian Sculptures), 1982, printed 1983
Photoetching and chine collé
  Atabey (Mother of the Waters), 5¼ × 3¾ in. (13.3 × 9.5 cm)
  Guabancex (Goddess of the Wind), 3¾ × 5⁵⁄₁₆ in. (9.5 × 13.5 cm)
  Guabancex (Goddess of the Wind), 3⁵⁄₈ × 5⁵⁄₁₆ in. (9.2 × 13.5 cm)
  Guacar (Our Menstruation), 5³⁄₁₆ × 3¹⁵⁄₁₆ in. (13.2 × 10 cm)
  Guanaroca (First Woman), 5¼ × 3¾ in. (13.3 × 9.5 cm)
  Guanaroca (First Woman), 5³⁄₁₆ × 3¹¹⁄₁₆ in. (13.2 × 9.4 cm)
  Itiba Cahubaba (Old Mother Blood), 5⁹⁄₁₆ × 3¹¹⁄₁₆ in. (14.2 × 9.4 cm)
  Iyare (Mother), 3⁷⁄₈ × 5⅛ in. (9.8 × 13 cm)
  Jaruco Caves (Cueva del Aguila), 3¹¹⁄₁₆ × 5¼ in. (9.4 × 13.3 cm)
  Untitled, 3¾ × 5⁵⁄₁₆ in. (9.6 × 13.5 cm)
Yale University Art Gallery, Leonard C. Hanna, Jr., Class of 1913, Fund, 2005.54.1.1–.10
Cat. 5

ABELARDO MORELL
Photographer
American, born Havana, 1948, active in Boston

Abelardo Morell and his family fled Cuba in 1962 after Fidel Castro came to power, and they eventually settled in the United States. Morell attended Bowdoin College on a scholarship, taking photography classes there. He later studied at the Yale School of Art, from which he received an M.F.A. in photography in 1981. Since then he has established himself as a successful photographer and teacher, notably as a professor at the Massachusetts College of Art and Design. He has experimented with various techniques throughout his career, such as photograms, with a special interest in optical effects. In the early 1990s he began a series of camera obscura photographs, transforming entire rooms into cameras by covering all of the windows—first in his own home, and eventually at other sites abroad. He received numerous awards, notably a Guggenheim Fellowship, and was the recipient of the International Center of Photography's Infinity Award in 2011. In 2014 the retrospective *Abelardo Morell: The Universe Next Door* was organized by the Art Institute of Chicago.

Camera Obscura: Houses Across the Street in Our Living Room, 1991
Gelatin silver print, 17⅞ × 22½ in.
(45.4 × 57.1 cm)
Yale University Art Gallery, The Allan Chasanoff, B.A. 1961, Photography Collection, 2004.130.84
Cat. 7

Camera Obscura: La Giraldilla de la Habana in Room with Broken Wall, 2002
Gelatin silver print, 18⅛ × 22⁷⁄₁₆ in. (46 × 57 cm)
Yale University Art Gallery, Gift of Robinson A. Grover, B.A. 1958, M.S.L. 1975, and Nancy D. Grover, 2016.26.23
Cat. 7, fig. 1

MU XIN
Painter, writer, and poet
Chinese, born Wuzhen, China, 1927, died Wuzhen, 2011

Mu Xin, born Sun Pu, grew up in a wealthy family and received an informal education in both the Chinese literati tradition and the classic Western literary canon. He attended the Shanghai Institute of Art in 1946 and began to write and paint prolifically. During the 1940s, Mu Xin was sympathetic toward Mao Zedong, but he quickly became disillusioned with the Communist Party. With the Cultural Revolution, the People's Republic of China declared him an enemy of the state and destroyed all of his early work. Similar to other members of the educated class during the Cultural Revolution, he was sanctioned with prison sentences and house arrest for "antisocial behavior" and

"counterrevolutionary tendencies." In 1971 and 1972, during his solitary confinement, he secretly wrote notes on sheets of paper that had been given to him for self-criticism. After the end of the Cultural Revolution, he was sentenced to hard labor at a factory and lived under house arrest, but he painted at night. Mu Xin left China in 1982 and settled in the United States. At this time, his writings, essays, and poems were "discovered," and he was recognized as an important writer both in Taiwan and by the Chinese diaspora. In 2001–2 the landscape paintings that he made while in confinement were the subject of a major traveling exhibition in the United States, notably at the Yale University Art Gallery. Shortly before his death, he moved back to Wuzhen. A museum dedicated to Mu Xin opened in 2015 in his hometown.

Autumn Colors at Jinling, 1977–79
Ink and gouache on paper, 12⅞ × 7⅞ in.
(32.7 × 20 cm)
Yale University Art Gallery, Gift of the Rosenkranz Charitable Foundation at the request of Alexandra Munroe and Robert Rosenkranz, B.A. 1962, 2010.84.7
Cat. 28

Dawn Mood at Bohai, 1977–79
Ink and gouache on paper, 6⁹⁄₁₆ × 13 in.
(16.7 × 33 cm)
Yale University Art Gallery, Gift of the Rosenkranz Charitable Foundation at the request of Alexandra Munroe and Robert Rosenkranz, B.A. 1962, 2010.84.6
Cat. 28

In Lonely Leisure, Seeking Beautiful Scenery, 1977–79
Ink and gouache on paper, 8⅛ × 13 in.
(20.7 × 33 cm)
Yale University Art Gallery, Gift of the Rosenkranz Charitable Foundation at the request of Alexandra Munroe and Robert Rosenkranz, B.A. 1962, 2010.84.10
Cat. 28

Noon Thunder in the Shade of a Banyan Tree, 1977–79
Ink and gouache on paper, 8¼ × 13 in.
(21 × 33 cm)
Yale University Art Gallery, Gift of the Rosenkranz Charitable Foundation at the request of Alexandra Munroe and Robert Rosenkranz, B.A. 1962, 2010.84.30
Cat. 28

Pure Mind amid Colored Clouds, 1977–79
Ink and gouache on paper, 5½ × 12⅞ in.
(14 × 32.7 cm)
Yale University Art Gallery, Gift of the
Rosenkranz Charitable Foundation at the
request of Alexandra Munroe and Robert
Rosenkranz, B.A. 1962, 2010.84.13
Cat. 28

SHIRIN NESHAT
Photographer and video artist
Iranian and American, born Qazvin, Iran, 1957,
active in New York

In 1974, at the age of seventeen, Shirin Neshat came
to the United States to complete her education and
study art. However, when the Islamic Revolution
of 1979 broke out, she could not return to Iran. She
attended the University of California, Berkeley, where
she received a B.A. in 1979, followed by an M.A. in 1981
and an M.F.A. in 1983. She then moved to New York to
work for Storefront Art and Architecture, a nonprofit
interdisciplinary organization. Her first visit back to
Iran, in 1990, marked the start of her artistic practice. In
the 1990s, Neshat began to produce a series of black-and-
white photographs, called *Women of Allah*, consisting
of symbolically charged portraits of women overlaid
with Islamic calligraphy. Her first solo exhibition was
at Franklin Furnace, in New York, in 1993. In 1996 she
was banned from visiting Iran because of the political
content of her work. She began to work on video and
film installations in 1998, starting with her first video
installation—the trilogy comprising *Turbulent*,
Rapture, and *Fervor*—that used dual video screens to
explore oppositions in gender and society; *Rapture* won
the International Award of the Venice Biennale in 1999.
In 2009 she made her first feature film, *Women Without
Men*, addressing the lives of women in Tehran amid
political upheaval; she won the Silver Lion Award at the
Venice Film Festival for best director the same year.
Neshat has also often collaborated with artists in other
disciplines, such as the author Shahrnush Parsipur and
the composer Philip Glass.

Untitled, from the series *Rapture*, 1999
Iris print, 15⅛ × 23 in. (38.4 × 58.4 cm)
Yale University Art Gallery, Gift of Susan
and Arthur Fleischer, Jr., B.A. 1953, LL.B. 1958,
2012.137.25
Cat. 29

Untitled, from the series *Rapture*, 1999
Gelatin silver print, 42½ × 67¹¹⁄₁₆ in.
(108 × 172 cm)
Yale University Art Gallery, Gift of Susan
and Arthur Fleischer, Jr., B.A. 1953, LL.B. 1958,
2012.137.26
Cat. 29

EMIL NOLDE
Painter and printmaker
German, born Nolde, Germany (now Denmark), 1867,
died Seebüll, Germany, 1956

Emil Nolde, born Emil Hansen, began an apprenticeship in
wood carving and draftsmanship in Flensburg, Germany,
in 1884. He started to teach drawing at the Industrie- und
Gewerbemuseum in St. Gallen, Switzerland, in 1892,
and created postcards of imaginary mountain views that
brought him financial success. Rejected from the Akademie
der Bildenden Künste in Munich, he subsequently studied
painting at the Hölzel-Schule in Dachau and briefly
took classes at the Académie Julian in Paris from 1899
to 1900. In 1902 he changed his surname to his place of
birth, Nolde. He joined the Expressionist artists' group
Die Brücke (The Bridge) in 1906, but resigned a year later.
Before the outbreak of World War I, he and his wife, Ada,
participated in a colonial expedition to German New
Guinea, which inspired many subsequent paintings and
graphic works. In the 1920s, his works were increasingly
shown in museums and exhibitions in Germany, but he
retreated from the artistic center of Berlin by settling in
1926 in the town of Seebüll. In 1931 his work was included
in the *Modern German Painting and Sculpture* exhibition
at the Museum of Modern Art, New York, and the first
volume of his autobiography was published. He was
supportive of the Nazi regime in the 1930s, expressing
his anti-Semitic views on several occasions, and joined a
regional national socialist group. However, in 1937, more
than one thousand of his works were confiscated from
public German collections, and his work was included
in the *Entartete Kunst* (Degenerate Art) exhibition.
In 1941 he was excluded from the Reichskammer der
bildenden Künste, a government agency that controlled
the German art world and to which each artist had to
apply for membership, and subsequently was forbidden by
the Nazi regime to exhibit or sell his work, or to engage
in any professional artistic activity. Retired to Seebüll,
he produced his *Ungemalte Bilder* (Unpainted Pictures)
from 1938 to 1945, a group of about 1,300 small watercolors
that he kept hidden. After the war, Nolde was exonerated
during the denazification process. In the last years before
his death, he received national honors and the graphic art
prize at the Venice Biennale in 1950.

Das Flötenspiel (The Flute Playing), ca. 1941–45
Watercolor on paper, 9¾ × 7½ in.
(24.8 × 19.1 cm)
Collection of Philip H. Isles
Cat. 2

Spiel (Play), ca. 1941–45
Watercolor on paper, 7¾ × 6¾ in.
(19.7 × 17.2 cm)
Collection of Philip H. Isles
Cat. 2

Sunset, ca. 1941–45
Watercolor on paper, 8¾ × 10 in.
(22.2 × 25.4 cm)
Collection of Philip H. Isles
Cat. 2

Two Women in a Park, ca. 1941–45
Watercolor on paper, 9¼ × 5⅝ in.
(23.5 × 14.3 cm)
Collection of Philip H. Isles
Cat. 2

URSULA von RYDINGSVARD

Sculptor
American, born Deensen, Germany, 1942,
active in Brooklyn

Ursula von Rydingsvard was born to a Ukrainian
father, who had been drafted for forced labor during
World War II in Germany, and a Polish mother. She
spent the first years of her childhood in a labor camp,
followed by postwar refugee camps in Germany, before
coming with her family to the United States in 1950.
She received a B.A. and an M.A. from the University
of Miami, Coral Gables, in 1965; she received an
M.F.A. from Columbia University in 1975 and had
her first solo exhibition that same year. Since then,
von Rydingsvard has primarily worked with wood,
creating large-scale, monumental sculptures, often
formed from intricate, labor-intensive assemblages
of cedar beams. Despite their abstract character, her
works draw from the real world, inspired by landscape,
architecture, or domestic objects. The artist has also
explored other materials in recent years, notably
bronze and resin. Von Rydingsvard was awarded an
honorary doctorate from the Maryland Institute
College of Art, Baltimore (1991), and her work has
garnered many awards, including an Academy Award
in Art from the American Academy of Arts and Letters
(1994), a Joan Mitchell Award (1997), and a Lifetime
Achievement Award from the International Sculpture

Center in Hamilton, New Jersey (2014). Her work has
been the subject of major exhibitions; most recently,
in 2014, her first exhibition in the United Kingdom
took place at the Yorkshire Sculpture Park, and in 2015
her work was shown in Venice.

Three Bowls, 1989
Cedar and graphite, 56¾ × 116 × 60 in.
(144.1 × 294.6 × 152.4 cm)
Yale University Art Gallery, Charles B.
Benenson, B.A. 1933, Collection, 2006.52.58
Josenhans, "(Re)Defining," fig. 14

LUCAS SAMARAS

Photographer, sculptor, painter, and installation artist
American, born Kastoria, Greece, 1936,
active in New York

After witnessing the violent uproar of the Greek Civil
War of 1946–49, Lucas Samaras and his family fled to
New York in 1948. From 1955 to 1959, Samaras studied
at Rutgers University on a scholarship, and in 1959
he was awarded a fellowship to study art history at
Columbia University. During that time, he also studied
acting at the Stella Adler Conservatory in New York. In
the 1960s, he created his first series of photographed
self-portraits, working with a Polaroid camera, and
later expanded into manipulating the emulsion of the
Polaroid print to create his *Photo-Transformations*.
Parallel to his activity as a photographer, he also began
to make sculptural boxes, using diverse media to create
highly complex works that convey images of beauty,
horror, and violence, and incorporate autobiographical
elements. The Museum of Contemporary Art, Chicago,
organized his first retrospective in 1971, highlighting
his boxes, and since then Samaras's work has been
the subject of numerous solo exhibitions and career
retrospectives, including a major show of his self-
portraits at the Whitney Museum of American Art
in 2004. He taught at Yale University and Brooklyn
College, and he has lectured at various American
universities. Samaras represented Greece in the Venice
Biennale in 2009.

Untitled, 1963
Mixed media on board, 15¾ × 11½ × 2⅝ in.
(40 × 29.2 × 6.7 cm)
Yale University Art Gallery, Richard Brown
Baker, B.A. 1935, Collection, 2008.19.250
Josenhans, "(Re)Defining," fig. 12

255

Photo-Transformation, 1974
Color instant print (Polaroid) with hand
additions, 3⅛ × 3⅛ in. (7.9 × 7.9 cm)
Yale University Art Gallery, Richard Brown
Baker, B.A. 1935, Collection, 2008.19.638
Cat. 27

KURT SCHWITTERS
Painter, sculptor, typographer, and writer
German and British, born Hanover, Germany, 1887,
died Kendal, United Kingdom, 1948

Kurt Schwitters pursued a traditional training at the
Königlich Sächsische Akademie der Bildenden Künste
in Dresden from 1909 to 1915. After experimenting
with Expressionism and abstraction, Schwitters
became famous in the 1920s with his *Merz* art, a
variation of Dada that encompassed collages of found
objects, assemblage, performance art, and poetry. His
most famous installation, a sculptural environment
called the *Merzbau*, built inside his studio in
Hanover, was destroyed in 1943 by Allied bombings.
Schwitters also published his own *Merz* magazine,
often collaborating with other artists such as Jean
(Hans) Arp, Theo van Doesburg, Raoul Hausmann,
and El Lissitzky. In 1937 his works were confiscated
from German museums, and his works were included
in the *Entartete Kunst* (Degenerate Art) exhibition.
Schwitters left Germany for Lysaker, Norway, in 1937 to
join his son Ernst, who had fled there earlier; his wife,
Helma, remained in Hanover, where she died in 1944.
Until the outbreak of war, Helma had periodically
visited her family in Norway and had helped to send
some of her husband's important artworks from
Germany to Lysaker. Following the German invasion
of Norway in 1940, Schwitters, along with Ernst and
his wife, fled to the United Kingdom, where both
men were interned in several different camps for
"enemy aliens" until 1941. After his release, Schwitters
moved to London, and in 1945 to the Lake District in
northwest England. During his exile, he supported
himself by painting portraits and landscapes, but he
also continued creating abstract works and began to
build a new *Merzbau*, first in Lysaker and then in the
English countryside, supported by a grant from the
Museum of Modern Art, New York. During the war,
Schwitters received support from American collectors
such as Katherine S. Dreier, who acquired several of his
works for herself and for the Société Anonyme, Inc.,
collection. His last years were marked by severe health
problems; in January 1948 he was granted British
citizenship, one day before his death.

Merzbild mit Regenbogen (*Merz* Picture with
Rainbow), 1920–39
Mixed media on plywood, 61⅝ × 47¾ × 10½ in.
(156.5 × 121.3 × 26.7 cm)
Yale University Art Gallery, Charles B.
Benenson, B.A. 1933, Collection, 2006.52.4
Cat. 16

Ohne Titel (Der Wunsch des Künstlers) (Untitled
[The Artist's Wish]), 1934
Collage; newspaper clippings, wrappers, tickets,
and mailing labels on paper, mounted on board,
12¾ × 10¼ in. (32.4 × 26 cm)
Yale University Art Gallery, Charles B.
Benenson, B.A. 1933, Collection, 2006.52.5
Cat. 16, fig. 1

For K S Dreier Viel Freude! (For K. S. Dreier
Much Joy!), 1937
Collage; paper and wax paper on board,
5⅜ × 2¹¹⁄₁₆ in. (13.6 × 6.8 cm)
Yale University Art Gallery, Gift of the Estate
of Katherine S. Dreier, 1953.6.196

White Blue C 5 [. . .], 1946
Collage; mailing label, letterpress text, graphite,
colored pencil, and tempera on board,
6⁷⁄₁₆ × 5¼ in. (16.4 × 13.3 cm)
Yale University Art Gallery, Gift of the Estate of
Katherine S. Dreier, 1953.6.75

47 20 Carnival, 1947
Collage; newspaper and magazine clippings,
painted paper, wove paper, and journal cover on
cardstock, 6⅛ × 4⅞ in. (15.6 × 12.4 cm)
Yale University Art Gallery, Gift of the Estate of
Katherine S. Dreier, 1953.6.76
Cat. 16

mean, 1947
Collage; wrapping paper, kraft paper, and
cardboard on paper, 7¹⁄₁₆ × 5⅝ in. (17.9 × 14.3 cm)
Yale University Art Gallery, Gift of the Estate of
Katherine S. Dreier, 1953.6.74

poco poco (Very Little), 1947
Collage; cardboard, fabric, paper, stamps, and
newsprint on board, 7⁹⁄₁₆ × 6 in. (19.2 × 15.2 cm)
Yale University Art Gallery, Richard Brown
Baker, B.A. 1935, Collection, 1991.10.1

KURT SELIGMANN
Painter, engraver, and illustrator
Swiss and American, born Basel, Switzerland, 1900,
died Sugar Loaf, New York, 1962

Kurt Seligmann first took painting lessons in Basel
before enrolling at the École des Beaux-Arts in
Geneva in 1918 and 1919, where Alberto Giacometti
was a fellow student. In the 1920s, he assumed the
management of his father's furniture store, a position
he quit in 1928 to travel to Florence and study at the
Accademia di Belle Arti. In 1929 he moved to Paris,
where he became acquainted with André Breton
and other Surrealists, and also became friends with
Jean (Hans) Arp. He joined the group of artists
called Abstraction-Création and contributed to their
publications. In 1932 he had his first solo exhibition
at Galerie Jeanne Bucher, Paris, and his work was
included in group shows abroad, such as the 1936
Fantastic Art, Dada, Surrealism exhibition at the
Museum of Modern Art, New York. In 1938 he spent
some time in British Columbia and Alaska and became
interested in Native American artifacts. Seligmann
left France in 1939 and settled in New York, where he
assisted fellow European artists who were trying to
immigrate to the United States. The following year
he was included in the *First Papers of Surrealism*
exhibition as well as in the *Artists in Exile* exhibition
at Pierre Matisse Gallery, and in 1941 he became a
contributor to *View* magazine. In 1948 he published
the book *The Mirror of Magic*—about the history
of magic, a topic that had long intrigued him and
informed his art—which was a critical success and
was translated into several languages.

The Myth of Oedipus, 1944
Etchings
 The Childhood of Oedipus, 17¹³⁄₁₆ × 11¹³⁄₁₆ in.
 (45.3 × 30 cm)
 The Marriage, 17¹³⁄₁₆ × 11⅝ in. (45.2 × 29.6 cm)
 Oedipus at Colonus, 17¾ × 11¾ in. (45.1 × 29.8 cm)
 The Riddle, 17¹¹⁄₁₆ × 11¹¹⁄₁₆ in. (45 × 29.7 cm)
 The Slaying of Laius, 17¾ × 11⅞ in. (45.1 × 30.1 cm)
 The Sphinx, 17⅝ × 11¹¹⁄₁₆ in. (44.7 × 29.7 cm)
Yale University Art Gallery, Gift of Mr. and
Mrs. R. Kirk Askew, Jr., 1970.32a–f
Cat. 22

Game of Chance, 1949
Oil on canvas, 22 × 22 in. (55.9 × 55.9 cm)
Yale University Art Gallery, Gift of Thomas F.
Howard, 1959.34.2
Cat. 22, fig. 1

HEDDA STERNE
Painter
American, born Bucharest, Romania, 1910,
died New York, 2011

Hedda Sterne, born Hedwig Lindenberg, first took
drawing lessons as a child in Bucharest and was
introduced to modern art by a family friend, artist
Victor Brauner. After taking art classes in Vienna
and in Bucharest, she began to spend time in Paris
in the 1930s, studying in the atelier of Fernand Léger
and becoming acquainted with the Surrealist group
through Brauner. In 1941 she narrowly escaped a
massacre of Romanian Jews in her apartment building
in Bucharest and subsequently obtained a visa to
travel to New York via Portugal. In New York, she
was included in several important group exhibitions
at Peggy Guggenheim's Art of This Century Gallery
during the 1940s, and she was later represented by
Betty Parsons Gallery. She met fellow Romanian
émigré and artist Saul Steinberg in 1943, and they
married the following year. At the same time, Sterne
became an American citizen. In 1950 *Life* magazine
named her one of the best artists under age thirty-
six, and she played an active part in the New York
School. As part of a group of modern artists dubbed
"The Irascibles," Sterne cosigned an open letter to
the director of the Metropolitan Museum of Art
protesting conservative group-exhibition juries. A
famous photograph of members of the Irascibles
taken by Nina Leen—which shows Sterne as the only
woman in the group—was published the following
year in *Life*. In 1963 she was awarded a Fulbright
fellowship in painting, which allowed her to spend
time in Italy. In the following decades, her work was
shown in both monographic and group exhibitions on
Abstract Expressionism.

Tondo, ca. 1953
Oil on canvas, DIAM. 30⅜ in. (77 cm)
Yale University Art Gallery, Gift of
Susan Morse Hilles, 1984.75.7
Josenhans, "Exiles in Art," fig. 8

DO HO SUH
Sculptor and installation artist
South Korean, born Seoul, 1962,
active in New York, London, and Seoul

Do Ho Suh grew up in Seoul, where he was exposed to
traditional Korean painting through his father, Suh
Se-ok (born 1929), an accomplished artist. Suh studied
traditional painting at Seoul National University

in the 1980s. He moved to the United States in 1991
to pursue his training, first studying painting at
the Rhode Island School of Design (B.F.A. 1994) and
subsequently gaining an M.F.A. in sculpture from the
Yale School of Art in 1997. Suh creates site-specific
installations and sculptures that explore questions
of identity, space, and transit. He has received
commissions from the Tate Modern, London (2011),
the University of California, San Diego (2012), and
the Museum of Modern and Contemporary Art,
Seoul (2013). In 2001 he represented South Korea at
the Venice Biennale, and he participated in the 2010
Venice Architecture Biennale, the 2010 Liverpool
Biennial, and the 2012 Gwangju Biennale. He has
studios in New York, London, and Seoul.

My Country, 2004
Lithograph with hand additions in watercolor,
6¹¹⁄₁₆ × 7¹⁵⁄₁₆ in. (17 × 20.2 cm)
Yale University Art Gallery, Gift of Bruce
Christopher Carr, 2009.131.5
Josenhans, "Exiles in Art," fig. 6

YVES TANGUY
Painter
French and American, born Paris, 1900,
died Woodbury, Connecticut, 1955

Born the son of a navy captain, Yves Tanguy briefly
joined the French merchant navy before being drafted
into the army. He settled in Paris in 1922, making a
living through various jobs before discovering the
work of Giorgio de Chirico, which triggered his desire
to become a painter, although he never underwent
formal training. Tanguy joined the Surrealist
group around André Breton in 1925 and soon began
practicing automatism. He participated in all the
major Surrealist exhibitions in Europe. In 1938 he met
the American-born artist Kay Sage, and they began
a relationship. He immigrated to the United States
in 1939, where his work was represented by Pierre
Matisse Gallery in New York, and he participated in
the 1942 exhibition *Artists in Exile*. He married Sage
in 1940 and became an American citizen in 1948.
He remained close to Surrealism and continued to
produce prolifically until his death a few years later.

Plusieurs ont vécu (Many Have Lived), 1939
Oil on canvas, 27⅝ × 21¾ in. (70.2 × 55.2 cm)
Yale University Art Gallery, Gift of Thomas F.
Howard, 1956.46.1
Cat. 18

De mains pâles aux cieux lasses (From Pale Hands to
Weary Skies), 1950
Oil on canvas, 35⅝ × 28⅛ in. (90.5 × 71.4 cm)
Yale University Art Gallery, Bequest of Kay Sage
Tanguy, 1963.43.4
Cat. 18, fig. 2

JACK TWORKOV
Painter
American, born Biała Podlaska, Russia (now Poland), 1900,
died Provincetown, Massachusetts, 1982

Jack Tworkov, born Yakov Tworkovsky, and his family fled
rising political tensions in Poland in 1913, immigrating to
the United States and changing their surname to Bernstein
to demonstrate their relationship with a relative already
living there. An aspiring poet, Tworkov entered Columbia
University as an English major in 1920 but abandoned his
studies in 1923 to attend classes at the Art Students League
and at the National Academy of Design. He and his sister
Janice, also an artist, reverted to their original family name,
modifying it slightly to Tworkov. In 1923 he spent some time
at the artists' colony in Provincetown, Massachusetts, where
he met the Modernist painter Karl Knaths, who became his
mentor. Tworkov became a naturalized American citizen
in 1928. From 1934 to 1941, Tworkov worked as part of the
Works Progress Administration (WPA) Federal Art Project,
where he met Willem de Kooning, Mark Rothko, and other
prominent artists. He joined the American Abstract Artists
group, founded in 1936, and had his first one-man exhibition
in 1939 at New York's ACA Gallery. In 1942 through 1945, he
took a hiatus from painting and worked as a tool designer
for the Eastern Engineering Company. Laid off in 1947,
Tworkov turned fully toward painting, and in 1949 he
was one of the founding members of the 8th Street Club,
which became the meeting place for the artists of the New
York School. After World War II, he taught at a variety of
American universities, including American University in
Washington, D.C., Black Mountain College, Queens College,
the Pratt Institute, University of Minnesota, and Columbia
University. He was chairman of the Art Department at the
Yale School of Art from 1963 to 1969. In the 1960s, his style
shifted away from Abstract Expressionism and toward more
geometric, structured works. In the last decades of his life,
his work was presented in numerous exhibitions in the
United States and abroad. He was awarded artist residencies,
as well as a Distinguished Teaching Award from the College
Art Association in 1976, and he was elected member of the
American Academy and Institute of Arts and Letters in 1981.

Drawing No. 3958, 1954
Charcoal on paper, 26⅛ × 19⅞ in. (66.3 × 50.5 cm)
Yale University Art Gallery, Richard Brown Baker,
B.A. 1935, Collection, 2008.19.81
Josenhans, "(Re)Defining," fig. 8

FRIEDRICH VORDEMBERGE-GILDEWART

Painter and typographer
German and Dutch, born Osnabrück, Germany, 1899,
died Ulm, Germany, 1962

Initially trained in the cabinetmaking craft at his father's
workshop, Friedrich Vordemberge-Gildewart developed
an affinity for sculpture after studying interior design at
the Kunstgewerbeschule und Technische Hochschule in
Hanover, Germany. In Hanover, he met members of the
avant-garde, notably through the Dada artist Kurt Schwitters
and the Constructivist El Lissitzky. These encounters
encouraged Vordemberge-Gildewart to use nonobjective
vocabulary in his paintings. Theo van Doesburg, the founder
of De Stijl, even invited him to join the Dutch artists' group,
which also included Piet Mondrian. He presented his works
in several exhibitions of abstract art in Germany and in
France, and founded, together with Schwitters, the group
Die abstrakten hannover in 1927. When the Nazis seized
power, Vordemberge-Gildewart's nonobjective art was labeled
"degenerate," leaving him unable to sell or exhibit his work,
and the artist subsequently left the country and settled in
Amsterdam, eventually gaining Dutch citizenship. After the
war, he returned to Germany and became the head of the
Department of Visual Communication at the Hochschule für
Gestaltung in Ulm in 1954.

Composition No. 126, 1941
Oil on canvas, 23¾ × 23¾ in. (60.3 × 60.3 cm)
Yale University Art Gallery, Gift of William S. Huff,
B.A. 1949, M.ARCH. 1952, 2014.123.2
Cat. 19

Composition No. 135, 1942
Oil on canvas, 21¼ × 29⅛ in. (54 × 74 cm)
Yale University Art Gallery, Gift of
Tom M. Schaumberg, B.A. 1960, and
Peter J. Schaumberg, 2010.139.1

Selected Bibliography

Aciman, André, ed. *Letters of Transit: Reflections on Exile, Identity, Language, and Loss.* New York: The New Press, in collaboration with the New York Public Library, 1999.

Addison Gallery of American Art. *European Artists Teaching in America.* Exh. brochure. Andover, Mass.: Addison Gallery of American Art, 1941.

Barron, Stephanie, ed. *"Degenerate Art": The Fate of the Avant-Garde in Nazi Germany.* Exh. cat. Los Angeles: Los Angeles County Museum of Art, 1991.

——————. *Exiles and Emigrés: The Flight of European Artists from Hitler.* Exh. cat. Los Angeles: Los Angeles County Museum of Art, 1997.

Behr, Shulamith, and Marian Malet, eds. *Arts in Exile in Britain 1933–1945: Politics and Cultural Identity.* Amsterdam: Rodopi, 2005.

Bloch, Ernst. "Disrupted Language, Disrupted Culture." *Direction* 2, no. 8 (December 1939): 16–17, 36.

Bordes, Philippe. *Jacques-Louis David: Empire to Exile.* Exh. cat. Williamstown, Mass.: Sterling and Francine Clark Art Institute, 2005.

Boym, Svetlana. *The Future of Nostalgia.* New York: Basic, 2001.

Braziel, Jana Evans, and Anita Mannur, eds. *Theorizing Diaspora: A Reader.* Malden, Mass.: Blackwell Publishing, 2003.

Buffalo, Audreen, ed. *Explorations in the City of Light: African-American Artists in Paris, 1945–1965.* Exh. cat. New York: Studio Museum in Harlem, 1996.

Carr, E. H. *The Romantic Exiles.* London: Penguin, 1933.

Chaffee, Cathleen, ed. *Eye on a Century: Modern and Contemporary Art from the Charles B. Benenson Collection at the Yale University Art Gallery.* New Haven, Conn.: Yale University Art Gallery, 2012.

Czaplicka, John, and David Mickenberg. *Emigrants and Exiles: A Lost Generation of Austrian Artists in America, 1920–1950.* Exh. cat. Evanston, Ill.: Mary and Leigh Block Gallery, Northwestern University, 1996.

Deutsche Nationalbibliothek. *Künste im Exil.* https://kuenste-im-exil.de.

Farrell, Jennifer, ed. *Get There First, Decide Promptly: The Richard Brown Baker Collection of Postwar Art.* New Haven, Conn.: Yale University Art Gallery, 2011.

Fleckner, Uwe, Maike Steinkamp, and Hendrik Ziegler, eds. *Der Künstler in der Fremde: Migration—Reise—Exil.* Berlin: De Gruyter, 2015.

Fort, Ilene Susan, and Tere Arcq, eds. *In Wonderland: The Surrealist Adventures of Women Artists in Mexico and the United States.* Exh. cat. Los Angeles: Los Angeles County Museum of Art, 2012.

Fréchuret, Maurice, and Laurence Bertrand Dorléac, eds. *Exils: Réminiscences et nouveaux mondes.* Exh. cat. Paris: Réunion des musées nationaux, 2012.

Gauguin, Paul. *The Writings of a Savage.* Edited by Daniel Guérin. Translated by Eleanor Levieux. New York: Viking, 1978.

Gross, Jennifer R., ed. *The Société Anonyme: Modernism for America.* Exh. cat. New Haven, Conn.: Yale University Art Gallery, 2006.

Grosz, George. *A Little Yes and a Big No.* Translated by Lola Sachs Dorin. New York: Dial Press, 1946.

Guilbaut, Serge. *How New York Stole the Idea of Modern Art.* Translated by Arthur Goldhammer. Chicago: University of Chicago Press, 1983.

Harithas, James, and Alan Schnitger, eds. *Iraqi Artists in Exile.* Exh. cat. Houston: Station Museum of Contemporary Art, 2010.

Held, Jutta. "Das Exil der deutschen Künstler in den dreißiger und vierziger Jahren." In *Aspekte der künstlerischen Inneren Emigration 1933–1945,* edited by Claus-Dieter Krohn, 191–99. Munich: Text and Kritik, 1994.

Herbert, Robert L., Eleanor S. Apter, and Elise K. Kenney. *The Société Anonyme and the Dreier Bequest at Yale University: A Catalogue Raisonné.* New Haven, Conn.: Yale University Art Gallery, 1984.

Hoffman, Eva. *Lost in Translation: A Life in a New Language*. New York: Penguin, 1989.

Horowitz, Frederick A., and Brenda Danilowitz. *Josef Albers: To Open Eyes*. London: Phaidon, 2006.

Hudson-Wiedenmann, Ursula, and Beate Schmeichel-Falkenberg, eds. *Grenzen überschreiten: Frauen, Kunst und Exil*. Würzburg, Germany: Königshausen und Neumann, 2005.

Lajer-Burcharth, Ewa. "The Self in Exile: David's Portrait of Sieyès." In *David after David: Essays on the Later Work*, edited by Mark Ledbury, 232–51. Conference proceedings. New Haven, Conn.: Yale University Press, 2007.

Luke, Megan R. *Kurt Schwitters: Space, Image, Exile*. Chicago: University of Chicago Press, 2014.

Madeline, Laurence, ed. *Gustave Courbet: Les années suisses*. Exh. cat. Paris: Éditions Artlys, 2014.

McCabe, Cynthia Jaffee. *The Golden Door: Artist-Immigrants of America, 1876–1976*. Exh. cat. Washington, D.C.: Hirshhorn Museum and Sculpture Garden, 1976.

McCloskey, Barbara. *The Exile of George Grosz: Modernism, America, and the One World Order*. Oakland: University of California Press, 2015.

Mercer, Kobena, ed. *Cosmopolitan Modernisms*. Cambridge, Mass.: MIT Press, 2005.

————. *Exiles, Diasporas, and Strangers*. Cambridge, Mass.: MIT Press, 2008.

Molesworth, Helen, ed. *Leap Before You Look: Black Mountain College, 1933–1957*. Exh. cat. Boston: Institute of Contemporary Art, 2015.

Nochlin, Linda. "Art and the Conditions of Exile: Men/Women, Emigration/Expatriation." *Poetics Today* 17, no. 3 (Fall 1996): 317–37.

Pierre Matisse Gallery, with essays by James Thrall Soby and Nicolas Calas. *Artists in Exile*. Exh. brochure. New York: Pierre Matisse Gallery, 1942.

Robinson, Marc, ed. *Altogether Elsewhere: Writers on Exile*. London: Faber and Faber, 1994.

Rose, Barbara. "Arshile Gorky and John Graham: Eastern Exiles in a Western World." *Arts Magazine* 50, no. 7 (March 1976): 62–69.

Rushdie, Salman. *Imaginary Homelands: Essays and Criticism 1981–1991*. London: Granta, 1992.

Said, Edward W. *Reflections on Exile and Other Essays*. Cambridge, Mass.: Harvard University Press, 2000.

Sawin, Martica. *Surrealism in Exile and the Beginning of the New York School*. Cambridge, Mass.: MIT Press, 1995.

Stephan, Alexander, ed. *Exile and Otherness: New Approaches to the Experience of the Nazi Refugees*. New York: Peter Lang, 2005.

Weber, Nicholas Fox, and Jessica Boissel, eds. *Josef Albers and Wassily Kandinsky: Friends in Exile, a Decade of Correspondence, 1929–1939*. Manchester, Vt.: Hudson Hills, 2010.

Woodall, Joanna, ed. *Portraiture: Facing the Subject*. Manchester, England: Manchester University Press, 1997.

Index

Page numbers in *italics* refer to illustrations; those in **boldface** refer to catalogue entries.

263

(1991), 76, 76, 253; *Camera Obscura: La Giraldilla de la Habana in Room with Broken Wall* (2002), 77, 253
Munroe, Alexandra, 229, 229n7
Museum of Modern Art (New York), 18–19, 152
Mu Xin, 24, **224–29**, 229n1, 229n4, 229n7, 229n8; *Autumn Colors at Jinling* (1977–79), 224, 228, 253; biography of, 253; *Dawn Mood at Bohai* (1977–79), 224, 225, 253; *In Lonely Leisure, Seeking Beautiful Scenery* (1977–79), 224, 227, 253; *Noon Thunder in the Shade of a Banyan Tree* (1977–79), 224, 226, 253; *Pure Mind amid Colored Clouds* (1977–79), 224, 225, 254; *Tower within a Tower*, 224, 253

N

Nabokov, Vladimir, 87, 88, 94–95, 98; *Drugie berega*, 94; *Lolita*, 96
Napoléon I, 17, 26n7, 102, 105, 186–89
narratives of exile, 22–25
nationalism, 24, 52, 58, 61, 72, 87–88. *See also* patriotism
Nauman, Bruce, 40; *Walking in an Exaggerated Manner around the Periphery of a Square* (1967–68), 39–40, 39
Naylor, Genevieve, *Josef Albers and Students at Black Mountain College Holding Out Their Pencils to Study Angles* (1946), 135
Nazism, Nazis, 31, 44, 45, 47n15, 212; artists targeted by, 122, 131, 139, 140n9, 142, 158, 189, 208, 212; Nolde and, 52, 57n1; refugees from, 15, 18, 22, 148, 185. *See also* Hitler, Adolf
Neoplasticism, 158
Neshat, Shirin, 25, **230–31**; biography of, 254; *Rapture* series (1999), 230, 230, 254
Netherlands, 36, 37, 158
New Bauhaus, 43
New York, 22, 23, 58, 66, 191; as art center, 18–19, 39, 42–43; exiles in, 94, 116, 132, 154, 168, 189, 195; Harlem, 65, 216
Nierendorf, Karl, *Specters 1939 A.D.—13 Variations on a Macabre Theme*, 172
Nochlin, Linda, 22, 24
Nolde, Emil, **52–57**; biography of, 254; *Cows in the Lowland* (1909), 52; *Das Flötenspiel* (The Flute Playing, ca. 1941–45), 52, 56, 255; *The Life of Christ*, 52; *Spiel* (Play, ca. 1941–45), 52, 53, 255; *Sunset* (ca. 1941–45), 52, 54, 255; *Two Women in a Park* (ca. 1941–45), 52, 55, 255; *Ungemalte Bilder* (Unpainted Pictures), 52, 57
Norway, 139, 142, 144
nostalgia, 36, 41, 72, 87–88, 100; as term, 33, 87–88; as theme of exile, 25, 84–125
Nuremburg, 36, 43

P

Panama, 48
Paris, 17, 39, 42, 48, 58, 62, 79, 110; as center of art world, 43, 154; exiles in, 22, 95, 197
Parler, Peter, 37

patriotism, 58, 61, 72. *See also* nationalism
peasants, 36–37, 48, 204
Pennsylvania College for Women, 43
Perlin, Bernard, 43
Peterlini, Domenico, *Dante in esilio* (ca. 1860), 16
photographs, photographers, 23, 35, 52, 79; abstraction in, 148–52, 222; camera obscura and, 76, 77, 77, 77n1; in *Life* magazine, 27n20, 148; women and, 22, 78–79, 148
Picasso, Pablo, 62, 120, 162; *Seated Woman* (1927), 120
Pierre Matisse Gallery (New York), 22, 23
Pittsburgh, 31, 34, 39, 43
Pliny the Elder, *Natural History*, 34
Poland, 44, 154, 168, 172, 204
Pollock, Jackson, 120, 166, 167n3
pomegranate (*grenade*), 80–81
portraits, 16, 17, 38, 38, 102–5, 148–50; identity and, 186–89, 215, 222
Postmodernism, 20
Potok, Chaim, 72
Poussin, Nicolas, 106
Prague, 37, 95
printmaking, 22, 48, 49, 58, 132, 135, 232
Protestant iconoclasm, 38

Q

Querschnitt, 191

R

race and racism, 24, 40, 52, 72, 216; segregation and, 62, 65, 216
Raeff, Marc, 95
Ramel de Nogaret, Ange-Pauline-Charlotte, *188*, 189
Ramel de Nogaret, Dominique-Vincent, 186–89, *187*, 206n6
Raphael, 106
Rasse de Gavre, François-Antoine, *104*, 105
realism, 105, 110
Redon, Odilon, 48
refugees, 21, 22, 25, 75n1, 76, 95, 132
Rembrandt van Rijn, 36
Renaissance, European, 19, 106
Renoir, Jean, 18
Riefenthaler, Josef, 44, 47n15
Romanticism, Romantics, 16, 41, 44, 87–88, 90, 92
Rome, 39, 106
Rosen, Aaron, 72
Roth, Philip, 72
Rudolf, Holy Roman Emperor, 37
Russia, 18, 31, 92; censorship in, 89, 91, 93; exile and, 25, 87–101; exiles due to, 89–94; immigrants from, 72, 94–95; Russian Revolution and, 18, 93–95. *See also* Soviet Union
Rutgers University, 222
von Rydingsvard, Ursula, 203–4; biography of, 255; *Three Bowls* (1989), 204, 203–4, 255

Photo Credits

Every effort has been made to credit the artists and the sources; if there are errors or omissions, please contact the Yale University Art Gallery so that corrections can be made in any subsequent editions.

© Robert Adams, courtesy Fraenkel Gallery, San Francisco: cat. 8, fig. 1

Josef Albers Papers (MS 32), Manuscripts and Archives, Yale University Library. Photo: Genevieve Naylor, Courtesy The Reznikoff Partnership: Luke, fig. 6

Photo courtesy The Josef and Anni Albers Foundation: Luke, fig. 1

© 2017 The Josef and Anni Albers Foundation/Artists Rights Society (ARS), New York: Luke, figs. 2–4, 7

© 2017 The Josef and Anni Albers Foundation/Artists Rights Society (ARS), New York. Photo: Tim Nighswander: Luke, fig. 5

Courtesy Albertina, Vienna: cat. 24, fig. 3

© 2017 Artists Rights Society (ARS), New York/VG Bild-Kunst, Bonn: pp. 85–86; cat. 15; cat. 15, fig. 2

© 2017 Artists Rights Society (ARS), New York/VG Bild-Kunst, Bonn. Digital Image © 2017 Museum Associates/LACMA. Licensed by Art Resource, N.Y.: cat. 30, fig. 1

© 2017 Artist Rights Society (ARS), New York/VG Bild-Kunst, Bonn. Digital Image © The Museum of Modern Art/Licensed by SCALA/Art Resource, N.Y.: cat. 15, fig. 1

© The Estate of Francis Bacon. All rights reserved/DACS London/Artists Rights Society (ARS), New York, 2017. Photo: Prudence Cuming Associates, Ltd.: cat. 30, fig. 2

General Collection, Beinecke Rare Book and Manuscript Library, Yale University. © 2017 Artists Rights Society (ARS), New York/VG Bild-Kunst, Bonn: Luke, figs. 8–9

bpk Bildagentur/Alte Pinakothek, Bayerische Staatsgemäldesammlunden, Munich, Germany/Art Resource, N.Y.: cat. 24, fig. 2

bpk Bildagentur/Nationalgalerie Staatliche Museen, Berlin, Germany. Photo: Andres Kilger/Art Resource, N.Y.: Koerner, fig. 8

bpk Bildagentur/Sprengel Museum Hannover. © 2017 Artists Rights Society (ARS), New York/VG Bild-Kunst, Bonn. Photo: Michael Herling/Aline Gwose/Art Resource, N.Y.: cat. 16, fig. 2

Reproduced with permission of the Charles E. Burchfield Foundation: cat. 24, fig. 4

Art © Catlett Mora Family Trust/Licensed by VAGA, New York, N.Y.: front flap; cat. 26

Art © Catlett Mora Family Trust/Licensed by VAGA, New York, N.Y. Photo: The Art Institute of Chicago/Art Resource, N.Y.: cat. 26, fig. 1

Art © Catlett Mora Family Trust/Licensed by VAGA, New York, N.Y. Digital Image © The Museum of Modern Art/Licensed by SCALA/Art Resource, N.Y.: cat. 26, fig. 2

Photo: Glenn Castellano: Josenhans, "(Re)Defining," figs. 2–3

Image © Sterling and Francine Clark Art Institute, Williamstown, Massachusetts, USA. Photo: Michael Agee: cat. 10 (p. 103)

© The Cleveland Museum of Art. © 2017 Artists Rights Society (ARS), New York/VG Bild-Kunst, Bonn: cat. 15, fig. 3

© CNAC/MNAM/Dist. RMN-Grand Palais/Art Resource, N.Y. Photo: Jacques Faujour: cat. 20, fig. 1

© CNAC/MNAM/Dist. RMN-Grand Palais/Art Resource, N.Y. Photo: Adam Rzepka: cat. 4, fig. 1

Permission granted by Marc Cousins and Danielle Godfrey (Cousins), owners of the estate of Harold Cousins: cat. 4

Dalí © Salvador Dalí, Fundació Gala-Salvador Dalí, Artists Rights Society (ARS), New York, 2017: Josenhans, "Exiles in Art," fig. 3

Courtesy Beauford Delaney Estate. Photo courtesy Bowdoin College Museum of Art: Josenhans, "(Re)Defining," fig. 9

© Succession Marcel Duchamp/ADAGP, Paris/Artists Rights Society (ARS), New York, 2017: cat. 3

© Succession Marcel Duchamp/ADAGP, Paris/Artists Rights Society (ARS), New York, 2017. Image courtesy the Mary Reynolds Collection, Ryerson & Burnham Libraries, Art Institute of Chicago: cat. 3, fig. 2

© Succession Marcel Duchamp/ADAGP, Paris/Artists Rights Society (ARS), New York, 2017. © CNAC/MNAD/Dist. RMN-Grand Palais/Art Resource, N.Y. Photo: © Phillippe Migeat: cat. 3, fig. 1

© Succession Marcel Duchamp/ADAGP, Paris/Artists Rights Society (ARS), New York, 2017. Image courtesy Philadelphia Museum of Art: cat. 3, fig. 3

Copyright © 1976 by Edmund Engelman. Image from *Berggasse 19: Sigmund Freud's Home and Offices, Vienna, 1938—The Photographs of Edmund Engelman* (Chicago: University of Chicago Press, 1981), pl. 13: Koerner, fig. 3

Courtesy Richard L. Feigen & Co., New York. © 2017 Artists Rights Society (ARS), New York/VG Bild-Kunst, Bonn: cat. 25

Gabinetto Fotografico delle Gallerie degli Uffizi: Josenhans, "Exiles in Art," fig. 1

Photo: Christopher Gardner: Josenhans, "(Re)Defining," fig. 5

Digital image courtesy the Getty's Open Content Program: cat. 14, fig. 3

© The Arshile Gorky Foundation/Artists Rights Society (ARS), New York: cat. 14; cat. 14, fig. 1

© The Estate of Arshile Gorky Foundation/Artists Rights Society (ARS), New York. Digital image © Whitney Museum, N.Y.: cat. 14, fig. 4

Art © Estate of George Grosz/Licensed by VAGA, New York, N.Y.: back cover, right; Josenhans, "(Re)Defining," fig. 4; cat. 24; cat. 24, fig. 1

Art © Estate of George Grosz/Licensed by VAGA, New York, N.Y. Photo courtesy Memorial Art Gallery of the University of Rochester: Josenhans, "(Re)Defining," fig. 6

Photo: Imaging Department © President and Fellows of Harvard College: Josenhans, "(Re)Defining," fig. 1

© Mona Hatoum: cat. 9; cat. 9, fig. 2

© Mona Hatoum. Photo courtesy the Museum of Fine Arts, Houston: cat. 9, fig. 3

© Mona Hatoum. Digital Image © The Museum of Modern Art/Licensed by SCALA/Art Resource, N.Y.: Josenhans, "Exiles in Art," fig. 5

With permission of the Renate, Hans & Maria Hofmann Trust/Artists Rights Society (ARS), New York: cat. 20

Courtesy Ipswich Museum and Gallery: Koerner, fig. 9

The Lotte Jacobi Collection, University of New Hampshire. Used with permission. © 2014 The University of New Hampshire: cat. 17

Photo: Alex Jamison: cat. 10 (p. 104)

Courtesy William Kentridge and Marian Goodman Gallery: Koerner, fig. 7

Courtesy the Estate of André Kertész: pp. 13–14; cat. 13

Copyright R. B. Kitaj Estate. Courtesy Marlborough Fine Art: cat. 6; pp. 236–37

Estate of Joan Koerner: Koerner, fig. 1

Estate of Joan Koerner. Photo: Christopher Gardner: Koerner, fig. 10

Kolar © 2012 Artist Rights Society (ARS), New York/ProLitteris, Zürich: cat. 23; cat. 23, fig. 1

Kunstmuseum Basel. Photo: Martin P. Bühler: Koerner, fig. 5

© An-My Lê: pp. 29–30; cat. 8

Copyright Leo Baeck Institute for the study of the history and culture of German-speaking Jewry. Alexina and Marcel Duchamp Papers, Philadelphia Museum of Art, Library and Archives: cat. 21, fig. 2

All rights reserved—Estate of Jacques Lipchitz: Josenhans, "Exiles in Art," fig. 4

© Estate of George Platt Lynes. Digital Image © The Museum of Modern Art/Licensed by SCALA/Art Resource, N.Y.: Josenhans, "Exiles in Art," fig. 7

Photo: Maher Mahmoud: Josenhans, "(Re)Defining," fig. 15

Courtesy the Collection of the Maryland State Archives: cat. 11, fig. 2

Matisse © 2017 Succession H. Matisse/Artists Rights Society (ARS), New York. Courtesy Musée Matisse, Nice. Photo: François Fernandez: cat. 9, fig. 1

Matisse © 2017 Succession H. Matisse/Artists Rights Society (ARS), New York. Digital Image © The Museum of Modern Art/Licensed by SCALA/Art Resource, N.Y.: cat. 6, fig. 2

Matta © 2017 Artists Rights Society (ARS), New York/ADAGP, Paris: back cover, top left; cat. 21; cat. 21, fig. 1

© The Estate of Ana Mendieta Collection, LLC. Courtesy Galerie Lelong, New York: cat. 5

© The Estate of Ana Mendieta Collection, LLC. Courtesy Galerie Lelong, New York. Photo courtesy the Smith College Museum of Art: Josenhans, "(Re)Defining," fig. 13

Image copyright © The Metropolitan Museum of Art. Image source: Art Resource, N.Y.: cat. 1, fig. 1

Courtesy Mildred Lane Kemper Art Museum. © 2017 Artists Rights Society (ARS), New York/VG Bild-Kunst, Bonn: cat. 19, fig. 1

© Abelardo Morell, Boston/Courtesy Edwynn Houk Gallery, New York and Zürich: cat. 7; cat. 7, fig. 1

Photo: Bonnie Morrison: cat. 12

Moviepix/Getty Images: Bozovic, fig. 4

© Musée d'art et d'histoire, Genève. Dom de Mme Necker-de Saussure, 1841, no. inv. 1841–0003. Photo: Flora Bevilacqua: Josenhans, "Exiles in Art," fig. 2

Musée Gustave Courbet/Photo: Pierre Guénat: cat. 12, fig. 1

© Musée du Louvre, Dist. RMN-Grand Palais/Angèle Dequier/Art Resource, N.Y.: cat. 11, fig. 1

Collection Musée de Tahiti et des Îles/J.-C. Bosmel. Image from Alastair Wright and Calvin Brown, *Gauguin's Paradise Remembered: The Noa Noa Prints*, exh. cat. (Princeton, N.J.: Princeton University Art Museum, 2010), fig. 21: cat. 1, fig. 2

Photograph © 2017 Museum of Fine Arts, Boston: cat. 12, fig. 2

Copyright Estate of Mu Xin, courtesy Mu Xin Art Museum: back cover, bottom left; cat. 28

© The National Gallery, London: cat. 6, fig. 1

Photograph © National Gallery in Prague 2017: Koerner, fig. 4

Photo © The Natural History Museum/The Trustees of the Natural History Museum, London: Koerner, fig. 2

Nauman © 2017 Bruce Nauman/Artists Rights Society (ARS), New York. Courtesy Electronic Arts Intermix (EAI), New York: Koerner, fig. 6

© Shirin Neshat. Courtesy Gladstone Gallery, New York and Brussels: front cover, bottom right; frontispiece; pp. 183–84; cat. 29

Neue Galerie New York/Art Resource, N.Y. © 2017 Artists Rights Society (ARS), New York/VG Bild-Kunst, Bonn: cat. 25, fig. 2

© Nolde Stiftung Seebüll: cat. 2

© Nolde Stiftung Seebüll. Digital Image © 2017 Museum Associates/LACMA. Licensed by Art Resource, N.Y.: cat. 2, fig. 1

Photo courtesy Ny Carlsberg Glyptotek: cat. 10, fig. 1

© 2017 Orange County Citizens Foundation/Artists Rights Society (ARS), New York. Image courtesy The Art Institute of Chicago/Art Resource, N.Y.: cat. 22, fig. 2

© 2017 Estate of Pablo Picasso/Artists Rights Society (ARS), New York. Digital Image © The Museum of Modern Art/ Licensed by SCALA/Art Resource, N.Y.: cat. 14, fig. 2

© RMN-Grand Palais/Art Resource, N.Y. Photo: Gerard Blot: Bozovic, fig. 1

© RMN-Grand Palais/Art Resource, N.Y. Photo: Hervé Lewandowski: cat. 4, fig. 2

© RMN-Grand Palais/Art Resource, N.Y. Photo: Benoît Touchard/Mathieu Rabeau: Bozovic, fig. 3

© RMN-Grand Palais/Art Resource, N.Y. Photo: Michel Urtado: Bozovic, fig. 2; cat. 20, fig. 2

© Ursula von Rydingsvard. Courtesy Galerie Lelong, New York: Josenhans, "(Re)Defining," fig. 14

© Lucas Samaras, courtesy Pace Gallery: Josenhans, "(Re)Defining," fig. 12; cat. 27

© Lucas Samaras, courtesy Pace Gallery. Digital Image © The Museum of Modern Art/Licensed by SCALA/Art Resource, N.Y.: cat. 27, fig. 1

Schalkwijk/Art Resource, N.Y.: Josenhans, "Exiles in Art," fig. 9

Photo: Scher/Süddeutsche Zeitung Photo: cat. 2, fig. 2

Smith College Museum of Art, Northampton, Massachusetts. © 2017 Artists Rights Society (ARS), New York/VG Bild-Kunst, Bonn: cat. 15, fig. 4

© Städel Museum—ARTOTHEK: cat. 25, fig. 1

© 2017 State Russian Museum, St. Petersburg: Bozovic, fig. 5

© Do Ho Suh: Josenhans, "Exiles in Art," fig. 6

© 2017 Estate of Yves Tanguy/Artists Rights Society (ARS), New York. Image courtesy Museo Thyssen-Bornemisza/ SCALA/Art Resource, N.Y.: cat. 18, fig. 1

Art © Estate of Jack Tworkov/Licensed by VAGA, New York, N.Y.: Josenhans, "(Re)Defining," fig. 8

Photo: Dmitry Vilensky: Bozovic, fig. 6

© The Estate of Friedrich Vordemberge-Gildewart. Courtesy Getty Research Institute, Los Angeles: cat. 19, fig. 3

© The Estate of Friedrich Vordemberge-Gildewart. Digital Image © The Museum of Modern Art/Licensed by SCALA/ Art Resource, N.Y.: cat. 19, fig. 2

© Wingate Studio and Ahmed Alsoudani: cat. 30

Visual Resources Department, Yale University Art Gallery, New Haven, Conn.: front cover, left and top right; Josenhans, "Exiles in Art," fig. 8; Josenhans, "(Re)Defining," figs. 7, 10–11; pp. 127–28; cat. 1; cat. 8, fig. 2; cat. 11; cat. 16; cat. 16, figs. 1, 3; cat. 18; cat. 18, fig. 2; cat. 19; cat. 22; cat. 22, fig. 1